A History of Music for Harpsichord or Piano and Orchestra

John M. Harris

The Scarecrow Press, Inc.
Lanham, Md., & London
1997

SCARECROW PRESS, INC.

Published in the United States of America
by Scarecrow Press, Inc.
4720 Boston Way
Lanham, Maryland 20706

4 Pleydell Gardens, Folkestone
Kent CT20 2DN, England

British Library Cataloguing in Publication Information Available

Library of Congress Cataloging-in-Publication Data

Harris, John M., 1939–
A history of music for harpsichord or piano and orchestra /
John M. Harris.
p. cm.
Discography: p.
Includes bibliographical references (p.) and index.
ISBN 0-8108-3257-7 (alk. paper)
1. Harpsichord with orchestra—History and criticism.
2. Piano with orchestra—History and criticism. I. Title.
ML1263.H37 1997
784.2′62′09—dc20

ISBN 0-8108-3257-7 (cloth : alk.paper)

∞ TM The paper used in this publication meets the minimum requirements of American National Standard for Information Sciences—Permanence of Paper for Printed Library Materials, ANSI Z39.48–1984.
Manufactured in the United States of America.

Contents

Tables

Abbreviations

ASCAP	American Society of Composers, Authors, and Publishers
bar	baritone voice
bd	band
bn	bassoon
br	brass (ensemble)
BWV	Schmieder's catalogue of J. S. Bach's music
ca.	circa
cel	celesta
cham	chamber (ensemble)
cl(s)	clarinet(s)
conc(s)	concerto(s)
D.	Deutsch's catalogue of Schubert's music
db	double bass
dbl	double (usually orchestra or chorus)
elec	electronic
Eng hn	English horn
ens	ensemble
fl(s)	flute(s), flourished if with a date
G.	Giazotto's catalogue of Viotti's music
H.	Helm's catalogue of C. P. E. Bach's music
hds	hands
hn	horn
Hob.	Hoboken's catalogue of Haydn's music
hp	harp
hpd	harpsichord
insts	instruments
ISCM	International Society for Contemporary Music
K.	Köchel's catalogue of Mozart's music or Kirkpatrick's catalogue of D. Scarlatti's music

kbd(s)	keyboard(s)
kl(s)	klavier(s)
mar	marimba
Mme	Madame
mod	modern
ms	manuscript
mvt(s)	movement(s)
n.d.	no date
no(s)	number(s)
ob	oboe
obbl	obbligato
op, opp	opus, opera
orch	orchestra
org	organ
perc	percussion
perf	performed
pf(s)	pianoforte(s)
pno(s)	piano(s)
prep	prepared
pseud	pseudonym
pub	published
qnt	quintet
rev	revised
RISM	Répertoire International des Sources Musicales
sax	saxophone
sop	soprano
sm	small
stg(s)	string(s)
sym	symphony, symphonic
tp	timpani
tr(s)	trumpet(s)
unfin	unfinished
va	viola
vars	variations
vc	cello
vers	version
vn(s)	violin(s)
W.	Wotquenne's catalogue of C. P. E. Bach's music or White's catalogue of Viotti's music

w, w/o	with, without
wds	winds (woodwinds and brass)
wk(s)	work(s) (musical compositions)
WoO	Werke ohne Opuszahl (works without opus numbers)
ww(s)	woodwind(s)

Preface

A History of Music for Harpsichord or Piano and Orchestra brings together much of the information concerning music composed for piano or harpsichord and orchestra. Previously individuals interested in reading about this music would have to cull the information from numerous sources because it has been treated as a component of symphonic literature or as part of the music for various solo instruments and orchestra.

Included in this study are compositions titled "concerto," compositions for any ensemble a composer considers an orchestra, and compositions accompanied by ensembles larger than those appropriate for chamber music.

The organization of the book follows the spread of the Baroque harpsichord concerto across countries. The book is in four parts each of which begins with Germany, followed by Italy. European countries east of the north-south line through Germany and Italy appear next, followed by countries west of that line. The consistent organization in each part allows a quick comparison of the growing number of concerted works for harpsichord or piano in each era. After Part I, the idea of concerted harpsichord or piano compositions spread rapidly, and in Part IV the phenomenon has global dimensions in the twentieth century. Generally, the four parts represent different eras of music: Part I the baroque era, Part II the classic era, Part III the romantic era and Part IV the twentieth century. Some countries are important in Parts I through IV, while other countries contribute little music for piano or harpsichord and orchestra until the twentieth century.

Composers appear in the country where they composed their significant works. Where compositions of equal importance are in two or more countries, the latest work determines the individual location. When an obvious placement is not possible, a composer's national significance decides the location. Composers appear in chronological order according to their birth dates.

Only the dates of well-known composers who have undergone numerous scholarly studies are normally acceptable. In a few cases in which a comparison of many sources strongly suggests dates, those dates have a question mark. Dates of composers may include a question mark if totally unknown (e.g., ? –1953) or questionable (e.g., 1767?–1807). Where sources list several dates and no single date can be determined as correct, a slash separates consecutive years (e.g., 1856/57/58–1919) and a hyphen separates the earliest and latest nonconsecutive years (e.g., 1855-62–1919). Dates of musical compositions appear in the same format as birth and death dates; when no date is available, no information appears in the text to save space.

Acknowledgments

A project of this size requires the assistance of many people. I would like to express my thanks to those kind individuals who helped in numerous ways. Most people are thanked in groups; otherwise, too many names would be listed.

Numerous faculty members and students at Texas A&M University-Commerce translated materials written in foreign languages and helped with the correct usage of names in various cultures. These people displayed good humor while translating materials and explaining cultural traditions.

The Graduate School at Texas A&M University-Commerce provided a computer program, a computer interface card and funding of grants to purchase library materials appropriate for this book. The Department of Music at Texas A&M University-Commerce provided a computer and computer hardware necessary to handle large amounts of information.

The staff in the Interlibrary Loan Office at Texas A&M University-Commerce was patient with numerous requests for interlibrary loan materials, and most helpful in their frequent devotion of time to computer searches.

The staff in the Reference Room helped in numerous ways. I learned much about library resources from all of these people.

Maurice Hinson took time from his own busy schedule to read an early draft of the book. His broad experience with publications proved helpful at a critical time.

I must thank one person whose name is unknown to me. A reviewer for Scarecrow Press wrote a critical assessment of the manuscript that provided many new ideas.

A special thanks goes to my family for their patience. My parents didn't see much of me while deadlines were pending. My wife, Sue, probably wondered if there can be a life without a book. She offered support and encouragement when the task seemed too great.

The following publishers allowed the use of their copyright-protected music:

A-R Editions, Inc.
Breitkopf & Härtel
Cathedral Music
C. F. Peters Corporation
Edito Musica Budapest
Foreign Music Distributors
G. Schirmer, Inc.
Harald Lyche & Co.

International Music Co.
Luck's Music Library
Max Eschig Editions Musicales
Music Treasure Publications
Musica Britannica Trust (Stainer & Bell Ltd.)
Stainer & Bell Ltd.

Part I

J. S. Bach to Mozart (ca. 1713–1770)

Chapter 1

Germany and Austria

Germany

Johann Linike (ca. 1680–1737) was from a musically active family living in northern Germany and the first violinist in the opera orchestra at Hamburg. He composed a harpsichord concerto after 1725 that probably is the first in Hamburg.

While working in Weimar, Johann Sebastian Bach (1685–1750) engaged in the widespread practice of transcribing other composers' music. His efforts resulted in the earliest harpsichord concertos, BWV 972–987 (ca. 1713-1716). Probably Bach composed the concertos for his own use or in response to requests from his employer Prince Johann Ernst for music in the fashionable style of the Venetian composers, namely Antonio Vivaldi and Alessandro Marcello.

Venetian concertos have three movements in an arrangement of fast-slow-fast. Frequently all movements are in the same key, but some slow movements are in the relative minor. The solo and tutti are distinctive and, occasionally, the solo has material not present in the tutti. Animated rhythms create an unrelenting rhythmic drive and homophonic textures dominate, with occasional imitative statements in accompanying parts.

The ritornello functions as the fundamental organizational device in the baroque concerto by presenting the first tutti material in various keys and finally in the tonic near the end of a movement. Bach adopted Vivaldi's practice of presenting the ritornello in a variety of near-related keys. Solo episodes, between the ritornellos, contain material from the ritornello or completely new material. Bach's concertos have four ritornellos: ritornello 1 (tutti) in the tonic, episode 1 (solo) moves from tonic to dominant; ritornello 2 (tutti) in the dominant, episode 2 (solo) modulates; ritornello 3 (tutti) in a near-related key, episode 3 (solo) moves from related keys to the tonic; and ritornello 4 (tutti) in the tonic.

Wolfgang Schmieder's *Thematisch-systematisches Verzeichnis der Musikalischen der Werke von Johann Sebastian Bach*[1] provides BWV numbers (Bach-Werke-Verzeichnis) or S numbers (Schmieder) for Bach's compositions. Peter Ryom's *Verzeichnis der Werke Antonio Vivaldis*[2] provides RV numbers for Vivaldi's music.

Bach's transcriptions of other composers' music into harpsichord concertos are seventeen in number: BWV 592a from an organ transcription of a violin concerto by Prince Johann Ernst of Saxe-Weimar; BWV 972 from Vivaldi's violin concerto, op. 3, no. 9, RV 230; BWV 973 from Vivaldi's violin concerto, op. 7, book 2, no. 2, RV 299; BWV 974, probably from Marcello's oboe concerto no. 2 in the *Concerti a Cinque;* BWV 975 from a lost Vivaldi violin concerto; BWV 976 from Vivaldi's violin concerto, op. 3, no. 12, RV 265; BWV 977 from an unknown source; BWV 978 from Vivaldi's violin concerto, op. 3, no. 3, RV 310; BWV 979 from an unknown source; BWV 980 from Vivaldi's violin concerto, op. 4, no. 1, RV 381, RV 383a, and RV 528; BWV 981 from an unknown source; BWV 982 from the violin concerto, op. 1, no. 1, by Prince Johann Ernst of Saxe-Weimar; BWV 983 from an unknown source; BWV 984 from a lost composition by Prince Johann Ernst of Saxe-Weimar; BWV 985 from a Telemann violin concerto; BWV 986 from an unknown source; and BWV 987 from a lost composition by Prince Johann Ernst of Saxe-Weimar.

The choice of key for a transcription is important. For known musical sources, Bach changes keys in the three concertos—BWV 976, BWV 978, and BWV 980. In Venetian violin concertos, the highest note is e3, and on Bach's harpsichord the highest pitch is c3. The decision to transpose the key appears to be determined by the musical importance of pitches above c3. When pitches above c3 are musically unimportant Bach keeps the original key and rewrites passages within the range of the harpsichord. When notes above c3 are musically important Bach transposes the concerto downward to accommodate the highest harpsichord pitches.

In concerto transcriptions, Bach places the original violin solo in the right hand, and the left hand has the orchestra bass line with figuration idiomatic to the harpsichord. Double stops in violin concertos become three-note chords in the harpsichord concertos. Sometimes melodic figuration appears in the left hand in the form of imitative material filling measures where the source concerto has a slowing rhythmic drive. In solo episodes, Bach occasionally writes original music instead of continuing material of the source concerto. Slow movements of violin concertos that contain embellished melodies remain the same for the harpsichord, and where slow movements lack embellishments, Bach adds figurations to the melody and a written accompaniment for the left hand.

From 1717 to 1723, Bach lived in Cöthen working as the *kapellmeister* for the Margrave Christian Ludwig of Brandenburg, for whom he composed the six *Brandenburg Concertos,* BWV 1046–1051. The *Brandenburg Concerto* no. 5, BWV 1050 (ca. 1720), is the first concerto with a solo harpsichord based on a composer's own musical material. This concerto *grosso* features flute, violin, and harpsichord in the concertino. Usually, the solo instruments share the musical material, but in this concerto the harpsichord has a dominant role and a sixty-five-measure cadenza near the end of the first movement. Harpsichord lines frequently double other concertino parts and the left-hand part often provides a bass line for the flute and violin during rests in the right-hand part. In ritornellos, Bach continues the practice of reinforcing the tutti violins with the concertino violin. Normally, Bach played violin in the orchestra and conducted from that location, but in the *Brandenburg Concerto* no. 5, he may have conducted from the harpsichord and intended the cadenza for himself.

Bach's harpsichord concertos, BWV 1052–1065, date between 1730 and 1740, when he and his sons probably needed harpsichord music for performances at the *Collegium Musicum* in Leipzig. While Bach's earlier concertos, BWV 972–987, are transcriptions of concertos by other composers, generally he based the later harpsichord concertos on his own concertos for other instruments. As with the earlier concerto transcriptions, Bach gives the original solo line to the right hand, and to the left hand an embellished version of the bass line. Concertos for two or more harpsichords come from concertos for two or more solo instruments, and the original solo parts appear in each right-hand part with each left-hand part having an embellishment of the bass line.

Generally, Bach based the solo concertos on his own musical compositions. They are: BWV 1044 with movement 1 from the *Prelude and Fugue,* BWV 894, and movement 2 from the *Trio Sonata,* BWV 527; BWV 1052 from a lost violin concerto (Vivaldi?); BWV 1053 from a lost violin concerto; BWV 1054 (1730–1733) from the violin concerto, BWV 1042; BWV 1055 from a lost violin concerto; BWV 1056 from a lost oboe concerto; BWV 1057 (1730–1733) from the *Brandenburg Concerto* no. 4, BWV 1049; BWV 1058 (1730–1733) from the violin concerto, BWV 1041; BWV 1059, incomplete, from a lost oboe concerto; BWV 1060 for two harpsichords from a lost oboe and violin concerto; BWV 1061 for two harpsichords, the original version; and BWV 1062 (1736) for two harpsichords from the concerto, BWV 1043, for two violins. The concerto BWV 1063 (1730–1733) for three harpsichords is on a violin and oboe concerto by an unknown composer, and the concerto BWV 1064 for three harpsichords is on a lost concerto for three violins. The concerto BWV 1065 (1730–1733) for four harpsichords is on Vivaldi's violin concerto *L'Estro Armonico,* op. 3, no. 10, RV 580. Bach changed keys to fit the harpsichord range in seven concertos: BWV 1054, BWV 1056, BWV 1057, BWV 1058, BWV 1062, BWV 1064, and BWV 1065.

The concerto BWV 1052 is an example of Bach's reuse of musical material. Originally, the music probably appeared in a lost Vivaldi concerto for viola d'amore that Bach apparently used as the source for the lost violin concerto BWV 1052a (ca. 1720) and the harpsichord concerto (1730/33). The first and second movements of the harpsichord concerto appear in the cantata no. 146 (1740).

In these harpsichord concertos, Bach usually follows the four-ritornello plan of Vivaldi. Characteristic rhythms and intervals of the ritornello appear in one or more solo episodes.

The earlier concertos, BWV 972–987, have middle movements in the key of the outer movements or sometimes in the relative minor. The *Brandenburg Concerto* no. 5 and the concertos BWV 1052–1065 have a middle movement in a relative major or minor key.

Bach's use of a continuo harpsichord in harpsichord concertos is unclear. Only the concerto BWV 1055 exists in original parts with a separate continuo part for a second harpsichord. The *Brandenburg Concerto* no. 5 is one of several concertos with a figured bass written in the ritornellos for the solo harpsichord. A lack of sufficient evidence leaves the possible role of a second harpsichord a matter of conjecture. In concertos for two or more harpsichords, there is no figured bass for an accompanying harpsichord.

Bach's orchestions usually include two violins, viola, cello, and bass. The concerto BWV 1057 has parts for two recorders, and the concerto BWV 1059 has an oboe part.

Harpsichord concertos appeared in several areas of Europe about the same time. There is no evidence Bach inspired other composers of concertos. Perhaps the time was right for such pieces.

Johann Kunzen (1696–1757) and his son Adolph Kunzen (1720–1781) continued Lübeck's strong oratorio tradition after Buxtehude. Johann became organist for the town of Leisnig at age 9 and worked in Zerbst, Wittenberg, Hamburg and Lubeck as organist at the *Marienkirche*. He left two harpsichord concertos. Adolph was a touring harpsichord and organ virtuoso, *konzertmeister* to the Duke of Mecklenberg-Schwerin and successor to his father as the organist at the *Marienkirche* in 1757. His five piano concertos possibly resulted from musical contacts in London.

Johann Molter (1696–1765) lived in the Thuringian-Saxon region and worked as a musician in Baden-Durlach, Saxe-Eisenach, and Karlsruhe. He composed about forty-four concertos, one of which is for keyboard, probably harpsichord.

Giovanni Platti (ca. 1700–1763) went to Wurzburg in 1722 to work as a teacher, composer, and performer. He composed six concertos, op. 2 (pub. 1742), for harpsichord obbligato, four harpsichord concertos, possibly as a set, and one additional concerto. His life spans the change of style from baroque to early classic. Platti's four-ritornello form suggests some concertos date prior to his use of classic elements; other concertos have *galant* melodic traits.

Johan Agrell (1701–1765), Swedish, was active in Kassal and Nuremburg from 1746. He composed three harpsichord concertos, op. 3 (1751), three harpsichord concertos, op. 4 (1753), four harpsichord concertos (1755–1761), and two harpsichord concertos. Lost are twelve or thirteen harpsichord concertos.

Johann Graun (1703–1759), brother of K. H. Graun, concertmaster in the court of Frederick the Great, composed at least six concertos for harpsichord or organ.

Johann Harrer (1703–1755) worked in the same court as Johann Goldberg. He probably composed two lost harpsichord concertos.

Georg Sorge (1703–1778) became the organist and cantor in the parochial schools of Lobenstein at age 18. Although he is remembered as a theorist, Sorge composed much music and perhaps one harpsichord concerto.

Karl Graun (1704–1759), brother of J. Graun, opera composer and *kapellmeister* in the court of Frederick the Great, left at least thirty-three harpsichord concertos following Vivaldi's structural ideas. Unclear indications concerning which composer wrote various concertos complicates the dating of concertos by Karl and Johann Graun. Both composers use Tartini's four-ritornello form, and occasional concertos have three or five ritornellos. The concertos appear important in the early evolution of a recapitulation.

Johann Leffloth (1704–1731), in Nuremberg, was a member of the Middle German Organ School with J. J. P. Kuffner and J. Agrell. Leffloth composed a lost harpsichord concerto.

Michael Scheuenstuhl (1705–1770) was the organist at St. Michael's church in Hof from 1729. He composed three harpsichord concertos (ca. 1738, ca. 1738–39, ca. 1740).

Johann Tischer (1707–1774) settled in Schmalkalden as the town organist and soon became the *konzertmeister* at the court of Saxe-Coburg-Meiningen. His musical compositions include two harpsichord concertos (ca. 1748), thirteen harpsichord concertos (ca. 1754), and six keyboard concertos.

Johann Janitsch (1708–1763), double-bass player, left at least six harpsichord concertos in J. G. Graun's style.

Franz Benda (1709–1786), concertmaster before and after J. G. Graun, composed three harpsichord concertos; however, Douglas A. Lee's *Franz Benda (1709–1786), A Thematic Catalog of His Works*[3] does not list any harpsichord concertos.

Franz Richter (1709–1789) sang in Mannheim until going to Strasburg in 1765. He composed six harpsichord concertos, probably before arriving in Mannheim, and there he composed eight lost harpsichord concertos. Extant harpsichord concertos are in four-ritornello form with the last ritornello not restating the first. Solos have some independent material, and a fermata in the last solo indicates an improvised cadenza.

Mannheim concertos are important in the evolution of the ritornello form into the concerto form with double exposition. Some concertos present a double exposition without a development and recapitulation, while other concertos have a full classic concerto form. The ritornello form continues as an important organizational force. Classic concerto form slowly emerges from new treatments of ritornello form. Ritornello 1, solo 1, and ritornello 2 become a single section resulting in a double exposition. Solo 2 evolves into the development, ritornello 3 becomes part of the development or recapitulation, depending on the composer's preference, and solo 3 and ritornello 4 become the recapitulation. Many concertos have features that suggest a partial evolution, where portions of a concerto have an exposition, development, or recapitulation and other parts maintain ritornello form. Among a composer's own works and works of different contemporary composers a lack of uniformity is the norm.

Christoph Schaffrath (1709–1763), composer and harpsichordist, composed at least twenty-nine harpsichord concertos and perhaps as many as forty. A harpsichord concerto in B-flat major has a slow movement (See ex. 1–1) with two embellished harpsichord versions (See ex. 1–2); these ornamented versions are important examples of improvisation in northern Germany.[4]

Christoph Schaffrath Concerto in B-flat for Cembalo and Strings. Edited by Karyl Louwenaar. By permission of A-R Editions, Inc.

Example 1–1. Schaffrath Concerto, mvt. 2, mm. 14–19

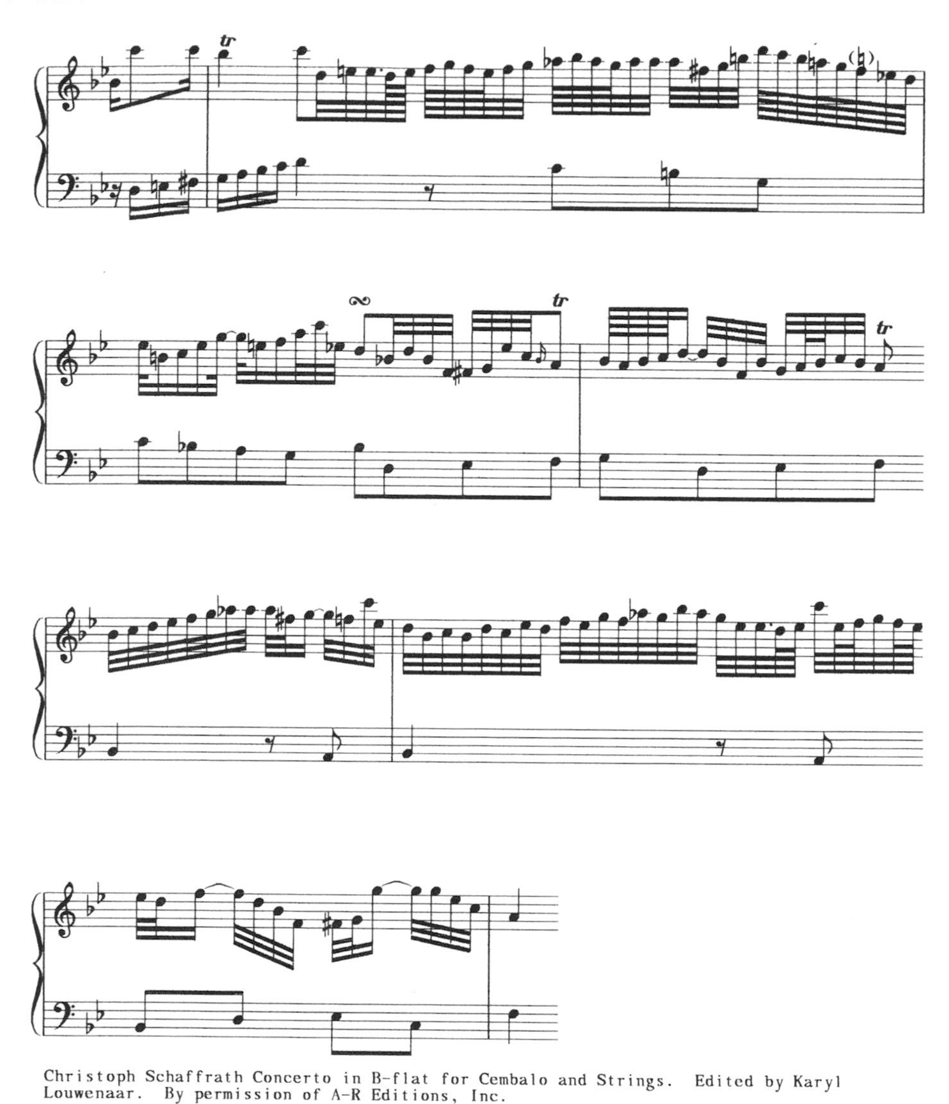

Christoph Schaffrath Concerto in B-flat for Cembalo and Strings. Edited by Karyl Louwenaar. By permission of A-R Editions, Inc.

Example 1–2. Schaffrath Concerto, mvt. 2, embellished version, mm. 14–19

Wilhelm Friedemann Bach (1710–1784), eldest son of J. S. Bach, revived Halle's musical life while the organist at the *Marktkirche*. Probably he was the most original and creative musician among J. S. Bach's sons, and contemporaries complained about his procrastination in writing down remarkable improvisations. Martin Falck's *Wilhelm Friedemann Bach, Sein Leben und seine Werke*[5] provides F. numbers for Bach's music. There are six harpsichord concertos—F.41 (1733–46), F.42 (1750s),

F.43 (before 1767), F.44 (1733–1746), F.45 (1733–1746)—with characteristics similar to concertos J. S. Bach composed in Dresden, and F.46 (?) for two harpsichords.

Joseph Umstatt (1711–1762), *kapellmeister* and court composer from 1752, composed six harpsichord concertos, three concertos for two harpsichords, and up to five lost concertos, all in a style similar to G. M. Monn. Umstatt changed Vivaldi's concerto style by making solo episodes weightier, longer, and virtuosic.

Johann Krebs (1713–1780), organist and composer, studied with J. S. Bach in Leipzig and became Bach's harpsichord assistant at the *Collegium Musicum*. He was an organist in Zeitz, Zwickau, and Gotha-Altenburg for Prince Friedrich. His concerto production is confusing, but there may be three harpsichord concertos: one for one harpsichord, one for one harpsichord with two manuals, and one for two harpsichords.

Christian Schale (1713–1800), cellist and composer, produced at least seven harpsichord concertos. Christoph Nichelmann (1717–1762), harpsichordist before and during part of C. P. E. Bach's era, left at least sixteen harpsichord concertos (ca. 1740–ca. 1759).

Carl Philipp Emanuel Bach (1714–1788), the "Berlin" Bach and third son of Johann Sebastian and Maria Barbara, studied music with his father through 1738, served Frederick the Great in Berlin from 1738 to 1767, and then succeeded Telemann as the *kantor* in Hamburg. Bach's harpsichord concertos span his entire life, with the largest number composed in Berlin.

Eugene Helm's *A New Thematic Catalog of the Works of Carl Philipp Emanuel Bach*[6] provides H. numbers to identify Bach's music, and Alfred Wotquenne's *Thematisches Verzeichnis der Werke von C. P. E. Bach*[7] provides W. numbers. H. numbers replace W. numbers.

In Leipzig, Bach composed the two lost concertos, H.403, W.1 (1733, rev. 1744), and H.404, W.2 (1734, rev. 1743). In Frankfurt, he composed the concerto H.405, W.3 (1737, rev. 1745).

At Frederick the Great's court, Bach composed thirty-four harpsichord concertos: H.406, W.4 (1738); H.407, W.5 (1739, rev. 1762); H.408, W.46 (1740), for two harpsichords; H.409, W.6 (1740); H.410, W.7 (1740); H.411, W.8 (1741); H.412–413, W.9–10 (1742); H.414, W.11 (1743); H.415–417, W.12–14 (1744); H.418–421, W.15–18 (1745); H.422–423, W.19–20 (1746); H.424, W.21 (1747, rev. 1775); H.425, W.22 (1747); H.430 and H.433, W.26–27 (1750); H.434, W.28 (1751); H.441, W.31 (1753); H.442, W.32 (1754); H.443, W.33 (1755); H.444, W.43 (1755) for organ or harpsichord based on the concerto H.445, W.169, for flute and strings; H.446, W. 35 (1759) for organ or harpsichord; H.447–448, W.36–37 (1762); H.454, W.38 (1763); H.465, W.39 (1765) based on the concerto H.466, W.164, for oboe and strings; and H.467, W.40 (1765) based on the concerto H.468, W.165, for oboe and strings. The slow movement of the concerto, H.444, W.43, displays Bach's *empfindsamer stil* (See ex. 1–3).

In Potsdam, Bach composed five concertos: H.427–428, W.23–24 (1748); H.429, W.25 (1749); and H.437 and H.440, W.29–30 (1753).

In Hamburg, Bach composed eleven concertos: H.469, W.41 (1769); H.470, W.42 (1770); H.471–476, W.43/1–6 (1771); H.477–478, W.44–45 (1778); and H.479, W.47 (1788) for harpsichord and fortepiano—the earliest concerto featuring these two

Example 1–3. C. P. E. Bach Concerto, H.444, W.43, mvt. 2, mm. 7–17

instruments. Bach's writing depends on the contrasting of the sound of the two instruments rather than a different style for each instrument (See ex. 1–4).

Bach's concertos often have an orchestra of two violins, viola, and bass, and a few concertos use two horns and two flutes. The accompanied harpsichord works *Sonatinas for Harpsichord and Diverse Instruments* require an orchestra of two horns, two flutes,

Example 1–4. C. P. E. Bach Concerto, H.479, W.47, for harpsichord and fortepiano and orchestra, mvt. 1, mm. 64–69[8]

two violins, viola, and bass. In concertos and sonatinas, "harpsichord concertato" means a composition presenting a harpsichord in contrast with other instruments.

In Berlin, 1762, Bach composed the sonatinas H.449, W.96; H.450, W.97; H.451, W.98; H.452, W.99; and H.453, W.109. In 1763, he composed the sonatinas H.455, W.100; H.460, W.101; H.456, W.102; H.457, W.103; and H.459, W.110. In Potsdam, 1764, he composed the sonatinas H.463, W.104, and H.464, W.105, and in Berlin, H.458, W.106; H.461, W.107; and H.462, W.108. The sonatina H.480 (1758) is for harpsichord, two flutes, and strings, and the sonatina H.481 (ca. 1762) for harpsichord, two flutes, and strings is a version of H.453, W.109. Georg Christoph Wagenseil of Vienna is the probable source of Bach's idea of sonatinas for harpsichord and orchestra.

The sonatinas have a south German, *galant* style with binary and French *rondeau* forms. Bach avoids virtuoso harpsichord writing in preference for passages where the solo and orchestra perform together or alternate. The sonatinas and a comparative lack of harpsichord concertos during this time suggest that Bach wanted a vehicle for musical experimentation unencumbered by tradition. Many new ideas appear first in the sonatinas and later in concertos Bach composed in Hamburg.

Although Bach's compositions follow the general musical characteristics of the Berlin composers, his harpsichord concertos show greater variety in the treatment of ritornellos and episodes. Characteristic of the concertos is the modulatory nature of ritornello 3, and ritornello 4 sometimes ends in tonic or never arrives on tonic. Some concertos have tutti and solo sections in a manner suggesting the double exposition or recapitulation of later eighteenth-century composers. The harpsichord writing is soloistic and eventually equality exists between the solo and tutti sections.

Bach's era is one of conflict between baroque influences and new musical ideas. Revisions of his concertos show a decided preference for new ideas, including more soloistic harpsichord writing and a rethinking of the ritornello form. Some revisions contain a written, embellished harpsichord part, possibly intended as a teaching tool or to communicate musical ideas to a friend or student in another city. Other revisions contain instruments added to the typical orchestra of two violins, viola, and bass. Two horn parts are in seven concertos, two flute parts are in two concertos, and horn and flute parts are in eight concertos. The concerto H.434, W.28, is the most heavily orchestrated, with parts added for two flutes, two oboes, two horns or trumpets, and timpani; added parts do not alter existing string or harpsichord lines. These revisions display Bach's willingness to improve and update compositions.

The intermingling of styles in Berlin caused fundamental musical changes. Baroque styles yielded to *galant* characteristics, and homophonic writing replaced contrapuntal styles. Polythematic sections supplanted monothematic solos, and ritornellos and short phrases superseded the spinning-out of melodies. A musically distinctive harpsichord part balanced the orchestra, and the continuo with figured bass became less important.

While Bach was a leader in the court of Frederick the Great, he was not totally happy with the situation. His relationship with his employer was not entirely pleasant, and several times he petitioned for a release. In 1768, he left Berlin to take the position of *kantor* in Hamburg.

The concertos Bach wrote in Hamburg reveal the influence of his experiments with the sonatinas. The Hamburg concertos have the expanded instrumentation of the sonatinas and more tonal variety in the middle movements, including tonalities outside the realm of near-related keys. The final ritornello frequently is a development of ritornello material in the style of a coda. Solos and tuttis are less contrasting and more cooperative without tutti interruptions of the solo. The solo has material from the tutti instead of new material. A standard practice in the Hamburg concertos is an inconclusive end of the slow movement, with the intent of continuing directly into the third movement.

The sonatinas influenced the six concertos H.471–476, W.43/1–6, in the popular south German style prevalent throughout most of the country. The concertos were for amateur performance and were published for subscription sales. Written cadenzas and ornamentations are in the slow movements.

Johann Stamitz (1717–1757) led the Mannheim orchestra to a level of exceptional virtuosity. His compositions elaborate on the sonata form and the sequence of movements in the symphony. While his most important contributions are in symphonic music, he composed six concertos, op. 10 (pub. ca. 1775), for harpsichord, organ, or piano. One additional harpsichord concerto may be lost.

Johann Kirnberger (1721–1783), violinist and theorist, may have composed a harpsichord concerto.

Musical activity in the court of Frederick the Great stimulated Frederick's favorite sister Wilhelmina (1709–1758) to write some compositions including a harpsichord concerto.

No information exists concerning the earliest harpsichord concerto composed at the court of Frederick the Great. An acknowledgement of Wilhelmina indicates that she received two harpsichord concertos by Schaffrath in 1736. K. H. Graun composed one concerto in 1736 and Janitsch probably completed some concertos in the 1730s.

Italian concerto composers, particularly Tartini, influenced musicians at the court of Frederick the Great. Many composers traveled to Italy for training or to southern Germany, where the Italian influence was strong. The infusion of Italian style into northern Germany places the Berlin concertos in a transitional position between the concertos of J. S. Bach and Mozart.

Berlin concertos display a combination of baroque and *galant* characteristics. Figured bass is common in the keyboard parts during tuttis, and short phrases replace baroque rhythms. Rhythms become more varied, with frequent appearances of triplets, syncopations, and dotted rhythms. Appoggiaturas appear as small notes when passages are in sixteenth notes. Melodies are in parallel thirds in the tuttis and solos, and the harpsichord has homophonic textures with accompaniments of single notes or chords. After 1740, extended unaccompanied solo passages had the importance of the tuttis.

Berlin composers often divided the first ritornello into as many as four sections, with some sections only four measures long. The ritornello opening presents thematic material used extensively in later portions of the movement. The second section treats the material sequentially. A contrasting third section—influenced by Tartini and where Berlin composers use a quiet dynamic level—has the melody in thirds in violins over repeated bass notes and suggests modulation. The fourth section, which ends the first ritornello, has a vigorous rhythm and style much like the first section. The modulatory third section is an important precursor of modulations in eighteenth-century orchestral expositions in concerto form.

The four-ritornello form in the Berlin concerto contains new ideas about tonality. Ritornello 1 appears in the tonic, ritornello 2 in the dominant or relative major or minor, ritornello 3 in the relative major or minor—or dominant if the second ritornello is in the relative major or minor—and ritornello 4 returns to tonic. Unlike J. S. Bach's practice of ending a movement with a complete ritornello, the Berlin composers shorten the final ritornello.

Berlin concertos typically use an orchestra of violins I and II, viola, and bass, with two players usually on each violin part. Some concertos have parts for flutes, oboes, horns, trumpets, and timpani.

Solo episodes contain new material or material taken from ritornello 1, modulations are completed during the episodes, and new keys are established before each ritornello. The harpsichord style is homophonic, with one-note lines typically in each hand, and some have three- or four-note chords. Solo episode 1 often emphasizes short *galant* phrases and lacks virtuosity; episode 2 shows a marked increase in virtuoso style, with long runs frequently passing through both hands, and material treated in an almost developmental manner; and episode 3 continues the virtuoso style of episode 2.

Several pianos built by Gottfried Silbermann (1683–1754) were in the court of Frederick the Great, and J. S. Bach played on one of those instruments during a visit in 1747. The strong position of the harpsichord as an instrument suitable for concertos and the weak sound of the contemporary piano resulted in virtually no piano concertos composed by Berlin composers. Not until C. P. E. Bach wrote the concerto H.479, W.47, for harpsichord and fortepiano, did a composer in the Berlin group consider the piano suitable for a concerto solo; Bach composed this concerto after moving to Hamburg.

In many Berlin concertos, a fermata prior to the last tutti indicates an improvised cadenza. Cadenzas may appear in any movement or several times in a single movement. Bach's concertos contain many cadenzas, and he composed cadenzas for many concertos in the same key. Apparently, Bach felt a need to provide cadenzas for musicians unable to improvise quality cadenzas.

Until Bach's concerto H.479, W.47 (1788), for harpsichord and fortepiano, the piano was not a solo instrument in concertos. Prior to this work, Bach composed only solo music for the fortepiano, and he was careful to distinguish between the harpsichord and fortepiano in the titles. While he preferred the clavichord or harpsichord, he knew the piano's musical possibilities. In the concerto, individual sonorities of the harpsichord and piano provide contrast instead of idiomatic writing for each instrument.

Although Bach believed the piano to be inferior to the harpsichord or clavichord, his piano music is a recognition of the growing public interest in the instrument. Paying for a costly periodic quilling of a harpsichord helped turn public attention toward less expensive pianos. Also, there was growing recognition of the piano's potential for a wider range of nuances than possible on harpsichords. The need for a keyboard instrument loud enough to be heard above an orchestra added to the growing demand for pianos. For economic reasons, composers began to write music for the increasingly popular piano. Undoubtedly, composers knew the differences between piano and harpsichords, but many publishers, interested in increased sales, indiscriminately titled music for piano or harpsichord and sometimes organ. Between ca. 1750 and ca. 1800 the piano emerged as the paramount keyboard instrument. The emerging musical style, with its emphasis on melody, stimulated interest in the piano's lyric potential. Pianos could produce dramatic dynamic changes; thus, the piano is the perfect keyboard instrument for pre-classic keyboard music. C. P. E. Bach began the German recognition of the piano.

Wilhelm Enderle (1722–1790), violinist and pianist, became the *konzertmeister* to Wilhelm Gottfried Enderle in 1753. He composed a harpsichord concerto.

Christlieb Binder (1723–1789), employed by Friedrich August III, composed three concertos (1767) for two harpsichords, eighteen concertos (1773?), twelve concertos (1775–1776), one concerto (1758), the adagio, and possibly three other concertos. The concertos have J. S. Bach's forms and C. P. E. Bach's style.

Johann Kehl (1725–1778) composed keyboard music while the organist at *Neustädter Kirche*. He was a fine harpsichordist; his only harpsichord concerto is in manuscript.

Peter August (1726–1787) composed fourteen harpsichord concertos, the divertimento for one harpsichord and the divertimento for two harpsichords. These *galant* works probably are from the late 1760s.

Johann Goldberg (1727–1756) was a highly praised German organist and the harpsichordist immortalized in the title of J. S. Bach's *Goldberg Variations*. In the court of Heinrich Brühl, he composed two harpsichord concertos; some sources mention "several" harpsichord concertos.

Johann Wilhelm Hertel (1727–1789) was born into a musical family. His father, Johann Christian Hertel (1697–1754), a famous gamba virtuoso, composed some lost keyboard concertos. Johann Wilhelm studied violin with Karl Hoeckh, *konzertmeister* of the Zerbst Court, and noticed Hoeckh's efforts to create a truly German musical style during an era of international musical crosscurrents. In Berlin, Hertel studied harpsichord with C. P. E. Bach, violin with F. Benda, and composition with K. H. Graun. He played violin and clavier at courts in Neustrelitz and Schwerin.

Hertel's fifteen keyboard concertos probably date between ca. 1755 and ca. 1775. From 1750, he liked the new Silbermann piano, and practiced on the piano more than any other keyboard instrument. Hertel may have used the term *cembalo* on title pages in a generic sense, while intending some concertos for piano.

Hertel used the fast-slow-fast scheme of movements and a four-ritornello form. Left-hand parts require greater facility in performing ornaments, particularly trills, than the concertos by Berlin composers. Improvised cadenzas are indicated by a fermata over a tonic six-four chord and terminated with a trill on the supertonic over a dominant chord. Orchestras are the usual two violins, viola, and bass, with occasional parts for horns and flutes.

Friedrich Graf (1727–1795) toured as a flutist, performed for Count Bentheim in Steinfurt, and directed music at the Protestant church and St. Anna's Gymnasium from 1779. He left two harpsichord concertos.

Johann Kuffner (1727–1786), in Nuremberg, left twelve keyboard concertos, probably for harpsichord.

Christian Cannabich (1731–1798) studied violin with Stamitz and succeeded him as the director of the Mannheim orchestra until going to Munich in 1778. As a conductor, he stressed synchronized violin bowing, and he composed about a hundred symphonies, many violin concertos, and other works. In Mannheim or Munich, he composed one concerto for harpsichord or piano.

Johann Seyfert (1731–1772), among the finest keyboard virtuosos in Europe, composed sacred music at the Lutheran *Kantorei* of St. Anna. He studied with Hass, C. P. E. Bach and Wagenseil. From 1753, he lived in Augsburg and composed several harpsichord concertos.

Anton Filtz (ca. 1733–1760) studied with Stamitz and eventually became a composer and second cellist in the Mannheim orchestra. His contributions to the improvement of the Mannheim orchestra equal the efforts of Stamitz and Richter. His music was in wide circulation and after his death it remained well-regarded. While much of his attention went to the symphony, he also composed a harpsichord concerto (1768), two harpsichord concertos (pub. ca. 1775) in the *Periodical Overtures,* and the *Favourite Concerto* for organ, harpsichord, or piano.

Johann Demmler (1748–1785) worked at the Augsburg cathedral as an organist, pianist, and conductor. He performed concertos as a pianist or violinist and played Mozart's three-piano concerto, K.242, with J. A. Stein and Mozart. Lost are some piano concertos with an Italian influence.

Austria

George Reutter (1707–1772) became the organist of the *Himmelspfort Concert* at age 14. After studies in Italy, he became the court composer, the *kapellmeister* at St. Stephen's Cathedral, and the *kapellmeister* at the court in 1741. He left two harpsichord concertos, one of which is incomplete.

Georg Wagenseil (1715–1777) was a highly praised harpsichordist and composer working in the court from 1739, and the music master to Maria Theresa, the future empress. Helga Schulz-Michelitsch cataloged Wagenseil's music in *Das Orchestrer—und Kammermusikwerk von Georg Christoph Wagenseil*[9]. He composed ninety-one concertos for one or two harpsichords and a fragment of a harpsichord concerto. Seventy-three concertos lack composition or publication dates, and twenty-eight concertos date between 1760 and 1781. Most of the concertos were published in London and Paris. Fifteen concertos are in versions with or without orchestra, six concertos are for two harpsichords, and one concerto is for fortepiano and harpsichord.

Georg Monn (1717–1750), better-known of the two Monns, worked in Vienna as the organist at the *Karlskirche*. With Wagenseil he was a leading Viennese counterpart to Johann Stamitz in Mannheim. Although known to musicians in Vienna and the surrounding area, he did not develop continental recognition. He is the first Viennese concerto composer to display traits of classic style while using ritornello form. In particular, the interplay between the solo instrument and orchestra is an important forerunner of Mozart's piano concertos. He composed seven harpsichord concertos (one in 1746). Arnold Schoenberg transcribed a Monn concerto in G minor (1932–33).

Jiri Linek (1725–1791) was born in Bohemia. Mozart was familiar with a concerto Linek possibly composed in Vienna.

Johann Monn (1726–1782), younger brother of G. M. Monn, lived in Vienna before leaving for Prague to be a music instructor to the count. He returned to Vienna in 1766. Three of his harpsichord concertos are in the collection of G. M. Monn at the *Staatsbibliothek der Stiftung Preussischer Kulturbesitz* in Berlin; concertos 2, 3, and 11 differ in style from the rest of the collection to such a degree that they are likely works of another composer, possibly J. C. Monn.

Notes

1. Wolfgang Schmieder, *Thematisch- systematisches Verzeichnis der Werke von Johann Sebastian Bach* (Leipzig: Veb Breitkopf and Härtel, 1966).

2. Peter Ryom, *Verzeichnis der Werke Antonio Vivaldis* (Leipzig: VEB Deutscher Verlag Für Musik, 1974).

3. Douglas A. Lee, *Franz Benda (1709–1786), A Thematic Catalogue of His Works* (New York: Pendragon Press, 1984).

4. See Christoph Schaffrath, *Concerto in B-Flat for Cembalo and Strings,* Ed. Karyl Louwanaar (Madison, A-R Editions, Inc.: 1977) for the two complete embellished versions by Schaffrath.

5. Martin Falck, *Wilhelm Friedemann Bach: Sein Leben und seine Werke* (Leipzig: C. F. Kahnt Nachfolger, 1913).

6. Eugene Helm, *A New Thematic Catalog of the Works of Carl Philipp Emanuel Bach* (New Haven: Yale University, 1989).

7. Alfred Wotquenne, *Thematisches Verzeichnis der Werke von C. P. E. Bach (1714–1788)* (Wiesbaden: Breitkopf & Härtel, 1972).

8. This example corrects an error in the published score where the keyboards are listed as two pianofortes rather than harpsichord and fortepiano.

9. Helga Scholz-Michelitsch, *Das Orchester—und Kammermusikwerk von Georg Christoph Wagenseil, Thematischer Katalog* (Wien: Ernst Becvar, 1972).

Chapter 2

Italy, Portugal, France, Belgium, the Netherlands, Norway, and England

Italy

Bologna's cosmopolitan environment was due to its location between important Italian musical cities to the south and German and Austrian cultural centers to the north. During an era of royal patronage, professional musicians controlled the Bolognese academies, particularly the *Accademia Filarmonica* founded in 1666.

Alessandro Scarlatti (1660–1725), famed *opera seria* composer, has six harpsichord concertos of doubtful authorship attributed to him. One harpsichord concerto may belong to G. Scarlatti (ca. 1718–1777), possibly Domenico's nephew. Alessandro's son Domenico is known for his highly idiomatic harpsichord sonatas.

Conrad Hurlebusch (ca. 1696–1765), noted German composer, theorist, and harpsichordist, spent time in Hamburg, Vienna, Brunswick, and many other major cities in Germany, Sweden, and Italy. While touring Italy as a harpsichord virtuoso he may have composed a harpsichord concerto (1718?).

Giovanni Predieri (fl 1730–1755) composed three concertos with harpsichord obbligato.

Antonio Gaetano Pampani (1705–1775) devoted most of his effort to *opera seria,* and he composed three or four harpsichord concertos.

Baldassare Galuppi (1706–1785), important composer of *opera buffa,* lived in St. Petersburg and gained a reputation as a brilliant harpsichordist. Contemporary reports treat his efforts in opera, but there are nine concertos for harpsichord. Galuppi may have composed the concertos in St. Petersburg or after returning in 1768 to Venice where he composed mainly keyboard music.

Giovanni Martini (1706–1784), known as Padre Martini, taught at the *Accademia Filarmonica* and gained an international reputation as the greatest Italian scholar of the time. His famous library of books and rare manuscripts is the basis of the present library at the *Conservatorio Musical G. B. Martini.* Many illustrious musicians, including J. C. Bach, Mozart, Jomelli, and Vogler, traveled to Bologna to study with Martini. Europe's luminaries sought his opinions, and he corresponded with many important people. Martini's musical compositions include symphonies, sacred works, and five harpsichord concertos (three in 1746, 1750,

1752). There is a concerto with harpsichord obbligato, and the *Symphonia* (1754) for violin and harpsichord obbligato. Only Martini's harpsichord concertos lack his usual signature F. G. B. M. (Frate Giovanni Battista Martini); possibly the secular usage of harpsichords caused this composer of sacred music to withhold his usual signature. Concerto movements are in ritornello and binary forms, and orchestra parts are for two violins, viola, basso continuo, and sometimes oboes, horns, or trumpets.

Giovanni Pergolesi (1710–1736) is famed for the comic opera *La Serva Padrona*. His concerto is for two harpsichords and strings.

Nicolò Jomelli (1714–1774), central to mid-eighteenth century changes in the singer-dominated opera, lived in Naples, Bologna, Venice, Rome, and Stuttgart. He left three harpsichord concertos.

Quirino Gasparini (1721–1778), student of Martini, became a composer of sacred vocal music. A concerto for harpsichord/organ shows *galant* traits.

Domenico Auletta (1723–1753), church organist and composer, left three harpsichord concertos.

Orazio Mei (1731–1788) was a fine harpsichordist and composer of church music. He composed three concertos for harpsichord/piano.

Vincenzo Manfredini (1737–1799), theorist and opera composer, settled with his brother Giuseppe in St. Petersburg at the court of Peter Fedorovich. In St. Petersburg, or during a trip to Italy, he may have composed one harpsichord concerto.

Giovanni Serini (fl 1740–1756) worked as the *kapellmeister* to Count Wilhelm zu Schaumberg-Lippe in Buckeburg, where he taught J. C. F. Bach. He composed six harpsichord concertos.

Allessandro Felici (1742–1772), known in some Italian cities as an opera composer, worked his adult life as a teacher in his father's music school. His harpsichord concerto with violin obbligato contains writing that is a precursor of Mozart's harpsichord style. Alessandro Felici is not the Turin composer Felice Allessandri.

Felice Alessandri (1747–1798), not the composer Alessandro Felici, lived mainly in Turin and a short time in Paris and Berlin. He gained recognition as an opera composer, conductor, and harpsichordist. He left six harpsichord concertos (pub. 1769).

Francesco Durante (1684–1755) helped establish and develop the Neapolitan school of composition. He left one harpsichord concerto (ca. 1750).

Portugal

Carlos de Seixas (1704–1742), organist at the royal chapel in Lisbon, was the leading musical person in Portugal. He was a friend of Domenico Scarlatti, and much of his fame rests on his sonatas for harpsichord. His concerto for harpsichord and strings has a thin texture, with most of the keyboard activty in the right-hand part. Much of Seixas' music was destroyed in the earthquake of 1755.

France

Keyboard concertos were important in Germany, England, and, to some extent, Italy and other isolated areas, but the suite so dominated French keyboard music that concertos found little acceptance among musicians. In 1739, someone known only as an *Ami du Clavier* printed a set of six concertos. Three concertos follow Vivaldi's model, but the middle movements have a suite-like character. The manuscript is in the *Bibliotheque National.*

The *Concert Spirituel,* established in 1725 by Anne Danican Philidor (1681–1728), was the important concert series noted for progressive music and the finest musicians of Europe. Violin concertos were the favored solo genre until Claude Balbatre performed an organ concerto with orchestra accompaniment in 1755. Afterward, musicians performed organ concertos frequently and probably performed the works at the harpsichord, as was the practice in England.

Michel Corrette (1709–1795), organist, teacher and author, is the earliest-known concerto composer in Paris. He left at least two keyboard concertos, op. 26 (pub. 1756), influenced by popular music, French baroque music, and a *galant* style similar to J. C. Bach. Probably, Corrette performed the concertos with the orchestra he conducted.

In the third quarter of the eighteenth century, Parisian audiences and musicians heard concertos by Wagenseil, Haydn, Eichner, and J. C. Bach. Concertos by north German composers found little reception in Paris and Parisians knew only one concerto by C. P. E. Bach. French audiences became interested in the keyboard concerto after the piano replaced the harpsichord in Viennese classic concertos. The lack of French interest in harpsichord concertos is apparent in music composed by foreign musicians in France. Italian composers found a receptive environment for stage works and violin concertos, and German composers a place for symphonic compositions. Many composers settled temporarily in Paris, but almost invariably they composed harpsichord concertos in countries more receptive to the genre. French musicians composed and performed operas because the government subsidized the genre and musicians could expect a reasonable income not easily available in other musical mediums.

The clavecin was the favored French keyboard instrument when musicians in other areas of Europe were adopting the piano. Johann Eckard (1735–1808) probably introduced the piano to Parisian audiences. While he did not compose piano concertos, he was the first composer in Paris to write sonatas specifically for the piano.

Giuseppe Jozzi (ca. 1710–1770), Italian castrato soprano, harpsichordist, and composer, sang in Rome, Venice, Milan, Bologna, and London. In London, he claimed to be a student of Alberti, whose sonatas he performed as his own. Walsh discovered the hoax and published the sonatas under Alberti's name. In London or Paris, Jozzi composed one harpsichord concerto (pub. 1758).

Johann Schobert (ca. 1720/40–1767), German harpsichordist and composer, arrived in Paris in 1760 and worked for Louis François de Bourbon, Prince of Conti. In 1908, a document provided his first name, and his birth place may be Silesia. Tragically, most of his family died after eating poison mushrooms. In Paris, he composed five harpsichord concertos: op. 11 (1767), op. 12 (1767), the *Pastorale,* op. 13 (ca.

1768), op. 15 (1774), and op. 18 (ca. 1776). One concerto (pub. ca. 1768) is in an edition without an opus number; some sources list the concerto as op. 19. The concertos have ritornello form and elements of classic concerto form with *galant* melodic characteristics. Schobert's style draws upon Italian, Austrian, German, and French styles. Orchestra parts include two violins, bass, and horns *ad libitum;* op. 18 omits horns. The brilliant keyboard style has arpeggios and scales moving over wide ranges. The cross-hand patterns of Schobert seem to have influenced young Mozart's music.

Friedrich Edelmann (1749–1794) possibly composed the earliest piano concerto (ca. 1774–1786) in France.

Belgium

Pieter van den Bosch (ca. 1736–1803), Dutch composer and organist at an Antwerp church, was one of Antwerp's leading musicians and a highly praised teacher. He composed six harpsichord/harp divertissements, op. 2 (pub. ca. 1762), and four harpsichord/organ concertos, op. 3 (pub. ca. 1769), in three movements.

The Netherlands

Nicolaas Lentz (ca. 1720–1780) composed at least one keyboard concerto.

Jean-Jacques Robson (baptized 1723–1785), south Netherlands composer and organist, directed choral music at the collegiate church of St. Germain. His harpsichord concerts, op. 4 (pub. 1762), and sonatas require an orchestra of two violins, viola, and bass.

Jean-Joseph Boutmy (1725–1782), organist, composer, and harpsichordist, worked in Ghent until the 1760s and then as an organist for the Portuguese ambassador at The Hague. Probably he composed six harpsichord concertos late in life. The concertos fit the piano and contain developmental passages, rondos or minuets as final movements and written cadenzas.

Norway

Johan Berlin (1714–1787), German-born organist and composer, was the head of the fire service and water works and a cartographer and architect. He served as the city musician and organist at the Trondheim Cathedral from 1740. He composed six harpsichord concertos.

England

England had a tradition of relying on foreign composers and performers, who made significant contributions to the concerto literature, while native English composers devoted less effort to the genre.

Giuseppe Sammartini (1695–1750), elder brother of composer Giovanni Battista Sammartini, arrived in London in 1728. He was the best oboist in Europe, and in London he ranked among the finest composers. Walsh printed Sammartini's four concertos (pub. 1754) as "Giuseppe St. Martini's Concertos for the Harpsichord or Organ." The concertos, op. 9, show the influence of the Italian concerto style of Corelli and Geminiana. The concerto no. 1 has movements in the slow-fast-slow-fast scheme similar to Corelli's church sonatas, and the other three concertos have the fast-slow-fast movements of Italian solo concertos. Baroque features include figured bass, ritornello form, and contrapuntal textures. Emerging *galant* style appears in written ornaments and the dominance of melodic right-hand parts in the keyboard writing. Orchestra parts include two violins for two players on each part, cello, and bass. His brother's name mistakenly appeared on this set of concertos; Giovanni Batista Sammartini did not compose harpsichord or piano concertos.

Giovanni Lampugnani (1706–1786) settled in London in 1743 to conduct the Italian Opera. He composed three harpsichord concertos.

Vincenzo Ciampi (1719–1762) arrived in London in 1748 to direct the Italian comic opera company. He composed six concertos, op. 7 (pub. 1756), for organ/harpsichord and two additional concertos for organ/harpsichord.

Karl Abel (1723–1787), student of J. S. Bach, was a noted viola da gamba player and composer of symphonies in the Dresden Court Orchestra. In 1759, he traveled to London and became a court musician of Queen Charlotte. By the time J. C. Bach arrived in London, Abel was an established gamba performer and composer. The two musicians quickly became friends and joined efforts for the important Bach-Abel Concerts at the Carlisle House, Almack's, and Hanover Square Rooms. Many harpsichord and piano concertos of Bach and Abel probably were performed at those concerts.

Abel composed six concertos, op. 11 (ca. 1770), for harpsichord or pianoforte. Judging by the numerous publications, these concertos enjoyed a degree of popularity. The two-movement concertos are for an orchestra of two violins and cello. First movements are an allegro and second movements usually are a *menuetto, tempo di menuetto* or rondo. The classic concerto form in the first movements has a variety of expositions, developments, and recapitulations.

Johann Christian Bach (1735–1782), youngest son of J. S. Bach and Anna Magdalena, became known as the "London" Bach. An early teacher of Johann Christian probably was Johann Schneider, a former student of J. S. Bach, or Johann Christoph Altnikol, who became J. S. Bach's son-in-law in 1749. His mother's inability to provide support after his father's death caused Johann Christian to live with his brother C. P. E. Bach in Berlin from 1750. He had a first-rate music education, and a variety of experiences with musicians and at events at the court of Frederick the Great. He went to Italy in 1754 to study with Padre Giovanni Battista Martini of Bologna, and he played organ at the Milan Cathedral; he become known as the "Milan" Bach. In 1762, he went to the King's Theatre in London and became the music master to the queen in 1763. He was the premiere pianist and composer in London, and his fame extended across much of Europe.

Charles Sanford Terry's *John Christian Bach*[1] provides T. numbers for Bach's music; T.298 means page 298. Since two or more unrelated concertos or other compositions may appear on the same page, some T. numbers are the same for unrelated works.

Concertos in two movements are unique to composers living in London. Bach composed eighteen concertos in three sets of six concertos: opp. 1 (1763), 7 (1770) and 13 (1777). In op. 1, T.292, concertos 1, 2, 3, and 5 are in two movements and concertos 4 and 6 are in three movements. In op. 7, T.293, concertos 1, 2, 3, and 4 are in two movements and concertos 5 and 6 are in three movements. In op. 13, T.295, concertos 1, 3, 5, and 6 are in two movements and concertos 2 and 4 are in three movements. Concertos in two movements typically have a fast first movement in *allegro* or *allegretto* and the second movement is a *menuetto, tempo di minuetto,* or *rondeau.* Concertos in three movements continue the Italian fast-slow-fast scheme. Both movements in two-movement concertos are in the same key, and in three-movement concertos the middle movement typically is in subdominant or relative minor.

In op. 1, T.292, concerto 6, "God Save the King" is the theme for variations in the third movement. In op. 13, T.295, concerto 4, Bach presents the Scotch air "The Yellow Haired Laddie" (See ex. 2–1) with variations (See ex. 2–2); Haydn liked this concerto so much he arranged it for solo piano in ca. 1792. In op. 1, concertos 4 and 6 have indications of "Concerto IV. o Sinfonia" and "Sinfonia," respectively, at the end of the third movements; three-movement concertos in opp. 7 and 13 lack these terms. Possibly, the terms reflect a difference in style, or Bach's conception of the works as symphonies he had completed as concertos to make a set of six concertos according to contemporary practice.

Most of Bach's concertos composed in London are in classic concerto form. Op.

Example 2–1. J. C. Bach Concerto, op. XIII, no. 4, mvt. 3, mm. 1–8

Example 2–2. J. C. Bach Concerto, op. XIII, no. 4, mvt. 3, mm. 44–53

1 contains transitional concertos with characteristics of classic concerto form and ritornello form. Opp. 7 and 13 are in classic concerto form with expositions containing first and second keys, developments built on material from the exposition and, in op. 13, recapitulations beginning in the orchestra. The last concertos contain fully established classic concerto form.

The concertos, op. 13, have Bach's largest concerto orchestra. Two oboes and two French horns *ad libitum* double and reinforce the string parts.

J. C. Bach composed the five concertos, T.298 (ca. 1750–1754), while living and studying with C. P. E. Bach in Berlin. These early works show a strong influence of his brother and other Berlin composers. In Bach's four-ritornello plan, ritornellos 2, 3, and 4 contain material from ritornello 1, and sometimes ritornello material appears in solo parts. Orchestra parts for the typical Berlin concerto are two violins, viola, and bass. Some sources list these concertos as P.390, meaning shelf 390 at the German Marburg Library; P. is for *partituren* (full score).

The harpsichord concerto, T.300 (1756–1762?), from Bach's years in Milan, has three movements and the four-ritornello form. In the three concertos, T.300, two are for harpsichord (one by ca. 1760) and one is for piano. Manuscript P.391 at the Berlin *Staabibliothek* is a version of T.284 and T.290. Two harpsichord concertos, T.297 (by 1760), may belong to J. C. F. Bach or C. P. E. Bach. The six harpsichord concertos, T.299 (?), in one movement and inscribed "Concerto de Bach" or "De Bach," may belong to F. Bach. Other concertos are T.301 for clavecin, T.301 for harpsichord, and one for keyboard; the harpsichord concerto may be a late work.

Bach intended many compositions, including the concertos, for performance by well-qualified amateurs. Charles Burney described Bach's piano music as "such as ladies can execute with little trouble"; at that time many people considered the piano an instrument for female performers. Bach described himself as composing to live, and his brother C. P. E. Bach as living to compose. Bach liked a life of style and usually spent money as fast as he earned it; thus, he composed music for people who might purchase the greatest number of copies, the public. Technical requirements include scales, arpeggios, thirds, and broken chords.

Notes

1. Charles Sanford Terry, *Johann Christian Bach,* 2nd ed. (London: Oxford University Press, 1967).

Part II

Mozart Through Beethoven (ca. 1770–1827)

Chapter 3

Germany and Austria

Germany

Carlmann Kolb (ca. 1703–1765), ordained priest and organist at the Benedictine Abbey, composed a sinfonia for harpsichord and orchestra.

Johann Seyffarth (1711–1796), highly regarded court composer and violinist, left a harpsichord concerto.

Gottfried Homiliu (1714–1785) was a German composer, organist, and *kantor* important in Protestant church music. Many of his works are religious, and there is one harpsichord concerto.

Johann Rolle (1716–1785) played organ and composed highly successful sacred vocal music. He left about seven keyboard concertos (ca. 1767–1778), including three published as "trois concerts," op. 1 (ca. 1782).

Anton Benda (1722–1795) joined many talented musicians drawn to Gotha because of the high-quality musical dramas. He composed two harpsichord concertos (1779), the concertino (ca. 1783), and seven harpsichord concertos, one of which is lost. His concertos display a considerable degree of virtuosity.

Jakob Kleinknecht (1722–1794) worked as a court composer, flutist, and *kapellmeister* in Bayreuth and Ansbach. His sinfonia concertant has a keyboard obbligato.

Johann Lang (1722–1798) played in the orchestra of the prince-bishop of Augsburg, and then worked for Clemens Wenzeslaus, elector of Trier, at Ehrenbreitstein and, eventually, Koblenz. Lang performed, composed and earned money publishing his own thirty-one easy harpsichord concertos (ca. 1766–1784) that appear intended for the keyboard-playing public. A complete list of concertos is in Shelley George Davis' dissertation, "The Keyboard Concertos of Johann Georg Lang (1722–1798)."[1] Many of his orchestrations include horns, flutes, oboes, and strings.

Johann Klöffler (1725–1790) performed as a musician in the courts at Bentheim and Steinfurt. His music in the Mannheim style circulated throughout Europe and England. He composed a concerto (pub. ca. 1784) for harpsichord/piano and a harpsichord concerto.

Georg Löhleim (1725–1781) worked as a German instrumentalist, teacher, composer, and frequent violin or piano soloist with the local orchestra. In 1779, he was the *konzertmeister* at Danzig (now Gdansk, Poland). He composed three harpsichord concertos (1775), three harpsichord/piano concertos (ca. 1781), the harpsichord concerto, op. 8, no. 1 (1781), and two harpsichord concertos, with one titled "Grand." His *Clavier-Schule* (part I, 1765; part II, 1788), based on C. P. E. Bach's *Versuch,* appeared in many editions for almost a hundred years.

Joseph Rouchemoulin (1727–1801), French violinist and composer, worked for the prince of Thurn and Taxis when he composed a harpsichord concerto. He also left three piano concertos.

Anton Adlgasser (1729–1777) worked as a court and cathedral organist and harpsichordist. He left two keyboard concertos.

Georg Gruber (1729–1796), violinist, composed two harpsichord concertos.

Franz Pokory (1729–1794) studied in Mannheim with J. Stamitz, Richter and Holzbauer, and worked as the *kapellmeister* at Wallerstein and the court of Thurn and Taxis in Regensburg. His music includes about fifty harpsichord concertos.

Johann Christoph Friedrich Bach (1732–1795), the "Bückburg Bach," was a chamber musician to Count Wilhelm of Schumberg-Lippe. He composed five harpsichord concertos (1765, ca. 1787 for harpsichord/piano, 1787 lost, ca. 1787, 1792). Two concertos require a string quartet, and others have parts for two horns, two oboes, or two flutes.

Nathaniel Gruner (1732–1792) was a composer, *kantor* and teacher. His music includes the *divertissement concertant,* op. 1, for harpsichord, the *divertissement concertant,* op. 2, for harpsichord/piano, the harpsichord/piano concerto, op. 3, the lost harpsichord concerto, op. 5 (ca. 1778), and two harpsichord concertos without opus numbers. Many of his harpsichord concertos were still popular ten years after his death.

Ignaz von Beecke (1733–1803) was a soldier in the Swabian army and welcome in many cultural cities and courts of Europe. His musical career was mainly in the court of Philipp Karl of Oettingen. He composed at least twenty piano concertos, and Mozart composed cadenzas for some of Beecke's concertos.

Joseph Lederer (1733–1796) lived as a monk, teaching and composing at the monastery. His strong religious views inspired him to berate local Protestants, forcing monastery officials to discipline him. Although he devoted much effort to musical comedies and operettas, he composed a harpsichord concerto and engraved it on copper plates; the concerto and plates appear to be lost.

Franz Buttstett (1735–1814) played organ at Weikersheim and the St. Jakob church in Rothenburg. Although many compositions seem lost, the extant music is similar to the pre-classic style of C. P. E. Bach. He composed many clavier concertos.

Ernst Wolf (1735–1792), respected composer of many instrumental and vocal works, was the *kapellmeister* to Anna Amalia, duchess of Saxe-Weimar from 1772. He composed about twenty-five piano concertos written in the Mannheim style: two concertos (pub. 1777), one concerto, op. 3 (pub. 1783), one concerto, op. 4 (pub. 1783), and two concertos, opp. 7 and 8. Most concertos date between ca. 1777 and ca. 1785 and some appear to be lost.

Johann Kellner (1736–1803), organist and composer at the Lutheran church, composed in the *galant* style with an influence of C. P. E. Bach. The harpsichord/piano concertos include one as op. 3, one as op. 4, three as op. 5, three as op. 7, three as op. 8 (lost), and one as op. 11 (pub. ca. 1782).

Carl Westenholz (1736–1789), tenor, conductor, and composer, worked as the *konzertmeister* and director of the *Hofkapelle.* Under his direction, the court orchestra was among the finest in Germany. He left two harpsichord concertos (one 1775).

Johann Beckmann (1737–1792) played organ at the Nevenhauser Church and the *Stadkirche,* taught singing, and conducted the town's orchestra. Contemporaries considered him a great keyboard player. The six concertos, opp. 1 and 2 (pub. 1779 and 1780), are for harpsichord.

Michael Haydn (1737–1806), younger brother of Joseph Haydn, enjoyed a successful musical career. He was the *kapellmeister* to the Bishop of Grosswardein in Hungary (now Oradea, Romania) and worked in Salzburg as a court musician and *konzertmeister* to Archbishop Sigismund Schrattenbach from 1762. Lothar Perger's catalog[2] provides P. numbers for Haydn's music. His concerto, P.55 (ca. 1761), is for organ/harpsichord and viola, and his harpsichord concerto, P.57 (ca. 1776), is a fragment. A recent find is a concerto for organ/fortepiano, possibly by Michael or Joseph Haydn.

Ernst Eichner (1740–1777), noted composer and virtuoso bassoonist, was born and probably trained at Mannheim, and performed in the court orchestra in Zweibrücken. Eichner most likely composed two harp/harpsichord concertos (1770–1771). He performed frequently in Paris and London, where publishers were eager for new works. From 1772, he worked in Berlin in the court of Frederick the Great's nephew, Prince Frederick William. Judging by the French titles of other works, some published concertos are from Paris, but the location of compositions cannot be determined. His harpsichord concertos are opp. 5, 6 (pub. 1773), and 9. Eichner adds flutes and/or horns to the usual concerto orchestra of two violins, viola, and bass.

Johann Schwanenberger (ca.1740–1804) was a *kapellmeister* at the court of the Duke of Brunswick. His highly praised keyboard works include four harpsichord concertos.

Andrea Lucchesi (1741–1801), Italian, was the leading musician in Bonn during Beethoven's childhood, and young Beethoven substituted for Lucchesi as a church organist. Lucchesi worked from ca. 1772 in Bonn where the lost harpsichord concerto (pub. 1773) appeared in print.

Johann Naumann (1741–1801) was an admired composer and conductor of stage works in Venice, Dresden, Stockholm, and Copenhagen. His harpsichord/piano concerto (pub. ca. 1793) displays an influence of Viennese classic style.

Johann Sievers (1742–1806) was a pianist, composer and organist at the Magdeburg Cathedral. His sinfonia is for harpsichord and orchestra.

Wolfgang Haueisen (1744–1801) was an organist, conductor, and composer in Frankfurt, and a music publisher in Offenbach. He published his own clavier concertos, opp. 5 and 6 (1772–1773).

George Ritschel (1744–1805) played violin in the Mannheim orchestra and the court orchestra in Munich. He composed two harpsichord concertos in Mannheim or Munich.

Johann Michael Bach (1745–1820), unrelated to the J. S. Bach family, composed six clavier concertos, op. 1 (pub. 1767). Another of his keyboard concertos has a fugue on *B-A-C-H.*

Friedrich Benda (1745–1814), son of Franz Benda, worked as a violinist in the

Prussian court. A harpsichord concerto thought to be Friedrich Ludwig Benda's (1752–1792) belongs to F. Benda.

Georg Druschetzky (1745–1819) served as a military and court musician to Count Grassalkovicz in Pressburg. His piano concerto is in the classic style.

Johann von Königslöw (1745–1833), important oratorio composer at the *Marienkirch* from 1772, composed the harpsichord concerto (1781).

George Kreusser (1746–1810) was a composer, violinist, and *konzertmeister*. He and Abbé Sterkel were the most important composers living in Mainz during the latter part of the century. Kreusser contributed one harpsichord concerto (ca. 1775).

Christian Uber (1746–1812), lawyer and virtuoso glass-harmonica performer, used his home as a meeting place for many cultured citizens. For harpsichord and orchestra, he composed the divertimento (1777), six divertimentos (1783), and two concertos.

Johann Hässler (1747–1822), pianist and organist, worked at the *Barfüsserkirche* and toured Germany as a performer in the 1780s. He lived in London, St. Petersburg, and his last years in Warsaw, but he stayed the longest in Erfurt. He left a "grand" concerto, op. 50. He composed solely for keyboard in a style influenced by C. P. E. Bach.

Carl Junker (1748–1797), pastor and writer on the arts, composed a lost piano concerto, op. 1 (pub. 1783), and the harpsichord concerto, op. 2 (ca. 1783).

Christian Neefe (1748–1798), Beethoven's teacher, worked as an organist in Leipzig, Dresden, and Bonn from 1776. Mainly, his creative effort was in lieder and *singspiels,* and he had a harpsichord concerto (1782) published in Bonn.

Theodor von Schacht (1748–1823) worked as a court musician to Prince Carl Anselm of Thurn and Taxis. He left seven harpsichord concertos, a concerto for two harpsichords, a concerto for harpsichord and harp, and two concertos for harpsichord, four-hands.

Joseph Schuster (1748–1812) conducted in the Dresden court church, worked as a *kapellmeister* to the elector and, by 1792, became an appreciated composer throughout Germany. His music includes a concerto (1773) for two harpsichords, the harpsichord concerto (ca. 1793), and perhaps two more harpsichord concertos.

Johann Forkel (1749–1818), music historian and founder of modern musicology, gained an enviable reputation as a keyboardist. He left two harpsichord concertos (1776, 1783).

Hugo Franz Karl Alexander von Kerpen (1749–1802) was an amateur church and theater musician in Mainz and Worms. His piano concerto, op. 9 (pub. ca. 1800), is op. 10 in some sources.

Georg Vogler (known as Abbé Vogler, 1749–1814) was a pianist, organist, composer, and teacher. He was ordained in Rome and settled in Mannheim as a court chaplain and *kapellmeister*. He was an important theorist and praised for his organ improvisations. For piano and orchestra, he composed six easy concertos (1778–1789), a concerto for four hands (1781), three concertos (pub. 1782–1784), and one concerto for two pianos. The variations are *L'Air de Marbrough* (pub. 1791), the *Dole Vise* (pub. 1791), and the *Ah Que Dirae-Je Mama* (pub. 1807).

Johann Just (ca. 1750–1791?), pianist, violinist, and composer, served Prince William V of Orange. As a respected performer and composer in the classic style his music circulated throughout Europe and England. For harpsichord and orchestra, he composed six *concerts,* op. 4 (pub. ca. 1773), and three concertos, op. 10 (pub. 1780).

Franz Rosetti (1750–1792) worked in the court as a double-bass player and, later, as the *kapellmeister*. Besides symphonies, oratorios, operas, and sonatas, he left five piano concertos including op. 2 (pub. ca. 1783), op. 3, one (pub. ca. 1788), and one as number 3 (pub. 1796).

Abbé Johann Sterkel (known as Abbé Sterkel, 1750–1817) was a chaplain and pianist to the elector of Mainz at Aschaffenberg. In 1791, Beethoven traveled to meet and hear Sterkel perform, and he was the best performer the young Beethoven had heard to date. He composed six piano concertos (pub. 1785–1792). Some concertos appeared under as many as three opus numbers: concerto, op. 20 (pub. 1785), also is op. 18; three concertos, op. 16 (pub. 1788), include op. 20; and sometimes op. 31 is op. 24 (pub. 1789). Two concertos are opp. 20 and 42 (pub. 1785 and 1792).

Carl Stegmann (1751–1826) worked as a tenor, harpsichordist, conductor, and composer in many German towns. The publication of most concertos occurred in Bonn, probably after 1801. Among the concertos is one for piano, oboe, and bassoon, one for two pianos and violin, one for three pianos, and several other possible concertos.

Johann Reichardt (1752–1814) was a well known *kapellmeister* in the court of Frederick the Great. He composed several works for harpsichord/piano and orchestra: for *l'usage du beaux sexe* the six harpsichord/piano *concerts,* op. 1 (pub. 1774), the concerto (pub. 1773), two concertos (1772, 1774), a concerto (1773) for two keyboards, and a concerto (ca. 1773) for harpsichord and violin.

Otto von Kospoth (1753–1817), amateur composer working as a royal chamberlain and canon, played cello with Frederick the Great, and became an accomplished keyboardist. His greatest successes were *singspiels* for the Berlin theater. He left a harpsichord concerto, op. 6 (pub. ca. 1788), and the *serenata,* op. 19 (pub. 1794), for harpsichord/piano. He had bizarre spiritual ideas, including beliefs of indestructibility, that contributed to his death during a fire at his castle.

Johann Schicht (1753–1823) lived mostly in Leipzig, working as cantor at the *Thomasschule*. His piano concerto appears lost.

Anton Stamitz (ca. 1753–1798/1809), son of Johann Stamitz, went to Paris with his brother Carl to perform in the *Concert Spirituel.* The brothers were among the finest violinists in Europe, and Anton worked at the Royal Chapel Orchestra in Versailles. He left three piano concertos (pub. 1783) and two in manuscript.

Anton Becvarovsky (1754–1823), Czech composer and teacher, played organ at the *Hauptkirche* and worked as a *kapellmeister* to the duke. He composed a concerto, op. 1 (1793), and a *concerto en rondo,* op. 2 (1794). The concertos are not technically or musically demanding and possibly were for amateur pianists. From ca. 1799, he worked in Berlin as a private music teacher, and there he composed the concerto, op. 5 (1800), for piano and orchestra. His concertos, opp. 5 and 6, are serious compositions intended for accomplished pianists. One other concerto is in E-flat major. These are transitional concertos with elements of classic and early romantic styles.

Christian Kalkbrenner (1755–1806), father of the nineteenth century pianist and composer Friedrich Kalkbrenner, was a court musician and opera composer at the queen's court in Berlin and the court of Prince Heinrich at Rheinsberg, and a choirmaster for the Paris *Opéra*. He left a harpsichord concerto.

Johann Sixt (1757–1797) served as a court musician and composer. He composed two harpsichord concertos (1811, 1815).

Christoph Nopitsch (1758–1824) worked as the town's organist and music director. Some of his piano concertos are lost.

Franz Bühler (1760–1823), Benedictine monk at Donauwörth, directed choirs at Balzen and the Augsburg Cathedral. For piano he composed a grand concerto, op. 4 (pub. 1794), and the eight variations on the tune *Nicht nur im Lenz des Lebens*.

Franz Neubauer (ca. 1760–1795), Czech violinist and composer, stayed in several German towns before settling in Bückburg to work at a court chapel. He became a rival of J. C. F. Bach and later succeeded him as the *kapellmeister*. Mozart and Haydn influenced Neubauer's music, and among his compositions is a harpsichord/piano concerto (pub. 1798).

F. S. Sander (ca. 1760–1796), Czech composer and keyboardist, earned a living teaching music. His keyboard sonatas were well received by contemporaries and three (six?) harpsichord concertos are in two volumes (1783).

Johann Abeille (1761–1838) was an orchestra director and court music director for the Duke of Württemberg. He composed a harpsichord/piano concerto, op. 5, and a concerto, op. 6, for piano duet.

Carl Agthe (1762–1797) directed music at Hündelberg and became a well-known organist and harpsichordist in the court of Prince Friedrich Albrecht of Anhall-Bernburg in Ballenstedt. He enjoyed a fine reputation as a composer of *singspiels*, songs, and instrumental works, including a concerto for violin and harpsichord.

Johann Amon (1763–1825), the music director in Heilbronn, composed a clavier concerto, op. 34 (1805).

Franz Danzi (1763–1826) began playing cello in the Mannheim orchestra at age 15. From 1783, he was in Munich composing opera. His music includes a piano concerto, op. 4 (pub. ca. 1800), another piano concerto, and a harpsichord concerto.

Johann Demar (1763-ca. 1832), organist and composer at Weissenburg, eventually directed the *Grand Concert D'amateurs* in Orleans. His clavier concertos are the "Chasse," op. 1, the "Cosaque," op. 48, and op. 54.

Peter Ritter (1763–1846) joined the Mannheim orchestra as a cellist, became the concertmaster, and rose to conductor in 1803. He composed two harpsichord concertos (1781, 1780s) and possibly one piano concerto.

Georg Grosheim (1764–1841) worked in Kassel as a violist, music director, teacher, writer, and publisher. In 1816 or 1817, he corresponded with Beethoven to encourage the adoption of the first movement of the "Moonlight" sonata to J. G. Seume's poem *Die Beterin*. Grosheim's three piano concertos are lost.

Friedrich Himmel (1765–1814) composed a piano concerto, op. 25 (1808), and two other piano concertos scored for small orchestra.

Gottlieb Köhler (1765–1833), flutist, left a clavier concerto.

Daniel Steibelt (1765–1823), brilliant pianist, composed extremely popular piano music known in Germany, Paris, London, and St. Petersburg. In Vienna, he had an uncomfortable experience in a musical contest with Beethoven, but this was the only low point in his musical career. Steibelt earned a fortune from his compositions and performances with his tambourine-playing wife; he would extemporize or play written music at the piano, while she danced and played the tambourine. Steibelt composed eight piano concertos in many different cities: no. 1 (pub. 1796); no. 2 (pub. ca. 1796); no. 3 *L'Orange,* op. 33 (1799), also called the "Storm Concerto"; no. 4 (pub. ca. 1800); no. 5 *A la chasse,* op. 64 (pub. 1802); no. 6 *Le Voyage au Mount St. Bernard* (pub. ca. 1816); no. 7 *Grand Military Concerto, dans le genre des Grecs* (pub. ca. 1816) with two orchestras; and no. 8 (1820) with chorus and the *Bacchanalian Rondo.* The "Storm Rondo" from concerto no. 3 was very popular and a model for Beethoven's symphony no. 6, *Pastoral.* The "Storm Concerto" has the most extensive orchestration for a concerto of its time: two flutes, two oboes, two clarinets, two bassoons, two horns, two trumpets, trombone, timpani, and strings. Generally, the winds double the string parts and play only in the tuttis. Probably, the slow movement of concerto no. 5 is on a musical theme by Mary, Queen of Scots. Steibelt knew more about the use of the piano pedals than anyone between Dussek and Chopin.

Johann Bürgmuller (1766–1824), theater musician, founded the Lower Rhine Music Festival in 1818 that still is an ongoing musical event. Probably, he composed his piano concerto in Weimar, considering his longevity in the city.

Johann Fleischmann (1766–1798) served as a cabinet secretary to Duke George I of Saxe-Meiningen. He composed a harpsichord/piano concerto, op. 1 (1794), the piano concerto, op. 4 (1797), and a concerto for keyboard and violin.

August Müller (1767–1817) was a composer and organist at various churches in Magdeburg and Leipzig and the court conductor in Weimar from 1810. He and his wife Elizabeth Catherina frequently soloed in Mozart's clavier concertos, and she may have assisted Müller in writing the first published guide to Mozart's clavier concertos, *Anweisung zum Genauen Vortrage der Mozartschen Clavierconcerto/hauptsächlich in Absicht Richtiger Applicatur* (Guide to the Accurate Performance of the Mozartean Piano Concertos/Principally with Respect to Correct Fingering).[3] Müller's concertos, opp. 1 and 21 (pub. ca. 1792 and 1802) show the influence of Mozart's concertos.

Christian Schwencke (1767–1822), composer, harpsichordist, mathematician, and editor, succeeded C. P. E. Bach as the Hamburg *stadkantor* in 1788. He composed two piano concertos and, at age 11, performed a harpsichord concerto by his father Johann Gottlieb Schwencke (1744–1823).

Friedrich Kuhlau (1768–1832) probably composed his concerto, op. 7 (1810), in Hamburg. He emigrated to Copenhagen in 1813 to avoid military conscription, and in Denmark he became the most important composer of music in the late classic, early romantic style. He probably composed the second concerto in Copenhagen; the concerto burned when fire destroyed his home.

Walburga Willman (1769–1835), possible piano student of Mozart, toured Europe as a pianist beginning at a young age. Her piano concerto (1808) is lost.

Georg Zulehner (1770–1841), music publisher, composed the concerto *facille,* op. 5, no. 2 (ca. 1817), for piano.

Anton Liste (1772–1832) toured as a concert pianist. His "grand" concerto, op. 13 (ca. 1822), is in the form of a fantasy.

Karl Zeuner (1775–1841) toured Europe as a pianist and taught in Paris, Vienna, St. Petersburg, and Dresden. He left two piano concertos, opp. 12 and 13.

Johann Nepomuk Hummel (1778–1837), a Hungarian born in Pressburg (now Bratislava, Czechoslovakia), is important in the evolution of the piano concerto of his teacher and friend Mozart from the classic to the romantic style of Chopin and other early nineteenth-century composers. Beginning in ca. 1787 with his first public performances as a child prodigy, Hummel rose to a position of great renown as a pianist and composer. Toward the end of his life, he faded quickly from public esteem because of his outdated classic style. He worked for Prince Esterhazy, lived in Vienna until 1816, worked in Stuttgart from 1816 to 1819, then resided in Weimar, where he composed many piano works.

Accurately dating Hummel's music is nearly impossible, and the publication of some works occurred up to ten years after composition. His concerto, op. 73, is an example of the dating problems. The piano concerto (pub. ca. 1816), based on the mandolin concerto (1799), contains elements of the mandolin version that are inconsistent with his later style: *ad libitum* oboes and horns, simple and straightforward Mozartian melodies and harmonies, and a thin orchestration from an era when orchestral color is less important in concertos.

Two concertos (1790s, 1790s?) are in manuscript. Seven concertos have opus numbers: op. 17 (pub. ca. 1805) for piano and violin; op. 34 (pub. ca. 1811), also published as op. 36; op. 73 (pub. ca. 1816), originally a mandolin concerto (1799); op. 85 (ca. 1816); op. 89 (1819), also published as op. 90, *Les Adieus;* op. 110 (1814), for Hummel's farewell concert in Paris; and op. 113 (1827). His concerto (1833) has the title *Posthumous Concerto* no. 1; the orchestration is lost. The variations are op. 6 (pub. ca. 1798) on a theme from Vogler's opera *Castor et Pollux;* op. 97 (ca. 1820); and op. 115 (1830) based on a *singspiel* theme from *Das Fest der Handwerker*. The "rondo Brilliants" are op. 56 (pub. ca. 1814); op. 98 (1823); and "Le Retour à Londres," op. 127 (1830). Other compositions are the fantasy *Oberons Zaberhorn,* op. 116 (1829), and the *Gesellshafts Rondo,* op. 117 (1829). The cadenzas, op. 4 (pub. 1798), are for seven Mozart concertos. Hummel arranged Mozart's piano concertos K.316a, K.456, K.466, K.482, K.491, K.503, and K.537.

To Mozartian melodies, Hummel adds grace notes and scale lines with various numbers of notes per beat. The melodic treatment is an outgrowth of improvisations contemporaries considered superior to his compositions. Harmony in the early works is simple and follows Mozart's models, while later works present highly chromatic harmonies. Frequently, accompaniments are eighth-note repeated chords in the left-hand part; this type of accompaniment is common in the concertos of Weber, Moscheles, Kalkbrenner, Field, and Chopin. Hummel contributed the arpeggio left-hand part that became a norm in nineteenth-century piano music. Hummel's concerto form follows Mozart's ideas, with features of Beethoven appearing in the first movements of the concertos, opp. 85 and 89. A rondo is the finale in all concertos. Hummel provides written cadenzas, and opp. 85 and 89 contain cadenzas with orchestra accompaniments. Hummel treats the orchestra as an accompaniment medium, as in concertos of Weber, Moscheles, Dussek, Kalkbrenner, Field, and Chopin.

The concerto, op. 85, remained popular through the nineteenth century and into the twentieth century. As a boy, Chopin learned the concertos, opp. 85 and 89, and in various solo works and concertos Chopin borrowed passages directly from Hummel's music.

In the *Pianoforte School* (ca. 1822–1825), Hummel explains his preference for light action Viennese pianos and certain fingerings. In the same era that Dussek and Clementi advanced pedal technique, Hummel believed pedals should be used only in slow movements.

Johann Clasing (1779–1829), teacher and composer, composed three *Fantasien* for piano and orchestra.

Johann Schmidt (1779–1853) trained in law and took a legal position with the government. Early in life he made some appearances as a pianist and his concerto (pub. 1798) was for his own use.

Conradin Kreutzer (1780–1849), successful opera composer and pianist, was a court conductor in Stuttgart and for Prince von Fürstenburg at Donaueberg. His works for piano and orchestra include the concerto, op. 42 (pub. 1819?), the concerto, op. 50 (pub. 1822?), the concerto, op. 65 (pub. 1825?), and a set of variations, op. 35.

Carl Eule (1783–1827) worked as a music director and composer of operas and piano music. His "Concertino Mêlé de Themes Favoris Variés," op. 7, is for clavier.

Conrad Berg (1785–1852) studied at the Paris *Conservatoire* and settled in Strausburg as a piano teacher. He composed three piano concertos; concerto no. 2, op. 21, is in an edition dated 1820.

Carl Marie von Weber (1786–1826) was one of the great pianists of his day. F. W. Jähns' *Carl Maria von Weber in seinen Werken*[4] provides J. numbers for Weber's music. For piano and orchestra Weber composed the concerto no. 1, op. 11, J.98 (1810); the concerto no. 2, op. 32, J.155 (1812); and the *koncertstück* (concerto no. 3), op. 79, J.282 (1821).

Weber's concertos display runs, arpeggios, leaps, and a variety of other idiomatic virtuoso techniques (See ex. 3–1). The concerto no. 2 shows the influence of Beethoven's concerto no. 5, with the first and third movements in E-flat major and the slow movement in B major. The *konzertstück* is important as the first one-movement concerto, an idea appreciated by Liszt. Originally, Weber intended the work to have a program: allegro—"separation," adagio—"lamento," and finale—"deepest grief, confused return, and jubilation." Weber disliked program music and now the composition is without a program. The *konzertstück* contains the first glissando (See ex. 3–2) and octave glissando (See ex. 3–3) in a concerto. In ca. 1852, Liszt arranged Weber's *Polacca brilliant,* op. 72, J.268 (1819), for piano and orchestra. Isidor Seiss (1840–1905), piano teacher at the Cologne Conservatory and composer of educational piano works, revised Weber's concerto no. 2.

Ludwig Böhner (1787–1860), called the "Thuringian Mozart" for his precociousness, resided in Gena from 1808. He knew Goethe and was the model for E. T. A. Hoffmann's *Capellmeister Kreisler* that inspired Schumann's *Kreisleriana.* In 1820, a serious emotional condition incapacitated his creative powers. His piano

Example 3–1. Weber *Konzertstück,* op. 79, mm. 44–51

concertos are op. 7 (1808), op. 11 (1812), op. 8 (1813), op. 13 (1815), op. 14 (ca. 1815), and the lost concerto (ca. 1819) for two pianos.

Johann Todt (fl. late eighteenth cent.) served Count Vollrath of Löwenstein as a valet and chamber musician. He composed about six harpsichord concertos (ca. 1780s).

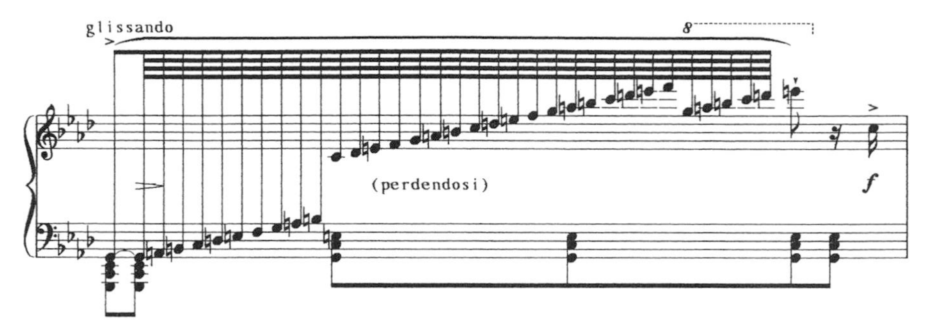

With permission of the International Music Company.

Example 3–2. Weber *Konzertstück,* op. 79, m. 52

With permission of the International Music Company.

Example 3–3. Weber *Konzertstück,* op. 79, "Tempo di Marcia," mm. 34–35

Carl Schnabel (1809–1881), esteemed pianist and composer, worked in the family piano manufacturing business that produced pianos prized by Hummel and Liszt. He composed a piano concerto.

Austria

Mozart's father Leopold Mozart (1719–1787) worked on a piano concerto, but only the autograph sketches are extant.

Joseph Steffan (1726–1787), Czech musician, studied harpsichord and composition with Wagenseil. After settling in Vienna in ca. 1741, he became a prominent teacher. His concertos are unusual in the use of expressive minor-key slow introductions shared by the orchestra and harpsichord. He is important in the evolution of the ritornello concerto into the sonata concerto, and his concertos are among the most advanced in Vienna before Mozart. Steffan composed six harpsichord/harp concertos, op. 3 (pub. ca. 1773), a lost harpsichord or piano concerto (1771), and thirty-seven concertos for harpsichord or piano. Haydn's arrangement of a Steffan harpsichord concerto is in the Hoboken catalog as XVIII:G2.

Franz Joseph Haydn (1732–1809) composed an insignificant number of compositions for piano and orchestra when compared with the volume and quality of his other instrumental works. Anthony van Hoboken's *Joseph Haydn: Thematisch-bibliographisches Werkverzeichnis*[5] provides Hob. numbers for Haydn's music. Hoboken's numbering system uses a Roman numeral for compositions of one genre and an Arabic number for a particular work. Group XVIII is Hoboken's number for Haydn's clavier concertos. Interesting inconsistencies of information in the Hoboken catalog may be found in Landon's *Haydn Chronicle and Works*.[6]

The organ/harpsichord concerto no. 1 (1765) may not be Haydn's. Landon lists the organ/harpsichord concerto no. 2 (1767) as the organ concerto (ca. 1752–1755). The concerto no. 3 (ca. 1765) is for harpsichord. The concerto no. 4 (1782) is in editions for clavecin/fortepiano/harp. Haydn named the concerto no. 5 (1763) a divertimento and Landon lists it as an organ concerto (ca. 1752–1755). The concerto no. 6 (1766) is for clavier and violin. Landon lists the concerto no. 7 (1766) as the organ concerto (ca. 1756). Haydn named the concerto no. 8 (1766) a divertimento and Landon calls it an organ concerto (ca. 1751–1755). Probably, the concerto no. 9 (1767) is for harpsichord. Landon lists the concerto no. 10 (1771) as an organ concerto (ca. 1752–1755). Publications of the concerto no. 11 (1782) are for clavecin or piano. Concertos of doubtful authenticity are Es1, F1, F2, F3 and F4. The concerto G1 may belong to Joseph Georg Haroldi and Steffan arranged the concerto G2 for two harpsichords/pianos.

An accurate count of Haydn's clavier concertos is difficult. Only three of approximately twelve authentic concertos reached publication during his lifetime, and many spurious works appeared under Haydn's name.

In the concertos, Haydn's keyboard writing is not at the high level of Mozart or Beethoven. The most difficult lines are in the right hand, with the left hand merely doubling the orchestra bass line. Technical demands include arpeggios and scale passages (See ex. 3–4).

Possibly, Haydn composed the early clavier concertos for organ instead of harpsichord. During the 1750s and 1760s, performances of organ concertos occurred during the middle of Sunday church services in the Austrian-Bohemian-Bravarian region. There is evidence Haydn planned some of his early clavier concertos for church services. The keyboard technique fits both the pedal-less *positive* organ and harpsichord—the keyboard ranges are similar.

In Haydn's early works, there is no clear distinction between concertos and chamber music. Some divertimentos are concertinos and some became concertos or concertinos in publications. Generally, concertinos have a fast-slow-fast order of movements, and divertimentos have a fast-minuet-fast pattern. Generally two violins and cello provide an accompaniment in divertimentos, as is common in concertos.

Group XIV is Hoboken's number for Haydn's clavier divertimentos. The divertimento no. 1 (1766) accompanied by violin, bass, and two horns is in an edition as the

Example 3–4. Haydn Concerto, Hob.XVIII/4, mvt. 1, mm. 174–186

sonata, op. 4 (1776), with accompaniment. The accompaniment for the lost divertimento no. 2 (1769) is barytonhorn and two violins. The divertimento no. 3 (ca. 1767) appeared as a concerto, a concertino-divertimento, or a concertino, and the divertimento no. 4 (1764) appeared as a concerto or concertino. Possibly, the accompaniment for the divertimentos nos. 5 (1766) and 6 (1767) is two violins and cello. Landon lists the divertimentos nos. 7, 8, and 9 (all 1766) as concertinos. Only the harpsichord part for the divertimento no. 10 (?) is extant. The divertimento no. 11 (1760) is in publications as a concerto and a concertino, and the divertimentos nos. 12 (1766) and 13 (?) are in publications as concertos. The divertimento C1 (1772) and C2 (?) may not be Haydn's. The divertimento C3 may be Wagenseil's and Es1 may be Steffan's. The accompaniment for the divertimento F1 is flute, viola, and cello, and it may belong to Joseph Aloys Schmillbaur. Oboe, violin, viola and cello provide the accompaniment in the divertimento F2, and the work may belong to J. C. Bach. The accompaniment for the lost divertimento G1 is two violins or violas(?) and bass. Not in the Hoboken catalog is the divertimento D1 of questionable sources.

Giovanni Matielli (ca. 1733–1805), student of Wagenseil, composed at least one piano concerto.

Leopold Hofmann (1738–1793) studied keyboard with Wagenseil and gained fame as a church musician at St. Peter's Cathedral and as a composer of instrumental music. He left close to sixty harpsichord concertos and a concerto for two harpsichords. In 1771, he composed a harpsichord concerto in collaboration with Joseph Haydn.

Carl Ditters von Dittersdorf (1739–1799) is important in the development of the Viennese classic style. Among his strongest compositions are many symphonies and *singspiels*. He left three concertos (pub. 1772), another concerto (1776), and his last concerto (1799). Some concertos display elements of the classic form mixed with features of baroque ritornello structure.

Jan Vanhal (1739–1813), Czech composer, traveled to Vienna in 1760 with Countess Schaffgotsch. He studied with Dittersdorf, and quickly became a musical favorite of the nobility. Many of his compositions appeared throughout Europe and, by 1800, in the United States. Early compositions are in *galant* style and later works in classic style. His writing is expressive (See ex. 3–5), and some passages are equally technical for both hands (See ex. 3–6). He composed five harpsichord/piano concertos (1785, op. 14 in 1788, 1788, ca. 1802, ca. 1809). Other compositions are three concertinos, several concertos, two concertos for harpsichord or organ, a harpsichord or organ concerto with solo violin, and a concerto for harpsichord and violin.

Marianne di Martínez (1744–1812), singer and pianist of Spanish descent, studied with Metastasio, Haydn, and Porpora. She composed two piano concertos.

Frantisek Adam Míca (1746–1811), Czech amateur composer, worked as a door-keeper and musician at the imperial court and later as a government official. Mozart and Emperor Joseph II liked his symphonies. He left a harpsichord concerto and a divertissement for harpsichord and orchestra.

Antonio Salieri (1750–1825), Italian composer and court *kapellmeister,* taught Beethoven, Schubert, Liszt, Czerny, Hummel, and Moscheles. He composed two concertos (1773).

Franz Hoffmeister (1754–1812), a German, settled in Vienna, where he opened a publishing house important for printing music by Mozart and Beethoven. His approximately fourteen harpsichord/piano concertos include op. 2, no. 1, op. 9 (pub. 1786), op. 16, and op. 24 (before 1784).

Wolfgang Amadeus Mozart (1756–1791) was an amazing child prodigy. His father Leopold, a noted violinist, composer, and teacher, took the young boy to perform

Example 3–5. Vanhal Concerto, op. 14, mvt. 2, mm. 30–43

before the empress in Vienna. The family proceeded on a three-year journey of Europe, with stops in important cities such as Paris, Versailles, and London. By age 12, Mozart was a serious composer and held the honorary position of concertmaster in the Salzburg Court. With his father, he went to Italy to meet Padre Martini and Jommelli, and after visiting Munich, Mannheim, and Paris, he settled in Salzburg and later in Vienna.

Ludwig von Köchel's *Chronologisch-Thematisches Verzeichnis Sämtlicher Tonwerke Wolfgang Amadé Mozarts*[7] provides K. numbers for Mozart's music. The

Example 3–6. Vanhal Concerto, op. 14, mvt. 1, mm. 47–51

noted Mozart scholar Alfred Einstein, brother of physicist Albert Einstein, revised Köchel's catalog in 1937 and again in 1947.

Mozart used the term clavier in the generic sense to mean keyboard. The earliest concertos are for harpsichord and later concertos are for piano. Some writers refer to all the clavier concertos as piano concertos, while others believe the harpsichord is the solo instrument in the concerto, K.365. Nathan Broder argues in *Mozart and the Clavier*[8] that piano concertos begin with K.414.

At age 4, Mozart composed the lost *Concerto per il Clavicembalo* (1760). The only information about the concerto is a description of Leopold Mozart's reaction to the young boy's effort.

Scholars considered the concertos, K.37, K.39, K.40, and K.41 (all 1767) original compositions by Mozart, but later findings indicate individual movements belong to other composers.[9] Borrowing musical material from other composers was a time-honored tradition, and usually such borrowings were taken from fashionable contemporary composers. Hermann Friedrich Raupach (1728–1778), German composer and conductor, met Mozart in Paris, where they improvised duets. Leontizi Honauer (ca. 1730–1790), German composer, performed in Paris and London as a pianist. Johann Gottfried Eckard (1735–1809), copper engraver, became a famous pianist in Paris. Johann Schobert (ca. 1720/40–1767), German harpsichordist and composer, lived in Paris from 1760. C. P. E. Bach (1714–1788) is the well-known "Berlin" Bach.

In the concerto, K.37, the first movement is from Raupach's harpsichord sonata, op. 1, no. 5, the second movement is from an unknown source, and the third movement is from Honauer's harpsichord sonata, op. 1, no. 3; possible composers of the unidentified movement may be Mozart himself, Le Grand, or Hochbrucker. In the concerto, K.39, the first movement is from Raupach's harpsichord sonata, op. 1, no. 1, the second movement is from Schobert's harpsichord sonata, op. 17, no. 2, and the third movement is from Raupach's harpsichord sonata, op. 1, no. 1. In the concerto, K.40, the first movement is from Honauer's harpsichord sonata, op. 2, no. 1, the second movement is from Eckard's harpsichord sonata, op. 1, no. 4, and the third movement is from C. P. E. Bach's *Musikalisches Mancherly;* a cadenza is in the first movement. In the concerto, K.41, the first movement is from Honauer's harpsichord sonata, op. 1, no. 1, the second movement is from Raupach's harpsichord sonata, op. 1, no. 1, and the third movement is from Honauer's harpsichord sonata, op. 1, no. 1. Mozart performed these concertos for several years.

When Mozart adapted sonata movements of other composers into concertos, he remained faithful to the original music; generally solo parts are like the original music. The concertos, K.37, K.39, K.40, and K.41, require a larger orchestra than the three concertos, K.107 (1771). These three concertos are adapted from J. C. Bach's sonatas, op. 5, nos. 1, 3, and 4, T.338–339, and include parts for strings, two oboes, or two flutes (the same person for oboe and flute), two horns, and, in K.40 two trumpets. Wind instruments support and double the string parts, as was common in contemporary concertos. Mozart uses only sonata forms from the sonatas, although he did use other forms in the concertos, K.107. In tuttis, the clavier part has a figured bass. Movements are transitional types, with features of ritornello and classic concerto form. Cadenzas are in movements 1 and 2.

The concertos, K.107, predate by one or two years the concertos, K.37–41. Mozart planned to perform the concertos, K.107, on a concert tour, and took care orchestrating the music for ensembles of two violins and bass available in most courts and towns. Mozart recognized the influence of his friend and mentor in the title *Tre Sonata del Sgr. Giovanni Bach Ridotte in Concerti dal Sgr. Smadeo Wolfgango Mozart*. J. C. Bach's concertos would have been unsuitable for the tour because the orchestrations include two oboes and two horns. The concertos, K.107, were useful to Mozart in performance and teaching. His practice of writing cadenzas for students is evidence of his use of these works well after 1770.

In Salzburg Mozart composed the concertos, K.175 (1773), K.238 (1776), K.242 (1776), K.246 (1776), K.271 (1777), and K.365 (1779). Mozart's first original piano concerto is K.175, and he performed the popular work until after 1782, when he composed the rondo, K.382 (1782), as a new final movement; *konzert-rondo* is another title for the rondo. In the original version of the concerto, all three movements are in sonata form during an era when rondos were becoming fashionable final movements. Some publications of the concerto contain the rondo, but the original final movement appears in later printings. Mozart composed two cadenzas for the first movement and two for the second movement.

Within a three-month period, Mozart composed the concertos, K.238, K.242, and K.246. Each concerto is in *galant* style with an orchestra of strings, two oboes, and two horns. Beginning with the concerto, K.238, final movements of Mozart's concertos are rondos or themes with variations. He composed the concerto, K.242, for three claviers, for Countess Lodron and her daughters Louise and Josepha; Mozart(?)

arranged the concerto for two claviers. The third clavier part is considerably easier than the other parts, suggesting that one daughter, probably Josepha, was not as proficient a player as the mother and other daughter. The final movement of the concerto, K.246, composed for Countess Lützow, is a rondo with the indication *Tempo di Minuetto,* a common direction in concertos of the London composers J. C. Bach and Abel. A copy of the concerto, K.246, at St. Peter's in Salzburg contains Mozart's realization of the continuo part in the tuttis of the first two movements.

Most modern writers consider the concerto, K.271, composed at the request of the French pianist Mlle. Jeunehomme, to be Mozart's first "great" concerto. Knowing Jeunehomme's advanced pianistic abilities, Mozart composed a concerto at the technical and musical level appropriate to his own talent (See ex. 3–7). The tutti and clavier phrases at the beginning of the first movement present an intimate relationship between the solo and orchestra. The clavier entry in measure two (See ex. 3–8) did not shock contemporary audiences because they were accustomed to hearing a harpsichord continuo in the orchestra sound. This concerto is Mozart's first with the middle movement in a minor key. The rondo contains a *minuetto* in the middle of the movement. Mozart composed cadenzas for each of the three movements.

Mozart intended the concerto, K.365, for two claviers, for his sister Nannerl and himself. The concerto presents equal difficulties for each performer, unlike the concerto for three claviers with unequal requirements for each soloist. This is Mozart's earliest piano concerto with bassoon parts.

In 1781, Mozart moved to Vienna for opportunities not available in Salzburg. Vienna was the cultural center of Europe, and many fine musicians were there, including Haydn, Kozeluch, Gluck, Salieri, and Vanhal, and many of Europe's finest performers visited to give concerts. Until Mozart arrived, the piano had not been a featured solo instrument in public concerts. Mozart referred to Vienna as "clavierland" in reference to the many pianos played by amateurs. During his first year there, he did not compose piano concertos, possibly because he carried several from Salzburg that were unfamiliar to Viennese audiences. The concerto, K.175, with its new rondo, K.382, became a much-admired work.

In the autumn of 1782, Mozart composed three clavier concertos—K.414 (1782), K.413 (1782–1783), and K.415 (1782–1783)—for subscription sales, but the venture was not successful. In 1785 Artaria published the three concertos with K.414 preceding K.413. Mozart composed the concertos in *galant* style, perhaps because he was unsure what type of music attracted cultured Viennese audiences who sometimes viewed his concertos as unusual and disturbing. The slow movement of the concerto, K.414, is one part of J. C. Bach's *Six Favourite Overtures,* T.272, no. 2. The concerto, K.413, is Mozart's first use of 3/4 meter in the first movement of a concerto. Of the concertos, K.413–415, the latter is for Mozart's largest orchestra of strings, two oboes, two bassoons, two horns, two trumpets, and two timpani. Possibly, the rondo, K.386 (1782), is the original finale for the concerto, K.414. Mozart composed cadenzas for the first two movements of K.413, two cadenzas for each of the three movements of K.414, and a cadenza for the first two movements of K.415.

In 1784, Mozart completed the six concertos K.449, K.450, K.451, K.453,

Example 3–7. Mozart Concerto, K.271, mvt. 1, mm. 259–272

K.456, and K.459. The concerto, K.449, for Barbara Ployer, is Mozart's first mature clavier concerto listed in his own catalog. The orchestration is for strings, two oboes, and two horns *ad libitum*. Mozart composed a cadenza for the first movement. Although the concerto is from the same year as the next five concertos, it is more akin to the concertos, K.414, K.413, and K.415.

The two concertos, K.450 and K.451, are for a large orchestra of strings, two oboes, two bassoons, and two horns. Mozart uses a flute in the finale of K.450, and a

Example 3–8. Mozart Concerto, K.271, mvt. 1, mm. 1–7

flute, two trumpets, and two timpani appear in all movements of K.451. The orchestra writing is symphonic and the clavier part is brilliant and difficult because Mozart composed for himself. At age 28, Mozart was at the height of his career as a pianist in Vienna, although perhaps not the most fashionable. The andante of K.451 has a thin texture in the piano part that Mozart used as a reminder while improvising (See ex. 3–9); contemporary listeners observed Mozart ornamenting and improvising during the slow movements. He sent his sister an ornamented version of this movement. The slow movement of K.450 is the first appearance of variation form in his clavier concertos. Mozart left cadenzas for the first and third movements in concertos, K.450 and K.451, two each for the first and second movements of K.453, two for the first movement, and one for the third movement of K.456, and one each for the first and third movements of K.459. Probably, the fragment, K.459a (1784), is an andante for the concerto, K.459.

In 1785, Mozart wrote three clavier concertos, K.466, K.467, and K.482. His first minor-key clavier concerto, K.466, remained popular well into the nineteenth century. Concertos in minor keys are unusual among *galant* and classic composers. He intended K.467 for the subscription concerts of 1785. Köchel lists the fragment, K.467a, as a possible symphony or overture, and Blume lists it as a movement for the concerto, K.467. Simultaneously, Mozart composed the concerto, K.482, and *The Marriage of Figaro* (1786) and, consequently, operatic melodies are in the piano concerto. The concerto was for a series of three subscription concerts and the andante movement was so well received that audiences demanded an immediate second performance. Mozart replaced oboes with clarinets, and winds have more independence than in earlier concertos.

In 1786, Mozart composed three clavier concertos, K.488, K.491, and K.503. The first two concertos were for subscription concerts, as were concertos of the previous year. In a letter dated 1786 to Sebastian Winter, Mozart wrote that K.488 requires two

Reprinted by Permission of G. Schirmer, Inc. (ASCAP)

Example 3–9. Mozart Concerto, K.451, mvt. 2, mm. 56–59

clarinets, and that Prince Furstenberg at Donaueschingen could substitute a violin and viola if clarinets were not available. The key of A major is uncommon in Mozart's clavier concertos, and F-sharp minor for the second movement is Mozart's only use of the key in a clavier concerto. The slow movement is an adagio in the autograph, but most editions have an andante. There are several fragments of clavier concertos: K.488a (1786) is an adagio for the concerto, K.488; K.488b (1786) and 488c (1786) are finales for the concerto, K.488; and K.488d (1786) may be a rondo for the concerto, K.488. The concerto, K.491, is the second concerto in a minor key, the other is K.466. The concerto, K.491, has the largest orchestration in Mozart's clavier concertos to date: strings, flutes, two oboes, two clarinets, two bassoons, two horns, two trumpets, and two timpani. The fragment, K.491a (1786), is a slow movement for the concerto, K.491. The concerto, K.503, is Mozart's "Emperor" because of the majestic character of the first movement. The fragment, K.502a (1786), may be for the concerto, K.503.

The *Szene mit rondo,* K.505 (1786), is for soprano, orchestra and clavier obbligato.

After 1786, Mozart's production of clavier concertos slackened considerably. He composed the concerto, K.537, known as the *Coronation,* for the 1790 coronation of Leopold II in Frankfurt. In the same concert, Mozart performed the concerto, K.459. Like many other concertos, the solo part in K.537 is sketchy, and many passages performed today are probably by another person, possibly Johann André. The trumpet and timpani parts may be for the Frankfurt performance or for a different concert. Mozart did not perform at the coronation festivities; he organized his own concert, thus the title is not accurate and it comes from the publisher André. Mozart's reliance on figuration over melodic structure makes the concerto less classic and more like a transitional concerto common between the classic and romantic eras. The fragment, K.537a (1788), is a possible first movement for the concerto, K.537.

In his final year, Mozart composed the concerto, K.595, for his own use and performed it at a concert given by clarinetist Joseph Bähr. The concerto is a comparatively quiet composition that avoids the virtuosity of Mozart's other clavier concertos. In the autograph, extensive portions of the left-hand part are missing, and the present version is from an unknown source, possibly André. Mozart composed cadenzas for the first and third movements.

Several fragments may be movements for clavier concertos. The fragment, K.43c (?), may be a concerto movement. The fragment, K.315f (1778), is for a concerto for clavier and violin. The fragments, K.452b (1784) and K.452c (1784), are concerto movements, and the fragment, K.537b (1788), is for an unidentified clavier concerto.

Some aspects of Mozart's clavier concertos leave unclear exactly when a soloist performs and several concertos contain sketchy notation completed by an unknown person. In performances, Mozart frequently embellished musical outlines, and there are examples of ornamented versions he considered acceptable. The direction "col basso"[10] means the clavier is to perform a continuo part and some concertos have figured bass. Soloists often used music in performance, and normally played the cello line in tutti sections (See ex. 3–10). To what extent Mozart intended a soloist to play a continuo role is unclear; generally, continuo playing in piano concertos was uncommon after 1775. A copy of a continuo part in Mozart's hand exists for the concerto, K.246, and Mozart probably intended a continuo part at least through the concerto, K.415. In concerto, K.414, Mozart's keyboard writing suggests piano instead of harpsichord.

Mozart's concertos contain two kinds of improvisation passages: lead-ins and cadenzas. A fermata over a dominant chord (See ex. 3–11) indicates a lead-in or *eingang* connecting sections of a composition with non-thematic, improvised scales and arpeggios on the dominant chord (See ex. 3–12). In many editions lead-ins are correctly composed by another person, but mistakenly identified as a cadenza (See ex. 3–13).

Example 3–10. Mozart Concerto, K.488, mvt. 1, mm. 1–4

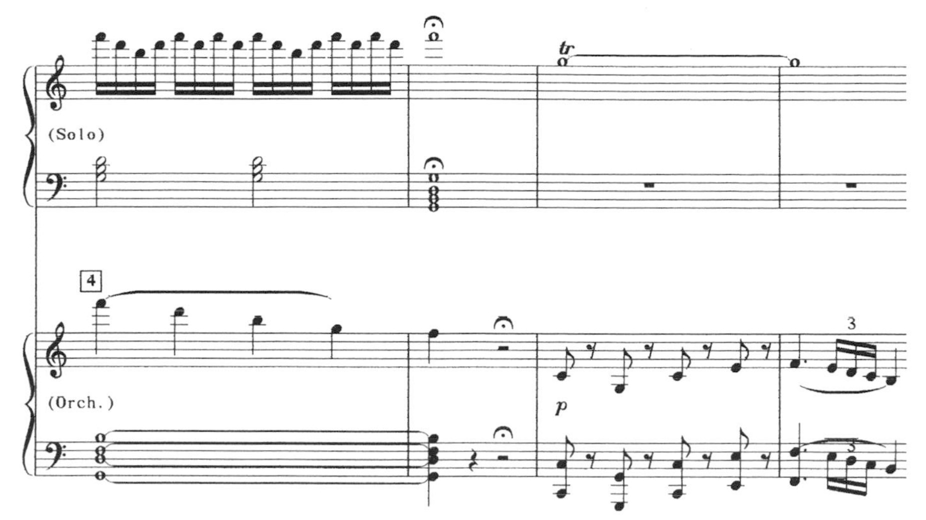

Example 3–11. Mozart Concerto, K.467, mvt. 1, mm. 78–81

A fermata over a tonic six-four chord in the orchestra part indicates a cadenza and, theoretically, a cadenza embellishes the cadential six-four chord with material from the movement (See ex. 3–14). The soloist signals the end of the cadenza, with a trill on the supertonic over a dominant chord. Cadenzas are longer and more harmonically varied than lead-ins, usually treat thematic material, and sometimes contain modulations. Mozart improvised cadenzas in performances, but most musicians need a prepared cadenza. Occasionally, pianists performed cadenzas inappropriate for the key or themes of a concerto.

When a cadenza by Mozart does not exist, a performer might use one composed by someone else, but often many such cadenzas are unsatisfactory due to stylistic and technical features not appropriate to Mozart (See ex. 3–15); the numerous trills, sometimes in both hands, are techniques of the generation of composers after Mozart. Another possibility is for a performer to compose a cadenza in Mozart's style. Information on cadenzas composed by Mozart can be found in Eva and Paul Badura-Skoda's *Interpreting Mozart at the Keyboard*.[11]

Mozart's cadenzas, K.624, are for his concertos. Also, he composed cadenzas for concertos by J. C. Bach, Honauer, Schröter, Beecke, and for some unidentified concertos.

Accompaniment patterns in Mozart's concertos include Alberti bass figures that span intervals larger than a fifth and repeated chords. The repeated chord pattern is common in the concertos of Mozart, Hummel, Weber, Chopin, and many contemporary composers. Accompaniment passages in the left hand that require a technique equal to

Example 3–12. Mozart Concerto, K.271, mvt. 3, mm. 228–236

Reprinted by Permission of G. Schirmer, Inc. (ASCA)

Example 3–13. Mozart Concerto, K.467, mvt. 1, mm. 77–84

Reprinted by Permission of G. Schirmer, Inc. (ASCAP)

Example 3–14. Mozart Concerto, K.246, mvt. 1, mm. 194–196

Reprinted by Permission of G. Schirmer, Inc. (ASCAP)

Example 3–15. Mozart Concerto, K.466, mvt. 3, cadenza by Beethoven, mm. 31–45

passages in the right hand and parallel octave passages are not common in the Mozart concertos; both techniques are ordinary features in the music of composers after Mozart's generation. Where Mozart wants octaves, he usually writes broken octaves.

In Mozart's lifetime, only seven of his clavier concertos reached publication: K.175, K.413, K.414, K.415, K.451, K.453, and K.595. After Mozart's death, André published K.467, K.481, K.488, K.491, K.503, and K.595 as the "Six grand concertos, dédié au Prince Louis Ferdinand de Prusse" (ca. 1801). For many years, most of Mozart's clavier concertos existed only in autograph form. Johann André and his family were caretakers of Mozart's autographs, and without their interest some clavier concertos might be lost. The only missing clavier concerto is the one Mozart composed at age 4.

Paul Wranitzky (1756–1808) was a Czech composer and violinist active in Vienna as a conductor of music by Haydn and Beethoven. His own music, in classic style, includes the sinfonia with solo piano and a symphony featuring solo harpsichord and violin.

Maria von Paradis (1759–1824) is the respected pianist for whom Mozart intended the concerto, K.456. Contemporary accounts mention that she had memorized about sixty piano concertos. Many of her compositions are missing, including two piano concertos.

Adalbert Gyrowetz (1763–1850), Czech composer and conductor, lived in Czechoslovakia, Italy, London, and Vienna as a court musician. Because some of his compositions imitate Haydn's style, several works appeared as Haydn's. He composed two concertos, opp. 26 and 49 (pub. 1796 and 1800). His interest in music faded when styles changed in the 1820s.

Anton Eberl (1765–1807) became a student of Mozart after producing several stage and instrumental works. Mozart's name appeared on publications of piano music by Eberl. Eberl's music includes four concertos: (1797), op. 32 (1803), op. 40 (1804), and op. 45 (1805) for two pianos. By 1800, Eberl's career as a pianist and composer peaked with the concertos, opp. 40 and 45 which received praise as equals of Beethoven's concertos. Contemporary writers cite Eberl's death as a tragic loss of one of Beethoven's strongest rivals.

Franz Kleingheinz (1765–1832), German composer and conductor, performed in Munich, Vienna, Brünn, and Budapest. His music, including a piano concerto, is in Viennese style.

Heinrich Marchand (1769–after 1812), violinist, keyboard player, and composer, pioneered performances of French light opera in Germany. He was a protege of Leopold Mozart, lived with the Mozarts, and worked as a musician at the court of Archbishop of Salzburg in Regensburg and the court of the Prince of Thurn and Taxis in Paris. He may have composed the *Rondeau* in Vienna.

Ludwig van Beethoven (1770–1827) is among the most important composers of music for piano and orchestra. George Kinsky and Hans Halm catalogued Beethoven's music in *Das Werk Beethovens*[12] and the catalog section "Werke ohne Opuszahl" provides WoO numbers for works lacking opus numbers. Willy Hess' *Verzeichnis der Nicht in der Gesamtausgabe Veröffentlichten Werke Ludwig van Beethovens*[13] provides numbers for two compositions.

For many years, Beethoven believed his birth date to be 1772. Perhaps Beethoven's father falsified the birth date to reap financial rewards from a son who seemed to be another musical prodigy like Mozart. Members of Beethoven's family believed he was born in December 1771, and possibly Beethoven himself thought December was close enough to the next year to use 1772 as his birth date. *Thayer's Life of Beethoven*[14] mentions a piano concerto composed in Beethoven's twelfth year; actually, the composition is the concerto, WoO 4 (1784), from his fourteenth year.

Beethoven composed the concerto no. 2, op. 19 (ca. 1793–1795, rev. 1798), before the concerto no. 1, op. 15 (1795–1798, 1800). Because he continued revising the concerto, op. 19, the concerto, op. 15, was the first of the two concertos published and now is the concerto no. 1. Beethoven reserved the two concertos for his own performances because composers faced serious problems of pirated scores due to a lack of legal protection. Both concertos are in the tradition of pleasurable music intended to be read at sight. At the first rehearsal of the concerto no. 2, Beethoven transposed the entire concerto up to C-sharp major so the piano would be in tune with the woodwinds. A quotation of the folk song *Die Katze Lässt das Mausen Nicht* (The Cat Will Catch Mice) appears in the rondo (See ex. 3–16) of the concerto no. 1. In concerto nos. 1 and 2, harmonic variety in the opening orchestra expositions is much greater than in concertos of contemporary composers.

Beethoven composed substantial portions of the concerto no. 3, op. 37 (1800), before the completion of concerto nos. 1 and 2. The first two concertos present the orchestra in an accompanying role, but in the concerto no. 3, the orchestra has a musical role equal to the solo. This is Beethoven's only concerto in a minor key and the work is more serious and expansive than his earlier concertos. Technical demands for the left hand are similar to those of the right hand. In the first movement, the continuation of the solo part through the coda after the cadenza is Beethoven's first use of the brilliant coda; the technique is in concerto nos. 4 and 5, and became the norm after Beethoven.

The concerto no. 4, op. 58 (1805), is the most difficult piano concerto to date, a fact quickly recognized by Beethoven's contemporaries. The concerto no. 4 and the concerto no. 5 "Emperor," op. 73 (1809), present the piano at the opening of the first movements. The practice is uncommon in classic concertos and common in concertos of the nineteenth and twentieth centuries. The title "Emperor" is not Beethoven's. Connecting the second and third movements of the concerto no. 5 is a transition leading directly into the third movement; this practice is unusual in earlier piano concertos, but common in concertos in the nineteenth century.

Beethoven composed concerto nos. 4 and 5 after writing the *Heiligenstädt Testament* (1802) in which he expresses profound feelings about his deafness. When he performed concertos with orchestras after becoming deaf, precision with the orchestra was possible because Beethoven could watch the violinist's fingerings, but judging volume and tone were performance problems.

Keys for Beethoven's concerto movements are daring for the time and show his fondness for distant key relationships. In the concerto no. 1 in C major the second movement is in A-flat major; in the concerto no. 3 in C minor the middle movement

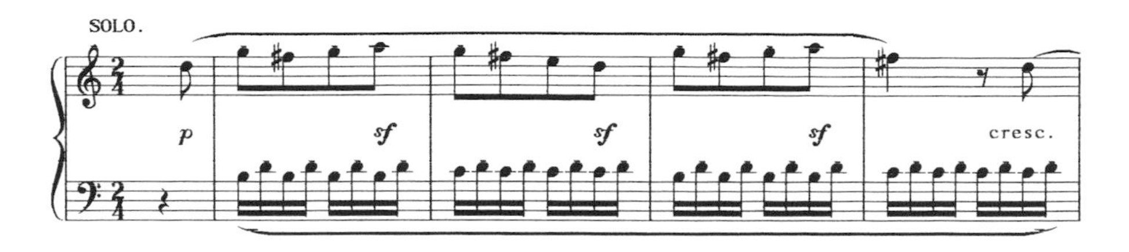

Used by permission of C. F. Peters Corporation: Beethoven (P144) Concerto no. 1, op. 15

Example 3–16. Beethoven Concerto no. 3, op. 15, mvt. 3, mm. 73–81

is in E major; and in the concerto no. 5 in E-flat major the middle movement is in B major.

In concerto nos. 1–4, a solo cadenza appears at the classic location in the first movement, after the recapitulation and before the coda. Ideally, pianists performed an improvised or prepared cadenza. By 1809, Beethoven composed cadenzas for the concertos. A written cadenza is in the concerto no. 5 and no other cadenza can be used. After the concerto no. 5, composers wrote a cadenza for the soloist. Composers ceased the practice of improvised cadenzas for a variety of reasons: pianists prepared musically poor cadenzas without any relationship to the concerto, pianists performed cadenzas that did not fit the concerto key, and written cadenzas gave musical control to the composer.

The triple concerto, op. 56 (1804–1805), for piano, violin, cello, and orchestra, is reminiscent of the baroque concerto *grosso* with a solo group or the symphonic *concertante* for multiple solo instruments like those of Navoigille in Paris in the late eighteenth and early nineteenth centuries. Concertos for piano and other solo instruments were rare in the nineteenth century, when piano virtuosity was important, but this type of concerto reappeared in the twentieth century.

The *Choral Fantasy,* op. 80 (1808), for piano, chorus, and orchestra, contains a theme Beethoven used again in the final movement of the symphony no. 9. This was a unique performance medium for the era, but an idea adopted by several later composers. The work begins with an extensive solo improvisation that probably is an accurate record of Beethoven's improvisational style. At the first performance, Beethoven improvised the piano part, and later he wrote it down.

Many extant examples demonstrate Beethoven's interest in music for piano and orchestra. The *Tempo di Concerto* (1788–1793) is an unfinished first movement of a concerto in D major; the theme is similar to Mozart's sonata, K.330, third movement. The adagio (ca. 1790) is for a concerto in A major. The romance *cantabile,* Hess 13 (ca. 1792–1793), is a fragment of a slow movement of a large work. The rondo, WoO 6 (ca. 1794–1795), is the original third movement of the concerto no. 3; Czerny completed the solo part. Probably, the adagio (ca. 1794) is the original middle movement of the concerto no. 3. Clementi suggested to Beethoven that he arrange the violin concerto, op. 61, as the piano concerto, op. 61A (1807). Beethoven left four fragments of unfinished concertos: one (1809) for a concerto in G major, one (1809) for a concerto in G major or E major, one (1911) for a concerto in D minor, and one (?) for a concerto in F minor. The sketch, Hess 15 (1814–1815), is an extensive 256-measure first movement in D major that would have been Beethoven's piano concerto no. 6.

Joseph Wölfl (1772/73–1812) studied music with Leopold Mozart and Michael Haydn. In the early 1790s, he began a musical career and soon gained respect as a composer and pianist. In Vienna, he developed a strong following of people preferring his gracious manner to Beethoven's rough demeanor. Wölfl toured Europe as a pianist and was admired by many. In 1801, performances in Paris resulted in praise for him as a leading pianist and composer, and he was the main musical attraction in London from 1805. There are nine piano concertos: op. 20 (ca. 1801), op. 26 (1803), op. 32 (ca. 1805), op. 36 (ca. 1806/1807), "The Calm," op. 43 (ca. 1799), the "Grand Concerto Militaire," op. 49 (ca. 1810), "The Cuckoo," op. 64 (ca. 1812), the "Concerto da Camera" (?), and one (1800–1802) with violin.

Franciszek Lessel (1780–1838), Polish composer and pianist, went to Vienna in 1797 to study medicine, but soon chose a career in music. He studied with Haydn and composed the adagio and rondo, op. 9, the "potpourri," op. 13 (pub. 1813), and the concerto, op. 14 (pub. 1813), with classic and romantic traits. His music contains features that influenced Chopin.

Mozart's son Franz Xaver Wolfgang Mozart (1791–1844) produced two piano concertos, op. 14 (by 1813) and op. 25 (perf. 1818). The "Introduction and Variations," op. 26, has the same opus number listed in some sources for two polonaises.

Johann Hugo Vorísek (1791–1825), Czech student of Tomásek in Prague, traveled in 1813 to Vienna where he made friends with Schubert, Moscheles, Beethoven, and Hummel, and conducted the *Gesellschaft der Musikfreunde* from 1818. He composed short piano pieces with poetic titles (e.g., "Impromptu," "Rhapsody," "Eclogue") prior to the character pieces of Schubert. His music for piano and orchestra includes the "Variations on the French Song *La Sentinelle,*" op. 6, the "Variations di Bravura," op. 14, the "Rondo Espagnol," op. 17, the "Introduction et Rondeau Brilliant," op. 22, and the grand *rondeau concertant,* op. 25, with violin and cello solo.

Carl Reissiger (1798–1859), German conductor and composer, performed his piano concerto (ca. 1821) in 1822 while a student of Salieri. Later he succeeded the opera composer Marschner as music director of the German Opera in Dresden.

Table 1 Additional Composers in Austria

Names	Dates	Compositions
Kauer, Ferdinand	1751–1831	3 Concertos, 1 for 2 kbds, 1 for 2 kls, 1 for kl & ob
Kozeluch, Leopold	1747–1818	27 Concertos
Krufft, Nikolas v.	1779–1818	*Fantaisie et Polonaise*
Mederitsch, Johann	1752–1835	4 Concertos
Preindl, Josef	1756–1823	Concertos, op 1 (pub 1797), op 2
Schenk, John	1753–1836	Concerto (1796)
Sgatberoni, Johann	ca. 1708–1795	4 Concertos, hpd
Struck, Paul	1776–1820	Concerto
Süssmayr, Franz	1766–1803	Concerto, pf
Teyber, Anton	1756–1822	4 Concertos, kbd Concerto, vn & kbd
Triebensee, Josef	1772–1846	Concertino (1798), pf Concerto, hpd other works, pf/hpd & orch
Ulbrich, Maxmillian	1741?-1814	Concerto
Umlauf, Ignaz	1746–1796	Concerto, pf concerto, 2 pfs

Notes

1. Shelley George Davis "The Keyboard Concertos of Johann Georg Lang (1722–1798)" (Ph.D. dissertation, New York University, 1971).

2. Lothar Herbert Perger. "Michael Haydn: Instrumentalwerke I." Vol. 29: *Denkmäler der Tonkunst in Österreich* (Graz: Akademische Druck-U. Verlagsanstalt, 1959).

3. Nathan Broder, "The First Guide to Mozart," *Musical Quarterly* 42 (April 1956): 223–229.

4. Friedrich Wilhelm Jähns, *Carl Maria von Weber in seinen Werken* (Berlin: Schlesinger'schen Buch- und Musikhandlung, 1871; reprint 1967).

5. Anthon van Hoboken, *Joseph Hayden: Thematisch-bibliographisches Werkverzeichnis,* Band I (Mainz: B. Schott's Söhne, 1957).

6. H. C. Robbins Landon, *Haydn: Chronicle and Works, 5 vols.* (Bloomington: Indiana University Press, 1980).

7. Ludwig Ritter von Köchel, *Chronologisch-thematisches Verzeichnis Sämtlicher Tonwerke Wolfgang Amadé Mozarts* (Wiesbaden: Breitkopf & Härtel, 1964).

8. Nathan Broder, "Mozart and the Clavier," *Musical Quarterly* 27 (October 1941): 422–432.

9. A. Hyatt King, "Introduction to Concerto, K.40, by W. A. Mozart." Edited by Arthur Balsam (London: Oxford University Press, 1966). Hyatt's introduction is in copies of Mozart's concertos, K.37, K.39, K.40, and K.41 by Oxford University Press.

10. Friedrich Blume writes in the prefatory material to the edition of Mozart's piano concerto, K.-V.466 (Edition Eulenburg, Inc., New York, 1933) ". . . although Mozart's handwriting is very exact—and as most interesting revelation the treatment of the piano as thorough-bass instrument throughout in those places where it has no

solo part. The directions of the autograph, in this respect, are by no means meant only in a conventional sense, but Mozart repeats the demand "col basso" for the piano page by page, and he explicitly writes rests where the thorough-bass accompaniment is not wanted."

11. Eva and Paul Badura-Skoda, *Interpreting Mozart on the Keyboard.* Trans. by Leo Black (New York: St. Martin's Press, 1957).

12. George Kinsky and Hans Halm, *Das Werk Beethovens. Thematisch-Bibliographisches Verzeichnis Seiner Sämtlich Vollendeten Kompositionen* (Munchen: G. Henle Verlag, 1955).

13. Willy Hess, *Verzeichnis der Nicht in der Gesamtausgabe Veröffentlichten Werke Ludwig van Beethovens* (Wiesbaden: Breitkopf & Hártel, 1957).

14. Elliot Forbes, ed., *Thayer's Life of Beethoven,* 2 vols. (Princeton, New Jersey: Princeton University Press, 1967): 53–54, 71–72.

Chapter 4

Italy, Hungary, Czechoslovakia, Poland, Russia, France, Spain, Belgium, the Netherlands, Denmark, England, Scotland, Ireland, and the United States

Italy

Opera dominated Italian musical activity from ca. 1770 to ca. 1827. The major opera and theater cities were Milan, Turin, Venice, Bologna, Florence, Rome, and Naples, and composers moved from city to city as their careers demanded. Most composers worked hardest in opera and church music, and dabbled in instrumental music because earning a living from such music was difficult. In this era, the Italian repertoire for harpsichord/piano and orchestra is meager.

Maddalena Sirmen (née Lombardini, 1735-after 1785) was one of Tartini's finest violin students and a highly praised virtuoso violinist in Italy, Paris, and London. In 1771, she performed an unidentified harpsichord concerto in London. Possibly, the concerto was part of six concertos Signor Giordani adapted for harpsichord in 1773 from Sirmen's violin concertos, op. 3.

Giovanni Paisiello (1740–1816), opera composer and rival of Puccini and Cimarosa, composed about fifty operas and some keyboard concertos. During his stay in St. Petersburg in the employment of Catherine the Great, he composed two harpsichord concertos (1766–1781). In Naples, he composed six harpsichord/piano concertos (1785–1788), and there may be several lost keyboard concertos.

Luigi Boccherini (1743–1805), important composer of string music in pre-classic style, is typical of the Italian instrumental composers who found appreciative audiences in other countries. After leaving home in Lucca, he lived in Florence, Vienna, Paris, and Madrid. Yves Gérard's *Thematic, Bibliographical, and Critical Catalogue of the Works of Luigi Boccerini*[1] provides G. numbers for Boccherini's music. The concerto, G.487 (ca. 1768), is for harpsichord. The piano concerto, G.488, is not Boccherini's.

Domenico Cimarosa (1749–1801) was the most important Italian opera composer in the late eighteenth century and a very popular opera composer before Rossini. He composed one harpsichord concerto, possibly in St. Petersburg or Italy.

Giovanni Giuliani (ca. 1760-after 1818) directed the orchestra at the *Teatro*

Table 2 Additional Composers in Italy

Names	Dates	Compositions
Agnesi, Maria	1720–1795	2 concs (one 1766), hpd 2 concertos, pf
Asiolo, Bonifazio	1769–1832	Concerto, hpd
Baldan, Angelo	1753–1803	Concerto, hpd
Bonesi, Barnaba	1745/46–1824	Concerto, hpd
Fortunati, Gian	1746–1821	Concerto (1785), hpd
Gatti, Luigi	1740–1817	Concertos, 1 for hpd
Gazzaniga, Giuseppe	1743–1818	3 concertos, pf
Grua, Grancesco de Paula	1753–1833	Concerto(s), pf
Puccini, Domenico	1772–1815	Concerto, hpd or pf
Rutini, Giovanni	1723–1797	Rondo, op 19 (pub 1795)
Sogner, Pasquale	1793–1842	Concerto, pf
Turini, Ferdinando	1749–1812	Concerto, pf?

degli Intrepidi and earned a living from instrumental music without emigrating to another country or composing theater or church music. The harpsichord concertos, op. 4 (ca. 1790), are three of six concertos.

Johann Mayr (1763–1845), German, pupil of Donizetti, became an important composer of Italian opera before Rossini. He composed two piano concertos in Bergamo, where he worked after 1802 as the *maestro di cappella,* and from 1805 he directed the S. Maria *Maggiore.*

Ferdinado Paer (1771–1839), pupil of Fortunati, and Mayr dominated Italian opera about the turn of the century. He lived in Vienna, Dresden, and, after some urging by Napoleon, in Paris, where he taught young Liszt in the 1820s. He left a harpsichord concerto.

Johan Pfeiffer (fl. 1780s), German, probably spent time in Venice and London during his last years; most of his published works are from Venice. He left a keyboard concerto.

Hungary

Anton Zimmerman (ca. 1741–1781), Austrian, developed a first-rate orchestra by 1778. He left the "Grand" concerto, op. 3 (1782), for harpsichord/piano and a harpsichord concerto.

Czechoslovakia

Franz Xaver Dusek (1731–1799), student of Waganseil in Vienna, was a highly regarded pianist and composer of piano concertos and sonatas, along with other instrumental works. Sometimes, F. X. Dusek is confused with the more famous Czech composer-pianist Jan Ladislav Dussek in London. F. X. Dusek's music for harpsichord/ piano includes six concertos (ca. 1773), an adagio (ca.1773), three lost concertos (1778, 1781, 1785–1787), four concertinos (ca. 1773–ca. 1780), two lost concertinos (ca. 1774, ca. 1782–1784), the concerto (ca. 1784), and one other concertino. As the most prominent native Czech composer in the late eighteenth century, Dusek's concertos are important in the evolution from harpsichord to piano.

Josef Smrcek (1751–1813) was a priest, composer, and music teacher in the order of the Merciful Brethren. He composed several lost piano concertos; only his sacred compositions survive.

Franz Götz (1755–1815) lived in Prague, Brno. and Knomeriz, and his music was popular in Bohemia. He left a piano concerto.

Vincenc Masek (1755–1831), piano student of J. L. Dussek, concertized in Berlin, Hamburg, Leipzig, and Dresden before settling in Prague to teach piano. His piano concertino (pub. 1803) is for four-hands. He left many concertos.

Bedrich Weber (1766–1842), champion and imitator of Mozart, founded and directed the Prague Conservatory where he taught Moscheles, Dessauer, and Kalliowada. His *Variazioni di bravura* is for piano and orchestra.

Johann Vitásek (1770–1839), composer and pianist, studied with F. X. Dusek and J. A. Kozeluch in Prague, where he directed the Prague Cathedral from 1814. He composed four piano concertos.

Jan Rösler (1771–1813), *kapellmeister* for Prince Lobkowitz, composed many piano sonatas and popular short piano works in a style similar to Beethoven. His concerto, op. 15, is one of several piano concertos.

Václav Jan Tomásek (1774–1850), composer of piano pieces prior to Schubert, was a highly praised organist, teacher to Prague nobility, and a well-paid composer in Count Bucquoy Longeval's household. He left two piano concertos, opp. 18 and 20 (1805, ca. 1805).

Nikolaus Kraft (1778–1853), cello virtuoso, performed (1789) with Mozart in Vienna at age 11, and worked as a chamber musician for Prince Lobkowitz from 1809. Although most of his concertos are for cello, the "Potpourri," op. 8 (1820), is for piano and orchestra.

Poland

Karl Birnback (1751–1805) conducted at the German Theater in Warsaw. He composed at least sixteen piano concertos.

Wenzel Würfel (1790–1832), Bohemian pianist, composer, teacher, conductor, and predecessor of Chopin, studied with Tomásek in Prague and composed music in his style. From 1815, he lived in Warsaw as a highly successful pianist. Würfel's music for piano and orchestra is the concerto, op. 28 (pub. 1825), the polonaise, and the *rondeau* "brilliant."

Russia

Carl-Gottlieb Richter (1728–1809) composed, played organ, and taught at the Königsberg Cathedral. He left eleven piano or harpsichord concertos, including the harpsichord concerto (ca. 1783), two piano or harpsichord concertos (pub. 1772), and two harpsichord concertos (pub. 1778).

Johann Palschau (ca. 1742–1813), highly praised German pianist, settled in Russia in the 1770s as a court musician. Two concertos (1771) appeared in publication.

Dmitri Bortnyansky (1751–1825) studied with Galuppi in St. Petersburg and worked in the imperial chapel composing operas and sacred vocal music. His *sinfonie concertante* (1790) is in classic style.

Daniil Kashin (1769–1841), composer and collector of folk songs, became important in music after his release from serfdom in 1798. As with other Russian composers, his music depends upon foreign styles. He left a piano concerto (perf. 1790).

Ludwig Berger (1777–1839), German composer and pianist, visited Clementi in St. Petersburg, stayed there for eight years, and composed the piano concerto, op. 34 (1808). After touring London in 1812, he returned to Berlin and taught Mendelssohn, Taubert, and Henselt.

John Field (1782–1837), born in Dublin, Ireland, studied piano with Tommaso Giordani from 1791, and moved to London as an apprentice demonstrator in Clementi's piano warehouse in exchange for piano lessons. At the end of the apprenticeship, he continued a musical association with Clementi, and they traveled together to Paris, Vienna, and St. Petersburg in 1802. Field viewed St. Petersburg's thriving musical life as the means to financial independence; Clementi's stinginess frequently caused Field to leave meals hungry and stay indoors during the Russian winter because he did not have a warm coat. In 1822, Field moved to Moscow and stayed there until his European tour in 1831 that included London, several cities in France, Geneva, and Naples. People eagerly anticipated his arrival and performances. Shortly after arriving in Naples, his deteriorating health required hospitalization for nine months and, after returning to Moscow in 1835, his health remained poor.

Cecil Hopkinson's *A Bibliographical Thematic Catalogue of the Works of John Field 1782–1837*[2] provides H. numbers for Field's music. The numerous editions of Field's music are evidence of his popularity.

The concerto no. 1, H.27 (1799), has James Hook's "T'was Within a Mile of Edinboro Town" (See ex. 4–1) as the theme for a set of variations (See ex. 4–2) in the second movement. The concerto no. 2, H.31 (ca. 1807), probably served Chopin as a model for his concerto no. 2. The second movement appeared separately as a "romance" or serenade for piano solo. The concerto no. 3, H.32 (ca. 1805), has two movements and Field probably performed one of his solo nocturnes in the place of a slow movement; the nocturne no. 5, H.37, exists in a version with orchestra accompaniment and the key is appropriate for the concerto. Field abridged the rondo to make a solo piece. The slow movement of the concerto no. 4, H.28 (by 1814), appeared as the piano solo "Siciliano." The concerto no. 5 "L'Incedie par L'Orage," H.39 (1817), appears to be modeled after Steibelt's concerto no. 3, "L'Orage." Steibelt presents his

Example 4–1. Field Concerto no. 1, H.27, mvt. 2, mm. 1–5[3]

Example 4–2. Field Concerto no. 1, H.27, mvt. 2, mm. 14–18

storm music in the final movement, while Field places the storm music in the development of the first movement. Both composers use a second piano to reinforce the solo piano during storm passages; twentieth century pianos make a second piano unnecessary. The concerto no. 6, H.49 (by 1819), features Field's first use of metronome markings, and the slow movement is the nocturne in F major, H.40 (pub. 1816). The concerto no. 7, H.58 (by 1822, third mvt. 1832), has metronome markings and is the first concerto Field did not perform as a solo work; the slow movement is the nocturne no. 12, H.12. Field referred to another concerto in a letter dated 1833 to his father, but there is no evidence he progressed further than thinking about the concerto that would have been no. 8.

First movements in Field's concertos have classic concerto form with a double exposition. Slow movements display the keyboard style of his nocturnes and the finales are rondos. Field followed contemporary practice when performing the concerto nos. 1–6 as solo pieces without orchestra accompaniment.

Gustav de Clavé (1784–after 1827?) authored an early Russian music theory book. His two-piano concerto (pub. 1812) is lost.

Franz Gebel (1787–1843), German, moved from Vienna to Moscow in 1817 and developed a fine reputation as a teacher, composer, and pianist. His first-hand knowledge of Viennese classic style was in great demand in Moscow musical circles. The *Fantaisie et Rondeau* for piano and orchestra is in the Viennese classic style.

Carl Arnold (1794–1877) was a German pianist, organist, conductor, and composer who toured Germany, Poland, and Russia. Publication of the piano concerto, op. 16, occurred in St. Petersburg. After settling in Berlin, he abandoned musical composition after the failure of his opera *Irene* in 1832.

Karl Hartknoch (1796–1834), student of Hummel, taught in St. Petersburg and Moscow. For piano and orchestra he composed the *Second Grand Concerto,* op. 14.

France

Jean-Jacques Beauvarlet-Charpentier (1734–1794), celebrated organist, succeeded his father as the organist at the *Hospice de la Charité* in Lyons and became the organist at St. Victor in 1771. He composed four harpsichord/piano concertos (two 1778).

Jean-Francois Tapray (1738–ca.1819), organist, composer, and keyboard teacher, settled in Paris in 1768. He is among the first composers in France to write specifically for piano, but in harpsichord style. He left six harpsichord/organ concertos, op. 1 (pub. 1758), the harpsichord concerto, op. 3 (pub. 1771), the piano and harpsichord *symphonie concertante,* op. 8 (ca. 1777), the harpsichord, piano and violin *symphonie concertante,* op. 9 (pub. 1778), the harpsichord *symphonie concertante,* op. 12 (pub. 1780), the harpsichord and piano *symphonie concertante,* op. 13 (pub. 1781), the harpsichord and piano *symphonie concertante,* op. 15 (pub. ca. 1782–1783), and two harpsichord symphonies, op. 21 (pub. 1784).

Henri-Joseph Rigel (1741–1799), German, studied with Jommelli in Stuttgart and emigrated in 1768 to Paris where he became a highly regarded teacher and composer. He composed two piano concertos, opp. 2 and 3 (pub. ca. 1770), published for harpsichord; the harpsichord concerto, op. 11 (pub. ca. 1773); the harpsichord concerto op. 19?; and the harpsichord and violin concerto *concertante,* op. 20 (pub. 1786). The symphonies, opp. 16 and 17, feature piano solo accompanied by an orchestra of two horns, two violins, and cello *ad libitum.*

Carl Stamitz (1745–1801), important composer and violinist, worked in Mannheim, went to Paris to play in the *Concert Spirituel* and became a court composer to Duke Louis of Noailes in Paris. He composed a harpsichord concerto (1783) in classic concerto form with clear features of double exposition, development, and recapitulation. His harpsichord concerto (1779) seems to be lost.

Giuseppe Cambini (1746–1825), Italian composer and violinist, arrived in Paris in the early 1770s. By 1800, he had composed nearly 600 instrumental works including three harpsichord/piano concertos, op. 15 (pub. 1780).

Ludwig Lachnith (1746–1820), Bohemian composer and horn player, moved to Paris in ca. 1780. The six harpsichord/piano concertos, opp. 9 and 10 (pub. ca. 1786), are in classic style.

Jean-Frédéric Edelmann (1749–1794), composer, harpsichordist, and pianist, made the piano a popular instrument in Paris. In a style influenced by Couperin, he composed the *sinfonie* (1776) for clavecin accompanied by two violins, two horns, and cello *ad libitum,* and the concerto, op. 12 (1782), for clavecin and orchestra of two violins, two oboes, two horns, and bass *ad libitum.* Joining the Jacobins during the revolution resulted in his execution by the guillotine.

Amedeo Rasetti (1754–1799), an Italian, arrived in France in 1760 to play in the *24 Violons du Roi* and organized performances for the *Concert Spirituel.* In ca. 1780 he began a successful career in Paris as a harpsichordist, pianist, and composer. The technically advanced *concerto arabe,* op. 14 (ca. 1800), sometimes appears as the *Nouveau concerto arabe.*

Antoine-Frédéric Gresnik (1755–1799), south Netherlands composer, is important for several *opéra comiques.* He composed keyboard concertos.

Baron von Adolph Münchhausen (ca. 1755–1811) was a German diplomat and musical dilettante living in Munich and Paris. Two of his harpsichord/piano concertos, op. 7, were published in Paris.

Giovanni Viotti (1755–1824), the most influential violinist between Tartini and Paganini, composed twenty-nine violin concertos in Paris and London that establish him as the founder of modern violin playing. Important features of his violin concertos are the linking of movements and first movement material in last movements. His music is in many editions, and the violin concertos were so popular that he or other composers arranged many as piano concertos. All piano concerto arrangements are in the key of the original violin concerto. Table 3 lists Viotti's violin concertos transcribed into piano concertos. For Viotti's music, Chappell White's *Giovanni Battista Viotti (1755-1824), A Thematic Catalogue of His Works*[4] provides W. numbers and Temo Giazotto's *Giovan*

Table 3 Viotti's Piano/Violin Concertos

Pf Concs	Vn Concs	W. Vn/kybd	G.	Remarks
1/1786	6/1782	I:6/Ia:1	34	Hpd/pf. By H. Montgeroult
2/1787	10/ca. 1783–86	I:10/Ia:2	56	Hpd/pf. By Steibelt
3/1789	9/1783–1786	I:9/Ia:3	51	Hpd/pf. By T. Labour. Vn obbl
4/1790	?/?	?/Ia:4	. . .	Lost? Advertised 1790 in *Journal de Paris*
5/1791	13/1788	I:13/Ia:5	65	Hpd/pf. By Dussek & pub as Dussek's
6/1792	17/1790–1791	I:17/Ia:6	86	Hpd/pf. By A. Adam
7/1794–1795	23/perf 1793–94	I:23/Ia:7	98	Pf. By Dussek & pub as Dussek's
8/1795	20/ca. 1792–1795	I:20,8/Ia:8	92/47	Pf. By Hullmandel & Dussek. 1st & 3rd mvts G.92, 2nd mvt G.47
9/ca. 1797	19/1791	I:19/Ia:9	91	Hpd/pf. By Steibelt
10/1796–1797	25/comp 1795–96	I:25/Ia:10	124	Pf. By Dussek
11/1803	10,14,12/ 1783–89	I:10,14, 12/Ia:11	56,63, 64	Pf. By Hullmandel. 1st mvt vn conc 10, 2nd mvt vn conc 14, 3rd mvt vn conc 12
12/ca. 1797	21/ca. 1792–1797	I:21/Ia:12	96	Pf. By N. Isouard. Pub as letter "A"
13/1813	27/ca. 1795	I:27/Ia:13	142	Pf. By J. B. Cramer
14/ca. 1801	24/ca. 1792–1797	I:24/Ia:14	105	Pf. By Viotti
15/ca. 1788	–/1787	I:30/Ia:15	76	Hpd/pf & vn obbl. By Steibelt. *Symphonie Concertante* no 1
16/n.d.	–/1786–88	I:31,IV: 124/ Ia:16	77 11	Pf. By Viotti. *Symphonie Concertante* no 2 & *Duet* no 24
20/ca. 1782–86	3/1769	I:3/Ia:20	25	Hpd/pf. Slow mvt omitted
Symphonie Concertante ca. 1788	1787	I:30/Ia:15	76	By Steibelt as Conc hpd/pf & vn. See pf conc 15
Symphonie Concertante 1780s?	1786–88	I:31/Ia:16	77	Pf. By Viotti. 2nd mvt from G.111. See pf conc 16

Battista Viotta[5] provides G. numbers. Publication dates follow each violin and piano concerto. In the column under W., numbers to the left of the slash are White's numbers for the violin concertos and numbers to the right of the slash are his numbers for the arrangements as piano concertos. Roman I is the section in White's book for concertos, and lower-case letters after the Roman I are arrangements as piano concertos. The gap between piano concerto arrangements 16 and 20 exists because numbers 17, 18, and 19 are concertos for other instruments. The piano concerto no. 12 has the identifying letter "A," and five violin concertos have identifying letters. Some arrangements are in editions as works of other composers, and some are for keyboard with or without added keys. About half the arrangements are for harpsichord or piano and half for piano.

Ignaz Pleyel (1757–1831) studied with Haydn in Vienna, opened a music store in Paris in 1795, and began manufacturing highly regarded pianos in 1807. His piano concerto (1789) is a version of his violin concerto (1785–1787) and the piano concerto (1796) is a version of his cello concerto (1788–1789). Other compositions are two concertos for piano, the divertissement for piano and a harpsichord concerto. His *symphonie concertante* (1791) is in a published version for piano and orchestra.

Bernard Vigueri (ca. 1761–1819) settled in Paris about 1783 and opened a music shop in 1795. He wrote the popular piano method *L'art de Toucher le Piano-Forte,* op. 6 (pub. 1795), and composed two concertos, opp. 5 and 7 (pub. 1795 and 1798).

Heinrich von Lentz (ca. 1764–1839) was a German piano virtuoso, composer, and teacher appreciated in Paris, London, and Warsaw. He probably was in Paris while composing the harpsichord concerto, op. 3, and two piano concertos, opp. 6 and 7.

Julie Candeille (1767–1834), pianist, harpist, singer, actress, composer, and author, was an impressive child genius who gained recognition while young, but lost public following when her considerable talents did not mature in adulthood. Candeille's music includes the piano/harpsichord concerto, op. 2 (pub. 1787), and the lost *symphonie concertante* (1786) for piano, flute, and horn.

Louis Jadin (1768–1853), brother of Hyacinthe Jadin, enjoyed a successful career as a composer of stage music and keyboard accompanist. His music for solo instrument(s) and orchestra includes the sinfonia *concertante* (pub. 1803) for two pianos, the sinfonia *concertante* (pub. ca.1819) for piano, flute, oboe, and clarinet, the fantasia *concertante* (pub. ca.1820) for piano and harp, and four piano concertos.

Hyacinthe Jadin (1769–1802), brother of L. Jadin and student of Hüllmandel, became an admired pianist. He performed one of his four piano concertos at the *Concert Spirituel.*

Antonine Reicha (1770–1836), Czech composer, arrived in Paris in 1799 and became an important theorist and teacher. His *Traité de Mélodie* (1814) presents an early description of sonata form. There are two piano concertos (1804, 1815) and the grand duo concertant for piano and violin. His *andante varié* for flute may exist in a version for piano and orchestra.

Ferdinand Hérold (1791–1833) composed several *opéra comiques* performed throughout the nineteenth century. His piano concertos are op. 25 (ca. 1812), op. 26 (ca. 1812), no. 3 (ca. 1813), and no. 4 (ca. 1813).

Joseph Hemmerlein (? –1799) was a pianist and composer in Frankfurt and a court organist in Coblenz and Paris, where most his compositions were published. He left the piano concertos, op. 6 (ca. 1786), op. 9, the lost op. 10 (1792), op. 11, op. 14 (1793), and op. 15.

Albert Walter (? -mid-nineteenth century), clarinetist, composer, and bandmaster, lived in Paris from 1795. He composed the piano concerto, op. 11.

Table 4 Additional Composers in France

Names	Dates	Compositions
Ancot, Jean	1799–1829	Concerto
Boieldieu, Fraçois-Adrien	1775–1834	Concerto (ca. 1792)
Chartrain, Nicolas	ca. 1740–1793	*Trois concertos,* op 14
Dreux, ?	? –1805	Concerto (pub. 1777), pf or hpd
Dumonchau, Charles-François	1775–1820	2 Concertos, opp 12 & 35 (or 33)
Hermann, Johann	ca. 1760–1846	6 Concertos (1780s). Two are opp 3 & 5
Jumentier, Bernard	1749–1828	Caprice
Kastner, Jean-Georges	1810–1867	Concerto (pub. 1827)
Lemoyne, Gabriel	1772–1815	2 Concertos. No 2 is op 20 (pub. 1813)
Navoigille, Guillaume	ca. 1745–1811	*Symphonie concertante* (ca. 1765–77), vn, pf, hp
Nonot, Joseph	1751–1840	3 Concertos, pf, lost
Pellegrini, Ferdinando	ca. 1715–1766	6 Concertos, op 9 (ca. 1768) hpd
Plati, Alessio	1750–1788	2 Concertos, hpd
Taskin, Henri	1779–1852	Concerto, op 2, pf

Spain

José Palomino (1755–1810) moved to Lisbon in 1774 to become a member of the Saint Cecilia Musicians and compose sacred music and stage works, particularly *tonadillas*. He composed a piano concerto/quintet.

Belgium

Ferdinand Staes (1748–1809) was an accompanist at the Grand Théâtre in Brussels and organist at the Madeleine Church. He composed a harpsichord/piano concerto, op. 6.

Jean-Englebert Pauwels (1768–1804), composer and conductor, founded the Belgian school of violin playing. With Lambert Godecharle, he established the *Société du Concerto* in 1799, and under his direction the group became the finest concert organization of its time. He composed a piano concerto.

The Netherlands

Johann Colizzi (ca. 1740–1790), born in Bohemia, probably settled at The Hague (1770s). His piano/harpsichord concertos probably are four in number, including op. 9, published at The Hague.

Carolus Fodor (1768–1848), brother of C. Emanuel Fodor, was a leading Amsterdam musician from 1795. His music for keyboard and orchestra includes three harpsichord/piano concertos, opp. 1, 8, and 12; op. 12 has a movement titled "Rondo á la Turque." For piano, there is the concertino, op. 24, and a concerto.

Jan Wilms (1772–1847), pianist, harpist, and organist, composer of the Dutch national song *Wien Neerlands Bloed,* arrived in Amsterdam in 1791 and soon became an important musician. He left the harpsichord/piano concerto, op. 3 (pub. 1799), and four piano concertos, opp. 12, 26 (ca. 1811), 36 (1814), and 55.

Ferdinand Hauff (? –1812) worked in a chapel in Delft in 1809. He left seven piano concertos.

Denmark

Gustaf Fredrici (1770–1801) probably is the fictitious creation of S. E. Svensson, director of music at Uppsala from 1939 to 1960 and known for his sense of humor. Supposedly, Fredrici studied with Haydn and Mozart, but no evidence supports the claim. Svensson claims that Fredrici composed a piano concerto.

England

Critics' harsh evaluations of piano concertos were partly due to the newness of the piano as a solo instrument, a lack of standard concerto literature for the piano, and the young composers unacceptable to conservative audiences. In 1796, the harpsichord lost its important position when it was replaced by the piano in a performance of the king's *Birthday Ode.*

Tommaso Giordani (ca. 1730–1806), renowned Italian composer of operas, toured London in 1753 and 1756 as a member of a strolling opera company made up solely of family members. From 1769, he conducted and composed at the King's Theatre and for the Dublin musical society. He composed fifteen concertos for piano or harpsichord: op. 14 (ca. 1775) is a set of six concertos; op. 23 (ca. 1785) is a set of six concertos titled *A Second Sett;* and op. 33a (before 1789) is a set of three concertos. The concertos are for an orchestra of two violins and cello, have structurally mixed features of ritornello and classic concerto forms, and contain the *galant* traits of J. C. Bach.

Giovanni Giornovichi (ca. 1735/1745–1804), known by the stage name Jarnowick, was an Italian composer of violin concertos (1791–1795) important in the evolution of piano concertos. His violin concertos are the source of the "romance" as a second movement and the rondo as the last movement. He did not compose piano concertos.

James Hook (1746–1827), organist, composer, and student of J. C. Bach, was a child prodigy who played concertos in public at age 6. His music is in *galant* style, with some use of Scottish idioms. Haydn influenced him from about 1800. Hook's music for keyboard and orchestra includes six harpsichord/piano concertos (ca. 1771); for harpsichord "A Favourite Concerto" (ca. 1772) containing twelve variations to "Lovely Nancy"; for organ/harpsichord/piano "Three Grand Concertos," op. 20 (ca. 1785); for organ/harpsichord "Six Grand Concertos," op. 55 (ca. 1790); and rondo for piano.

Johann Schröter (1750–1788) traveled from Germany to London in 1772 with his sister and father to perform concerts. As a student of Hiller in Leipzig, Schröter developed an impressive command of the piano and, beginning with his debut in 1772 at a Bach-Abel concert, he became the leading pianist, eclipsing J. C. Bach. When Bach died in 1782, Schröter succeeded him as the music master to the queen. Schröter's highly praised legato and colorful tone helped make the piano a popular instrument in England. In London, Schröter composed twelve piano or harpsichord concertos, opp. 3 and 5 (both ca. 1774), in two sets of six concertos. On the continent, op. 3 is opp. 4 or 5, and op. 5 is opp. 6, 7, or 8. Mozart liked op. 3 and wrote cadenzas, K.626a, for the first, fourth, and fifth concertos. Schröter is the source for Mozart's Alberti-bass figures spanning an octave instead of a fifth, and Mozart's blending of scales and arpeggios in rapid passages.

From 1776, Schröter and Mozart share credit for solidifying the double exposition in the piano concerto. To date, Schröter is the most "classical" composer of keyboard concertos in England. Sometime after ca. 1774 he arranged Buigi Borghi's violin concerto, op. 2, no. 2, as a piano concerto.

Muzio Clementi (1752–1832), Italian, settled in England in 1766 and began a successful musical career as a harpsichordist, pianist, teacher, composer, publisher, and piano manufacturer. During the era in which London audiences enjoyed the pianistic skills of J. C. Bach, Hüllmandel, and Schröter, Clementi's efforts were at the harpsichord, until he turned to the piano in the mid-1790s. He had a bravura style of quick scale lines, thirds, and other double-note passages, altered pitches common in the next generation of composers and, with Dussek, an early appreciation and exploration of the new pianos. The inscription "The Father of the Piano-Forte" on Clementi's gravestone at Westminster Abbey dates from 1877.

Clementi's only extant piano concerto (1796) is a manuscript by the Viennese composer Johann Schenk; no information exists about Schenk's copy. The concerto is a sonata, op. 33, no. 3 (1794), with passage work in both hands that suggests an orchestra accompaniment is necessary. Elaborate cadences frequently end solo sections in concertos, and a cadenza ending a first movement suggests a concerto written as a sonata. The concerto version seems to predate the sonata version. Considering the practice of Dussek and other composers of writing concertos with or without orchestra, Clementi's concerto-sonata makes sense. Often, when a concerto is available as a sonata, it lacks the opening orchestra tutti and has shorter inner tuttis.

Programs and advertisements list Clementi performing piano concertos presumed to be his. These works are not extant in concerto form, but exist as piano sonatas. The sonata, op. 23, no. 3, contains bravura writing that suggests an orchestral accompaniment and elaborate cadences with trills commonly found at ends of solo passages in concertos. The sonata, op. 24, shows some concerto features, and Clementi possibly performed other sonatas composed about 1790 as concertos. The sonata, op. 25, no. 1, has cadences prepared with a tonic six-four chord and finished with trills on the supertonic over the dominant chord. The sonata, op. 33, no. 3, was a concerto prior to being a sonata, and Clementi's pupil Ludwig Berger wrote that the sonata, op. 34, no. 1, originally was a concerto. Clementi left cadenzas (pub. ca. 1787) in appropriate keys for those sonatas.

Wilhelm Friedrich Ernst Bach (1759–1845), son of J. C. F. Bach of Bückburg, was the only grandson of J. S. Bach to receive recognition as a composer. Willhelm studied with his father, visited C. P. E. Bach in Hamburg, traveled to London and became a virtuoso pianist while living with J. C. Bach. London's musical life probably inspired him to write three piano concertos and a concerto for two pianos. He left Bückburg before his father composed harpsichord concertos.

Jan Ladislav Dussek (1760–1812), Czech pianist and composer, was among the earliest pianists, along with Clementi, to earn a living performing public concerts in Europe. Dussek concertized in the mid-1780s, and from 1800 to 1804, and toured from 1781 to 1784. He left Bohemia in 1778, lived in Belgium, went to Hamburg in 1782, and in 1786 traveled to Paris where he became a favorite of Marie Antoinette. In 1789, he went to London, married, became a business partner of his father-in-law, and composed many piano concertos. From 1804 to 1806, he worked for Prince Louis Ferdinand of Prussia until the Prince fell in battle. By 1807, Dussek was in Paris teaching and playing concerts.

Howard Allen Craw's dissertation, "A Biography and Thematic Catalog of the Works of J. L. Dussek (1760–1812)"[6] provides C. numbers for Dussek's music. Publications display more than one opus number for a concerto or misleading information when numbers are in the title, as in the "Fourth Concerto"; this concerto is number 8 in order of composition. During the era, composers were fond of the term "grand" in titles.

The concerto, C.1 (1779), has at least two movements. For piano or harpsichord Dussek composed the concerto, op. 1, C.2–4 (by 1783) and the concerto, op. 3, C.33 (1787). The concerto, op. 15/26, C.53/265 (1789), is the harp concerto, C.265, published as the piano concerto, opp. 15 and 26. The rondo theme is from William Shield's opera *The Farmer* and published as *The Plough Boy*. The concerto, op. 14, C.77 (1791?), called the "Second Concerto," is for harpsichord or piano. The concerto, op. 17, C.78/266 (ca. 1792), called the "Fourth Concerto," is for harpsichord/piano; C.266 is the harp concerto no. 2. Dussek arranged the last movement as the "Duet," op. 26, C.102, for harp and one or two pianos. The concerto, op. 22, C.97 (1793), called the "Grand Concerto," appeared as the piano sonata (1818). The second movement of C.97 and two movements from C.104 form the piano concerto, op. 66, and the third movement is in a version for piano solo. The concerto, op. 27, C.104 (1794), is the "Second Grand Concerto." The concerto, op. 29, C.125 (1795), called the "Third Grand Concerto," sometimes is op. 20. The concerto, op. 30, C.129/267 (1795), called the "Grand Concerto," is a version of the harp concerto no. 3. The concerto, op. 40, C.153 (1798), called the "Grand Military Concerto," has two fast movements. The concerto, C.158 (1798?), for piano or harp, is the "Favorite Concerto." The concerto, op. 49, C.187 (1801), called the "Sixth Grand Concerto," also is op. 50. The title in the autograph of the two-piano concerto, op. 63, C.206 (1805–1806), is "Concertante per due Cembali." The piano concerto, op. 70, C.238 (1810), is the "XIIth Grand Concerto." The concertos, D.7 and D.8, may be by F. X. Dusek.

In 1781, Dussek encouraged Broadwood to extend the piano range from five to five and a half octaves (from FF-f3 to CC-c4), and in 1794 to six octaves. Several of Dussek's concertos are in two versions, one for the smaller keyboard and one for the larger. The concertos, C.97, C.104, C.125, and C.129/267, are in two versions.

As a young man in Paris, Dussek's attractive profile caused people to call him "le beau Dussek." In the early days of concertizing in large halls, the problem of placing the piano on stage came to the forefront. By sitting with his right side facing the audience, Dussek could project the piano sound toward the audience and place his handsome profile before the public. In time, he lost his profile to gluttony.

Dussek is important as a transitional composer writing first in classic style and, eventually, developing striking romantic traits. His music is innovative, with full chords, chromatic chords, modulations to distant keys, and a wide choice of keys. The harmony is more chromatic than Mozart, Haydn, or Beethoven, and Dussek employs virtuoso elements of octaves, thirds, and scales in the style of later nineteenth-century composers. He obtained a smooth legato, like Chopin, by shifting fingers on a key to hold notes or connect passages for a singing style. Dussek was among the first to play the melody louder than the accompaniment. He advanced the use of the damper pedal to new artistic levels, and his music from about 1798 contains occasional pedal indications. His music has contemporary stylistic features and passages that predate Schumann and Chopin.

Dussek's concertos are in a tradition of light and unimportant orchestra parts, so the compositions could be performed as solo pieces; *ad libitum* is written in the orchestra part. Partly, this was a practical matter of concertizing in towns without orchestras or unsuitable orchestras, so a pianist could still perform an advertised concerto as a solo work. Dussek's business sense prompted him to publish music in simplified solo editions for amateur pianists.

In "Dussek and the Concerto,"[7] Truscott finds Dussek's piano concertos to be the first conceived in a truly pianistic idiom, rather than harpsichord concertos titled for piano. Mozart and some contemporaries composed piano concertos with features of harpsichord style and transitional technical devices common during the change from harpsichord to piano. All of Dussek's concertos are pianistic, regardless of publishers' claims that the concertos also were for harpsichord. Truscott believes Dussek, not Beethoven, should be credited with eliminating the improvised cadenza and creating the bravura coda. Dussek understood the tonal possibilities of the new pianos, and addressed these potentials in his piano music. Dussek arranged four of Viotti's violin concertos as piano concertos.

Felix Janeiwicz (1762–1848), Polish composer and popular violinist, went to Vienna, where he met Haydn and Mozart. He established a music business in Liverpool, and in London he composed *A Favorite Concerto* (ca. 1805).

Thomas Wright (1763–1829), organist, composer, and inventor, was famous for organ improvisations. His harpsichord/pianoforte concerto (1795) may be the earliest concerto with metronome markings. Wright used a weighted string arcing over a measured scale to establish tempos.

T. Latour (1766–1837/40) worked in London as a court pianist to the Prince of Wales. He composed *A Military Concerto* (pub. 1810) and the *Second Concerto* (pub. ca. 1810).

Franz Dussek (1766–1816), brother of J. L. Dussek, composed several piano concertos in London or Italy.

Veronika Dussek (1769–1833), sister of J. L. Dussek, became a successful teacher and performer. She composed two piano concertos.

John Cramer (1771–1858), German, was born into a family of violinists working in the Mannheim orchestra and then in London. English audiences knew Cramer as "Glorious John," and Beethoven remarked that Cramer was the only pianist worth mention and "all the rest count for nothing." Like his teacher Clementi, Cramer began as a harpsichordist and switched to the piano. He was a renowned performer important in the development of an idiomatic pianistic style. With Dussek and Clementi, Cramer led the way with the legato touch, and was among the earliest pianists to feature music of other composers on programs. His publishing business may have appended the title "Emperor" to Beethoven's concerto no. 5. Cramer's influence is due to the two sets of the *studio per il pianoforte* (1804, 1810) that are fundamental in the evolution of piano technique.

Cramer's music for piano and orchestra is the nine concertos: op. 10 (pub. 1795), op. 16 (pub. 1797), op. 26 (pub. ca. 1801), op. 38 (pub. ca. 1806), op. 48 (ca. 1812), op. 51 (pub. ca. 1813), op. 56 (pub. ca. 1815), op. 70 (pub. ca. 1822), and the *Concerto da Camera* (ca. 1813). Cramer's music is in the classic style and, like Clementi, he lived longer than his music remained popular. Cramer was a legend in his own time due to a smooth playing style.

Joao Bomtempo (1775–1842), Portuguese pianist and composer, studied in Paris, where he became popular until the Napoleonic invasion forced him to London in 1810. In Paris he composed the three piano concertos, opp. 2, 3, and 7 (1804, 1805, 1809). In London he composed the concerto, op. 12 (1810), and the concertos, opp. 5 and 6 (ca. 1818–1820). There is the grand *fantaisie,* two divertimentos, and a fragment of a fantasy. In 1835, he settled in Lisbon and reformed Portuguese music by establishing a conservatory and breaking the influence of Italian opera.

Valentino Nicolai (fl. 1775–1798?) lived in Paris and London, where he probably published his music. In this era, a publisher commonly printed a composition with different opus numbers or assigned the same opus number to unrelated works. His music includes the four lost harpsichord/piano concertos, op. 9 (ca. 1788), that appeared as opp. 3–6 (ca. 1790); the harpsichord/piano concerto, op. 12 (1788); and, for harpsichord/piano and violin, the three lost concertos, op. 13 (ca. 1795), and the three concertos, op. 14 (ca. 1795). The rondo for piano and violin might be from op. 3 and the two piano concertos are opp. 14 and 15 (both ca. 1799). Possible other piano concertos are opp. 17 and 18.

Philip Corri (1784–1832), composer, singer, teacher, and brother-in-law of J. L. Dussek, helped establish the Philharmonic Society of London in 1813. Sometime between 1813 and 1817, he settled in Baltimore, United States, and changed his name to Arthur Clifton, possibly to avoid creditors. In London, he composed the *Concerto da Camera* (pub. 1812). His opera *The Enterprise* (1822) is among the earliest American operas.

Ferdinand Ries (1784–1838), German, student of Beethoven, who influenced his style, and Albrechtsberger, was a popular pianist and made a fortune touring Europe, Russia, and England. Dates for his compositions are lacking, but his retirement in 1824 suggests most of his works are earlier. Ries was in London from 1813 to 1824.

Ries composed eight(?) piano concertos: no. 2, op. 42 (pub. 1812), based on the violin concerto no. 1; nos. 3 and 4, opp. 55 and 115 (pub. 1815 and 1823); no. 5, "Pastoral," op. 120 (pub. 1823); no. 6, op. 123 (pub. 1824); no. 7, "Farewell to London," op. 132 (pub. 1823); no. 8, "Salut au Rhin," op. 151 (pub. 1826); and no. 9, op. 177 (pub. ca. 1834–1835). Possibly, the concerto no. 1 is for another instrument. Other works are the variations, op. 52 (pub. 1814), based on Swedish national songs; the variations on "Rule Britannia," op. 116/117 (pub. 1824); the rondo "Introduction and Rondo Brilliant," op. 144 (pub. 1825); the variations "Variations Brillantes," op. 170 (pub. 1832); and the polonaise "Rondo Polacca," op. 174 (1833). Works without opus numbers are the rondo "Introduction and Rondo Brilliant," WoO.54 (pub. 1835), and the lost concertino, WoO.88, mentioned in an 1836 letter of Ries. Cecil Hill's *The Music of Ferdinand Ries: A Thematic Catalogue*[8] provides WoO numbers for compositions without opus numbers

William Smetergell (fl. late eighteenth century and early nineteenth century), pianist, organist, theorist, violinist, and composer, composed two-movement concertos in the London tradition of J. C. Bach and Abel. For harpsichord or piano he composed the "6 Concertos" (pub. ca. 1775) and "A Favorite Concerto" (pub. 1784).

Table 5 Additional Composers in England

Names	Dates	Compositions
Barber, Robert	ca. 1750-	"A Favorite Concerto" (ca. 1785), hpd or pf
Beckwith, John "Christmas"	ca. 1750–1809	"A Favourite Concerto" (ca. 1795), org or hpd or pf
Broderip, Robert	ca. 1758–1808	"A Favourite Concerto" op 7 (ca. 1785), hpd or pf
Corri, Domenico	1746–1825	Concerto (pub 1800), pf
Crotch, William	1775–1784	Concerto (pub 1784), hpd or pf
Dale, Joseph	1750–1821	Concerto, op 4, pf or hpd Concerto, op 5
Ferrari, Giacomo	1763–1842	2 Concertos, pf
Griesbach, John	1798–1875	Capriccio (1822), pf
Griffin, George	1781–1863	2 Concertos (ca. 1790s), pf
Guest, Jan Mary	ca. 1765-ca. 1814	Concertos, pf
Haigh, Thomas	1769–1808	6 Concertos, op 1 (ca. 1783), hpd or pf
Kollmann, Christoph	1756–1829	Concerto (1804), pf
Mazzinghi, Joseph	1765–1844	*Concertante,* op 42 (pub 1800), fl, pf
Moller, Johann	1755–1803	2 Concertos, pf
Park(e), Maria	1775–1822	Concerto, op 6 (Pub ca. 1795), pf or hpd
Rawlings, Thomas	1775-ca. 1850	Concerto (pub ca. 1800), pf
Ross, John	1763–1837	6 Concertos, op 1, pf
Rush, George	fl. ca. 1760–1780	4 Concertos (ca. 1770–77), hpd
Smith, Theodore	ca. 1740-ca. 1810	6 Concertos, op 6 (pub 1782), hpd or pf 6 Concertos, op 13 (ca. 1782)
Webbe, Samuel	1740–1816	Concerto, hpd
Wesley, Charles	1757–1834	"Six Concertos," op 2, org or hpd
Wesley, Samuel	1766–1837	2 Concertos (ca. 1774), hpd
Worgan, John	1724–1790	"A New Concerto" (pub ca. 1785), hpd

Scotland

Johann Schetky (1737–1824), German cellist and composer, moved from Hamburg to Edinburgh in 1772. He became the principal cellist for the Edinburgh Musical Society, and composed a concerto published as *A Select Collection of Choice Music for the Harpsichord or Pianoforte* (ca. 1790).

Ireland

Philip Cogan (1748–1833), composer, organist, pianist, teacher, and performer, was among the earliest composers in Ireland to use Irish rhythms in keyboard music. He left the concerto, op. 5 (pub. 1790), and the concerto, op. 6 (pub. ca. 1790?-1795).

The United States

Alexander Reinagle (1756–1809), English musician and friend of C. P. E. Bach, emigrated in 1786 to the United States, where he taught music to wealthy families. The lost *Concerto on the Improved Pianoforte with Additional Keys* (1794) is the earliest American piano concerto. Reinagle was the first composer in America to use the piano in the orchestra, instead of the harpsichord, and, when conducting, he sat at the piano.

Notes

1. Yves Gérard, compiler, *Thematic Bibliographical and Critical Catalogue of the Works of Luigi Boccherini,* Trans. by Andreas Major (London: Oxford University Press, 1969).
2. Cecil Hopkinson, *A Bibliographical Thematic Catalogue of the Works of John Field 1782–1837* (London: printed for the author, 1961. Bath: Harding & Curtis, n.d.).
3. The marking "solo pianoforte" indicates the composition is played as a solo work when an orchestra is not available.
4. Chappel White, *Giovanni Battista Viotti (1755–1824), A Thematic Catalogue of His Works* (New York: Pendragon Press, 1985).
5. Temo Giazotto, *Giovan Battista Viotti* (Milano: Edisioni Curci, 1956).
6. Howard Allen Craw, "A Biography and Thematic Catalog of the Works of J. L. Dussek (1760–1812)" (Ph.D. dissertation, University of Southern California, 1964).
7. Harold Truscott, "Dussek and the Concerto," *Music Review* 16 (February 1955): 29–53.
8. Cecil Hill, *Ferdinand Ries, A Thematic Catalogue* (Armidale, Australia: University of New England, 1977).

Part III

After Beethoven Through Brahms (ca. 1827–1897)

Chapter 5

Germany and Austria

Germany

Franz Fröhlich (1780–1862) was a teacher, critic, theorist, conductor, composer, and organizer of musical events. He composed a piano concerto.

August Klengel (1783–1852) worked as a pianist, composer, and organist at the Roman Catholic Court Church. The cleverness of his canons resulted in the complimentary nickname "Kanon-Klengel." In the classic style he composed two piano concertos.

Friedrich Schneider (1786–1853) was the organist at the university church and the *Thomaskirche* and the music director of the city theater. He probably premiered Beethoven's concerto no. 5 in 1811. He worked on eight piano concertos: no. 1 (1804) with an unfinished first movement; no. 2 (1805); no. 3 as op. 18 (1808); no. 4 (1809) with the second and third movements lost; no. 5 as op. 22 (1809); no. 6 (1809); no. 7 (1812) with the second and third movements lost; and no. 8, with an unfinished first movement and no work completed on other movements.

Christian Rummel (1787–1849) was a composer, conductor and an excellent pianist. The concerto *militaire,* op. 68, quotes a Beethoven theme.

Aloys Schmitt (1788–1866), pianist and composer, settled in Frankfurt in 1816. He composed four piano concertos: op. 14b, op. 43, op. 60 (1824), and op. 56. Other works are the variations "Noch ist Polen," op. 41, the *concertino brillant* "Retour a Frankfurt," op. 75, and the concerto *rondeau* "Souvenir de Field," op. 101. Three concertos and two *concertstücks* exist in manuscript.

Karl Loewe (1796–1869), composer, singer, organist, and conductor, is an important composer of songs between Schubert and Brahms. He composed two concertos for piano and orchestra.

Johann Kalliwoda (1801–1866), Bohemian composer and violinist, led musical activities for Prince Karl Egon II of Fürstenberg for forty years, ending in 1848. His music includes the violin and piano concertino, op. 15 (1830), the *grosses rondo,* op. 16 (1830), and the "Introduction and Variations," op. 128 (1844).

Jakob Schmitt (1803–1853), brother of Georg Aloys Schmitt, left the concerto, op. 300.

Felix Mendelssohn (1809–1847) was a pianist, organist, composer, and conductor born to a wealthy family that brought famous performers, composers, writers, and artists into their home. He composed most of his music for piano and orchestra before leaving on an ambitious tour of Italy, France, and England from 1830 to 1833. He worked as a music director in Dusseldorf and the director of concerts at the *Gewandhaus* in Leipzig. In 1843, he became the director of the Leipzig Conservatory, the first of many such schools founded in Germany during the nineteenth century. Much of Mendelssohn's music is in a forty-four-volume collection he organized and bound. The Mendelssohn family placed the collection in the Berlin State Library in 1877.

For piano and orchestra, Mendelssohn composed a concerto (ca. 1822), a piano and violin concerto (1823), two concertos for two pianos (1823, 1824), the capriccio or capriccio *brillant,* op. 22 (1825–1826), the concerto, op. 25 (1831), the rondo or rondo *brilliant,* op. 29 (1834), the concerto, op. 40 (1837), and the serenade or serenade and allegro *gioioso,* op. 43 (1838). The concerto G minor, op. 25, is in three movements to be performed without stops between the movements. The style is similar to Weber's style, with a repeated chordal accompaniment with eighth-note and sixteenth-note passages at a quick tempo (See ex. 5–1).

Robert Schumann (1810–1856) read widely from early childhood and spent much time writing about music. He started work toward a law degree to meet his mother's wishes, but a strong love of music caused him to give full attention to composition.

Schumann completed his concerto, op. 54 (1845), using the *fantasie* (1841) as the first movement and composing the intermezzo second movement and the third movement in 1845. The *fantasie* does not have a double exposition, and in the concerto Schumann kept the single exposition with the piano entering in the introduction and continuing through the exposition. The first movement is monothematic (See exs. 5–2, 5–3, 5–4, and 5–5) with tonalities of sonata-concerto form and a written cadenza at the end of the movement. Opening themes of the second and third movements (See exs. 5–6 and 5–7) are from the opening theme of the first movement (See ex. 5–2) and the second movement leads directly into the third movement without a pause.

At the end of the cadenza, a trill on the dominant takes the place of the classic trill on the supertonic (See ex. 5–8). This change is possible because of the written cadenza. Beethoven ends the cadenza in his concerto, no. 5, movement 1, with a trill on the supertonic followed by a trill on the dominant (See ex. 5–9).

Schumann's writings on music evidence a keen awareness of the differences between musically worthwhile compositions and shallow contemporary piano concertos. Unlike virtuoso concertos commonly performed as solo pieces because the orchestra has only an accompanying role, Schumann's concerto integrates the orchestra and piano parts so tightly that the work must be performed with the orchestra part. In passages where virtuoso composers might have octaves in both hands, Schumann writes an octave for one hand and a single line for the other hand (See ex. 5–10).

Schumann's other compositions for piano and orchestra are the *concertstück* or "Introduction and Allegro Appassionato," op. 92 (1849), and the "Introduction and Allegro," op. 134 (1853). Incomplete compositions are the three concertos (1829, 1829–1831, 1839) and the "Introduction and Variations" (ca. 1830) on a theme of Paganini.

Schumann's style of piano writing comes from Hummel and Moscheles. Gone are the repeated eight-note chordal accompaniments common in Hummel, Moscheles, Weber, Field, and Chopin, and instead Schumann's chordal accompaniments sometimes duplicate the rhythm of the melody. Hummel's arpeggio accompaniments are an

Used by permission of C. F. Peters Corporation: Mendelssohn (P2896a) Concerto, op. 25.

Example 5–1. Mendelssohn Concerto, op. 25, mvt. 1, mm. 21–32

important feature in Schumann's concerto. Rarely does Schumann write parallel octaves for both hands; instead, one hand has octaves and the other hand single notes doubling the octave line.

Ferdinand Hiller (1811–1885) was an eminent conductor, composer, and teacher in Paris, Frankfurt, Italy, Dresden, and Cologne from 1850. Among his friends were Beethoven, Hummel, Chopin, Liszt, Berlioz, Mendelssohn, and Wagner. Mendelssohn and Spohr influenced his conservative musical style. Hiller composed

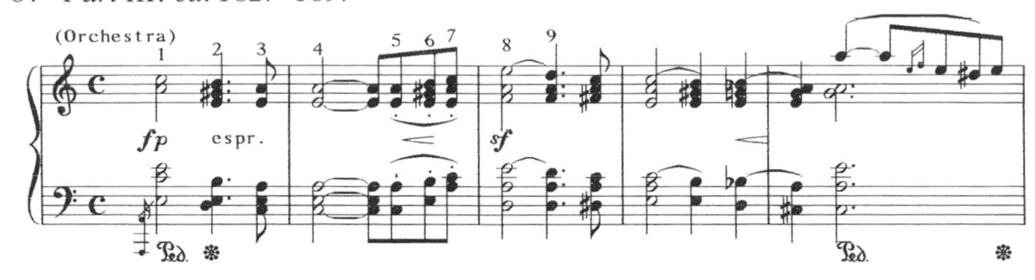

Example 5–2. Schumann Concerto, op. 54, mvt. 1, mm. 4–11[1]

Example 5–3. Schumann Concerto, op. 54, mvt. 1, mm. 67–69

Example 5–4. Schumann Concerto, op. 54, mvt. 1, mm. 157–159

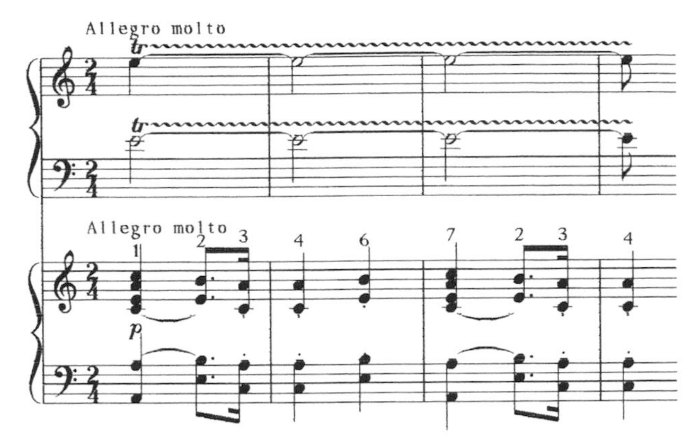

Example 5–5. Schumann Concerto, op. 54, mvt. 1, mm. 347–350, coda

Example 5–6. Schumann Concerto, op. 54, mvt. 2, mm. 1–3

the concerto, op. 5 (ca. 1835), in Paris and the concerto, op. 69 (1860–1861), and the *konzerstück,* op. 113 (ca. 1865), in Cologne.

Franz Liszt (1811–1886) heard Paganini's violin virtuosity in 1831, and resolved to become equally accomplished at the piano. Liszt composed all of his music for piano and orchestra prior to 1870 with the harmonic vocabulary of Chopin and

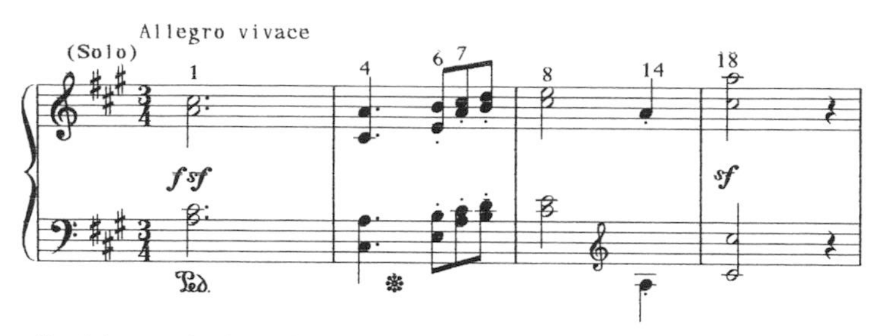

Used by permission of C. F. Peters Corporation: R. Schumann (P2898) Concerto, op. 54.

Example 5–7. Schumann Concerto, op. 54, mvt. 3, mm. 1–4

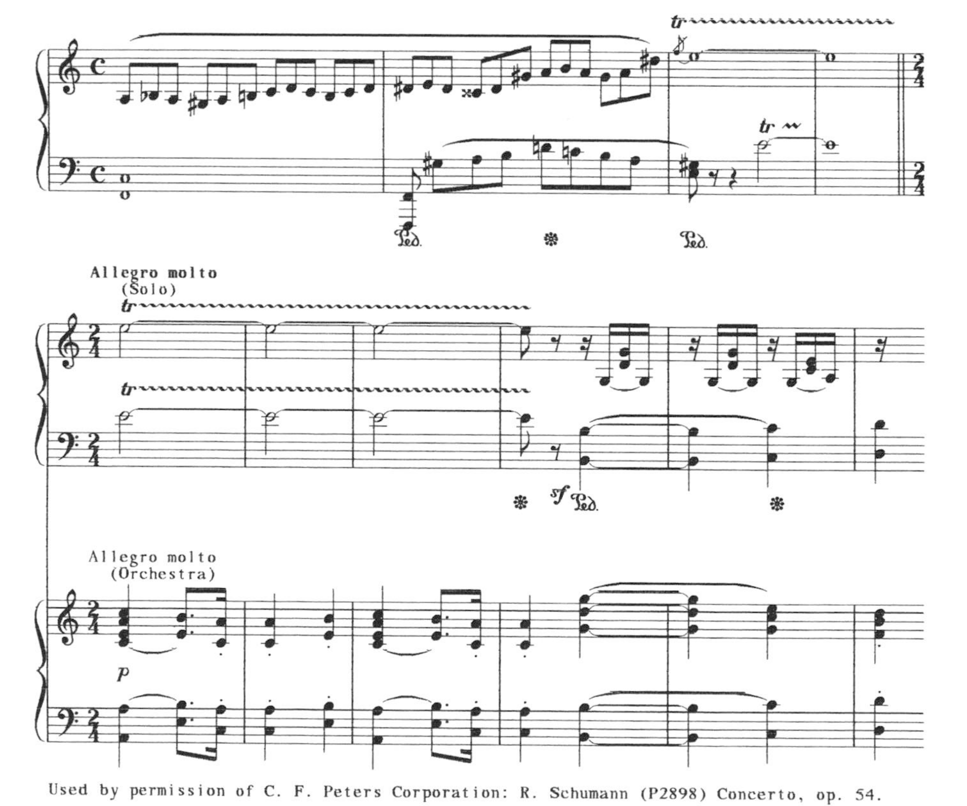

Used by permission of C. F. Peters Corporation: R. Schumann (P2898) Concerto, op. 54.

Example 5–8. Schumann Concerto, op. 54, mvt. 1, mm. 347–352

Example 5–9. Beethoven Concerto no. 5, op. 73, mvt. 1, mm. 495–499

Example 5–10. Schumann Concerto, op. 54, mvt. 1, mm. 39–41

late Beethoven. Humphrey Searle's *The Music of Liszt*[2] provides S. numbers for Liszt's music, and Peter Raabe's *Liszt Schaffen*[3] provides R. numbers.

The *grand fantasy symphonique,* S.120, R.453 (1834), has material from Berlioz's opera *Lélio*. The title *Malédiction,* S.121, R.452 (ca. 1840?), comes from words Liszt jotted in the music, and a sketch of a concerto (1827) provides the material for the musical ideas of ca. 1830. The opening theme of the *Malédiction* bears a strong resemblance to "Orage" in the *Années de Pèlerinage* "Suisse." The musical source for Liszt's *fantasie,* S.122, R.454 (1848?-1852?), is Beethoven's *Ruins of Athens*. The *Fantasie on a Hungarian Folk Melody,* S.123, R.458 (1852?), is a version of the *Hungarian Rhapsody* no. 14 for solo piano.

The concerto no. 1, S.124, R.455 (1849, rev. 1853 and 1856), displays a cyclic influence of Schubert's *Wanderer Fantasy,* D.760, with four movements performed without a break. Together, the four movements are in sonata form without a development. Liszt realized the striking changes introduced in the concerto, and he would sing to the opening motive, "Das versteht ihr alle nichts" (This none of you understand, See ex. 5–11). The opening motive (See ex. 5–12) with the original rhythm appears in the transition, *Un poco marcato,* between the third and fourth movements. The motive in the second movement (See ex. 5–13) appears with a different rhythm at the beginning of the fourth movement (See ex. 5–14). The dedication to Henry Litolff offers insight into interesting aspects of the work. Litolff used the triangle in his concerto *symphonique*

Example 5–11. Liszt Concerto no. 1, S.124, mvt. 1, mm. 1–2

Example 5–12. Liszt Concerto no. 1, S.124, mvt. 1, mm. 1–4

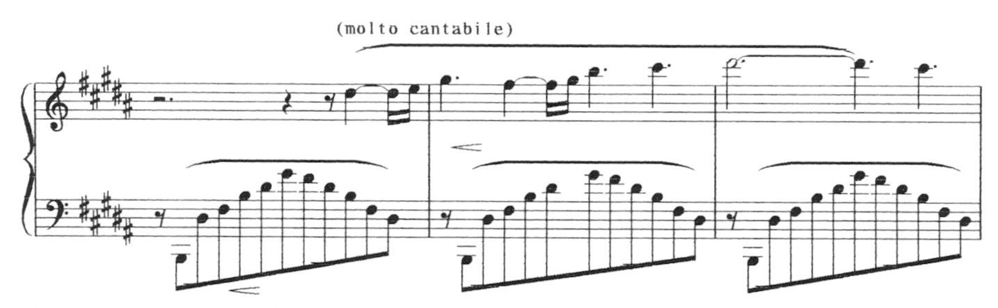

Example 5–13. Liszt Concerto no. 1, S.124, mvt. 2, mm. 10–12

Example 5–14. Liszt Concerto no. 1, S.124, mvt. 4, mm. 1–3

no. 3, op. 45 (1846), three years before the first completed version of Liszt's concerto. When the music critic and philosopher Hanslick heard Liszt's concerto, he derided it as the "triangle concerto." Other ideas Liszt may have observed in Litolff's music are monothematicism, four-movement compositions for piano and orchestra, and octave passages in both hands. The concerto no. 2, S.125, R.456 (1839, rev. 1849–1861), is cyclic.

The inspiration for the *Totentanz,* S.126, R.457 (1849, rev. 1853 and 1859), is the *Orcagna* fresco *The Triumph of Death*. The music is a set of variations based on the chant "dies irae" (day of wrath, See ex. 5–15). Variation IV is an unaccompanied canon (See ex. 5–16) composed by the Berlin teacher and writer Karl Friedrich Weitzmann. Liszt's use of a new theme (See ex. 5–17) with variations in the middle of the composition is unusual in a work based on theme and variations.

In 1894, Busoni arranged Liszt's *Spanish Rhapsody,* S.254, for piano and orchestra. The *grand solo de concert,* S.365, R.18 (1850?), is on the *Grosses Konzertsolo* (1849?) and the early title is the *Concerto Pathetique*. For piano and orchestra, Liszt arranged Schubert's Wanderer Fantasy, D.760, as the *Wandererfantasie,* S.366, R.459 (by 1852), and the *Hexameron,* S.392, R.377. Material from the unfinished *De Profundis,* S.691, R. 668 (ca. 1834), appears in the "Pensée des Morts" in the *Harmonies Poetiques et Religeuses*. Musical material from two lost concertos, S.713 (ca. 1821–1825), appears in the *Malédiction*. Sometimes, Liszt's use of material in later compositions is the only remaining information about his early music.

Many sources list the "Concerto in the Hungarian Style," S.714, as lost, but recent research[4] suggests Liszt gave the work to his pupil Sophie Menter who carried it to Tchaikovsky for orchestration. Because Tchaikovsky did not care for Liszt, Menter did not tell him that Liszt composed the work. For many years, credit for the concerto went to Menter.

The "Concerto in the Italian Style," S.715, is lost. Another unfinished concerto differs from the concertos that are sources for the *Malédiction*. A discovery[5] in ca. 1988 is the *Concerto Opus Posthumous*.

A work associated with Liszt is the lost "Ambrosia Concerto," probably composed by the German scholar A. W. Ambros at Prague University. Ambros composed the concerto by 1871 because Liszt mentioned it in a letter of that date. In the letter Liszt makes a play on the composer's name, so the concerto became known as the "Ambrosia."

Carl Gradener (1812–1883) was a cellist, composer, teacher, and conductor. His music, including a piano concerto (ca. 1852), shows the influence of Schumann and German folk music.

Niels Gade (1817–1890), composer, conductor, and educator, was the most important Danish composer in nineteenth-century music. He met Schumann and Mendelssohn and admired their music. He went to Leipzig, where he conducted the Gewandhaus Orchestra. While in Leipzig, he composed the "Spring Fantasy" (1852) as an engagement gift for his future wife, and the symphony no. 5 (1852) as a wedding gift for her. The symphony has an obbligato piano part that frequently accompanies the orchestra parts and sometimes has important parts that tend not to be virtuosic.

Example 5–15. Liszt *Totentanz,* S.126, mm. 3–11

Example 5–16. Liszt *Totentanz,* S.126, Variation IV, mm. 1–16

Fritz Spindler (1817–1905) was a pianist and composer with more than 400 published musical compositions. He left one piano concerto.

Theodor Kullak (1818–1882), outstanding piano teacher, founded a conservatory in 1850 with Julius Stern and Bernard Marx. Due to a disagreement, Kullak established a separate music school, *Neue Akademie der Tonkunst* which enjoyed great popularity and became known as "Kullak's Academy." He composed the concerto, op. 55 (ca. 1850).

Example 5–17. Liszt *Totentanz*, S.126, mm. 466–483

Clara Schumann (1819–1896), wife of Robert Schumann, achieved considerable eminence as a concert pianist. Her music for piano and orchestra is the concerto, op. 7 (1835/36), and an unfinished concerto (1847). She composed cadenzas for Mozart's concerto, K.466, and Beethoven's concerto nos. 3 and 4. The concerto, op. 7, contains melodic and accompaniment patterns common to the era (See ex. 5–18).

Joseph Raff (1822–1882) experienced such financial difficulties that he gave up a music career for many years until moving to Weimar in 1850 to study with Liszt. Before moving to Weimar, he composed a *concertstück* (perf. 1848) and in Weimar he composed the *Ode au Printemps,* op. 76 (1857), the concerto, op. 185 (1873), and the suite, op. 200 (1875). His concerto has a motive at the beginning of the first movement (See ex. 5–19) that appears in the three movements (See exs. 5–20, 5–21, and 5–22). From 1877, he directed Hoch's Conservatory in Frankfurt.

Carl Reinecke (1824–1910) was a noted pianist, conductor, composer, and teacher at Hiller's Conservatory in Cologne and at the Leipzig Conservatory. His

Example 5–18. Clara Schumann Concerto, op. 7, mvt. 1, mm. 38–51

concertos are op. 72 (pub. 1879), op. 120 (pub. 1873), op. 144 (pub. 1878), and op. 254 (pub. ca. 1900). Other works are the *concertstück,* op. 33 (pub. 1853), and the suite, op. 7 (pub. 1878). Publication dates have little relationship with composition dates. Reinecke wrote forty-two cadenzas, op. 87, for various classic concertos.

Georg Schmitt (1827–1902), son of Aloys Schmitt, composed the *konzertstück,* op. 23.

Example 5–19. Raff Concerto, op. 185, mvt. 1, mm. 1–2

Example 5–20. Raff Concerto, op. 185, mvt. 1, mm. 9–12

Example 5–21. Raff Concerto, op. 185, mvt. 2, mm. 1–4

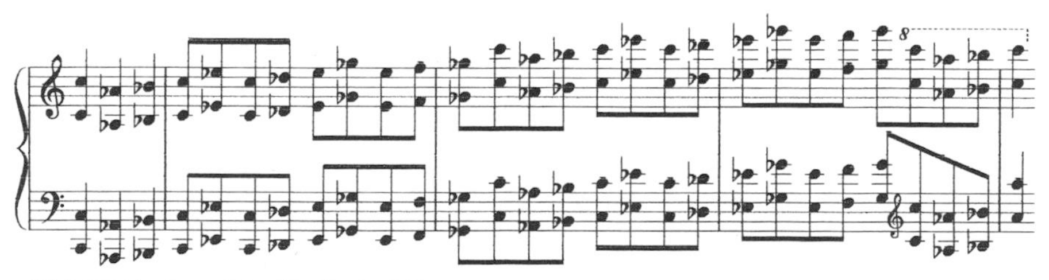

Example 5–22. Raff Concerto, op. 185, mvt. 3, mm. 2–6

Hans von Bronsart (1830–1913), student of Kullak and Liszt, was an active pianist and composer. He followed the "new German" school of Liszt and Wagner, and Liszt dedicated his concerto no. 2 to Bronsart. Bronsart's two concertos are opp. 10 (ca. 1873) and 18. The concerto, op. 10, has an eclectic style common in the music of the era. In 1861, Bronsart married the Swedish composer Ingeborg Starck , who also composed a piano concerto.

Karl Klindworth (1830–1916), pianist, conductor, and teacher, co-founded with Scharwenka the Klindworth-Scharwenka Conservatory. Klindworth orchestrated Chopin's concerto no. 2, and condensed and orchestrated Alkan's concerto.

Salomon Jadassohn (1831–1902), author of theory books used in Europe and the United States, composed two concertos, opp. 89 (pub. 1887) and 90.

Johannes Brahms (1833–1897) championed German classic musicians opposing the futuristic "new German" school led by Liszt and Wagner. His music has classic formal structures blended with late nineteenth-century harmonic and melodic traits. At early performances, audiences were cool to the concertos, opp. 15 (1854–1858) and 83 (1878–1881), possibly because both compositions lack the expected bravura styles.

Material in the concerto no. 1 appeared first as an unfinished symphony, then as a two-piano sonata. The first and slow movements of the sonata are in the concerto, while a somber scherzo is in the requiem. Brahms composed the rondo for the concerto. In the concerto version, Brahms composed a lengthy orchestra exposition of symphonic proportions for the first movement. After about 1825, the double exposition in concertos was generally avoided. The original concept as a symphony resulted in a concerto with a close musical relationship between the orchestra and piano. The somber mood of the first movement stems from Schumann's attempted suicide. At the beginning of the slow movement in the symphonic version, Brahms wrote "Benedictus qui venit in nomine Domini" (Blessed is he who cometh in the name of the Lord), a reference to Schumann's return from attempted suicide to the love of Clara and their children.

The concerto no. 2 is in four movements with generally calmer moods than in the concerto no. 1. Four movements suggest a parallel between concerto and symphonic forms. In a letter, Brahms called the second movement a scherzo and the music has the appropriate meter, tempo, and style. Only Brahms' symphony no. 1 has a scherzo as the second movement, and the last three symphonies and the three piano sonatas have a scherzo or scherzo-like movement as the third movement. The use of a scherzo as the second movement in the concerto is an aesthetic decision. Brahms wanted to make this concerto different from the concerto no. 1; the scherzo is the difference.

Felix Draeseke (1835–1913) was an important composer of the "new German" school of Liszt and Wagner. He left the piano concerto, op. 36 (1885–1886).

Bernhard Scholz (1835–1916) taught theory at the Royal School of Music at Munich, conducted at the Hanover Court Theatre, went to Berlin and Breslau, and taught at Hoch's Conservatory in Frankfurt. He composed the capriccio, op. 35 (1872), and the concerto, op. 57 (1883).

Heinrich Schulz-Beuthen (1838–1915) studied with Moscheles and Hauptmann and became an important composer in the style of Liszt and Wagner. The *Symphonisches Konzert* is for piano and orchestra.

Ferdinand Thieriot (1838–1919), composer, teacher and student of Rheinberger, spent the greatest portion of his active musical life in Graz. He composed a two-piano concerto in Graz, Hamburg, or Leipzig.

Friedrich Gernsheim (1839–1916) was a pianist, composer, and conductor. While on the faculty at the Cologne Conservatory, he composed the concerto, op. 16 (1869).

Josef Rheinberger (1839–1901), composer, organist, and teacher, studied with Bülow at the Munich Conservatory and taught there. While known as a composer of organ music, he also composed the piano concerto, op. 94 (1876).

Hermann Goetz (1840–1876), pianist, conductor and composer, studied with Bülow at the Stern Conservatory while composing a one-movement concerto (1861). He moved to Zürich, Switzerland, in 1863, and composed the concerto, op. 18 (1867), influenced by Schubert, Schumann, and Mendelssohn.

Carl Tausig (1841–1871), Polish pianist, composer, and favorite piano student of Liszt, left a concerto, originally titled "Fantasy," adapted from a two-piano sonata. He probably composed the concerto in Dresden or Vienna.

Martin Wallenstein (1843–1896), pianist and composer, probably composed a concerto in Leipzig or Frankfurt or while on tour.

Martin Wegelius (1846–1906), born in Helsinki, studied with Sibelius at the Helsinki University and with Richter, Reinecke, and Jadassohn in Leipzig. He composed the *Phantasie* (1872) in Leipzig; some sources list the work as a rondo. After returning to Helsinki, he became an opera coach at the National Theater and the director of the newly founded Helsinki Conservatory in 1882.

Xaver Scharwenka (1850–1924), German-Polish pianist and composer, studied at Kullak's Academy. In 1881, he opened a conservatory in Berlin, and merged it in 1893 with the Klindworth Conservatory as the Klindworth-Scharwenka Conservatory. Scharwenka's four concertos are op. 32 (pub. 1876), op. 56 (pub. 1881), op. 80 (pub. 1899), and op. 82 (pub. 1908). Scharwenka's style follows Schumann and other German romantic composers.

Anton Urspruch (1850–1907), student of Raff and Liszt, composed the concerto, op. 9 (pub. 1870s).

James Kwast (1852–1927) was a famous German pianist and teacher at the Cologne Conservatory, where he composed a concerto (1881–1882).

Eugenio Pirani (1852–1939), Italian pianist and composer, studied and taught at Kullak's Academy. The *Venetian Scene,* op. 44, is in an edition dated 1892.

Moritz Moszkowski (1854–1925), German pianist and composer of Polish descent, studied at the Dresden Conservatory, the Stern Conservatory, and the Kullak Academy in Berlin. He taught at the Kullak Academy while enjoying a highly successful career as a pianist. The last movement of the concerto, op. 59 (1898), quotes Chopin's "Black Key" *Etude,* op. 10, no. 5. The right-hand part in Moszkowski's concerto is similar to the right-hand in Chopin's *Etude* and the orchestra part in the concerto has the left-hand part of the etude.

Edward MacDowell (1860–1908), America's most popular nineteenth-century composer, composed two piano concertos in Germany. After completing the concerto

Table 6 Additional Composers in Germany

Names	Dates	Compositions
Anzoletti, Giuseppe	1823–	Concerto *in stitle antico,* 4 vns, pno
		Insogno, vn, pno
Berger, Wilhelm	1861–1911	*Konzertstück* (1888)
Birnbach, Heinrich	1793–1879	6 Concertos (4 in 1821)
Brambach, Kaspar	1833–1902	Concerto, op 39
Brassin, Gerhard	1844–1884	2 Concertos, no 2, op 22 (1865)
Brassin, Leopold	1843–1890	Concertos
Brendel, Franz	1833–1874	Concerto
Bürgmuller, Norbert	1810–1836	Concerto, op 1 (pub 1865)
Buths, Julius	1851–1920	Concerto, op 7
Destouches, Franz	1772–1844	Concerto
Dorn, Alexander	1833–1901	Concerto
Dreyschock, Alexander	1818–1869	*Morceau de Concert,* op 27
		Gruss an Wien, op 32 (1865)
Frank, Eduard	1817–1893	Concerto
		Concerto, op 13 (1850)
Gleitz, Karl	1862–1920	*Irrlichter Fantasie,* op 9 (pub 1895)
Hummel, Ferdinand	1855–ca. 1924	Concerto, op 5 (ca. 1884–1945)
Kauffmann, Fritz	1855–1934	Concerto, op 25 (pub 1892)
Kiel, Friedrich	1821–1885	Concerto, op 30 (pub 1864)
Levi, Herman	1839–1900	Concerto, op 1 (1861)
Limbert, Frank	1866–1938	*Concertstück,* op 3 (1890)
Marschner, Heinrich	1795–1861	Concerto, unfin
Mayer, Emilie	1821–1883	Concerto
Petzet, Walter	1866–1941	2 Concertos
Puchat, Max	1859–1919	Concerto
Raif, Oskar	1847–1899	Concerto, op 1 (pub 1878)
Ritter, August	1811–1885	Concerto
Schneider, Julius	1805–1885	Concerto
Sormann, Alfred	1861–1913	Concerto, op 7
Taubert, Wilhelm	1811–1891	2 Concertos, opp 18 & 189
Vierling, Georg	1820–1901	Capriccio
Wendt, Ernst	1806–1850	Variations
Wolf, Leopold	?–	Serenade, op 7 (pub 1884)

no. 1, op. 15 (1882), he performed it for Liszt with Eugene d'Albert playing second piano. MacDowell began the concerto no. 2, op. 23 (1884–1886), in Frankfurt, completed it in Wiesbaden, and debuted it in the United States with the Boston Symphony Orchestra in 1889. Both works display the influence of German romantic composers, with Liszt and Schumann being obvious models for style and technique. The main theme from the first movement of Edward Grieg's concerto influenced some melodies in MacDowell's concertos. The concerto no. 2 has cyclic features, with first-movement elements appearing in the third movement. A revision of the concerto no. 1 appeared in 1910, with suggestions of the concert pianist Teresa Carreño.

Bernhard Stavenhagen (1862–1914) was a pianist, conductor, composer, court musician, and one of Liszt's favorite students. He composed the concerto, op. 4 (1894), a concerto still in manuscript, and cadenzas for Beethoven's concertos nos. 2 and 3. The concerto, op. 4, begins with a motive that is in the subject of a fugue in the first movement and appears at the beginning of the third movement.

Eugene d'Albert (1864–1932), German pianist and composer of British birth, was *le petit allemand* (the litte German) in Paris, and Liszt called him "young Tausig" due to his amazing piano technique. D'Albert composed two single-movement concertos, opp. 2 (1883–1884) and 12 (1893), and cadenzas to Beethoven's concerto no. 4. The concerto, op. 12, is in four sections approximating movements to be performed without a pause. D'Albert's popularity in England dropped dramatically after he expressed his support for Germany during World War I.

Emil Kronke (1865–1938) taught piano at the Dresden Conservatory while actively performing as a concert pianist. The symphonic variations, op. 14, is on a Norse theme.

Felix von Rath (1866–1905) studied with Reinecke and Thuille. In Munich, he composed the piano concerto, op. 6 (1901).

Percy Sherwood (1866–1939) was an Anglo-German pianist, composer, and teacher at the Dresden Conservatory. There he may have composed a piano concerto.

Austria

Karl Czerny (1791–1857) studied with Beethoven, Hummel and Clementi and taught Liszt, Thalberg, and Kullak. He gained respect as a performer of Beethoven's music, particularly the concerto no. 1. Czerny's compositions include two concertos, opp. 28 and 214, the four-hand concerto, op. 153, two concertinos, opp. 28 and 210, three unpublished concertos, and three cadenzas for Beethoven's piano concertos. He completed 798 opus numbers and many works without opus numbers.

Franz Schoberlechner (1797–1843), pianist and composer, went to Hummel for piano instruction at age 10. Hummel composed his concerto no. 2 for Schoberlechner, whose music is strongly influenced by his teacher's style. For piano and orchestra, Schoberlechner left two concertos and three sets of variations. He probably composed these works in Vienna, but St. Petersburg and Florence need to be considered.

Sigismond Thalberg (1812–1871) studied with Hummel, Pixis, Kalkbrenner, and Moscheles, and became a renowned pianist and rival of Liszt. His pianistic trademark was writing the bass part in the left hand, an accompaniment in the upper register of the piano for the right hand, and, simultaneously, a melody in the middle of the keyboard for the thumbs of both hands; the concerto, op. 5 (1829–1830), has this technique. The ill feeling between Thalberg and Liszt ended when both agreed to join Pixis, Herz, Czerny, and Chopin in contributing variations to the *Hexaméron*.

Ignaz Brüll (1846–1907), close friend of Brahms, studied in Vienna and Dessoff before settling in Vienna after extensive European recital tours. His music for piano and orchestra is the concerto, op. 10 (1877), the concerto, op. 24, the rhapsody, op. 65 (pub. 1892), and the *concertstück* "Andante and Allegro," op. 88 (1903).

Table 7 Additional Composers in Austria

Names	Dates	Compositions
Assmayr, Ignaz	1790–1862	2 works, titles?
Bagge, Selmar	1823–1896	Concerto (1849, rev 1878)
Blahetka, Marie	1811–1887	*Souvenir d'angleterre,* op 38
		Variations *brillantes*
Fuchs, Robert	1847–1927	Concerto, op 27 (1880)
Gradener, Hermann	1844–1929	Concerto, op 20 (1900)
		Concerto
Labor, Josef	1842–1942	*Konzertstück*
Rèe, Louis	1861–1939	Concerto, 2 pnos
Reinhold, Hugo	1845–1935	Suite, op 7
Riotte, Philip	1776–1856	Concertos, opp 4, 8, & 15
		2 Concertos
Rufinatscha, Johann	1812–1893	Concerto
Schaden, Nanete von	? –	2(?) Concertos
Schutt, Eduard	1865–1933	2 Concertos, op 7 (perf 1882), op 47 (by 1896)
Stein, Andreas	1797–1863	2 Concertos
Tyrell, Agnes	1846–1883	Concerto
Wolf, Ludwig	1804–1859	Concert variations
Zeller, Julius	1832–1900	Concerto, op 12 (pub 1872)

Ludvig Schytte (1848–1890), Danish pianist and composer, gave up a career as a pharmacist to pursue music. He studied with Gade and Liszt and settled in Vienna (1887). The concerto, op. 28 (pub. ca. 1890), displays a strong influence of Schumann and the barcarolle, op. 60, requires a string orchestra.

Ignaz Paderewski (1860–1941), internationally famous Polish pianist and diplomat, composed music for piano and orchestra early in life before becoming concerned about Poland during the tumultuous years of the early twentieth century. He composed the "Polish Fantasy on Original Themes," op. 19 (1893), during a concert tour to England and the Americas. While a student of Leschetizky in Vienna he composed the concerto, op. 17 (1888). Both works exhibit traits of Polish folk music. Paderewski helped produce a complete edition of Chopin's piano music.

Notes

1. Notes are numbered in Examples 5–2, 5–3, 5–4, 5–5, 5–6, and 5–7 to facilitate comparisons.
2. Humphrey Searle, *The Music of Liszt,* 2nd revised ed. (New York: Dover Publication, 1966).
3. Peter Raabe, *Liszt Schaffen* (Tutting: Hans Schneider, 1968).
4. Maurice Hinson, "Long Lost Liszt Concerto?," *Journal of the American Liszt Society* XIII (June 1983): 53–58.
5. Anon., "A Chicago Grad Student Strikes a Career High Note, Finding a Long-Lost Liszt," *People* 31 (April 10, 1989): 113.

Chapter 6

Italy, Poland, Czechoslovakia, Hungary, Russia, France, The Netherlands, Belgium, Denmark, Switzerland, Norway, Sweden, Finland, Spain, England, Ireland, and the United States

Italy

Between the deaths of Beethoven and Brahms, Italian composers concentrated primarily on opera. Italian audiences and composers did not have opportunities to hear music for piano and orchestra or other forms of instrumental music. German musical culture, particularly the music of Liszt and Wagner, influenced Italian composers and performers. Therefore, there was little development of an Italian style of instrumental music.

Francesco Basili (1767–1850), famous for church music and operas, worked in Foligno, Macerata, and Loreto. He left a piano concerto.

Tommaso Marchesi (1773–1852), composer, conductor, organist, and member of the *Accademia Filarmonica Bologna,* left a concerto for piano and strings.

Giovanni Pacici (1796–1867) was a quick and facile composer, with more than eighty operas popular in Rome, Milan, and Naples before Bellini and Donizetti. The sinfonia *Dante* (1863) is for piano and orchestra.

Marianna Bottini (1802–1858), harpist, composed an indeterminate number of piano concertos.

Disma Fumagalli (1826–1893) taught piano at the Milan Conservatory from 1857. His 334 piano compositions include the concerto, op. 83 (pub. 1856), with string orchestra.

Giovanni Sgambati (1841–1914) studied with Liszt and learned the music of Bach, Beethoven, Liszt, and Wagner. With his friend Pinelli, he founded the *Liceo Musicale* in association with the *Accademia di Santa Cecilia* and taught there from 1868. He introduced Italian audiences to instrumental music and composed the concerto, op. 10 (1878–1880), and the lost *Cola de Rienzo* (1866).

Antonio Scontrino (1850–1922) was a virtuoso double-bass performer in Milan and Palermo. He left a piano concerto.

Henrique Oswald (1852–1931), Brazilian, composed a concerto (1888) and an andante *e variaçoes*. In 1911, he returned to Rio de Janeiro to teach.

Alfonso Rendano (1853–1931), student of Thalberg and Mathias, enjoyed success as a pianist. His greatest contribution was the *pedale independente,* also known as the *pedale Rendano* or *sostenuto pedal,* that allows notes or chords to be held while playing and using the damper pedal for other passages. He composed a piano concerto.

Giuseppe Martucci (1856–1909) was the most prolific Italian composer of music for piano and orchestra. He left the concerto, op. 66 (1884–1885), an unpublished concerto (1878) and the *tema con variazioni*. From 1880, he taught piano at the Naples Conservatory, and later he directed the Bologna and the Naples conservatories.

Giuseppe Ferrata (1865–1928), one of Liszt's last piano students, emigrated to the United States in 1892 and taught at Tulane University in New Orleans. He left the concerto, op. 5.

Elmérico Fracassi (1874–1930) went to Buenos Aires as a child and returned to Naples in 1890 to study at the conservatory. He toured Europe as a pianist before settling in Buenos Aires in 1904. He composed one piano concerto.

Poland

Frédéric Chopin (1810–1849) is Poland's most important composer of piano music in the nineteenth century. He was born near Warsaw, where he received musical training based on Bach and Viennese classic masters. His talent was evident early, and by 1817 he was composing and performing for aristocrats.

Maurice Brown's *Chopin, An Index of His Works in Chronological Order*[1] provides BI (Brown Index) numbers for Chopin's music. In 1829, Chopin debuted in Vienna with the variations, op. 2, BI 22 (1827), the *Fantasy on Polish Airs,* op. 28, BI 13 (1828), and improvisations on a Polish folk melody. The theme for the variations is Mozart's melody *Là ci Darem la Mano* (Extend Me Thy Hand, My Love) from *Don Giovanni*. This is the musical composition that inspired Schumann to write, "Hats off, gentleman, a genius!" The *Fantasy on Polish Airs* is on the Ukrainian folk song "Already the Moon Had Set, the Dogs Were Asleep," an air by Karol Kupinski, and a slow mazurka *Kujawiak* from the Kujawia district of Poland.

After returning to Warsaw, Chopin composed two piano concertos, op. 11, BI 53 (1830), and op. 21, BI 43 (1929–1930), and performed the concerto no. 2 and the *Fantasy on Polish Airs*. Five days later, he played the concerto no. 2 and the *Krakowiak,* op. 14, BI 29 (1828); a *Krakowiak* is a Polish dance in 2/4 meter from the Cracow district of Poland. The concerto no. 1 is the second concerto Chopin composed. Delays in publication due to problems with the orchestra parts caused the first concerto to be published as the concerto no. 2.

Both concertos are in three movements, with the first movements in sonata form with a double exposition. In the developments, Chopin presents new material and melodic elaborations of previous material. Chopin's developments are not developmental in the sense of Beethoven's treatment of motives; Chopin treats the musical material much as it is treated in other sections of the movements. Because cadenzas are essentially developmental treatments of previous material, Chopin probably chose not to write cadenzas or places for them. Also, Chopin's improvisational style provides substantial virtuoso material of the kind common in cadenzas. The first edition of the concerto no. 2 contains figured bass in the tutti sections.

Slow movements of both concertos are lyric and embellished. A "romance" is the slow movement of the concerto no. 1, and the simple melody appears in elaborated forms. The slow movement in the concerto no. 2 is a ternary form, and Chopin wrote an additional left-hand part for mm. 43–70 for when the movement is a solo work. The final movements of both concertos are rondos and the mazurka is a strong influence. The nocturne, BI 49 (1830), contains material from the concerto no. 2, and in Poland it is the "Remembrance Nocturne" due to its reference to the concerto. The nocturne has a quotation of Chopin: "For my sister Louise to play, before she practises my second concerto."

The polonaise, op. 22, BI 58 (1830–1831), is the grand polonaise and the andante spinato, op. 22, BI 88 (1834), is for piano solo. In 1836, Chopin merged the two works into the *grande polonaise brillante précédée d'un andante spinato* with orchestra accompaniment. Chopin arranged the composition for solo piano (pub. 1838).

Chopin planned the Allegro *de Concert,* op. 46, BI 72 (1830?–1841), as a third piano concerto or a concerto for two pianos. The composition is a piano solo work with recognizable tutti and solo sections. Material from 1830 may not appear in the finished version. Jean Louis Nicode (1835–1919) arranged the work for piano and orchestra (pub. 1880).

The source of Chopin's style is a matter of controversy. Modern research suggests a complex mixture of local, regional, and foreign composers important in the evolution of his style. Citing influences on Chopin's style is easier than pinpointing exact sources. Essentially, the style is a product of many creative minds, and the idea that Chopin created his own style is erroneous. This view is popular because Chopin's style comes from forgotten predecessors and contemporaries. Throughout Europe, many individuals used musical elements identifiable as Chopin's, but Chopin used those features better than other composers.

In his article "Some Slavic Predecessors of Chopin,"[2] Georges S. Golos lists a number of local musicians who might have influenced Chopin. They include Wojciech Zywny (1756–1842), Jozef Jawurek (1756–1840), Wenzel Würfel (1791–1832), Karol Kupinski (1785–1857), Jozef Elsner (1769–1854), and Feliks Ostrowski (1802–1860), who composed polonaises and other piano works with characteristics similar to Chopin's style. Franciszek Lessel[3] (1780–1838) composed music with elements similar to Chopin's style, and predated Chopin's practice of writing a mazurka as the final movement of a concerto. Maria Szymanowska (1789–1831) toured Europe as a concert pianist and composed much piano music. Chopin heard her elegant pianistic style in concerts of her own music and works of contemporary European composers. Her etudes, nocturnes, and mazurkas are important precursors of Chopin's similar compositions. Also, Prince Michal Kleofas Oginski (1765–1833) composed polonaises with features similar to Chopin's early polonaises.

Chopin was familiar with the music of the Bohemian composers Vaclav Jan Tomásek and Jan Hugo Vorisek. Although Dussek's productive years were in England and France, his music contains stylistic features probably known to Chopin.

Also influencing Chopin's style were Hummel,[4] Moscheles, Field, Weber, and Kalkbrenner. Chopin's concerto, op. 11, has strong similarities to Hummel's concerto, op. 85 (See ex. 6–1), in the melodic design and the accompaniment pattern, and to Moscheles' concerto, op. 60. Chopin's concerto no. 2 suggests an influence of Hummel's concerto, op. 89, and he was fond of Field's concerto no. 2. Hummel, Moscheles, Weber, and Field demonstrate Chopin's characteristics of florid and elegant melodies above repeated left-hand chords or arpeggios and melodic elaboration with appoggiaturas, suspensions, and passing notes.

The tradition of writing concerto orchestrations as mere accompaniments to the piano begins with J. C. Bach and continues through Dussek, Kalkbrenner, Field, Hummel, Ries, and others. Unlike the concertos of J. C. Bach, concertos of the other composers were popular in Poland when Chopin was composing concertos. Composer's knew that an orchestra might not be available, orchestra players might be unable to perform the parts, or available instruments might be unsuitable for a concerto. Also, many touring pianists prepared concertos as solo works. Chopin's concerto orchestrations conform to established practice. Only when established orchestras become the norm do performances of concertos as solo works become unnecessary and unacceptable.

Several composers attempted to improve Chopin's orchestrations and some-

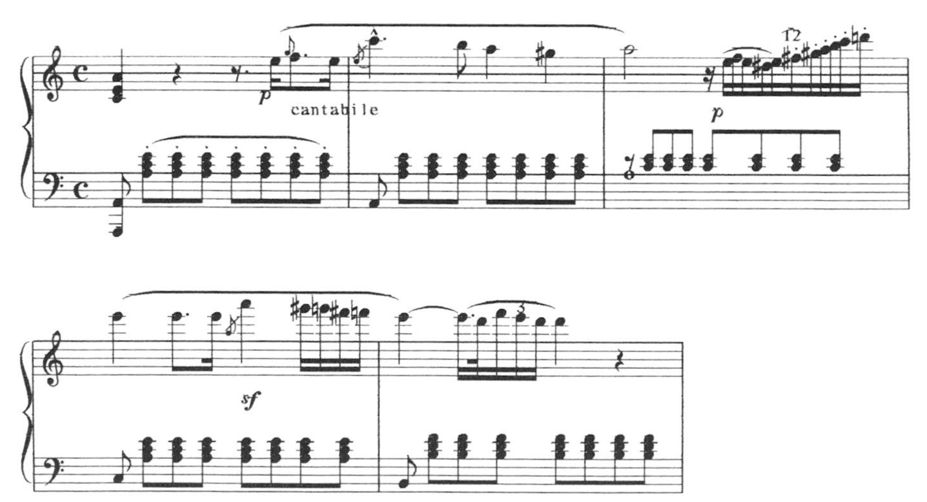

Example 6–1. Hummel Concerto, op. 85, mvt. 1, mm. 152–156

Table 8 Additional Composers in Poland

Names	Dates	Compositions
Bergson, Michal	1820–1898	Concerto, op 62
Brzowski, Jözef	1805–1888	Grand *rondeau* (1837)
		Grand allegro (1846)
Czerwinski, Wilhelm	1837–1893	Concerto
Deszczynski, Józef	1781–1844	Concert brillant, op 25
		2 Concertos
Grabowska, Clementine	1771–1831	Concerto
Grossman, Ludwik	1835–1915	Concerto
Illinski, Jan	1795–1860	2 Concertos
Janotha, Natalia	1856–1932	Cadenzas, Beethoven Conc, no 4
Jeske-Choinska-Mikorska, Ludmila	1849–1898	*At the Castle*
Katski, Antoni	1817–1899	Concerto(s?)
Kazimierz, Wernik	1828–1859	Concerto (pub 1853)
Krogulski, Jozef	1815–1842	2 Concertos (1830/1831)
Markowska-Garlowska, Eliza	? –	Concerto
Melcer-Szczawinski, Henryk	1869–1928	2 Concertos (1895/98)
Pachulski, Henryk	1859–1921	Fantasia, op 17
Soltys, Mieczyslaw	1863–1929	Concerto "Religioso"
Stolpe, Antoni	1851–1972	Concerto (1869)
Zarzycki, Aleksander	1834–1895	Grand Polonaise, op 7
		Concerto, op 17 (ca. 1859)
Zelenski, Ladislaw	1837–1921	Concerto, op 60 (1890s?)

times the piano writing, but none of the "improved" versions have a place in the standard performing literature. Perhaps these failed efforts prove the appropriateness of Chopin's orchestrations. Karl Klindworth orchestrated the concerto no. 2 (1868), Karl Tausig orchestrated a concerto (pub. 1866), Adam Minchejmer (1830–1904) orchestrated the concerto no. 1, Balakirev orchestrated and partly rewrote the concerto no. 1 (1910), and Granados tried orchestrating the concerto no. 2. A publication in Paris of the concerto no. 1 is for orchestra or string quartet accompaniment.

Czechoslovakia

Bedrich Smetana (1824–1884) was the first important nationalistic composer of Bohemia. He arranged his polka (ca. 1862) for piano and orchestra and wrote cadenzas for Mozart's concertos, K.491, K.466, and K.595, and Beethoven's concerto no. 3 (1861).

Ivan Zajc (1832–1914) left musical compositions numbering up to opus 1202, including three works for piano and orchestra: the *sinfonicka glazbena slika* (symphonic tone painting), op. 343, the *Frühling-Sonata* (Spring-Sonata), op. 457, and the *fantasia polacca,* op. 617b.

Antonin Dvorák (1841–1904) composed symphonic music displaying the Czech national character. The concerto, op. 33 (1876–1879), is conservative considering the

Table 9 Additional Composers in Czechoslovakia

Names	Dates	Compositions
Hampel, Hans	1822–1844	Cadenza, Beethoven Conc no 3
Kanka, Jan	1772–1863	Concerto (pub 1804)
		Grand Concerto
Kovarovic, Karel	1862–1920	Concerto (1887)
Novák, Vitezslav	1870–1949	Concerto, op 10 (1895)
Rieger, Gottfried	1764–1855	2 Concertos
Trnecek, Hanus	1858–1914	Concerto
Vitäsek, Jan	1770–1839	Concerto

composition date. Dvorák's awkward keyboard writing prompted Rudolf Firkusny and Franz Reizenstein to revise the concerto in two versions.

Hungary

Ferenc Erkel (1810–1893) composed the Hungarian national anthem in 1844 and helped create a Hungarian operatic style. He influenced Liszt's use of the cadential melodic figure with grace notes and Hungarian musical features, including the Hungarian scale, as in the opening bass line of the sonata in B minor. As the foremost pianist in Pest, his repertoire included concertos by Moscheles, Hummel, Herz, Thalberg, and Field. For piano and orchestra, Erkel composed the lost *Fantasy and Variations on the Transylvanian Rákóczi Song* (1838) and sketches of variations (1839). His style is similar to Viennese classic composers.

Mihály Mosonyi (1815–1870), composer, teacher, and writer on music, lived in Pozsony (now Bratislava) and, from 1842, in Pest as one of Hungary's first independent musicians important in the development of a Hungarian national musical style. His concerto (1844) predates Liszt's single-movement works with cyclic treatment of material in movement-like sections, passages similar to the Schumann concerto, op. 54, where one hand has octaves and the other hand has single notes, and a variety of techniques in relatively short passages.

Robert Volkmann (1815–1883), friend of Schumann and Mendelssohn, lived mostly in Budapest and taught at the National Academy of Music. The four-movement *concertstück,* op. 42, is cyclic, with the same material appearing in the first and fourth movements. The first movement functions as a slow introduction to the second movement, a theme and variations. Volkmann's style shows a German classic influence, namely the music of Schumann and Brahms, with some of the Hungarian *verbunkos* style.

James Major (1858–1925) was a noted pianist, conductor and composer in the generation following Erkel, Liszt, and Mosonyi, and preceding the national turn to folk music for inspiration. Volkmann represents the German romantic influence in Major's music. Among Major's compositions is the concerto (1882?), the *concert symphonique,* op. 12 (1888?), the concerto, op. 49 (ca. 1902), and the concert fantasies, op. 63 (1905?).

Arpád Szendy (1863–1922), piano teacher at the Academy of Music, studied piano with Liszt in 1881 and played in the manner of Liszt. He composed a concerto (1888) and the concert *phantasie,* op. 13 (1907?).

Russia

Alexey Zhilin (ca. 1766–ca. 1848), blind at age 6, was the *kapellmeister* at the Institute for Blind Works in St. Petersburg, and he lived in Kursk and Moscow. He probably composed a concerto for piano and orchestra.

Adolf von Henselt (1814–1889), German composer and brilliant pianist, performed at least as well as Liszt, but his nervousness prevented him from pursuing a concert career. He settled in St. Petersburg in 1838, and became a decisive influence on Russian piano music. The *variations de concert,* op. 11, is on "Quand je quittai la Normadie" from the Meyerbeer opera *Robert le Diable*. The concerto, op. 16 (1838), is a virtuoso work featuring Henselt's speciality of wide extensions (See ex. 6–2).

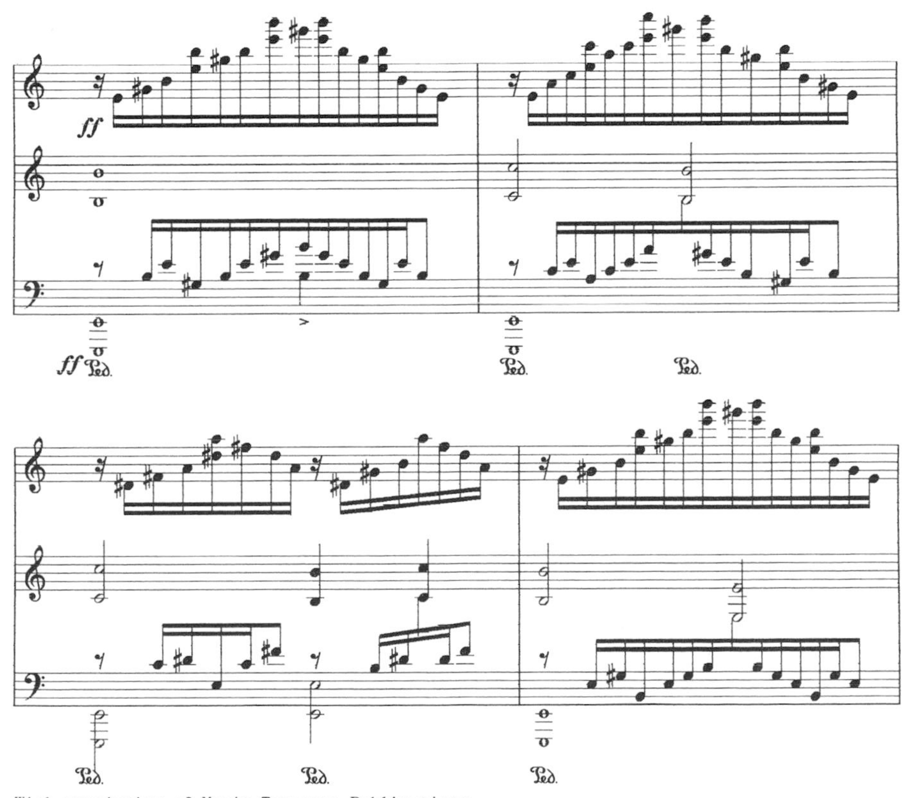

Example 6–2. Henselt Concerto, op. 16, mvt. 1, mm. 218–221

Example 6–3. Rubinstein Concerto no. 4, op. 70, mvt. 1, mm. 54–58

Otto Deutsch (ca. 1823–1863) was a conductor, choral director, and theory teacher at the conservatory from 1862. The sonata is for two pianos and orchestra.

Anton Rubinstein (1829–1894), brother of pianist Nicholas Rubinstein and teacher of pianist Josef Hoffmann, was a pianist equal to Liszt. In a period of 240 days, he performed 215 concerts during an American tour. His early training was on music by Hummel, Hertz, Moscheles, Kalkbrenner, Czerny, Diabelli, and Clementi, and his eclectic musical compositions (See exs. 6–3 and 6–4) contain influences of Schumann, Mendelssohn, Chopin, and Liszt.

Rubinstein was the most prolific nineteenth-century Russian composer of music for piano and orchestra. When he tried to enter Russia after a concert tour, suspicious border police confiscated his luggage that contained his early musical works. Again, he composed music as op. 1; thus, there is a lost set of opus numbers and the same opus numbers for extant works. The first movement of his concerto (1847) is lost, and the concerto (1849) became the octet (1856).

There are five extant concertos by Rubinstein: op. 25 (1850), op. 35 (1851), op. 45 (1853–1854), op. 70 (1864), and op. 94 (1874). Other works are the fantasia, op. 84 (1869), the *caprice russe,* op. 102 (1878), and the *concertstück,* op. 113 (1889). He composed cadenzas for Mozart's concerto, K.466, and Beethoven's concertos nos. 1–4.

Mily Balakirev (1837–1910) composed the piano solo work *Islamey* that blends Oriental elements with contemporary Western techniques. His music for piano and orchestra includes the *grand fantaisie,* op. 4 (1852), based on Russian folk songs, the one-movement concerto no. 1 (1855–1856), and the concerto no. 2 (1861–1862, 1906–1909) completed by Liapunov in ca. 1910. Simultaneously Balakirev composed the slow movement of the concerto no. 2 and a thematically related requiem that is incomplete. The inscription "Finis del prima parte" at the end of the *grand fantaisie* suggests he intended to continue the work. The grand fantaisie is on the Russian folksongs "The Sun Is Not Eclipsed" and "Down in the Vale." Balakirev's reverence for Chopin is evident in his orchestration of Chopin's concerto no. 1.

Eduard Nápravnik (1839–1916), Czech-born, was a naturalized Russian conductor and composer important in the revitalization of Russian court opera. In a musical style influenced by Tchaikovsky and Glinka, he composed the concerto, op. 27

Example 6–4. Rubinstein Concerto no. 4, op. 70, mvt. 1, mm. 91–94

(1877), and the *Fantasia on Russian Themes,* op. 39 (1881), that contains the "Volga Boat Song."

Peter Tchaikovsky (1840–1893) is an important cosmopolitan representative of Western influence, notably Liszt and Chopin, on Russian music. His music includes the concerto no. 1, op. 23 (1874–1875), the concerto no. 2, op. 44 (1879–1880), and the concerto fantasy, op. 56 (1884). The one-movement concerto no. 3 (1893) sometimes has the titles "*Allegro de Concerto*" or "*Konzertstück*"; Taneyev completed and orchestrated the andante and finale (1893) movements in 1897. Originally Tchaikovsky intended the concerto no. 3 and the andante and finale as the symphony no. 6; the present symphony no. 6 would be no. 7. Except for the piano part, orchestrations in the concerto and the andante and finale are identical with Tchaikovsky's last symphonies, but he felt the musical material to be unsuitable for a symphony.

The concerto no. 1 did not receive a warm reception from N. Rubinstein or other noted musicians. Rubinstein's unkind comments caused Tchaikovsky to change the dedication to von Bülow. Musicians considered the music difficult and unwieldy, and during the first performances of the concerto listeners found the large introduction offensive (See ex. 6–5). Eventually, Tchaikovsky agreed the concerto needed revision and he completed work on the present version in 1889. The first-movement theme beginning at the "Allegro con Spirito" (See ex. 6–6) is on a tune Tchaikovsky heard blind beggars perform at a fair in Kamenka. The second movement follows the Russian practice of writing in one key, D-flat major, then moving to the key one-half step above, D major (See ex. 6–7). In the prestissimo the melody in the orchestra part is "Il faut s'amuse, danser et rire" (See ex. 6–8) which soprano Désirée Artôt sang, the woman Tchaikovsky wanted to marry. The third movement is a sonata-rondo based on the Ukrainian folk song "Come, Come, Ivanka" (See ex. 6–9).

Nikolay Rimsky-Korsakov (1844–1908) led the nationalistic "Mighty Five" that included Cui, Borodin, Balakirev, and Mussorgsky. "Mighty Five" comes from V. V. Stassov's written description of an 1868 concert for the All-Russian Ethnographical Exhibition in Moscow. Stassov called the group of composers the "mighty handful," and the term became "Mighty Five." Rimsky-Korsakov taught Glazunov, Liadov, Arensky, Ippolitov-Ivanov, Gretchaninov, N. Tcherepnin, and Stravinsky. His one-movement

Example 6–5. Tchaikovsky Concerto no. 1, op. 23, mvt 1. mm. 25–29

Example 6–6. Tchaikovsky Concerto no. 1, op. 23, mvt. 1, mm. 108–110[5]

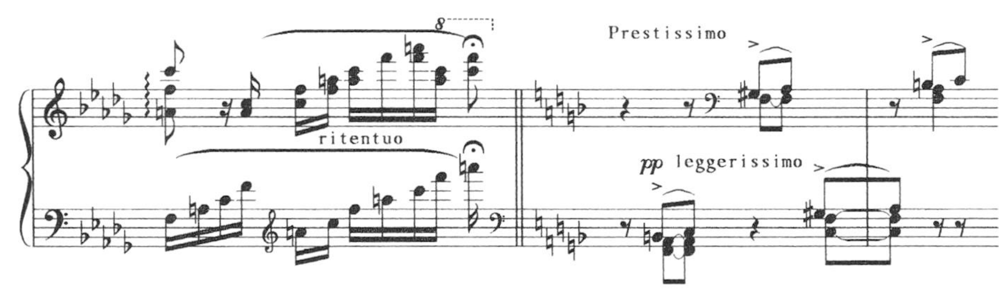

Example 6–7. Tchaikovsky Concerto no. 1, op. 23, mvt. 2, mm. 58–60

concerto, op. 30 (1882), has thematic transformation, keyboard techniques similar to Liszt and the melodic material that begins the first movement (See ex. 6–10) also begins the second (See ex. 6–11) and third movements (See ex. 6–12).

Anton Simon (1850–1916), French conductor and composer, studied at the Paris *Conservatoire* and settled in Moscow in 1871. He conducted at the *Bouffe* theater and

Example 6–8. Tchaikovsky Concerto no. 1, op. 23, mvt. 2, mm. 80–82

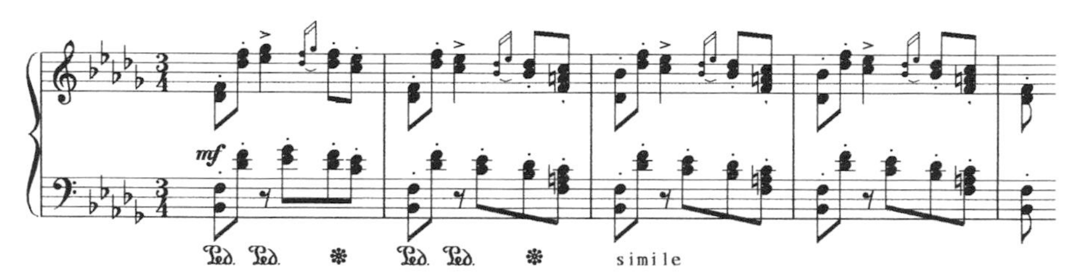

Example 6–9. Tchaikovsky Concerto no. 1, op. 23, mvt. 2, mm. 5–9

taught piano at the music school of the Moscow Philharmonic Society. He composed the concerto, op. 19.

Paul Pabst (1854–1879) studied piano with Liszt and taught piano at the Moscow Conservatory. His concerto, op. 82, is in an edition dated 1883.

Sergey Taneyev (1856–1915), student and friend of Tchaikovsky, completed some of Tchaikovsky's music and premiered all of Tchaikovsky's piano concertos, except the original version of the concerto no. 1. Taneyev's fame comes from teaching Scriabin, Rachmaninoff, Lyapunov, and Glier. His concerto (1876) has two of three movements completed.

Sergey Lyapunov (1859–1924) studied piano with Klingworth and Pabst, and composition with Tchaikovsky, Hubert, and Taneyev. His compositions display Russian musical characteristics and influences of Schumann, Chopin, Mendelssohn,

With permission of the International Music Company.

Example 6–10. Rimsky-Korsakov Concerto, op. 30, mvt. 1, mm. 1–10

With permission of the International Music Company.

Example 6–11. Rimsky-Korsakov Concerto, op. 30, mvt. 2, mm. 1–11

Example 6–12. Rimsky-Korsakov Concerto, op. 30, mvt. 3, mm. 1–10

Henselt and Liszt. Lyapunov's *Transendential Etudes,* op. 11, imitate Liszt works of the same title. His music includes the concerto, op. 4 (1890), the "Rhapsody on Ukrainian Themes," op. 28 (1908), and the concerto, op. 38 (1909).

Anton Arensky (1861–1906) was a friend of Tchaikovsky, Rimsky-Korsakov, and Taneyev and the teacher of Rachmaninoff, Scriabin, and Glier. His eclectic musical style is influenced by Chopin and Tchaikovsky. In St. Petersburg, he composed the concerto, op. 2 (1882), and in Moscow the *Fantasy on Russian Folksongs,* op. 48 (1899), based on themes of Russian folklorist Trophim Riabinine. The concerto displays Chopin's cantabile style.

Vasily Wrangell (1862–1901), friend of Glazunov, championed contemporary Russian music as the editor of the journal *Nuvelist.* He left a fantasy (1893).

Felix Blumenfeld (1863–1931) studied with Rimsky-Korsakov at the St. Petersburg Conservatory, and taught at conservatories in St. Petersburg, Kiev, and Moscow. He was a virtuoso pianist, accompanist for many fine singers, and friend to A. Rubinstein, Rimsky-Korsakov, Glazunov, Rachmaninoff, and Shalyapin. He left the *allegro de concerto,* op. 7 (1888).

Ivan Kryzhanovsky (1867–1924), theorist and composer, worked as a researcher on conditioned reflexes in Pavlov's laboratory. He composed a concerto.

Alexander Scriabin (1872–1915) left early works that display an influence of Chopin (See ex. 6–13), and later compositions that evidence ideas about theosophy and mysticism that led to the mystic chord. He composed the concerto, op. 20 (1896), and *Prometheus, The Poem of Fire* (1908–1910), with solo piano in an orchestra work.

Used by permission of C. F. Peters Corporation on behalf of M. P. Belaieff, Frankfurt. Scriabin (BEL189) Concerto, op. 20.

Example 6–13. Scriabin Concerto, op. 20, mvt. 3, mm. 1–13

France

Sigismund von Neukomm (1778–1858), student of Haydn, was a composer, teacher, conductor, pianist, and scholar in Vienna, St. Petersburg, Paris, Rio de Janeiro, and London. He composed at least one concerto for piano. Neukomm participated in the

1842 unveiling of the Mozart monument in Salzburg, and he delivered the main address and conducted Mozart's *Coronation Mass,* K.317, and requiem, K.626.

Friedrich Kalkbrenner (1785–1849), German, was a virtuoso pianist and composer born on a stagecoach between Kassel and Berlin. After settling in Paris in 1824, he enjoyed a successful career as a pianist, teacher, and piano maker. He encouraged Chopin to study piano with him, but Chopin declined, although he held Kalkbrenner's pianistic abilities in high esteem; Chopin dedicated his concerto no. 1 to Kalkbrenner. To the advancement of piano playing, Kalkbrenner contributed finger and wrist technique, octave-playing, left-hand technique, and a better understanding of the damper pedal.

Kalkbrenner composed five piano concertos: op. 61 (1823), op. 85 (1826), op. 107 (1829), op. 125 (1835) for two pianos, and op. 127 (1835). Other works are the *grand rondeau "Gage d'Amitié,"* op. 66 (1823); the *grand Rondeau Brillant "Les Charmes de Berlin,"* op. 70 (1824); the fantasy and grand variations, opp. 72 and 70 (1824), based on "My Lodging is on the Cold Ground"; the *variations brillantes,* op. 83 (1826), based on Rossini's *Di Tanti Palpiti;* the variations, op. 99 (1828), based on *God Save the King;* the *adagio e allegro de bravura,* opp. 100 and 102 (1928); the *introduction et rondeau brillant,* op. 101 (1828), based on *Frère Jacques;* the *fantaisie Le Rêne,* op. 113 (1833); and the *grand rondeau brillant "Les Charmes de Carlsbad,"* op. 174 (1845). Some works have more than one opus number.

Johann Pixis (1788–1874) was a German piano virtuoso and famous piano teacher in Paris after 1825. Among his friends were Beethoven, Meyerbeer, Schubert, Cherubini, Moscheles, Liszt, Berlioz, and Rossini. He contributed a variation to the *Hexaméron* based on a theme from Bellini's *I Puritani.* Before opus 100, his musical models are Beethoven, Haydn, and Mozart, and after opus 100 he follows Weber and Hummel. Pixis' compositions for piano and orchestra are the *Grandes Variations sur un Thême Favori de l'Opéra du Barbiero de Seville de Rossini,* op. 36; the *rondo brillant,* op. 61; the *Introduction and Grand Rondeau Hongrois,* op. 64; the *grandes variations militaires,* op. 66, for two pianos; the concertino, op. 68 (pub. 1830s); the *grand concerto,* op. 100 (pub. 1830s); *Les Troise Clochettes rondo brillant,* op. 120; the *fantaisie militaire,* op. 121 (pub. 1833); and the concerto for piano and violin.

Giacomo Meyerbeer (1791–1864), German, was the most important composer of French opera after 1831. His music for piano and orchestra dates before success in opera turned his attention away from the piano. Among his piano compositions are two concertos (1811, 1812), a concert piece, and a set of variations.

Jean-Amédée de Méreaux (1802–1874) was a pianist, musicologist, and composer. He was among the first musicians to present performances of early keyboard music in Paris and Rouen. In 1855, he gave the first performance in Paris of Mozart's concerto, K.365, for two pianos. He composed the *60 Grandes Études* which the Paris *Conservatoire* adopted as part of the pianistic regime. Chopin influenced Méreaux's *grand concerto symphonique* for piano and orchestra.

Wojciech (Albert) Sowinski (1803–1880) was a Polish pianist, piano teacher, writer, and composer. After settling in Paris in 1830, he composed over a hundred compositions with classic traits. His important contribution is the *Les Musiciens Polonaise et Slaves, Anciens et Modernes: Dictionnaire Biographique.* His music for piano and orchestra is the concert variations, op. 14; the grand polonaise, op. 16; the "Heroic March," op. 24; the *Piesn Legionów* (The Song of the Legions), op. 31; and the concerto, op. 36.

Louise Farrencs (née Dumont, 1804–1875) was a pianist, teacher, scholar, composer and the only woman with a permanent teaching position at the Paris *Conservatoire* in the nineteenth century. Some musicians praised her symphonic works as equals of her male contemporaries. The grand *fantaisie et variations,* op. 25 (ca. 1838), is on a theme by Count Gallenberg. The first and second movements of a piano concerto are complete and the third movement is incomplete. Her lasting musical contribution was the continuation of the historically important periodical *Le Trésor des Pianistes* after her husband's death.

Henri Herz (1806–1888), German, was a teacher, brilliant pianist, and composer identified by Schumann as a musical "philistine" due to the shallowness of his music. He settled in Paris in ca. 1821, taught piano at the *Conservatoire* in 1842, and toured the United States, Mexico, and the West Indies from 1845 to 1851. He modeled his music on Moscheles' style, and openly intended it for the public.

Herz's music for piano and orchestra lacks dates of composition. He composed eight piano concertos: opp. 34, 74, 87, 131, 180, 192, 207, and 218. Other works are the *rondeau brillant,* op. 11; the *rondo de concert,* op. 27; the rondo, op. 37, based on Rossini's *Moses;* the *variations de concert,* op. 57, based on a march from Rossini's *Guillaume Tell;* the rondo, op. 67, based on Rossini's *Otello;* the variations, op. 76, based on a trio from Herold's *Le Pré aux Clercs;* the rondo, op. 90, based on Belini's *Norma;* and the rondo, op. 163, based on Donizetti's *La Fille du Régiment.*

Alkan (Charles Henri Valentin Morhange, 1813–1888) was the "Berlioz of the piano," and praised by Liszt, Busoni, and others for his pianistic abilities. He was a friend of many contemporary writers and composers, including Victor Hugo, George Sand, and Chopin. The *concerto da camera* no. 1, op. 10 (ca. 1832), and the *concerto da camera* no. 2 (1834) are for piano and orchestra. Late in life, he became a recluse and he died when a bookcase fell on him.

Émile Prudent (1817–1863) entered the Paris *Conservatoire* at age 10 and became a successful touring pianist in the tradition of Thalberg. He composed the concerto (perf. 1814), the *concerto-symphonie,* op. 34 (1850), the concerto, op. 48 (1856), and the *concerto-symphonie,* op. 67 (1863).

Charles Gounod (1818–1893) was the most important composer of French opera in the third quarter of the nineteenth century. For piano and orchestra, he composed the waltzes *Le Rendez-Vous* (1886?), the *Fantaisie sur l'Hymne National Russe* (1886), and the *suite concertante* (1888). The *Fantasie sur l'Hymne* is on Alexei Fyodorovich Lvov's melody "God Preserve the Tsar" that appears in Tchaikovsky's *1812 Overture.*

César Franck (1822–1890) played organ at several churches before teaching at the Paris *Conservatoire.* He became a powerful force in the establishment of French instrumental music, and taught the important organists of the next generation. With d'Indy, Bordes, and others, Franck founded the *Schola Cantorum* and later some of those same individuals formed the *École Cesar Franck.*

Franck's music for piano and orchestra is the *variations brillantes* (1834) based on Herold's opera *La Pre-aux-Clercs;* the *variations brillantes,* op. 8 (1834–1835), based on a favorite rondo of Gustave III; two concertos, both op. 11 (ca. 1835); *Les Djinns* (The Spirits, 1884); and the symphonic variations (1885). *Les Djinns* is on Victor Hugo's poem *Les Orientales,* and Franck's designation as a symphonic poem and the obbligato piano writing demonstrate his desire to place the orchestra and piano on equal terms. The symphonic variations is a continuation of his effort to treat the piano and orchestra as equals. The composition is on two distinct themes followed by six variations and a finale.

Édouard Lalo (1823–1892) was an esteemed French composer of Spanish descent whose *symphonie espagnole,* op. 21 (1874), is important in violin literature. The piano concerto (1888–1889) is a three-movement cyclic composition with the motive that is presented at the beginning of the first movement appearing in each movement.

Thomas Tellefsen (1823–1874), Norwegian pianist and composer, studied with Kalkbrenner and performed Chopin's music. He is an important forerunner of Grieg, Svendsen, and Sindling in the use of Norwegian folk music. Chopin thought highly of Tellefsen and designated him to finish his Pianoforte Method. He left two concertos, opp. 8 and 15 (1852, 1854). He composed the concerto, op. 15, under Chopin's direction.

Georges Mathias (1826–1910) studied privately with Kalkbrenner and Chopin, and taught piano at the *Conservatoire*. He composed two concertos and the *5 morceaux symphoniques*.

Georges Pfeiffer (1835–1908) was a successful pianist and chamber musician. He composed three concertos, opp. 11, 21, and 86 (pub. 1859, 1864, and 1883), and the *Legende, fantaisie symphonique,* op. 58 (pub. 1894). The concerto no. 3 had several performances in Paris.

Camille Saint-Saëns (1835–1921) made a significant contribution to the establishment and recognition of a French school of symphonic writing prior to Franck. His concertos are five in number: op. 17 (1858), op. 22 (1868), op. 29 (1869), op. 44 (1875), and the "Egyptian," op. 103 (1896). The music of Mozart, Weber, Mendelssohn, and Beethoven influenced the concerto no. 1. The concertos nos. 2 and 3 show an influence of Beethoven, Liszt, Mozart, and Mendelssohn. The slow movement of the concerto no. 5 is based on an Oriental theme, and the finale is the toccata no. 6 in the *Etudes,* op. 111.

The "Carnival of the Animals" (1886), subtitled *grand Fantaisie Zoologique,* is Saint-Saëns' popular work for piano and orchestra. The score is for two pianos, flute, clarinet, harmonica, xylophone, celesta, and strings. In modern performances, the glockenspiel often replaces the glass harmonica that was popular in the nineteenth century. The work is in fourteen sections: 1. "Introduction and Royal March of the Lions," 2. "Cocks and Hens," 3. "Mules," 4. "Turtles," based on two melodies from Offenbach's "Orpheus in the Underworld" performed at the slow speed of a turtle, 5. "Elephants," based on melodies of Berlioz's sylphs from "The Damnation of Faust," op. 24, and Mendelssohn's fairies from the "Midsummer Night's Dream," 6. "Kangaroos," 7. "Aquarium," 8. "Personages with Long Ears," 9. "The Cuckoo in the Deep Woods," 10. "Aviary," 11. "Pianist," based on the types of exercises young pianists practice, 12. "Fossils," based on Saint-Saëns' own *Danse Macabre,* four French folks songs—*J'ai du Bon Tabac, Ah*! *Vous Dirai-Je Maman, Au Clair de la Lune,* and *Partant Pour la Syrie,* and the aria *Una Voce Poco Fa* for Rosina from Rossini's "The Barber of Seville," 13. "The Swan," and 14. "Finale."

The original idea for the "Carnival of the Animals" dates between 1861 and 1865, when Saint-Saëns planned a musical diversion for his students at the *École Niedermayer*. The first performances occurred at the annual *Shrove Tuesday* concert, then at the mid-lent concert of *La Trompette,* a prestigious chamber music society. Saint-Saëns' concern for his musical reputation resulted in a strict prohibition on the work's publication during his lifetime. Only "The Swan" appeared in a publication before his death.

Other compositions for piano and orchestra are the *allegro appassionato,* op. 70 (1874), also in a version for piano solo; the *Rapsodie d'Auvergne,* op. 73 (1884), structured in three main sections—andante, allegretto, and allegro; the *Wedding Cake,* op. 76 (1885), that was a wedding gift; and the fantasy *Africa,* op. 89 (1891), based on Oriental resources. Saint-Saëns wrote cadenzas for Beethoven's concerto no. 4 (ca. 1878) and Mozart's concertos, K.482 and K.491. A cadenza of doubtful authenticity exists for Mozart's concerto, K.365, for two pianos.

Ernest Guiraud (1837–1892) was a friend and classmate of Bizet at the *Conservatoire* and composition teacher of Debussy and Dukas. He contributed recitatives to Bizet's opera *Carmen* and arranged the *L'Arlésienne* suite. His *allegro de concert* (1885) is for piano and orchestra.

Alexis de Castillon (1838–1873), student of Franck and important pioneer of French song, founded with Saint-Saëns and Duparc the *Société Nationale de Musique* and served as its first secretary. The concerto, op. 12 (ca. 1872), begins with a piano solo with the main theme.

Elie-Miriam Delaborde (1839–1913) was Alkan's brilliant piano student and probable illegitimate son. The *Morceau romantique,* op. 3 (pub. 1880s), is for piano and orchestra.

Victor Duvernoy (1842–1907) was a pianist, composer, and teacher at the *Conservatoire.* He composed the *concertstück,* op. 20 (1876), the *Scene de bal,* op. 28 (1885), the *fantaisie symphonique* (1906), and two fragments of a *symphonique.*

Emile Bernard (1843–1902) was a noted organist at the *Notre Dame des Champs* and composer of popular salon pieces for the piano. For piano and orchestra, there are the nocturne, op. 51 (pub. 1902), the *concertstück,* and the fantasy.

Louis Diemer (1843–1919), virtuoso pianist and composer, taught piano at the *Conservatoire* and presented piano recitals of early keyboard music. He left the *concertstück,* op. 31, and the concerto, op. 32.

Charles Widor (1844–1937) was the creator of the organ symphony, an organ virtuoso, composer and teacher at the *Conservatoire,* and a music critic under the pen name "Aulétès." For piano and orchestra, he composed the concerto, op. 39 (pub. 1876), the *fantaisie,* op. 62 (pub. 1889), and the concerto, op. 77 (pub. 1906).

Garbiel Fauré (1845–1924) was a brilliant student of Saint-Saëns at the *École Niedermeyer,* successful organist, holder of several important French music offices, and the most advanced French composer until Debussy's *Pelléas et Mélisande.* In 1909, he revised the *ballade,* op. 19 (1881), originally for piano solo, for piano and orchestra. Fauré's ambidexterity is apparent in the equal technical and musical treatment of the two hands (See ex. 6–14). Due to his organ training, his piano music requires finger substitutions. The music has highly chromatic harmony with expanded tonality

Example 6–14. Fauré *Ballade,* op. 19, mm. 195–196

and modality, traditional dissonances treated as consonances, quick and distant modulations, and free treatments of major and minor thirds within chords.

Benjamin Godard (1849–1895) studied violin with Vieuxtemps and composition with Reber at the *Conservatoire*. He was a popular violinist in Paris during the *Concerts Populaires*. For piano and orchestra, he composed two concertos, opp. 31 and 148 (1870, 1899), and the introduction and allegro, op. 49 (1881).

Vincent d'Indy (1851–1931) established the *Schola Cantorum* and championed French instrumental music in the style of Franck. His music for piano and orchestra is the *Symphony on a French Mountain Air,* op. 25 (1886), the *Summer Day on the Mountain,* op. 61 (1905), and the concerto, op. 89 (1927), for piano, flute, and cello. Another title for the *Symphony on a French Mountain Air* is *Symphony Cévenole,* after the Cévenole mountains d'Indy loved. The English horn presents the folk song (See ex. 6–15) from the Ardèche region of France in the first movement before the melody undergoes many variants (See ex. 6–16) in the three movements.

Ernest Chausson (1855–1899) studied with Franck and Massenet, and was a friend of Debussy, Albéniz, and Cortot. Franck recognized Chausson as an influential member of Franck's circle. His concerto, op. 21 (1889–1891), is for piano, violin, and string quartet, and the unfinished concerto (1897) is for piano, oboe, viola, and string quartet.

Cécile Chaminade (1857–1944), pianist and composer, performed her piano music in numerous concerts in France and England. The *concertstück,* op. 40, is a conservative work with triads and seventh chords.

Frederick Delius (1862–1934), English, settled in Grez-sur-Loing, about 30 miles from Paris. In 1886, he went to the Leipzig Conservatory to study with Reinecke, Sitt, and Jadassohn. Grieg and Wagner were powerful influences on Delius' work. His harmonic vocabulary includes triads, secondary function chords, dominant discords and chromatic alterations. Among his musical compositions is the unfinished *Sagen* (Legends, 1890) and the concerto (1897, rev. before 1904, 1906–1907, 1909) that is the "Fantasy for Orchestra and Pianoforte" in the autograph. The revision of 1906–1907 is the version performed today.

Charles Bordes (1863–1909) studied with Franck and joined Guilmant and d'Indy to establish the *Schola Cantorum* to promote sacred music. After collecting numerous examples of early Basque music, he composed the *Rhapsodie Basque* (1890).

With permission of the International Music Company.

Example 6–15. d'Indy *Symphony on a French Mountain Air,* op. 25, mvt. 1, mm. 2–11

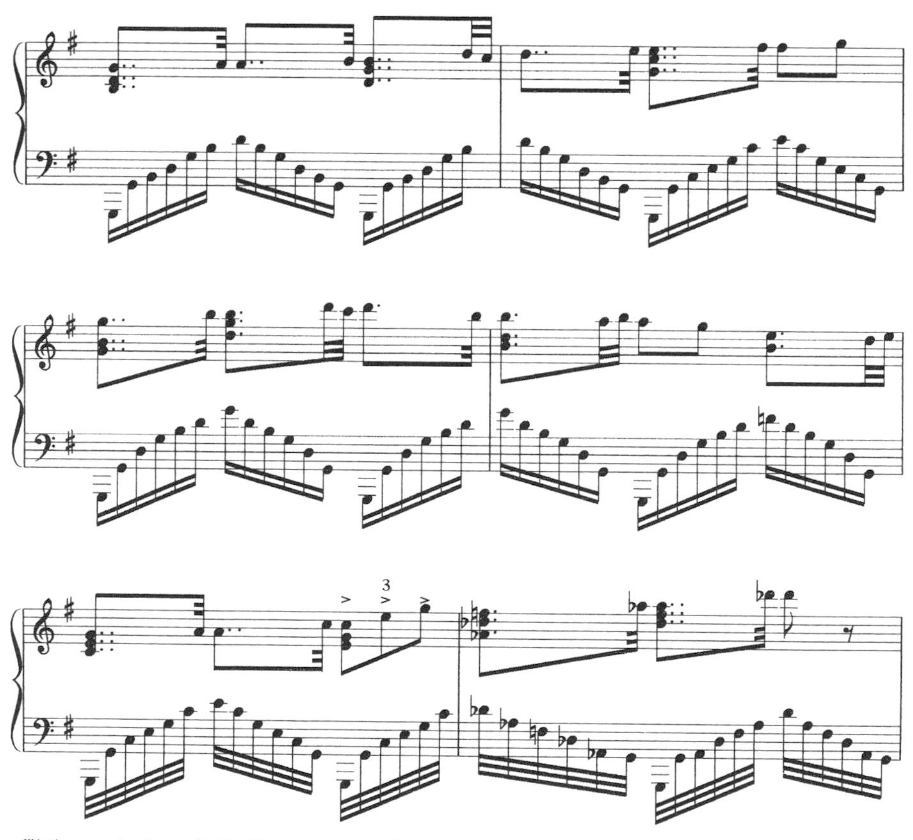

With permission of the International Music Company.

Example 6–16. d'Indy *Symphony on a French Mountain Air,* op. 25, mvt. 1, mm. 43–48

Table 10 Additional Composers in France

Names	Dates	Compositions
Bériot, Charles-Wilfride de	1833–1914	4 Concertos (by 1881)
Blondeau, Pierre	1784–1865	Concerto
Bonis, Melanie	1858–1937	Fantasy
Bordier, Jules	1846–1896	Scherzo Oriental
Domange, Mme Albert	. . .	See Melanie Bonis
Dubois, Theódore	1837–1924	Concerto-Capriccios (1876)
		Concerto no 2 (1897)
Dupont, Auguste	1827–1890	*Concertstück,* op 42 (pub 1883)
		Concerto, op 49 (pub 1882)
Flotow, Friedrich	1812–1883	2 Concertos (ca. 1830/31)
Hillemacher, Paul	1852–1933	*Retraite* (1885)
Hopekirk, Helen	1856–1945	Concerto (1887–89)
		Konzertstück (1894)
Isouard, Nicol	. . .	See Nicol Ninette
Jaéll, Alfred	1832–1882	Concerto (1875)
Jaéll-Trautmann, Marie	1846–1925	Concerto (1870s?)
Lacombe, Paul	1837–1927	Divertissement, op 40 (1885)
		Suite, op 52 (by 1896)
Laurens, Edmond	1852–1925	*Silhouettes*
Lenormand, René	1846–1932	Concerto, op 51
Maréchal, Henri	1842–1924	*Feuillets d'Album*
Mihevec, Georg	1805–1882	Concerto (pub 1839)
Nicolò, Ninette	1814–1876	Concerto, lost
Perilhou, A.?	? –	Second *Fantaisie* (pub 1895)
Rigel, Henri-Jean	1772–1852	4 Concertos
Stamaty, Camille	1811–1870	Concerto, op 2
Street, Joseph	? –	2 Concertos, opp 20 & 24 (pub ca. 1868)
Thomas, Ambroise	1811–1896	*Fantaisie brillante,* op 6 (1836)
Voss, Charles	1815–1882	Concerto
Wolff, Edouard	1816–1880	Concerto, op 39
Zimmerman, Pierre- J.-G.	1785–1853	2 Concertos

Gabriel Pierné (1863–1937) studied at the *Conservatoire* with Marmontel for piano, Franck for organ, and Massenet for composition. He succeeded Franck as the organist at *Sainte-Clotilde.* For piano and orchestra, he composed the *Fantaisie-Ballet,* op. 6 (1885), the concerto, op. 12 (1887), the scherzo-*caprice,* op. 25 (1890), the *Poeme Symphonique,* op. 37 (1901), and the *concertstück,* op. 39 (1903), for harp or piano.

Holland (now the Netherlands)

Henry Litolff (1818–1891), born in England, studied piano with Moscheles. In parts of Europe he was called the "English Liszt," and eventually he lived in Paris, Brussels, Leipzig, Prague, Dresden, Berlin, Amsterdam, and Braunschweig.

Litolff composed five compositions for piano and orchestra: a lost concerto

Example 6–17. Litolff *Concerto Symphonique* no. 3, op. 45, mvt. 2, mm. 98–113

(1839–1841) in Brussels; the *concerto-sinfonie* no. 2, op. 22 (1844), in Leipzig; the *concerto symphonique* no. 3, op. 45 (1846), in Amsterdam; the *concerto symphonique* no. 4, op. 102 (1851–1852), in Braunschweig; and the *concerto symphonique* no. 5, op. 123 (ca. 1867), in Paris. In Holland, Litolff enjoyed great musical success with the *concerto symphonique* no. 3, "National Hollandais," that contains the Dutch song *Al Is One Prinje Nog Zoo Klein* (Even Though Our Little Toddler Is Little, See ex. 6–17) in the second movement. The Dutch national song "Wien Neèrlands Bloed" (Whose Dutch Blood Flows in the Veins, See ex. 6–18) is in the fourth movement.

In Blair's dissertation, "Henry Charles Litolff: (1818–1891): His Life and Piano Music,"[6] Litolff represents a probable musical link between Schumann's concerto and Liszt's concerto no. 1. Particularly significant is Liszt's dedication of his concerto to Litolff and adoption of Litolff's use of triangle and piccolo. Liszt and Litolff were friends, and the influence of the first movement of Litolff's *concerto symphonique* no. 4 on the

Example 6–18. Litolff *Concerto Symphonique* no. 3, op. 45, mvt. 4, mm. 67–83

first movement of Liszt's concerto seems more than coincidental. Litolff uses a scherzo movement in the *concerto symphoniques* to give four-movement symphonic proportions to compositions having an intimate relationship between an obbligato piano and orchestra. Many passages in Litolff's piano writing display the virtuoso flair of a soloist (See ex. 6–19), but frequently the piano assists the orchestra in treating thematic material.

Hermina Amersfoordt-Dyk (1821–1891), pianist and composer, left a piano concerto.

Samuel de Lange (1840–1911), an organist, composer, and conductor, taught at the Rotterdam Music School and later in Basel, Cologne, and Stuttgart. He left a piano concerto.

Hendrikus de Waart (1863–1931) taught piano and organ at the conservatory and played organ at the English Church. His fantasy is for piano and orchestra.

Example 6–19. Litolff *Concerto Symphonique* no. 3, op. 45, mvt. 1, mm. 299–300

Belgium

François-Joseph Fétis (1784–1871), scholar, critic, teacher, and composer, wrote the important *Biographie Universelle des Musiciens* and the *Histoire Generale de la Musique* in five volumes. His systematic portrayal of music history as a sequence of related events is an important contribution, as are his comments about contemporary performing musicians. He believed top-caliber pianists should perform not only their own compositions, but also the best music from the past and present. Fétis' two lost piano concertos are early works from before 1800.

Peter Benoit (1834–1901), conductor, teacher, and composer of vocal music, studied with Fétis and Hanssens, established the Royal Flemish Conservatory of Music, and attempted to raise the level of Flemish music to the quality of the main musical centers of Europe. Beethoven, Mendelssohn, Liszt, Chopin, and Weber influenced his early compositions, and Berlioz and Meyerbeer influenced the later works. The concerto, op. 43 (1864), listed in some sources as a symphonic poem, has rich harmonies of the late romantic era.

Jozef Wieniawski (1837–1912), Polish composer-pianist and brother of the violinist Henryk Wieniawski, taught for a short time in Warsaw and Moscow before settling in Brussels to teach piano at the conservatory. He composed the concerto, op. 20 (1873), in Moscow and probably the fantasia for two pianos and orchestra and the cadenza to Beethoven's concerto no. 3 in Brussels.

Julius Rontgen (1855–1932), German-born, settled in 1878 in Amsterdam where he helped establish the Amsterdam Conservatory. He was a friend of Grieg and Brahms, and Schumann influenced his music. Most of his seven piano concertos are in manuscript, and only his concerto, op. 18 (1880), appeared in publication. He wrote cadenzas for Beethoven's concerto no. 4.

Arthur De Greef (1862–1940) studied with Brassin at the Brussels Conservatory, with Liszt in Weimar, and with Saint-Saëns in Paris. He was a highly regarded interpreter of Grieg's music, and helped popularize Grieg's concerto. De Greef composed two piano concertos and possibly other music for piano and orchestra.

Table 11 Additional Composers in Belgium

Names	Dates	Compositions
Brassin, Louis	1840–1884	2 Concertos
Gregoir, Jacques	1817–1876	Concerto, op 100
Hanssens, Charles-Louis	1802–1871	Concerto
Huberti, Gustave-Leon	1843–1910	Concerto
Kufferath, Hubert-Ferdinand	1818–1896	Concertos
Ledent, Félix-Étienne	1816–1886	*Adagio et rondo*
Paque, Désiré	1867–1939	2 Concertos, opp 4 & 127 (1888/1935)
Stadtfeld, Alexandre	1826–1853	2 Concertinos

Denmark

Erik Siboni (1828–1892), student of Moscheles and Hauptmann in Leipzig, became the organ teacher at the Royal Academy of Sorö in 1864 and settled in Copenhagen in 1883. He left a piano concerto (1864).

August Winding (1835–1899), student of Gade, taught at the Copenhagen Conservatory and became the director in 1891. He composed a piano concerto and cadenzas for concertos by Beethoven and Mozart.

Emil Hartman (1836–1898), composer and organist of German descent, studied with Gade and followed Mendelssohn's style. He left the piano concerto, op. 47.

Edvard Grieg (1843–1907), Norway's most famous and popular composer, followed Ole Bull's advice by training at the Leipsig Conservatory. After the Norwegian government denied Grieg's request for a stipend to support his musical activities, he settled in Copenhagen and received Gade's encouragement. Until then, his musical experiences were Danish and German, but in Copenhagen Grieg met Rikard Nordraak, a champion of Norwegian nationalism, and together they formed the *Euterpe Society* to further national features of Scandinavian music. Nordraak's premature death at age 23 left Grieg as the principal proponent of the Norwegian musical character.

The concerto, op. 16 (1868, rev. 1906–1907), is Grieg's only completed work for piano and orchestra; his concerto in B-major (1882–1883) exists in sketches. The structure of Grieg's concerto bears a strong resemblance to Schumann's concerto, but the musical content of both works is distinctive. Both concertos begin with a short introduction (See ex. 6–20), the first melodic material is chordal (See ex. 6–21), and the following material has a quarter-note melody over a sixteenth-note accompaniment (See ex. 6–22). Liszt's style and technique are obvious throughout the concerto, particularly in the bravura cadenza (See ex. 6–23) which is strikingly similar to a portion of Grieg's sonata, op. 7 (1865, See ex. 6–24). A Norwegian folk dance rhythm appears in the third movement (See ex. 6–25).

Otto Malling (1848–1915) studied with Gade and Hartmann at the Copenhagen Conservatory, and later taught theory there. He left the concerto, op. 43 (1890).

Example 6–20. Grieg Concerto, op. 16, mvt. 1, mm. 1–6

Example 6–21. Grieg Concerto, op. 16, mvt. 1, mm. 19–22

Victor Bendix (1851–1926), student of Gade and Liszt, conducted at the Royal Theatre and became a highly regarded pianist and teacher at the Royal Academy of Music. Gade, Liszt, Wagner, and Nielson influenced his musical compositions, including the piano concerto, op. 17 (ca. 1884).

Siegfried Langgaard (1852–1914), father of the Danish composer and organist Rued Langgaard, taught at the Royal Academy of Music after studying piano with Liszt. His concerto (pub. 1889) appeared in Copenhagen and Leipzig.

Robert Hansel (1860–1926), cellist in the court orchestra, lived in Leipzig and settled in Denmark in 1918. He composed a piano concerto.

Example 6–22. Grieg Concerto, op. 16, mvt. 1, mm. 23–26

Example 6–23. Grieg Concerto, op. 16, mvt. 1, m. 178, Cadenza

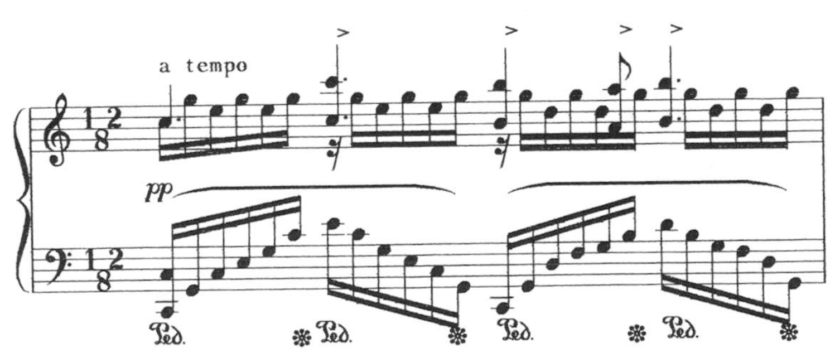

Example 6–24. Grieg Sonata, op. 7, mvt. 2, m. 30

Example 6–25. Grieg Concerto, op. 16, mvt. 3, mm. 10–19

Louis Glass (1864–1936) was among the finest pianists in Copenhagen until paralysis of an arm forced his retirement. He composed the *fantasie,* op. 47.

Switzerland

Xaver von Wartensee (1786–1868) taught in Pestalozzi's singing school after learning that his philanthropic father spent his inheritance. He received a considerable income from many publications of his musical compositions. Among his works in a romantic style are a set of variations for piano and orchestra and cadenzas for piano concertos by Mozart and Beethoven.

Hans Huber (1852–1921), the most important Swiss composer during the second half the nineteenth century, studied with Richter, Reinecke, and Wenzel at the Leipzig Conservatory. Brahms, Liszt, and R. Strauss influenced his music. From 1889, he taught at the conservatory in Basel. He composed four piano concertos: op. 36 (1878), op. 107 (1891), op. 113 (1899), and no. 4 (1910).

Norway

Agathe Backer-Grondahl (1847–1907), important woman composer, studied with Kullak, Bülow, and Liszt. Among her approximately 250 musical compositions is the andante for piano and orchestra.

Christian Sindling (1856–1941), pianist and finest national composer after Grieg, studied at the Leipzig Conservatory with Reinecke and Jadassohn. He settled in Christiania (now Oslo), where a government stipend allowed time for musical composition. The "Rustle of Spring," op. 23, no. 3, earned Sindling a fortune. His concerto, op. 6 (1887–1888), is cyclic, with musical material at the beginning of the concerto appearing in each of the three movements.

Sweden

Edvard Passy (1789–1870), of French parentage, was a renowned pianist who studied with Field in St. Petersburg. His fantasy and two piano concertos are in manuscript.

Franz Berwald (1796–1868) directed music at the University of Uppsala, taught at the academy and the conservatory, and ran a successful sawmill and glassworks factory. In a romantic style influenced by Spohr, Chopin, Mendelssohn, and Liszt, he composed a concerto (1855). Berwald wrote the piano part to play continuously throughout the concerto, because he also intended the piano part to stand as a solo work. This practice was common at the end of the 1700s and the beginning of the 1800s, when established orchestras were not always available to touring pianists, but at the time Berwald composed his concerto, composers were writing concertos with an indispensable orchestra part.

Jacob Ahlström (1805–1857), conductor and composer at various Stockholm theaters, left a concerto for piano and orchestra.

Ludvig Norman (1831–1885) studied with Moscheles, Hauptmann, and Rietz at the Leipzig Conservatory, and returned to Stockholm to conduct the Philharmonic Society. The German musical tradition of Mendelssohn and Schumann is strong in his music which includes the *konsertstücke,* op. 54 (1875), two marches, and a concerto.

Lago (pseud. of Laura Netzell, 1839–1927) lived in Vienna, Paris, and Stockholm. She composed a piano concerto.

Karl Wohlfart (1874–1943) worked as a church organist and musician before founding his own music school in 1913. His *concertstück* is for piano and orchestra.

Finland

Ernst Mielck (1877–1899) studied piano in St. Petersburg and composition with Bruch in Berlin. Although he died two days before turning 22, he left two concertos (1895, 1898); some lists show the second concerto as a *konzertstück.*

Spain

Isaac Albéniz (1860–1909), important composer and pianist, helped establish a Spanish national musical style. For piano and orchestra, he composed the *Spanish Rhapsody,* op. 70, the *concerto fantastico,* op. 78 (1887), and the *catalonia* (1899); a *catalonia* is a rhapsody displaying the Spanish national character. Chopin, Schumann, and Liszt influenced Albéniz's style.

England

Richard Cudmore (1787–1840) performed as the soloist in concertos for violin, piano, and cello in one concert. For quite a while, he lived in London, before settling in Manchester. He composed several piano concertos.

Cipriani Potter (1792–1871), pianist, conductor, composer, and teacher, studied with Loelffle for five years before going to Vienna and meeting Beethoven. From 1822, he taught at the Royal Academy of Music. He introduced Beethoven's piano concerto nos. 1, 3, and 4 to English concert audiences. As a composer Potter was appreciated by audiences, but soon after his death his compositions dropped from the performing repertoire. Much of his music exists only in manuscript, and a few published works are without manuscripts. Due to a lack of opus numbers, manuscript numbers identify compositions. The definitive study of Potter is Philip Henry Peter's dissertation, "The Life and Work of Cipriani Potter (1792–1871)."[7]

An article (1863) on Potter mentions four piano concertos. The concerto no. 1? (ca. 1828) is lost. The concerto no. 2, MS 11 (1832), has "Second Concerto" on the title page. A watermark on the manuscript dates the concerto no. 3?, MS 12 (1833). The 6/4 meter in the first movement predates Brahms' 6/4 meter in the first movement of his concerto no. 1. The concerto no. 4? is MS 13 (1835). The *duo concertant,* op. 14 (pub. 1827–1828), for piano, violin, and orchestra exists only in published form. The introduction and rondo, MS 7 (1827), is the "Alla Militaire." The bravura variations, MS 8 (1829), is on Rossini's theme "Ah! Come Nascondere" from *Coradino*. The *concertante* "Les Folies d'Espagne," MS 9a (1829), is for solo violin, cello, string bass, piano, and orchestra. The *Ricercate,* op. 24, MS 10 (1830), based on a "Favorite French Theme," is an introduction, theme, and variations.

Ignaz Moscheles (1794–1870), German pianist, conductor and composer of Czech descent, settled in Vienna and became a close friend of Beethoven. He toured Europe and London, worked in London championing Beethoven's music, and settled in Leipzig to teach at the conservatory.

He composed many musical compositions in the style of Beethoven and Weber while touring or living in London. Left-hand accompaniments have eighth-note chords, and sometimes the left hand duplicates technical demands placed on the right hand. Passages appear with parallel octaves, thirds, and sixths, and runs span the keyboard with varying numbers of notes. Harmonies occasionally move as abruptly as Beethoven's, and there are frequent diminished-seventh chords. Slow movements display ornamented melodies similar to those of Hummel.

Moscheles composed eight piano concertos: the "Concert de Société," op. 45 (1819); op. 56 (1825); op. 60 (1820), published as op. 50; op. 64 (1823); op. 87 (1826); the "Fantastique," op. 90 (1833); the "Pathetique," op. 93 (1835–1836); and the "Pastorale," op. 96 (1838). The seven fantasies are the *Fantaisie et Variations sur l'aire favori: Au Clair de le Lune,* op. 50 (1821); the *Souvenirs d'Irlande,* op. 69 (1826), with the melodies "The Groves of Blarney," "Garry Owens," and "St. Patrick's Day"; the *Anklänge aus Schottland,* op. 75 (1826); the *Fantaisie sur des Airs des Bardes Cossais,* op. 80 (1828); and the *Souvenirs de Danemarc,* op. 83 (1830). Other compositions are the variations *La Marche d'Alexandre,* op. 32 (1815); the *Franzsisches Rondo,* op. 48 (1819); and, in collaboration with Mendelssohn, the two-piano *duo concertante,* op. 87b (1833), with variations on a tune from Weber's *Preciosa.*

Julius Benedict (1804–1885), German composer, conductor, and teacher, studied with Weber and Hummel at Weimar, and moved to Naples and London in 1835. He devoted much time to conducting *opera buffa* and became a first-rate pianist. He composed two concertos, opp. 89 and 90 (both 1867). Originally, the first movement of the concerto, op. 89, was the concertino no. 2, op. 29 (ca. 1833), and the first movement of the concerto, op. 90, was the concertino no. 1, op. 18 (1833). Benedict's concertos show the influence of Field, Hummel, and Weber.

George Macfarren (1813–1887), blind from 1823, student, and later a teacher at the Royal Academy of Music, composed a concerto (perf. 1835). He was the only English composer of this era to write symphonies.

Sterndale Bennett (1816–1875), pianist, conductor, composer, and teacher at the Royal Academy of Music, enjoyed a close friendship with Mendelssohn and Schumann. Despite public taste, he composed quality music in the style of Mozart and Mendelssohn, but the necessity of earning a living forced him to other activities. His four published piano concertos are op. 1 (1832), op. 4 (1833), op. 9 (1834), and op. 19 (1837–1838). Originally, the unpublished concerto (1836) had a second movement titled "A Stroll Through the Meadows," and now the second movement is the "Barcarolle." Also, there is the *caprice,* op. 22 (1838), and the three-movement *concertstück* (1841–1843).

Henry Wylde (1822–1890), conductor and composer, established and taught at the Royal Academy of Music, and played organ at various London churches. His concerto (perf. 1852) is for piano and orchestra.

Frederick Jewson (1823–1891), Scottish pianist, composer, and teacher, was a friend of Mendelssohn, Wagner, Chopin, and Moscheles, and taught at the Royal Academy of Music from 1834. He left the concerto nos. 1 (perf. 1838?) and 2, op. 33 (perf. 1882).

Edouard Silas (1827–1909), Dutch pianist, organist, and composer, studied in Paris with Kalkbrenner and Halévy, and assisted Berlioz in preparing *L'Enfance du Christ* for publication. After settling in London in 1850, he composed the fantasia (perf. 1865), the *Elégie* (perf. 1873), and a concerto.

Francis Bache (1833–1858), organist at All Saints Church on Gordon Square, studied with Bennett in England and with Hauptman at the Leipzig Conservatory. For piano and orchestra, he composed two concertos (one perf. 1852), the polonaise, op. 9 (1854), and the *Morceau de Concerto.*

Oscar Beringer (1844–1922), German born, studied with Moscheles, Richter, and Reinecke in Leipzig and with Tausig in Berlin. He began teaching at Tausig's Music

Table 12 Additional Composers in England

Names	Dates	Compositions
Aguilar, Emanuel	1824–	Allegro *maestoso* (1852)
Allison, Horton	1846–	2 Concertos (1870/perf 1894)
Ashton, Algernon	1859–1937	Concertos, lost
Banister, Henry	1831–	Fantasia (1863)
Barnett, John	1837–	Concerto, op 25 (1869)
Beaumont, Alexander	? –	Suite
Bennett, George	1863–	Concerto (ca. 1880–84)
Booth, Robert	1862–	Waltzes, titles?
Borton, Alice	? –	Andante and Rondo
Bunnett, Edward	1834–	Andante and Rondo
Cianchettini, Katerina	1779–1883	2 Concertos
Cianchettini, Pio	1779–1851	Concertos
Clarke, James	1840–	Concerto, op 78
Cowen, Frédéric	1852–1935	Concerto (1869)
		Concertstück (1898)
Cusins, William	1833–1893	Concerto
Ellicott, Rosalind	1857–1924	Fantasia (1895)
Evans, Edwin	? –	Concerto (perf 1882)
Faulkes, William	1863–	Concerto (1891)
Goldschmidt, Otto	1829–1907	Concerto
Holmes, William	1812–	Concerto "The Jubilee"
Horrocks, Amy	1867–	Variations, op 7 (ca. 1892)
Horsley, Charles	1822–1876	Concerto (1848)
Hurlstone, William	1876–1906	Concerto (perf 1896)
Jackson, Arthur	1852–	Concerto
Jervis, St. Vincent	? –	Adagio and Rondo (perf 1854)
Kerrison, Davenport	1841?–	Concerto
		Concerto-caprice
King, Oliver	1855–1923	Concerto (1885)
Macfarren, Walter	1826–1905	*Concertstück* (ca. 1852)
		Concerto
Macpherson, Charles	1865–	*Concertstück* (1893)
Nixon, Henry	1842–1904	*Concertstück*
O'Leary, Arthur	1934–	Concerto
Orger, Caroline	. . .	See Caroline Reinagle
Parry, Charles	1848–1918	Concerto (1878–79)
Pauer, Ernst	1826–1905	Concerto
Reinagle, Caroline	1818–1892	Concerto
Richard, Richard	1858–	Concerto
Richards, Henry	1817–1885	Concerto
Ryan, Desmond	1851–	Symphony (1885)
Saint-George, Henry	1866–	Concerto
Salaman, Charles	1814–	Rondo *al capriccio*
Schachner, Rudolf	1821–1896	2 Concertos
Shakespeare, William	1849–1931	*Capriccio* Concerto (1879)
Smith, Alice	1839–1884	Introduction and Allegro (1865)
Sullivan, Arthur	1842–1900	Cadenzas, Mozart Conc, K.488
Surenne, John	1814–1878	Rondo *de concert*
Thouless, A. H.	? –ca. 1839	Concerto (1873)

Table 12 Additional Composers in England—Continued

Names	Dates	Compositions
Trickett, Arthur	? –	Sketches of wks
Waley, Simon	1827–1875	Concerto
Warner, Harry	1859–	Romance
Wesché, Walter	1857–	Concerto (1886)
		Andante and Allegro
White, Alice	. . .	See Alice Smith
Wingham, Thomas	1846–1893	Concert-Capriccio (1885)

School, and returned to England to establish the Academy for the Higher Development of Pianoforte Playing. He gave the first performance in England of Brahms' concerto no. 2 and his own andante and allegro (perf. 1880).

Arnold Dolmetsch (1858–1940), leader in the performance of early music on original instruments, wrote the book *The Interpretation of the Music of the 17th and 18th Centuries*. He composed the suite (1893) for piano and strings and arranged some of Purcell's music as the "Suite of Five Pieces for Piano and Strings."

Arthur Friedheim (1859–1932), German pianist, composer, and conductor, was a close friend of Liszt and a champion of Liszt's music. He taught piano at the Royal College of Music, the Chicago Musical College, and in New York City. He left a piano concerto.

Dora Bright (1863–1951) was the first person to give a recital of all English music. She left two concertos (1888, 1892).

Alfred Kaiser (1872–1917), Belgian-born, changed his name to De Keyser during World War I to avoid hostile English feelings about the kaiser of Germany. He left a piano concerto.

Richard Walthew (1872–1951) studied with Parry at the Royal College of Music, joined the faculty at Queen's College, and became the conductor of the South Place Orchestra. In 1894, he performed his own concerto at Queen's Hall.

Ireland

Johann Logier (1777–1846), German pianist, teacher specializing in group instruction, author, and composer, invented the *chiroplast* in Ireland as an aid in teaching piano and became widely known for his theory and piano-teaching books. His grand concerto, op. 13, appeared in a publication in London.

The United States

Louis Moreau Gottschalk (1829–1869), the earliest American composer to gain lasting fame in piano music, studied music in his native city of New Orleans, and traveled to Paris to seek admittance to the *Conservatoire*. After rejection by the *Conservatoire* he began lessons with various teachers. In Europe he enjoyed considerable fame as a pianist, went to Spain where the success continued, returned to France, and sailed in 1852 to the United States, where he experienced success as in Europe.

Robert Offergeld's *The Centennial Catalogue of the Published and Unpublished Compositions of Louis Moreau Gottschalk* [8] provides RO numbers for Gottschalk's music. The American pianist Eugene List commissioned the *Grande Fantaisie Triomphale sur l'Hymne National Bresilien,* op. 69, RO.108 (1869), originally for solo piano, for piano and orchestra. Gottschalk composed the original version in Rio de Janeiro, and performed it at the court of Pedro II, Emperor of Brazil. The *Grande Marche de Faust* (Gounod), RO.111 (ca. 1864), is for 31 pianists at 16 pianos and for orchestra. In 1850, Gottschalk planned an "American Concerto," but lucrative concert engagements caused him to put the concerto aside. In 1853, he worked on part of the lost concerto, RO.197, but any performances were under the title *Fragment de Concerto.* The *Grand Tarantelle,* op. 67, RO.259 (1868), is the same as the *Célèbre Tarantelle,* op. 67. Eugene List commissioned a version of the work for piano and string quintet (perf. 1969), and Hershy Kay reconstructed and orchestrated the composition for a publication in 1964. Eugene List commissioned Samuel Adler to prepare *L'Union,* op. 48, RO.269 (1862), originally for solo piano, for piano and orchestra. *L'Union* contains passages in the virtuoso style of Liszt (See exs. 6–26 and 6–27) and the songs *The Star-Spangled Banner* and *Hail Colombia.* The *Variations de Concert sur l'Hymne Portugais,* RO.289

Example 6–26. Gottschalk *L'Union,* op. 48, mm. 1–4

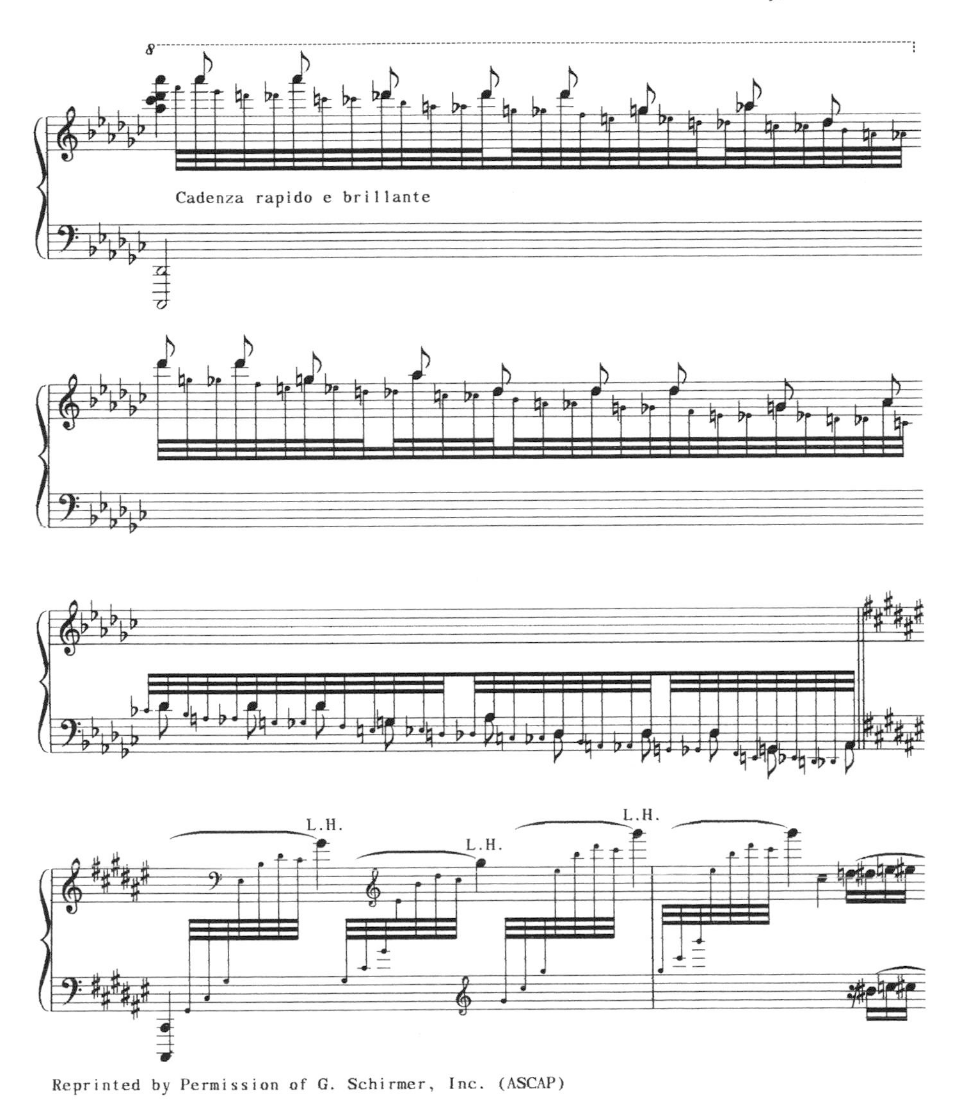

Example 6–27. Gottschalk *L'Union,* op. 48, mm. 36–37

(1869?), appeared under two titles, as the *Fantasia Sobre o Hymno de Luis I* and the *Grandes Variacoes de Concerto Sobre Hymno de D. Luis* I; Gottschalk probably composed the work in Rio de Janeiro. Gottschalk's success with Weber's *concertstück* resulted in his arranging it for piano quintet under the original title *Concertstück,* RO.199 (1851).

Table 13 Additional Composers in the United States

Names	Dates	Compositions
Boise, Otis	1845–1912	Concerto, op 36 (1874)
Buck, Dudley	1839–1909	*Andante et Allegro de Concert,* op 12
Devries, Herman	1858–1949	Titles?
Florio, Caryl	. . .	See William Robjohn
Gilchrist, William	1846–1916	Suite (ca. 1882–1911)
Gleason, Frederick	1848–1903	Concerto, op 18 (ca. 1898)
Hopkins, Jerome	1836–1898	Concerto no 1 (1872)
Huss, Henry	1862–1953	Rhapsody, op 3 (1885)
		Concerto, op 10 (1898)
Klein, Oscar	1858–1911	Concerto or *Konzertstück*
Maasa, Louis	1852–1889	Concerto, op 12 (1887)
Nicholl, Horace	1848–1922	Concerto, op 10 (perf 1888)
Nová, Ottokar	1866–1900	*Concerto Eroico,* op 8 (1894)
Pattison, John	1845–1905	Concerto-fantasia
Paur, Emil	1855–1932	Concerto (1896)
Pease, Alfred	1838–1882	Concerto (perf 1876)
Ritter, Frédéric	1824–1891	Concerto
Robjohn, William	1843–1920	Concerto (1875–86, rev 1915)
Singer, Otto	1833–1894	2 Concertos
Wels, Charles	1828–1906	Concerto?
Whiting, Arthur	1861–1936	Concerto (1888)
		Fantasy, op 11 (1897)
Whiting, George	1840–1923	Concerto
Zech, Frederick	1858–1926	4 Concertos
Zeuner, Charles	1795–1857	Variations

Notes

1. Maurice J. E. Brown, *Chopin, An Index of His Works in Chronological Order,* 2nd revised ed. (New York: Da Cape Press, 1972).
2. George S. Golos, "Some Slavic Predecessors of Chopin," *Musical Quarterly* 46 (January 1950): 39–61.
3. See Chapter 3 for Franciszek Lessel's music for piano and orchestra.
4. For examples of Chopin's use of piano passages from Hummel's music, see Hans Engel, *The Solo Concerto* (Cologne: Arno Volkk Verlag, 1964), 44.
5. The score lacks a slur in the fourth beat, right-hand part.
6. Ted M. Blair, "Henry Charles Litolff: (1818–1891): His Life and Piano Music" (Ph.D. dissertation, University of Iowa, 1968).
7. Philip Henry Peter, "The Life and Work of Cipriani Potter (1792–1871)," Vols. I and II (Ph.D. dissertation, Northwestern University, 1972).
8. Robert Offergel, *The Centennial Catalogue of the Published and Unpublished Compositions of Louis Moreau Gottschalk,* Prepared for *Stereo Review* (New York: Ziff-Davis, 1970).

Part IV

After Brahms to the Present (ca. 1897–1992)

Chapter 7

Germany and Austria

Germany

Max Bruch (1838–1920), famed composer of violin concertos and the *Kol Nidrei* for cello and orchestra, had an active musical life in Koblenz, Liverpool, Breslau, and Berlin. He composed the "Concerto for Two Pianos," op. 88a (1912–1915), in response to a request in 1911 from Rose and Ottilie Sutro for a duo concerto. In 1915, he gave the sisters the composition with the stipulation that performances occur only in the United States. Unbeknownst to Bruch, the sisters revised the concerto into a simpler version, including a reduction from four movements to three movements, because they could not play the original piano parts. They performed the corrupted version in Philadelphia in 1916 and in New York City in 1917. The concerto disappeared until the sale of Ottilie Sutro's estate in 1971. Among the items auctioned was an original copy of the concerto. The duo-pianists Martin Berkofsky and David Hagan performed the original version in Hamburg in 1977.

The concerto has four movements, with the opening motive of the first movement also beginning the fourth movement. An unusual feature of the concerto is a fugue in the first movement; fugues in piano concertos tend to be in later movements.

Louisa Lebeau (1850–1927) studied with Clara Schumann and Kalliwoda. She composed the *fantasie,* op. 25, and two concertos, opp. 7 and 37.

Richard Burmeister (1860–1944) studied with Liszt in Weimar and traveled with him to Rome and Budapest. While on the faculty at the conservatory, he composed the concerto, op. 1 (pub. 1890). He wrote orchestra parts for Chopin's concerto no. 1, Liszt's Hungarian rhapsody no. 5, and Weber's *konzertstück.*

Emil von Sauer (1862–1942), pianist, composer, and editor of Brahms' piano music, studied with Liszt and at the Moscow Conservatory with N. Rubinstein. He toured while composing the two concertos (pub. 1900 and 1901) in four movements. The concerto no. 1 is reminiscent of Tchaikovsky's concerto no. 1, and the concerto no. 2 does not have pauses between the thematically related movements.

Hugo Kaun (1863–1932), pianist and choral conductor, composed music in the style of the late nineteenth-century German composers. He composed the concerto, op. 19 (1889), in Milwaukee, and the concerto, op. 50 (1903), the *konzertstück,* op. 74 (by 1923), and the concerto, op. 115 (1923), in Berlin. Schumann, Mendelssohn, Brahms, and Reger influenced the *konzertstück.*

Richard Strauss (1864–1949) is famous for symphonic poems and operas in the chromatic style of the late-nineteenth century. Erich H. Mueller von Asow's *Richard Strauss, Thematisches Verzeichnis*[1] provides AV numbers for works without opus numbers. Strauss composed three works for piano and orchestra: the *Burleske,* AV.85 (1885–1886), originally titled *Scherzo,* composed in Meiningen; the *Parergon zur Symphonia Domestica,* op. 73 (1924); and the *Panathenaenzug,* "symphonic studies in the form of a passacaglia," op. 74 (1927). The *Rhapsodie,* AV.213 (1886), remains a fragment. The cadenza, AV.179 (1885), is for Mozart's concerto, K.491. The *Burleske,* the *Rhapsodie,* and the cadenza were written when Strauss was a performing pianist. The *Burleske* contains broad musical ideas common to the romantic era.

Strauss composed the *Parergon zur Symphonia Domestica* and the *Panathenäenzug* for left hand, for pianist Paul Wittgenstein, who lost his right arm in combat. For the *Parergon zur Symphonia Domestica,* Strauss chose a melodic fragment from his own *Symphonia Domestica,* op. 53 (1903), for the portrayal of his son Bubi's serious illness and recovery. Later, Wittgenstein modified the work with, he claimed, the approval of Strauss. The *Panathenäenzug* has 55 variations on a ground bass, introduction, and finale. Strauss created the composition in remembrance of the *Panathenaea,* an ancient Greek festival commemorating the birthday of the goddess Athena. Perhaps he chose the passacaglia to depict with musical variations numerous events and sights in the ancient pageant.

Ferruccio Busoni (1866–1924), Italian pianist, composer, and editor of Bach's keyboard works, was a friend of many famous musicians, including Brahms, Rubinstein, Franz, Malher, Delius, and d'Albert. He lived in Italy, Leipzig, Helsingfor, Moscow, several cities for short periods, and Berlin from 1894. The opus numbers of Busoni's music require clarification. As a youth, he assigned numbers to works without regard to publication. At age 17, having reached op. 40, he started again with op. 1. Sometime later, he began numbering from op. 30 with the letter "a" for opp. 30–36. Beginning with op. 41, the numbering is nearly correct. His music for piano and orchestra is the *konzertstück* (introduction and allegro), op. 31a (1890); the concerto, op. 39 (1903–1904); the *Indianische Fantasie,* op. 44 (1913), based on music of the North American Indians; and the *Romanze e Scherzoso,* op. 54 (1922), also performed under the title "Concertino." Busoni's transcriptions for piano and orchestra include Bach's concerto, BWV 1052 (1899); Liszt's "Spanish Rhapsody" (1894), which Busoni performed using his own contrapuntal introduction on the theme *Folies d'Espagne,* and Mozart's rondo *concertante* (1919) from the finale of the concerto, K.482.

The concerto, op. 39, is Busoni's monumental contribution to the piano literature. The work has five movements with Italian melodies, a lengthy cadenza, and an offstage male chorus singing words from Adam Gottlob Oehlenschlaeger's poem *Aladdin.* Audiences did not care for a concerto they considered another symphony with piano obbligato, like Brahms' concerto no. 2. The piano part is technically and musically difficult.

Busoni's style displays influences of Bach, Mozart, and Liszt; he wanted to combine their styles with late-romantic and post-romantic harmony. While his music gained little recognition in the performing repetoire, his compositional efforts are part of a historical line adopted by Hindemith and other mid-twentieth-century composers.

Busoni composed cadenzas for Mozart's concertos K.271 (pub. 1916), K.453 (pub. 1922), K.459 (1920), K.466 (two pub. 1907), K.467 (pub. 1922), K.482 (1919), K.488 (pub. 1919), K.491 (pub. 1919), and K.503 (1922). In 1900, he arranged

Beethoven's cadenzas for the concerto nos. 1, 3 and 4, and composed two cadenzas (1890) for Beethoven's concerto no. 4.

Siegfried Kallenberg (1867–1944), writer on music, settled in Munich in 1910 and composed the neo-romantic *konzertante fantasie.* The Kallenberg Society promotes Kallenberg's musical contributions.

Akos Buttykay (1871–1935), Hungarian, composed music in a late-romantic style. While studying with Stavenhagen in Berlin, he may have composed the fantasy, op. 6 (perf. 1897). In 1907, he settled in Budapest to teach at the Academy of Music.

Paul Juon (1872–1940), Russian-born, trained at the Moscow Conservatory with Taneyev and Arensky. A successful blending of Russian and German idioms earned him the name "Russian Brahms." From 1906, he taught at the *Hochschule für Musik* in Berlin, where he composed the concerto, op. 45 (1912), for violin, cello, piano, and orchestra.

Max Reger (1873–1916) studied with Riemann, who directed him to the music of Beethoven, Brahms, Bach, and Wagner. His thickly textured concerto, op. 114 (1910), has the contrapuntal style of J. S. Bach and the chromatic harmony of Wagner. Perhaps Reger's lasting influence is on the next generation of German composers, who continue his love of contrapuntal textures.

Josef Hoffmann (1876–1957), legendary pianist of Polish birth, studied with Moskowski and was the only pianist to study piano with A. Rubinstein. He began concertizing at an early age, and performed Beethoven's concerto no. 1 with the Berlin Philharmonic under von Bülow at age 10. He wrote on music and held more than 70 patents for scientific and mechanical inventions. His more than 100 musical compositions include five concertos (no. 2 1903, others 1898–ca. 1906) in a conservative romantic style and the one-movement *Chromaticon* (ca. 1915) that merges sonata form and concerto structure in a style akin to Liszt's sonata. Hoffmann composed the *Chromaticon* in response to the stylistic challenge he perceived in Scriabin's music. The musical influences are Scriabin, Rachmaninoff, Debussy, Bruch, and Bloch.

Ernö Dohnányi (1877–1960) was a Hungarian composer, conductor, teacher, brilliant touring pianist and the most influential individual in Hungarian music during this century. His concerto, op. 5 (1897–1898), is from when he was in Budapest, Weimar, and London. His popular work for piano and orchestra is the "Variations on a Nursery Song," *Ah, Vous Dirai-Je, Maman,* op. 25 (1913), from when he taught at the Berlin *Hochschule für Musik.* This witty composition begins with a lengthy and serious introduction by the orchestra. The piano presents the theme and eleven variations follow. The tenth variation is a passacaglia, and there is a fugato finale. In 1919, Dohnányi became the director of the Budapest Conservatory of Music, and there he composed the concerto, op. 42 (1946). He moved to Argentina in 1948, and settled in the United States in 1949 to teach at Florida State University in Tallahassee. Although Dohnányi composed music for piano and orchestra mainly while outside Hungary, his influence on Hungarian music should not be understated. Dohnányi composed cadenzas (1906–1942) for all of Mozart's piano concertos and Beethoven's concerto nos. 1–4 (1897–1951).

Siegfried Karg-Elert (1877–1933) gave up a brilliant pianistic career to compose. His real name is Karg, which means "avaricious," and at the suggestion of his concert agent he added the hyphenated Elert. While his most important contribution is to organ literature, he also composed two piano concertos, op. 6 (1901), and one (1913). The piano concertos contain elements of impressionism and an influence of Reger. Grieg encouraged him and influenced Karg-Elert's early works.

Halfdan Cleve (1879–1951), Norwegian composer and pianist, studied in Berlin with Raff and the Scharwenka brothers. In Berlin, he concertized as a pianist and, depending on the source, returned to Oslo between 1910 and 1914 to teach and perform. His late-romantic, virtuoso concertos are five in number: op. 3 (1902), op. 6 (1904), op. 9 (1906), op. 12 (1910), and op. 20 (1916). The premiere of the concerto, op. 3, occurred in Berlin and the other premieres were in Oslo. The concertos, opp. 3 and 9, have four movements and the concertos, opp. 6, 12, and 20, have three movements. Sometimes performers use the concerto, op. 9, as a quintet. In Norway, he received a state salary of arts to allow time for musical composition.

Julius Weismann (1879–1950) played piano and conducted in Freiburg from 1902, and moved to Nussdorf to compose in 1939. In the 1920s and 1930s, his music was popular in Germany. For piano and orchestra, he left three concertos, opp. 33, 138, and 141 (1909–1910, rev. 1936, 1941–1942, 1942–1948), and the suite, op. 97 (1927).

Kurt von Wolfurt (1880–1957), Baltic-German composer and conductor, spent the early part of his life in St. Petersburg. His neo-classic concerto, op. 25 (1933), is from his stay in Stockholm. Wolfurt's use of contrapuntal devices comes from his studies with Reger.

Walter Braunfels (1882–1954), student of Leschetizky and Thuill, taught at the *Hochschule für Musik*. His style has romantic features similar to Brahms and Berlioz. For piano and orchestra, he composed the *Hexensabbath,* op. 8, the concerto, op. 21 (1911), the concerto, op. 29, the *konzertstück,* op. 64 (1946), the *Hebriden-Tänze,* op. 70 (ca. 1950), and the divertimento (1950).

Hermann Waltershausen (1882–1954), accomplished pianist, lost his left arm in a childhood accident. While on the faculty at the Munich State Academy, he composed the *Krippenmusik,* op. 23 (1926), for chamber orchestra and harpsichord obbligato.

Manfred Gurlitt (1890–1973), opera conductor, helped popularize German opera in Japan after arriving there in 1939. His chamber concerto (1927) is for piano and chamber orchestra.

Fidelio Finke (1891–1968) began composing in a style similar to Brahms and Reger, and adopted traits of Schoenberg and neo-classicism as of 1930. The capriccio (1930), based on a Polish folk song, is for piano and small orchestra, and the suite for *Blaserquintet* (1960–1961) is for two pianos and string orchestra. He probably composed the capriccio in Czechoslovakia while on the faculty at the German Academy of Music in Prague.

Heinrich Lemacher (1891–1966) composed in the style of Bruckner and Reger, and later made freer use of tonality. Although church music was his main compositional interest, he composed the concerto, op. 46, for piano and strings, the *Leuzbacher Tänze,* op. 114, for piano duet and orchestra, and the duo concerto (pub. 1956) for piano, four-hands, and string orchestra.

Alois Hába (1893–1973), Czech microtonal composer, founded the department of microtonal music at the Prague Conservatory. He composed the twelve-tone symphonic fantasy, op 8 (1920–1921), while a student at the Berlin *Hochschule für Musik*. At the *Hochschule,* or while studying with Schrenker at the Vienna Academy, he composed the overture, op. 5 (1920). Hába's interest in Oriental folk music led him to create a system of microtonal symbols.

Paul Hindemith (1895–1963) moved from Germany to the United States, where he became the head of the Music Department at Yale University and a faculty member at the Berkshire Music Center in Massachusetts. His concern about the widening gap between music of twentieth-century composers and audiences led him to write *Gebrauchsmusik* (workaday music), a term Hindemith disliked, aimed at audience understanding, and *Hausmusik* (house music) for amateurs to perform at home. Hindemith's style uses harmonic ideas according to a personal concept of fundamentals and overtones. "Harmonic fluctuation" refers to increasing and decreasing harmonic tension according to a classification of chords and chord constructions.

Hindemith's music for piano and orchestra is the *Klaviermusik mit Orchestra,* op. 29 (1923), for left hand, the *Kammermusik* no. 2 (piano concerto), op. 36/1 (1925), the *Konzertmusik,* op. 49 (1930), for piano, brass, and two harps, and a concerto (1945). *The Four Temperaments* (1940) is a ballet and concert piece for piano and strings describing in theme and variations the four moods of melancholy, sanguine, phlegmatic, and choleric. Hindemith's style shows an influence of Busoni, who believed in musical craftsmanship, a back-to-Bach aesthetic in contrapuntal writing, a fondness for classic ideas, and expanded harmonies using quartal and chromatic chords.

Carl Orff (1895–1982) successfully worked in the music education of children, and developed the Orff instruments. Among his musical compositions is the frequently performed *Carmina Burana* (1937) for chorus and orchestra. He has withdrawn the concertino (1927) for wind instruments and harpsichord.

Edwin Bodky (1896–1958), musicologist, harpsichordist and pianist, studied with Dohnányi, Juon, Busoni, and R. Strauss. His concerto (1922) is from the years he studied composition with Strauss. He taught at the Scharwenka Conservatory, and moved to the United States in 1938 to teach at the Longy School of Music in Cambridge. His book *The Interpretation of Bach's Keyboard Works* appeared in publication in 1960, two years after his death.

Eduard Erdmann (1896–1958), Latvian-German, composed the concerto, op. 15 (1930), while a student of Ansorge in Berlin, and the *konzertstück* (*rhapsodie* and rondo), op. 18 (1946), for his own use as a pianist.

Karl Pillney (1896–) completed Bach's unfinished *Art of the Fugue*. For piano and orchestra, he composed a *divertimento* (1929), the *Musik* (1932), the *Parodistische Variationen über einen Gassenhauer* (1945), and the *Kammermusik* (1972) for oboe, harpsichord, and string orchestra.

Marta von Kriegner (1898–), Hungarian virtuoso violinist, conductor, and composer, was the first woman conducting student at the Berlin *Hochschule für Musik* and she remained there as a faculty member. Among her compositions is the Hungarian Capriccio for violin or piano and orchestra.

Walter Rehberg (1900–1957) studied piano with d'Albert and taught at the *Hochschule für Musik*. His *konzertante musik* (1912) is for clarinet, French horn, piano, and string orchestra.

Hermann Reutter (1900–1985) composes music influenced by classic thinking and the neo-romantic styles of Pfitzner, Hass, Hindemith, and Honegger. For piano and orchestra, he composed three concertos, opp. 19, 36, and 62 (1926, 1929, 1944); the *Sinfonishche Fantasie* (piano concerto), op. 50 (1938); the one-movement concerto, op. 63 (1949), for two pianos; the one-movement concertino, op. 69 (1947), with string orchestra; the concert variations (1952); and the *capriccio, aria e finale* (1963). Reutter premiered most of his own piano compositions, and taught at the *Hochschule für Musik*.

Friedrich Wührer (1900–1975) was a prominent Austrian pianist who made the first complete recordings of Schubert's sonatas and eventually recorded 35 LP records of Viennese and German classic and romantic composers. He taught in Vienna and Salzburg, and in Munich he wrote cadenzas for Mozart's concertos K.467, K.491, and K.537. He arranged Schmidt's left-hand concerto for two keyboards.

Wilhelm Maler (1902–1976) used stylistic elements of Hindemith, Reger, and Busoni, classic and baroque techniques, and tonal harmony. He composed the concerto (1927) for harpsichord and chamber orchestra, the *concerto grosso* (1928) for two woodwinds, piano, and strings, and the concertino (1940) for violin, cello, and piano.

Miroslav Ponc (1902–1976), Czech violinist and conductor, probably composed his piano concerto (1930) in Berlin while studying with Schoenberg. Hába and the Berlin avant-garde group *Der Sturm* influenced his music. In 1932, he settled in Prague as a theater conductor.

Boris Blacher (1903–1975) taught at and directed the *Hochschule für Musik* from 1970. In about 1948, he began using the twelve-tone method of Schoenberg mixed with tertian, quartal, and quintal harmonies and bitonality. His piano textures are often thin, and the rhythms show the influence of Stravinsky. He evolved a system of variable meters based on mathematical permutations resulting in varying numbers of eighth notes in each measure. Variable meters are in Blacher's music of the 1950s and 1960s.

Blacher's music includes the lost concerto (1935); the concerto no. 1, op. 28 (1947–1948); the *dialog* (1950) for flute, violin, piano, and string orchestra; the concerto no. 2 "In Variable Meters," op. 42 (1952); and the *Variations on a Theme of Muzio Clementi,* op. 61 (1961), sometimes called the concerto no. 3. The *Variations* has 16 neo-classic variations on the theme C-D-E-F-G-F-E-flat-D.

Rudolf Wagner-Regeny (1903–1969), Hungarian-born, arrived in Germany in 1920 to study in Leipzig and Berlin, and lived in or near Berlin from 1924. He directed the *Musikhochschule* in Rostock and the State Conservatory in Berlin. The *Ochestermusik mit Klavier* (1935) is a concerto with solo piano.

Hans Brehme (1904–1957) studied piano with Kempff and taught at the *Hochschule für Musik*. His compositions follow the German romantic style and contain twentieth-century techniques. He left the concerto, op. 32 (1936), the chamber concerto, op. 43 (1946), for violin, cello, and piano, and the twelve-tone concerto, op. 58 (1954).

Hermann Schroeder (1904–) helped reform Catholic church music by blending musical features of the Middle Ages and twentieth-century ideas. For piano and orchestra, he composed the concerto, op. 35 (1955), and the concertino, op. 42 (ca. 1965–1970).

Kurt Thomas (1904–1973), important in Protestant church music, began teaching theory and composition at the Leipzig Conservatory at age 21. He left the concerto, op. 30.

Karl Hartmann (1905–1963), student of Webern in Vienna, founded the *Musica Vina* concerts in Munich. He composed the concerto (1953) for piano, winds, and percussion using rhythmic and harmonic mirroring, and Blacher's ideas on variable meter. Influences on Hartmann's concerto (1955) for viola, piano, winds, and percussion are Berg, Stravinsky, Bartók, Reger, expanded tonality, polytonality, and atonality.

Johannes Thilman (1906–1973) was a student and follower of Hindemith in writing music for amateurs. He composed the left-hand concertino, op. 65; the "Little Concerto" (1968) for harpsichord and small orchestra; the double concerto (1968) for bass clarinet and piano with string orchestra and percussion; and the concerto (1968) for two pianos.

Günter Bialas (1907–) began composing music with folk songs, traditional idioms, and ideas from Hindemith and Stravinsky. He adopted the twelve-tone method in about 1945, and experimented with timbres and aleatoric techniques in 1970. His music for piano and orchestra is the *Kleine Konzertmusik* (1935), the *Jazz-Promenade* (1956), the *Concerto Lirico* (1967), and the chamber concerto (1973) for harpsichord and thirteen instruments.

Wolfgang Fortner (1907–1987) is an important German composer influenced by neo-classic ideas, Hindemith, and Stravinsky. He studied at the Leipzig Conservatory and began teaching at the Institute of Sacred Music in Heidelberg. He used his own organ concerto when composing his piano concerto (1932). His concerto (1943) is for piano and orchestra, and the *Fantasy on B.A.C.H.* (1950) is for two pianos, nine solo instruments, and orchestra. The concertos for harpsichord and piano are in a dissonant contrapuntal style following the general ideas of neo-baroque style. Since 1945, Fortner has used the twelve-tone method. The *Fantasy on B.A.C.H.* is on the row technique, with the notes B-A-C-H appearing in all presentations of the row. Besides two pianos, the first-chair players of the orchestra perform the other nine solo parts. Fortner began teaching at the North-West German Music Academy in Detmold in 1954 and there he composed the atonal *Mouvement* (1954) in sections marked "Prologue," "Etude I," "Etude II," and "Epilogue." He taught at the Freiburg *Musikhochschule* and became the director of the *Musica Vina* concerts in Munich in 1964, taking over from Hartmann. In Munich, Fortner composed the *Triplum* (1966) for three pianos and orchestra. Not only has Fortner contributed important literature to the piano and orchestra repertoire, he is important as the teacher of many important German composers to emerge since 1950.

Willy Schneider (pseud. Matthias Burger, 1907–) taught at the *Hochschule für Musik*. The concertino (1964) is for alto-flute, piano, and string orchestra.

Fred Lohse (1908–) has been teaching at the Institute of Musicology at the Leipzig University since 1952. He has the concerto (1937–1938), the concertino (1950–1951) with string orchestra, the concerto (1963) for clarinet, trumpet, piano, timpani, percussion, and strings, and the concerto (1970).

Edward Staempfli (1908–), born in Switzerland, studied in Cologne and with Dukas in Paris. After hearing Berg's violin concerto, Staempfli followed the twelve-tone method in his own compositions. In Switzerland, he composed two concertos (1932, 1933), the concerto (1940) for two pianos, and the concertino (1947) with chamber orchestra. In Berlin, he composed two concertos (1954, 1963), the *Tripartita* (1969) for three pianos and twenty-three winds, and the *Satze und Gegensätze* (1972) for vibraphone, piano, percussion, and fifteen strings.

Erwin Dressel (1909–1972) studied composition with Juon and worked as a freelance pianist and arranger. For piano and orchestra, he composed the *allegro brioso* (pub. 1950), the *Preludio Antico* (pub. 1950), and the *Variationen-Serenade* (1962).

Jan Koetsier (1911–), Danish, conducted many orchestras in Europe and joined the faculty at the *Hochschule für Musik* in 1966. In a musical style with baroque and modern techniques, he composed the *Musical Sketch* (1956), the fantasy *Kreisleriana concertino* (1965) for two pianos, and the concerto *capriccioso* (1975).

Herbert Collum (1914–) gave highly praised organ performances of music by Bach and modern composers. He composed in the manner of Fortner before 1945, and afterward he turned to the twelve-tone method. Among the works dating from before 1945 that survived destruction are five concertos (three ca. 1939) for harpsichord and string orchestra, the concerto (1967–1968), and the *Hymnus im Alten Stil* (concerto).

Hans Poser (1917–1970) was in Canada as a prisoner of war when the Red Cross arranged for him to study composition by mail with Hindemith and Grabner. He left the concertino, op. 19, for piano, trumpet, string orchestra, and percussion.

Jürg Baur (1918–) taught at the Düsseldorf Conservatory from 1946 and became the head of the composition department at the *Musikhochschule* in Cologne in 1971. His style shows the influence of Reger, Hindemith, Lutheran neo-classicism, and, from 1958, the twelve-tone method of Webern. For piano and orchestra, he composed the *koncertante musik* (1958) in four neo-classic, atonal movements, and the concerto (1970).

Bernd Zimmermann (1918–1970) began his musical career as a dance band musician and taught at the *Hochschule für Musik* from 1958. He committed suicide soon after completing the *Requiem für Einen Jungen Dichter* based on texts of poets who committed suicide. His music for piano and orchestra is expressionistic and chromatic. The two-piano concerto *Dialoge* (1960, rev. 1965) is an homage to Debussy. His opera *Die Soldaten* is the most important German opera after Berg.

Johannes Driessler (1921–) taught at the *Nordwestdeutsche Musik Akademie* and became known for his church music. The concerto, op. 17 (1953), is in a traditional tonal style.

Erhard Karkoschka (1923–), follower of Webern since 1960, teaches at the *Musikhochschule*. His *Polyphonic Studies* are for orchestra with piano obbligato.

Wolfgang Steffen (1923–) studied at the conservatory and the *Musikhochschule,* conducted at the Berlin Free University, and taught at the Staatlich *Hochschule für Musik*. His main interest is avant-garde music. Among his compositions are the *Dance Impressions I* (1950); the concerto, op. 16 (1956); the harpsichord concerto

(1969); the *Dance Impressions II* (1970) for piano, percussion and string orchestra; the *Polychromie,* op. 38 (1970), for piano and ten instruments, arranged for piano and orchestra as op. 38a (1971); the *Klangseqmente,* op. 41 (1973–1975), for cymbal, harp, harpsichord and orchestra; and the "Music for Piano and 7 Players," op. 44 (1975).

Giselher Klebe (1925–) studied composition with Blacher and taught at the *Nordwestdeutsche Musik Akademie* from 1957. He writes music similar to Schoenberg and Webern. His music includes the concerto (1971–1972) for electronically altered harpsichord and small orchestra, and the sinfonia, op. 16 (1953), with a melody from Mozart's concerto, K.491. With Henze, Klebe has been important in German opera since the mid-1950s.

Günter Kochan (1930–), student of Blacher and a teacher at the *Hochschule für Musik,* composes in a neo-classic style with modern techniques. His music includes the concerto, op. 16 (1957–1958), the "Variations on a Theme of Mendelssohn" (1971–1972), and the "Variations on a Ventian Canzonetta" (1972).

Siegfried Kurz (1930–) conducted at the Dresden State Academy and the Dresden State Opera. His music has classic elements mixed with dissonant counterpoint and expanded tonality. He composed the divertimento (1950) with strings and the concerto, op. 32, (1964).

Vinko Globokar (1934–), Yugoslavian trombonist, lived in Paris before going to the *Hochschule für Musik.* The *Vendre le Vent* (1972–1973) is for piano, percussion, five woodwinds, and four brass, and the *Drama* (1972) is for piano and percussion.

Arvo Pärt (1935–) is the first Estonian composer trained at the Tallin Conservatory to adopt the twelve-tone method. He began writing in a traditional style, and after exposure to avant-garde techniques turned toward contemporary ideas. The *Collage on B-A-C-H* (1964) is for harpsichord, oboe, and strings. The *Credo* (1968) has a solo piano, mixed chorus, and orchestra, and the revision (1980) is for harpsichord and twenty strings. Version B of the *Mirror in Mirror* (1980) is for violin, piano, and strings. *If Bach Had Raised Bees,* based on the theme "B-A-C-H," is in a version (1978) for harpsichord, electric bass guitar, electronic tape, and ensemble, and a version (1980) is for harpsichord and strings.

Maki Ishii (1936–), Japanese composer, studied at the Berlin *Hochschule für Musik* with Blacher and Rufer, and settled in Germany, possibly in Berlin. His music joins sonorities of Japanese music with serialism and electronic techniques. The *Kyo-o* (1968) is for piano, orchestra, and tape.

Rainer Kunda (1936–) composes light opera and ballet. He has the one-movement concerto, op. 45 (1969), and the concerto (1970) for harpsichord, piano, ionica, celesta, strings, and percussion.

Marc Neikrug (1946–), American, studied with Klebe at the *Nordwestdeutsch Musik Akademie* and plays violin duos with Pinchas Zukermann. His piano concerto (1966) has atonality and chromaticism.

Liana Alexander Saptefrati (1947–), Romanian, teaches at the University at Darmstadt with Xenakis and Stockhausen. She has composed the *Music* (1974).

Table 14 Additional Composers in Germany

Names	Dates	Compositions
Abendroth, Walter	1896–	*Konzertante Phantasie,* op 23, hpd
Abrosius, Herman	1897–	5 Concertos, one op 51 (1927), one (1946)
Angorge, Conrad	1862–1930	Concerto
Aschenbrenner, Johannes	1903–	Divertimento
Barbe, Helmut	1927–	Concerto (pub 1973)
Baumann, Max	1917–	Concerto, op 36 (1952)
Bayer, Friedrich	1902–	Concerto (1935)
Beckerath, Alfred v.	1901–	Concerto
Beeboth, Max	1904–	Concerto
Behm, Eduard	1862–1946	Concerto
Behrend, Fritz	1889–	*Am Rhein,* op 8 (perf 1913)
		Fantasie, op 9 (perf 1919)
Berger, Jean	1909–	Concertino
Blumer, Theordor	1882–1964	Concerto
Bohnke, Emil	1888–1928	Concerto, op 14
Borck, Edmund von	1906–1944	Concerto, op 20 (1941)
Borris, Siegfried	1906–	Concerto, op 58 (1962)
		Conc (1952), hpd, fl, bn
Bredemeyer, Reiner	1929–	*Piano Une 72*
Bremen, Alexander	1930–	Concerto (1953)
Brüggemann, Alfred	1873–1944	Concerto, op 17
Brugk, Hans	1909–	*Für die Jugend,* op 16
		Karneval, op 24
Buch, Wolfgang	? –	*Notturno in Blue* (1961)
Büchtiger, Fritz	1903–1978	Concertino II
Bullerian, Hans	1885–1948	2 Concertos, opp 4 & 5
Busch, Adolf	1891–1952	Concerto, op 31 (1925)
Butting, Max	1888–1976	Concerto, op 110 (1964)
Chop, Max	1862–1929	3 Concertos
Cilensek, Johann	1913–	Concerto (1950)
		Konzertstück (1966)
Courvoisier, Walter	1875–1931	Cadenza, Beethoven Conc no 2
Czernik, Willi	1901–	*Dionysisches Fest*
Degen, Helmut	1911–	Concerto (1940)
		Concertino (1942), 2 pnos
		Little Concerto (1942)
		Concerto (1945), hpd
		Symphonisches Spiel II (1957) vn, vc, pno
Deutsch, Peter	1901–	*The Magic Picture* (perf 1950)
Dimov, Bojidar	1935–	*Raumspiel* (1968–69)
Döhl, Friedhelm	1936–	Sound-Scene III "Zorch" (1972), 3 pnos
Erdmann, Dietrich	1917–	Concerto (1950)
		Concertino (1956)
Faltis, Evelyn	1890–1937	Concerto, op 3
Fiebig, Kurt	1908–	Concerto, hpd
Fischer, Ernst	1900–	*Toccata* (pub 1947)
Fortig, Peter	1934–	*Konzertstück* (1966)
Friebe, Wolfgang	1909–	*Slawische Rhapsodie* (pub 1959)
Friedrichs, Günter	1935–	*Bewegangen*

Table 14 Additional Composers in Germany—Continued

Names	Dates	Compositions
Fromm-Michaels, Ilse	1888–	20 Cadenzas, Mozart concs
Frommel, Gerhard	1906–	Conc, op 9 (1934), pno, cl
Funk, Heinrich	1893–	*Romantic Variations,* op 60 (by 1943)
Furst, Paul	1926–	Conc, op 30 (1960), 2 pnos
Furtwängler, Wilhelm	1886–1954	*Sinfonisches Konzert* (1924–36)
Fussan, Werner	1912–	Music for Strings, Piano, Percussion and Timpani (1950)
Gebhard, Hans	1897–1947	Concerto, op 25 (ca. 1933)
Gebhardt, Rio	1907–1944	Concerto
Geissler, Fritz	1921–	Concerto
Gerhard, Fritz	1911–	*Rhapsodisches Konzert* (1950)
		Concerto *con Unisono*
Gerster, Ottmar	1897–1969	3 Concertos (1932/48/55)
Gilse, Jan van	1881–1944	*3 Tanzkizzen* (Dance Sketches) (1925–26)
Girnatis, Walter	1894–	Rondo-Bolero (pub 1928)
		Concerto *Retrosspectif* (pub 1955)
Gmeindl, Walther	1890–1958	Concerto, op 16 (1938)
Göhler, Karl	1874–1954	Concerto (1925)
Goodman, Alfred	1920–	*3 Essays* (1972), hpd
Görner, Hans-Georg	1908–	Concerto (1959), hpd
Graener, Paul	1872–1944	Concerto, op 72 (by 1943)
Grenz, Artur	1909–	*Manhattan-Capriccio,* op 13 (pub 1955)
Gress, Richard	1893–	Concerto, op 81
Griesbach, Karl-Rudi	1916–	*Blues-Impressions* (1962)
		Konzertante Musik (1964)
Grosz, Wilhelm	1894–1939	*Symphonic Dance,* op 24 (1928)
		Concerto, op 24 (1930)
Gürsching, Albrecht	1934–	*Konzert* (1972)
Halaczinsky, Rudolf	1920–	Concerto (1973–74)
Halm, August	1869–1929	Concerto (1913), pno obbl
Hannenheim, Norbert v.	1898–1940	2 Concertos (perf 1932)
Hartig, Heinz	1907–1969	Concerto, op 30 (1959)
Hartzer-Stibbe, Marie	1880–1961	Concerto
Hasse, Karl	1883–1960	Concerto, op 61 (1938)
		Toccata, Passacaglia and Fugue, op 70 (perf 1939)
Heider, Werner	1930–	*Capriccio* (pub 1955)
		Glimpses (1958), sop, pno
		Bezirk (1969)
Heilmann, Harald	1924–	Concerto (1953–61), pno
		Concerto (1969–73), tr, pno
Heinemann, Alfred	1908–	Concerto (1941)
Helm, Everett	1913–	2 Concertos (1951/56)
Herrman, Hugo	1896–1967	Conc, op 76 (1931), hpd
		Concertmusic, op 79b
Herrmann, Peter	1941–	*Klavierkonzert für die Jugend* (1969)
Herz, Maria	1878–	Concerto (1927–28)
Hespos, Hans-Joachim	1938–	*Break* (1968)
		Blackout (1972)

Table 14 Additional Composers in Germany—Continued

Names	Dates	Compositions
Hessenberg, Kurt	1908–	Concerto, op 3 (1931), hpd Conc, op 21 (1939), pno Conc, op 50 (1950), 2 pnos
Höffer, Paul	1895–1949	2 Concertos, opp 8 & 45 (1939)
Höller, Karl	1907–	Concerto, op 19 (1934, rev 1958), hpd *Bamberger Concerto,* op 63 (1972)
Humel, Gerald	1931–	Chamber Concerto (1966), hn, pno
Jacobi, Wolfgang	1894–1972	Concerto (1954), hpd Capriccio (1956)
Jentzsch, Wilfried	1941–	*Transformationen* (1970), 2 pnos
Jung, Helge	1943–	Concerto, op 11 (pub 1973)
Kaminski, Heinrich	1886–1946	Concerto (1936)
Kempff, Wilhelm	1896–	Concerto (1915)
Killmayer, Wilhelm	1927–	Concerto (1955)
Klees, Gabriele	1895–	Concerto
Klein, Richard	1921–	Chamber Concerto IV (1967), hpd or org
Kletzke, Paul	1900–1973	Concerto, op 22 (1931)
Knapp, Arno	1913–1960	Concertino (1952)
Knorr, Ernest-Lothar von	1896–1973	Chamber Concerto, pno, sax, chorus
Köhler, Siegfried	1927–	Concerto, op 46 (1971–72)
Komma, Karl	1913–	Concertino (1938), hpd Concerto (1958)
Kraft, Karl	1903–	*Concerto breve* no 4, pno obbl
Krauze, Zygmunt	1938–	Concerto (1974–76) *Suite de dances et de chansons* (1977), hpd
Kreuder, Peter	1905–	Concerto
Kröll, George	1934–	*Cerchi* (1960)
Künneke, Eduard	1885–1953	2 Concertos, one op 36 (1920s)
Kurzbach, Paul	1902–	Concerto (1965), hpd
Lachenmann, Helmut	1935–	*Klagschatten* (1972) 3 pnos
Lampe, Walther	1927–1964	Theme and Variations (1933)
Lang, Hans	1897–1968	*Tafelmusik,* op 40 (pub 1935)
Langstroth, Ivan	1887–1971	Concerto, op 1 (1915)
Lehner, Franz	1904–	Little Concerto
Leimer, Kurt	1920–	4 Concertos (one perf 1956), one for left hand
Linke, Norbert	1933–	Concerto (1971)
Lothar, Mark	1902–	Concertino (1972), 2 pnos
Loy, Max	1913–	Concerto
Ludwig, Franz	1889–1955	Concerto
Mach, Constantin	1915–	Concerto, op 19 Suite
Mackeben, Theo	1897–1953	Concerto (1945)
Marz, Karl	1897–	2 Concertos, opp 9 (1930, rev 1959) & 24 (1936?)
Matthus, Siegfried	1934–	Concerto (1970)
Mauke, Wilhelm	1867–1930	Concerto
Merath, Siegfried	1928–	*Concerto d'Amore* (1964)
Meyer, Ernst	1905–	*Konzertante Sinfonie* (1961) *Konzert* (1974), pno obbl
Mikorey, Franz	1873–1947	Concerto (perf 1905)

Table 14 Additional Composers in Germany—Continued

Names	Dates	Compositions
Mohaupt, Richard	1904–1957	Concerto (1938, rev 1942)
Mohler, Philipp	1908–	Concerto, op 16 (1937)
Motte, Diether de la	1928–	Concerto (1965)
Müller, Gottfried	1914–	Concertino (1963), 3 pnos
		Concerto (1967), 2 pnos
		Concerto (1969), 1 pno
Niemann, Walter	1876–1953	Concerto, op 153
Nowka, Dieter	1924–	Concerto (1963), left hand
		Concerto (1971)
Oertzen, Rudolf von	1910–	*Concert Lyrique,* op 32 (pub 1965), hpd
Pepping, Ernst	1901–	Concerto IV (1931)
		Concerto (1950–51)
Perpessas, Charilaos	1907–	*Dionyssos-Dithyramben* (by 1934)
Pferdemenges, Maria	1872–	Concerto, op 31, 2 pnos
Pfitzner, Hans	1869–1949	Concerto, op 31 (1922)
Pittrich, George	1870–1934	Fantasy
Polaczek, Dietmar	1942–	Concerto (1967–68)
Raecke, Hans-Karsten	1941–	*Estrakte* 1–4 (1970)
Rasch, Kurt	1902–	Concertino, op 30
Reimann, Aribert	1936–	2 Concertos (1961/72)
Reinhold, Otto	1899–1965	*Tänzerishche Suite* (1954)
Reuss, August	1871–1935	Concerto, op 48 (1924)
Richter-Hasser, Hans	1921–	Conc, op 28 (perf 1935)
Riethmüller, Helmut	1912–1966	2 Concertos, no 2 is op 37 (1951)
Rohwer, Jens	1914–	Concerto (1963)
Rosenfeld, Gerhard	1931–	Concertino (1962) pno qnt
		Concerto (1969)
Rosenstengel, Albrecht	1912–	Concertino (1958), pno duet
Roter, Ernst	1892–1961	3 Concertos (by 1950)
Röttger, Heinz	1909–1977	Concerto (1950)
Rüdinger, Gottfried	1886–1946	Concerto, op 138
Ruff-Stohr, Herta	1904–	Concerto
Ruzicka, Peter	1948–	*Emanazione* (1972)
Sachsse, Hans	1891–1960	Concertino, op 30 (after 1925)
Samter, Alice	1920s/30s–	*Konzerstück*
Schäfer, Karl Heinz	1899–	Concerto, op 37 (perf 1960)
		Concerto (1960), fl, vn, tr, pno
Schenker, Friedrich	1942–	Triple Concerto (1971) ob, bn, pno
Schick, Philippine	1893–1970	Concerto, op 10
Schnabel, Arthur	1882–1951	Concerto (1901)
		Cadenzas, Mozart Concs K.467 & K.491
Schnabel, Karl	1909–	Concerto, 2 pnos
Schönback, Dieter	1931–	Concerto (1958)
		Concert Variations (1960)
Schroder, Hanning	1896–	*Music* (1975), fl, pno
Schubert, Heinz	1908–1945	*Abrosianisches Concerto* (perf 1944)
Schumann, Georg	1866–1952	*Fantasie-Scherzo,* op. 68/1
Schuster, Elfrieda	1894–	Concerto
Schweinitz, Wolfgang von	1953–	Concerto, op 18 (1978)
Simon, James	1880–1944	Concerto

Table 14 Additional Composers in Germany—Continued

Names	Dates	Compositions
Skop, V. F.	? –	Suite, op 32 (pub 1909), pno, harmonium
Spies, Leo	1899–1965	*Divertimento notturno* (1941)
Sthamer, Heinrich	1885–	Concerto, op 9 (pub 1913)
Stockmeier, Wolfgang	1931–	Concerto (1957)
		Variations, pno trio
Straube, Karl	1873–1950	Concerto (pub 1926)
Suder, Joseph	1892–	Concerto (1936)
Thaerichen, Werner	1921–	Concerto, op 29 (1950)
		Concerto no 2
Thiele, Siegfried	1934–	Concerto (1962)
Thieme, Karl	1909–	*Mascherata piccola* (1958)
		Rapsodia festina (1960), alto sax, pno
Tiessen, Heinz	1887–1971	*Konzertante Variationen über eine eigene Tanzmelodie,* op 60 (1962)
Trapp, Max	1887–1971	Concerto, op 26 (1931)
Trede, Ynge	1933–	Capriccio
Trexler, Georg	1903–	Concerto
Unger, Hermann	1886–1958	Concerto, op 47
Vetessy, Georg	1923–	Concerto
Vogt, Hans	1911–	Concerto (1952)
		Concertino (1963)
		Divertimenti concertante (1969)
Wahren, Karl Heinz	1933–	Concerto (1965)
		Wechselspiele (1967), fl, pno
Waldenmaier, August-Peter	1915–	*Skizzen,* op 19
		Arabeske, op 21
Walter, Fried	1907–	Concerto (perf 1951)
		Divertimento
Weber, Heinrich	1901–1970	2 Concertos (1939/67–68)
Wenzel, Eberhard	1896–	Concerto (1936)
Werner, Fritz	1898–1977	Concerto, op 12 (1937–38)
Windsperger, Lothar	1885–1935	Concerto, op 30 (1925)
Wohlfahrt, Frank	1894–1971	Concerto (1966), hpd
Wohlgemuth, Gerhard	1920–	Concertino (1948)
Wolf, Hellmuth	1906–	Concerto (1948)
Wolpert, Franz	1917–1979	*Banchetto Musicale* no 2 (1953)
Wolter, Detlef	1933–	Ritornello (1962)
Wunsch, Hermann	1884–1954	Concerto, op 22 (1923)
Wurm, Mary	1860–1938	Concerto, op 21
Wüsthoff, Klaus	1922–	Concertino (pub 1961)
		Drei Russische Fantasien (1964)
Zechlin, Ruth	1926–	*Thoughts on a Piano Piece of Prokofiev* (1968)
		Kristalle (1975), hpd
Zender, Hans	1936–	Concerto (1956)
Zieritz, Grete von	1889–	Symphonic Music (1928)
		Dances Macabres (1951–52) vn, pno
Zilcher, Hermann	1881–1948	*Nacht und Morgan,* op 24 (1917)
		Concerto, op 20 (1918–19)
		Concerto, op 102

Table 14 Additional Composers in Germany—Continued

Names	Dates	Compositions
Zimmermann, Udo	1943–	*Musik* (1972), 2 pnos
Zimmermann, Walter	1949–	*Akkord-Arbeit* (1971)
Zipp, Friedrich	1914–	*Festliche Musik,* op 11A
		Chamber Concerto, op 15, pno, cl, vc

Austria

The Second Viennese School of twelve-tone composers led by Schoenberg, Berg, and Webern is a strong force in twentieth-century music. Although examples of tone rows can be found before Schoenberg's *Suite für Klavier* (1924), it is the first complete work in this method. Due to twists of history, Schoenberg composed his piano concerto in the United States.

Alban Berg (1885–1935), student and close friend of Schoenberg, felt a loyalty to the classical-romantic traditions of German-Austrian music and saw his own music in a historical perspective. The chamber concerto (1923–1925) for piano, violin, and thirteen wind instruments displays Schoenberg's compositional thinking about rows. The first movement is a set of variations on a thirty-measure theme and the entire movement is a sonata form. The theme and variation 1 constitute the exposition, variations 2, 3, and 4 are the development using retrograde, inversion, and inverted retrograde, and variation 5 is the recapitulation. The second movement is in two halves of ABA/ABA, and the second half is a retrograde inversion of the first half. The final movement, "Rondo Ritmico," is a recapitulation of the first two movements and structurally similar to the rhythmic symmetry of the rondo and sonata forms.

Berg viewed the chamber concerto as a single movement with various connecting devices. Berg's *Hauptrhythmus* refers to rhythms functioning as motives in the structural design. In the third movement, the rhythm undergoes various modifications. Immediately before the first movement, Berg wrote musical representations of the names Arnold Schoenberg in the clavier part, Anton Webern in the *geige* (violin) part, and Alban Berg in the horn part. Due to treatments of the row, these references frequently occur. Berg's chamber concerto contains references to Schoenberg's chamber symphony through musical quotes and the same instrumentation.

Jan Brandts-Buys (1868–1939) settled in Vienna in 1893 to work for Universal Edition preparing vocal scores. While mainly an opera composer, he composed two piano concertos, opp. 3 (pub. 1901) and 15 (1897).

Franz Schmidt (1874–1939), piano student of Leschetizky and composition pupil of Bruckner, is an important Austrian composer of symphonies in the style of Schubert and Bruckner. His music for piano and orchestra is the *Variations on a Theme of Beethoven* (concerto no. 1, 1923), based on a violin sonata, and the concerto no. 2 (1934). Both compositions are for the one-armed pianist Paul Wittgenstein, and Schmidt's student F. Wührer transcribed both works for piano, two hands. The *phantasiestück* is in manuscript.

Sergey Bortkiewicz (1877–1952), born in Russia, composed music with elements of Russian romantic traditions, folk music, Liszt, and Chopin. He trained at the St. Petersburg Conservatory before going to Germany. His concerto no. 1, op. 16, received a performance (1912) in Berlin. In Vienna, he composed the concerto no. 2, op. 28 (perf. 1930), for the left-hand pianist Paul Wittgenstein and the concerto no. 3, op. 32 (1927). Some sources suggest the existence of at least one additional concerto.

Karl Weigl (1881–1949), composer of songs and chamber music, studied in Vienna, coached opera under Mahler, and taught at the New Vienna Conservatory and the University of Vienna. He composed the concerto (1924) for left hand and the concerto, op. 21 (1931), in the tradition of Brahms and Reger. In 1938 he settled in New York City and composed a rhapsody (1940).

Josef Hauer (1883–1959), theorist and composer, claimed to precede Schoenberg in evolving the twelve-tone method of composition when he wrote the theories in *Deutung des Melos* (1923). The claim strained his relationship with Schoenberg. Hauer left the concerto, op. 55 (1928).

Friedrich Frischenchlager (1885–1970) taught at the *Mozarteum* from 1918 to 1945. The *7 Tanzmythen* is for piano and orchestra.

Ernst Toch (1887–1964) composed the lost concerto (1904), the concerto, op. 38 (1926), with dissonant counterpoint, and the symphony (concerto no. 2), op. 61 (1932), for piano and orchestra.

Edward Steuermann (1892–1964), student of Busoni in Berlin and Schoenberg in Vienna, participated in the first performance of Schoenberg's *Pierrot Lunaire* and in the premieres of most of Schoenberg's compositions with piano parts. In 1938, he emigrated to the United States where he taught in New York City at the Juilliard School of Music from 1952. He probably composed the concerto, op. 42, in Vienna.

Joseph Messner (1893–1969) was a musicologist, conductor, composer in the tradition of Bruckner, and famed for organ improvisations at the Salzburg Cathedral. He left two *sinfoniettas,* opp. 10 and 55 (ca. 1922, ca. 1942), for piano and orchestra.

Hans Erich Apostel (1901–), student of Schoenberg and Berg, adopted the twelve-tone method in 1951. He freely combines tonal harmony with the row, and at times he uses more than one row. In the three-movement concerto, op. 30 (1958), each movement is an ABA structure, and a solo cadenza is in the final movement. All the themes appear in the third movement. Due to the blend of tonal and twelve-tone elements, the level of dissonance is gentler than in many compositions based solely on a row.

Jacques de Manasce (1905–1960), American composer of Austrian birth, studied in Vienna with Sauer, Marx, Pisk, and Berg. He toured Europe as a concert pianist, probably lived in Vienna, and left two concertos (1935, 1939) for piano and orchestra. In 1940, he emigrated to the United States and in New York City he composed the *Divertimento on a Children's Song* (1940) for piano and strings.

Cesar Bresgen (1913–), best known for musical fairy tales and school operas, settled in Salzburg in 1939 and taught at the *Mozarteum.* Webern, Hindemith, Bartók, and Stravinsky are models for his music. For piano and orchestra, he has the two-piano concerto, op. 13 (1934), the *Sinfonisches Konzert,* op. 21 (1936–1937), the neo-classic *Mayenkonzart* (1937), the twelve-tone concerto (1951), and the *Totentanz* (1958).

Table 15 Additional Composers in Austria

Names	Dates	Compositions
Angerer, Paul	1927–	Concerto (1962)
Bach, Maria	1896–	Concerto
Badura-Skoda, Paul	1927–	Cadenzas, Mozart Concs, K.453, K.456, K.459
Berger, Theodor	1905–	Concerto *Manuale* (1950), 2 pnos, mar, perc
Bijvanck, Henk	1909–1969	Concerto (1943)
Blochs, Waldemar	1906–	Concerto no 2 (1963)
Braun, Rudolf	1869–1925	Concerto, left hand
Eder, Helmut	1916–	Concerto (1952)
		Concerto (1958)
		Concerto *semiserio* (1960), 2 pnos
Fischer, Emma	1876–	Concerto
Füssl, Karl Heinz	1924–	Refrains, op 13 (1972)
Gary, Marianne	1903–	Concerto (1966)
Gattermeyer, Heinrich	1923–	Concertino, op 53
Gulda, Friedrich	1930–	2 Concertos (1972)
Heiller, Anton	1923–1979	Conc (1971–72), hpd, org
Holenia, Hanns	1890–1972	Concerto, op 15 (1925)
Jelinck, Hanns	1901–1969	*Phantasie* (1951)
		Rai buba, op 34 (1956–61)
Jentsch, Max	1885–1918	Concerto
Kattnigg, Rudolf	1895–1955	Concerto, op 15 (1934)
		Concertino (1940), pno, fl
		4 Konz-Stücke
		Exotische Hirtenballade (pub 1972)
Kaufmann, Armin	1902–	Concerto (1970)
Kern, Frida	1891–	Variations, op 7 (1930)
		Concerto, op 36 (1940)
Kickinger, Paula	1899–	Concerto
Kleiber, Erich	1890–1956	Concerto
Kont, Paul	1920–	*Concerto des Enfants* (1928)
Korngold, Erich	1897–1957	Concerto, op 17 (1923), left hand
Kotik, Petr	1942–	*Spontano* (1964)
Kropfrieter, Franz	1936–	Concerto (1960), hpd
Marx, Joseph	1882–1964	Romantic Concerto (1919)
		Castelli Romani (1931)
Mojsisovics, Roderich von	1877–1953	2 Concertos, opp 55 & 57
Nessler, Robert	1919–	Chamber Concerto (1962)
Peters, Guido	1866–1937	*Walzer* (1930)
Petyrek, Felix	1892–1951	2 Concs (1931/49), 2 pnos
Schiske, Karl	1916–1969	Concerto, op 11 (1938–39)
Schollum, Robert	1913–	Concerto, op 43 (ca. 1950)
Schönherr, Max	1903–1984	Concertino (1964)
Senn, Karl	1878–1964	Concerto, op 22
		Concertino, op 168 (1954)
Siegl, Otto	1896–	*Kleine Unterhaltungsmusik* (1930)
		Concerto, op 90 (1935)
		Chamber Concerto (1960)
Singleton, Alvin	1940–	*Kwitana* (1974)
Skorzeny, Fritz	1900–1965	Double Concerto, pno, vn

Table 15 Additional Composers in Austria—Continued

Names	Dates	Compositions
Stolz, Robert	1880–1975	*Traume an der Donau,* op 162 (pub 1955)
Szell, George	1897–1970	Rondo (perf 1908)
Urbanner, Robert	1936–	Concerto (1958)
		Dialogue (1965)
		Concerto "76"
Vogel, Ernst	1926–	Concerto (1962)
Weissensteiner, Raimund	1905–	Concerto (1941), hpd, fl
		Concerto (1949), pno
		Concerto, pno, fl
Wellesz, Egon	1885–1974	Concerto, op 49 (1934)
Wolf, Winfried	1900–	Concerto, op 13 (pub 1958)

Gottfried von Einem (1918–), student of Blacher in Berlin, settled in Salzburg in 1948 and Vienna in 1960. He composes neo-classic operas with contemporary dissonance and polytonality. For piano he has the concerto, op. 20 (1955), and the *Arietten,* op. 50 (1977).

Roman Haubenstock-Ramati (1919–), Polish-born composer of experimental music, read philosophy at the University of Cracow, directed music for Radio Cracow and the State Music Library in Tel-Aviv, Israel, and worked for Universal Edition in Vienna from 1957. In Tel-Aviv, he composed the *Recitativo and Aria* (1954) for harpsichord and orchestra, and in Vienna the concerto (1973) for three pianos, percussion, trombone, and orchestra.

Gerhard Wimberger (1923–), conductor and composer of comic operas, studied and taught at the *Mozarteum.* His concerto (1955) is for piano and fifteen strings.

Heimo Erbse (1924–) studied with Blacher in Berlin and settled in Salzburg as a composer. Among his works is the capriccio, op. 4 (1952), for piano, strings, and percussion, the dialog, op. 11 (1955), the *Miniaturen* (1954), the atonal concerto, op. 22 (1962), and the triple concerto, op. 32, for piano, violin, and cello.

Friedrich Cerha (1926–), avant-garde composer, follows his own theory of "atomization of thematic materials" that emphasizes the compositional possibilities of tiny musical features. He used the theory when composing the *relazioni fragili* (1957) for harpsichord and chamber orchestra.

HK Gruber (given name Heinz Karl, 1943–) studied at the Vienna Academy of Music and with Gottfried von Einem. From 1969, he played double-bass in the Austrian Radio Symphony Orchestra. He has the suite (1960) for two pianos, winds, and percussion, and the cadenzas (1965) to Domenico Puccini's piano concerto.

Notes

1. Erich H. Mueller von Asow, *Richard Strauss, Thematisches Verzeichnis,* 3 vols. (Vienna: Verlag L. Doblinger, 1974).

Chapter 8

Italy, Yugoslavia, Greece, Cyprus, Turkey, Malta, Israel, Egypt, Lebanon, and South Africa

Italy

The dominant role of opera in Italy lessened in the twentieth century. No longer are many composers of instrumental music neglected in their own country or settling in other countries for recognition. Instrumental music attracted only small audiences until about 1915, when Alfredo Casella returned to Italy from France. Casella's *Societá Italiana di Musica Moderna* (1917–1919) offered a musical springboard to young composers such as Respighi, G. F. Malipiero, Castelnuovo-Tedesco, and Gui. Casella, along with Malipiero and Labroca, founded the *Corporzione delle Nuove Musiche* (1923–1928) to bring new musical ideas to Italy, including Schoenberg's *Pierrot Lunaire* and Stravinsky's *The Wedding*. About 1930, the Ricordi publishing firm, which dominated Italian music with opera, began accepting contemporary instrumental compositions for publication. The success of new publishing houses handling contemporary instrumental music undoubtedly helped change the policy at Ricordi and other firms. The extreme conservatism of the recording industry hampered Italian instrumental music at home and abroad. In the twentieth century Italian instrumental music has achieved a position in music equal to opera.

Ettore Pozzoli (1873–1957), pianist, composer, and theory teacher at the Milan Conservatory, edited keyboard works of Bach, Beethoven, Liszt, and Weber. In a nineteenth-century romantic style, he composed the concert allegro and a concerto.

Franco Alfano (1875–1954) began a concert career before concentrating on chamber music performance and accompanying. He completed Puccini's opera *Turandot* and composed the lost neo-classic concerto (ca. 1900) and the divertimento (1934) with piano obbligato.

Ottorino Respighi (1879–1936), noted composer of the *Fountains of Rome* and *Pines of Rome,* studied with Torchi, Martucci, and Rimsky-Korsakov in St. Petersburg. He taught at the Santa Cecilia Academy and used sensual orchestrations in his compositions. His music for piano and orchestra is a concerto (1902), a fantasia (1907), the *Concerto in Mixolydian Mode* (1925), and the *Concerto a Cinque* (1933) for oboe, trumpet, violin, double bass, piano, and string orchestra. The *Concerto in Mixolydian Mode* contains melodies similar in style to the early Christian *Graduale Romanum.* The score contains the psalm quotation "omnes gentes plaudite manibus" (clap your hands, all ye nations), the introit "Viri Galilei" from the Ascension Day liturgy is quoted, and the second movement begins with modal material.

Gian Malipiero (1882–1973), internationally acclaimed composition teacher, directed the Marcello Conservatory and worked on editions of music by Vivaldi and Monteverdi. His music displays influences of the Venetian baroque, impressionism, romanticism, modality, traditional diatonic ideas, atonality, and a sharp level of dissonance. Malipiero is the most prolific Italian composer of music for piano and orchestra during the twentieth century. Those works are the *Variazioni Senze Tema* (1923), with the statement in the score " . . . the component parts of this work actually possess the character of variations on an absent theme"; the one-movement concerto no. 1 (1934) in three sections; the concerto no. 2 (1937); the *concerto a tre* (1938) for violin, cello, and piano; the *sinfonia* V, "Concertant in Eco" (1947), for two pianos "in echo"; the concerto no. 3 (1948) in three movements to be performed without a pause; the concerto no. 4 (1950); the *fantasie concertant* no. 4 (1954) for piano trio; the "quasi concerto" *dialogo* no. 6 (1956) for harpsichord; the *dialogo* no. 7 (1956) for two pianos; the *fantasie concertant* no. 6 (1956) for harpsichord; the *fantasie concertant* no. 7 (1957?) for two pianos; the concerto no. 5 (1958) with a higher dissonance level than Malipiero's previous similar works; and the concerto no. 6 "Delle Machine," (1964) in three cyclic movements.

Riccardo Pick-Mangiagalli (1882–1949), Czech-born pianist and composer, studied at the Conservatory Giusseppe Verdi and directed the institution from 1936. His fondness for ballet and dance rhythms is evident in the *Humoresque,* op. 35 (1916), the *Poema Sinfonico,* op. 39 (1916), the concerto, op. 72 (1944), and the *Sortilege* (Sorcery).

Alfredo Casella (1883–1947) was the most important composer in Italy between the two wars, and a friend of Fauré, Debussy, Enesco, and Ravel. R. Strauss, Mahler, Bartók, Stravinsky, and Schoenberg are strong influences on his music. Casella's style is neo-classic with elements of impressionism and free tonality. From 1932, he taught piano at the Santa Cecilia Academy in Rome, and he made a valuable contribution to piano literature through editions of piano music. Casella's music for piano and orchestra is *A Notte Alta,* op. 30 (1917–1921); the *Partita,* op. 42 (1924–1925); the *Scarlattina,* op. 44 (1926), based on sonatas of D. Scarlatti; the triple concerto, op. 56 (1933), for piano, violin, and cello; and the concerto, op. 69 (1937). For piano and orchestra, he arranged the *Serenata,* op. 46 (1930), and Albeniz's *Spanische Rhapsodie.* He wrote two cadenzas (1920) for Mozart's concerto, K.466.

Luigi Perrachio (1883–1966) was a composer in the French impressionistic style, a pianist, writer on music, and teacher at the *Turino Liceo Musical.* He left a concerto (1931–1932).

Gino Tagliapietra (1887–1954) studied with Busoni in Berlin and taught at the *Liceo Benedetto Marcello.* He abandoned a pianistic career due to neuritis in his right arm. Busoni influenced Tagliapietra's music, which includes the concerto (1913) with a chorus, as does Busoni's concerto, op. 39 (1909); the concertino (1922); the *Parafrasi* (1922); and the *variazioni a fantasia* (1930).

Guido Guerrini (1890–1965), conductor, critic, and teacher at the Cherubini Conservatory, studied with Torchi and Busoni and followed the styles of R. Strauss and Ravel. He composed the "3 Pieces" (1931) for piano, percussion, and strings; the *due tempi di concerto* (1936), published as the "Two Concerto Movements"; *Il Lamento di Job* (1938) for bass voice, piano, gong, and strings; the *Theme with Variations* (1940); and the *7 Variations on a Sarabande* by Corelli (1940).

Giorgio Ghedini (1892–1965), teacher and later director of the Milan Conservatory, was influenced by Stravinsky and conservative styles. He composed the concerto (1946), the concerto (1947) for two pianos, the fantasia (1958), and the *Concerto Dell'Albatro, da "Moby Dick" di Hermann Melville* (ca. 1949) for piano, violin, cello, narrator, and orchestra, Ghedini's finest musical composition. The text for the fourth and fifth movements is from the novel *Moby Dick.*

Mario Castelnuovo-Tedesco (1895–1968), composer of guitar music for Segovia, lived in Florence until emigrating to the United States in 1939, first to Larchmont, New York, and, in 1941, to Beverly Hills, California, where he wrote film music. The *Ninna Nanna,* op. R4a (1914), is for piano and orchestra. The R comes from Rossi's *Catalogue of Works by Mario Castelnuovo-Tedesco*[1] and the "a" indicates the work is after op. 4 and before op. 5. Two concertos, opp. 46 and 92 (1927, 1936–1937), show clear forms, chromatic harmonies, flowing melodies containing chromatic lines, contrapuntal treatment of two melodies, and a strong romantic influence.

Achille Longo (1900–1945), son of Alessandro Longo, who produced an edition of Domenico Scarlatti's harpsichord works, composed the suite (1924) for piano and brass and the concerto (1932).

Luigi Dallapiccola (1904–1975), leading twelve-tone composer, taught at the Cherubini Conservatory and in the United States. The *Piccolo Concerto per Muriel Couvreux* (1939–1941) is a twelve-tone work with traditional chords and harmonic progressions.

Giacinto Scelsi (1905–), composition student of Respighi and Casella, enjoyed recognition in Paris for the *Rotative* (1930) for three pianos, winds, and percussion. He probably composed the concertino (1934) in Vienna or Italy. His international travel and residences produced a cosmopolitan view of music, including serial writings and a strong interest in Eastern music and philosophy. He became interested in relating scales and rhythms to the human psyche.

Sandro Fuga (1906–), pianist, organist, and teacher at the Turino Conservatory, composed the toccata (1952) and the concerto (perf. 1970).

Franco Margola (1908–) studied with Casella and taught at the conservatories in Cagliari and Parma. He composed a concerto (1943); the *Concerto di Oschiri* (1950) for two pianos; the *Fantasia su Tema Aramico* (1951) for two trumpets and piano; the double concerto (1960) for violin and piano; the passacaglia (1970); and a concerto for a pianist (child) with small hands.

Raffaele Gervasio (1910–) taught at the Conservatory N. Piccini and composed the *Preludio e Allegro Concertant* (perf. 1968).

Nino Rota (1911–1979) composed large musical compositions at age 11, taught at and directed the *Liceo Musicale,* and wrote film music. In a dodecaphonic style, he composed the *Fantasia sue 12 Note del Don Giovanni di Mozart* (1961), the concerto *soirée* (1961), and the concerto *Piccolo Mondo Antico* (1979).

Gino Gorini (1914–), composer mainly of piano music, teamed with pianist Sergio Lorenzi to bring two-piano music to Italian audiences. He studied with Malipiero, and taught at the Venice Conservatory. He composed the suite (1934), the *Cinque Studi* (1959) for two pianos, strings, and timpani, and two concertos (1948, 1960).

Bruno Maderna (1920–1973), student of G. F. Malipiero, toured Italy as a young violinist under the name of "Brunetto." He may have composed a piano concerto (before 1946) under the direction of Malipiero at the Venice Conservatory. His atonal concerto (1948) for two pianos and orchestra of two harps, celesta, vibraphone, xylophone, timpani, and several other percussion instruments has one movement in four sections. The serial concerto (1959) requires the pianist to slam the piano lid closed at the orchestra climax. Maderna taught at the Venice Conservatory and the Darmstadt, summer courses. He is an important influence on Nono, Berio, Donatoni, Aldo Clementi, and other Italian composers of their generation.

Camillo Togni (1922–) was among the first Italian composers to forsake neoclassicism for the twelve-tone method, and eventually he evolved a personal style he called "panchromatic." The panchromatic style appears in his variations, op. 27 (1945–1946).

Franco Mannino (1924–), touring pianist and opera conductor, directed music at the *Teatro San Carlo*. He composed the concerto (1954); the *concertino lirico* (1956) for cello, piano, and strings; the *Music for Angels* (1965); the concerto (1969) for piano and three violins; the concerto, op. 100 (1974); the *Olympic Concerto* (1979) for six violins and piano; and the concerto (1980) for six violins and two pianos.

Hans Werner Henze (1926–), best known for operas, is a German avant-garde composer with his own ideas on the twelve-tone method. He studied with Fortner, followed ideas of Hindemith, Stravinsky, and Bartók, and now lives at Forio d'Ischia in the Bay of Naples. While studying with Fortner, he composed the neo-baroque chamber concerto (1946) for piano and flute, and the concertino (1946–1947) for piano and wind instruments. Other works are the concerto (1950); the *Jeuz des Tritones* (from *Ondine*, 1956–1957, rev. 1967); the concerto (1967); and the *Tristan* (1973) preludes for piano, electronic tapes, and orchestra, based on Wagner's Tristan and with a quotation from Brahms' symphony no. 1 in the third movement. *Tristan* is in six parts: I. "Prologue," II. "Lament," III. "Prelude and Variations," IV. "Tristan's Folly," V. "Adagio" in five parts, and VI. "Epilogue."

Niccolò Castiglioni (1932–) composes music using neo-classic elements, twelve-tone ideas and, eventually, romantic elements. The *moveimento continuo* (1959) is for piano and eleven instruments. He completed the *Ode* (1966) the year he moved to Buffalo, New York, to teach at the State University. After retiring to Milan, he composed the *Arabeschi* (1971–1972) for flute and piano, and the *Quodlibet* (1976).

Teresa Procaccini (ca. 1932–) trained at the Giordano Conservatory of Music in Foggia and at the Santa Cecilia Conservatory. Bartók and Stravinsky are inspirations for her music and French, Italian, and American music are resources for her ideas. Her style is tonal with formal ideas influenced by classic models. Works for orchestra and concertant piano are the *Sonata in Tricromia*, op. 11 (1957), and the *Musica Barbara*, op. 20 (1959).

Table 16 Additional Composers in Italy

Names	Dates	Compositions
Abbado, Marcello	1926–	Double Concerto (1967), vn, pno
		Quadruple Concerto (1969), pno, vn, va, vc
Abbiate, Louis	1886–1933	Concerto *Italien,* op 95 (pub 1925)
Agostini, Mozio	1875–1944	Concerto
Alderighi, Dante	1898–1968	2 Concertos (1925/38)
		Fantasia (1932)
		Divertimento (1940)
Ambrosi, Alearco	1931–	*Dialoghi Notturni*
Amendola, Ugo	? –	Concerto (pub 1975)
Azfred, Mario	1922–	Triple Concerto, vn, vc, pno (1954)
		Concerto (1959)
		Concerto (1961), 2 pnos
Bartolucci, Domenico	1917–	Concerto (1943)
Bettinelli, Bruno	1913–	2 Concertos (1953/68)
		Concerto (1962), 2 pnos
Bianchini, Emma	1891–1928	Concerto
Bormioli, Enrico	1895–	Symphonic Variations
		Concerto Allegro
Braga, Antonio	1929–	*Concerto Exotique* (1959)
Brugnoli, Attilio	1880–1937	Concerto (1905)
		Pezzo da concerto, op 6
Bucchi, Valentino	1916–1976	Concerto in Rondo (1957)
Bugamelli, Bario	1905–	*Sinfonietta*
Cammarota, Carlo	1905–	Concerto (1958)
		Preludio, Adagio e Toccata (1961)
		Twelve Studi da Concerts
Canino, Bruno	1935–	*Concerto da Camera* no 2 (1961)
Castagnone, Riccardo	1906–	Toccata
Castaldi, Paolo	1930–	*L'esercizio* (1973)
		Invenzione (pub 1971)
Cesi, Napoleone	1867–1961	*Concertstück*
		Concerto
Chiari, Giuseppe	1926–	Concerto (1970)
Clementi, Aldo	1925–	Concerto (1967), pno 4 hds
		2 Concertos (1970/75)
Confalonieri, Giulio	1896–1972	Concerto (pub 1961)
Corini, Gino	1914–	Concerto (1953)
Dionisi, Renato	1910–	Concerto (1958), 2 pnos
Donatoni, Franco	1927–	*Portrait* (1976–77), hpd
Engelmann, Ulrich	1921–	*Trias,* op 24 (1962)
Fano, Guido	1875–1961	*Andante e allegro con fuoco* (pub 1900)
Ferrari, Giogrio	1925–	*Piccolo Concerto* (1965)
Franci, Carlo	1927–	Concerto
Furgeri, Bianca,	1935–	*Antifonie* (1975)
Gargiulo, Terenzio	1903–1972	Concerto
Gaudioso, Mario	1906–	Capriccio
Gentilucci, Armando	1939–	Concerto (1962)
Ghisi, Federico	1901–1975	*3 Canzoni Strumentali*
Giuranna, Elna	1902–	*Episodi* (1947)

Table 16 Additional Composers in Italy—Continued

Names	Dates	Compositions
Gorli, Sandro	1948–	*Flottaison Blême* (1977)
Grattarola, Gruno	? –	Concerto no 2 (pub 1945)
Grecate, Luigi	1884–1964	Cadenza, Mozart Rondo, K.386
Guarino, Carmine	1893–1965	Concerto
Gubitosi, Emilia	1887–	Concerto
Incontrera, Carlo de	1937–	Concerto (pub 1968)
Jachino, Carlo	1877–1971	2 Concertos (1952/57)
Jesi, Ada	1912–	Concertino (1934)
Labroca, Mario	1896–1973	Sonata (1927–33), pno obbl
Lorenzini, Danilo	1952–	Concerto (1976)
Macchi, Egisto	1928–	*Morte all'orecchio di Van Gogh* (1964), amplified hpd
Malipiero, Riccardo	1914–	2 Concertos (1937/55)
		Piccolo Concerto (1945)
		Conc for Dimitri (1960)
		Concerto (1971), pno trio
		Concerto (1974), 2 pnos
Mannino, Vincenzo	1913–	Concerto
Marinuzzi, Gino	1920–	Concertino (1936), pno, ob, sax
		Suite concertant (1945)
		Concerto
Masetti, Enzo	1893–1961	*If Gioco del Cucu*
Medici, Mario	1913–	Concerto (1930s)
Mortari, Virgilio	1902–	Fantasia (1933)
		Double Concerto, vn, pno
Neilsen, Riccardo	1908–	*Capriccio Sinfonia* concertant (1931)
Nono, Luigi	1924–	2 Concertos (1972/75)
Novak, Jan	1921–	Concerto (1955), 2 pnos
		Concerto (1976), pno duo
Pannain, Guido	1891–1977	Concerto (1968)
Panni, Marcello	1940–	*Allegro Brillante* (1975)
Pedrollo, Arrigo	1878–1964	*Allegro da concerto* (1951)
		I Castelli di Giulietta e *Romeo* (pub 1960)
Peragallo, Mario	1910–	2 Concertos (1949/51)
Perosi, Lorenzo	1872–1956	Concerto (1916)
Petrassi, Goffredo	1904–	Concerto (1936–39)
Pezzati, Romano	1939–	*Dialoghi* (1967)
Piccioli, Giuseppe	1905–	Concerto (1950)
		Sinfonietta Concertant (1947)
		Burlesca
Pilati, Mario	1903–1938	Suite (1924–25) Concerto (1932)
Pinelli, Carlo	1911–	Concerto, pno, va
Pizzetti, Ildebrando	1880–1968	*Concerto Canti della stagione alta* (1930)
Porena, Boris	1927–	Concerto (1952), pno obbl
Porrino, Ennio	1910–1959	Sonata drammatica, op 35 (1947)
Prosperi, Carlo	1921–	*Concerto dell' arcobalens* (1972–73)
Quaranta, Felice	1910–	Capriccio Concertant (1946)
		Concerto
Ramous, Gianni	1930–	Concerto (1964)

Table 16 Additional Composers in Italy—Continued

Names	Dates	Compositions
Razzi, Fausto	1932–	*Movimento* (1963)
Renosto, Paolo	1935–	Concerto (1976)
Ripa, Virgilio	1897–	*Rapsodia Italica*
Sanders, Robert	1906–1974	Suite for Large Orchestra (1928), pno obbl
Scarpini, Pietro	1911–	Concerto (1934)
Sciarrino, Salvatore	1947–	*Clair de Lune,* op 25 (1975)
		Concerto (1976)
Setaccioli, Giacomo	1868–1925	Concerto Allegro
Silvio, Omizzolo	1906–	Concerto
Sinopoli, Giuseppe	1946–	Concerto (1974–75)
Tacchinardi, Guido	1840–1917	Concerto (1917)
Testi, Flavio	1923–	*Musica da Concerto* no 3 (1961)
		Double Concerto (1959), vn, pno
		Opus 23 (1972), 2 pnos
Tocchi, Gian	1901–	Concerto (1935), 2 pnos
Tommasini, Vincenzo	1870–1950	Duo concertant (1948)
Tosatti, Vieri	1920–	Concerto (1945)
		Il Concerto Della Demenza
Trythall, Richard	1939–	Composition for Piano and Orchestra (1965)
Veretti, Antonio	1900–	Divertimento (1936)
		Concerto (1949), hpd
Viozzi, Giulio	1912–	Concerto II
Vlad, Roman	1919–	*Variazioni concertanti* (1954–55)
Wassil, Bruno	1920–	Concerto II (1942–43)
Wigglesworth, Frank	1918–	Concertino (1952)
Zanella, Amidlcare	1873–1948	*Concerto sinfonico* (1897–98)
		Fantasia e grande fugato sinfonico, op 25 (1902)
Zanettovich, Danièle	1950–	*Invenzione sopra un Tritono*
Zecchi, Adone	1904–	*Caleidofonia* (1963), vn, pno

Yugoslavia[2]

Bozidar Sirola (1889–1956) is a Croatian musicologist recognized by the Yugoslav Academy of Sciences for his work in ethnomusicology. While he is remembered mainly for operas and extensive research and writings on Croatian music, he also composed the *symphonie concertant* (1952) for piano and orchestra.

Slavko Osterc (1895–1941), important leader in Yugoslavian music, studied with Novák, Juák, and Hába at the Prague Conservatory and taught at the Ljubljana Academy of Music. His early works are in a late-romantic style, and later works are atonal, twelve-tone, quarter-tone, and athematic. He probably composed the concerto (1933) in Prague or Ljubljana.

Lucijan Skerjanc (1900–1973) studied with Marx in Vienna and d'Indy in Paris and taught at the Ljubljana Academy of Music. His music displays neo-romantic elements with impressionistic colors. While studying with d'Indy, he probably composed the concerto (1940). Other works are the fantasy (1944), the concertino (1949), and the concerto (1963) for left hand.

Blaz Arnic (1901–1970), teacher at the Ljubljana Academy of Music, liked music with programmatic ideas and musical features of his native Slovenia. He composed the symphony II (symphonic rhapsody), op. 12 (1933), and the concerto *The Devil's Serenade.*

Boris Papandopulo (1906–) is an important composer using Croatian musical devices. He composed four concertos (1938, 1942, 1947, 1958), the concerto (1962) for harpsichord, the *phantasie,* op. 14 (1939), and the *Vrizino kolo* (1958). His fourth concerto contains elements of jazz.

Milan Ristic (1908–) is a Serbian composer of instrumental music influenced by neo-romantic and neo-classic ideas, the twelve-tone method, and quarter-tone techniques. After studying with Slavenski in Belgrade and Hába in Prague, he took a position with Belgrade radio in 1940. He has two concertos (1954, 1973).

Pavel Sivic (1908–) is a composer, pianist, accompanist, writer on music, and teacher at the Ljubljana Conservatory and the Academy of Music. He adopted the newest musical trends in his compositions. For piano and orchestra, he composed the divertimento (1949), the suite (1954), the *Emotions Fugatives* (1969), and the concerto (1972).

Bruno Bjelinski (1909–) taught at the Academy of Music and composed in a style influenced by German romanticism, neo-classic elements, and Mediterranean folk songs. He has the chamber concerto (1948), the concertino (1956), the serenade (1957) for trumpet and piano, the *sinfonietta concertant* (1967–1968), and the *petit concert* (1975).

Ljubica Maric (1909–) studied quarter-tone music with Hába, and taught at the Belgrade Music Academy. Her main interest is ancient Byzantine chants, and she realized some Serbian *Octoichos*. Several *Octoichos* influenced the *Vizantijski koncert* (Byzantine Concerto, 1959). Along with Rajicic, Ristic, and Vuckovic, Maric helped raise music standards in Belgrade during the 1930s.

Natko Decic (1914–) graduated from the Zagreb Music Academy in 1963 and joined the faculty in 1968. He studied with Marx in Vienna and Rivier in Paris. His compositions contain folk music idioms, and later works have electronic sounds and other avant-garde techniques. His music includes the *Balada* (1953), the *Panta Rei* (1973), and the *8 Minutes* (1965).

Primoz Ramovs (1921–) studied at the Academy of Music and with Casella and Petrassi in Rome. He worked at the library of the Slovene Academy of Sciences and Arts, and taught at the Ljubljana Conservatory. His style is neo-classic with rich sonorities; among his works is the concertino (1948), the concerto (1949) for two pianos, the scherzo (1958), the *Parallels* (1965), the *Antiparallels* (1966), and the symphony (1970).

Milko Kelemen (1924–), avant-garde Croatian composer, studied at the Zagreb Academy of Music and with Messiaen and Aubin at the Paris *Conservatoire*. He composed the neo-classic concerto (1952) while a student at the Zagreb Academy of Music and the serial *Transfiguration* (1960) while on the faculty. He composed the two-piano *Composé* (1967) at the Siemens electronic music studio in Munich, and the *Sonabilé* (1972) for piano and ring modulator at the Schumann Conservatory in Düs-

Table 17 Additional Composers in the Former Yugoslavia

Names	Dates	Compositions
Cossetto, Emil	1918–	*Obrati u scherzu* (Transformations in Scherzo, 1971), cl, pno
Dumicic, Petar	1901–	Concerto (1937)
Fribec, Kresimir	1908–	Concerto (1964)
Gagic, Bogdan	1931–	Concertino (1956)
		2 Concertos (1962/70)
Hrictic, Stevan	1885–1958	Rhapsody (1944)
Josif, Enriko	1924–	Concerto (1959)
Kirigin, Ivo	1914–1964	Concertino (1946)
Kostic, Dusan	1925/26–	Concerto (1967)
Krnic, Boris	1900–	*Koncertna etida* (Concert Etude, 1949)
Lang-Beck, Ivana	1912–	Concerto (1946–56)
Logar, Mihovil	1902–	*Dve tokata* (Two Toccatas, 1933)
Lovec, Vladimir	1922–	Concerto
Majer, Milan	1895–1965	Concerto (1942, rev 1962)
Markovic, Adalbert	1929–	*Diptih* (Diptych, 1962), 2 pnos
		Concertino (1962), 2 pnos
Mihelcic, Slavko	1912–	Concertino
		Fantasy
Milenkovic, Jelena	1944–	Concerto
Mokranjoac, Vasilije	1923–	Concertino (perf 1960)
Nilovic, Janko	1941–	Concerto (1978)
Njiric, Niksa	1927–	Concertino (1954)
Obradovic, Aleksander	1927–	Concerto (1956)
Odak, Krsto	1888–1965	Concerto (1963)
Ozgijan, Petar	1932–	*Concerto solenne* (1952)
		Meditacije (1962), 2 pnos
Pejacevic, Dora	1885–1923	Concerto, op 33 (1913)
		Fantasie Concertant, op 48 (1919)
Pibernik, Zlatko	1926–	*Koncertantna Musika* no. 2 (1961), 2 trs, pno
Prosev, Toma	1931–	2 Concertos (1958/69)
Radenkovic, Milutin	1921–	Concerto (1958)
Radica, Ruben	1931–	*Extensio* (1973)
Rajicic, Stanojlo	1910–1942	3 Concertos (1940/42/50)
		Concerto (1972), bn, pno
Savin, Dragutin	1915–	Concerto (1960)
Sistek-Djordjevic, Mirjana	1935–	Concerto (1969)
Slavenski, Josip	1896–1955	Concerto (1951), unfin
Stibilj, Milan	1929–	*Skladja* (Congruences, 1963)
Stojanovic, Petar	1877–1957	Concerto (1950), pno, vn
Stuhec, Igor	1932–	Concertino (1953–58)
		Minikoncert (1967)
Ulrich, Boris	1931–	2 Concertos (1961/64)
Vidosic, Tchomil	1902–1973	Rondo capriccioso (1942)
		Intrada (1959)
Zivkovic, Mirjana	1935–	*Koncertante Metamorfoze* (1974)

seldorf. While on the faculty at the *Hochschule für Musik* in Stuttgart, he composed the *Mirabilia* II (1977) for piano, ring modulator, and two orchestra groups. The ring modulator is an electronic sound-producing device that derives its name from the ring-like arrangement of diodes in its schematic.

Stanko Horvat (1930–) studied at the Zagreb Academy of Music and joined the faculty in 1961. When he entered the Paris *Conservatoire,* he used traditional compositional elements, and there he learned atonal and classic ideas. He has the concerto (1966) and the *Taches* (1968).

Ivo Petric (1931–) studied at the Ljubljana Music Academy, led a new music group, and began working for the Union of Slovenian Composers in 1969. His *Music Concertant* (1970) is neo-classic with modern features.

Dane Skerl (1931–) graduated from the Music Academy. Serialism and neo-classicism influenced his two concertinos (1949, 1958–1959).

Darijan Bozic (1933–) probably composed his concerto (1956) while studying at the Music Academy. The *Elongation and Audiostructures* (1973) is for piano and orchestra. Early compositions show an influence of jazz, and later works have serial techniques.

Dubravko Detoni (1937–), leader of *ACEZANTEZ* (Ensemble of the Center for New Tendencies in Zagreb), studied piano with Cortot in Paris, composition with Lutoslawski in Warsaw, and avant-garde trends with Stockhausen and Ligeti at the summer courses in Darmstadt. Serialism, aleatory, and neo-classic materials appear in his passacaglia (1962) for two pianos and the experimental *Elucubrations* (1969).

Greece

Manolis Kalomiris (1883–1962), highly praised composer, teacher, and administrator, studied at the Vienna Conservatory, taught piano in Kharkov, Russia, and stayed in Greece from 1910 teaching at the Athens School of Music and establishing the Hellenic Conservatory and the Conservatory of Athens. Greek folk songs influenced most of his music, and the harmony and instrumentation evidences the German-Austrian romantic tradition and his years in Russia. He composed the *Greek Rhapsody* (1925) and a symphonic concerto (1934–1935). A variation, fugue, and finale on a Greek folk song constitutes the second movement of his two-movement concerto.

Dimitri Levidis (1886–1951) studied at the Athens Conservatory, the Lausanne Conservatory and the Munich Academy of Music. He settled in Paris in 1910 and returned to Athens in 1939. The impromptu (1903) and the prelude (1904) come from his student years at the Athens Conservatory. He composed a sonata (1907) in Lausanne or Munich.

Petros Petridis (1892–1978), Turkish-born, composed music with features of Greek folk music and Byzantine music. He studied with Roussel in Paris, where he composed the concerto (1934, rev. 1948). After 1937, he lived in Paris and Athens. He left the concerto (1937) and the concerto (1973) for two pianos.

Georges Poniridas (1892–), composer and violinist, studied at the Brussels Conservatory and the *Schola Cantorum* in Paris with d'Indy and Roussel. After returning to Athens he worked in the Music Division of the Greek Ministry of Education. His piano concerto (1968) relies on authentic Greek motives.

Andreas Nezeritis (1897–), piano teacher at the Athens Conservatory, composed nationalistic music dependent on Greek modal melodies. He has the concertino (1938) and the *5 Dances* (perf. 1965).

Antiochos Evanghelatos (1903–), follower of Kalomiris, taught composition and counterpoint at the Hellenic Conservatory. His concerto (1957–1958) displays a dependence on Greek folklore.

Theodore Karyotakis (1903–1978) composed music in a neo-romantic style influenced by Greek folk music. He left the ballade (1939) for piano, strings, and percussion. In 1957, he became the general secretary of the Union of Greek Composers.

Nikos Skalkottas (1904–1949), one of Schoenberg's most gifted composition students, used the twelve-tone method until about 1938, when he began experiments with tonality and authentic Greek modalities. After 1935, he worked in obscurity because musicians deemed his music to be extremely radical, but since his death there has been a growing recognition of his talent. The Skalkottas Archive provides A/K numbers for his music. While a student of Schoenberg, Skalkottas composed the lost concerto, A/K 21 (1930), for piano, violin, and chamber orchestra. Also in Berlin, he composed the concerto no. 1, A/K 16 (1931). After returning to Athens in 1935, he composed the two-piano concertino, A/K 20 (1935), the concerto no. 2, A/K 17 (1937–1938), and the concerto no. 3, A/K 18 (1938–1939), in a serial style.

Yannis Papaioannou (1911–) studied at the Hellenic Odeon in Athens and in Paris with Honegger. Since 1953, he has been teaching at the Hellenic Odeon. Some compositions are neo-classic and other works venture into dodecaphony and serialism. He has two concertos (1940, 1950), the *Koursarikoi Horoi* (Corsair Dances, 1952), the concertino (1962) for piano and string orchestra, and the concerto (1972–1973) for violin, piano, and orchestra.

Georges Georgiadis (1912–) studied piano and composition at the Conservatory of Athens and taught piano there from 1943. His concertino (1959) was inspired by Greek folk music.

Menelaos Pallantios (1914–), student of Mitropoulos in Greece and Casella in Rome, taught at the Athens Conservatory. He composed the concerto (1958).

James Haliassas (1921–), Greek(?), has the concerto (1977).

Marie Kalogridou (1922–), pianist and composer, has a concerto.

Yorgos Sicilianos (1922–) studied at the Santa Cecilia Academy in Rome, the Paris *Conservatoire,* Harvard University, and the Juilliard School of Music, and joined the faculty of Pierce College in Athens. The *6 Etudes,* op. 38 (1975), is on the piano solo work *Etudes Compositionnelles,* op. 32 (1973–1974).

Jani Christou (1926–1970) studied at King's College in Cambridge, England, and lived on the family estate on the island of Skyros in the Aegean Sea. His music combines human experience and metaphysical expression. He added the term "meta" to words to mean "beyond," as in meta-serialism. Dice determine events in some aleatoric works. He left the concerto (1962) and the toccata (1962).

Cyprus

Solon Michaelides (1905–1979), musicologist, conductor, and composer, studied at the Trinity College of Music in London and in Paris with Boulanger at the *École Normale de Musique* and the *Schola Cantorum.* He returned to Cyprus in 1934 and became the director of the Salonica State Conservatory in 1957. The concerto (1966) shows his appreciation of Greek musical tradition and the modal *cantilena* of Greek folk music.

Turkey

Cemal Rey (1904–) studied in Paris and taught at the Istanbul Conservatory. He composed the concerto (1960) and the chromatic concerto (1933). While the principal conductor of the Istanbul Radio Orchestra, he composed the *Variations on an Istanbul Folksong* (1961). Turkish melorhythms influenced his music.

Ulvi Erkin (1906–1972) went to Paris to study piano with Philipp and composition with Boulanger. He returned to Turkey to teach piano at the State Conservatory and later he directed the institution. His music includes the concertino (1932), the concerto (1942), and the concertant symphony (1966). For the concerto, Erkin received the Music Prize of the People's Party. His wife performed the work in Ankara and Berlin.

Ahmed Saygun (1907–) received a scholarship from the Turkish government to study composition with d'Indy at the *Schola Cantorum.* His musical style displays an influence of Ravel and Bartók, and among his compositions are two concertos, opp. 29 and 34 (1952, 1957).

Bulent Arel (1919–), composer and musicologist, composed the concerto (1946). He settled in the United States to teach at Yale University, Columbia University, and the State University of New York at Stony Brook.

Ertugrul Firat (? –) has the concerto *Upheaval,* op. 46 (1969–1972).

Malta

Charles Camilleri (1931–) draws on the musical ideas from the East and West. Folklore is an important subject in his life and a source of inspiration for his music. European structures are often used with Afro-Asian musical elements. The *Maqam* (1968) is based on Afro-Oriental melodies, rhythms and structures. Camilleri took the title *Maqam* for the Arabic term "maqámát," meaning short melodic motifs serving as the basis for improvisation. His concerto I is titled "Mediterranean."

Israel

Max Brod (1884–1968), Czech-born composer, was a colleague of Kafka. In 1939, he moved to Tel-Aviv, where he composed the *2 Israeli Peasant Dances,* op. 30 (perf. 1947), for piano and small orchestra.

Paul Ben-Haim (1897–1984) studied at the State Academy of Munich (1915–1920) and conducted opera in Munich (1920–1924) and Augsburg (1924–1931). In the 1930s, he emigrated to Palestine, where he became the president of the Israeli Composers' Association. His compositional style is neo-classic, with a pastoral aesthetic, and he frequently uses Jewish and Oriental folk tunes. The concerto (1949) is in three movements titled "Vision," "Voices in the Night," and "Dance." The capriccio (1960) is on a Sephardic love song presented in the score. King David inspired the *Sweet Psalmist of Israel* (perf. 1956) for harpsichord, harp, and orchestra that won the Israel State Prize. His rhapsody (1971) is for piano and strings.

Marc Lavry (1903–1967), born in Riga, Latvia, studied at the Leipzig Conservatory, and conducted in Germany and Sweden. In 1935, he moved to Palestine, and in 1951 he joined the music section of the Jerusalem Broadcasting Service. He composed the first opera in Hebrew that has been performed, and he is the first composer in Israel to write symphonic music for the public taste. His music is imbued with influences of local music and custom. He composed two concertos (1945, 1947).

Franz Crzellitzer (1905?–), German-born, composes in a post-romantic style with elements of popular music. He settled in Tel-Aviv in 1934. Among his musical compositions are the concerto (1966) for two pianos and orchestra and the capriccio (1970) for piano and chamber orchestra.

Verdina Shlonsky (1905/13–) trained in Russia, at the Berlin *Hochschule für Musik* with Petri and Schnabel, and in Paris (1930–1932) with Boulanger, Varèse, and Milhaud. Since 1929, her residence has been in Israel, and recently she taught at the Tel-Aviv Academy. She is Israel's first woman composer. Her two-movement concerto (1942–1944) is in a contrapuntal style.

Oedoen Partos (1907–1977) was born in Hungary, where he studied with Kodály at the Royal Academy of Music in Budapest. He settled in Palestine in 1938, and played violin in the Israel Philharmonic. In 1951, he became the director of the Tel-Aviv Academy of Music, and emigrated to the Netherlands in 1971. The *Hezionot* (Visions, 1957) for flute, piano, and strings displays an influence of Israeli folk music.

Table 18 Additional Composers in Israel

Names	Dates	Compositions
Brandmann, Israel	1901–	*Variations on a Theme by Engle* (1934)
Kaufman, Fredrick	1936–	Triple Concerto (1975), pno, tenor sax, jazz bd
Klepper, Leon	1900–	Concertino (pub 1962), pno, fl Concertino (1964), pno 4 hds
Ma'ayani, Ami	1936–	Concerto (1969), 2 pnos
Marinescu-Schapipa, Ilana	1935–	*Burlesque* Concerto
Miron, Issachar	1920–	*Seven Syncopated Preludes* *Profiles of Soul*
Salmon, Karel	1892/97–	1974 *Sinfonia Concertante* (1947)
Singer, George	1908–	Concertino (1965)
Wohl, Yehuda	1904–	*Discussione* (1956) *With Mixed Feelings* (1970) Concerto

Joseph Tal (1910–), born in Poland, was influenced by the serialism he learned in Germany and, later, by electronic music. In 1937, he began teaching at the Academy of Music in Jerusalem, and in 1965 he became the director of the Institute for Electronic Music at Hebrew University. He has six concertos: no. 1 (1944), no. 2 (1953), no. 3 (1956), no. 4 (1962), no. 5 (1964), and no. 6 (1970). The concerto no. 3 uses a tenor voice, and the concerto no. 4 is with a tape player instead of an orchestra. *The Mother Rejoices* (1949) is for chorus, piano, and orchestra, and the concerto (1964) is for harpsichord and orchestra.

Artur Gelbrun (1913–), Polish-born, trained at the Warsaw Conservatory and Santa Cecilia Academy in Rome. He played violin and viola in the Warsaw Philharmonic Orchestra, the Radio Lausanne Orchestra, and the Zürich Tonhalle Orchestra. In 1949, he emigrated to Israel and began teaching at the Academy of Music. For piano and orchestra, he composed the variations (1955) and a concerto.

Sergiu Natra (1924–) was born in Rumania and studied at the Bucharest Conservatory. He settled in Israel and teaches at the Rubin Academy of Music at Tel-Aviv University. Hindemith, Prokofieff, and Stravinsky influenced his musical compositions. The *Music* (1964) is for harpsichord and six instruments, and the variations (1966) is for piano and orchestra.

Ram Da-Oz (1929–) immigrated from Germany to Palestine with his parents in 1939. He was blinded during the Palestine War in 1948. The *Rhapsody on a Jewish Yemenite Song* (1971) for piano and strings is also known as the *Song*.

André Hajdú (1932–), born in Hungary, studied with Kodály at the Budapest Music Academy and in Paris with Milhaud and Messiaen. He taught at the conservatory in Tunis, and he moved to Israel, where he has been on the faculty at the Tel-Aviv Academy of Music since 1967. His compositions are expressionistic, with some influence of folk music. He has the concerto (1968) for piano and orchestra.

Egypt

Jenö Takács (1902–), born in Hungary, taught and performed in numerous locations, including the Cairo Conservatory, the University of the Philippines in Manila, the Conservatory of Music at Pecs, Hungary, in Switzerland at the conservatories of Lausanne and Geneva, and in the United States. Concert tours carried him around the world and he composed at least two compositions for piano and orchestra while touring. The concerto no. 1 (1932) is from the period Takács taught in Cairo. Both the tarantella, op. 39 (1937), and the concerto no. 2, op. 61 (1937), were completed during concert tours. The partita, op. 55 (1949–1950), for guitar or harpsichord, is from Geneva. His musical style shows the variety of his experiences. There is a mixture of Hungarian folk elements, tonal harmonic structures, and Oriental influences from trips to China and Japan.

Abu-Bakr Khaïrat (1910–1963) studied at the Paris *Conservatoire,* and in Cairo he founded and directed the conservatory. He was the first Egyptian composer to use sonata form, and he was among the first composers to use Western musical methods. The concerto, op. 10, employs Western techniques, and later he began using Egyptian musical traits. As an architect, he designed the Academy of Arts and the Darwish concert hall.

Table 19 Additional Composers in South Africa

Names	Dates	Compositions
Clough, Robert	? –	Concertino (1972)
Gerstman, Blanche	1910–	*Serenade to Starlight*
Grové, Stefans	1922–	*Darstallung* (1972), fl, hpd or 2 pnos tuned quarter tone apart.
		Concerto Grosso (1974), vn, vc, pno
		Maya (1976), vc, pno
Hallis, Adolph	1896–	Concerto (by 1968)
Klatzow, Peter	1945–	*Interactions* I (1971)
Loots, Joyce	1907–	*Concertstück*
Stephenson, Allan	? –	Concerto (1977)
Wyk, Arnold van	1916–	*Fantasie*

Aziz Shawwan (1916–) changed his studies from violin to piano due to injuries sustained in an accident. He studied with European musicians living in Cairo, then he went to Moscow for additional training. His music displays the influence of Egyptian music, Russian and European romantic music, and the Oriental harmony of Egyptian folk music. His concerto (1955–1956) is one of his finest compositions.

Lebanon

Arkadie Kouguel (1898–) studied at the Leningrad Conservatory and, while living in Beirut, composed the concerto (1930) and the concerto for the left hand (1934). He moved to Paris, and in 1952 settled in New York City to teach piano.

South Africa

Gideon Fagan (1904–1980) studied at the College of Music in Cape Town and at the Royal College of Music in London, England. In 1926, he settled in Johannesburg, where he composed the suite *Heuwelkruin* (Hill Crest, 1954) for piano and orchestra.

Thomas Rajna (1928–) studied with Kodály at the Liszt Academy in Budapest, Hungary, and at the Royal College of Music in London, England. He probably was in London while composing the concerto (1960–1962). In 1970, he moved to Cape Town, where he composed a concerto (1984). He is an accomplished pianist.

Notes

1. Nick Rossi, compiler and ed., *Catalogue of the Works by Mario Castelnuovo-Tedesco* (New York: International Castelnuovo-Tedesco Society, 1977).

2. Due to the unresolved political turmoil, the composers are listed within the borders of the former Yugoslavia.

Chapter 9

Bulgaria, Hungary, Czechoslovakia, Romania, and Poland

Bulgaria

Pantcho Vladigerov (1899–1978), student of Juon and Georg Schumann in Berlin, conducted and composed at the Max Reinhardt Theater in Berlin and taught at the conservatory. His musical style blends Western European harmonic traditions with Bulgarian folk melodies, meters, and harmony. Often, meters in Bulgarian folk music are asymmetrical: 5/8, 7/8, 8/8, 9/8, 10/8, etc. Vladigerov composed five piano concertos: op. 6 (1918), op. 22 (1930), op. 31 (1937), op. 48 (1953), and op. 58 (1963).

Boyan Ikonomov (1900–1973) studied music in Sofia, in Paris with d'Indy, and in Basel with Weingartner, and was the head of the music department at Sofia Radio. His concerto (1958) contains Bulgarian folk songs, modal melodies, and asymmetrical rhythms.

Lubomir Pipkov (1904–1974), music administrator, studied with Boulanger and Dukas at the *École Normale de Musique* in Paris. His music follows Bartók and folk music styles of the Balkans and Macedonia. The concerto, op. 9 (1930), is for winds, percussion, and piano, the concerto, op. 48 (1954), is for piano and orchestra, and the symphony no. 3 (1965) features two pianos.

Marin Goleminov (1908–) taught at the Bulgarian Conservatory and composed in a style that incorporates Bulgarian folk elements, including the national fondness for asymmetrical rhythms. He has the *Prelude, Aria and Toccata* (1947) and the concerto (1975).

Lazar Nikolov (1922–) is one of a few Bulgarian composers to experiment with the newest compositional ideas including atonality and polytonality. He composed two concertos (1947–1948, 1954–1955), the symphony no. 2 with two pianos (1960–1961), and the concertino (1964). In 1961, he joined the faculty at the Sofia Conservatory.

Konstantin Iliev (1924–) conducted the State Opera and the Sofia Philharmonic Orchestra and taught at the State Conservatory. His concerto *grosso* (1950) is for strings, piano, and percussion, and the *Tempi concertanti II* (1969) is for flute, harpsichord, and twelve instruments. His style blends Balkan rhythms, Oriental melodic practices, and serial techniques.

Table 20 Additional Composers in Bulgaria

Names	Dates	Compositions
Christoskov, Peter	1917–	Concerto (1972)
Filev, Ivan	1941–	2 Concertinos (1963/67)
Ivanov, Georgi	1924–	Divertimento (1962), cl, vn, hpd Concerto
Kazandjiev, Vasil	1934–	Conc (1957–60), pno, sax
Khristov, Dimiter	1933–	Concerto (1954)
Kiurkchiysky, Krasimir	1936–	Concerto (1958)
Minchev, George	1939–	Concerto (1976), pno, hpd, synthesizer
Nenov, Dimiter	1902–1953	Concerto (1932–36) 2 Ballads (1942/43)
Pekov, Michael	1941–	Concerto (1965)
Pironkov, Simeon	1927–	*Muzika* (Music, 1973), 2 pnos
Raichev, Alexander	1922–	Concerto (1947)
Remenkov, Stefan	1923–	2 Concertos (1953/70)
Spasov, Ivan	1934–	Concerto (1976)
Stoikov, Todor	1932–	Concerto
Stoyanov, Vesselin	1902–1969	3 Concertos (1942/53/66)
Tanev, Alexander	1928–	Concerto (1976)
Tzvetanov, Tzvetan	1931–	Concertino (1971)
Yossifov, Alexander	1940–	Concerto (1970), 2 pnos Concerto (1971–72)

Hungary

Geza Zichy (1849–1924), student of Volkmann and Liszt, was the president of the National Conservatory. At age 14, he injured his right arm in a hunting accident, but he still enjoyed a brilliant career as a virtuoso pianist. He performed literature for the left hand and composed piano works for the left hand, including a concerto (1902).

Albert Siklós (until 1910 his name was Schönwald, 1878–1942) was a cellist, musicologist, composer, and important writer of educational literature, including the first Hungarian treatise on musical composition. He became an important teacher at the Budapest Academy of Music. His style follows German romanticism; for piano and orchestra he composed the rondo *capriccioso*.

Bela Bartók (1881–1945) is the most widely known Hungarian composer of the twentieth century. He auditioned as a piano student at the Vienna Conservatory, but Dohnányi advised him to attend the Budapest Academy of Music to study piano with Thomán, one of Liszt's finest piano students, and composition with Janos Koessler, who exposed young Bartók to German romantic composers, particularly Wagner. By 1902, R. Strauss influenced Bartók with *Also Sprach Zarathustra* and *Ein Heldenleben,* which Bartók played brilliantly as a piano solo work. Growing Hungarian nationalism led Bartók to dress in clothes of the national style and write music displaying Hungarian features. In 1904, he completed the rhapsody, op. 1, for piano solo, influenced by Liszt's *Hungarian Rhapsodies,* and a version (1904?) for piano and orchestra. The same year, he composed the scherzo (Burlesque) for piano and orchestra. By 1904, Bartók realized the use of popular folk-like melodies was not an accurate reflection of Hungarian folk music. From 1906, Bartók began touring the country to search for authentic examples of Hungarian folk music, and in the following years he researched folk music of the surrounding countries. He joined the piano faculty at the Budapest Academy of Music in 1907, and began using folk elements in his music in 1908.

Bartók's three piano concertos (1926, 1930–1931, 1945) have the traditional three-movement scheme of fast-slow-fast. First movements are sonata forms, second movements are ternary forms, and the last movement of the concerto no. 1 is a sonata form, while the concerto nos. 2 and 3 have rondos. Recapitulations show considerable variety when compared with the expositions, instrumentation is changed, and melodic material varied. The concerto nos. 1 and 2 have arch forms, with music from the first movements appearing in the third movements. Bartók intended concerto nos. 1 and 2 for his own use and premiered both works. In New York City, he composed the concerto no. 3 for his wife Ditta. Tibor Serly completed the last seventeen measures of the concerto using Bartók's spoken directions, and in 1946 György Sándor premiered the work with the Philadelphia Orchestra. In the concerto no. 1, the right-hand thumb presses an F double-sharp simultaneously with the adjacent G-sharp.

Bartók transcribed the sonata for two pianos and percussion (1936) into the concerto for two pianos and orchestra (1940), and he premiered it with his wife. He performed some Mozart piano concertos, and composed cadenzas for K.482. In 1944, Bartók received a commission to write a duo-piano concerto, but no composition resulted.

Bartók's style integrates the character and spirit of folk music instead of using quotations or imitations. Classic forms of Mozart and Beethoven and the polyphony of J. S. Bach undergird Bartók's early music, which incorporates romanticism and impressionism. While tonality is present, there is extreme dissonance, bitonality, simultaneous use of diatonic and chromatically altered pitches, and modality. Other elements are percussive sevenths and ninths, clusters of non-resolving dissonant pitches, and repeated notes. Ostinato figures, syncopations, and changing meters are common. Frequently, he uses intervals of fourths, outline melodies, and chord structures. Tonality is not a factor in Bartók's form.

Tibor Kazacsay (1892–1977) taught at the Scharwenka Conservatory in Berlin and the National Conservatory in Budapest. The concerto rhapsody (1957) is for oboe, piano, and orchestra.

György Kósa (1897–) began a decade of piano study with Bartók at age 7, and entered the Budapest Academy of Music at age 13 to study with Dohnányi and Kodály. He successfully toured Europe as a concert pianist, taught at the Academy of Music, and composed music influenced by Bartók. His concerto (1973) is for piano and violin.

Pal Kadosa (1903–), pianist, teacher, and internationally recognized composer, taught at the Fodor School and the Academy of Music. Bartók, Stravinsky, Hindemith, and Brecht influenced his early compositions, and later works feature his original use of the twelve-tone method. His style displays a strong kinship with Hungarian folk music. The concertos are four in number: op. 15 (1931); op. 29 (1938), sometimes listed as a concertino; op. 47 (1953, rev. 1955); and op. 63 (1966).

Istvan Szelenyi (1904–1972), student of Kodály, successfully toured as a pianist and contributed to the sophistication of Hungarian music by introducing the music of Schoenberg, Hindemith, Casella, and others. He taught at the State Music High School, the Bartók Conservatory, the State Musical Gymnasium and the Liszt Academy. He composed the triple concerto (1933) for violin, cello, piano, and wind orchestra; the *Summa vitae* (1956) on a motive by Liszt; the concertino (1964); the variations *concertante* (1965); and the concerto (1969).

Ferenc Farkas (1905–) studied at the Academy of Music in Budapest and the Santa Cecilia Academy in Rome with Respighi. He composed the fantasy (1929) while studying with Respighi. After returning to Hungary, he held several teaching posts, organized the State Conservatory in Székesfehérvár, and taught at the Budapest Superior Music School, where he composed the concertino (1947), rewritten for harpsichord (1949). Respighi, Bartók, and Kodály influenced his music.

György Ránki (1907–), student of Kodály, received the title "Merited Artist of the Hungarian People's Republic," allowing him time for musical composition. The fantasy "1514" (1959) is a piano solo depicting the Hungarian peasant uprising of 1514, based on woodcuts by Derkovits. He prepared a version of the "1514" (1961) for piano and orchestra. Hungarian folk music influenced most of Ránki's music.

Mihály Hajdu (1909–) studied with Kodály at the Academy of Music, and taught there from 1961. He writes music in a clear tonal style with traditional forms and an influence of Hungarian folk music. He has the concerto (1968) and a concertino.

Gabor Darvas (1911–) studied with Kodály at the Liszt Academy of Music in Budapest. His musical style draws from Bartók, serialism, and aleatoric techniques. Among his compositions are the *Improvisations Symphoniques* (1963), the *Piano Concertanto* (1968), and the concerto (1969) for two pianos.

Endre Szekely (1912–), influenced by the twelve-tone method, studied at the Budapest Academy of Music, conducted choral ensembles, and taught at the Budapest Training College for Teachers. He has the concerto (1957–1958), the sinfonia *concertante* (1960–1961) for piano and violin, and the *musica notturna* (1967) with an orchestra of wind quintet and string quintet.

Erzsébet Szonyi (1924–) studied at the Franz Liszt Academy of Music and the Paris *Consersatoire* with Boulanger and Messiaen. From 1948, she worked with Kodály implementing his teaching methods. The *Trio Concertino* (1958) for violin, cello, and piano is a pedagogical work. Her book, *Kodály's Principles in Practice* (1973), is an important contribution to music education.

Zsolt Durkó (1934–) studied with Farkas at the Academy of Music and Petrassi at the Santa Cecilia Academy in Rome. In 1959, Durkó and other composers began a search for compositional possibilities to break Kodály's strong influence on Hungarian music. His style blends traditional Hungarian musical elements and tonal techniques. Durkó has the *Cantilene* (1968–1969, rev. 1970–1973).

László Vidovszky (1944–) studied at the Academy of Music with Farkas and in Paris with Messiaen. In 1970, he helped establish the New Music Studio, and has been teaching at the Teacher's Training College of the Academy of Music since 1972. The "405" (1972) is for prepared piano, chamber ensemble, and tape.

Table 21 Additional Composers in Hungary

Names	Dates	Compositions
Berg, Lily	?–	Suite
Borgulya, András	1931–	Concerto (1968)
Decsényi, János	1927–	Divertimento (1959), hpd
		Variations (1976), pno obbl
Dubrovay, László	1943–	Concerto (1982), pno, synthesizer
Gaál, Jenö	1906–	Concerto (1951)
Gyulai-Gaál, Janos	1924–	*The Fountain* (1961)
		Concertino
Hajdú, Lóránt	1937–	Concerto (1966)
		Concertino (1972)
Hidas, Frigyes	1928–	Concerto (1972)
Horusitsky, Zoltan	1903–	2 Concertos (1938/59)
Huzella, Elek	1915–	Rhapsody (1959)
Kalmár, Lásló	1931–	Toccata *concertante* (1968–70)
Karai, József	1927–	Concertino (1967), pno, children's voices
Kardos, István	1891–1975	2 Concertos (1856/62–63)
Lendvay, Kamillo	1928–	Concertino (1959)
Litkei, Ervin	1921–	*Peace and Remembrance*
Lorand, István	1933–	Concertino (1976)
Mihály, András	1917–	2 Concertos (1954/59). No 2, vn, pno obbl
Papp, Lajos	1935–	*Dialogo* (1965–66)
Patachich, Iván	1922–	4 Concertos (1963/68/69/72). No 3, vn, pno.
Sárközy, István	1920–	*Confessioni* (*Anno 1853*)
Sugár, Rezsö	1919–	Rondo (1952)
Sulyok, Imre	1912–	*Concertino da Camera* (1963)
Szokolay, Sándor	1931–	Concerto Rondo (1955)
		Concerto, op 7 (1958)
		Deploration (1964), pno, chorus
Szollosy, Andras	1921–	2 Concertos (1957/78), 2nd hpd
Tardos, Béla	1910–1966	Concerto (1954)
		Fantasy (1961)
Vécsey, Jenö	1909–1966	Concertino (1953–56)
Vincze, Imre	1926–1969	*Rapsodia concertante* (1969)
Viski, Janos	1906–1961	Concerto (1952–53)
Weiner, László	1916–1944	Concerto
Weiner, Leó	1885–1960	Concertino, op 15 (1923)
		Cadenzas (1949),
		Beethoven Concs 1–4

Czechoslovakia

Leos Janácek (1854–1928), representative of the Czech national style, composed the concertino (1925) and the capriccio (1926) for left hand. The concertino uses a chamber orchestra of two violins, viola, clarinet, horn, and bassoon, and the capriccio requires an orchestra of piccolo, flute, two trumpets, three trombones, and tenor tuba. At some point during the composition of the concertino, Janácek planned it as a suite titled *Spring* with movements titled "The Beetle," "The Deer," "The Cricket," and "The Stream." The

Capriccio was for pianist Otakar Hollmann, who lost the use of his right hand in combat. Originally, the work was to be titled *Defiance* for reasons not made clear by the composer.

Karel Jirak (1891–1972) conducted in Europe prior to settling in the United States in 1947. The one-movement concerto, op. 55 (1946), displays mid-twentieth century romantic qualities of middle European composers.

Jaroslav Kvapil (1892–1958), student of Janácek in Brno and of Reger in Leipzig, directed the Philharmonic Society and taught at the Janácek Academy of Music. Janácek's romantic Czech style and Reger's fondness for polyphony influenced Kvapil's music. He left the *Burlesa* (1933) and the concerto (1950).

Osvald Chlubna (1893–1971) taught at the Brno Conservatory and the Janácek Academy of Music. His compositions merge features of the Czech national style with a rhapsodic flair akin to Janácek. He left the concerto, op. 46 (1937), and the etude (1970) for harpsichord and twelve strings.

Pavel Borkovek (1894–1972), teacher at the Academy of Musical Arts, blended neo-classic and baroque elements with modern dissonant counterpoint. His two concertos (1931, 1949–1950) follow the styles of Honegger, Hindemith, and Stravinsky. The concerto *grosso* (1941–1942) is for two violins, cello, and piano obbligato.

Erwin Schulhoff (1894–1942), piano teacher and performer, studied with Debussy, Reger, Friedberg, and Hába. Two of his three concertos, opp. 12, 43, and 72, date 1913 and 1923. The double concerto, op. 63 (1927), is for flute and piano. He wrote five cadenzas for a Beethoven concerto.

Josef Kohout (1895–1958) taught French horn at the Brno Conservatory and the Janácek Academy. He left the concertino (1947–1948) for piano and orchestra.

Stefan Németh-Samorinsky (1896–1975), student of Schmidt at the Vienna Music Academy and of Bartók, taught at the City School of Music in Bratislava, then at the conservatory. His style is late-romantic with folk elements and modern features. The concerto (1958) is one of his finest compositions.

Emil Burian (1904–1959) had many abilities, including composition, drama, poetry, fiction, piano accompanying, singing jazz, acting, and stage managing. He studied with Foerster at the Prague Conservatory before directing the avant-garde theater *D34* and the *Dada* theater. The symphony (1948) includes solo piano.

Theodor Schaefer (1904–1969) taught at the Brno Conservatory and the Janácek Academy, and composed music following his "diathematic" principle, in which themes incorporate previous musical fragments. He composed the concerto, op. 10 (1937–1943), and *The Barbarian and the Rose*, op. 27 (1957–1958).

Jaroslav Jezek (1906–1942) studied quarter-tone music with Hába, and wrote music for the Prague satirical show Liberated Theatre. Jazz and popular music influenced his music, which includes the concerto (1927) with orchestra and jazz band and the fantasy (1930). In 1939, he settled in New York City.

Alexander Moyzes (1906–) taught regional folk idioms to a generation of Czech composers. He was teaching at the Prague Academy of Music while composing the concertino, op. 18 (1933, rev. 1942), and living in Prague or Bratislava when composing the *sonatina giocosa* (1962) for violin, harpsichord, and chamber orchestra.

Dalibor Vackár (1906–), son of composer Vaclav Vackár, studied at the Prague

Conservatory, played violin in the Prague Radio Orchestra, and produced films. After retirement he composed the *Czech Concerto* (1952) and the *Legenda o Cloveku* (Legend of Men, 1966).

Miloslav Kabelác (1908–1979) directed music at Czech Radio and taught at the conservatory. His compositions contain contemporary devices, including the twelve-tone method, and Oriental techniques. He left the fantasy (1934) and the Variations on the Chorale "Hospodine, Pomilujny" (Our Lord, Forgive Us, 1978).

Eugen Suchon (1908–) studied with Novák at the Master School at the Prague Conservatory. From 1933, he taught at various music institutions in Bratislava, where he worked toward a national Slovak style that blends authentic folk music and contemporary trends. His music includes the *Balladic Suite* (1935) and the *Rapsodicka Suita* (Rhapsodic Suite, 1965).

Rudolf Firkusny (1912–) studied at the Prague Conservatory, where he may have composed the concerto (perf. 1930). His concert career began with a performance of a Mozart piano concerto at age 8. He settled in New York City in 1940, and taught at the Juilliard School of Music. He championed Dvorák's piano concerto and the music of Czech composers.

Simon Jurovsky (1912–1963) studied at the Bratislava Academy of Music and with Marx at the Vienna Academy of Music. He became the manager of the Bratislava Opera and worked for the radio station. His music for piano and orchestra includes the *Muskát* (Nutmeg, 1946) for soprano and piano; the *3 Uspávanky* (3 Lullabies, 1947) for soprano, piano, harp, and strings; the symphony no. 1 *Mirova* (Peace, 1950); and the concertino (1962).

Josef Páleníček (1914–), born in Yugoslavia, is a highly praised interpreter of Janácek's piano music. He debuted in a piano recital at age 11. He toured as the pianist in the Czech Trio after studies with Sin and Novák at the Prague Conservatory and with Roussel and Cortot in Paris. In 1963, he joined the faculty of the Prague Conservatory. He composed three concertos (1939, 1952, 1961), and intended the last concerto for young pianists.

Vítezslava Kaprálová (1915–1940), conductor and composer, died young of tuberculosis. She composed the concerto, op. 7 (1935), during her student years at the Brno Conservatory. At the Paris *Conservatoire,* she received help from Martinu while composing the polytonal partita, op. 20 (1939).

Zbynek Precechtel (1916–) worked as a musician at the E. F. Burian Theatre, and later as the music manager of Czechoslovakia Radio. Regional folk song traditions are a strong influence on his music, which includes a rhapsody (1954).

Tibor Freso (1918–) directed the Slovak National Opera from 1953. The fantasia (1969) and the "Little Concerto" display late romanticism and impressionism with traits of Slovak folk music.

Stepan Lucky (1919–), critic, teacher, writer, and important composer of film music, studied quarter-tone composition with Hába at the Prague Conservatory. Lucky's music blends a romantic style with elements of Czech and South American folk songs, jazz, and dance music. He has the concerto, op. 13 (1947), and the double concerto (1971) for violin and piano.

Jan Fischer (1921–) studied with Ridky in the Master Class at the Prague Conservatory. His compositional style incorporates the neo-classicism of Stravinsky, Czech and Slavic folk song elements, and jazz. He composed the *Esej* (Essay, 1947) for piano and jazz orchestra, the *Lidová suita* (Popular Suite or Folk Suite), op. 19 (1950), and the fantasy, op. 22 (1953).

Vladimír Sommer (1921–) writes music influenced by Prokofieff, Shostakovich, Stravinsky, and Honegger. The concerto (1952) was his graduation work at the Academy of Music, and the symphony no. 2 "Anno Mundi Ardenti" (1970) with piano solo was composed when he taught at Charles University.

Jan Tausinger (1921–), Romanian-born composer, conductor, and teacher, worked at Prague Radio and the conservatory. His music contains many influences including neo-classic techniques and dodecaphony. He has the *Praeludium, Sarabande and Postludium* (1967) for winds, harp, piano and percussion, the *Improvisation* (1970), and the sinfonia *Bohemica* (1973–1975) for bass, male chorus, trumpet, harpsichord, and orchestra.

Ilja Hurník (1922–), student of Ridky and Novák at the Prague Conservatory, composes stage works and chamber music with classic forms and impressionistic techniques. His concerto (1972) is for piano and small orchestra.

Mirí Válek (1923–) studied at the Prague Conservatory, was the secretary of the Guild of Czech Composers, edited music programs for Czech Radio and recently taught theory at the Prague Conservatory. The symphony no. 1 *Rok 1948* (The Year 1948, 1948) is for trumpet, piano, and orchestra. The symphony no. 10 *Barokni* (Baroque, 1973) is a concerto for violin and piano celebrating the 300th anniversary of the death of the Czech baroque painter Karel Skreta and the 150th anniversary of Bedrich Smetana's birth. The symphony no. 11 *Revolucni* (Revolutionary, 1974) for piano trio, wind quintet, and orchestra commemorates the 30th anniversary of the Czech liberation.

Ivan Rezác (1924–1977) graduated from the Prague Academy of Music in 1953 and joined the faculty in 1966. His three concertos (1955, 1964, 1972) and the introduction and allegro (1969) show an influence of Prokofieff, Shostakovich, and Honegger.

Jindrich Feld (1925–) studied at the Prague Conservatory, the Academy of Music, and Charles University, and joined the faculty at the Prague Conservatory. Bartók and serialism influenced his music. The *konzertsuite* (1972) is for bass clarinet, piano, strings, and percussion, and the concerto (1973) is for piano and orchestra.

Alois Pinos (1925–) studied forestry at Brno University, music at the conservatory and the Janácek Academy, and joined the faculty at the Janácek Academy. The double concerto (1965–1966) is for cello, piano, winds, percussion, and tape, and the "Concerto on the Name B-A-C-H" (1968) is for bass clarinet, cello, and piano. His music from the 1960s evidences the twelve-tone method, aleatoric style, and his experiences at the Darmstadt summer courses.

Cestmir Gregor (1926–) composed the three-movement rhapsody *Nikdo Neni Sám* (No One is Alone, 1955) and the *Concerto Semplice* (1958). His ideas on form and counterpoint come from Novák, rhythms and textures from Janácek, and other influences are jazz and dance music.

Ivan Jirko (1926–1978), psychiatrist, studied music at the Prague Conservatory. His music shows the influence of Czech folk songs, Shostakovich, and Borkovec. He left four concertos (1949, 1951, 1958, 1966) and the double concerto (1976) for violin and piano.

Ján Zimmer (1926–), student of Farkas at the Liszt Musical Academy in Budapest, accompanied for the Bratislava Opera and taught at the conservatory. His piano concertos are op. 1 or 5 (1949), op. 10 (1952), op. 29 (1958), op. 36 (1960), and op. 50 (1962–1964) for left hand. Other works are the concerto *grosso,* op. 7 (1950–1951), for two pianos, two orchestras, and percussion; the two suites *Tatry,* opp. 11 and 25 (1952, 1956); the rhapsody, op. 18 (1954); the concertino, op. 19 (1955); the small fantasy (1960); and the concerto (1967) for two pianos. The music is neo-classic, polyphonic, harmonically structured in thirds and fourths, and intended for the composer who is a virtuoso pianist.

Karel Kupka (1927–) follows the musical styles of Janácek and Bartók, and he worked at the Ostrava Theater from 1951. He composed two concertos (1951, 1960–1961).

Miloslav Istvan (1928–) began composing with elements of folk music, and later turned to avant-garde ideas. In 1963, he joined the advanced music organization Creative Group A. While a student at the Brno Academy of Music, he composed the concerto (1949) for horn and piano, and when he was on the faculty he composed the concerto-symphony (1957–1958). The *Zimni Suita* (Winter Suite, 1956) is for strings, piano, and percussion.

Zdenek Lukás (1928–) began writing music in a romantic style containing elements of Czech folk songs. He composed the concerto (1955), possibly in Pilsen, the serial sonata *concertanta* (1966–1967) for piano, winds, and percussion, and the variations (1970).

Pavel Blatny (1931–) follows Martinu's style and that of the Second Viennese School. While a student at the Brno Conservatory or the Prague Conservatory, he composed the *Huba* (Music, 1955). He tried "third stream" ideas in the *In Modo Archaico* (1973).

Lubos Fiser (1935–) studied at the Prague Conservatory and the Prague Academy of Music where he composed the chamber concerto (1963–1965, rev. 1970) for piano and twelve instruments. Beginning in 1971, he was a composer-in-residence with the American Wind Symphony Orchestra in Pittsburgh, Pa. Possibly, he composed his concerto (1980) in the United States.

Zdenek Pololáník (1935–) joined the avant-garde group Creative Group A in 1963. His music depends on medieval polyphonic forms, Moravian folk music and elements of Janácek's style. The *Musica Spingenta* II (1962) is for harpsichord and strings, the concerto *grosso* (1966) is for flute, guitar, harpsichord, and string orchestra, and the concerto (1966) is for piano and orchestra.

Dusan Martincek (1936–) studied at the Bratislava Conservatory and later joined the faculty at the Pedagogical Institute at Trnava. In a style influenced by Prokofieff, he composed the *Dialogues in the Form of Variations* (1961) and the rhapsody (1965–1966).

Table 22 Additional Composers in Czechoslovakia

Names	Dates	Compositions
Axman, Emil	1887–1949	Concerto (1938–39)
Babusek, Frantisek	1905–1954	Concerto (1950)
Bárta, Lubor	1928–1972	Concerto (1958–59)
Bartos, Jan	1908–1981	*Concerto per due Boemi* (1975), bass, cl, pno
Bartovsky, Josef	1884–1964	Concerto (1934)
		Concerto (1950), left hand
Bedrich, Jan	1932–	Concerto (1956)
Bohác, Josef	1929–	Concerto (1974)
Ceremuga, Josef	1930–	Concerto (1961–62)
Chaun, Frantisek	1921–1981	*Ghiribizzo* (1969)
Cikker, Jan	1911–	Concertino, op 20 (1942)
Drejsl, Radim	1923–1953	Concerto (1948–49)
Dvorácek, Jirí	1928–	*Ex Post* (1963)
Eben, Petr	1929–	Concerto (1961)
Felix, Vaclav	1928–	Double Concerto (1978), pno, bass cl
Ferenczy, Oto	1921–	Capriccio (1957)
Folprecht, Zdenek	1900–	Concerto, op 20 (1940)
Gresák, Jozef	1907–	Concerto (1963)
Hatrík, Juraj	1941–	Concertino in mode classico (1968)
Horky, Karel	1909–	*Fateful Preludes* (1972)
Hrusovsky, Ivan	1927–	Concerto (1957–58)
Hudec, Jiri	1923–	Rhapsody (1949)
Juchelka, Miroslav	1922–	Burlesque (1958)
		Concert Valse (1958)
Kalabis, Viktor	1923–	Concerto, op 12 (1953–54)
		Conc, op 42 (1975), hpd
Kapr, Jan	1914–	2 Concertos (1938/53)
Kardos, Dezider	1914–	Concerto, op 40 (1969)
Kopelent, Marek	1932–	*Appassionato* (1970–71)
Krejcí, Isa	1904–1968	Concertino (1935)
Krivinka, Gustav	1928–	2 Concertos
		Concerto Grosso I, op 3 (1949–50, rev 1960)
Kucera, Václav	1929–	*Obraz* (Picture, 1966–70)
Mácha, Otmar	1922–	Double Concerto (1975–76), vn, pno
Macudzinski, Rudolf	1907–	*Variazioni Olimpiche* (1960)
Malovec, Jozef	1933–	Suite (1974), hpd
Mastalír, Jaroslav	1906–	2 Concertos (1932/34)
Matej, Josef	1922–	*Kazak Intermezzo*
Mazourova, Jarmila	1941–	*Symphonic Dialogue* (1963)
Navrátil, Karel	1867–	2 Concertos
Neumann, Veroslav	1931–	Concerto (1959)
Novácek, Blahoslav	1911–	Concerto Fantasy
Obrouska, Jana	1930–	2 Concertos (1955/60)
		Concerto facile (1966), va, hpd
		Concerto da tasca (1973)
Ocenás, Andrej	1911–	Concerto (1959)
Palkovsky, Pavel	1939–	Symphony no 2 (1968–69)
Parsch, Arnost	1936–	Concertino (1968), vn, pno, guitar
Perina, Hubert	1890–1964	Concerto
		Concertino

Table 22 Additional Composers in Czechoslovakia—Continued

Names	Dates	Compositions
Podést, Ludvik	1921–1968	2 Concs (1951–53/58–59)
Podesva, Jaromír	1927–	2 Concertos (1949/73)
		Triple Concerto (1956–57) vn, vc, pno
Rauch, Frantisek	1910–	Concertino
Reiner, Karel	1910–1979	Concerto (1932)
Ridky, Jaroslav	1897–	Concerto, op 46 (1951–53)
Salva, Tadeás	1937–	Concerto (1970)
		Ballad-Fantasy (1972), sop, pno
Satra, Antonin	1901–	Concerto (1956)
Slavicky, Klement	1910–	Fantasy (1931)
Sluka, Lubos	1928–	Variation Fantasy (ca. 1964)
Smatek, Milos	1895–	*Château Melník*
Smutny, Jirí	1932–	*Tristia* (1969)
Soukup, Vladimir	1930–	Concerto "An Ode to Youth" (1960–61)
Srnka, Jirí	1907–	Concerto (1968)
Srom, Karel	1904–	Concerto (1961)
Strniste, Jirí	1914–	Burlesque (1954), 2 pnos
Sust, Jirí	1919–	Romantic Fantasy (1950)
Sykora, Václav	1918–	Cadenzas, Concs by F. X. Dussek & Jan Zach
Thomsen, Geraldine	1917–	Concerto (1960)
Tomásek, Jaroslav	1896–1970	Symphonic Rondo (1962)
Ullmann, Vikto	1898–1944	Concerto, op 25 (1940)
Urbanec, Bartolomej	1918–	Concertino (1969)
Vorlova, Slávka	1894–1973	*Korelace* (Correlations), op 75 (1968), bass cl, pno
Vrana, Frantisek	1914–	Concerto, op 18 (1941)
		Concerto (1957)
Zeljenka, Ilja	1932–	Concerto

Milos Stedron (1942–) likes to use bass clarinet and jazz in his musical compositions. The *Dyptich* (1967) is for bass clarinet, piano, strings, and percussion. For piano and jazz orchestra, he composed *To the Memory of Gershwin* (1971) and the *Diagram* (1971).

Romania

George Enesco (1881–1955) brought Romanian music to a high level with his neoromantic compositions. He composed the fantasy (1896) and the incomplete concerto (1897) while studying in Paris with Fauré and Massenet. After returning to Bucharest, he composed the symphony no. 3, op. 21 (1916–1921), for chorus, solo piano, and orchestra. In honor of his contributions to Romanian music, the village where he was born became Enesco.

Alexandru Zirra (1883–1946) studied and taught at the Cernauti Conservatory. He used aspects of Romanian history in stage works, and many instrumental compositions relate to Moldavia. The *Sinfonic Dichtung* (Symphonic Poem, 1930) is for piano and orchestra.

Sabin Dragoi (1894–1968) taught at the conservatory and lived in Clug and Bucharest. The concerto (1940–1941) displays the influence of Romanian folk music.

Sigismund Toduta (1908–) studied at the Cluj Conservatory and the Santa Cecilia Academy in Rome, and joined the faculty of the Cluj Conservatory. He is important in raising the musical level of the city to that of Bucharest. His music uses romantic melodies with rich orchestra colors, baroque forms, polyphony, and folk music elements. He has the concerto (1943).

Sergiu Celibidache (1912–) moved to Berlin in 1945 to play in the philharmonic. He composed a concerto.

Domnica Constantinescu (1930–) studied at the Bucharest Conservatory and taught at the Ciprian Porumbescu Conservatory from 1955. She has the concerto, op. 4 (1963).

Cornel Taranu (1934–) studied at the Cluj Conservatory and in Paris with Boulanger and Messiaen, and now teaches at the Cluj Conservatory. His music is austere, formal, atonal, influenced by experiences at the Darmstadt summer courses, and

Table 23 Additional Composers in Romania

Names	Dates	Compositions
Barberis, Mansi	1899–	Concerto (1954)
Bentoiu, Pascal	1927–	2 Concertos, opp 5 & 12 (1954/60)
Brîndus, Nicolae	1935–	Concerto (1964), pno, perc
		Cantus firmus (Phtora III, 1970), elect org or pno
Capoianu, Dumitru	1929–	Concerto
Ciortea, Tudor	1903–	*Variatiumi pe o tema de colind* (Variations on a Christmas Carol, 1969)
Constantinescu, Dan	1931–	Concerto (1963)
		Concerto (1972), 2 pnos
Constantinescu, Paul	1909–1963	*Burlesca* (1937)
		Concerto (1952)
		Conc (1963), vn, vc, pno
Cuclin, Dimitri	1885–1978	Concerto (1939)
Dandara, Liviu	1933–	Concerto (1972)
Demian, Vilmos	1910–	Concertino (1953)
Gheorghiu, Valtntin	1928–	*Burlesca* (1964)
		Concerto (1959)
Glodeanu, Liviu	1938–	Concerto (1960)
Jerea, Hilda	1916–	Concerto (1945)
Marbe, Myriam	1931–	*Inevitable Time* (1971)
		Concerto, hpd, 8 insts
Mendelsohn, Alfred	1910–1966	2 Concertos (1946/49)
Miereanu, Costin	1943–	*Finis coronat opus* (1966)
		Espace II (1967–69)
Petra-Bascopol, Carmen	1926–	Concerto, op 17 (1961)
Ratiu, Adrian	1928–	Concerto (1973)
Stroe, Aurel	1932–	*Muzica de concer* (1964)
Vieru, Anatol	1926–	*Jocuri* (Games, 1963)
		Muzeu muzical (Museum music, 1968), hpd

contains elements of Romanian folk rhythms, melodies, and whistles. He composed the concerto (1966) while at the Paris *Conservatoire,* and the *Intercalarei* (Intercalations, 1967–1969) probably in Cluj.

Ede Terényi (1935–), of Hungarian descent, studied and taught at the Cluj Conservatory. He has the concerto (1968).

Poland

Witold Maliszewski (1873–1939) began orchestration lessons with Rimsky-Korsakov at the St. Petersburg Conservatory at age 13. He taught Lutoslawski and became the head of the Music Department at the Ministry of Culture. For piano and orchestra, he composed the *Kujavian Fantasy,* op. 25 (1928), and the concerto, op. 27 (1931), displaying Russian romanticism influenced by Polish folk music.

Felix Nowowiejski (1877–1946) studied with Bussler at the Stern Conservatory in Berlin and with Dvorák in Prague, and taught organ and church music at the State Conservatory in Poznan. Among his musical compositions in the German romantic style is the symphonic poem *Ellenai* (1915), after J. Slowacki, and the concerto, op. 60 (1941).

Adam Wieniawski (1879–1950), nephew of the Polish violinist Henri Wieniawski, learned French impressionism from d'Indy and Fauré in Paris. After returning to Warsaw, he directed the Chopin High School of Music and collaborated with Zurawlew in organizing the Chopin International Competition for pianists. He left a concertino (1932).

Karol Szymanowski (1882–1937) composed the neo-baroque symphony no. 4, op. 60 (1931–1932), for piano and orchestra. *Symphonie concertante* is another name for the work. There are sketches of an incomplete concerto (1925) and an incomplete and lost concertino (1934).

Ludomir Rózycki (1884–1953) is an important Polish composer of music with German, Russian, Italian and Polish influences. In 1926, he founded the Polish Composers' Union and was its first president. The *Ballade,* op. 18 (1904), is a product of his student years at the Warsaw Conservatory. He composed the concerto no. 1, op. 43 (1917–1918), in Berlin and the concerto no. 2 (1942) while a teacher at the Warsaw Conservatory.

Piotr Rytel (1884–1970) taught Baird, Panufnik, and Tansman at the Warsaw Conservatory. His one-movement concerto (1907) has neo-romantic features.

Apolinary Szeluto (1884–1966), pianist and composer, helped organize the progressive musical group Young Poland. He left five concertos (1937, 1939, 1940, 1943, 1948). Later, he moved to Ufa, U.S.S.R., to work as a lawyer.

Boleslaw Szabelski (1896–1979), organ virtuoso and teacher at the State School of Music, influenced the direction of modern Polish music by using polyphonic techniques. For piano and orchestra, he composed two concertinos (1946, 1955), two concertos (1956, 1978), and the *Wiersze* (Verse, 1961).

Tadeusz Szeligowski (1896–1963), director of the State Opera School, left the concerto (1939) for piano and orchestra.

Witold Friemann (1899–) composed nearly 100 compositions, including 24 concertos. For piano and orchestra, he has five concertos (1911, 1951, 1952, 1956,

1960–1963) and the *Cien Chopina* (Shadow of Chopin, 1937). All of his musical compositions have romantic features.

Jan Maklakiewicz (1899–1954) was a music critic, teacher, and composer. The *Concerto Quasi una Fantasia* (1928–1929) for piano, soprano, and orchestra is from when he experimented with harmony and polytonality.

Boleslaw Woytowicz (1899–1980) studied philology, mathematics, and law until a growing interest in music led to a career change. He studied with Boulanger in Paris and, upon returning to Poland, took a teaching position at the Chopin High School of Music in Warsaw. He gained considerable prominence as a concert pianist, and in 1932 he won the first prize from the Warsaw Philharmonic for his lost concerto (1932). He composed the symphony no. 3 *Concertante* (1963) while a faculty member at the State College of Music.

Walerian Gniot (1902–) taught at the Poznan Music School from 1945. His *Variations on a Folk Theme* (1957) contains elements of folk music.

Arthur Malawski (1904–1957), violinist, teacher, conductor, and avant-garde composer, helped move Polish composers away from German romanticism toward a national style. His music blends modern idioms with Polish folk songs, and among his works is the *Symphonic Studies* (1947) and the *Toccata and Fugue in Variation Form* (1949). His radical style that was too removed from public taste resulted in hostility and neglect.

Jadwiga Helena Szajna-Lewandowska (1912–) taught music and performed in theaters. Her music for piano and string orchestra includes the *Funerailles* (1971), the *Polish Capriccio* (1973), the *Three Fragments* (1968), and the *Two Etudes* (1962).

Witold Lutoslawski (1913–), pianist and conductor, composed the *Variations on a Theme by Paganini* (1977), based on Paganini's *Caprice,* op. 1, no. 24, for unaccompanied violin. The piano has the theme and the orchestra accompaniment has chords with a contemporary level of dissonance (See ex. 9–1).

Tadeusz Paciorkiewicz (1916–) composes music in a late-romantic tradition. He has two concertos (1952, 1954).

Eleonora Grzadzielowna (1921–), teacher of secondary school music, has two concertinos (1951, 1963), the *Five Miniatures* (1965) with solo trumpet, and the concerto (1969).

Stanislaw Wislocki (1921–) conducted the Philharmonic Orchestra in Poznan and taught conducting at the State College of Music in Warsaw. His concerto (1948) is for piano and orchestra.

Kazimierz Serocki (1922–1981) began composing works in a neo-classic style and later in Webern's style. His compositions for piano and orchestra are the concerto (1947), the *Romantic Concerto* (1950), the *Forte e Piano* (1967) for two pianos, and the *Pianophonce* (1976–1978).

Krystyna Moszumanska-Nazar (1924–), teacher at the Cracow Conservatory, merges classic forms with dense dissonant harmony. She has the concertino (1954).

Wlodzimierz Kotonski (1925–) is an avant-garde composer and researcher in Polish folk music at the State Institute of Art. His *Concerto per Quattro* (1965) is for harp, harpsichord, guitar, piano, and chamber orchestra. Since 1955, his musical interest has been atonality and serialism.

Reprinted by Permission of G. Schirmer, Inc. (ASCAP) on behalf of J. & W. Chester Ltd., London

Example 9–1. Lutoslawski *Variations on a Theme by Paganini,* mm. 1–16

Table 24 Additional Composers in Poland

Names	Dates	Compositions
Bacewicz, Grazyna	1909–1969	Concerto (1949)
		Concerto (1966), 2 pnos
Barbag, Seweryn	1891–1944	Concerto
Brzezinski, Franciszek	1867–1944	Concerto, op 9 (1914–15)
Buczek, Barbara	1940–	Concerto (1969)
Bukowski, Ryzard	1916–	Concertino (1949)
Bury, Edward	1919–	*Czech Fantasy* (1948)
Czerniawski, Cornelius	1888–	*Notturno*
Ekier, Jan	1913–	Concerto (1949)
Gablenz, Jerzy	1888–1937	Concerto
Garztecka, Irena	1913–1963	Concerto (1952)
		Concertino (1959)
Haas, Pavel	1899–1944	Variations (1944)
Halski, Czeslaw	1908–	Concerto (1950–51)
Hundziak, Andrzej	1927–	Concertino (1972)
Iszkowska, Zofia	1911–	Concerto
Izbicki-Maklakiewicz, Franciszek	1915–1939	*Wycinankilowickie* (Paper Cut-outs from Lowicz)
Lachowska, Stefania	1898–1966	Concertino (1953)
		Variations (1960)
Langeron, Irena de	1891–1951	Concerto (1914)
Lopuska-Wylezynska, Helna	1887–	*Legenda*
Machl, Tadeusz	1922–	Concerto (1962), hpd
		Concerto (1965), pno
		Double Concerto (1967), pno, hpd
		Triple Concerto (1971), 2 pnos, org
Morawski-Dabrowa, Eugen	1876–1948	2 Concertos
		Finale
Moss, Piotr	1949–	Concertino (1973)
Mycielski, Zygmunt	1907–	Concerto (1954)
Nawrocki, Stanislaw	1894–1950	5 Concertos
Palubicki, Konrad	1910–	Concerto IV
Perkowski, Piotr	1901–	Concerto (1925), lost
		Fantasy (1926), lost
Prószynski, Stanislaw	1926–	Concerto (1949)
Rudzinski, Witold	1913–	Concerto (1936)
		Music Concertante (1959)
Rybicki, Feliks	1899–	Concerto, op 53
Sandelewski, Wiaroslaw	1912–	Concerto (1974)
Sokorski, Jerzy	1916–	Concerto (1941)
Sternicka-Niekraszowa, Ilza	1898–1932	*Basn* (1927)
Swierzynski, Adam	1914–	Concerto (1950)
Szlowski, Antoni	1907–1973	Conc (1930), withdrawn
Szymanska, Iwonka	1943–	*Third Sonnet* (1972), 2 pnos
		Wiosanny Koncert
Szymonowicz, Zbigniew	1922–	Concerto (1956)
Turski, Zbigniew	1908–	Concerto (1937), lost
		Symphonic Variations (1939), lost
Twardowski, Romuald	1930–	Concerto (1956)
		Little Symphony Concertante (1958)
		Nomopedia (1962), pno duet
Wiechowicz, Stanislaw	1893–1963	Suite (1948)
Wielhorski, Aleksander	1889–1952	Fantasy (Polonaise)

Jan Krenz (1926–) was a noted conductor of the Lodz Philharmonic, the Poznan Philharmonic, the Polish Radio Symphony in Katowice, and the Warsaw Opera. The toccata (1943) is from his student years at the Lodz State Music College, and the concertino (1952) he composed in Katowice.

Juliusz Luciuk (1927–) taught at Jagiellonian University and the State College of Music. His music contains folk music, elements of jazz, and neo-classic structures. He has the *So Pass Five Years* (perf. 1972) for prepared piano and chamber ensemble, and the concertino (1973).

Tadeusz Natanson (1927–) studied and taught at the State College of Music. He has the concerto (1956), the symphony no. 1 *Symphony Concertante* (1961), and the concerto (1966).

Tadeusz Baird (1928–) helped Serocki and Krenz establish the Group 49, named after the year of inception, to promote uncomplicated music in accord with government policy on socialist music. His concerto (1949) has neo-classic traits.

Boguslaw Schaeffer (1929–), the first Polish twelve-tone composer, has numerous works with the melo-rhythms of Polish folk songs up to 1953, when he turned toward avant-garde techniques. Later compositions include serial features and "third stream" practices. He has the concerto for two pianos (1951); the *Quattro Movimenti,* no. 32 (1957); the *Tertium Datur,* no. 38 (1958), for harpsichord and chamber orchestra; the *Concerto for 6 and 3,* no. 50, for changing solo instruments, including clarinet, saxophone, violin, cello, percussion, and piano, with three orchestras; the *Musica,* no. 56 (1961), for harpsichord; the *Azone a* 2, no. 60 (1961), for piano and eleven instruments; the *piano concerto,* no. 110 (1967); the concertino *Mare,* no. 142 (1971), for piano and nine instruments; the *Experimenta,* no. 144 (1971), for one pianist on two pianos; and the *Concerto for 3 Pianos* (1972). A cadenza is for Beethoven's concerto no. 3.

Wojciech Kilar (1932–) writes film music containing modern techniques and classic forms. While a student at the Cracow Academy, he composed the sinfonia *concertante* (symphony no. 2, 1956) and the concerto (1958) for two pianos and orchestra.

Boguslaw Madley (1932–) studied at the Academy of Music in Poznan and the Guildhall School of Music in London, conducted the Warsaw Opera, taught at the State College of Music, and directed music at the Grand Theater of Opera and Ballet in Lodz. His concerto, op. 12 (1957), is a student work from the Academy of Music.

Henryk Gorecki (1933–) follows Webern's serialism and is among the most original Polish composers. In 1959, he wrote a version of the *Piesni o Radosci i Rhtmie* (Songs of Joy and Rhythm), op. 9 (1956), for two pianos and orchestra.

Tomasz Sikorski (1939–) studied composition with Boulanger in Paris, and as a pianist he specializes in new music. He composed the *concerto breve* (1965) for two pianos, the *Architektury* (Architectures, 1965) for piano, winds, and percussion, and the *Music in Twilight* (1977).

Grazyna Pstrokonska-Novratil (1947–), musicologist and composer at the State Music College, has the *concerto grosso* (1971) for clarinet, horn, piano, percussion, and strings, and the *Music* (1973).

Chapter 10

Estonia, Latvia, Lithuania, Russia, Belarus, Ukraine, Moldava, Georgia, Azerbaijan, Armenia, Uzbekistan, and Kazakhstan

Estonia

Arthur Kapp (1875–1952) studied with Rimsky-Korsakov at the St. Petersburg Conservatory, and directed the Tallinn Conservatory. He is the earliest composer to use Estonian folk music in concert music. He left the *Concerto-Rhapsodie* (1944–1945).

Artur Lemba (1885–1963) studied and taught at the St. Petersburg Conservatory and returned to Tallinn, his birthplace, to work. He composed at least two concertos, one is op. 2. Fragmentary information suggests several other piano concertos.

Eugen Kapp (1908–) studied with his father at the Tallinn Conservatory where he later joined the faculty. He composed the concerto (1969).

Lydia Auster (1912–) has been the music supervisor with Estonian television and radio since 1949. She has the concerto, op. 18 (1952).

El's Aarne (pseud. for El'ze Janovna, 1917–) graduated from the Tallinn Conservatory. While on the conservatory faculty she composed the concerto (1945) and the *Ballad* (1955).

Ester Miagi (1922–), teacher at the Tallinn Conservatory, composed the concerto (1951–1953) and the variations (1972) for piano, clarinet, and string orchestra.

Jan Koha (1929–) has the concerto, op. 6 (1958).

Jaan Rääts (1932–) composes music influenced by the neo-classic style, Estonian folk music, and jazz. He has three concertos (1958, 1968, 1971).

Latvia

Janis Medins (1890–1966), with Alfreds Kalnins, is important in establishing Latvian opera. While on the faculty at the Riga Conservatory, he composed the concerto (1934).

Lucia Garuta (1902–) graduated from the Riga Conservatory (1924), studied with Philipp, Dukas, and Cortot in Paris, and returned to Riga to teach at the conservatory. She composed a concerto (1951).

Janis Ivanos (1906–) uses Latvian folk music as a source of inspiration. He has the concerto (1959).

Janis Kepitis (1908–) was a member of the Jazeps Vitols trio and a faculty member at the conservatory. He has three concertos (1934, 1953, 1973) and the variations (1973) for two pianos.

Stasys Vainiunas (1909–) studied and taught at the conservatory. His piano concertos are op. 15 (1946), op. 22 (1952), op. 33 (1965), and op. 40 (pub. 1977). His *rhapsodie* (1947) is for two pianos.

Margers Zarins (1910–), secretary-general of the Union of Latvian Composers, writes music using elements of Latvian folk songs. For piano and orchestra, he has the concerto (1937), the suite *Greek Vases* (1946, rev. 1960), and the concerto *grosso* for harpsichord and piano.

Romualdo Grinblat (1930–) graduated from the Riga Conservatory. He has a concerto (1963).

P. Plakidis (1947–) composed the *Music* for piano, percussion and strings that is in a version for guitar instead of piano. Also, there is a concerto.

Lithuania

Balis Dvarionas (1904–) studied with Karg-Elert and Petri in Berlin, taught at the Lithuanian Conservatory from 1933, and conducted the Lithuanian Philharmonic Orchestra. He composed two concertos (1958, 1962).

Vytautas Barkauskas (1931–) has been on the faculty of the Lithuanian State Conservatory since 1960. Contemporary western European techniques are in his style. Among his works is the *Poem* (1960).

Russia

Georgi Catoire (1861–1926) studied with Rimsky-Korsakov and Liadov in St. Petersburg, and in Berlin with Klindworth, who guided him toward Wagner. His books laid the foundation of music theory in Russia. While on the faculty at the Moscow Conservatory, he devoted himself to musical composition. Among his works is the concerto, op. 21 (1909).

Arseny Koreshchenko (1870–1921) studied with Taneyev and Arensky at the Moscow Conservatory, and later joined the faculty. About 1919, he settled in Kharkov to teach piano and composition at the music school. His music, including the concerto fantasy, op. 3, shows influences of Tchaikovsky and Arensky.

Sergei Rachmaninoff (1873–1943) is among the few composers of the twentieth century to have three compositions for piano and orchestra firmly established in the performing repertoire; they are the concerto nos. 2 and 3 and the *Rhapsody on a Theme of Paganini*. His musical style has roots in the music of Tchaikovsky, Scriabin, Chopin, and the Russian romantic school. Although Rachmaninoff lived until the middle of the twentieth century, he never gave up romantic compositional features in favor of contemporary techniques. Young Rachmaninoff's talent so impressed Tchaikovsky, that he advised study with the famous teacher Taneyev. He also studied with Arensky.

Rachmaninoff's first effort at writing a piano concerto resulted in an unfinished sketch (1889). He started the concerto no. 1, op. 1 (1890–1891, rev. 1917), while a student at the Moscow Conservatory, and completed it during a vacation in Ivanovka.

A negative reception to the symphony no. 1 caused Rachmaninoff to experience depression and a psychological block of his creative powers. With the help of Dr. Nikolay Dahl, a hypnotist and amateur musician, Rachmaninoff's mood improved, and he began the concerto no. 2, op. 18 (1900–1901). He composed the second and third movements in Italy, and after receiving an encouraging audience response, he composed the first movement in Moscow.

Rachmaninoff started the concerto no. 3, op. 30 (1909), in Ivanovka, finished it in Moscow, and immediately took it on tour to the United States. The opening theme of the first movement stimulated interesting conjecture as to its possible musical source. Joseph Yasser suggests in the article "The Opening Theme of Rachmaninoff's Third Piano Concerto and Its Liturgical Prototype"[1] that a similarity exists between Rachmaninoff's theme and a Russian orthodox chant used in the vesper services at the *Kievan-Petchersk Lavra* (Abbey on the Caves) since the twelfth century. Yasser demonstrates striking similarities between the two melodies, and places Rachmaninoff near the *Kievan-Petchersk Lavra* during rehearsals of his opera *Aleko* in Kiev in 1893. The distance from Kiev to the *Kievan-Petchersk Lavra* is short. When Yasser first became aware of a possible relationship between the concerto theme and the church chant, he wrote to Rachmaninoff in Switzerland. In a letter dated April 30, 1935, Rachmaninoff responded to Yasser's questions concerning a liturgical or national musical source or influence on the concerto theme. In Rachmaninoff's words, the theme "wrote itself," and no other music of any type influenced the melody. Biographies on Rachmaninoff describe a devoted Russian orthodox home, where the young boy entertained his maternal grandmother with chants performed at the piano. Yasser believes Rachmaninoff's subconscious held the chant during the conception of the concerto theme.

Rachmaninoff started the concerto no. 4, op. 40 (1914–1927), in Russia, finished it in the United States, and revised it between the first performance and the publication date. He dedicated the concerto to his friend Medtner, who returned the compliment by dedicating his concerto no. 2, op. 50, to Rachmaninoff.

In Switzerland, Rachmaninoff composed the *Rhapsody on a Theme of Paganini,* op. 43 (1934), based on Paganini's *Caprice,* op. 1, no. 24, for unaccompanied violin. The rhapsody begins with a short introduction followed by variation I, marked "Precedente," the "Tema," then variations II through XXIV. Variation VII contains the plainsong chant *dies irae*. The melody in variation XVIII begins with an inversion of Paganini's theme.

Alexander Gedike (1877–1957) was a brilliant piano student of Safonov at the Moscow Conservatory, and later he taught piano at the conservatory. His compositions follow the classic traditions in Russian music. Some lists show the concerto, op. 11, as a *concertstück*.

Nikolay Medtner (1880–1951), composer and pianist of German descent, is the "Russian Brahms" because of his fondness for polyrhythms and neo-classic features. His music blends the German romanticism of Schumann and Brahms with Russian features. Superficially, Medtner's music suggests an influence of Rachmaninoff, but Medtner's concertos have stronger elements of classicism, frequent meter changes, and greater rhythmic inventiveness and complexity. Medtner's melodic affinity for Rachmaninoff and Rimsky-Korsakov comes from a shared Russian-European musical heritage. He learned his contrapuntal skills from Taneyev, who was one of Russia's finest contrapuntists. For piano and orchestra, Medtner composed an incomplete *kontsertshtyuk;* the concerto no. 1, op. 33 (1914–1918), in Moscow; the concerto no. 2, op. 50 (1920–1927), begun in Moscow and completed in Paris; and the concerto no. 3 *Ballade,* op. 60 (ca. 1940–1943), in London. He wrote two cadenzas, op. 55, no. 2 (ca. 1910), for Beethoven's concerto no. 4.

Anatoly Alexandrov (1888–1982) studied with Taneyev, Vassilenko, and Igumov at the Moscow Conservatory and taught composition there from 1923. Scriabin, Medtner, and Rachmaninoff influenced his musical style. He left the concerto, op. 101 (1974).

Samuel Feinberg (1890–1962), pianist and teacher, studied and taught at the Moscow Conservatory. His music is post-romantic, with influences of Chopin and Scriabin. He composed three concertos, op. 20 (1931), op. 36 (1944), and op. 44 (1947, rev. 1951), and cadenzas for concertos of Mozart and Beethoven.

Serge Prokofieff (1891–1953) began composition lessons with Gliere in Moscow at age 6, and attended the St. Petersburg Conservatory for studies with Rimsky-Korsakov, Wihtol, Liadov, and N. Tcherepnin. He composed the one-movement concerto no. 1, op. 10 (1911–1912), based on a youthful concertino. In 1923, he revised the four-movement concerto no. 2, op. 16 (1912–1913), because the original score accidentally burned in his apartment. In the concerto no. 1, the piano and orchestra are equals, and in the concerto no. 2, the piano dominates.

Prokofieff's concerto no. 3, op. 26 (1911–1918), is among the finest piano concertos of the twentieth century. He considered writing a large virtuoso concerto in 1911 while working on the concerto no. 1; the parallel triads in the recapitulation of the first movement date from that year. In 1913, he composed the theme for the second movement, and in 1916–1917 the opening themes of the first movement and two variations on the second-movement theme of 1913. Two themes from an unfinished quartet of 1918 are in the finale. To finish the concerto he composed the subordinate theme of the first movement, the third theme of the finale, and joined the completed sections.

In 1931, the left-hand pianist Paul Wittgenstein commissioned Prokofieff to compose a concerto. When Wittgenstein received the four-movement concerto no. 4, op. 53 (1931), he did not like the work and told Prokofieff he would not perform it. Prokofieff considered rewriting the work as a concerto for two hands.

Prokofieff began the five-movement concerto no. 5, op. 55 (1932), while traveling in Europe. Initially, he considered titling the concerto *Music for Piano and Orchestra,* but his interest in producing a virtuoso work resulted in a concerto. The composition has motor rhythms, wide leaps, hand-crossings, and orchestra timbres of a metallic machine.

In 1952, he planned a concerto for two pianos and orchestra. The sketch is op. 133.

Leonid Polovinkin (1894–1949), student of Gliere, Vassilenko and Catoire at the Moscow Conservatory, successfully wrote music for the Moscow Central Children's Theater. In a style influenced by Scriabin, *Les Six,* Schoenberg, and Russian music, he composed the concerto (1933).

Boris Liatosinsky (1895–1968) taught at the Kiev and Moscow conservatories. His music merges Russian traditions and folk songs with European late-romanticism, polytonality, and polyrhythms. He left the *Slavic Concerto,* op. 54 (1953).

Joseph Schillinger (1895–1943) studied with Tcherepnin at the St. Petersburg Conservatory, taught at the State Academy of Music in Kharkov, and taught and composed in St. Petersburg. He composed the *Oktyabar,* op. 19 (1927), and the symphonic rhapsody (1927) to commemorate the tenth anniversary of the U.S.S.R. In 1928, he moved to New York City, where his mathematical training became the basis of *The Schillinger System of Musical Composition.* Gershwin studied composition with Schillinger.

Alexander Mosolov (1900–1973), composer and pianist in Moscow until 1937, adopted the modern techniques of Prokofieff, Steinberg, and Hindemith. He left the concerto no. 1 (1927) and the concerto no. 2 (1932), based on Kirghiz themes he heard on a visit to Kirghiz.

Boris Shekhter (1900–1961) studied with Vassilenko and Miaskovsky at the Moscow Conservatory, and taught there from 1929. In 1940, he began teaching at the Conservatory of Ashkhabad, Turkestan. He tried to create a musical style using Turcoman folk scales, melodies, rhythms, and forms, while avoiding influences of European music. He left the concerto (1932/1938).

Aram Khachaturian (1903–1978), Armenian composer, studied with Miakovsky and Vassilenko at the Moscow Conservatory and composed music with elements of Rimsky-Korsakov, Balakirev, Borodin, and the Oriental color and Caucasian folk elements of Azerbaijan and Georgia. His music has a biting level of dissonance and stronger rhythms than his Russian predecessors. His concerto (1936) immediately became popular with international audiences. The theme of the second movement is on a Transcaucasus song "Khachaturian" heard in Tbilisi. The concert-rhapsody (1969) did not achieve nearly as much popularity as the concerto.

Dmitry Kabalevsky (1904–1987) studied with Vassilenko and Catoire at the Scriabin Music School, and later at the Moscow Conservatory. His music follows socialistic realism—it is mainly triadic and based on traditional musical forms. For piano and orchestra, he left the concerto no. 1, op. 9 (1928), the concerto no. 2 (1935), the concerto no. 3 *Youth,* op. 50 (1963), the *Rhapsody on a Theme of the Song "School Years,"* op. 75 (1964), that is a theme and variations, and the concerto no. 4 *Prague* (1974).

Boris Alexandrov (1905–), composition student of Gliere at the Moscow Conservatory, evolved a style using twelve-tone techniques with harmonic practices. His interest in Ukrainian folk music is evident in the concerto (1929) and the concerto-fantasy (1955) for piano and folk orchestra.

Boris Arapov (1905–) ceased his career as a concert pianist due to a hand ailment. He composed a concerto (1938) for three pianos and the concerto (1973) for piano and violin. His interest in Uzbekistan folk music is evident in his concert music.

Dimitry Shostakovich (1906–1975) composed the concerto no. 1, op. 35 (1933), for piano, solo trumpet, and orchestra, and the concerto no. 2, op. 102 (1957), for his teenage son Maxim to use as an audition piece. Shostakovich's style in the second concerto is triadic, with some nonfunctional harmony, and has parallel octaves performed with each hand taking one note of the octave. The slow movement employs a single-note melody over a simple accompaniment. The final movement returns to parallel octaves, with each hand playing one note in the octave, and contains changing meters.

Ivan Dzerzhinsky (1909–1978), best known for the opera *Quiet Flows the Don,* composed the concerto (1932) influenced by Grieg, Rachmaninoff, and Ravel, a concerto (1934) influenced by Shostakovich, and the concerto (1945).

Orest Evlakhov (1912–1973) studied at the St. Petersburg Conservatory and later joined the faculty. He composed the concerto (1939) and the concerto *Triptych,* op. 40 (pub. 1977), displaying elements of Shostakovich.

Vadim Salmanov (1912–1978) taught composition and orchestration at the St. Petersburg Conservatory. Prokofieff and Shostakovich influenced his music. His sonata (1961) for piano and orchestra has sonata and symphonic form.

Tikhon Khrennikov (1913–), head of the Soviet Composers' Union for twenty-five years, follows socialist realism by writing music of immediate appeal using characteristics of Russian folk songs. The concerto, op. 1 (1932–1933), is a student work from the Moscow Conservatory. The concerto, op. 21 (1971), won the Lenin Prize. There is also the concerto no. 3 (1982).

Julian Krein (1913–) composes music that blends the French style he learned from Dukas and nineteenth-century Russian romanticism, particularly Scriabin. He composed the concerto (1929) in Paris and two concertos (1942, 1943) in Moscow.

Valery Zhelobinsky (1913–1946) graduated from the St. Petersburg Conservatory, taught at the Tambov Music School and returned to St. Petersburg to pursue a career as a pianist. He composed three concertos (1933, 1934, 1938–1939) in the romantic style.

Albert Leman (1915–) composed a concerto (1939) while studying at the St. Petersburg Conservatory. While a teacher at the Kasan Conservatory, he composed two concertos (1943, 1953).

Georgy Sviridov (1915–) follows socialist realism by writing music using Russian romantic traditions and folk music. He has the concerto (1936).

Nikolay Peyko (1916–), student and teacher at the Moscow Conservatory, received a commission to research folk songs in Yakutsch, Siberia. Folk songs, Stravinsky, Prokofieff, and Shostakovich influenced Peyko's concerto (1943–1947, rev. 1954).

Andrey Eshpay (1925–), student of Khatchaturian, developed a love of folk music of the Mari area from his musicologist father Yakov Eshpay. His music includes two concertos (1954–1955, 1972) and the concerto for orchestra (1967) for trumpet, vibraphone, piano, and double bass.

Sulkhan Tsintsacze (1925–) has been teaching at the Tibilis Conservatory since 1963. Georgian folk music and Russian art music influence his compositions. He has two concertos (1952, 1968) based on Georgian themes, and the fantasia (1954).

Mstislav Rostropovich (1927–), cellist and conductor, taught at the Moscow and St. Petersburg conservatories. Since 1971, he has directed the National Symphony Orchestra in Washington, D.C. He composed two piano concertos.

Otar Gordeli (1928–), Georgian composer, has been on the faculty at the Tbilisi Conservatory since 1959. His compositional style uses Georgian folk elements in polyphonic textures. The concerto (1952) is from his student years at the Moscow Conservatory.

Evgeny Svetlanov (1928–) conducted the Bolshoi Theater orchestra and the State Orchestra of the U.S.S.R. He composed the concerto (1951) while a student of Gnesin in Moscow.

Edison Denisov (1929–), named after Thomas Alva Edison by his father, who was an electrical engineer, writes music that joins Russian folk music materials, serial techniques, aleatory practices, electronic music, microtones, and experimental instrumental ideas. He has the concerto (1963) for flute, oboe, piano, and percussion, the *crescendo e diminuendo* (1965) for harpsichord and twelve string instruments, and the concerto (1974) for piano and orchestra. The score of the *crescendo e diminuendo* is in graphic notation.

Nikolay Sidelnikov (1930–) studied and taught at the Moscow Conservatory. The *Dueli* (Duels, 1973) is a concerto-symphony for cello, two pianos, and percussion.

Aleksandr Baltin (1931–) probably composed the *concerto-ballade* (1959) in Moscow.

Sofia Gubaidulina (1931–) composed the concerto (1959) using tonality, polyphony, and snappy rhythms. The concerto (1978) is in an avant-garde style, with twelve-note serialism.

Rodion Shchedrin (1932–) composed the concerto no. 1 (1954) while studying with Schaporin at the Moscow Conservatory. The concerto has rich piano and orchestra colors, the Russian tune *chastushka,* and Vologda folk material. The concerto no. 2 (1966), commissioned for the 125th anniversary of the New York Philharmonic in 1968, employs motor rhythms, Western dissonances (See ex. 10–1) and features of jazz (See ex. 10–2). The concerto is in three movements titled "Dialoge," "Improvisationen," and "Kontraste." His latest concerto is no. 3 (1973).

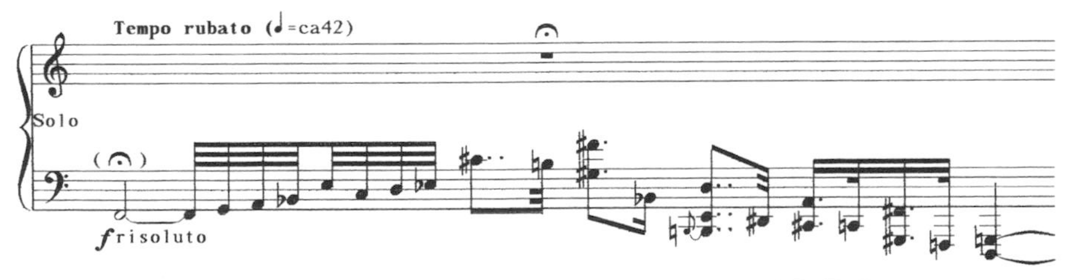

Example 10–1. Shchedrin Concerto no. 2, mvt. 1 *Dialoge,* m. 1

Example 10–2. Shchedrin Concerto no. 2, mvt. 3, *Kontraste,* mm. 40–43

Alfred Schnittke (1934–), composition teacher at the Moscow Conservatory, is a bold experimenter with a style based on serialism and dynamic gradations as thematically important elements. He has the concerto (1960), the *Music* (1964) for piano and chamber orchestra, the concerto *grosso* no. 1 (1977) for two violins, piano, harpsichord, and strings, and the concerto (perf. 1977) for piano and string orchestra.

Gennadi Banshchikov (1943–), serial composer on the faculty of the St. Petersburg Conservatory since 1973, composed the concerto (1963) while a student at the Moscow Conservatory.

Table 25 Additional Composers in Russia

Names	Dates	Compositions
Abramsky, Alexander	1898–	Concerto (1941)
Avetisian, Aida	1932–	Concerto (1955)
Biriukov, Yuri	1908–1976	3 Concertos (1941/45/70)
Bogdanov-Berezovsky, Valerian	1903–1971	Concerto, op 17 (1936) *Partita,* op 32 (1962)
Brazinskas, Algis	1937–	Concerto, op 2 (pub 1964)
Bunin, Revol	1924–	2 Concertos (one 1963)
Bunin, Vladimir	1908–1970	Concerto (1965)
Evseyev, Sergei	1893–1956	2 Concertos (both 1932)
Finko, David	1936–	Concerto (1971)
Galynin, Herman	1922–1966	2 Concertos (1945–46/65)
Gasanov, Gotfrid	1900–1965	2 Concertos (1949, pub 1960)
Gauk, Alexander	1893–1963	Concerto
Golub, Marta	1911–	*Yanosheski Concerto* (1960) Concerto (1962)
Golubev, Evgenii	1910–	3 Concertos, opp 24, 30, 40 (1943–44/48/54)
Iakhin, Rustem	1921–	Concerto (pub 1959)
Khachaturian, Karen	1920–	Concerto (1974)
Khodzha-Einatov, Leon	1904–1954	2 Concertos
Kikta, Valerii	1941–	Concerto (pub 1970)
Klyuzner, Boris	1909–	Concerto (1939)
Kornakov, Juri	1938–	Concerto (pub 1970)
Kotschetow, Nikolay	1864–1925	Concerto (1922)
Kozakievich, Anna	1914–	Concerto (1938)
Kriukov, Vladimir	1902–1960	Concerto, op 55 (1959)
Levina, Zara	1906–1976	2 Concertos (1945/75)
Lukomskii, Leopold	1898–	*Concerto in the Classical Style* (pub 1960)
Molchanov, Kirill	1922–	3 Concertos (1945/47/53)
Moralev, Oleg	1922–	Concerto (pub 1968)
Nikolayeva, Tatiana	1924–	2 Concertos, opp 10 & 32 (1950/76)
Nikolskaya, Lyubov	1909–	2 Concertos (1939/52)
Osetrova-Yakovlieva, Nina	1923–	Concerto (1951)
Ovchinnikov, Viacheslav	1936–	Concerto
Poliakov, Valerie	1913–1970	Concerto (pub 1958)
Rakov, Nikolay	1908–	2 Concertos (both 1969)
Shaposhinkov, Adrian	1888–1967	Concerto (1947, rev 1953)
Simonian, Nadezhda	1922–	Concerto (pub 1963) *Poem-Concerto* (1968)
Sink, Kuldar	1942–	*Kontrasti* (1963)
Solov'yov-Sedoy, Vasily	1907–1979	Concerto (1934)
Sorokin, Konstantin	1909–	Concerto, op 42 (pub 1970) *Youth Concerto,* op 50 (pub 1972)
Spadavecchia, Antonio	1907–	Concerto (1944)
Stepanov, Lev	1908–	2 Concertos (1947/55)
Strelnikov, Nicolai	1888–1939	Concerto
Tchaikovsky, Boris	1925–	Concerto (1971)
Tishchenko, Boris	1939–	Concerto, op 21 (1962) Concerto, op 54 (1972), fl, pno

Table 25 Additional Composers in Russia—Continued

Names	Dates	Compositions
Tolstoy, Dmitri	1923–	Concerto I, op 44
Tsfsman, Alexander	1906–1971	Concerto
Ustvolskaya, Galina	1919–	Concerto (1946)
Vinogradova, Vera	? –	Concerto Ballade
Voronina, Tatiana	1933–	Concert Ballad (1961)
Yakhnina, Yevgenia	1918–	Concerto (1953), ob, pno
Zaranek, Stefania	1904–1972	Concerto (1930)
Zeidmann, Boris	1908–	2 Concertos (1931/35)
Zhubinskaya, Valentina	1926–	Concerto (1950)
Znantakov, Iurii	1926–	Concerto, op 9 (pub 1955)

Tat'iana Saliutrinskaya (? –) possibly composed the concerto (pub. 1958) in Moscow.

Belarus

Evgeny Tikotsky (1893–1970), important in the establishment of Belarusan concert music, was the musical director of the Philharmonic concerts. His compositional style contains elements of Belarusan folk music he heard in Bobruysk. In 1954, he arranged the concerto, op. 47 (1953), originally for piano and Belarusan folk orchestra, for piano and symphony orchestra.

Eta Turmand (1917–) studied and taught at the Belarusan Conservatory. He has the concerto (1952).

Henrikh Wagner (1922–) graduated from the Warsaw Conservatory in Poland and taught piano at the Belarusan Conservatory. Among his compositions influenced by Belarussian folk music is the concerto (1956) for piano and Belarussian folk orchestra and the concerto (1964) for piano and symphony orchestra.

Ukraine

Henry Bobinski (1861–1914), Polish, studied at the Warsaw Conservatory and joined the faculty at the Russian Musical Society School in Kiev. He composed the concerto, op. 8 (pub. 1901), and the concerto, op. 12.

Lev Revutsky (1889–1977) studied composition with Gliere at the Kiev Conservatory and taught at the Music-Dramatic Institute and the conservatory. The two concertos (1914, 1934), the second is op. 18, show the influence of Tchaikovsky and Rachmaninoff in a romantic style with regional folk elements.

Victor Kossenko (1896–1938), pianist, composed music displaying influences of Tchaikovsky, Rachmaninoff, Chopin, Schumann, and Ukrainian and Moldavian folk songs. He started the concerto (1928–1937) in Moscow and finished it in Kiev.

Andrei Shtogarenko (1902–), rector of the Kiev Conservatory, writes music with colorful orchestrations and influences of Borodin, Bartók, Mussorgsky and Ukrainian music. He has the concerto-suite (1957), the concertino (1972), and the *Partyzans'ki Kartynky* (Partisan Scenes).

Igor Boelza (1904–), composer and musicologist, authored the *Handbook of Soviet Musicians*. He composed at least one piano concerto.

Herman Zhukovsky (1913–1976) wrote music influenced by Ukrainian folk songs. While a student at the Kiev Conservatory, he composed a concerto (1938).

Mikolai Silvansky (1915–) has the concerto no. 3 (pub. 1967), the *Pioneer Concerto* (pub. 1969), and the *Petit Concerto*.

Nykolai Dremiuha (1917–) left a concerto (pub. 1967).

Zhanna Kolodub (1930–) studied and taught at the Kiev Conservatory. He has the concerto (1972).

Valentin Sil'vestrov (1937–) uses ideas from the twelve-tone method. For piano and orchestra, he has the *Mododia* (1965) and the symphony no. 2 (1965).

Vladimar Zagortsev (1944–) merges serial techniques with Ukrainian folk elements. He composed the *Mysteries* (1965) and the *Sonata for Strings, Piano, and Percussion* (1969).

Moldava

Mark Kopytman (1929–), born in the Ukraine, studied at the Lwow Academy of Music and the Moscow Conservatory. While on the theory and composition faculty at the Moldavian State Academy of Music, he composed the concerto (1971). He emigrated to Israel in 1972, and joined the faculty at the Rubin Academy of Music in Jerusalem.

Georgia

Andrei Blanchivadze (1906–), brother of the American choreographer George Balanchine, studied with Ippolitov-Ivanov at the Tbilisi Conservatory. He contributed to the development of Georgian art music by using elements of local folk music. The concerto no. 1 (1934) brought him quick recognition, while the neglected concerto no. 2 (1946) does not meet the requirements of socialist realism. The three-movement programmatic concerto no. 3 (1952) is so popular it is in thirty editions. The concerto no. 4 (1967) is a set of programmatic sketches of locations in Georgia; eight movements are in the first edition and six movements in later editions.

Table 26 Additional Composers in Georgia

Names	Dates	Compositions
Chkeidze, Dali	1927–	2 Concertos (1949/55)
Davitashvili, Meri	1924–	Concerto (1946)
		Fantasy (1956)
Dolidse, Victor	1890–1933	Concerto (1932)
Eksanishvili, Eleonora	1919–	2 Concertos (1943/53–55)
Gabuniya, Nodar	1933–	2 Concertos (1961/76)
Kereseldize, Archil	1912–1971	2 Concertos (1941/49)
Kvernadze, Alexander	1928–	2 Concertos (1950/65)
Mailian, Elza	1926–	Concerto (1949)
Matschawariani, Alexei	1913–	Concerto (1944)
Shaverzashvili, Alexander	1919–	2 Concertos (1946/49)
Slianova-Mizandari, Dagmara	1910–	Concerto (1938)
Taktakishvili, Shalva	1900–1965	Concertino
Tumanishvili, Ketevana	1919–	2 Concertos (1943/52)

Otar Taktashvili (1924–) composes music with characteristic melo-rhythms of the Caucasus. His post-romantic concerto (1950) brought him recognition. Other works are the concerto no. 2, *Melodies of the Mountains* (1973), and the concerto no. 3.

Sulkan Nasidze (1927–) studied at the Tbilisi Conservatory and joined the faculty and became the artistic director of the State Philharmonic of Georgia in Tbilisi. His music, in a modern style, incorporates Georgian melo-rhythms. The concerto no. 1 (1955) is a diploma work and the concerto no. 2 (1961) is a symphonic composition.

Giya Kancheli (1935–) studied at the Tbilisi Conservatory and joined the faculty. He writes music in a radical style for a Georgian composer, and favors Oriental sounds and folk music of the Caucasas. The "Largo and Allegro" (1963) contains modal elements of Georgian folk music.

Azerbaijan

Nina Karnitskaya (1906–) taught at the Baku Conservatory and worked for the government of the Azerbaijan Soviet Socialistic Republic. She has a piano concerto and the double concerto for violin and piano.

Fiket Amirov (1922–1984) blends folk song features of the Azerbaijan region with Russian and European concert music. He has the double concerto (1946) for violin and piano, and collaborated with Elmira Nazirova (1922–) when composing the *Concerto on Azerbaijanian Themes* (1956).

Azer Rzaev (1930–), probably living in Baku, has the concerto (pub. 1965) and a concertino.

Vasif Adigezalov (1935–) composed the concerto (pub. 1962) in Baku.

Armenia

Aro Stepanian (1897–1966) studied at the St. Petersburg Conservatory and joined the faculty at the Erevan Conservatory. He contributed to the foundation of Armenian concert music during the 1930s and 1940s, and composed two concertos (1947, 1955) and the rhapsody (1962).

Alexander Harut'unyan (1920–) was the music director of the Armenian Philharmonic Society and a teacher at the Erevan Conservatory. His music uses lyric elements of Armenian folk songs in concert works that include the concerto (1941) and the concertino (1951).

Arno Babadjanyan (1921–1983) studied and taught at the conservatory. Khachaturian, Rachmaninoff, Bartók, and Prokofieff influenced his musical style. He left the concerto (1944) and the *Heroic Ballad* "Symphonic Variations" (1950) for piano and orchestra.

Eduard Abramiam (1923–) has the concerto no. 1 (1950).

Uzbekistan

Sergey Vassilenko (1872–1956) studied with Grenchaninov and Conus, and at the Moscow Conservatory with Taneyev and Ippolitov-Ivanov. He taught at the conservatory, then went to Tashkent to assist regional composers in establishing a musical style based on Uzbekistan music. He left the concerto, op. 128 (1949).

Georgy Mushel' (1909–), colleague of Vassilenko, studied at the Tambov Musical Technical College and the Moscow Conservatory. His concert music uses features of Uzbek folk music. He composed six concertos (1936, 1943 rev. 1958, 1943, 1950, 1951, 1952). Prokofieff praised the 1936 concerto as a graduation piece at the Moscow Conservatory. Mushel's music shows influences of Debussy, Ravel, Prokofieff, Uzbek folk music, and European music.

Kazakhstan

Evgeny Brusilovsky (1905–1981), student of Steinberg at the St. Petersburg Conservatory, received a commission to study the regional folk music of Kazakhstan. From 1933, he researched at the Kazakh Music and Drama Technical College and later joined the faculty at the conservatory. His research efforts developed a union between Kazakh folk music and traditional European music. The concerto (1947) shows the influence of Kazakh music.

Table 27 Additional Composers in the Former Soviet Union[2]

Names	Dates	Compositions
Aisberg, Ilya	1872–	Capriccio Concerto, op 15 (1928) *Hebraique,* op 20 (pub 1931)
Bagirov, Zakir	1916–	Concerto
Barsukov, Sergei	1908–	Concerto no 2 (ca. 1950)
Berkovich, Isak	1902–	3? Concertos, opp 44 & 48 (pub ca. 1968)
Binkin, Zinovii	1913–	Concertino
Blagoi, Dmitrii	1930–	Capriccio (1960)
Chicherina, Sofia	1904–	Concerto (1945)
Chichkov, Iurii	1929–	*Concerto on Kabardino Themes* (pub 1965)
Conus, Sergei	1902–	Concerto
Dhabadary, Erekle	? –	Georgian Rhapsody
Dolukhanian, Aleksandr	1910–	Concerto
Eiges, Oleg	1905–	Concertino (1960) Concerto
Gan, Nikolai	1908–	Concerto no 3
Kagan, Simon	1909–	Concertino (1963)
Kaminsky, Dimitrii	1907–	2 Concertos (1948/77) Concertino Concerto-Fantasia
Kokoity, Tatarklan	1908–	Azau-Concert Fantasia
Kortes, Sergei	1935–	Concerto (1969)
Kos-Anatolsky, Antollii	1909–	2 Concertos (1955/61)
L'vov-Kompanetts, David	1915–	Concert Waltzes
Levitin, Iurii	1912–	2 Concertos (one pub 1958)
Liavova, Ludmila	1925–	*Poem Osvobozhdennaya Korea* (1951)
Luppov, Anatolii	1929–	Concerto-Toccata
Magidenko, Mikhail	1915–	Concerto
Makarov-Rakitin, Konstantin	1912–1941	Concerto, op 8
Mamedov, Nariman	? –	Concerto
Mamisashvily, Nodar	1930–	Concerto "Pioneer"
Nakhabin, Vladimir	1910–	Concerto
Nikolskaya, Olga	1916–	Concerto (1952)
Nurymov, Chary	1941–	Concerto
Okunev, German	1931–1973	Concerto, op 38 (1972)
Partskhaladze, Merab	1924–	Concerto, op 12 (pub 1959)
Pikul, Vladimir	1937–	Concerto
Podkovyror, Petr	1910–	Concerto
Prawossudowitsch, Natalia	1899–	Concerto
Ratsevichius, Aleksas-Ramvidas	1935–	Concerto
Repnikov, Albon	1932–	Concertino
Romm, Rosa	1916–	Concerto (1971)
Saigun, Akhmed	1907–	Concerto
Shukailo, Lyudmila	? –	Concertino (pub 1977), vn, pno
Sinisalo, Helmer-Rayer	1920–	Concerto (1958)
Sosnovtsev, Boris	1921–	Concerto (pub 1972)
Tchesnokoff, Alexandre	? –	Ballade, op 41
Trotsyuk, Bogdan	1931–	Concerto-Suite

Table 27 Additional Composers in the Former Soviet Union[2]—Continued

Names	Dates	Compositions
Tsytovich, Vladimir	1931–	Concerto (1960)
Uspenskii, Vladislav	1937–	Concerto, 2 pnos
Valfenzon, Sergei	? –	Concerto

Notes

1. Joseph Yasser, "The Opening Theme of Rachmaninoff's Third Piano Concerto and Its Liturgical Prototype," *Musical Quarterly* 55 (July 1969): 313–328.

2. Scarce information about these composers makes their precise placement in any of the republics of the former Soviet Union impossible.

Chapter 11

France and Switzerland

France

Georges Witkowski (1867–1943) studied with d'Indy at the *Schola Cantorum,* founded the *Sociéte des Grands Concerts* and became the director of the Lyons Conservatory in 1924. He left the *Mon lac: prelude, variations et finale* (1921).

Albert Roussel (1869–1939) composed music in a style influenced by Debussy's impressionism and d'Indy's classicism. His concerto, op. 36 (1927), shows the classic influence in the sonata and rondo forms.

Francis Casadesus (1870–1954), uncle of pianist Robert Casadesus, founded and directed the American *Conservatoire*. He left an intermezzo.

André Bloch (1873–1960) studied with Guiraud and Massenet at the Paris *Conservatoire* and conducted the orchestra at the American *Conservatoire*. He composed the concerto-ballet (1946).

Maurice Ravel (1875–1937) studied with Fauré at the Paris *Conservatoire* and was a friend of many contemporary French composers, including Debussy, d'Indy, Schmitt, Chabrier, and Roussel. Ravel is a foremost French contributor to the repertoire for piano and orchestra. As early as 1906, he thought about writing a piano concerto titled *Zaspiak-Bat,* based on Basque folk themes. In ca. 1909, he worked on the concerto but problems of merging folk elements into his style of art music caused him to abandon the composition. The title in Basque means "the seven are one," referring to the union of four Spanish and three French Basque provinces. Parts of *Zaspiak-Bat* appear in the concerto in G major.

After thinking about composing a piano concerto in 1928, he started the concerto in G major (1929–1931). A commission from the Austrian pianist Paul Wittgenstein to write a concerto for the left hand interrupted Ravel's work on the concerto in G major. After completing the concerto (1930) for left hand, Ravel returned to the concerto in G. Composing both concertos simultaneously produced many similarities between the works, although the styles are contrasting. Some melodic motives are the same in both concertos, but the accompaniments make those motives appear dissimilar. Evidence of Ravel's fondness for jazz appears as the "blue" notes, sliding chromatic neighbor chords, passing tones suggesting sliding pitches in brass sections of jazz bands, and the simultaneous major and minor thirds in accompaniments. Similarities between the concertos are the shortened recapitulations, glissandos, and cadenzas with the left-hand thumb having the melody. Many passages in the concerto in G suggest Ravel's admiration of Gershwin's *Rhapsody in Blue* and *Concerto in F.*

To learn the possibilities of left-hand technique, Ravel examined Saint-Saëns' *Six Etudes pour la Main Gauche,* op. 139; Godowsky's transcriptions for the left hand of Chopin's *Etudes;* Czerny's *Ecole de la Main Gauche,* op. 339, and the *24 Etudes pour la Main Gauche,* op. 718; Alkan's *Etude,* op. 76, no. 1; and Scriabin's *Prelude* and *Nocturne,* op. 9. When working on the concerto in G, Ravel studied the piano concertos of Mozart and Saint-Saëns. He found composing the slow movement a laborious experience that drew inspiration from the slow movement of Mozart's quintet, K.581, for clarinet, two violins, viola, and cello. The slow movements of Ravel and Mozart have major modes, 3/4 meter, similar melodic features, eight-note accompaniments, and moods of serenity.

Henry Filleul (1877–1959) studied at the Paris *Conservatoire* and directed the *École Nationale de de Musique* in St. Omer. He left the *Fantasie concertante* (1950).

Paul Ladmirault (1877–1944) taught at the Nantes Conservatory. He composed the *Valse triste* in a style influenced by Brittany and Celtic musical ideas.

Jean Cras (1879–1932) followed a naval career that culminated in the rank of vice-admiral. His musical interests included composition lessons with his friend Henri Duparc. His last musical composition is the virtuoso piano concerto (1931).

Édouard Flament (1880–1958) played bassoon in many important European orchestras. For piano and orchestra, he composed the *concertstück,* op. 15; the concerto, op. 121; the *Nocturne,* op. 148; the concerto no. 3, op. 150, with military orchestra; and the concerto no. 4, op. 158.

Igor Stravinsky (1882–1971) was born in Oranienbaum, Russia, on the coast of the Gulf of Finland. In Stravinsky's early childhood, his father practiced opera roles at home and took young Stravinsky to the ballet to hear music of Russian composers. His parents insisted on law studies at the university, but Igor's interest in musical composition grew stronger than his interest in law.

Stravinsky lived in France from 1920 to 1939, and again later. He composed the concerto (1923–1924), the capriccio (1928–1929), and the *movements* (1958–1959). He worked on an unfinished *konzertstück* (1910) in Russia.

The concerto is in three movements and the premiere in 1924, with Koussevitsky conducting, was Stravinsky's debut as a pianist. His interest in the piano comes from the success of the piano version of *Petrushka* that he arranged for Artur Rubinstein and the final instrumentation of *The Wedding*. Nineteenth-century styles of piano playing did not attract Stravinsky. The concerto requires a dry, percussive sound without lyric lines. Neo-classic features are the rhythmic elements, the treatment of instruments, and the sequence of movements. Shifting accents, changing meters, and syncopations are common. The orchestration is for winds, timpani, and string bass. For five years Stravinsky reserved the performance rights for himself, and during those years he performed the concerto about forty times. In 1950, he made slight revisions to the score.

After many performances of the concerto, Stravinsky felt a need for a new composition for piano and orchestra. He began writing a movement titled "Allegro capriccioso" that eventually became titled *Capriccio.* Although he composed the "Allegro Capriccioso" movement first, it is the final movement in the finished work. Strings appear with a concertino string quartet and a ripieno string quartet along with various winds. The *Capriccio* is more lyric than the concerto because of the musical influence of Tchaikovsky and Chopin and the addition of strings to the orchestra.

The concerto and the capriccio display Stravinsky's keen interest in the piano as a solo instrument. The *movements* (1958–1959), originally titled *Concerto for Piano and Group of Instruments,* is one of Stravinsky's serial works. In each movement the serial features have considerable freedom. The piano functions more as an ensemble instrument than a solo instrument. *Movements* contains five movements with musical material appearing between them.

Charles Chaix (1885–1973) studied in Paris and Geneva, worked as a church organist, and taught at the Lyon Conservatory. The symphony no. 2, op. 8 (1928), has a piano obbligato.

Nadia Boulanger (1887–1979), student of Fauré, is the famous composition teacher of a generation of important French and American composers. Among her musical compositions is a rhapsody.

Louis Durey (1888–1979), oldest member of *Les Six,* chose an anti-romantic musical path. After joining the French Communist Party, his music follows the principles of the Prague Manifesto of 1948 that calls on artists to avoid individualism and to compose music based on national folk songs. The concertino (1956) is for piano, sixteen winds, double bass, and timpani, and the *mouvement symphonique* (1963) is for piano and strings.

Bohuslav Martinu (1890–1959), Czech-born, studied at the Prague Conservatory and played violin in the Czech Philharmonic Orchestra. He spent many years in Paris composing musical compositions. He went to New York City in 1941, and returned to Europe in 1953 to live in Nice, Rome, and Schönenberg. His music follows neo-classic models, impressionism, and has characteristics of the Czech national musical style.

In Paris, Martinu composed eight compositions for piano and orchestra. The concerto no. 1 (1925) has a percussive piano style that lacks lyric lines and is similar to Scarlatti's harpsichord writing. He disowned the work due to the dull piano part. In 1928, Martinu changed the title of the left-hand divertimento (1926) to concertino. The keyboard style is not idiomatically comfortable for the hand. The four-movement concertino no. 1 (1933) for violin, cello, and piano is a neo-baroque work with ritornellos and other similarities to the concerto *grosso*. The concertino no. 2 (1933) for violin, cello, and piano is similar to the concertino no. 1 in the treatment of themes in ritornellos, but the musical content is different. The concerto no. 2 (1934, rev. 1935 in New York City) displays the Czech fondness for long melodic lines. The concerto (1935) is for harpsichord and a small ensemble of piano, flute, bassoon, three pairs of violins, two violas, two cellos, and bass. The harpsichord, with eighteenth-century figuration and twentieth-century dissonance, is in concertant to the ensemble. In the concertino (1938), the piano has a percussive style. The *Sinfonietta Giocosa* (1940, rev. 1941), originally titled *Sinfonia Gaie,* has the piano in two-part polyphony.

In New York City, Martinu composed the concerto (1943) for two pianos, one of his favorite compositions. The concerto no. 3 (1947–1948) is for the pianist Rudolf Firkusny and the orchestration is by Jan Novák. The Musical Arts Society of La Jolla, Calif., commissioned the *Sinfonietta La Jolla* (1950) for piano obbligato and small orchestra. The concerto (1953) is for violin and piano. Sometimes the two-movement concerto no. 4 "Incantation" (1955–1956) appears as the *Incantation.* In Schöenberg-Pratteln, Switzerland, he composed the *Fantasia Concertante* (concerto no. 5, 1957).

George Migot (1891–1976), more famous as a painter than as a composer, used old French polyphony in his musical compositions. He composed the *Suite en Trois Parties* (1925–1926), the *Deux Pieces* (1934) for piano, voice, and orchestra, the concerto (1962), the harpsichord concerto (1964), and an orchestra part to accompany the piano in Chopin's *Fantasie on Polish National Airs* (1913).

Alexis Roland-Manuel (pseud. for Roland Alexander Manuel Lévy, 1891–1966) studied with Roussel and d'Indy at the *Schola Cantorum* and privately with Ravel. The concerto (1938) follows French neo-classic style.

Arthur Honegger (1892–1955), member of *Les Six,* composed the *Entree, Nocturne et Berceuse* (1919) and the concertino (1924–1925) based on jazz. He followed German musical thinking more than French musical traditions.

Arthur Louré (1892–1966) trained as a composer at the St. Petersburg Conservatory and settled in Paris in ca. 1922. He composed the *Sonata Liturgique* (1928) and the *Concerto Spirituel* (1929), both for orchestra, piano, and chorus. Busoni's concerto may be the model for both works.

Darius Milhaud (1892–1955), member of *Les Six,* is the most prolific French composer of music for piano and orchestra in the twentieth century. He viewed his music in a historical line running through Couperin, Rameau, Berlioz, Bizet, and Chabrier, and displaying the intimate relationship between solo and orchestra in the French tradition. Prominent features in the music are elements of Brazilian music, polytonality, pandiatonicism, counterpoint, intervals of ninths and tenths in the left hand, and *glissandos,* sometimes in thirds. Many compositions have traditional concerto instrumentation, others have instrumentations common to chamber music, and some have non-traditional instrumentations with harps and a variety of percussion instruments.

Milhaud composed seventeen works featuring the piano as a solo instrument with orchestra. Until 1964, he held the manuscript for the *Poleme sur un Cantique de Camargue,* op. 13 (1913–1914). The one-movement *ballade,* op. 61 (1920), has elements of Fauré's *ballade,* Debussy's *fantasie* and Brazilian music. In the *Cinq Etudes,* op. 63 (1920), the "Etude" no. 3 has four simultaneous fugues. His most popular work is the twelve-movement *Le Carnaval d'Aix,* op. 83b (1926), subtitled *Fantasie pour Piano et Orchestra d'Apres "Salade,"* based on his ballet *Salade,* op. 83 (1924), and influenced by jazz and Brazilian music. The concerto no. 1, op. 127 (1933), uses a variety of percussion instruments. Movements one and two of *Scaramouche,* op. 165b (1937), for two pianos and orchestra, are on *Le Médecin Volant,* op. 165a (1937), and a theme in the middle movement comes from music Milhaud composed for Superville's *Bolivar.* The one-movement *Fantasie Pastorale,* op. 188 (1938), is for a non-traditional orchestra. Milhaud composed the concerto nos. 2 and 3, opp. 225 and 270 (1941, 1946), in Oakland, Calif., where he taught at Mills College. The concerto, op. 228 (1941), is for two pianos. The suite *concertante,* op. 278a (1952), is on the marimba concerto, op. 278. *L'Apotheose de Moliere: Suite d'Apres Baptiste Anet,* op. 286 (1948), is for harpsichord and orchestra. The concerto no. 4, op. 295 (1949), and the concerto no. 1 are the two virtuoso compositions Milhaud composed for piano and orchestra. The five-movement *Suite Opus 300,* op. 300 (1950), is for two pianos, and the *Concertino d'Automne,* op. 309 (1951), is for two pianos and eight instruments. The concerto no. 5, op. 346 (1955), is for piano and orchestra and the *Concert de Chambre,* op. 389 (1961), is for piano and wind quintet.

Nicolas Obouhov (1892–1954), experimenter with twelve-tone ideas prior to Schoenberg, studied at the St. Petersburg Conservatory with N. Tcherepnin and Steinberg, and in Paris with Ravel. His lifelong effort is the 2000-page *Le Livre de Vie* for solo voices, chorus, two pianos, and orchestra. As a mystic, he signed manuscripts *Nicolas l'Illumine* and marked portions of scores with his blood. The incomplete *Duexieme Intronisation* is for piano duet and orchestra.

Germaine Tailleferre (1892–) is the only female member of *Les Six.* For piano and orchestra, she composed the *ballade* (1922), the concerto (1924), the concerto (1934) for two pianos and chorus, the concertino (1953) for flute, piano and strings, and the partita (1964) for two pianos and percussion.

Henri Cliquet-Plegel (1894–1963) studied with Gédalge and Koechlin at the Paris *Conservatoire.* His concerto is for the right hand.

Filip Lazar (1894–1936), Romanian, trained at the Bucharest and Leipzig conservatories and settled in Paris where he helped found the musical society Triton for the advancement of modern music. Romanian music influenced the four concertos: *Concerto Grosso in the Old Style,* op. 18 (1930); op. 19 (1931) with small orchestra; op. 23 (perf. 1934); and op. 24 (1934).

Marguerite Sara Roesgen-Champion (pseud. for Jean Delysse, 1894–1976), born in Switzerland, studied with Bloch and Dalcroze at the Geneva Conservatory and joined the faculty to teach harpsichord and piano. After settling in Paris in 1926, she promoted the harpsichord and composed music in a neo-romantic style. Her compositions for harpsichord and orchestra are the *Aquarelles* (1929); the *Concerto Moderne* (1931); the concerto *grosso* (1931) for harpsichord, violin, and cello; five concertos (1931–1959); the introduction, sarabande et toccata (1933); two concertos (1938, 1945) for alto saxophone, harpsichord, and bassoon; and the concertino (1947). For piano and orchestra, she composed the rhapsody (1944), the concerto *romantique* (1961) and three concertos.

Jean Rivier (1896–) was an associate of Milhaud at the Paris *Conservatoire* and a member of the Triton group to promote modern music. Among his compositions in a French classic and impressionistic style are the concerto (1940), the concerto *brève* (1953), and the *Climats* (1968) for celesta, vibraphone, xylophone, piano, and strings.

Jean Wiener (1896–1982), friend of *Les Six* and champion of contemporary music, is among the earliest French composers to incorporate jazz into concert music. He used jazz in the concerto *Franco-Americain* (1924), the concerto (1970), and the cadences.

Alexandre Tansman (1897–), Polish, settled in Paris about 1918, Hollywood in 1940, and returned to Paris in 1946. His compositions contain influences of Chopin, Szymanowski, Stravinsky, Ravel, Polish music, and jazz. His compositions for piano and orchestra are the neo-classic concerto no. 1 (1925) in four movements; the concerto no. 2 (1927); the two-piano suite (1928) with a double fugue and the *Finale on un Theme Slave;* the concertino (1931); the symphony no. 3 (*Symphonie Concertante,* 1931) for piano, violin, viola, and cello; and the *Fantasie* (1937).

Marcel Delannoy (1898–1962), student of Gédalge and Honegger, was successful in ballet and opera. He composed *La Romani* (perf. 1928), the *Concerto de Mai,* op. 50 (1949–1950), and the *Ballade Concertante,* op. 59 (1954), with an ensemble of twelve instruments.

Marcel Mihalovici (1898–), Romanian, settled in Paris in 1919 where he studied with d'Indy at the *Schola Cantorum* and helped found the music society Triton to promote modern music. His music blends French and eastern European elements. Among his works are the *Chindia* (1929) for piano and thirteen winds; the toccata, op. 44 (1938–1940, rev. 1940), for piano and orchestra; the *Etudes en Deux Parties* (1951) for piano, seven winds, celesta, and percussion; the *Periples* (1967); and the *Rhapsodie Concertante* (1951).

Robert Casadesus (1899–1972), pianist, composed three concertos, opp. 7, 37, and 63 (1926, 1944–1945, 1961?), and the *concertstück,* op. 27 (1937–1938). The concerto, op. 17 (1931), and the capriccio, op. 49 (1933), are for his wife Gaby and himself. The three-piano concerto, op. 65 (1964), is for his wife, son Jean, and himself. Casadesus wrote cadenzas for Beethoven's concerto nos. 1, 3, and 4, Mozart's concertos, K.365, K.466, K.482, K.503, and K.595, and Haydn's concerto, Hob. XVIII:11.

Francis Poulenc (1899–1963), member of *Les Six,* identified Chabrier, Satie, Stravinsky, and Ravel as strong influences on his style. He opposed the vagueness of French impressionism and the lure of sophistication in contemporary French music. His music has memorable melodies of symmetrical lengths, a predilection for homophony and avoidance of polyphony, an influence of jazz and French dance hall music, little rubato, meter changes, and a liberal use of the "wrong note" technique. Some textures suggest the romantic era, and Poulenc is fond of short passages reminiscent of his favorite composer, Mozart. Orchestrations in the concertos feature lightness and clarity, while the keyboard writing resembles techniques common in chamber music.

In 1923, Ricardo Vines invited Poulenc to the Paris premiere of Falla's pantomime-ballet *El Retable de Maese Pedro* (Master Peter's Puppet Show). Wanda Landowska played the harpsichord during the performance, and later she asked Poulenc and Falla to compose music for the instrument. For Poulenc, musical ideas for a harpsichord composition did not develop until he visited Landowska's home at Saint-Leu-la-Forêt, a suburb north of Paris, where in the spring of each year she presented *concerts champetres*. Country (*champetres*) concerts have a long history in French music. The result of that chance experience is Poulenc's *concert champetre* (1926) for harpsichord and orchestra. Neo-classic characteristics draw from François Couperin's and Rameau's clavecin techniques of rolled chords, staccato chords, mordents on beats, lightness, *galant* style, and constant eight-note activity. Twentieth-century elements are chords with added sixths, sevenths, and ninths, meter changes, percussive sound, and dry style. Poulenc strived for simplicity, variety, and a dialogue between the orchestra and harpsichord. At times the harpsichord is a solo instrument and at times an accompanying instrument. Although Poulenc preferred performances with harpsichord, occasionally he performed the work at the piano.

The complete title of the *Aubade* (1929) for piano and eighteen instruments is *Aubade: Concerto Choregraphique*. The original version is a ballet on the myth about Diana, but the ballet version appeared only a few times. The composition is neo-classic, by the nature of its subject, the influence of the Fontainebleau school of painting and the *galant* musical style. The piano functions in a chamber music role, sometimes carrying the melody and sometimes accompanying other instruments. Poulenc's use of eight continuous movements suggests a suite instead of a traditional concerto of three or four movements. However, none of the movements is in a baroque binary form. The movement titles are "Toccata," "Récitatif," "Rondeau," "Presto," "Récitatif," "Andante," "Allegro Feroce," and "Conclusion." In the *Aubade* Poulenc used a melody in Mozart's sonatina no. 5, K.439b.

The two-piano concerto (1932) and the one-piano concerto (1949) have several similarities. The mood of both works is light and non-virtuoso, the first and second movements are in ternary form, the finales are in rondo form, and the piano begins and ends most movements. Poulenc's fondness for Mozart's music is evident in the slow movement of the concerto for two pianos. The third movement of the concerto for one piano has a quotation from Stephen Foster's "Old Folks at Home" and a fragment of French dance hall music.

Alexander Tcherepnin (1899–1977), son of Nikolay Tcherepnin, blends traditional Russian compositional techniques with modern features of Prokofieff. Ostinatos and motor rhythms are common, textures are uncluttered, traditional forms maintain freshness, and, generally, there is a sense of tonality.

The *Bagatelles,* op. 5 (1913–1918), originally a piano solo work, is in versions (1958–1959) for piano and orchestra and piano and string orchestra. The only change, in the orchestra version compared with the solo version, is the return of the "bagatelle" at the end of the composition in later versions.

The one-movement concerto no. 1, op. 12 (1919–1920), composed in Tbilisi, shows the influence of Russian music heard in the Tcherepnin household. In Paris, Tcherepnin evolved his theory of the nine-step scale and ideas of polyphony he called "interpoint" that emphasize the independence of various voices. These two techniques exist in the one-movement concerto no. 2, op. 26 (1922, rev. 1950), the four-movement concertino, op. 47 (1931, rev. 1965), for violin, cello, and piano, and the two-movement concerto no. 3, op. 48 (1931–1932). About 1934, Tcherepnin's interest turned to folk music and the pentatonic scale. Two works of this era are the *suite Georgiene,* op. 57 (1938), and the fantasy (concerto no. 4), op. 78 (1947). Each movement in the suite is on a popular Georgian folk song. The titles of the three movements in the concerto are "Eastern Chamber Dream," "Yan Kwei Fei's Love Sacrifice," and "Road to Yunnan." In the cyclic concerto nos. 5 and 6, opp. 96 and 99 (1963, 1965), composed in the United States, Tcherepnin employs the eight-step scale and his own "novella concept" that treats sections of a composition as leading to the end of the work without resolving internal parts.

George Antheil (1900–1959), *enfant terrible* of modern music, made the machine age the inspiration for compositions with titles like the *Airplane Sonata* and the *Ballet Mechanique*. He studied with Bloch in New York City and went to Berlin. After settling in Paris in 1923, he established a considerable reputation and was among the first American students of Boulanger. He composed the concerto no. 1 (1922) in Berlin and the concerto (1926) in Paris. The concerto no. 2 caused considerable criticism because Antheil repudiated radicalism for a neo-classicism akin to Stravinsky. Eventually he settled in the United States.

Henry Barraud (1900–) studied with Dukas at the Paris *Conservatoire* and school officials expelled him for composing a radical string quartet. From 1948, he directed the *Programme National* for *Radiodiffusion Française* and helped found the progressive music group Triton. He has the concerto (1939) and the concertino (1954) for piano and four winds.

Henri Sauguet (1901–), born Henri-Pierre Poupard, chose his mother's maiden name of Sauguet. He studied with d'Indy and Koechlin, knew Milhaud and other members of *Les Six,* and joined with other musicians in the group *L'Ecole d'Arcueil* to show admiration for Satie's music. Koechlin and Satie influenced Sauguet's music. The incomplete concerto no. 1 (1933–1934) has one movement, the concerto no. 2, *Rêverie Concertante* (1947) is on the film score *Les Amoureuz Sont Seuls au Monde,* and the *Concerto des Mondes Souterrains* (1961–1963) sometimes appears as the concerto no. 3.

Claude Arrieu (pseud. for Louise Marie Simon, 1903–) studied with Long, Caussade, and Dukas. In a Parisian neo-classic style, she composed the concerto (1932), the concerto (1938) for two pianos, *Les Jongleurs* (1962), the *Menuet Vif* (1961), and the *Scherzo Valse* (1961).

Nicolas Nabokov (1903–1978), born in Russia, trained in St. Petersburg, with Ribikov in Yalta, at the Stuttgart Conservatory, and with Busoni and Juon at the Berlin *Hochschule für Musik.* He spent time in Paris and Germany and probably was in Paris while writing his concerto (1932). His music evidences Russian folk songs and compositional ideas learned in Germany.

Eugene Bozza (1905–) conducted the *Opéra Comique* in Paris. While the director of the *École National de Musique,* he composed a concerto (1955).

André Jolivet (1905–1974) was an avant-garde composer strongly influenced by Varèse and Schoenberg's atonality. With Baudrier, Messiaen, and Lesur, Jolivet established the progressive music group *La Jeune France* to promote contemporary music. He composed the concertino (1948) for trumpet, piano, and strings, and the concerto (1954) for bassoon, harp, piano, and strings. French *Radiodiffusion* commissioned the concerto (1949–1950), originally titled *Equatoriales,* as "a work of colonial inspiration." The first movement treats musical elements of Africa, the second movement relates to Polynesia, and the third movement refers to the Far East. Throughout the concerto, Jolivet wrote important music for the percussion instruments.

Edward Lockspeiser (1905–1973), English, studied in Paris with Tansman and Boulanger. In London, he wrote music criticism for the *Yorkshire Post* and his musicological interest culminated in a two-volume publication, *Debussy: His Life and Mind.* The concerto (1935) for piano and winds is a product of his work with Tansman.

Maxime Jacob (1906–1977) took Catholic holy orders under the name Clement. He composed more than 500 songs influenced by modal and plainsong practices, and a concerto (1961) for piano.

Roman Palester (1907–), Polish, studied at the Lwow Conservatory and the Warsaw Conservatory. After settling in Paris in 1925, he adopted contemporary compositional techniques used there. He composed the lost concerto (1935), the concertino (1942), the concertino (1955) for harpsichord and chamber ensemble, and the *Music* (1957) for two pianos.

Oliver Messiaen (1908–1992) entered the Paris *Conservatoire* at age 11 for studies with Jean and Noël Gallon, Dupré, Maurice, and Dukas. To promote modern French music, Messiaen joined with Jolivet, Baudrier, and Daniel-Lesure in 1936 to form the musical group *La Jeune France*. After two years in a German prisoner-of-war camp in Silesia, he joined the faculty at the Paris *Conservatoire* in 1942.

Messiaen's musical style depends on old devices like Greek rhythms, Hindustani rhythms of northern India, Carnatic rhythms of southern India, fourteenth-century isorhythms, and plainchant. Modern musical influences are Debussy, rhythmic features in Stravinsky's *Rite of Spring,* his own modes, polymodal writing, modes of limited transposition, his device of "added resonance," resulting from playing a chord quietly over a louder chord or note, and an equation of sound to color.

Messiaen considers birds to be among the world's finest musicians. He based the *Reveil des Oiseaux* (1953) solely on bird songs for melodic and rhythmic material. Various musical instruments depict bird songs, and the composition is an arch form with the "dawn chorus" being the highest point of the arch. He dedicated the first part of the work to the ornithologist Jacques Delamain, the second part to the music editor Yvonne Loriod, and the third part to "the blackbirds, thrushes, nightingales, orioles, robins, warblers, and all the birds of our forests." The bird songs are of a single region of France.

The *Oiseaux Exotiques* (1956) uses bird songs from many parts of the world. Changes in timbre and texture give a variety of sounds not available in bird songs.

The *Sept Haïkaï* (1962) employs Japanese music and bird songs Messiaen heard during a visit to Japan. A *Haïkaï*, or haiku, is a three-line poem with five syllables in the first line, seven syllables in the second line, and five syllables in the third line. Messiaen generally follows the Japanese musical tradition of reserving specific musical material to each instrumental group.

The *Couleurs de la Cié Céleste* (1963) contains many features of Messiaen's style: Christian symbolism, plainchant, bird songs, Greek and Indian rhythms, and an equation of sound and color. Messiaen's perception of trombones as having an apocalyptic sound led him to read the *Apocalypse*. The preface to the score contains quotations from the *Apocalypse* and the score has Messiaen's indications about which colors to perform, as in "play blue" or "play red."

Jean Françaix (1912–) studied piano with Phillip and composition with Boulanger. His music is light-hearted, suggesting spontaneity and neo-classic balance and control. He has the concertino (1932), the concerto (1936), the variations (1950) for cello, piano, and orchestra, the concerto (1959) for harpsichord, flute, and strings, and the double concerto (1965) for two pianos. His music style is light and cheerful.

René Leibowitz (1913–1972), born in Poland of Russian parents, studied with Schoenberg in Berlin and Vienna, and with Webern. He led the French twelve-tone composers in the revival of the technique. He composed the chamber concerto, op. 5 (1942), for violin, piano, and seventeen instruments, the concerto, op. 32 (1954), and *A Legend,* op. 82 (1968), for soprano, piano, and orchestra. Leibowitz's chamber concerto strongly suggests Berg's chamber concerto.

Maurice Ohana (1914–), French composer and pianist of British parentage, studied with Lévy and Lesur in Paris and with Casella in Rome. He composed the sarabande (1947) for harpsichord; the *Tombeau de Claude Debussy* (1961) for piano, soprano, zither tuned in one-third tones, and orchestra, based on quotations from Debussy's

Preludes, Etudes, and *En Blanc et Noir;* the *Synaxis* (1966) for four percussion instruments, two pianos and orchestra; and the *Chiffres de Clavecin* (1968) for harpsichord and twenty-one instruments. He preferred artistic liberties to established practices.

Michal Spisak (1914–1965), Polish, studied at the Katowice Conservatory, the Warsaw Conservatory and the Paris *Conservatoire* with Boulanger. In a style based on Stravinsky's neo-classic and neo-baroque practices, he composed the concerto (1947), the divertimento (1948) for two pianos, and the suite *Musique Légère* no. 2 (1952) for strings and piano.

Jean Hubeau (1917–) entered the Paris Conservatoire at age 9 and won the second *Grand Prix de Rome* at age 17. While the director of the Versailles *Conservatoire,* he composed the *Concerto Heroique* (1946), based on two hymns.

Dinu Lipatti (1917–1950), Romanian, studied piano with Flocia Musicesco at the Bucharest Conservatory. He won an international piano competition in Vienna in 1933, and studied in Paris with Cortot, Dukas, and Boulanger. He composed the *Concertino in Classical Style,* op. 3 (1935), and the *3 Romanian Dances* (1945) for two pianos and string orchestra. Originally, the *Romanian Dances* were for two solo pianos. He wrote cadenzas for several Mozart concertos and a Haydn concerto. He joined the faculty at the Geneva Conservatory in 1943, and established a reputation for sensitive performances of Chopin's piano music.

Rolande Flacinelli (1920–) played organ at the *Sacré Coeur de Montmartre* and taught at the American *Conservatoire*. He composed the *Polska Suite,* op. 8, based on well-known Slavic themes, and *D'un Ame, Poeme en Dix Chantes,* op. 15.

Serge Lancen (1922–) trained at the Paris *Conservatoire*. He composed the concertino (pub. 1953) in the style of Françaix, the *Fantasie Creol* (pub. 1969) using Creole rhythms, the concerto-rhapsodie (pub. 1974) influenced by the blues, and the concerto (1947).

Serge Nigg (1924–) studied at the Paris *Conservatoire* and privately with Leibowitz for the twelve-tone method. He was among the earliest composers in France to use the twelve-tone method, but later he returned to a neo-classic style more accessible to the public. His musical compositions include the concertino (1946) for piano, winds, and percussion, influenced by Messiaen, the variations (1946), the concerto (1947) for piano, strings, and percussion, the concerto (1971), and the *Scenes Concertantes* (1975), influenced by expressionism. The concerto (1947) is one of his finest works.

Marius Constant (1925–), Romanian-born, studied at the Bucharest Conservatory and in Paris with Messiaen, Boulanger, and Honegger. His musical style began with impressionism and later included serialism and aleatoric techniques. The concerto (1954) was for the Aix en Provence Festival in 1957 and the *Candide* (1971) is for amplified harpsichord and orchestra.

Pierre-Max Dubois (1930–) composes music influenced by Françaix, Prokofieff, and his teacher Milhaud. He has the concertos I (n.d.), II (1957), III (pub. 1967), and IV (pub. 1971); the *Concerto Italien* (1962) for two pianos; and the concertino (1962) for piano and violin that sometimes appears on lists as the double concerto.

Roger Boutry (1932–) studied with Boulanger, Long, and Aubin at the Paris *Conservatoire* and performed piano concerts in Europe, Russia, and Australia. In a

Table 28 Additional Composers in France

Names	Dates	Compositions
Aaron, Yvonne	1897–	*Reflects sur un Même Théme* (1965)
Acart (-Becker), Eveline	1921–	2 Concertos (1945/74) No 2, fl, tr, pno
Alix, Rene	1907–1966	Concerto, op 16 (pub ca. 1959)
Ancelin, Pierre	1934–	Concerto, op 14 (1962)
Arma, Paul	1904–	Concerto (1939)
Aubert, Louis	1877–1968	*Fantasie,* op 8 (1899)
Auclert, Pierre	1905–	2 Concertos (pub 1951/54)
Bancquart, Alain	1934–	*La Naissance du Geste*
Barraine, Elsa	1910–	*Fantasie concertante* (1933)
Bartos, Josef	1902–	Theme and Variations, op 5 (1935)
Belaubre, Louis	1932–	2 Concertos (one 1970)
Bernard, Robert	1900–1971	Concerto
Beugniot, Jean-Pierre	1935–	Concerto, pno, tr
Bienvenu, Lily	1920–	Concerto (1957)
Bitch, Marcel	1921–	2 Concertos (1950/53) Concertino (1953)
Bizet, Jean	1924–	Concerto II "Da Camera"
Boisselet, Paul	? –	Jazz-Concerto (1946)
Bonnal, Joseph	1880–1944	*Fantasie Landaise*
Borchard, Adolphe	1882–1967	*Es Kual Herria* (perf 1922)
Borne, Fernand le	1862–1929	Symphonic-Concerto, op 37
Boucourechliev, André	1925–	Concerto (1974–75)
Boulez, Pierre	1926–	*Symphonie concertante* (1947), 2 pnos *Repons* (ca. 1982), 2 pnos
Brenet, Thérèse	1935–	*Concerto pour un Poeme Inconnu* (pub 1968) *Fragor,* 2 pnos
Canteloube, Joseph	1879–1957	*Pièces françaises* (1934–35)
Capdenat, Philippe	1934–	*Concerto Italien* (1969–70), pno, cel, org
Capdevielle, Pierre	1906–1969	*Conc del Dispetto* (1959)
Casanova, André	1919–	Concertino, op 8 (1952)
Casinière, Yves de la	1897–1971	Symphony no 2 (1930)
Castéra, René de	1873–1955	Concerto, fl, cl, vc, pno
Castérède, Jacques	1926–	2 Concertos (1954/70) Conc "Images pour un jour d'étè" (1969), 2 pnos
Cecconi-Botella, Monic	1909–	Concerto
Chardon, Julien	1909–	Concerto (1941)
Charpentier, Jacques	1933–	Concerto no 3 (1971), hpd Concerto no 4 (1971), pno
Chaynes, Charles	1925–	Concerto (1961)
Chretien-Genaro, Hedwige	1859–1944	*Danse Rustique, Soir d'Automne,* vn, pno or vc, pno *Source*
Ciry, Michel	1919–	Concerto (1948)
Cools, Eugène	1877–1936	*Symphonique Poem,* op 94
Coppola, Piero	1888–1971	*Poeme* Concerto no 4
Cotron, Fanou	1936–	Suite *concertante* (1959)

Table 28 Additional Composers in France—Continued

Names	Dates	Compositions
d'Ollone, Max	1875–1959	*Fantasie* (1899)
Damase, Jean-Michel	1928–	2 Concertos (1949/62)
		Variations sur un Theme de Rameau (1962), hpd
		Rhapsodie de Printemps (1959)
Dandelot, Georges	1895–1975	2 Concertos (1932/51)
Dautremer, Marcel	1906–	Double Concerto (1961), fl, pno
Debussy, Claude	1862–1918	*Fantasie* (1889–90)
Delerue, Georges	1925–	Concertino
Delmas, Marc	1885–1931	*Le Bateau Ivre* (perf 1923)
Delune, Louis	1876–1940	Concerto
Déré, Jean	1886–1970	*3 Esquisses*
Dervaux, Pierre	1917–	Concerto
Desportes, Yvonne	1907–	2 concertos (1957/60)
Doire, René	1879–1959	*Dramatico* (1923)
Doyen, Albert	1882–1935	*Suite Russe* (pub 1926)
Dumas, Louis	1877–1952	*Fantasie*
Dupont, Jacque	1906–	Concerto, op 2 (1932)
		Fantasie, op 20
		Concertino
Dupré, Marcel	1886–1971	*Fantasie,* op 8 (1912)
Fédorov, Vladimir	1901–1979	Concerto (1928)
Ferrand-Teulet, Denise	1921–	Concerto (1957)
Flem, Paul Le	1881–	*Fantasie* (1911)
France, Jeanne	1898–	Concerto
François, Samson	1924–1970	Concerto (1950)
Gaillard, Marius-François	1900–1973	*Images d'Epinal* (1929)
		Tombeau Romantique (1954)
Gallo, Gérard	? –	Concerto
Gallois-Montbrun, Raymond	1918–	Concerto (1964)
Gallon, Noël	1891–1966	*Fantasie* (1909)
Gartenlaub, Odette	1922–	Concertino
Gédale, André	1856–1926	Concerto, op 16 (1899)
Goeffray, César	1901–1972	Concerto (1966), hpd
Golestan, Stan	1875–1956	Concerto "Sur les Cimes Carpathiques" (1938)
Gradstein, Alfred	1904–1954	Concerto (1929), unfin
Grassi, Eugene	1881–1941	*Les Equinoxes*
Grovlez, Gabriel	1879–1944	*Fantasia Iberica* (1941)
Gruenwald, Jean-Jacques	1911–	Concerto (1940)
		Concert d'été (1944)
Guillou, Jean	1930–	Concerto (1970)
Guinjoán, Juan	1931–	Concerto (1963)
Harsányi, Tibor	1898–1954	*Concertstück* (1930)
		Concertino (pub 1932)
Hartmann, Thomas	1885–1956	Concerto, op 61 (1940)
Hossein, André	1907–	3 Concs (pub 1957/58/74)
Houdy, Pierick	1929–	Concerto (1961), pno or hpd
Hugon, Georges	1904–1980	Concerto (1962)
Huré, Jean	1877–1930	Nocturne (1908)

Table 28 Additional Composers in France—Continued

Names	Dates	Compositions
Husa, Karel	1921–	Concertino, op 10 (1949–50)
Jarre, Maurice	1924–	*Polyphonies concertantes* (1959), pno, tr
Jolas, Betsy	1926–	*Stances* (1978)
Joly, Suzanne	1916–	*Fantasie concertante* (1944–46)
Kartum, Leon	1895–	*Poème Rhapsodie*
Keller, Ginette	1925–	Concerto (1962–63)
Koechlin, Charles	1867–1950	*Ballade,* op 50 (1911–15)
Kullman, Alfred	? –	*Poéme Concertante*
Labey, Marcel	1875–1968	*Poeme*
Lalauni, Lila	1918–1952	2 Concertos
Landowska, Wanda	1897–1959	Cadenzas, Mozart conc & Haydn conc
Landowskii, Marcel	1915–	*Poeme* (Conc no 1, 1938–40)
		Concerto no. 2 (1963)
Langlais, Jean	1907–	Concerto (1936),pno
		Conc (1949), org or hpd
Lantier, Pierre	1910–	Concerto (pub 1953)
		Concertino (pub 1954)
		Concertinetto (pub 1960)
Laparra, Raoul	1876–1943	*Un Dimanche Basque*
Larmanjat, Jacques	1878–1952	Divertissement (1927)
		Fantasie Romantique (1932)
Lavagne, André	1913–	*Concert dans un Parc* (1941)
Lazarus, Daniel	1898–1964	Concerto (1928)
Lazzari, Sylvio	1857–1944	*Concertstück*
Leleu, Jeanne	1898–1980	Suite *Symphonique* (1925)
		Concerto (1935)
Lenot, Jacques	1945–	Concerto (1975)
Lesur, Daniel	1908–	*Passacaille* (1937)
		Variations (1943)
		Concerto da Camera (1953)
Litaize, Gaston	1909–	Concertino (1937)
Loudova, Ivana	1941–	Partita (1975)
Mache, François-Bernard	1935–	*Rambaramb* (1972)
Manen, Christian	1934–	Concertino (pub 1968)
Manziarly, Marcelle de	1899–	Concerto (1933)
		Incidences (1966)
Marcel, Luc-André	1919–	3 Concertos (1967/67/70)
Mariotte, Antonine	1875–1944	*Kakemonos*
Markevich, Igor	1912–1983	Concerto (1929)
		Partita (1930)
Martelli, Henri	1895–1980	Concerto, op 56 (1948)
		Fantasie sur un Théme Malgache (1945)
Martinet, Jean-Louis	1912–	*Mouvement Symphonique* no 4 (1955)
		Divertissement Pastoral (1966)
Martinon, Jean	1910–1976	*Symphoniette,* op 16 (1936)
Massenet, Jules	1842–1912	Concerto (1903)
Massias, Gerard	1933–	*Concert Bref* (1956)
Maticic, Janez	1926–	Concerto (1965)
Maurice, Paule	1910–1967	2 Concertos (1950/55)
		Suite

Table 28 Additional Composers in France—Continued

Names	Dates	Compositions
Mawet, Lucien	1875–1947	Suite *Symphonique*
Méfano, Paul	1937–	*Incidences* (1960)
Mel-Bonis, (Melanie)	1858–1937	Fantasy
Ménil, Félicien de	1860–1930	Espero (1928)
Meynaud, Michel	1950–	2 Concs (no 1, 1977–78)
Mirouze, Marcel	1906–1957	Concerto (1948)
Moreau, Léon	1870–1946	Concerto (1899)
Nat, Yves	1890–1956	Concerto (1953)
Noogaard, Per	1932–	Concerto, op 21 (ca. 1957)
Paray, Paul	1886–1979	Fantasy (1909)
		Fantasy (1923)
Pascal, Claude	1921–	Concerto (1958)
Passani, Emile	1905–1974	*Rhapsodie Provençale* (1939)
Petit, Pierre	1922–	Concertino
		Concerto
Philippart, Renée	1905–	*Three Preludes* (1938), 2 pnos
Pinchard, Max	1928–	Concerto, hpd
Ple-Caussade, Simone	1897–	Concerto, pno, tr, vn
Presle, Jacques de L.	1888–1969	Concerto (1949)
Pugno, Raoul	1852–1914	*Concertstück* (pub 1900)
Quef, Charles	1873–1931	Fantasie (1912)
Rabaud, Henri	1873–1949	Prelude and Toccata (1945)
Rhené-Baton	1879–1940	Variations (*Sun un Mode Éolien*), op 4 (1902)
Richapin, Elaine	1919–	*Fantasie*
Robert, Lucie	1936–	2 Concertos (1961/63)
		Divertissement (1966)
		Double Conc (perf 1969), pno, alto sax
Rogalski, Theodor	1901–1954	*2 Romanian Dances* (1925), pno duet
Roger, Roger	1911–	Jazz Concerto
		"Concerto Romantique" (pub 1974)
Roget, Henriette	1910–	*Concerto da Camera* (1934)
		Sinfonia *Andovana* (1938)
		Concerto Sicilien (1943)
Rokseth, Yvonne	1890–1958	*Fantasie "La Latiére et le Pot au Lait"* (1922), 2 pnos
Rollin, Jean	1906–1977	Concerto (1947)
Roos, Robert de	1907–1976	*5 Etudes* (1929)
		Concerto (1943–44)
Samuel-Rousseau, Marcel	1882–1955	*Variations a Danser* (1916)
Sancan, Pierre	1916–	Cadenzas (1948), Mozart Conc, K.466
		2 Concertos (1955/63)
		Concertino (1967)
Sarnette, Eric	1898–	Concerto, 2 pnos
Schmitt, Florent	1870–1958	Symphonic *concertante,* op 82 (1928–31)
Schulé, Bernard	1900–	Concertino, op 88 (1971)
Siohan, Robert	1894–	Concerto, op 15 (1939)
Spitzmueller, Alexander	1894–1962	2 Concertos (1937/53)
Sutter, Toussaint de	1889–1959	Concerto
Swanson, Howard	1907–1978	Concerto (1956)
Tessier, Roger	1939–	Suite *concertante* (1969), fl, pno

Table 28 Additional Composers in France—Continued

Names	Dates	Compositions
Theodorakis, Mikis	1925–	Suite no 1 (1954)
		Concerto (1958)
Thiriet, Maurice	1906–1972	Concerto, unfin
Tisne, Antoine	1932–	3 Concertos (1958/61/63)
		A une Ombre (1972)
Tournier, Franz	1923–	Concerto
Vantoura, Suzanne	1912–	*Rhapsodie Israelienne*
Vaubourgoin, Marc	1907–	Concerto (1947)
Vierne, Louis	1870–1937	*Poem,* op 5 (1925)
Vieu, Jane	1871–	*Colombine, Air de Ballet*
		Griserie de Caresses, Valse Chantee
		Ivresse des Parfums, Valse
		Marquis Bergers, Chanson Louis XV
		Nymphes et Papillons
		Tarantelle
Weber, Alain	1930–	Concertino (1961)
Werner, Jean-Jacques	1935–	3 Concertos (1960/62, pub 1963)
Will, Madeleine	1910–	Divertissements
		Concertino, hpd
Wissmer, Pierre	1915–	3 Concertos (1937/47/72)
		Concertino Crosière (1966), fl, pno

style influenced by Debussy and Ravel, he composed the concerto (1954), the rhapsodie (1956), the concerto-*fantasie* (1966–1967) for two pianos, and the berceuse and rondo (pub. 1968).

René Koering (1940–) studied with Boulez, Maderna, and Stockhausen, and has been teaching at the *Ecole des Beaux Arts* since 1969. He composed the *Triple et Trajectoires* (1965) for piano and two orchestras with two conductors; the *Combat T3N* (1970) with the pianist playing the strings inside the piano; and the *Jeuz et Enchantements* (pub. 1974).

Switzerland

Emanuel Moór (1863–1931), Hungarian pianist, composer, and inventor, actively composed until about 1916, when he turned to the development and production of the double-keyboard, which he first called the duplex-coupler pianoforte (1921). The instrument increased the possibilities for wider sonorities than a conventional piano, and simplified some technical problems, such as chords spanning wide intervals and hand crossings. The instrument had two keyboards similar to a two-manual harpsichord or organ and pedals coupled the two keyboards. Moór's wife Winifred Christie-Moór, an accomplished pianist, devoted much of her life to promoting the instrument before abandoning the effort in 1941.

Moór's published works have opus numbers and the unpublished compositions have catalog numbers in Max Pirani's book *Emanuel Moór.*[1] He composed the two concertos, nos. 164 and 171 (both 1886), in the United States, and two concertos, opp. 46A and 57 (1888, 1893), in England. The concerto, op. 57, is Moór's most frequently performed work for piano and orchestra. In or near Lausanne, Switzerland, Moór composed the triple concerto, op. 70 (1907), for violin, piano, and cello; the concerto, op. 85 (1908); two *concertstücks,* opp. 88A and 113 (1909, 1910); the concerto, no. 183 (1911), for piano and violin; the rhapsody, no. 143B (1912); and two suites, nos. 170 and 175 (both 1914).

Joseph Lauber (1864–1952) studied at the Music School of Zürich, in Munich with Rheinberger and in Paris with Massenet and Diémer, and taught at the Zürich Conservatory. His musical influences are Massenet and other French composers of the late nineteenth century. He left at least two piano concertos.

Emile Blanchet (1877–1943) studied with Busoni in Weimar and Berlin and taught at the Lausanne Conservatory. He left the *konzertstück,* op. 14 (pub. 1912), and the *ballade* scored by Ansermet.

Fritz Brun (1878–1959) studied in Lucerne and Cologne and lived in Berlin, London, Dortmund, and Bern, where he taught at the conservatory and conducted the symphony orchestra. Brahms and Bruckner influenced his music. The *Variationen über ein Eigenes Thema* (1944) comes from his teaching years, and after retirement, he composed the concerto (1946).

Volkmar Andreae (1879–1962) settled in Zürich in 1902 as a conductor, composer, and administrator. His concerto (perf. 1898) and *konzertstück* (perf. 1900) are in a romantic style influenced by R. Strauss.

Henri Gagnebin (1886–1977) studied with Vierne and d'Indy at the *Schola Cantorum* in Paris, worked as a church organist in Paris and Lausanne, and directed the Geneva Conservatory. He liked the classic ideas and stylistic features of Franck, d'Indy, and Stravinsky. He left the concerto (1951), the *fantaisie* (1960), and the concerto, op. 57.

Frederick Hay (1888–1945) studied medicine and then music with Huber in Basel, with Widor in Paris, and with Schalk in Vienna, and taught musicology at the University of Geneva. His musical compositions include the *Notturno, Intermezzo e Capriccio* for piano and woodwind orchestra, and a number of piano concertos.

Emil Frey (1889–1946) studied with Fauré and Widor in Paris and taught at the Imperial Conservatory (now the Moscow Conservatory) until the 1917 revolution forced his return to Zürich, where he joined the faculty at the conservatory. For piano and orchestra, he composed the concerto, op. 17, two *konzertstücks,* opp. 24 and 60, and the capriccio, op. 78, with chamber orchestra.

Aloys Fornerod (1890–1965) studied at the Lausanne Conservatory and the *Schola Cantorum* in Paris. While on the theory faculty at the *Institut de Ribaupierre,* he composed the concerto, op. 29 (1943–1944).

Frank Martin (1890–1974) composed music that blends Schoenberg's twelve-tone method with tonality, chromaticism, and quartal, quintal, and hybrid chords. He felt a musical kinship with classic and romantic compositional practices and contemporary techniques such as frequent meter changes, ostinatos, and Stravinsky-like irregular accents. Some compositions show thematic development on a small scale, with a motive expanded in various ways.

Martin studied in Geneva, Rome, and Paris, and taught at the Institute Jaques-Dalcroze in Geneva. He founded and directed the *Technicum Moderne de Musique* and moved to the Netherlands and, simultaneously, took a teaching post at the *Hochschule für Musik* in Cologne, Germany.

Martin composed the concerto no. 1 (1934) using romantic influences and the twelve-tone method, the *ballade* (1938) for piano, saxophone, and strings, the *ballade* (1939), and the highly acclaimed *Petite Symphonie Concertant* (1944–1945). In Cologne, Amsterdam, or Naarden he composed a concerto (1952) for harpsichord that has an unusual passage for the right hand in the harpsichord part accompanied by cello, bass, and viola, with the clarinet given melodic material. Possibly, he composed the concerto no. 2 (1968–1969) in the Netherlands.

John Hilber (1891–1973), church musician, critic, and editor for *Der Chorwachter,* composed the concerto (1915) in Stans and the concertino (1933) in Lucerne.

Rudolf Moser (1892–1960) settled in Basel after studying theology at Basel University and musicology at the Leipzig Conservatory. His religious training and work as a choir master at the Basel Cathedral kindled an interest in combining old forms and ecclesiastical modes with contemporary techniques. Possibly, he composed the concerto, op. 61 (1934), while on the conservatory faculty.

Werner Wehrli (1892–1944) taught music at the *Lehrerseminar* from 1918. The sinfonietta, op. 20 (1921), is for flute, piano, and string orchestra.

Walter Lang (1896–1966) studied with Jaques-Dalcroze and taught at the Jaques-Dalcroze Institute, the Wolff Conservatory in Basel, and the Zürich Conservatory. The main influences on his music are Bartók, late romanticism, and neo-classicism. He composed the concerto, op. 34 (1940), the etude-caprice, op. 49 (1947), and the *konzertante suite,* op. 65 (1954), for two pianos and strings.

Walther Geiser (1897–) studied and later taught violin, counterpoint and composition at the Basel Conservatory. He writes music in a neo-baroque style influenced by his teacher Busoni at the Berlin Academy of Arts. He composed the fantasy no. 1, op. 31 (1942), for piano, strings and timpani, the *Concerto da Camera,* op. 50 (1957), for two violins, harpsichord, and strings, and the concerto, op. 53 (1959).

Albert Moeschinger (1897–), teacher at the Bern Conservatory, composed music influenced by German neo-romanticism and French impressionism. He composed more than 100 opus numbers, including at least four piano concertos: op. 18 (1929) with chamber orchestra is the same as op. 77, with large orchestra; op. 23 (1930) with chamber orchestra; op. 42 (1938) with string orchestra; and op. 96 (1953). There may be another piano concerto (1970).

Roger Vuataz (1898–) trained with Jaques-Dalcroze and Otto Barblan at the Geneva Conservatory, worked as a church organist, music critic, staff member at Radio Geneva, and taught at the conservatory. His concerto, op. 112 (1963–1964), is neo-classic with expanded tonality and impressionistic colors.

Walter Müller (1899–1967) directed the Basel Conservatory. He composed the *Musik,* op. 24 (1931), for string orchestra, harpsichord, violin, and viola; the *Overture im Alten Stil,* op. 29 (1933), for string orchestra and piano; and the concertino, op. 83 (1965).

Hans Haug (1900–1967) studied with Petri and Levy in Basel and Busoni at the Munich Academy of Music. He seems to have been in Lausanne when composing the two concertos (1938, 1962) and a concertino. In 1947, he wrote an orchestral part for Chopin's rondo, op. 73.

Robert Oboussier (1900–1957) used the neo-classicism of Busoni, contrapuntal techniques, atonality, and polytonality. Possibly, he composed the concerto (1932–1933, rev. 1944) in Paris. He lived in Switzerland and directed the Central Archive of Swiss Music. He composed the concerto (1952–1953), cadenzas for Mozart's concerto, K.467, and two cadenzas for Haydn's concerto, Hob.XVIII:9.

Conrad Beck (1901–) studied at the Zürich Conservatory and in Paris with Honegger and Lévy. He writes music in a neo-classic style with considerable counterpoint and influences of Roussel and Honegger. He composed the concertino (1927) in Paris. In 1932, he moved to Basel and conducted for Radio Basel from 1939. Other compositions are the concerto (1933), the *rhapsodie* (1936) for piano, four woodwinds, and strings, and the chamber concerto (1942) for harpsichord and string orchestra.

Bernhard Reichel (1901–) taught at the *Institut Jaques Dalcroze* and played organ at the *Tempe des Eaux-Vives*. Besides church music, he composed the concertino (1949), the concerto (1961) for harpsichord and small orchestra, and the concerto, op. 68.

André-François Marescotti (1902–) studied at the Geneva Conservatory and in Paris, directed choir, and taught at the conservatory from 1931. His concerto (1956) has some twelve-tone features, atonality, and neo-classic elements.

Rudolf Wittelsbach (1902–1972) studied at the Zürich Conservatory, studied piano with Casadesus in Paris and Schnabel in Berlin, and studied composition with Hindemith. The concerto (1937–1941, rev. 1962) displays an influence of Debussy, Ravel, Hindemith, and Stravinsky.

Will Eisenmann (1906–) taught music and worked in drama and stage management. Since 1952, he has lived in Lucerne, where he composed the concerto (1953) for piano and string orchestra.

Peter Mieg (1906–) is a pianist, writer for several Swiss and foreign newspapers and magazines, and successful painter. His compositional style follows his teacher Martin, Bartók, and Stravinsky, and he likes polyphonic textures, chromaticism, and bright sounds. He has the concerto (1941) for two pianos, two concertos (1947, 1961) for one piano, the *Concerto da Camera* (1952) for strings, piano, and timpani, and the concerto (1956) for harpsichord or piano.

Hans Schaeuble (1906–) follows the styles of Hindemith, Stravinsky, Bartók, Martin, and the twelve-tone method. He composed the concerto (1931), the capriccio, op. 30 (1946), the *sinfonisch-konzertante variationen,* op. 33 (1949), for string orchestra with piano obbligato, and two concertos, opp. 34 and 50 (1949, 1967).

Franz Brenn (1907–1963) was in Basel or Lucerne when he composed the symphony, op. 7 (1938), for orchestra and two *concertante* pianos.

Sandor Veress (1907–), Hungarian pianist, studied at the Budapest Royal Academy of Music with Bartók and Kodály, and went to Berlin in 1934. He worked with Bartók editing folk songs and taught at the Bern Conservatory. His work with Bartók and his research and travels through Modava learning regional folk music are shaping forces in his musical compositions. He has the concerto (1950–1952) and the *Hommage à Paul Klee* for two pianos and strings.

Heinrich Sutermeister (1910–), living on the north shore of Lake Geneva, attained recognition as an opera composer in the 1940s. He studied at the Sorbonne in Paris, at the Academy of Music in Munich, and joined the faculty at the Hanover *Musikhochschule*. For piano and orchestra, he composed three concertos (1942–1943, 1953, 1961), the *Marche Fantasque* (1950) for one-half piano, and the *Orzione per Orchestra* (1951).

Raffaele d'Alessandro (1911–1959) studied organ with Dupré, composition with Boulanger in Paris, and composed music in a tonal style with traditional forms. He left three concertos (1939, 1945, 1951), the concertino (1938), and the symphonietta (1944) for string orchestra with piano obbligato.

Hans Studer (1911–), composer of church music, was influenced by the Swiss composers Burkhard, Bartók, Hindemith, Stravinsky, and neo-classicism. He has the chamber concerto (1948) and the little concerto (1951) for piano duet, flute, and string orchestra.

Ernst Hess (1912–1968), authority on Mozart's music, helped found the Zürich *Mozart Geselschaft* and became the president of the *Zürich Allgemeine Musikgesellschaft*. His love of Mozart's music shows in the concertino, op. 48 (1957), for flute, violin, piano, and string orchestra, and the sinfonia *concertante,* op. 55 (1964), for violin and piano.

Nikita Magaloff (1912–), Russian-born student of Philipp at the Paris *Conservatoire,* is a noted interpreter of Chopin's music. Lipatti studied with him at the Geneva Conservatory. He wrote cadenzas for some Mozart concertos.

Hermann Haller (1914–) settled in Kusnacht after teaching at the Zürich Conservatory. His music draws from the baroque era and impressionism, and it includes two concertos (1959, 1962).

Julien-Francois Zbinden (1917–) was the assistant director of Radio Lausanne. He has the concerto, op. 3 (1944), the *Concerto da Camera,* op. 16 (1950–1951), for piano and string orchestra, and the *Concerto de Gibraltor* for piano and brass.

Robert Suter (1919–) taught at the conservatory. His *Kleines Concerto* (1948) is for piano and chamber orchestra.

Armin Schibler (1920–) studied with Rubbra and Tippett in England and at the Darmstadt summer courses. His music evidences Vivaldi and Bach as models and the twelve-tone method. He has the concertino, op. 4 (1943), the *Concerto 1959,* op. 59 (1959), for trumpet, horn, trombone, piano, harp, percussion, and double string orchestra, the concerto, op. 76 (1962–1963), and the concerto (1963) for piano, percussion, and string orchestra.

Jacques Wildberger (1922–) taught at the Bad Karlsruhe Academy of Music, Germany, and the Basel Academy of Music. About 1948, he adopted the twelve-tone method. His divertimento is a neo-classic work.

Rudolf Kelterborn (1931–) read musicology at Basel University and studied composition with Blacher in Salzburg. In 1960, he joined the faculty at the Music Academy in Detmold, and there he composed the concertino (1958–1959) for piano, percussion, and strings. In 1968, he returned to Switzerland to teach at the *Musikhochschule* in Zürich. The *Musik* (1970) is for piano and eight wind instruments. In 1975, he went to work with Basel Radio. He uses the twelve-tone method and serializes the durations of notes and tempos.

Table 29 Additional Composers in Switzerland

Names	Dates	Compositions
Ansermet, Ernest	1883–1963	*Ballade*
Balmer, Luc	1898–	Concertino (1956)
		Concerto
Blume, Robert	1900–	Concerto
Brunner, Adolf	1901–	Partita (1938–39)
Burkhard, Willy	1900–1955	Concertino, op 94 (1954), 2 fls, hpd
David, Karl	1884–1951	2 Concertos (one 1929)
Denzler, Robert	1892–1972	Concerto
Ermatinger, Erhart	1900–1966	Concerto, op 4 (pub ca. 1922)
Flury, Richard	1896–1967	2 Concertos (1927/43)
		Concerto (1940), vn, pno
Futterer, Carl	1873–1927	Concerto (1927)
Gerber, René	1908–	2 Concertos (1933/66–70
Kuhn, Max	1896–	*Concierto de Tenerife*
Kunz, Ernst	1891–	Concerto (1929)
Leutwiler, Toni	1923–	*Fantasia Romantica,* op 56 (pub 1954)
		Gnomentanz, op 91 (pub 1957)
		Konzert (pub 1957)
		Reminiscence (1966)
Nussio, Otmar	1902–	*Rubensiana* (perf 1950), hpd, fl, vn
		Concerto *Classico* (1955) hpd or pno
		Concerto (1960)
Pfister, Hugo	1914–1969	*Concertanti* (1954)
Roger, Denise	1924–	Concerto (1962)
Ryterband, Roman	1914–1979	Concertino
		Toccata, hpd
Schulthess, Walter	1894–1971	Concerto
Tischhauser, Franz	1921–	Concertino (1945)
Wendel, Martin	1925–	Concerto, vn, pno
		Drei Konzertante Skizzen, pno, fl
		Musik

Jacques Guyonnet (1933–) trained at the Geneva Conservatory and with Boulez at Darmstadt. In 1959, he established the *Studio de Musique Contemporaine* and taught at the conservatory. *En 3 Eclats*! (1964) is for piano and chamber orchestra.

Jurg Wyttenbach (1935–), piano teacher at the Berne Conservatory, composes in a style influenced by Bartók and Stravinsky. He has the concerto (1963–1964, rev. 1966) and the *Divisions* (1964) for piano and nine solo strings, plus a version (1965) for piano and string orchestra.

Notes

1. Max Pirani, *Emanuel Moor* (London: P. R. MacMillan, 1959).

Chapter 12

Spain and Portugal

Spain

Emilio Serrano y Ruiz (1850–1939) studied at the Madrid Conservatory and joined its faculty. Through various musical posts, he exerted a powerful influence on Madrid's musical life. He left a concerto (1924).

Joaquin Cassadó (1867–1926) directed choir at the *Basilica of Nuestra Señora de la Merced,* played organ in San José, and established the chorus *Capilla Catalana* (1890). He left the *Hispania* (*Fantasia Española,* 1911) and a concerto.

Enrique Granados (1867–1916) composed music displaying romantic and Spanish idioms. The *Elisende* (ca. 1910) is a suite based on a poem by Granados' librettist Apeles Mestre. Granados orchestrated Chopin's concerto no. 2.

Eduardo Lopez-Chavarri (1871–1970) taught and conducted at the Valencia Conservatory. For piano and orchestra, he composed the *Rapsodia Valenciana;* the concerto *Espanol* with string orchestra; the *Concierto Breve* with chamber orchestra; the *Concierto Hispanico;* and the *Rapsodia de Pascua* (concertino).

Manuel de Falla (1876–1946) began the *Nights in the Gardens of Spain* "Impressions Symphoniques" (1911–1915) in Paris, where he enjoyed the friendship and encouragement of Debussy, Ravel, and Dukas. The French influence on the *Gardens* is the parallel chords, unresolved dissonances, piano writing similar to the technical demands in the piano music of Debussy and Ravel, and colorful orchestrations reminiscent of Debussy, Ravel, and Dukas. The Spanish character comes from Falla's use of Andalusian folk music. The original idea was a set of nocturnes for solo piano, but the Spanish pianist Ricardo Viñes convinced Falla to write for piano and orchestra. After leaving Paris in 1914 due to political events, Falla worked on the *Gardens* in Madrid and Barcelona, and finished it in Sitges while visiting the Spanish painter Santiago Rusiñol.

Nights in the Gardens of Spain contains three movements with descriptive titles. "En el Generalife" depicts the Moorish palace gardens in Alhambra. Titles of other movements are "Danze Lejana" and "En los Jardins de la Sierra de Córdoba." While the titles suggest programmatic intent, the music follows the French impressionistic practice of vague musical gestures. Falla wrote that the orchestration has "certain effects peculiar to popular instruments" of Andalusia, and at times the entire orchestra sounds like a guitar.

Simultaneously with Falla's work on *Gardens,* the Spanish composer Amades Vives composed a zarzuela, a Spanish musical composition. While the two composers worked on their respective compositions in the same neighborhood, a blind violinist played out-of-tune melodies in a location where each composer could hear him. The violin melodies influenced Falla and Vives.

Falla's concerto (1923–1926), for harpsichord (or piano), flute, oboe, clarinet, violin, and cello treats each instrument as a solo. However, the harpsichord has the most important role. The composition is a product of the revival of harpsichord music due to Wanda Landowska's encouragement. The musical style is similar to Stravinsky's *The Soldier's Tale* and some elements suggest an influence of D. Scarlatti. Textures vary between harsh and sensuous. An important source for the melodic material is the fifteenth- or sixteenth-century song *De Los Almos Vengo, Madre* (I Come From the Poplar Wood, Mother) by Juan Vázquez. The song appears three times in the first movement, with the last time in augmentation in the oboe, violin, and cello parts. The same musical material appears in the opening of the second movement and the main theme of the third movement, where meters alternate between 3/4 and 6/8, relating to the toccata-like figure in the first movement.

Conrado del Campo (1878–1953) taught at the Madrid Conservatory, where he became the most important composition teacher in Spain. R. Strauss, Wagner, Spanish nationalism, and folk songs and scales influenced his music. For piano and orchestra, he composed the *Evocación de Castilla* (1931) and the *Fantasia Castellana* (1939).

Joaquin Turina (1882–1949) studied with Tragó at the Madrid Conservatory and with d'Indy at the *Schola Cantorum* in Paris and worked with Debussy, Ravel, and Schmitt. Turina and Falla are in the generation of Spanish composers after Albénz and Granados. His compositions feature a personalized use of Andalusian and Sevillian music. The one-movement rhapsody *sinfonica,* op. 66 (1931), has a strong Spanish flavor. The concerto, op. 88 (1935), erroneously appears in some sources as having orchestra accompaniment; it is for solo piano.

Juan Manén (1883–1971) settled in Germany in 1908 as a successful concert pianist. The *Juventus,* op. 5, is a *concerto grosso* for two violins and piano. The suite, op. 22 (pub. 1889), is in a copy as op. A-1. The concerto, op. A-13, is the concerto *symphonique* in some copies. The significance of the letter "A" could not be determined. He composed the *rapsodia catalana* (1968) at age 85.

Oscar Esplá (1886–1976) was the first president of the *Junta Nacional de Musica* and a teacher at the Madrid Conservatory. He developed his own musical scale, and was influenced by the native Spanish music found along the Mediterranean coast and the Debussy and Stravinsky scale. He composed the *musica instrumental* (1940) and the *Sonata del Sur,* op. 52 (1943–1945), influenced by Spanish music and Ravel.

Manuel Palau (1893–1967) taught at the Valencia Conservatory. His musical style uses Mediterranean folk music, polytonality, atonality, and modality. He composed the *Valencia* (1936) and the *concierto dramatico* (1946).

Manuel Blancafort (1897–) was a traveling representative for the Victoria piano-roll company founded by his father. Influences on his music are Catalan musical elements, *Les Six,* impressionism, Stravinsky, and modern techniques. For piano and orchestra, he composed the *concerto omaggio* (1944) and the *concierto ibérico* (1946).

Salvador Bacarisse (1898–1963) helped lead the *Grupo de los Ocho* along a musical path similar to *Les Six* in Paris. His early works display harsh dissonance and polytonality, and later compositions show a neo-romantic leaning influenced by traditional Spanish music. He composed the concertino (1929), the *balada* (1935–1936), three piano concertos (1933, 1957, 1958), and the harpsichord concerto (1962). In 1939, he settled in Paris due to political conditions in Spain.

Rodolfo Halffter (1900–) joined *Grupo de los Ocho* to promote traditional Spanish musical characteristics. After settling in Mexico in 1939, he founded *Ediciones Mexicanas de Musica,* edited the journal *Nuestra Musica,* and directed the music department at the National Institute of Fine Arts. The overture *concertante,* op. 5 (1932), is a product of Halffter's years in Madrid.

Joaquin Rodrigo (1902–), student of Dukas in Paris, held the Manuel de Falla Chair created for him at the Madrid University. Spanish folk music influenced his compositions. The *Concierto Heróico* (1941–1942) musically describes aspects of the heroic character without having specific programatic elements. The second movement is a scherzo set in an uncharacteristic duple meter instead of the traditional triple meter.

Javier Alfonso (1904–) studied and later taught at the Madrid Conservatory. He studied piano with Cortot at the *École Normale de Musique* in Paris, pursued a career as a concert pianist, and championed the music of Bartók. He composed the *concierto-fantasia* (1939).

José Valls (1904–) studied in Barcelona and with d'Indy and Roussel at the *Schola Cantorum* in Paris. His musical style merges renaissance polyphony, Gregorian chant, Catalan folk music, and contemporary techniques. His suite is for piano and strings.

Jose Munoz Molleda (1905–) studied with Campo in Madrid and teaches at the San Fernando Academy. Ravel, neo-romanticism, and Andalusian music influenced the concerto (1935).

Joaquin Homs (1906–), influenced by Catalan folk music, has the concertino (1946).

Gustavo Pittaluga (1906–), composition student of Esplá, stressed the value of music independent of nationalism or folk music. He composed the *capriccio alla romantica* (1936).

Federio Elizalde (1907–1979) studied at the Madrid Conservatory, where he received first prize in piano at age 14. During the 1920s and 1930s, he performed jazz in England. Falla influenced Elizalde's sinfonia *concertante* (ca. 1936) and the concerto (1947).

Xavier Montsalvatge (1912–) taught at the Barcelona Conservatory, wrote music criticism for the weekly *Destino,* followed the styles of *Les Six,* Stravinsky, and Catalan music, and used ninth and eleventh chords, polychords, and elements of jazz. He composed the *concerto breve* (1952) and the *concerto per un virtuose* (1977) for harpsichord.

Francisco Escudero (1913–) taught at the San Sebastian Conservatory from 1948. Falla, impressionism and Basque popular music influenced the *concierto vasco* (1947).

Manuel Valls (1920–) taught at the Adriá Gual School of Dramatic Arts and at Barcelona University. In a style influenced by *Les Six* and Catalan music, he composed the *estudios concertantes* (1958).

Ramón Barce (1928–), influenced by Messiaen and Ligeti, helped found the

Table 30 Additional Composers in Spain

Names	Dates	Compositions
Barbosa, Elena	1880–	*Balada de Castilla*
Blanco, Jose Pegro	? –1920	Concerto no 2
Gómez, Julio	1886–1973	*Concierto lirico* (1945)
Guridi, Jesú	1886–1961	Fantasia
Moreno Gans, José	1897–	Concerto
Pablo, Luis de	1930–	Concerto (1956), hpd
Remacha, Fernando	1898–	*Rapsodia de Estella* (1958)
Villa, Ricardo	1873–1935	Fantasia *Espanola*

New Music Group and the *Zaj* to promote contemporary music. From 1967, he composed music using his personal system of chords based on levels of harmony related to polar notes. He has the concerto (1971).

Manuel Castillo (1930–), influenced by French music and folk music around Seville, has two concertos (1958, 1966).

Cristóbal Halffter (1930–) studied with Tansman in Paris, taught at the Madrid Conservatory, worked at *Radio Nacional de Espana,* and conducted the Falla Orchestra. Early works show the influence of Falla and music from the mid-1960s displays an avant-garde style with dodecaphonic techniques. For piano and orchestra, Halffter composed the concerto (1953), the *rhapsodie Española de de Albéniz* (1960), the *Tiempo para Espacios* (1974) for harpsichord and twelve strings, and the *Procesional* (1973–1974) for two pianos, winds, and percussion.

Xavier Benguerel (1931–), influenced by French impressionism, has the concerto (1955).

José Soler (1935–), teacher at the Barcelona Conservatory, composes music that blends techniques from the fourth through fourteenth centuries, serialism and rhythmic ideas of Messiaen and Bartók. The concerto (1969) is for piano and the concerto (1969) is for harpsichord with a small ensemble of oboe, English horn, bass clarinet, viola, and cello.

Cecily Foster (? –) studied with Casella in Rome and Boulanger in Paris, and was a close friend of Falla. Among her musical compositions is a concertino.

Portugal

Lucien Lambert (1858–1945) studied at the Paris *Conservatoire* with Dubois and Massenet and joined the composition faculty at the Oporto Conservatory in 1914. He probably composed *Les Cloches de Porto* (1912) in Paris, and the *Andante et Fantaisie Tzigane* and a concerto in Oporto.

Luis Freitas Branco (1890–1955) studied in Berlin with Humperdinck and in

Paris. From 1916, he taught at the Lisbon Conservatory, where he influenced an entire generation of Portuguese composers and established a distinctive Portuguese symphonic style. The *balada* (1917) is for piano and orchestra.

Ruy Coelho (1891–) studied in Lisbon with Humperdinck, with Bruch and Schoenberg in Germany, and in Paris. He championed Portuguese music by drawing upon its folk music. Elements of folk music are in the two concertos (1909, 1948), the *Noites nas Ruas da Mouraria* (Nights in the Streets of Mouraria, 1943), which is similar to Falla's *Nights in the Gardens of Spain,* and the *Rapsódia Portugueza.*

Claudio Carneyro (1895–1963) studied with Lambert at the Oporto Conservatory and in Paris with Widor and Dukas. He returned to Oporto to teach at the conservatory. His music merges Portuguese musical heritage with impressionism he learned in Paris. He left the *Catavento* (1942).

Ivo Cruz (1901–) founded and conducted the Lisbon Philharmonic Orchestra and directed the National Conservatory. His two concertos, *Coimbra* (1945) and *Lisbon* (1946), appear as the symphonic poems *Coimbra* and *Lisbon* and the concertos *Português Coimbra* and *Lisbon.*

Maria Antonietta de Lima Cruz (1901–1957), musicologist, was a music critic with the daily newspaper *A Voz* and a curator for the Museum Instrumental and the library of the National Conservatory. She composed the *Poemas,* op. 19, and the *Ritmos Lusitanos,* op. 26.

Ernesto Halffter (1905–), brother of Rodolfo Halffter, studied with Falla and Adolfo Salazar who influenced his musical style. The *Rapsodia Portuguêsa* (1940, rev. 1951) evidences features of Ravel and Portuguese folk material.

Armando Fernandes (1906–) composed music mostly for the national broadcasting station. Popular music influenced the *Fantasia Sobre Temas Populare Portuguêses* (1945), the concerto (1952), and the *suite concertante* (1967) for harpsichord and chamber orchestra.

Fernando Lopes-Garça (1906–) is an important Portuguese composer whose style contains elements of Falla, Stravinsky, Schoenberg, Bartók, and Iberian folk music. For piano and orchestra, he composed two concertos (1940, 1942), the concertino (1954), and the fantasia (1974) based on a religious song.

Jorge Croner de Vasconcelos (1910–1974) studied with Dukas, Boulanger, and Cortot in Paris, and taught piano at the Lisbon Conservatory. He left the suite *concertante.*

Joly Braga Santos (1924–), important contributor to Portuguese symphonic style, follows the musical ideas of his teacher Branco. He was the assistant conductor with the Portuguese National Symphony Orchestra. The concerto (1973) is in a neoclassic style with cyclic elements.

Filipe Pires (1934–) studied at the Lisbon Conservatory and at the Darmstadt summer courses. He composed the *Mobiles* (1968–1969) while on the faculty at the Oporto Conservatory.

Alvaro Cassuto (1938–) studied composition with Ligeti, Messiaen, and Stockhausen, and conducting with von Karajan. He conducted in Lisbon and New York, and taught in Lisbon and Irvine, Calif. He probably composed the concertino (1964) in Lisbon, Hamburg, or Vienna.

Candido Lima (1939–) taught at the Oporto Conservatory. The *Epitáfio para Franz Kafka* (1970) is for orchestra with piano obbligato.

Jorge Peixinho (1940–) studied with Webern, Boulez, Nono, and Stockhausen, and now leads Portuguese avant-garde music. He may have started the *Diafonia* (1963–1965) in Basel, Switzerland, and possibly finished it in Lisbon; some sources list the composition as *Diafonia* 2.

Chapter 13

The Netherlands, Denmark, Belgium, and Luxemburg

The Netherlands

Willem Landré (1874–1948) edited music for the *Nieuwe Roterdamsche Courant* and taught at the Rotterdam Conservatory. He is one of the earliest Dutch composers to adopt French musical style, as opposed to German teachings. He left the romantic concerto (1935).

Henri Zagwijn (1878–1954) was a self-taught composer who followed impressionism and contemporary French music. From 1916, he taught at the Rotterdam Academy of Music and joined the faculty at the Rotterdam Conservatory in 1931. He composed two *concertantes* (1939, 1946) and the concerto (1939).

Sem Dresden (1881–1957) studied with Pfitzner at the Stern Conservatory in Berlin, and taught at the Amsterdam Conservatory and the Royal Conservatory at the Hague. His music displays influences of German neo-romanticism, impressionism, and Dutch music. From 1935 to 1950, he composed many pieces for solo instruments and orchestra, including at least two piano concertos (no. 2, 1942–1946).

Daniel Ruyneman (1886–1963) helped establish the Society of Modern Dutch Composers. While a student, he had an international reputation as one of the boldest young Dutch composers, and his studies of Javanese music brought exotic sonorities to many of his compositions. He left a concerto (1939).

Willem Andriessen (1887–1964) studied at the Amsterdam Conservatory and later directed the institution. His concerto (1908) is a student work and he wrote cadenzas to Beethoven's concerto nos. 3 and 4. He was the finest Dutch pianist of his day.

Johanna Bordewijk-Roepman (1892–1971), mainly a composer of choral and carillon music, lived in or near Rotterdam. His concerto (1940) is in a late romantic style.

Oscar van Hemel (1892–1981) was influenced by the neo-romanticism of the German and Austrian symphonic composers, Pijper, and dodecaphonic techniques late in life. He composed the concerto (1941–1942) in Bergen op Zoom and the divertimento (1974) in Hilversum.

Willem Pijper (1894–1947) is the most important Dutch composer of the first half of this century. Up to 1920, his style had elements of Brahms, Mahler, Fauré, and Debussy, and from 1920 on he followed the "germ-cell theory" he evolved after reading biological documents on germ cells. In Pijper's germ-cell theory, the first chord or motive functions as the compositional source for all harmonic and melodic activity. His personal scale of alternating whole and half steps, known in the Netherlands as the

"Pijper scale," is in the music of Rimsky-Korsakoff. Another influence on Pijper is the polyphony of past Dutch contrapuntal composers. The *Orchestral Music with Pianoforte* (1915), originally titled concerto no. 1, is confused with the later and only concerto (1927). In 1940, the divertimento (1916) for strings and piano burned in a fire caused by war. Sometimes, the one-movement concerto (1927) in seven sections appears on lists as the concerto no. 2. The composition has polyrhythms, polymeters, and bitonality. He wrote the cadenza (1915) for a Beethoven concerto, and in 1923 he orchestrated one of Haydn's clavier concertos.

Henriette Rosmans (1895–1952), student of Dopper and Pijper, composed music influenced by neo-classicism and French impressionism. She probably intended the concertino (1928) and concerto (1929) for her own use as a pianist.

Alexander Voormolen (1895–1980) studied with Wagenaar at the Utrecht Conservatory and with Roussel in Paris and worked as a librarian at the Royal Conservatory in the Hague. His music has neo-classic and neo-baroque elements. The concerto (1950) for two harpsichords or pianos and orchestra is a contrapuntal work.

Marius Monnikendam (1896–1977) studied at the Amsterdam Conservatory and the *Schola Cantorum* in Paris, and taught composition at the Rotterdam Conservatory. He left the concerto (1973–1974).

Ignace Lilien (1897–1964) was a respected performer of mainly his own piano music. His concerto (1954) is for violin and piano.

Hugo Godron (1900–1971) taught in music schools in Amsterdam, Bussum, Hilversum, and Utrecht. His music includes the *7 Miniatures* (1933) for piano and strings; the concerto (1938–1939); the *Ambile Suite* (1943) for clarinet, piano, and small orchestra; the concert suite (1945–1947) for piano and string orchestra; the suite *Aubade Gaudeamus* (1966–1968) for piano, string orchestra, and percussion; the *Hommages Classiques* (1950) for flute, piano, and strings; and a concerto for harpsichord and orchestra. In 1949, Godron received a government prize for the concert suite.

Emile Enthoven (1903–1950) left music in the style of R. Strauss and Mahler. Possibly, he composed the *Praeludium, Intermezzo en Variaties* (1920) while studying with Wagenaar.

Geza Frid (1904–), Hungarian by birth, studied composition with Kodály and piano with Bartók at the Budapest Conservatory. He became a highly praised interpreter of Bartók's piano music. His own music shows the influence of Hungarian folk music and Ravel. In 1929, he settled in Amsterdam and taught at the Utrecht Conservatory from 1964. For piano and orchestra, he composed the concerto, op. 14 (1934), with chorus; the *Variaties op een Nederlands Volkslied* (Variations on a Dutch Folksong), op. 29b (1949), for piano, brass, men's chorus, and orchestra; the concerto, op. 55 (1957), for two pianos; and the concertino (1961) for violin, cello, and piano.

Guillaume Landré (1905–1968) trained in jurisprudence, taught economics, and became the president of the Society of Netherlands Composers. His musical compositions blend Flemish renaissance style with twentieth-century elements including serialism. The suite (1936) for strings and piano represents a major change of style—

from a Pijper-like use of short motifs to a lyric, long-melody romanticism. The suite has an elegy as a memorial for Belgium's Queen Astrid.

Leon Orthel (1905–) studied with Wagenaar at the Royal Conservatory in the Hague, at the *Hochschule für Musik* in Berlin, and with Pijper in Rotterdam. He taught piano and theory at the Royal Conservatory in the Hague. He composed the scherzo, op. 10 (1927), the concertino *alla burla,* op. 12 (1930), and the symphony no. 4 "Sinfonia Concertante," op. 32 (1949), with a piano solo part.

Kees van Baaren (1906–1970) studied at the *Hochschule für Musik* in Berlin and with Pijper in Rotterdam, directed the Amsterdam Music Academy, and taught at the Conservatory of Utrecht and the Royal Conservatory in the Hague. His music shows influences of Schoenberg, Webern, Pijper's germ-cell theory, a rejection of tonality for serialism, dissonances of seconds and sevenths, pointillism, metrical ordering of pitches, and irregular meter signatures such as 3+2/8, 3+2/4, and 2+3+2/8. The three-movement concerto (1934) is on one motive and the piano and orchestra are autonomous equals. The serial concerto (1964) is a one-movement work in eight sections.

Henk Badings (1907–), self-taught with a little help from Pijper, composes music with elements of Brahms, Reger, and Hindemith. His concerto no. 1 (1939) is from the era in which he co-directed the Amsterdam Music Lyceum. The concertino (1942) for piano trio (violin, cello, and piano) and chamber orchestra dates from when he directed the State Conservatory in the Hague. He composed the concerto no. 2 "Atlantic Dances" (1955). He experimented with scales of six or eight notes, harmonic or subharmonic series, and micro-intervals.

Gerald Hengeveld (1910–), student of Friedberg, became an acclaimed concert pianist and teacher at the conservatory. He composed the concertino (1946) and the concerto (1947).

Hans Osieck (1910–) composes music influenced by Dutch folk songs and classic models. He composed three concertinos (1937, 1950, 1971); the fantasy on *In een Blauw Geruite Kiel* (In a Blue-Check Blouse, 1936); the concerto (1942) for two pianos; the variations on *De Bloempjes Gingen Slapen* (The Little Flowers Went to Sleep, 1942); the concerto (1954); and the suite *concertante* (1959) for piano duet and orchestra.

Herman Strategier (1912–), esteemed composer of liturgical music for Roman Catholic rites, taught at the Institute for Catholic Church Music and at Utrecht University. He has the concerto (1947–1948) and the *triptych* (1960) for piano and wind orchestra.

Hans Henkemans (1913–), respected interpreter of piano music of Mozart, Debussy, and Ravel, forsook concertizing to pursue the dual careers of musical composition and psychiatric medicine. From studies with Pijper, he adopted the "germ cell" and evolved a complex concept of formal structures. In the *Passacaglia and Gigue* (1941–1942), the passacaglia is in sonata form with fourteen statements of the bass theme. Common elements in his style are modality, bitonality, polyrhythms, and polymeters. Henkemans composed his first major work, the concerto (1932) with string orchestra, while a medical student at the University of Utrecht. He received a prize from the Union of Dutch Composers for his concerto (1936).

Jan Masséus (1913–) trained at the Rotterdam Conservatory and recently taught at the Leeuwarden Music School. In Rotterdam, he composed the concerto (1945) and the symphonic variaties (1949). He composed the concerto, op. 37 (1966), in Leeuwarden.

Marius Flothius (1914–) is a noted Mozart scholar who contributed to the Mozart clavier concertos in the *Neue Ausgabe Sämtlicher Werk* and composed cadenzas to several Mozart concertos and the Haydn concerto, XVIII:11. His own music includes the neo-classic concerto, op. 30 (1946–1948), for piano and small orchestra.

Cor de Groot (1914–) is a famous pianist praised for interpretations of concertos by Beethoven, Chopin, Liszt, Tchaikovsky, and Ravel. His own music for piano and orchestra includes the concerto no. 1 (1931), the *concerto classico* (1932), the concertino (1939), the concerto (1939) for two pianos, the "Minuten" concerto (1950), the *capriccio* (1955), the *Variations Imaginaires* (1960–1962) for left hand, and the *Bis* (Evocation, 1972).

Luctor Ponse (1914–) trained at the Conservatory in Valenciennes, France, settled in the Netherlands in 1936, and taught at the Utrecht University from 1964. He is a noted interpreter of contemporary music, particularly Bartók. In a dodecaphonic style, he composed the divertissiment, op. 13B (1946), the concerto, op. 17 (1955), and the concerto, op. 33 (1962), for two pianos.

Jan van Dijk (1918–) adopted a thirty-one-tone scale developed by the Dutch physicist Adrian Fokker. He was a student of Pijper at the Rotterdam Conservatory and a teacher at the Brabant Conservatory in Tilburg and the Royal Conservatory at the Hague. Among his compositions are the concertino (1938) for flute, percussion, piano, and strings; the *cassatio* (1943) for strings with piano obbligato; four concertinos (1948–1949, 1953, two 1966); the neo-classic concertino (1949) for two pianos with string or wind orchestra; the serenade (1959) for piano, winds, and percussion; the concerto (1963) for piano, four hands and small orchestra; the triple concerto (1968) for flute, recorder and harpsichord; the *2 Résumés* (1970) for piano and small orchestra; and *Touch After Finish* (1971) for trumpet, organ, piano, and strings.

Lex van Delden (1919–), trained in medicine, was self-taught in composition and worked as a music editor for the daily paper *Het Parool*. He composed the scherzo (1949), the introduction and allegro (1951), which is a small concerto for violin, piano, and orchestra, and the concerto (1960).

Wim Franken (1922–), pianist and teacher, composed the concertino (1952) and three concertos (one 1975).

Jurriaan Andriessen (1925–1964), son of the composer Hendrik Andriessen, studied with Messiaen in Paris and with Copland in the United States and followed Stravinsky's early neo-classic style. For piano and orchestra, he composed the concertino (1943); the concerto (1948); the *Trelleborg concerto* (1967) for harpsichord and three instrumental groups; the *Omaggio à Sweelinck* (1968) for harpsichord and twenty-four strings; and the Dutch rhapsody for two pianos.

Rudolf Perdeck (1925–) studied with H. Andriessen at the Amsterdam Conservatory and attended the Royal Conservatory in the Hague. He has the scherzo (1968).

Hans Kox (1930–) taught at the Doetinchem Music School. His concern with

Table 31 Additional Composers in the Netherlands

Names	Dates	Compositions
Andriessen, Cornelius	1865–1947	Fantasy
Bank, Jacques	1943–	Alexandre's Conc (1978)
Bois, Rob du	1934–	*Cerle* (pub 1963)
		Concerto (1960, rev 1968)
		Le Concerto pour Hrisanide (1971)
Boogaard, Bernard van de	1952–	Concerto (1976)
Bruins, Theo	1929–	Concerto (1952)
Emmer, Huib	1951–	*Montage* (1977)
Escher, Rudolf	1912–1980	Concerto (1952)
Geraedts, Jaap	1924–	*Concerto da Camera* (1956)
Keuris, Tristan	1946–	Concerto (1952)
Lichtveld, Lou	1903–	Concertino (1932)
Maessen, Antoon	1919–	Concertino (1962)
Manassen, Alex	1950–	*Double Helix* (1978)
Milandolle, Ludovicus	1904–	Concerto (1949)
Mul, Jan	1911–1971	2 Concertos (1938/62)
		Divertimento (1967)
Mulder, Ernest	1898–1959	Concerto (1935)
Mulder, Herman	1894–	Concerto, op 37 (1943)
		Concertino, op 131 (1964)
		Concerto, op 151 (1968), 2 pnos
Pouwels, Jan	1898–	Concerto (1967)
Rötterging, Martin	1926–	Concerto (pub 1972)
Schat, Peter	1935–	*Concerto da Camera* (1960), 2 cls, pno
Schooenbeek, Kees	1947–	Concerto (1975–1976)
Schuyt, Nicolass	1922–	3 Preludes (1973)
Somer, Louis	1901–1966	*Burlesque Louis*
Stallaert, Alphonse	1920–	Concerto (by 1950), 2 pnos
		Concerto (1950)
Vries, Klaas de	1944–	Refrains (1970), 2 pnos
Wegner, Emmy	1901–1973	Rhapsody
Wertheim, Rosy	1888–	Concerto

mathematical possibilities in music led to his adoption of the 31-note scale formulated by the Dutch physicist Adrian Fokker. The strongest influences on his compositional style are Berg, Malher, and Badings. For piano and orchestra, he composed the concerto (1961–1962) and the *cyclophony* no. 6 (1967) for violin, trumpet, piano, vibraphone, and sixteen strings. The nine *cyclophonies* (Sound Cycles) are short *concertante* pieces featuring various solo instruments in experimental structures.

Tera de Marez Oyens (1932–) studied at the Amsterdam Conservatory and taught at Utrecht University and recently in Hilversum. *In Exile* (pub. 1977) is a concertino.

Joep Straesser (1934–) has been teaching at the Utrecht Conservatory since 1969. He composed the *Canterbury Concerto* (1969) and *Just a Moment Again* (1969).

Jan van Vlijmen (1935–) studied with van Baaren and uses elements from Schoenberg and Berg. The sonata (1966), sometimes called a concerto, for piano and three instrumental groups, is on Pijper's germ cell theory. Theo Bruins premiered van Vlijmen's new concerto (perf. 1991).

Louis Andriessen (1939–), son of organist and composer Hendrik Andriessen, studied with his father at the Utrecht Conservatory, with van Baaren at the Royal Conservatory at the Hague, and with Berio in Milan and Berlin. He co-founded the Amsterdam Charles Ives Society and is a leading avant-garde composer. The *Ittrospezions III* (Concept I, 1964) is for two pianos and three instrumental groups.

Willem Bon (1940–1983) studied with van Baaren at the Conservatory in the Hague and conducted the Eindhoven Baroque Ensemble and the *Concertgebouw Orchestra* in Amsterdam. He composed the *Dialogues and Monologues,* op. 17 (1967), and the *Games* (1970) for six winds, piano, and string orchestra.

Denmark

Flemming Weis (1898–1981) studied at the Royal Conservatory and the Leipzig *Hochschule für Musik.* His early compositions follow German romanticism and later works have elements of French impressionism and neo-classicism. The Introduction Grave (1939) is a neo-classic work.

Finn Høffding (1899–), opera composer, taught at the Royal Danish Conservatory from 1931. He studied with Marx in Vienna and follows the styles of Nielsen, Stravinsky, and Bartók. The symphony no. 3, op. 12 (1928), is for two pianos and orchestra.

Otto Mortensen (1907–) studied at the Copenhagen Conservatory and with Milhaud in Paris before returning to Copenhagen in 1942 to teach at the conservatory. Mortensen composes mainly vocal music, but he has the *koncertstykke* (1935) for flute, cello, piano, and orchestra, and the concerto (1945).

Herman Koppel (1908–), brilliant pianist with tours throughout Europe and the former Soviet Union, taught at the Copenhagen Conservatory from 1949. His compositions include elements of jazz, contemporary French music, Bartók, and Stravinsky. He has four concertos: op. 13 (1931–1932), influenced by jazz; op. 30 (1936–1937); op. 45 (1948), influenced by Neilson, Schubert, and Brahms; and op. 69 (1960–1963). The *Eight Variations and Epilogue,* op. 89 (1972), is for piano and thirteen performers.

Svend Tarp (1908–) studied and taught at the Copenhagen Conservatory and at the University of Copenhagen. He is a member of the Danish Composers Society and worked for *Edition Dania* and the Society for Publication of Danish Music. French neo-classicism influenced his concertino (1930).

Gunnar Berg (1909–) studied in Copenhagen and with Honegger in Paris, where he learned ideas of Messiaen and Webern. Readings in cellular biology led him to write musical cells of five to ten notes as the source for various themes. His compositions include the *Essai Acoustique III* (1954) for piano and orchestra; the *Pour Piano et Orchestra* (1959); the Frise (perf. 1961) for piano and chamber orchestra; and the *Uculang* (1967).

Vagn Holmbor (1909–), follower of Kodály's and Bartók's lead in studying folk music, is the most important Danish composer of symphonies after Neilson. He taught at the Royal Conservatory in Copenhagen and the Royal Danish Institute for the Blind. Sibelius and Nielsen are the main musical influences on his compositions. He uses a personal concept of "germ themes" that grow into larger musical ideas, folk songs, modified major-minor systems, chromaticism, and polymodalities. His contribution to the literature is the chamber concerto no. 1, op. 17, M.113 (1939) for piano, strings, and percussion; and the chamber concerto no. 4, op. 33 or 30?, M. 139 (1940), also called the Triple Concerto, for violin, cello, piano, and chamber orchestra. The letter M from the Greek word "meta," meaning beside or after, is in Paul Rapoport's *Vagn Holmbor: A Catalogue of His Music, Discography, Bibliography, Essays.*[1]

Svend Schultz (1913–) taught piano, conducted choral music, and wrote criticism for the newspaper *Politiken.* While his main interest is chamber music, he has two concertos (1943, 1951), the concertino (1953), and the introduction and rondo (perf. 1964), all in the neo-classic style.

Niels Bentzon (1919–) performed as a pianist in Scandinavia, Europe, and the United States, and has been on the faculty at the Royal Danish Conservatory since 1950. He is the best-known and most often performed Danish composer after Nielson. In a style based on tonality, dissonance, polymeter, polytonality, and dodecaphony, he composed seven concertos: op. 49 (1945), one (1952), op. 94 (1954), op. 149 (1963), op. 195 (1966), one (1967–1969), and op. 243 (1982). Other compositions featuring piano are the symphony no. 2 (1944–1945); the chamber concerto no. 1, op. 52 (1948), for three pianos, two trumpets, clarinet, bassoon, double-bass, and percussion; the *Piccolo-Concerto*[2] (1950); the rhapsody (1961); the symphonic fantasy, op. 119 (1958–1963), for two pianos; the *Busonism* (1971) with audio-visual effects; the *Leipziger Tage* (1976) with strings; the double concerto (1965) for violin and piano with percussion; the *brillantes concertino* on "Ein Mädchen oder Weibchen," op. 108 (1956); the *Still's* (1975) for piano, orchestra, and jazz band; and the *Variations Without a Theme* (1980).

Poul Olsen (1922–1982), composer and ethnomusicologist, studied with Jeppesen at the Royal Conservatory in Copenhagen and Boulanger in Paris. He left the concerto, op. 31 (1953–1954), and the concertino (1973) for clarinet, violin, cello, and piano.

Peder Holm (1926–) conducted the West Jutland Symphony Orchestra from 1949 and taught at the Esbjerg Conservatory. In a contemporary tonal style, he composed three concertos (1953, 1963, 1967), the *KHEBEB* (1968) for two pianos, and the concertino II.

Henning Christiansen (1932–) advocates avant-garde techniques and he led the movement *Den Ny Enkelhed* (The New Simplicity) to promote music accessible to many listeners. The *Danish Summer,* op. 98 (1975), is for piano and orchestra.

Thomas Koppel (1944–) studied piano and theory with his father Herman Koppel at the Royal Danish Conservatory. His avant-garde concerto *Héroique* (perf. 1967) is for three pianos, orchestra, chorus, and wind machine.

Table 32 Additional Composers in Denmark

Names	Dates	Compositions
Amberg, Johan	1846–1914	*Mazurek* (pub 1903)
Emborg, Jen	1876–1975	Concerto, op 72 (1930)
Salomon, Siegfried	1885–1962	Concerto (1947)
Sandby, Herman	1881–1965	Triple Concerto, vn, va, pno
Schierbeck, Poul	1888–1949	*Natten* (The Night)
		Symfonish Scen (1935–36)
Schmidt, Ole	1928–	Concerto (1956)
Simonsen, Rudolph	1889–1947	Concerto (1915)
Thybo, Leif	1922–	Concerto (1961–62)

Belgium

Emile Mathieu (1844–1932) studied with Fétis at the Brussels Conservatory and directed the Ghent Conservatory. He composed the *koncertstück* (1905).

Arthur de Greef (1862–1940), brilliant pianist in the tradition of Liszt, met Liszt in Weimar and adopted his musical style and some of Wagner's musical features. De Greef is important for popularizing Grieg's concerto. He studied at the Brussels Conservatory and later taught piano there. He composed two concertos (one 1914), the concertino (1928–1929), the *Menuet Varié,* the *Chant Polonais de Chopin,* and the *Polonaise de Liszt.*

Charles Smulder (1863–1934) was well known as a composer, author, critic, scientist, and teacher at the Liége Conservatory. He left at least two concertos.

August de Boeck (1865–1937) was influenced by the composition teacher Paul Gibson and the Russian Five. He introduced impressionism to Belgian audiences and composed the concerto (1929) for two pianos and orchestra.

Paul Gibson (1865–1942) taught composition at the Brussels Conservatory and composed music influenced by romantic styles, classic forms, the Russian Five, and a rejection of twentieth-century techniques. He left the *Scherzando* (1941).

Henri Theibaut (1865–1959) was on the faculty of the *Institute des Hautes Etudes Musicales et Dramatiques*. The suite is for piano and orchestra.

Théophile Ysaye (1865–1918), younger brother of violinist Eugène Ysaye, studied in Berlin with Kullak and in Paris with Franck, who influenced his style, as did Debussy. He probably was in Belgium while composing the concerto, op. 9 (pub. 1907).

Juliette Folville (1870–1946), teacher at the Liége Conservatory, left a concerto.

Joseph Jongen (1873–1953) followed the chromaticism of R. Strauss, Wagner, and Franck, and ideas of Debussy, Ravel, and d'Indy. From 1920, he taught counterpoint and fugue at the Brussels Conservatory. He composed the *piece symphonique,* op. 84 (1928), the *piece symphonique* (1930), and the concerto, op. 127 (1943).

François Rasse (1873–1955) studied and taught at the Liege Conservatory. While a conductor he composed the *Poème concertant* (1918).

Albert Dupuis (1877–1967) conducted the *concerts d'Harcourt* in Paris and directed the Verviers Music School. He followed the compositional style taught at the *Schola Cantorum* and Franck's cyclic ideas. He left the concerto (1940).

Leon Jongen (1884–1969), brother of Joseph Jongen, toured as a concert pianist and taught at the Brussels Conservatory. He probably intended the prelude, divertissement, and finale (1937) and the fantasie (1938) for his own use.

Arthur Meulemans (1884–1969) conducted the radio orchestra, joined the Royal Flemish Academy of Fine Arts, and followed French impressionism. He composed three concertos (1941, 1956, 1960), the concerto (1959) for two pianos, and the concerto (1958) for harpsichord.

Lodewijk de Vocht (1887–1977) established the *Royal Chorale Caecilia* that became famous in Belgium and taught at the Royal Flemish Conservatory. He left at least one piano concerto.

Rene Barbier (1890–) uses compositional ideas of Dukas and Wagner. He was on the conservatory faculty during the composition of the two concertos, opp. 22 and 43 (1922, 1934).

Francis de Bourguignon (1890–1961) was a concert pianist who toured Australia, Canada, South America, Asia, and Africa. In 1925, he settled in Brussels, where he joined the faculty at the conservatory. He composed the concertino, op. 25 (1927), the *Fantasy on Two Themes of Eugéne Ysaye,* op. 57 (1938), the concerto, op. 89 (1949), and the concertino, op. 99 (1952), with string orchestra. After 1939, his style became neo-classic.

Marius de Jong (1891–), pianist with tours in Europe and the United States, settled in Belgium in 1926 and joined the faculty of the Antwerp Conservatory in 1931. His compositional style uses Gregorian melodies and twentieth-century harmonies in a neo-impressionistic style. He composed three concertos, opp. 21, 80, and 105 (1924, 1952, 1956–1957), and the Flemish Rhapsody no. 3 (1971).

Jules Strens (1892–1971), organist, studied with Gibson and helped establish the Group des Synthetistes to promote contemporary compositional techniques using old structures. The fantaisie concertante (1938) is for piano and orchestra.

Jean Absil (1893–1974) directed music at the Academy of Etterbveek and simultaneously taught at the Brussels Conservatory. His concerto, op. 30 (1937), was a composition for the *Concours Ysaye,* later known as the Queen Elisabeth International Competition, won by pianist Emil Gilels. Two concertos are opp. 131 and 162 (1967, 1973). Other compositions are the allegro *brillante,* op. 133 (1967), the *ballade,* op. 156 (1971), for saxophone, piano, and small orchestra, and *La Zodiaque, Variations Symphoniques,* op. 70 (1949), based on poems in *La Zodiaque* by Thomas Braun, for piano, chorus, and orchestra. *La Zodiaque* is in three movements presenting various signs of the zodiac.

Godefroid Devreese (1893–1972), father of composer-pianist Frederic Devreese, was the director of the conservatory during the composition of his concerto (1938), which has elements of romanticism and impressionism.

Clement D'Hooghe (1899–1951), virtuoso organist at several churches, taught at the Antwerp Conservatory. His piano concerto (1949) has classic and romantic traits.

Raymond Chevreuille (1901–1976) worked as a sound engineer with Belgian Radio. He was an autodidactic composer influenced by French impressionism, the twelve-tone method, atonality, and tonality. The concerto no. 2, op. 50 (1951–1952), was a performance requirement at the 1952 Queen Elizabeth International Competition. Other compositions are the concerto no. 1, op. 10 (1937), the double concerto, op. 34 (1946), for piano and viola or alto saxophone, and the concerto no. 3, op. 88 (1968).

Suzanne Daneau (1901–1971) taught music history at the conservatory. She composed the *Poème de Rosaire* (1938) and the variation, lied et finale for violin, piano, and orchestra.

Willem Pelemans (1901–) is a composer, music critic for the newspaper *Het Laatste Nieuws,* and a follower of expressionism. He composed two concertinos (both 1931) for harpsichord, three concertos (1945, 1950, 1967), and the concerto (1973) for two pianos.

Marcel Poot (1901–) taught at the Brussels Conservatory. The concerto (1959) was the required piece at the 1960 Queen Elizabeth International Competition. Other compositions are the rondo (1935), the *Epic Legend* (1938), the *concerto grosso* (1964) for piano quartet and orchestra, and the concerto (1975).

Gaston Brenta (1902–1969) studied with Gibson and helped found the *Groupe des Synthetistes* to promote contemporary music. He worked for Belgian Radio and as the musical director of the French Service in Brussels. The concerto no. 2 (1968) was the required piece at the Queen Elizabeth International Competition. Other compositions are two concertos (1949, 1953) and the *Pointes Sèches de la Belle Epoque* (1964).

Flor Peeters (1903–) is a famous organist, organ teacher at the Antwerp Conservatory, and composer of organ works. For piano and orchestra, he composed the concerto, op. 74 (1954).

Wladimir Woronoff (1903–) arrived in Brussels in 1922 and destroyed much of his early music, including a *concert lyrique* for piano and orchestra. There remains the *Strophes concertantes* (1964).

Rene Defossez (1905–), conductor, joined the faculty at the Brussels Conservatory in 1959. In a neo-classic style, he composed the variations (1938), the piano concerto (1951) revised as the concerto (1954) for two pianos, the concerto (1956), and the concerto *romantique*.

Jef Maes (1905–), violist in several Antwerp orchestras, studied and taught at the Flemish Conservatory. In a light style accessible to many audiences, he composed two concertos (1946, 1975) for piano and the concerto (1955) for harpsichord and string orchestra.

Norbert Rosseau (1907–1975) studied with Respighi in Italy. An injury to his right hand forced him to turn from performance to composition. The concertino, op. 85 (1963), for piano, double string quartet, and double bass, has serial and expressionist elements.

Calmille Schmit (1908–1976) was a well-known Belgian composer and organist. He adopted the twelve-tone method in 1949 and used the technique in the concerto (1955).

Richard de Guide (1909–1962) taught at the conservatory. He composed the concerto *Le Temeraire,* op. 26 (1952).

Franz Constant (1910–), duo pianist with his wife Jeanne Pellaerts, joined the faculty at the Brussels Conservatory in 1947. His music has elements of classic Belgian style and colorful modern sonorities. The *Expressions* (1973) is for violin, piano, and strings.

Robert Darcy (1910–1967), French-born, was a prize winning cello student at the Lyons Conservatory in 1928. The piano concerto (1951) has neo-classic elements blended with atonal procedures.

Renier van der Velden (1910–) worked with the French service of Belgian Radio from 1945. In an autodidactic style with elements of expressionism, Hindemith, and Stravinsky, he composed the concertino (1949) for clarinet, bassoon, piano, and string orchestra, the concerto (1965) for two pianos and brass quintet, the *balletmuziek* (1972) for piano and nineteen winds, the concerto (1973), which is in some sources as a concertino, and the *Judith Ballet* (1951, rev. 1953) for two pianos.

Jacques Stehman (1912–1975), student and then a teacher at the Brussels Conservatory, adopted contemporary techniques and older jazz styles. He left the *Escapades* (1968) and the concerto (1965–1972).

Jan Decadt (1914–) taught counterpoint and fugue at the Antwerp Conservatory and composition at the Ghent Conservatory. He composed two concertos (1953, 1971).

Jean Louël (1914–) joined the faculty at the Brussels Conservatory in 1943 and has been an inspector of music schools in the Flemish area of Belgium since 1956. He has two concertos (1945, 1949).

Marcel Quinet (1915–) studied at the Mons and Brussels Conservatories and privately with Absil. Since 1943, he has been teaching at the Brussels Conservatory and the *Chapelle Musicale Reine Elisabeth.* He composed three concertos (1955, 1964, 1966), the concertino (pub. 1960) for piano and woodwinds, and the two-piano *Dialogues* (1975) featuring musical dialogues between the pianos and the orchestra and between the two pianos. He composed the concerto (1964) for the 1964 Queen Elizabeth Composition Competition.

Berthe di Vito-Delvauz (1915–) taught at the Royal Conservatoire from 1938. He composed the *Improvisation et Finale,* op. 30 (1944–1946), and the concerto, op. 120 (1968–1969).

David van de Woestijne (1915–) studied with Gibson and Esplà, then took a position with Belgium Radio. He composed music in a neo-baroque style with contemporary compositional techniques. He has the double concerto (1935) for piano and cello, the concerto (1938), the *ballade* (1940), the serenade (1946) for piano and wind ensemble, the concerto (1972) for two pianos, and the *Eenentwintig* (1976) for piano, nineteen winds, and double bass.

Herman Roelstraete (1925–) likes Gregorian modes, baroque forms, and counterpoint. He composed the sinfonia *concertante,* op. 36, no. 1 (1957), while a student at the Ghent Conservatory.

Nina Bulterijs (1929–) studied and taught at the Royal Flemish Conservatory. Her concerto (1962) is in a dodecaphonic style.

Frederic Devreese (1929–) writes music using irregular metric pulses in the style of Stravinsky. While a student at the Brussels Conservatory, he composed the

Table 33 Additional Composers in Belgium

Names	Dates	Compositions
Antoine, Georges	1892–1918	Concerto, op 5 (1914)
Bertouille, Gérard	1898–	2 Concertos (1946/53)
Bruzdowicz, Joanna	1943–	Impression (1966), 2 pnos
		Episode (1973)
		Concerto (1974)
Delcoix, Leon	1880–1938	Serenade, cl, pno
Dupriez, Christian	1922–	Concerto
Durme, Jef van	1907–1965	2 Concertos (1943/45)
Freson, Armande	1896–	Concerto (1963)
Glorieux, François	1932–	*Mouvements* (1962)
		Manhattan (1973–74)
Herberigs, Robert	1886–1974	2 Concertos (1932/52)
Leduc, Jacques	1932–	Concerto, op 31 (1970)
Legley, Victor	1915–	Concerto, op 39 (1952)
Meester, Louis de	1904–	2 Concertos (1952/56)
Middelleer, Jean de	1908–	2 Concertos (one 1953)
Moulaert, Raymond	1875–1962	Concerto (1938)
		Rhapsodie Ecossaise (1940)
Peeters, Emil	1893–1974	Concerto, op 27 (1934), fl, hpd
		Concerto, op 31 (1934)
		2 Concs (1949/51), 2 pnos
		Studie (1971)
Souffrianu, Arsène	1926–	Concerto
		Concertino
Tolkowsky, Denise	1918–	Concerto
Velthuysen, Annie v.	1887–1965	*Fantaisie*
Vigneron-Ramakers, C.- J.	1914–	Concertino, op 5 (1970), ob, Eng hn, hpd

concerto (1949) with elements of jazz and Gershwin. As a student at the Santa Cecilia Academy in Rome, he composed a concerto (1952). His concerto (1955–1956) is a student work from the Vienna State Music Academy.

Henri Pousseur (1929–), serial composer, studied with Stockhausen in Cologne and Berio and with Maderna in Milan. He composed the concerto (1949), *Les Ephemerides d'Icare II* (1970), and the Midi-Minuet (1970) for orchestra, piano, jazz group, pop group, chorus, children's chorus, and folk singers.

Jacqueline Fontyn (1930–), wife of Camille Schmit, taught at the Antwerp Royal Conservatory and the Brussels Conservatory. She composed the two-movement *mouvements concertante* (1957) for two pianos and strings and the concerto (1967).

Jeanne Lemaire-Sindorff (1931–) taught at the Music Academy. She has a piano concerto.

Philippe Boesmans (1936–), composer of serial music, wrote music for Belgian Radio from 1961. The *Multiples* (1974) is for two pianos and the *Element-Extension* (1975) is with chamber orchestra.

Claude Coppens (1936–), autodidactic composer, studied at the Brussels Conservatory and taught at conservatories in Brussels, Antwerp, and Ghent. His style is influenced by dodecaphony, serialism, and electronic techniques. He composed at least one piano concerto.

Frederic Rzexski (1938–) studied with Piston at Harvard University, with Babbitt and Sessions at Princeton, and with Dallapiccola in Florence. In 1960, he settled in Berlin and Rome and joined the faculty at the Royal Conservatory in 1977. The *Long Time Man* (1979) is a theme and variations.

Frederik van Rossum (1939–) studied and later taught at the Brussels Conservatory. He writes music with elements of Prokofiev, Stravinsky, Rachmaninoff, Goréchi, and Lutoslawski. The *symphonie concertante,* op. 11 (1967), for horn, piano, percussion, and orchestra, is a product of the era in which he taught at the Liege Conservatory. He composed the concerto "Slavic Soul," op. 30 (1975), in Brussels.

Luxemburg

Victor Vreuls (1876–1944) studied with d'Indy at the *Schola Cantorum* in Paris and directed the Luxembourg Conservatory. He left the suite *pastorale* (pub. 1925).

Notes

1. Paul Rapoport, *Vagn Holmbor: A Catalogue of His Music, Discography, Bibliography, Essays* (London: Triad Press, 1974).
2. Piccolo in this title means little.

Chapter 14

Norway, Sweden, and Finland

Norway

Johannes Haarkou (1847–1925) studied music in Oslo, in Leipzig with Richter and Jadassohn, and in Berlin. He received praise for his organ improvisations at the Old Akers Church. The piano concerto, op. 47 (1917), shows influences of Grieg and Norwegian folk song.

Hjalmar Borgstrøm (1864–1925), important for symphonic poems, wrote criticism for the *Aftenposten* and influenced Norwegian music during the first quarter of the century. For piano and orchestra, he composed *Hamlet* (1903) and the concerto (1910).

Eyvind Alnaes (1872–1932) studied with Ivar Holter in Oslo, with Reinecke in Leipzig, and played organ at various churches in Drammen and Oslo. Besides highly regarded solo and choral songs in a late-romantic style, he composed the piano concerto, op. 27 (1914).

Fartein Valen (1887–1952) spent much of his childhood in Madagascar, where his father was a missionary. After studying in Oslo and with Reger in Berlin, he evolved an atonal style of polyphony akin to Schoenberg. Valen's last completed composition is the concerto, op. 44 (1949–1951), with chamber orchestra, for the English pianist Alexander Helmman, who died before performing the work.

Monrad Johansen (1888–1974) gave piano recitals and wrote music criticism for the *Afterposten*. His musical compositions join Norwegian musical traditions, the lyricism of Grieg, and Russian and French traits. He left the concerto, op. 29 (1952–1954).

Sverre Jordan (1889–1972) studied with Ansorge in Berlin and directed music at the National Theater. The concerto, op. 45 (1945), and the concerto piccolo, op. 77 (1963), show the influence of Norwegian folk songs.

Marius Ulfrstad (1890–1968) studied at the Oslo Conservatory, with Humperdinck in Berlin, and with Ravel in Paris. He wrote music criticism for the *Morgenposten,* and opened a music school in 1921. He composed the concerto (1935).

Issay Dobroven (1894–1953), Russian conductor, settled in Oslo in the 1930s. He made a concert debut at age 5, and entered the Moscow Conservatory at age 9. As a pianist, he enjoyed much success performing his concerto, op. 20.

Eivind Groven (1901–) composed music in a nationalistic style based on Norwegian folk music. The concerto no. 1 (1950) is for piano and orchestra.

Harald Lie (1902–1942) received musical training in Olso before going to the United States and later to Leipzig for work with a piano manufacturer. He returned to Oslo in 1929 and studied with Valen in 1930. His compositional style has elements of

Bruckner and Norwegian national traits. He rejected several early compositions, including a concerto for piano and orchestra.

Klaus Egge (1906–1979) received the State Salary of Art from 1949 for his musical contributions to Norway. Some of his compositions contain his musical signature E-g-g-e. The concerto no. 1, op. 9 (1937), has conventional forms, features of folk music and functional harmony. The one-movement concerto no. 2, op. 21 (1944), subtitled *Variations and Fugue on a Norwegian Folktune,* begins with the Nowegian folk song (See ex. 14–1), followed by seven variations (See ex. 14–2) and the "Finale," with the piano in concert with a fugue in the orchestra (See ex. 14–3). The concerto no. 3 (1974) uses the twelve-tone style while maintaining some sense of tonality.

Geirr Tveitt (1908–1981) studied with Schmidt and Honegger, concertized as a pianist, received the Norwegian State Salary of Art to allow time for musical composition, and composed a concerto for the national Hardanger fiddle. For piano he composed the concerto, op. 5 (1930), the one-movement concerto, op. 11 (1933), the concerto (1947), the concerto *Hommage à Brahms* (1947), the concerto *Northern Lights,* op. 156 (1954), and the concerto (1960). The *Variations on a Folk Tune from Hardanger* (1937) is for two pianos and orchestra.

Anne-Marie Ørbeck (1911–) studied in Norway, Berlin, and with Boulanger and Milhaud in Paris. Her concertino (1938) displays late-romantic and nationalistic influences.

Finn Arnestad (1915–) composed music in a neo-classic style with some French impressionism and a touch of dodecaphony. The *Conversation* (1950) is an intermezzo of about four minutes. There also is a neo-classic concerto.

Per Albertsen (1919–) played organ at the Church of Our Lady and taught at the university. In a musical style influenced by Palestrina, Haydn, *Les Six,* and Bartók, he composed the concerto, op. 33 (1969), for piano and school orchestra.

Bjørn Fongaard (1919–1980) studied at the Oslo Conservatory and taught guitar there. His music contains microtonal elements, bitonality, polytonality, a restructured scale, and other contemporary practices. He composed the concertino, op. 11 (1953), the Space Concerto (1971), and twenty-three concertos (1973–1976) for piano and orchestra.

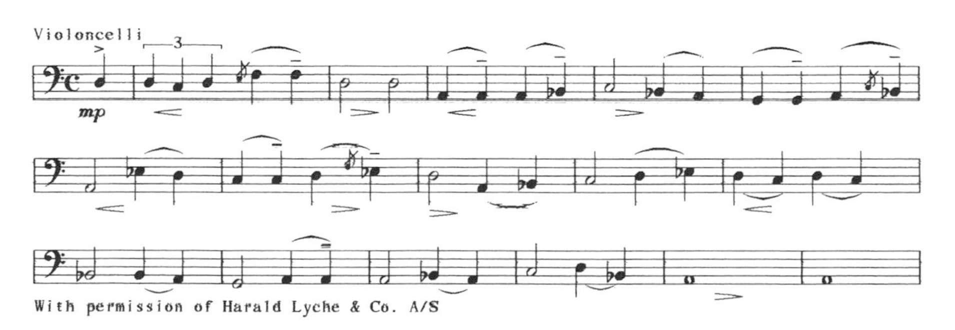

Example 14–1. Egge Concerto no. 2, op. 21, mm. 2–18

Example 14–2. Egge Concerto no. 2, op. 21, "Var. 1," mm. 1–12

Antonio Bibalo (1922–), born and trained in Trieste, Italy, studied in London with Lutgen, and settled in Larvik in 1956. His compositional style uses the twelve-tone method, neo-classic elements and features of Bartók. Bibalo probably composed the concerto (1953) and the chamber concerto no. 1 (1954) for piano and strings under Lutgen's guidance. The concerto (1971) has a modified twelve-tone row, and the chamber concerto no. 2 (1974) is for harpsichord, violin, and strings.

Example 14–3. Egge Concerto no. 2, op. 21, "Finale," mm. 1–6

Finn Mortensen (1922–) taught at the Oslo Conservatory and followed his teacher Egge as the chairman of the Norwegian Society of Composers. His compositional style has polyphony, diatonic melodies, motivic development, dodecaphonic features, and classic forms. He composed the concerto, op. 25, and the fantasy, op. 27 (1956–1957).

Edvard Baein (1924–1976) studied in Paris and conducted choirs and orchestra. In a conservative style, he composed the capriccio, op. 9 (1956–1957).

Egil Hovland (1924–) played organ at the Glemmen Church. Although most of

Table 34 Additional Composers in Norway

Names	Dates	Compositions
Bull, Edward	1922–	Divertimento, op 15 (1954) *Sonata con Spirito* (1970)
Evje, Johan	1874–1962	*Quo Vadis, Introduction and Fugue*
Gjerstrom, Gunnar	1891–1951	Concerto (perf 1931) *Sea Moods* (perf 1965)
Hvoslef, Ketil	1939–	Concerto
Rypdal, Terje	1947–	Concerto
Saeverud, Harold	1897–	Concerto, op 31 (1948–50)
Strømholm, Folke	1941–	Concerto

his compositional efforts are in church music, he has the concerto, op. 91 (1976–1977), for piano and orchestra.

Ketil Vea (1932–), trained at the Oslo Conservatory, became a music teacher and head of the Northern Norway Music Council. His concerto is in a neo-romantic style.

Ketil Saeverud (1939–), son of composer Harold Saeverud, taught at the conservatory and composed the concertino (1964).

Sweden

Henning Mankell (1868–1930) composed mainly piano compositions influenced by French impressionism, the formal structures of Chopin, and the harmonies of Liszt, Grieg, and Sjögren. His compositions for piano and orchestra are the andante, op. 17, for violin and piano, and the concerto, op. 30 (1917).

Wilhelm Stenhammar (1871–1927), pianist and chamber music performer, conducted the Gottenborg Symphony Orchestra. His musical style results from studies of Beethoven, Haydn, and Mozart. The two concertos, op. 1 (1894) and op. 23 (1904–1907), have a special kinship with Brahms' style. Both compositions avoid obvious technical displays in favor of musical content (See ex. 14–4). In 1894, critics praised the concerto no. 1 as a masterpiece. In 1964, Kurt Atterberg reconstructed the lost orchestra score of the concerto no. 2 from a piano reduction and his recollections of Stenhammar's performances.

Natnael Berg (1879–1957) studied veterinary medicine until enrolling in the Stockholm Conservatory to learn singing. The late-romantic style of R. Strauss influenced his concerto (1931).

Gustaf Heintze (1879–1946) trained at the Stockholm Conservatory and played organ at the Maria Magdalena Church from 1910 until his death. In a romantic style requiring a virtuoso pianistic technique, he composed two concertos, opp. 15 and 21 (1919, 1925), the *concertstück* (1931), and the concerto (1933) for two pianos.

Sigurd von Koch (1879–1919) was a piano accompanist and music critic. The *ballade* (1919) is in a rhapsodic style based on late-romantic practices.

Example 14–4. Stenhammar Concerto, no. 2, op. 23, mvt. 1, mm. 1–18

Adolf Wiklund (1879–1950) composed music influenced by Brahms and Stenhammer. The *concertstück* (1902) is a student work from the Stockholm Conservatory, and the concerto, op. 10 (1906, rev. 1935), is a student work from his time in Germany. Brahms influenced the concerto, op. 17 (1916). The third movement of the first concerto has a coda based on a theme from the first movement, and the second concerto is a three-movement work to be performed without pauses between the movements. Wiklund's two concertos are among the finest by a Swedish composer.

Edvin Kallstenius (1881–1967) studied science at Lund University before pursuing music at the Leipzig Conservatory. He worked in Stockholm as a critic for the *Svenska Dagbladet,* as a music librarian with Radio Sweden, and as a board member of the Society of Swedish Composers. The concerto or sinfonia *concertante,* op. 12 (1922), is in the romantic tradition of Scandinavian music. He became a pioneer of contemporary compositional techniques, including the twelve-tone method.

Henrik Melchers (1882–1961), violinist, trained at the Stockholm Conservatory and the Paris *Conservatoire,* and taught at the Stockholm Conservatory from 1925. He composed two concertos for piano and orchestra.

Ture Rangström (1884–1947) composed the ballad (1937) using elements of Scandinavian music, Wagner, and Nielson. He wrote music criticism for Stockholm newspapers, conducted the Göteborg Symphony, and directed the Stockhlom Opera.

Johan Haquinius (1886–1966), one of Sweden's finest pianists, studied at the Stockholm Conservatory and with Moszkowski in Paris and Friedman in Berlin. The concerto (1940s) displays a leaning toward Scandinavian romantic traditions.

Kurt Atterberg (1887–1974) worked as a certified civil engineer in the patent office while maintaining an active musical career as a composer, critic and conductor. The rhapsody, op. 1 (1909), and the concerto, op. 37 (1927–1935), display his fondness for German and Scandinavian romanticism and Swedish folk music. He reconstructed Stenhammer's concerto no. 2.

Knut Håkanson (1887–1929) directed the Boras *Orkesterforening* and wrote music criticism for the Gottenborg *Handels-orch Sjofartstidning*. The *Svensk svit* no. 1, op. 18 (1923), for piano and orchestra or string trio, displays influences of Reger, Brahms, and Swedish folk music.

Gösta Nystroem (1890–1966) studied with d'Indy in Paris and wrote music criticism for the Gottenborg *Handels-orch Sjofartstidning*. An early concerto disappeared in 1920. The *Concerto Ricercante* (1947) displays romantic and impressionistic influences and ideas of cell theory.

Hilding Rosenberg (1892–), Swedish composer and teacher, trained at the Royal Academy of Music and in Dresden, and worked as a church organist and assistant conductor of the Stockholm Opera. The *5 Pieces* (1933, rev. 1965) with string orchestra and the concerto (1950) exhibit Scandinavian romanticism and neoclassicism.

Nils Bjorkander (1893–1972) studied at the Stockholm Conservatory before establishing a music school in 1917. In a style based on impressionism and Swedish romanticism, he composed the *Festpolonas,* op. 17, the *Gavotte-Caprice* with string orchestra, and the concert-fantasy.

Moses Pergament (1893–1977), Finnish-born composer, conductor, and music critic, studied violin at the St. Petersburg Conservatory. Sibelius, Russian music (mainly Mussorgsky), German expressionism, and *Les Six* influenced his concerto (1951).

Gustaf Paulson (1898–1966), organist at the Gustav Adolf Church, used musical ideas of Sibelius, his teacher Nielsen, and twelve-tone serialism. The two concertos, opp. 26 and 115 (1940, 1961), are for piano.

Yngve Sköld (1899–) trained at the Brno Conservatory in Czechoslovakia and worked in the Swedish Film Industry Orchestra and as a librarian for the Association of Swedish Composers. His concertos, opp. 7, 46, and 67 (1917, 1946, 1967), and the concerto-fantasy, op. 21, merge Scandinavian romanticism with conservative contemporary elements.

Gunnar Ek (1900–), organist, played cello in the Swedish film industry orchestra. Swedish folk songs influence his musical compositions, which include the piano concerto (1944–1945).

Albert Henneberg (1901–) studied at the Stockholm Conservatory and in Vienna and Paris before becoming active as a conductor in Stockholm. He composed the concerto, op. 8 (1925), in Stockholm or Vienna.

Hilding Hallnäs (1903–) trained at the Royal Academy of Music in Stockholm and worked in Gottenborg as a church organist and teacher. His music has romantic features of Scandinavian music. During the 1950s, he adopted the twelve-tone method, and in about 1970 he rejected the technique. He has the concerto (1956) and the triple concerto (1972–1973) for violin, clarinet, and piano.

Hans Holewa (1905–), Austrian-born, studied in Vienna and settled in Stockholm in 1937 as a pianist and teacher. He is the first composer in Sweden to use Schoenberg's twelve-tone method. He has the variations (1942), the concerto (1972), and the concerto (1975) for two pianos and string orchestra.

Eduard Tubin (1905–1982), born in Estonia, studied with Kapp at the Tartu Conservatory and with Kodály in Budapest. After settling in Sweden in 1942, he composed the concerto (1944–1946). With his formative years spent in Hungary, his style contains elements of Hungarian folk music, Kodály, and Bartók.

Dag Wiren (1905–) studied at the Stockholm Conservatory and in Paris, worked as music critic for the *Svenka Morgonbladet* and became the vice-president of the Society of Swedish Composers. His concerto, op. 26 (1947–1950), displays Scandinavian romanticism and neo-classicism akin to Stravinsky and Prokofieff.

Ingemar Liljefors (1906–), pianist, organist, and composer, taught at the conservatory from 1938. He composed the rhapsody, op. 5 (1936), the concerto, op. 11 (1940), and the concertino, op. 22 (1949).

Gunnar de Frumerie (1908–) is a highly regarded teacher, pianist, and composer with studies at the Royal College of Music in Stockholm, and with Sauer in Vienna and Cortot in Paris. In 1945, he joined the piano faculty at the Royal College of Music. His concertos, opp. 3 and 17 (1929, 1935), and the *variations and fugue,* op. 11 (1932), show a strong baroque influence. The symphonic ballad, op. 31 (1934–1944), and the concerto, op. 46 (1953), for two pianos display Scandinavian romanticism with elements from Chopin, Brahms, and Tchaikovsky.

Lars-Erik Larsson (1908–) studied at the Royal Academy of Music and with Berg in Vienna. While a conductor of the Swedish Radio Orchestra, he composed the *Gustavian suite,* op. 28 (1944), based on the film score *Kungajakt.* While on the faculty at the Royal Academy, he composed the concertino, op. 45, no. 12 (1957). Each of the twelve concertinos is for a different solo instrument.

Sixten Eckerberg (1909–), pianist with concerts in Sweden, Germany, Paris, and London, conducted the Gottenborg Symphony Orchestra from 1937. In a style influenced by Poulenc, Eckerberg composed three concertos (1943, 1949, 1971) and the concertino (1962).

Werner Glaser (1910–), German-born, trained in Cologne and in Berlin with Hindemith and settled in Vesteras in 1943. In the neo-classic style influenced by Hindemith, he composed the capriccios III (1964), the *Transformation* (1966), the *Arioso e Toccata* II (1969), and the *concerto lirico* (1971) for soprano, piano, timpani, and strings.

Erland von Koch (1910–), son of Sigurd von Koch and a piano student of Arrau, merged the twelve-tone technique with Swedish Dalecarlian folk music. As a student in Germany, he composed the neo-classic concerto, op. 11 (1936). While on the faculty at the Royal College of Music in Stockholm, he composed the concerto (1962) and the concerto (1970) with wind orchestra and, later, full orchestra (1972). The concerto (1974) is for violin and piano.

Bjorn Johansson (1913–), music critic with the Gottenborg *Handels-och Sjofartstdning,* composed two concertos (one 1966).

Carl-Olof Anderberg (1914–1972), pianist, free-lance composer, and conductor of the *Hippodromen* (Malmö operetta theater), composed music influenced first by the French and later by the twelve-tone method. There are two early concertos, the concerto, op. 66 (1968), that quotes the *Internationale* and *Horst Wersel Lied,* the *Music* (1970) for piano, winds, and tape, and the *Concerto for a Ballet* (perf. 1972).

Karl Blomdahl (1916–1968) taught at the Royal College of Music and directed music for Swedish Radio. The chamber concerto (1953) for piano, winds, and percussion is for the Swedish pianist Hans Leygraf.

Ingvar Wieslander (1917–1963) follows Scandinavian romanticism and contemporary techniques. While a choir master at the Malmö Municipal Theater, he composed the *Mutzaioni* (1962) for two pianos.

Sven-Eric Johanson (1919–) played organ in churches in Uppsala and Gottenborg, and taught organ and harmony at the conservatory. Reger and Hindemith influenced his compositional style and later works contain atonal techniques. He has the concerto *Gottenborg* (1970).

Hans Leygraf (1920–), performer of Mozart's piano music, has been on the faculty of the Salzburg Mozarteum since 1956. He has the concertino (1938).

Torbjorn Ludquist (1920–), accordionist and composer of concert music for the accordion, composed music influenced by romanticism and Scandinavian styles, Lapland folk songs, and modern compositional techniques, including what he terms "organized spontaneity." The *Hangarmusik* (1967) appears in various sources as the concerto sinfonico or concerto I.

Torsten Nilsson (1920–), respected composer of liturgical music, played organ at the Oscar Church. For piano and orchestra, he composed the *Eurhytmical Voyage* (1970) and the *Steget över Tröskelm* (Over the Threshold), op. 67 (1975), which is a concerto for piano, winds, and percussion.

Ingvar Lidholm (1921–), recently in Rönninge, directed chamber music for Swedish Radio. The serial and improvisational *Poesis* (1963) has a central piano cadenza.

Erik Blomberg (1922–) was a music teacher with Swedish Radio. The *Dialogue* features a concertant relationship between piano and orchestra.

Lars Werle (1926–) studied at Uppsala University and taught at the National School of Music Drama. The *Summer Music 1965,* op. 4 (1965), is for piano and strings.

Gunnar Bucht (1927–) served in the Swedish diplomatic service. The *Meditation,* op. 5 (1950), has traditional forms and contemporary techniques.

Hans Eklund (1927–) studied with Larsson at the Royal Academy of Music and has been teaching counterpoint and harmony at the Stockholm *Musikhögskolan* since 1964. His leanings toward baroque forms appear in the *Musica da Camera* no. 2 (1956), titled "Art Tatum in Memoriam," for trumpet, piano, percussion, and strings. Other compositions are the *Musica da Camera* no. 4 (1955–1959) and the introduction and allegro (1972) for harpsichord and string orchestra.

Maurice Karkoff (1927–) trained at the Royal Academy of Music and has been teaching theory and composition at the Stockholm Training College for teachers since 1965. His experimental techniques appear in the concerto, op. 28 (1957, rev. 1960), and the suite, op. 67 (1962), for harpsichord and strings.

Bengt Hambraeus (1928–), organist, teacher, musicologist, and administrator, evolved a personal musical style with ideas from medieval music, non-European music (especially Japanese), and avant-garde styles. The *Notazioni* (1961) is for harpsichord and chamber orchestra.

Eberhard Eiper (1932–), Polish-born, played violin in the Royal Opera House Orchestra. He has the *Petite Nocturne* (1972) for double bass, harpsichord, and string orchestra, and the concerto (1974).

Bengt Hallberg (1932–), jazz pianist, composer and arranger, wrote music for television, film, and stage. He composed the *Lyrisk Ballad* (1968) for two pianos and the *Ivory Concerto* (1976).

Bo Linde (1933–1970) has a compositional style influenced by Scandinavian music, neo-classic techniques of Larsson, Britten, and Shostakovich, and polytonality. He composed two concertos, opp. 12 and 17 (1954, 1956).

Gunnar Valkare (1943–) uses avant-garde techniques in his musical compositions. The *Kanske en Pastoral om Det Får Tina Upp* (Perhaps a Pastorale if It Will Thaw, 1968) is for percussion, piano, and strings.

Lars-Erik Rosell (1944–) composes music that provides performers with opportunities to improvise. The *Moments of a Changing Sonority* (1969) is for harpsichord, Hammond organ, and strings.

Table 35 Additional Composers in Sweden

Names	Dates	Compositions
Blohm, Sven	1907–1956	*Konsertstycke*
Boldemann, Laci	1921–1969	Concerto, op 13 (1956)
Lundkvist, Per	1916–	Mountain Rhapsody (1960)
		Concertos I, II (1976)
Maciejewski, Roman	1910–	Allegro *concertante* (1944)
		Concerto, 2 pnos
Norre, Dorkas	1911–	Concerto (1946)
Ottoson, David	1892–	*Konsert*
Wahlberg, Rune	1910–	Concerto (1938)
		Concert Fantasy (1967)
		Ballade
		Karneval
Welander, Waldemar	1899–	*Concerto da Camera*
Westin, Karl	1913–	*Legend*

Finland

Pekka Hannikainen (1854–1924), father of the composer Ilmari Hannikainen, was a conductor, writer, chemist, and autodidactic composer. He depended on folk melodies of the Karelien region in his concert works and the concerto, op. 7. His educational efforts established a Finnish musical identity.

Selim Palmgren (1878–1951), student of Busoni, was among the finest Finnish pianists of his time. Features in his piano music are impressionism, the whole-tone scale, moderate dissonance, and characteristics of his own proficiency at the keyboard. While Palmgren achieved popularity with *May Night* for piano solo, he also contributed five concertos: op. 13 (1903), composed in Helsinki; *The Stream* or *The River,* op. 33 (1913), composed in Turko; *Metamorphoses,* op. 41 (1915), with variations; *April,* op. 85 (1928), composed while on the faculty at the Eastman School of Music in the United States; and op. 99 (1939–1940), composed while on the faculty at the Sibelius Academy of Music, Helsinki.

Erik Furuhjelm (1883–1964) studied with Sibelius and in Vienna with Fuchs. While on the faculty at the Helsinki School of Music (now the Sibelius Academy of Music) he composed the *konzertstück* (1911).

Armas Maasalo (1885–1960) was a choirmaster, organist, teacher at the Church Music Institute, and leader of Finnish church music. The *Ricordanze* (1919) is for cello, piano, and orchestra, and the concerto (1919) is for piano.

Carl Hirn (1886–1949) trained in Vienna, Berlin, and Paris. For piano and orchestra, he composed the *Hoang-ho,* the *Valse-Champagne,* and the *Tête-à-Tête.*

Ernest Pingoud (1888–1942) trained in Germany with Riemann and Reger, and directed the Helsinki Municipal Orchestra from 1924. He composed three concertos, opp. 8, 22 and 23 (1917, 1921, 1922), and the *Suurkaupungin Kasvot* (The Fact of the

Big City, 1936–1937). Pingoud's compositional style has coloristic elements of Scriabin, including mystical titles and orchestra effects.

Ernst Linko (1889–1960) changed his name from Lindroth in 1906, studied piano at the Helsinki School of Music (now the Sibelius Academy of Music), in Berlin, and in St. Petersburg. After pursuing a concert career, he joined the faculty at the Sibelius Academy in 1936. Four concertos (1916, 1920, 1931, 1957) are for piano and orchestra.

Väinö Raitio (1891–1945), student of Merikanto in Helsinki, learned Scriabin's harmony in Moscow, expressionism in Berlin, and impressionism in Paris. The concerto, op. 6 (1915), is a student work from the *Musikinstitut.*

Bengt Törne (1891–1967), writer on music, studied with Sibelius and lived in London, Paris, and Rome. He left a concerto.

Ilmari Hannikainen (1892–1955) studied in Helsinki, St. Petersburg, and Paris with Cortot. He was one of Finland's finest pianists, with highly regarded performances of music by Sibelius and Rachmaninoff. He and his brothers Avro and Tauno made up the highly praised Hannikainen Trio. He left the concerto (1919).

Aarre Merikanto (1893–1958) learned polyphony with Reger in Leipzig, studied with Vassilenko in Moscow, and found attractive the German Romantic tradition and Schoenberg's twelve-tone method. In 1951, he followed Palmgren as head of composition at the Sibelius Academy of Music. He left three concertos (1913, 1935–1937, 1955).

Uuno Klami (1900–1961), music critic, composed music in a style influenced by the folk music of the Karelian region, Sibelius, and impressionism which he learned from Ravel in Paris. He composed the concerto *Night in Montartre,* op. 8 (1925), influenced by Ravel, and the concerto, op. 41 (1950). Compositions with string orchestra are the *4 Folksongs,* op. 12 (1930), the *2 Waltzes,* op. 16, and the *Hommage à Haendel,* op. 21 (1931).

Sulho Ranta (1901–1960), conductor, musicologist, critic, and writer, studied at the Helsinki Conservatory (now the Sibelius Academy of Music) and in Germany, Italy, and France. He was among the earliest composers to bring impressionism, expressionism, and Asian musical ideas to Finland. He composed the *sinfonie rhapsodie* (1930), the concertino (1932) with string orchestra, the concerto or partita sinfonia (1938–1939), and the *Tuntematon Maa* (The Unknown Land).

Helvi Leiviskä (1902–), female composer of symphonies, worked as a librarian at the Helsinki Academy (now the Sibelius Academy of Music). The concerto (1935) is in the German romantic style.

Eino Roiha (1904–1955), musicologist and music critic, taught at the *Pädagogischen Hochschule* and the Sibelius Academy of Music from 1948. He composed the concertino (1939).

Lauri Saikkola (1906–) trained at the Viipuri School of Music and played violin in the Viipuri Philharmonic and the Helsinki Philharmonic Orchestra. The *Concerto da Camera* (1957) with chamber orchestra follows classic-romantic traditions.

Erkki Aaltonen (1910–) studied at the Helsinki Conservatory and privately with Raito and Palmgren. He played violin in the Helsinki City Symphony Orchestra until he became the music director for the city of Kemi in 1966. He composed two concertos (1948, 1954).

Nils-Eric Fougstedt (1910–1961), symphony and choral conductor, adopted elements of Hindemith's *Gebrauchmusik,* late-romantic Nordic music, and Bartók. He left the concerto, op. 30 (1944).

Tauno Marttinen (1912–) conducted the city orchestra and directed the music school from 1950. He began composing in a style reflecting Scandinavian nationalism, and, about 1955, adopted serial techniques that are in the concertos, opp. 23 and 74 (1964, 1972).

Jouko Tolonen (1912–), musicologist and pianist trained at the University of Helsinki, directed the Finnish National Opera, and joined the faculty at the University of Turku in 1972. The andante (1950) is for piano and strings.

Bengt Johansson (1914–) studied composition with Palmgren and cello at the Sibelius Academy of Music, where he joined the music history faculty. His music shows the influences of neo-classic techniques, quartal and quintal harmonies, irregular meters, and traditional chord constructions. The concerto (1951) is for piano and orchestra.

Ahti Sonninen (1914–), best known for small musical compositions influenced by Finnish folk songs and modern techniques, studied composition and conducting at the Sibelius Academy of Music, and conducted for Finnish Radio. He composed the concerto (1944–1945) while serving in the Finnish army.

Einar Englund (1916–) studied composition with Copland and at the Sibelius Academy of Music, where he later joined the faculty. His activities as a jazz musician and the neo-classicism of Bartók and Stravinsky influenced his two concertos (1955, 1974).

Erik Fordell (1917–1981) studied at the Sibelius Academy of Music and the Helsinki Institute of Church Music. Much of his compositional effort went toward the completion of forty-five symphonies. He left four concertos, opp. 16, 41, 42, and 117 (1961, 1962, 1962, 1962 rev. 1970), and the *Lasten Savelkuvia.*

Heikki Suolahti (1920–1936), promising composer who died at age 16, left several unfinished musical compositions including a concerto for piano and orchestra.

Matti Rautio (1922–) studied composition and piano at the Sibelius Academy of Music. While the director of the institution, he composed the concerto (1968–1971).

Einojuhani Rautavaara (1928–) trained at the Sibelius Academy of Music, in the United States with Copland, Persichetti, and Sessions, and in Switzerland with Vogel for dodecaphonic techniques. He composed the concerto, op. 45 (1969), and *The Water Circle* (perf. 1972) for chorus, piano, and orchestra.

Osmo Lindeman (1929–), pianist, studied at the Sibelius Academy of Music and taught there. He is a leader in computer and electronic music composition. His two concertos (1964, 1965) are in a traditional, romantic style.

Usko Meriläinen (1930–), choral conductor with the Finnish National Opera and piano teacher at the Sibelius Academy of Music, composes music with features of Hindemith, Bartók, Stravinsky, and the twelve-tone method from 1958. He has two concertos (1955, 1969), the *Dialogues* (concerto no. 3, 1977), and the *Kinetic Poem* (perf. 1982).

Jorma Panula (1930–) trained at the Helsinki School of Church Music, the

Sibelius Academy of Music, and with Dean Dixon at Lund. The jazz capriccio (1965) has contemporary devices.

Aulis Sallinen (1935–) directed the Finnish Radio Symphony, taught at the Sibelius Academy of Music, and became a Finnish State Arts Professor. The *Metamorphoses* (1964) is for piano and chamber orchestra.

Paavo Heininen (1938–), conductor and writer, taught at the Juilliard School of Music in New York City, in Turku, Finland, and at the Sibelius Academy of Music from 1966. Two concertos (1964, 1966) show elements of motivic development and twelve-tone ideas.

Erkki Salmenhaara (1941–) studied at the Sibelius Academy of Music and with Ligeti in Vienna. The *9 Improvisations* is a serial concerto for piano, strings, and timpani.

Pehr Nordgren (1944–) studied musicology at Helsinki University and composition and Japanese music at Tokyo University of Arts and Music. He uses tone clusters, serialism, and tonal devices. For piano and orchestra, he composed the concerto, op. 23 (1975).

Leif Segerstam (1944–), conductor of the Finnish National Opera, composed the Two; Onward, Inwards, Outwards (Upwards, Downwards) . . . Aroundwards . . . Towards . . . (1974) for two pianos and orchestra. The concertino fantasia is for violin, piano, and thirteen or thirty-one players.

Mikko Heiniö (1948–) studied at the Sibelius Academy of Music. Possibly, his two concertos, opp. 4 and 13 (1971, 1973), are student works.

Chapter 15

England and Wales, Scotland, Ireland, and Iceland

England and Wales

Charles Stanford (1852–1924) taught composition at Cambridge University and the Royal College of Music in London. Among his many students were Wood, Lambert, Vaughan Williams, Holst, Coleridge-Taylor, Ireland, Bridge, Butterworth, Bliss, Benjamin, and Howells. Schumann and Brahms influenced Stanford's music (See ex. 15–1). For piano and orchestra, he composed three concertos, opp. 59, 126, and 171 (1895, 1915, 1919), and the concert variations, op. 71 (1898), based on the old English tune "Down Among the Dead Men." Stanford had the unusual ability to revise his compositions mentally before writing the finished version.

Tobias Matthay (1858–1945), student and teacher at the Royal Academy of Music, gained international fame for his teaching methods set forth in *The Act of Touch*. Among his more than one hundred piano compositions is the *konzertstück,* op. 12 (pub. 1909), and a cadenza for Beethoven's concerto no. 1.

Arthur Somervell (1863–1937) taught at the Royal College of Music and served as an inspector of music for the Board of Education. He worked toward the establishment and recognition of music in the public schools. While his most important musical compositions are song cycles, for piano and orchestra he composed the symphonic variations (ca. 1912) and the concerto *The Highland* (1921). The music contains elements of German classicism of the nineteenth century, namely Mendelssohn and Brahms.

Herbert Bedford (1867–1945), highly regarded painter of miniatures, composed military band music and unaccompanied songs. The divertimento (1926) is for piano and strings.

Frederick Dawson (1868–1940), a precocious child who learned by memory the two volumes of Bach's *Well-Tempered Clavier* by age 10, was a respected pianist with duties at the Royal Manchester College of Music and the Royal College of Music. He studied Grieg's concerto with Grieg, and composed cadenzas for Beethoven's concerto nos. 3 and 4.

Frédéric d'Erlanger (1868–1943) wrote under the pseudonym Regnal, formed by the retrograde of the last six letters of his last name. He was a banker in London and he directed the Covent Garden Opera. The concerto symphonique (1921) is for piano and orchestra.

Example 15–1. Stanford Concerto no. 2, op. 126, mvt. 1, mm. 63–75

Henry Walford Davies (1869–1941) was the organist and choir director at the Temple Church. His music for piano and orchestra has descriptive titles. The Conversations, op. 43 (1914), is in four movements titled *Congenial Company, A Moment in Passing, Intimate Friends,* and *Playmates.* The memorial suite, op. 50 (1923), is in five movements titled *Memorial Melody* (1919), *Personal Memories, Arrows of Desire, Leisure,* and *Envoy.* Davies composed a children's symphony, op. 53 (1927), while on the faculty at the University of Wales. For his popular radio series "Music Lessons in Schools," he composed *London Calling the Schools* (1932) for piano, orchestra, and radio announcer.

Eugénie-Emilie Folville (1870–1946), praised pianist, violinist, and conductor, taught piano at the Liège Conservatory and settled in Bournemouth to teach. The concerto (1924) is for piano and orchestra.

Ralph Vaughan Williams (1872–1958) studied with Wood at Cambridge, Parry and Stanford at the Royal College of Music, and Bruch in Berlin. In 1919, he joined the faculty of the Royal College of Music. As a nationalist, he broke the traditional English ties with the music of Germany and Italy. He composed the first two movements (1926) of a concerto, and later the third movement (1930–1931). In 1933, Adrian Boult suggested that Vaughan Williams score the concerto for two pianos, because one piano did not seem to balance the orchestra. Pianist Joseph Cooper produced the two-piano version (perf. 1946) with the approval and help of the composer. Most of the right-hand part of the original version is for one piano and the left-hand part is for the other piano. The work is percussive, and a fugue is in the finale.

Edward Elgar (1875–1934) worked on the scherzo (1909) that remains a fragment and the incomplete concerto, op. 90 (1909, 1914, 1917, 1925, 1932).

Albert Ketèlbey (1875–1959) was a precocious child who composed and played his own piano sonata at Worcester Town Hall. At age 13, he entered the Trinity College of Music as a Queen Victoria scholar, and he became a music director at the Vaudeville Theater at age 22. He composed a caprice and the *concertstück.*

Cyril Rootham (1875–1938) played organ at St. John's College. The miniature suite (1921) is for piano and orchestra or strings.

Donald Francis Tovey (1875–1940) was a music scholar, pianist, author of the six-volume *Essays in Musical Analysis,* and editor of Beethoven's sonatas for piano. He left the cadenzas (pub. 1937) for Beethoven's concerto no. 4.

William Whittaker (1876–1944), choral conductor and writer, taught at Edinburgh University. The orchestral concerto (1933) is for piano and strings.

Kathleen Bruckshaw (1877–1921), student of Stavenhagen and Busoni, conducted English orchestras in Berlin. At age 9, she performed Rubinstein's concerto no. 4, op. 70. She may have composed her piano concerto in London.

Roger Quilter (1877–1953) is a member of a group of English composers sometimes known as the Frankfurt group because he, Grainger, Scott, Gardiner, and O'Neil studied at the Hoch Conservatory in Frankfurt. While Quilter received praise mainly for his songs, for piano and orchestra he composed *Moonlight on the Lake* (intermezzo from Where the Rainbow Ends, pub. 1937) and the *Water Nymph* (pub. 1937).

Harry Farjeon (1878–1948) taught piano at the Royal Academy of Music from 1903. The concerto, op. 64 (1903), sometimes appears as the *Phantasy Concerto.*

Joseph Holbrooke (1878–1958) studied at the Royal Academy of Music before conducting ballet and various orchestras. His piano concertos are op. 36 (1896–1900), *The Song of Gwyn ap Nudd,* op. 52 (1907), also known as the *Poem Concerto,* and *L'Orient,* op. 100 (1928).

Thomas Beecham (1879–1961), conductor, established the London Philharmonic Orchestra and brought it to world renown. He probably intended the concerto (ca. 1903) for his career as a pianist, but an injury forced a change in plans.

Frank Bridge (1879–1941), teacher, conducted the Marie Brema Opera at the

Savoy Theater and the Promenade Concerts at Covent Garden. He had difficulty obtaining recognition as a mainstream composer. The rhapsody *Phantasm* (1931) has tritones (See ex. 15–2), wholetone scales (See ex. 15–3), and bitonality.

Hamilton Harty (1879–1941), conductor, orchestrated Handel's *Water Music* and *Firework's Music*. His concerto (1922) is from the years he conducted the Hallé orchestra.

John Ireland (1879–1962) entered the Royal College of Music at age 13, taught Arnell, Britten, Bush, Moeran, and Searle there, and played organ at St. Luke's in Chelsea. His two-movement concerto (1930) has French impressionistic leanings, and both themes of the first movement appear in the second movement. The *Legend* (1933) reflects Ireland's interest in Arthur Machen's pagan mysticism, and the *Dies Irae* is the basis for the "Quasi Recitando."

Cyril Scott (1879–1970) composed music influenced by Scriabin, Delius, and Ravel. His chromatic style depends on a high level of dissonance in chords, unresolved chords and pitches, and a rhapsodic character. Piano parts have thick textures instead of quick bravura lines. Among his musical compositions for piano and orchestra are the two concertos (1913–1914, 1950); *Early One Morning* (1931), which is a set of variations on the tune "Early One Morning"; the concerto (1937) for harpsichord; and the *passacaglia festevole* for two pianos. In 1931, Scott revised *Early One Morning* for one piano from the original version for two pianos.

Edgar Bainton (1880–1956) taught piano and composition at the Conservatory of Newcastle-upon-Tyne and directed the New South Wales State *Conservatorium* in Sydney, Australia. The concerto-fantasia (ca. 1917) is in a late-romantic style.

Example 15–2. Bridge *Phantasm,* mm. 78–84

Example 15–3. Bridge *Phantasm,* mm. 13–23

Irene Wieniawski (1880–1932), daughter of Polish violinist Henryk Wieniawski, by marriage Lady Dean Paul, used the pseudonym Poldowski. She studied at the Brussels Conservatory and with Gédalge and d'Indy in Paris, where she adopted impressionistic traits. For piano and orchestra, she composed *Pat Malone's Wake*.

Edward Isaacs (1881–1953), teacher, performed weekly Friday afternoon piano recitals from 1917 to 1923. Even after becoming blind, he continued an active life of concert work, including performances of concertos with major orchestras. He probably planned the concerto (1907) for his own use.

Arthur Willner (1881–1959), German, studied with Reinecke at the Leipzig Conservatory and with Rheinberger and Thuille at the Munich Academy. He taught at the Stern Conservatory in Berlin and moved to London in 1938. For piano and strings, he composed the concerto, op. 53, the concerto *Bagpipes,* op. 78 (copyright 1939), and the suite, op. 80.

George Dyson (1883–1964) directed music at Winchester College and the Royal College of Music. The concerto *leggiero* (1951) is for piano and strings.

York Bowen (1884–1961), brilliant pianist, taught at the Royal Academy of Music. He composed three concertos (no. 1 ca. 1899, no. 3 ca. 1906).

Montague Phillips (1885–1969) studied and taught at the Royal Academy of Music. He left two concertos, opp. 5 and 32 (1908–1909, 1919).

Frank Merrick (1886–1981) studied with Leschetizky in Vienna. He edited works by Chopin, worked on the John Field piano concertos for *Musica Britannia,* and championed Field's piano concertos. Merrick composed two concertos.

Norman Peterkin (1886–) worked with the Oxford University Press from 1925. He was an autodidactic composer with at least one concerto for piano and orchestra.

Harold Darke (1888–1976) studied with Stanford at the Royal College of Music and worked as the organist at St. Michael's Church. For fifty years he performed a midday recital at the church each Monday. The *Phantasie* for piano and orchestra is a student work.

Cecil Gibbs (1889–1960) studied at Trinity College in Cambridge and the Royal College of Music, where he later joined the faculty. For piano and string orchestra, he composed the dance fantasy *Enchanted Wood,* op. 25 (1919), the concertino, op. 103 (1942), and *A Simple Concerto* (1955).

Julius Isserlis (1889–1968), Russian, studied piano with Safonov and composition with Taneyev at the Moscow Conservatory. He taught at the Moscow Philharmonic Institute of Music in Vienna, and settled in London in 1928. His piano recitals in Europe and America included Russian music and works of Chopin. He left two *Poèms* for piano and orchestra.

Arthur Bliss (1891–1975) studied at the Royal College of Music with Stanford, Holst, and Vaughan Williams. He began composing as an "enfant terrible," and soon gravitated toward a romantic style influenced by Elgar. The concerto (1923, rev. 1923) for piano, tenor, strings, and percussion disappeared during the war. In 1924, he revised the concerto for two pianos and orchestra and, in 1968, arranged it for two pianos, three hands. This is the earliest English concerto for two pianos in the twentieth century. He composed the concerto (1938–1939) for British Week at the 1939 World's Fair in New York City and dedicated it "to the People of the United States of America."

Herbert Howells (1892–1983) composed the concerto, op. 4 (1913), while a student of Stanford and Parry at the Royal College of Music. Howells' music blends English musical style, modal counterpoint, and influences of Elgar and Vaughan Williams. While on the faculty at the Royal College of Music, he composed the concerto, op. 39 (1924), that drew much attention due to outbursts of an audience member.

Alec Rowley (1892–1958), pianist and teacher, studied at the Royal Academy of Music, where he was a fellow from 1934. He composed the concerto, op. 49 (1938), with band accompaniment; the concerto (perf. 1938); the *Miniature Concerto* (1947); the *Legend* (1947), with solo violin and string orchestra; and the concerto (1956) for piano or harpsichord with small orchestra.

Kaikhosru Shapurji Sorabji (1892–), born Leon Dudley, placed no importance on public acceptance or rejection of his music. About 1950, he published a prohibition against performances of his musical compositions because of bad interpretations, but legally he could not prohibit performances of published works. He evolved a complex style with extreme technical problems, textural difficulties, asymmetric rhythmic patterns, Oriental and Western musical ideas, and four and five staves of music. Many works are extremely long and intended as entire concert programs. Due to his reclusive behavior, a complete and accurate list of compositions is difficult to obtain. He destroyed the concerto no. 1 (1917, rev. 1918) or another concerto of about the same era. Other concertos are no. 2 (1920) in one movement; no. 3, *Simorg-Anka* (1924) with chamber orchestra; and nos. 4 and 5 (ca. 1925, 1927–1928). The symphony (1922) is for chorus, orchestra, organ, and piano, and the symphony (1933) remains incomplete. The symphony *Jami* (1942–1951) for large orchestra, double chorus, organ, piano, and baritone solo is more than 1000 pages in length. There are the symphonic variations (1951–1955) and the symphony *High Mass* (1955–1961) for solo violin, chorus, orchestra, organ, and piano. His last works are the *Opus Clavisymphonicum* (1957–1959) and the *Opus Claviorchestrale* (1973–1975).

Arthur Benjamin (1893–1960), Australian pianist, taught at the Royal College of Music, where Britten was one of his students. He claimed Gershwin's *Rhapsody in Blue* inspired his concertino (1926). Other compositions are the *Concerto Quasi una Fantasia* (1949), the *Caribbean Dance* (1949), and the *North American Square Dances* (1955), arranged from an orchestra version (1951) for duo pianists Vronsky and Babin.

Edric Cundell (1893–1961) conducted various orchestras including the Stock Exchange Orchestra. He founded the Edric Cundell Chamber orchestra, taught at the Trinity College of Music, and directed the Guildhall School of Music. While most of his energy went to administrative duties, he composed a concerto for piano and orchestra.

Hugo Anson (1894–1958), born in New Zealand, studied in London at the Royal Academy of Music and Trinity College, and taught at the Royal College of Music from 1925. His concerto (pub. 1941) for two pianos and strings is in two sections, with the theme of the first section appearing in the second section.

Gordon Jacob (1895–1984), conductor, teacher, and author, taught at the Royal College of Music. He composed two concertos (1927, 1956), the concerto (1969) for piano duet, three hands, and the concertino (1957).

Arnold Foster (1896–1963) studied with Vaughan Williams at the Royal College of Music and taught at the Westminister School. The *Concerto on Country Dance Tunes* (1930) is on English folk songs.

Roberto Gerhard (1896–1970), Spanish, studied with Granados in Barcelona and Schoenberg in Vienna and in Berlin before settling in England. His music has Spanish elements and employs the twelve-tone method. The concerto (1950–1951) has serialism; the concerto (1955–1956) is for harpsichord, strings, and percussion.

Norman Demuth (1898–1968), writer on music and teacher at the Royal Academy of Music, used musical techniques of d'Indy, Franck, and Roussel. He composed the *Two War Poems* (1940), the concerto (1943), the concertino (1947) with small orchestra, the concerto (1947) for left hand, the *Legend* (1949) for left hand, and the sinfonietta (1958).

Alan Bush (1900–) studied with Matthay, Schnabel, and Ireland, and adopted the socialist-realist philosophy as a basis for musical composition. He believes each note must have thematic significance akin to Schoenberg's twelve-tone method. His music includes the concerto, op. 18 (1962), with baritone solo and men's chorus in the last movement, the *Variations, Nocturne and Finale on an English Seasong,* op. 60

(1962), and the symphonic movement *Africa,* op. 73 (1971–1972). Compositions of the 1920s and 1930s employ contemporary central European styles, and later compositions have simpler harmonic and melodic ideas.

David Wynne (1900–) studied in Cardiff where he stayed to pursue musical interests. The concerto (1962) for two pianos, three hands has free chromaticism and a Bartók influence.

Gerald Finzi (1901–1956), influenced by Elgar, Vaughan Williams, and English folk music, attended the Royal Academy of Music and taught there. He owned the finest private library of music from the years 1740–1784; now the collection is at St. Andrews University in Fife. For piano and orchestra, he composed the eclogue, op. 10 (1920s, rev. 1940s), and the grand fantasie and toccata, op. 38 (1928, rev. 1953).

Edmund Rubbra (1901–) had an uncle who owned a music store where young Edmund demonstrated pianos for customers. He studied composition with Ireland, Goossens, Scott, Holst, and Vaughan Williams. Rubbra's music shows an influence of romanticism, a fondness for lyricism, and a rich harmonic vocabulary. He composed the concerto, op. 30 (1931), and the sinfonia *concertante,* op. 38 (1934, rev. 1943), based on a discarded piano concerto. The concerto, op. 85 (1956), is from his teaching years at Oxford University.

Hubert Hales (1902–1965) taught at several schools in England. He left the ballad *Merseyside,* op. 19.

Freda Swain (1902–), champion of contemporary English music, composed the *Airmail Concerto* (1939) for her husband Arthur Alexander, who was stranded in South Africa at the outbreak of the war. While composing the concerto in England, she copied each page of music on lightweight paper and airmailed it to him.

William Walton (1902–) used jazz in music written for the Savoy Orpheus Band and that influence is seen in the fantasia *concertante* (1923–1924) for two pianos, jazz band, and orchestra. The composition existed in 1928, when the Oxford University Press planned its publication, but Walton destroyed the manuscript. The sinfonia *concertante* (1926–1927, rev. 1943) is for orchestra with piano obbligato.

Ralph Wood (1902–), businessman, is mostly self-taught, with only a few lessons with Howells and Jacob. His primary musical contributions are articles for periodicals. He has the concerto (1946).

Lennox Berkeley (1903–) studied French and philosophy at Merton College in Oxford and composition with Boulanger in Paris. He worked in the Music Department of the BBC and taught composition at the Royal Academy of Music. His music is diatonic, with "wrong note" techniques akin to Poulenc, neo-classic and neo-baroque elements, and influenced by Stravinsky, Mozart, Chopin, Fauré, and Ravel. He composed the introduction and allegro, op. 11 (1938), for two pianos, the concerto, op. 29 (1947), the concerto, op. 30 (1948), for two pianos (See ex. 15–4), the concerto, op 46 (1958), with double string orchestra, and the sinfonia *concertante* (pub. 1973).

Avril Coleridge-Taylor (1903–), daughter of composer Samuel Coleridge-Taylor, promoted her father's music. Much of her compositional effort was in songs. Her concerto (1938) is for piano and orchestra.

Richard Hall (1903–) taught at the Royal Manchester College of Music, where his students included Stevenson, Butterworth, Goehr, Davies, Birtwistle, and Ogdon.

Example 15–4. Berkeley Concerto, op. 30, mvt. 1, mm. 1–8

These composers are known as the Manchester New Music Group. Hall's music shows the influence of Hindemith, serialism, atonality, and contrapuntal devices. While a church organist in Leeds, he probably composed the rhapsody (1932) for saxophone, piano, and strings. He composed the concerto (1949) in Manchester.

Leighton Lucas (1903–1982) danced with the Diaghilev Russian Ballet in Paris and conducted the Birmingham Repertory Theatre. He composed the partita (1934), with chamber orchestra, and the *Five Sonnets* (1937).

Robin Milford (1903–1959) studied with Holst, Vaughan Williams, and Morris at the Royal College of Music. His compositional style depends on diatonic materials similar to English folk music. The miniature concerto (1929) is for harpsichord and small orchestra, and *Fishing by Moonlight* (1952) is for piano and strings.

Thomas Pitfield (1903–) trained at the Royal Manchester College of Music and later joined the faculty. The concerto no. 1 (ca. 1951) is in the eighteenth-century style and the concerto no. 2 (pub. 1960) has the title *The Student.*

Richard Addinsell (1904–1977) composed the popular *Warsaw Concerto* (1941) for the film *Dangerous Moonlight,* which appeared in the United States under the title *Suicide Squadron.* The concerto is stylistically similar to Rachmaninoff's concerto no. 2. Also, the *Smokey Mountains* (1950) is in Rachmaninoff's style.

William Alwyn (1905–), flautist and teacher at the Royal Academy of Music, composed the concerto (1930) using neo-classic practices. From Indian music, he learned the idea of "limited modes" of four to eight notes to create melody and harmony similar to Schoenberg's twelve-tone method.

Francis Chagrin (1905–1972), administrator and conductor of Romanian birth, studied engineering in Zürich and worked in the family business in Bucharest. He studied at the *École Normale* with Boulanger and Dukas, and settled in London in 1936. He composed theater and film music and the concerto (1948).

Christian Darnton (1905–1981) studied at the Brighton School of Music, the Matthay School, and with Jacob at the Royal College of Music. He enjoyed a degree of recognition in England during the 1940s and 1950s. For piano, he composed the concerto (1933) and the concertino (1952) with strings. He eventually ceased musical composition in favor of writing philosophy.

Constant Lambert (1905–1951), conductor of the Vic-Wells ballet, is the first English composer to have a composition commissioned by Diaghilev. While a student at the Royal College of Music, he composed the concerto (1924) for piano, two trumpets, timpani, and strings. The work has three titled movements—"Overture," "Intermède," and "Finale"—and contains changing meters, cross accents, and a strong rhythmic drive. Probably his most successful composition is the jazz-influenced *Rio Grande* (1927), with orchestra and chorus, based on a poem by Sacheverell Sitwell. Lambert believed the concerto (1930–1931) to be superior to the *Rio Grande.* Lambert arranged one of Handel's organ concertos as a concerto for piano and small orchestra.

Walter Leigh (1905–1942) composed the concerto (1936) while a student in Cambridge. He perished in combat in North Africa.

Michael Tippett (1905–) studied with Morris, Boult, and Sargent at the Royal College of Music. His compositional style draws upon neo-romantic ideas, dense polyphony, and rhapsodic passages. Both works for piano and orchestra are products of his teaching years at Morley College. He composed the *Fantasy on a Theme by Handel* (1939–1941) and the concerto (1955) based on intervals of fourths similar to Hindemith's style and structurally akin to Beethoven's Concerto no. 4. In the first movement, Tippett writes parts for both hands in a high register and in a style that accompanies the orchestra, and in the third movement the piano part has rhythmic passages independent of the orchestra.

Arnold Cooke (1906–) studied in Berlin with Hindemith and adopted the idea of *Gebrauchsmusik.* He composed the concerto (1939–1940) while serving in the British navy.

Benjamin Frankel (1906–1973) trained as a watchmaker before studying music in Germany. When he returned to London, he played piano and violin in restaurants, wrote film music, and taught at the Guildhall School of Music and Drama from 1946. He follows the communist philosophy of socialist realism. The twelve-tone serenata *concertante,* op. 37 (1961), is for piano trio.

Elisabeth Lutyens (1906–1983), daughter of architect Edwin Lutyens, studied at the Royal College of Music and in Paris. Her early musical compositions had a strong romantic expression, then she gravitated toward a personal concept of expressionist style with a reliance on twelve-tone ideas. The chamber concerto no. 2, op. 8 (1940–1941), is for clarinet, tenor saxophone, piano, and strings. The symphony, op. 46 (1961), is for piano, winds, two harps, and percussion. Other works are the *Music,* op. 59 (1964), and the *Nox,* op. 118 (1977), for piano and two chamber orchestras.

Grace Williams (1906–1977), Welsh, trained at the University of Wales, Cardiff, and the Royal College of Music with Vaughan Williams and Jacob. She intended the sinfonia *concertante* (1941) to be a concerto influenced by Vaughan Williams and in the tradition of Liszt and Tchaikovsky. In Barry, she composed the *Variations on a Swedish Tune "The Shoemaker."* She worked on the concerto (1948) using material from sketches for other works. One movement has an orchestration and the rest is incomplete.

Elizabeth Maconchy (1907–) studied with Vaughan Williams at the Royal College of Music and in Prague, where expressionism captured her interest. Her music includes the concerto (1928) with chamber orchestra, the concerto (1928) with string orchestra, the *Dialogue* (1940), and the concertino (1949).

Howard Ferguson (1908–), editor, musicologist, and pianist, taught at the Royal Academy of Music and settled in Cambridge. Some of his important contributions have been in early keyboard music and include the book *Keyboard Interpretation.* Mozart's music influenced the concerto, op. 12 (1950–1951), and possibly the concerto (1939).

George Linstead (1908–), Scottish pianist, wrote criticism for the *Sheffield Daily Telegraph* and taught at Sheffield University from 1947. He has two concertos (1939, 1941).

Brian Easdale (1909–), trained at the Royal College of Music, composed music for the theater and the film *The Red Shoes.* His concerto (ca. 1936) displays influences of Britten, Bax, and Bridge.

Franz Reizenstein (1911–1968), born in Germany, studied with Hindemith at the State Academy of Music in Berlin and with Vaughan Williams at the Royal College of Music in London. He gained a fine reputation as a pianist in performances of chamber music and concertos. He taught at the Royal Academy of Music and the Royal Manchester College. He left the concerto, op. 16 (1941), which has a neo-romantic style, and the concerto, op. 37 (1956–1961). The comical *Concerto Populare,* or *Piano*

Concerto to End All Piano Concertos (1956), contains parts of concertos by Tchaikovsky, Grieg, and Rachmaninoff, and elements of Gershwin, Beethoven, popular tunes, and fragments of other compositions. The work begins with the orchestra performing the tutti introduction of Tchaikovsky's concerto no. 1, while the pianist plays the introduction of Grieg's concerto. After musical disagreements about which concerto to perform, the orchestra and piano settle on the same composition at approximately the same time. The concerto was one of several humorous compositions performed at a Hoffnung Concert.

Daniel Jones (1912–), lifelong friend of the poet Dylan Thomas, uses traditional forms, tonality, and the Welsh propensity for complexity and lyricism without including features of folk music. He evolved meters such as 9+2+3/8. He has a concerto (1943).

Percy Young (1912–) directed Wolverhampton College of Technology from 1944. The *Fugal Concerto* (1954) is for two pianos and strings. The *Poco andante* movement is for a concerto for piano and strings.

Stanley Bate (1913–1959), pianist and painter, studied with Vaughan Williams, Boulanger in Paris, and Hindemith in Berlin. He created a considerable reputation for himself on the London stage. Among his compositions are the concerto, op. 21 (perf. 1939), for piano and chamber orchestra; the *concertante,* op. 24, for piano and strings; the two concertos, opp. 28 and 61 (1941, 1952); the concerto *grosso* (1952) for piano and strings; and the harpsichord concerto (1953). Much of the music displays influences of Vaughan Williams and Hindemith.

Benjamin Britten (1913–1976) revised the concerto, op. 13 (1938, rev. 1945), by discarding the original third movement and using different music for the movement. He retracted the *Young Apollo,* op. 16 (1939), for piano, solo string quartet, and strings. The work has two motives: the first is the scale passages in the piano part that span an octave, with each octave note repeated, and the second in the string parts with distinctive leaps, repeated notes, and grace notes played on the beat. Britten dedicated the left-hand *Diversions on a Theme,* op. 21 (1940), to Paul Wittgenstein. The composition has a theme and eleven variations: "Recitative" for solo piano, "Romance," "March," "Rubato," "Chorale," "Nocturne," "Bádineríe," "Ritmico" (discarded 1951), "Toccata," "Toccata II," "Adagio," and "Tarantella." In the United States, Britten composed the one-movement *Scottish Ballad,* op. 26 (1941), for two pianos and orchestra. The work contains the psalm tune "Dundee" from the *Scottish Psalter* (1615), which is known today as "Let Saints on Earth in Concert Sing" and "God Moves in a Mysterious Way." Other tunes include "The Flowers of the Forest," describing Scottish soldiers killed in the Battle of Flodden, "Turn Ye to Me," and a Scottish reel. The cadenza (1966) is for Mozart's concerto, K.482.

Miriam Hyde (1913–), Australian, studied with Benjamin, Morris, and Jacob at the Royal College of Music. She performed the concertos, opp. 27 and 32 (1934, 1935), with the BBC Orchestra and the London Philharmonic Orchestra. She has the fantasy-romantic, op. 49 (1941), and cadenzas for some Mozart concertos.

George Lloyd (1913–) writes music in a tonal style with romantic and twentieth-century features. He has four concertos, with one titled *Scapegoat.* He orchestrated the concerto no. 4 (1970) in 1983.

Andrej Panufnik (1914–), Polish conductor, studied at the Warsaw Conservatory and settled in England as the music director of the Birmingham Symphony Orchestra. His concerto (1962, rev. 1972) is for piano and orchestra.

William Bardwell (1915–) studied with Morris and Jacob at the Royal College of Music and Boulanger in Paris. He played first trumpet with the London Philharmonic Orchestra. His concerto (1954) for harpsichord and small orchestra has neoclassic traits.

Pamela Harrison (1915–) studied at the Royal College of Music with Benjamin, Howells, and Jacob. The *concertante* (1954) is for piano and orchestra.

Humphrey Searle (1915–1982) was a Liszt scholar and author of *The Music of Liszt*[1], which contains an accepted numbering system for Liszt's music. He studied with Jacob, Morris, and Ireland, and in Vienna with Webern, who turned Searle's interest toward atonal music. Searle composed two concertos, opp. 5 and 27 (1943–1944, 1955), and the *concertante,* op. 24 (1954). He was a composer-in-residence at Stanford University in California, and taught at the University of Southern California in Los Angeles and the Royal College of Music in London.

Denis Aplvor (1916–), Irish of Welsh parentage, studied in London with Hadley and Rawsthorne. The concerto, op. 13 (1948), marks the begining of his use of the twelve-tone method. The themes have rows, but the music is chromatic within a tonal idiom. The concertino, op. 18a (1951), contains musical material from the ballet *A Mirror for Witches.*

David Cox (1916–) writes and plays organ for the BBC and in church. The *Majorca, a Balearic Impression* (1955) is for two pianos and orchestra.

Ian Parrott (1916–) composed music influenced by Welsh musical elements. While a faculty member at Birmingham University, he composed the concerto (1948) for piano and string orchestra.

Richard Arnell (1917–), praised for stage works, composed the divertimento I, op. 5 (1939), while a student of Ireland at the Royal College of Music. The romantic concerto, op. 44 (1946), and the concerto (1967) were composed when he taught at Trinity College. Other compositions are the *Sections* for piano and chamber orchestra and a harpsichord concerto.

Anthony Burgess (1917–), author of the novel *A Clockwork Orange,* is a jazz pianist with serious musical training. He has the *Song of a Northern City* (1947), the concerto (1976), and the concertino (1951) for piano and percussion.

John Gardner (1917–) writes in a diatonic style dependent on contrapuntal techniques. While a student at Exeter College, Oxford, he composed the serenade (1944) for oboe, piano, and string orchestra. While on the faculties of Morley College and the Royal Academy of Music, he composed the concerto, op. 34 (1955–1957).

John Addison (1920–) schooled at Wellington College and the Royal College of Music, where he joined the staff in 1951. He wrote incidental scores and music for more than sixty films. The variations (1949) display impressionism and a concertino contains contemporary influences of syncopation, meter changes, and chromaticism. Other works are the *Conversation Piece* and the *Wellington Suite.*

Geoffrey Bush (1920–), organist, teacher, and writer on music, composes in a traditional tonal style. While on the faculty at the University of London, he composed the concertino no. 1 (1953) and the concerto (1962) for piano, trumpet, and strings. Since 1969, he has been at King's College, London, where he composed the concertino no. 2 (1976).

Peter Fricker (1920–), influenced by Bartók, Berg, Hindemith, and Schoenberg, trained at the Royal College of Music and followed Tippitt as the director of Morley College. In 1964, he joined the faculty at the University of California at Santa Barbara. The four-movement *concertante* no. 2, op. 15 (1951), for three pianos, timpani, and strings is on a three-clavier concerto of J. S. Bach. The concerto, op. 19 (1954), has a chromatic middle movement titled *Air and Variations,* and there is the toccata, op. 33 (1959).

Malcom Arnold (1921–), principal trumpeter with the London Philharmonic, achieved international recognition as a composer of more than eighty film scores. Compositions for piano and orchestra are the concerto, op. 32 (1951), for piano duet, the *Concerto for Phillis and Cyril,* op. 104 (1969), for two pianos, three hands, and the *Fantasy on a Theme of John Field,* op. 116 (1975).

Ruth Gipps (1921–) studied with Vaughan Williams and Matthay. While a conductor in Birmingham, she composed the concerto, op. 34 (1948).

Robert Simpson (1921–), Carl Nielsen scholar, produced music programs for the BBC. The music of Beethoven and Nielsen influenced Simpson's concerto (1967).

Peter Wishart (1921–) taught music at Birmingham University. The concerto, op. 32 (1958), displays a fondness for ostinatos and motor rhythms.

Ian Hamilton (1922–), Scottish composer influenced by Webern, trained at the Royal College of Music and taught at Morley College and several institutions in the United States. He has the concerto no. 1 (1959–1960, rev. 1967) and the concerto no. 2 (1960).

Stephen Dodgson (1924–) studied and taught at the Royal College of Music from 1965. He composed the concerto (1959), the *Concerto da Camera IV,* and a concertino for piano and percussion.

Joseph Horovitz (1926–) arrived in London from Austria in 1938. He studied at the Royal College of Music and with Boulanger in Paris and worked on the humorous *Hoffnung Concerto*. The jazz concerto (1965) for harpsichord or piano follows the concerto structure of J. S. Bach.

John Dankworth (1927–) is a jazz clarinetist, saxophonist, and band leader. His concerto (1972) displays characteristics of jazz and concert music.

Wilfred Josephs (1927–) trained as a dental surgeon before entering the Guildhall School of Music. He adopted a compositional style having elements of the twelve-tone method, atonality, and tonality. He composed the *Concerto da camera,* op. 25 (1959–1960), for violin, harpsichord, and strings; the concerto, op. 48 (1965); the concerto, op. 77 (1971), with chamber orchestra; and the *Concerto da Camera,* op. 82a (1972), for guitar, harp, harpsichord, and chamber orchestra.

John Joubert (1927–), born in South Africa and a student of Ferguson at the Royal Academy of Music, writes music aimed at pleasing audiences. He composed the concerto, op. 25 (1958), for piano and strings during the years he taught at the University of Hull. *Threnos,* op. 78 (1974), is for harpsichord and twelve strings.

Francis Routh (1927–), pianist and writer, mixes English musical ideas with neo-classic elements of Stravinsky. He has the concerto, op. 32 (1976).

Gerard Schurmann (1928–), born in Indonesia, combines neo-baroque ideas with serial techniques. His concerto (1972–1973) follows the romantic traditions of Liszt and Rachmaninoff. In 1981, he moved to Hollywood, Calif.

Roy Teed (1928–) studied with Berkeley at the Royal Academy of Music and now teaches there. His concerto (1952) is a student work.

Philip Cannon (1929–) studied with Vaughan Williams and Jacob at the Royal College of Music and taught at the institution. He has a concertino for piano and strings.

Alun Hoddinott (1929–) taught at the University College of South Wales, Cardiff. The main influences on his style are Rawsthorne and Bartók. He has three concertos, opp. 19, 21, and 44 (ca. 1960, 1960, 1966). In op. 19, the palindrome technique appears in various movements.

Kenneth Leighton (1929–) trained at Queen's College, Oxford, and with Petrassi in Rome. He began composing in a chromatic style like Bartók and Hindemith, and moved toward a twelve-tone style similar to Berg and Dallapiccola. He composed the concerto, op. 11 (1951), in Rome or Oxford. The concerto, op. 26 (1954), is for two pianos, timpani, and strings. In Edinburgh, he composed the concerto, op. 37 (1960), using elements of tonality and serialism. While in Oxford, he composed the concerto *Estivo,* op. 57 (1969).

Christopher Headington (1930–), pianist and writer, studied with Berkeley at the Royal Academy of Music. He taught in the London schools until joining the BBC in 1964. The variations (1950) is for piano and orchestra.

Anthony Hedges (1931–), pianist, taught at the University of Hull. He has the concertante music (1968).

Malcolm Williamson (1931–), Australian, trained with Goossens at the Sydney Conservatory and in London. He played organ in London churches, taught at Westminster College in Princeton, N.J., and served as the Master of the Queens *Musik* from 1975. The concerto no. 1 (1957–1958) is a virtuoso work that drew attention to Williamson's abilities. The concerto no. 2 (1960) with string orchestra is akin to the style of Stravinsky. The concerto no. 3 (1961) is a virtuoso composition. Other works are the sinfonietta *concertante* (1960–1962) for piano, three trumpets, and strings, the concerto (1962) for two pianos and strings, and the concerto (1965) for two pianos, eight hands, and wind quintets.

Robert Johnson (1932–) adopted the compositional elements of his teacher Messiaen and authored the book *Olivier Messiaen.* While on the faculty at the University of York, he composed the *Trika* (1968–1969).

Malcolm Lipkin (1932–) taught at Liverpool College, the Royal College of Music, and Oxford University. His concerto (1957) attracted considerable attention when premiered at the Cheltenham Festival in 1959.

David Harries (1933–), Welsh, trained and taught at the University College in Aberystwyth. His concerto, op. 43 (1977), is a chromatic, bitonal work.

William Mathias (1934–), Welsh pianist and teacher, studied at the University

College of Wales and with Berkeley at the Royal Academy of Music. The concerto, op. 2 (1955), is a student composition from the University College of Aberystwyth. In Bangor, he composed the two concertos, opp. 13 and 40 (1960, 1968), in a style influenced by Tippett. The concerto, op. 56 (1971), is for harpsichord, strings, and percussion. For piano and orchestra, Mathias arranged *Hunting the Hare* (1957), the *Five Welsh Dances* (1957), and the *Festival Dance* (1961). Important piano writing is in the symphony, op. 31 (1966), the sinfonietta, op. 34 (1966), and the *Litanies,* op. 37 (1967).

Gordon Dale (1935–) works as a violin teacher. His concerto, op. 37, is for piano, percussion, and strings.

Bernard Rands (1935–) studied with Dallapiccola in Florence, and joined the faculty at York University. The *Mesalliance* (1971) is an abstract work influenced by Berio.

André Tchaikowsky (1935–1982) studied at the State Music School in Lodz, the Paris *Conservatoire* with Boulanger, the Warsaw Conservatory, and the American Conservatory before settling in London in 1957. He presents non-conventional interpretations of Mozart's piano concertos. His concerto, op. 4 (1966–1971), is a tonal work comprising an introduction, passacaglia, capriccio, and finale.

Richard Rodney Bennett (1936–), successful film composer, studied with Berkeley and Ferguson at the Royal Academy of Music and with Boulez in Paris. During his teenage years, he delved into the twelve-tone method at a time when most English composers avoided the technique. The concerto no. 1 (1968) displays an influence of jazz. Other compositions are the *Party Piece* (1970) for young pianists and school orchestras, the concerto no. 2 (1976) with chamber orchestra, and the harpsichord concerto (1980).

John Ogdon (1937–1989), internationally acclaimed concert pianist, won the 1961 Tchaikovsky Competition in Moscow. His compositional style contains elements of Liszt, Busoni, and Ravel. The *Concerto of Love* (1966–1968) has a cadenza for piano and trumpet.

John McCabe (1939–), composer of film and television music, directed the London College of Music from 1983. He recorded the complete piano compositions of Haydn and Nielsen, and by age 11 he had composed thirteen symphonies. His musical style draws from many contemporary techniques. For piano and orchestra, he has the *concertante* (1965) for harpsichord, the concerto, op. 43 (1966), the *Metamorphoses* (1968) for harpsichord, the concertino (1968) for piano duet, and two concertos (1970, 1976).

Patric Standford (1939–) studied with Rubba at the Guildhall School of Music, Malipiero in Italy and with Lutoslawski in Darlington, and joined the faculty at the Guildhall School of Music and Drama in 1967. He has the *concertante* (1967) for piano and small orchestra and the concerto (1979).

Edward Cowie (1943–), recognized for his paintings, composed the concerto (1976–1977) while on the faculty at the University of Lancaster.

John Tavener (1944–), student of Berkeley at the Royal Academy of Music, composed music with features of Lassus, Victoria, Messiaen, Cage, Stockhausen, Stravinsky, Indian transcendentalism, and avant-garde techniques. While he is most

Table 36 Additional Composers in England and Wales

Names	Dates	Compositions
Ames, John	1860–1924	2 Concertos
Arlen, Albert	1905–	*Alamein Concerto*
Brent Smith, Alexander	1889–1950	Concerto Concerto, 2 pnos
Bridgewater, Leslie	1893–	2 Concertos
Broome, Ray	? –	*Lineaments* (1964), 2 pnos
Bryan, Gordon	1895–	2 Concertos
Busch, William	1901–1945	Concerto (1937–38)
Carhart, David	1937–	Concerto
Carwithen, Doreen	1922–	Concertina Concertino
Coke, Roger	1912–	5 Concertos
Dalley-Scarlett, Robert	1887–1959	Concerto
Dring, Madeleine	1923–1977	Festival Scherzo
Ellinger, Albert	? –	Concerto
Erhart, Dorothy	1894–1971	Variations (1929)
Farrar, Ernest	1885–1918	*Variations on an Old British Sea Song* (ca. 1916)
Fulton, Norman	1909–	Waltz Rhapsody (1961)
Gatty, Nicholas	1874–1946	Concerto
Geehl, Henry	1881–1961	Concerto
Haendel, Ida	1924–	Concerto
Head, Michael	1900–1976	Concerto
Hinton, Arthur	1869–1941	Concerto, op 24
Howell, Dorothy	1898–1982	Concerto (1923)
Lara, Adelina de	1872–1961	2 Concertos (ca. 1938/39)
Lyon, John	1938–	Concerto (1964)
McEwen, John	1868–1948	Concerto (1914)
Pehkonen, Ellis	1942–	*Concerti with Orch* (1968)
Phillips, Donald	1913–	Concerto in Jazz
Posford, George	1906–	*Broadcasting House* (1933)
Prescott, Olivera	1842–1919	Concerto
Proctor, Charles	1906–	Concerto
Redman, Reginald	1892–1972	Concerto
Richardson, Alan	1904–1978	Junior Concerto
Rutter, John	1945–	Six Beatles Impressions (1980), 2 pnos The Beatles Conc (1980), 2 pnos
Speaight, Joseph	1868–1947	Concerto
Spinner, Leopold	1906–1980	Concerto, op 4 (1947)
Still, Robert	1910–1971	Concerto (1970)
Waddington, Sidney	1869–1953	Concerto
Weber, Svend	1934–	Concerto, op 2 (1975)
White, John	1936–	Concerto (1966)
Wood, Haydn	1882–1959	Concerto (1908)
Young, Douglas	1949–	Concertino (1972–74)

productive in sacred cantatas, he also composed the concerto (1962–1963) with chamber orchestra and the *Palintropos* (1977).

Michael Finnissy (1946–) studied with Stevens and Searle at the Royal College of Music, and joined the faculty at the London School of Contemporary Dance. While on the faculty at the Chelsea School of Art, he composed three concertos (1975, 1975–1976, 1978) and the *Long Distance* (*concertante,* 1977–1978) with chamber orchestra.

David Branson (? –) works as a performing musician and wrote the book *John Field and Chopin.*[2] As a composer, he has the *pavane and toccata* (1944) and the *Mediterranean* (1946) with string orchestra.

Scotland

Alexander Mackenzie (1847–1935) studied at the Sondershausen Conservatory in Germany and taught at the Royal Academy of Music. The *Scottish Concerto,* op. 55 (1897), reflects Mackenzie's lifelong interest in his Scottish heritage. Other influences on his music are Mendelssohn, Schumann, and Liszt.

Hans Gál (1890–), Austrian pianist, musicologist, and writer, taught at the Vienna University and the Conservatory at Mainz before settling in Edinburgh. His compositional heritage is the music of Brahms and R. Strauss. He composed the concertino, op. 43 (1934), in Vienna and the concerto, op. 57 (1947–1948), while on the faculty at Edinburgh University.

Ian Whyte (1901–1960) studied with Stanford and Vaughan Williams at the Royal College of Music and joined the BBC, Scotland, in 1935. He tried to establish the bagpipe as an orchestra instrument. The concerto (1946) is for piano and orchestra.

Eric Chisholm (1904–1965) studied with Tovey in Edinburgh and held various music positions until going to South Africa in 1946. He composed the *Straloch Suite* (1933) with string orchestra, the concerto (1940), and the *Hindustani Concerto* (1949) with Hindustani themes and scales.

William Wordsworth (1908–) studied with Tovey at the University of Edinburgh. Late in life, he became interested in composition and among his finest works is the one-movement concerto, op. 28 (1946).

Davie Thorpe (1913–) taught at the Royal Scottish Academy of Music. The concerto (1943) is with string orchestra.

Thomas Wilson (1927–) studied and later taught at the University of Glasgow. After the concertino (1949), his musical interests turned to serialism.

Ronald Stevenson (1928–) studied at the Royal Manchester College and the Santa Cecilia Academy in Rome, and lectured at Edinburgh University and the University of Cape Town. The concerto *Faust Triptych* (1960) is on themes from Busoni's opera *Doktor Faust.* The poem *Die Kind* (The Child), by the Afrikaans writer Ingrid Jonker, inspired the concerto *The Continents* (1972), based on musical material from African, Asian, American, and European traditions. Stevenson's DSCH motif in the concerto and other works is based on letters from Dimitri Shostakovich's name (D, E-flat, C, and B).

Ireland

Arnold Bax (1883–1953) lived along the coast of Ireland and Scotland and studied with Matthay at the Royal Academy of Music. His music completed prior to 1920 displays Liszt's thematic transformation, influences of R. Strauss, Russian romanticism, and elements of Ravel, Debussy, and Elgar. In the 1920's, Bax turned toward counterpoint and colorful sonorities. Most of his compositions for piano and orchestra were for pianist Harriet Cohen, who injured her right hand in 1948. His compositions for piano and orchestra are the symphonic variations (1918), the *Winter Legends* (1930), the *Saga Fragment* (1932), the concertino (1939), with two movements written in pencil and the third movement in ink, the *Morning Song* (Maytime in Sussex, ca. 1946), and the *concertante* (1949), sometimes called a concerto, for left hand, missing the orchestra score. The symphonic variations has a theme and six titled variations with an intermezzo: I. "Youth[3]," II. "Nocturne," III. "Strife," IV. "The Temple," V. "Play," intermezzo "Enchantment," and VI. "Triumph." Variation V. "Play," is a scherzo.

Ernest John Moeran (1894–1950) found inspiration in the modal folk music of Delius, Vaughan Williams, Holst, Bax, Warlock, and his teacher Ireland. The rhapsody no. 3 (1943) is his only work for piano and orchestra.

James Potter (1918–1980) taught at the Royal Irish Academy of Music from 1955. While a student at Dublin University, he composed the *Concerto da Chiesa* (1952) based on a chorale melody in the baroque style.

Gerald Victory (1921–) has been on the staff of Irish Radio and Television since 1948. Irish folk music is the basis for two concertos (1954, 1972).

James Wilson (1922–) trained with Rowley at Trinity College, London. The concerto (1960) displays elements of Vaughan Williams, Holst, and French impressionism.

Sean O'Riada (1931–1971) was the music director of the Abbey Theatre. The *Nomos* no. 4 (1957–1958) has features of the twelve-tone method and tonality.

Iceland

Jórunn Vioar (1918–) composed at least one concerto for piano and orchestra.

Thorkell Sigurbjörnsson (1938–) studied at the Reykjavik School of Music and in the United States at Hamline University and the University of Illinois. The *Wiblo* (1976) is for horn, piano, and strings, and the *Duttlungar* (caprice) is for piano and orchestra.

Notes

1. Humphrey Searle, *The Music of Liszt,* 2nd revised ed. (New York: Dover Publications, 1966).
2. David Branson, *John Field and Chopin* (New York: St. Martin's Press, 1972).
3. In the score, the titles of each variation and the intermezzo appear in parenthesis. Example: Variation I (Youth).

Chapter 16

The United States

Gilda Ruta (1853/56–1932), Italian, studied with Liszt and pursued a career as a pianist, teacher, and composer. At age 12, she debuted a Beethoven concerto in Naples. She arrived in New York City in 1896. Among her compositions is a concerto and, for piano and string orchestra, the andante rondo, and the bolero.

Alfred Robyn (1860–1935) played organ in various churches. Besides the light opera *The Gypsy Girl* and several successful Broadway comic operas, he composed a concerto for piano and orchestra.

Charles Loeffler (1861–1935), born in Schöneberg, Germany, was the second concertmaster with the Boston Symphony Orchestra, and he settled in Medfield in 1905. His style displays German and French traditions, and he championed contemporary American composers. *A Pagan Poem,* op. 14 (1901), based on Virgil's *Eighth Ecologue,* first appeared as a chamber work, then in a revision (1906) for piano and orchestra with English horn and three trumpets obbligato; another version (1903) is for two pianos and three trumpets. His music received criticism for its bizarre and sinister moods. Loeffler arranged Albeniz's *Spanish Rhapsody* for piano and orchestra.

Mrs. H. H. A. Beach (1867–1944), maiden name Amy Marcy Cheney, was the first American woman to compose a symphony. She performed Moscheles' concerto no. 3 and, at age 17, Chopin's concerto no. 2 with the Boston Symphony Orchestra. Her eclectic, nineteenth-century compositions draw from Chadwick, Foote, others in the Boston area, Brahms, and Wagner, and, eventually, MacDowell and Debussy. Her harmonic style includes altered chords, Neapolitan chords, enharmonic modulations, and half-diminished seventh chords. The four-movement concerto, op. 45 (1899, See ex. 16–1), received praise in Europe. She wrote the cadenza, op. 3, for her performance in 1888 of Beethoven's concerto no. 3. Some sources list the piano quintet, op. 67, as a concerto.

Zygmunt Stojowski (1869–1946), Polish, traveled to Paris to study with Massenet, Saint-Saëns, and Delibes. While a student at the Paris *Conservatoire,* he won first prize in piano and composition. He composed the Concerto no. 1, op. 3 (1891), in Paris and the rapsodie symphonique, op. 23 (1906), in New York City. His teacher Paderewski frequently performed the rapsodie symphonique. Saint-Saëns influenced Stojowski's concerto no. 2, op. 32 (1910), which appeared in publications under the title of sections in the work "Prologue, Scherzo, and Variations."

Felix Borowski (1871–1956) studied in London and at the Cologne Conservatory, joined the faculty at the Chicago Musical College to teach violin, composition, and history, and built the music collection at the Newberry Library. His concerto (1913–1914) is in the style of late German romanticism.

Frederick Converse (1871–1940) graduated from Harvard University and the

Example 16–1. Beach Concerto, op. 45, mvt. 1, mm. 132–143

Royal Academy of Music in Munich, taught at the New England Conservatory and Harvard University, and administered the Boston Opera Company. His early music shows the influence of his training in Germany, and some later compositions have elements of jazz. The *Night and Day,* op. 11 (1905), for piano and orchestra is inspired by Walt Whitman's poems *A Clear Midnight* and *Youth, Day, Old Age and Night*. Converse attempted to capture the mood of the poems and not simply portray night and day. He wrote two mottos from Whitman's poems into the score: for *Night,* "This is the hour o soul, thy free flight into the wordless," and for *Day,* "Day full blown and splendid—day of the immense sun, action, ambition, laughter." His fantasy (1922) has an influence of jazz. Converse considered the concertino (1932) to be among his finest compositions, but he was disappointed by the first performance.

Henry Hadley (1871–1937), associate conductor of the New York Philharmonic Orchestra, studied with Emery and Chadwick at the New England Conservatory of Music in Boston and in Vienna. He left the one-movement concertino, op. 131 (1932).

Ernest Hutcheson (1871–1951) studied at the Leipzig Conservatory with Reinecke and Jadassohn and taught piano at the Peabody Conservatory and the Juilliard School of Music, where he became the president. At one concert in 1915, he performed the Tchaikovsky concerto no. 1, a Liszt concerto, and a MacDowell concerto, and in 1919 he performed three Beethoven concertos in one concert. He composed the concerto (perf. 1898, Berlin) and for two pianos a concerto and the *March.* He wrote the book *The Literature of the Piano.*

Arthur Farwell (1872–1952) championed American music in the first half of the twentieth century, founded the Wa-Wan Press to publish music of contemporary American composers, and attempted to break the European dominance over American composers. Most of his music treats topics indigenous to the United States. While at the Wa-Wan Press, he composed the incomplete *Symbolistic Study* no. 2 "Perelion" (1904). A version of the *Dawn-Fantasy on Indian Themes,* op. 12 (1901), originally for solo piano, is for piano and orchestra (1926), as are versions (1931) of the *Symbolistic Study* no. 6 "Mountain Vision," op. 37 (1912). He also left the concerto (1938) for two pianos and orchestra.

Edward Burlingame Hill (1872–1960) trained at Harvard University and later joined the faculty. Other studies were with Chadwick and Whiting, and with Widor in Paris, where he learned musical techniques of French impressionism. The scherzo (1923–1924) is in versions for one piano and orchestra and two pianos and orchestra. The one-movement concertino, op. 36 (1931), has influences of jazz. Other works are the divertimento (1927) and the concertino no. 2 (1938).

Leo Ornstein (1872–) studied at the St. Petersburg Conservatory and emigrated in 1907 to the United States where he attended the New England Conservatory of Music. His early musical compositions were so dissonant that he earned the name "Stormy Petrel" identifying him as a musical problem child. From 1920, he taught at the Philadelphia Music Academy until he established the Ornstein School of Music. The concerto, op. 44 (1923), is for piano and orchestra, and the concerto, op. 89, is for two pianos and orchestra.

Daniel Mason (1873–1953) studied with Paine at Harvard University, with Whiting, Goetschius, and Chadwick in Boston, and with d'Indy in Paris. He taught at Columbia University and became the MacDowell Professor of Music in 1929. His music follows Austro-German romantic and classic traditions, and in the United States he is called a Boston classicist. The prelude and fugue, op. 20 (1914, rev. 1932), is for piano and orchestra. The opening melody in the prelude has distinctive intervals that appear in the fugue.

Mary Carr Moore (1873–1957), born in Memphis, Tenn., studied music in San

Francisco and taught in Los Angeles at the Olga Steeb Piano School and the California Christian College (renamed Chapman College). The concerto, op. 94, no. 1 (1933–1934), for piano and orchestra is in a version as the quintet, op. 94, no. 2, for piano and string quartet. The concerto received at least three performances, one in 1936 and two in 1940.

T. (Thomas) Carl Whitmer (1873–1959), known for religious music dramas, was on the faculty at the Pennsylvania College for Women when he composed the *Poem of Life* (1914) for piano and orchestra.

Charles Ives (1874–1954) received international recognition for his creative musical ideas. Two unfinished or lost compositions for piano and orchestra are the *Emerson Overture* (1907) and the *Hawthorne Concerto* (1910?). The *Emerson Overture* is a musical imitation of Emerson's literary style, and Ives planned what he called a "centrifugal cadenza." Material from the sketches of both works appears in other compositions.

Arne Oldberg (1874–1962) studied piano with Leschetizky in Vienna and composition with Rheinberger in Munich. On returning to the United States, he became the head of the piano department at Northwestern University. The symphonic concerto, op. 17 (pub. 1907), won the Hollywood Bowl prize. Other compositions are the variations, op. 40, for piano, harp, and orchestra and the symphonic variations (1930).

Arnold Schoenberg (1874–1951) changed the course of music history with his twelve-tone method. After immigrating to the United States, he taught at the University of California at Los Angeles from 1936. The concerto, op. 42 (1942), is on a row containing two perfect fifths, three thirds, a minor sixth, and a major triad. There is a strict treatment of the row, octave doubling, and tonal elements. The concerto has four interconnected movements, with the first movement being a theme and five variations ending with a coda containing the B-A-C-H motive. The second movement is scherzo-like with a diminutive return of opening material. The third movement begins with the inverted B-A-C-H motive, and the fourth movement is a five-part rondo.

John Alden Carpenter (1876–1951) took musical training at Harvard University, then joined his father's shipping business. The concertino (1916, rev. 1947) received frequent performances in the United States and Paris. His compositions show the influence of popular music, jazz, and ragtime. Other works for piano and orchestra are the *Patterns* (1932) and the *Carmel Concerto* (1948).

Ernest Schelling (1876–1939) performed a piano recital at the Academy of Music in Philadelphia at age 4 1/2. When he entered the Paris *Conservatoire,* the minimum entrance age was 9, but due to his remarkable talent he was admitted at age 7. He studied with Mathias, Moszkowski, Bruckner, Leschetizky, and Paderewski. As an adult, he performed an amazing musical feat by presenting three performances with the New York Symphony Orchestra in 1923. On January 23, he performed Beethoven's concerto no. 5, Chopin's concerto no. 2, and Liszt's concerto no. 1. On January 30, he played Schumann's concerto, Franck's symphonic variations, Paderewski's concerto, op. 17, and the Liszt-Busoni *Spanish Rhapsody*. On February 6, he performed Chopin's concerto no. 1, Mozart's concerto, K.488, Liszt's concerto no. 2, and Paderewski's *Polish Fantasy*. Artur Rubinstein praised Schelling's performance of the Beethoven concerto no. 5 as the finest he had ever heard. Schelling performed his four-movement suite *fantastique,* op. 7 (1906– ?), several times early in the century. The last movement titled *Virginia Reel* contains the tunes *Dixie, Old Folks at Home,* and a reference to *Yankee Doodle.* The symphonic variations *Impressions from an Artist's Life* (1913) is a theme and variations depicting places, personalities, and events. Schelling was one of only four piano students Paderewski admitted teaching.

Rudolph Ganz (1877–1972), Swiss pianist and conductor, studied with Busoni in Berlin and settled in Chicago, where he taught at the Chicago Musical College. He composed the *konzertstück,* op. 4 (1892), possibly at the Lausanne Conservatory, and the concerto, op. 32 (1941). The basis of the scherzo in the concerto is the numbers on Ganz's 1940 and 1941 car license plates and Frederick Stock's 1940 car license.

Heinrich Gebhard (1878–1963) studied with Leschetizky in Vienna and gave the first American performances of some of d'Indy's compositions. He performed the piano part in Loeffler's *A Pagan Poem* about one hundred times with various orchestras, and appeared with the Boston Symphony thirty-six times. In an impressionistic style, he composed the fantasy (1925) and the divertimento (1927) with chamber orchestra.

Rudolf Friml (1879–1972) trained at the Prague Conservatory and settled in the United States in 1906. Part of his fame rests on the musical *Rose-Marie* and the song *Indian Love Call.* As a pianist, he successfully toured Europe and the United States, and his improvisations were praised. He composed two concertos (one perf. 1906) for his own use.

Jacob Weinberg (1879–1956) studied at the Moscow Conservatory with Igumnov, Taneyev, and Ippolitov-Ivanov. He taught at the Odessa Conservatory in Russia, in Palestine, and at Hunter College in New York City. He left at least one concerto for piano and orchestra.

Ernest Bloch (1880–1959), Swiss, composed the concerto *grosso* no. 1 (1924–1945) while the director of the Institute of Music in Cleveland, Ohio. The composition contains neo-classic and neo-baroque techniques and ideas from Stravinsky and Schoenberg. The score is for string orchestra with piano obbligato and in four parts: "Prelude," "Dirge," "Pastorale and Rustic Dance," and "Fugue." While on the faculty at the University of California, Berkeley, Bloch composed the concerto symphonique (1946–1948) and the scherzo fantasque (1948).

John Homer Grunn (1880–1944) trained at the Stern Conservatory in Berlin and taught at the Chicago Music College. He may have composed the *March Heroique* in Los Angeles.

Arthur Shepherd (1880–1958) studied with Goetschius and Chadwick at the New England Conservatory of Music. While on the conservatory faculty, he composed the Fantasie-Humoresque (1916) with influences of Wagner, Brahms, and French composers.

Gena Branscombe (1881–1977) studied with Ganz at the Chicago Musical College and with Humperdinck in Berlin. She settled in New York City and taught at the Musical College in Chicago. She probably composed the one-movement *concertstück* (1906–1907) in Chicago.

Charles Wakefield Cadman (1881–1946) worked as a music critic for the

Pittsburgh Dispatch and, after arriving in Los Angeles, he founded the Hollywood Bowl. He devoted much time to researching, lecturing, and writing about music of the American Indians. His compositional style blends a stylized concept of Indian music, European romanticism and American nationalism. The *Dark Dancers of the Mardi Gras* (1932), originally titled *Dance of the Scarlet Sister Mary,* with piano obbligato, is a fantasy based on a motive stated by the tuba in the first two measures. Cadman's close friend, librettist Nelle Eberhart, suggested the title *Aurora Borealis: Impressionistic Fantasy* (1940–1942) for a programmatic work concerning a journey through the arctic. He composed the work at the MacDowell Colony after studying MacDowell's concertos. The *Aurora Borealis* contains features of MacDowell's style and melodies similar to sea chanties available in the colony library.

Fannie Dillon (1881–1947) studied with Godowsky in Berlin and with Goldmark in New York City. She composed *A Western Concerto,* op. 117, while at Pomona College.

Percy Grainger (1882–1961), Australian, studied with Busoni in Frankfurt while he composed the *Tribute to Foster* (1899, 1905, rev. 1915, 1921) for five solo voices, mixed chorus, piano solo, musical glasses, and orchestra with a second piano. In London, he composed the four-movement suite *In a Nutshell* (1905–1911) and the *Handel in the Strand* (1911–1912), originally titled *Clog Dance*. The four movements of the *Handel in the Strand,* named for the home of the London musical theater, are "Arrival Platform Hamlet" (1908), "Gay but Wistful" (1912), "Pastoral" (1915–1916), and "The Gum-Suckers March" (1905, 1917) which originally had the title "Cornstalkers March." Gum-suckers are Australians in the state of Victoria who chew the gum of Eucalyptus trees in the summer for its refreshing taste. The children's march *Over the Hills and Far Away* (1916) is for piano and band. In 1914, Grainger moved to the United States, where he composed *The Merry King* (1936–1939) for piano and strings, originally planned for chorus (ca. 1905), and the *Gardineriana Rhapsody* (1947) sketched for piano and small orchestra and based on works of H. Balfour Gardiner. Grainger arranged J. S. Bach's *Brandenburg Concerto* no. 3 (pub. 1913) for two pianos, six violins, three violas, three cellos, and double-bass. Grainger's "elastic scoring" presents many compositions in numerous different instrumentations to make the music available for skilled and unskilled performers. He strongly believed academic institutions should not give his music serious consideration because they displayed "non-education."

Mary Howe (1882–1964), educated at the Peabody Conservatory in Baltimore and in Germany, settled in Washington, D.C., in 1915. She was important in various musical organizations, including the Friends of Music at the Library of Congress and a member of the board of directors of the National Symphony Orchestra. The *Castellana* (1930) was for the two-piano team of Ann Hull and the composer.

Ralph Lyford (1882–1927) entered the New England Conservatory at age 12. In 1916, he began teaching at the conservatory and became the associate conductor of the Cincinnati Symphony Orchestra in 1925. His concerto (1917) is from his years on the conservatory faculty.

Lazare Saminsky (1882–1959), born near Odessa, Russia, learned mathematics at the University of St. Petersburg and music at the St. Petersburg Conservatory with Liadov and Rimsky-Korsakoff. He settled in New York City in 1920 and directed music at Temple Emanu-El. The *Vow* (1943) follows romantic traditions.

Louis Gruenberg (1884–1964) helped establish the League of Composers in 1923, won several academy awards for film scores, and is among the first American composers to use jazz in serious music. He composed the concerto no. 1, op. 8 (1914), while on the faculty at the Vienna Conservatory. In Los Angeles, he composed the concerto no. 2, op. 41 (1938, rev. 1963), and the concerto for strings and piano (1955).

Lily Strickland (1884–1958) studied at Converse College and the Juilliard School of Music. In India, she composed *From a Caravan* (1924) in sections titled "Prelude," "The Well in the Desert," "At Ouled-Nail," "Night on the Nile," and "Song to the Crocodiles." In New York City, she composed the concerto (ca. 1948) and probably the *Chivalric Suite* for two pianos and orchestra.

Emerson Whithorne (1884–1958) studied with Leschetizky in Vienna, worked as executive editor of the Art Publications Society of St. Louis, and settled in New York City as the vice-president of the Composers' Music Corporation. Among his musical compositions is the *Poem,* op. 43 (1927).

Werner Josten (1885–1963), born and trained in Germany, taught composition and counterpoint at Smith College. In a German romantic style, he composed the *Concerto Sacro* I and II (1925) that he intended as a large four-movement concerto divided into two halves, so either half could be performed separately. The *Concerto Sacro* I has two movements titled "Annunciation" and "The Miracle," and the *Concerto Sacro* II has two movements titled "Lament" and "Sepulchre and Resurrection."

Wallingford Riegger (1885–1961) studied with Goetschius at the Institute of Musical Art (now the Juilliard School) and the *Hochschule für Musik* in Berlin. After several years of conducting and teaching he turned to musical composition and became a leader in avant-garde styles. The atonal and dodecaphonic concerto, op. 53 (1953), for piano and woodwind quintet is one of his finest compositions. The variations, op. 54 (1952–1953), is in a version for two pianos and orchestra as op. 54b (1953). The *Machine Ballet,* op. 28 (1938), for piano and orchestra remains in manuscript, and the *Duo,* op. 75 (1960), is among his last musical compositions.

John Becker (1886–1961) trained at the Wisconsin Conservatory in Milwaukee and taught at Notre Dame University. He began composing in a style reflecting German romanticism, and in the 1920's he moved toward the dissonant atonal thinking of Ives, Ruggles, Cowell, and Riegger. While serving as the chairman of the Fine Arts Department at the College of St. Thomas, he composed the *Concerto Arabesque* (1930) for piano and chamber orchestra or full orchestra and the scherzo *Mockery* (1933) for piano and dance orchestra or chamber orchestra. The *Soundpiece* I (1935) for piano and orchestra is the same work as the *Soundpiece* IA for piano and string quintet. The concerto no. 2 *Satirico* (1938) contains material from the *Mockery*. Other works are the *Dance Masque* and a concerto for piano, violin, and orchestra. After serving as the director of Federal Music in Minnesota, he joined the faculty of Barot College of the Sacred Heart at Lake Forest, Ill.

George Boyle (1886–1948), born in Australia, studied with Busoni in Berlin and settled in the United States in 1910. He taught at the Peabody Conservatory in Baltimore, the Curtis Institute of Music in Philadelphia, and the Institute of Musical Art (now the Juilliard School). His concerto (1911), which is in a nineteenth-century romantic style, received frequent performances early in the century. In New York City, he composed the concertino (1935).

Ethel Leginska (1886–1970), family name Liggins, used a Polish-sounding name, believing it would help her musical career. She studied at the Hoch Conservatory in Frankfurt and with Leschetizky in Vienna. She organized the Boston Philharmonic Orchestra, which became the Women's Symphony Orchestra of Boston. Eventually, she acquired the title "disappearing pianist" for not appearing at some of her own concerts. Her only work for piano and orchestra is the fantasy (perf. 1926).

Marion Bauer (1887–1955) studied with Boulanger in Paris and taught at the Institute of Musical Arts (now the Juilliard School of Music). She composed the *American Youth* concerto, op. 36 (1943), for the New York High School for Music and Art.

Philip Greely Clapp (1888–1954) studied with Spalding, Converse, and Hill at Harvard University and Schillings in Stuttgart, Germany. In 1919, he became the director of the Music Department at the University of Iowa. He is important for improving undergraduate and graduate music study in the United States. Wagner, Mahler, R. Strauss, and Debussy influenced his music. He composed the concerto (1922, rev. 1936) for one piano and a version (1941) for two pianos. The symphonic poem *Norge* (1908) has an obbligato piano.

Karl Hajos (1889–1950), born in Hungary, mainly composed operettas. He left the fantasy for piano and orchestra.

Clarence Loomis (1889–1965) studied at the American Conservatory in Chicago and with Godowsky in Vienna. He composed light opera in a chromatic, romantic style. While a teacher of piano and organ at Highland University, he composed the fantasy (1954) for piano and orchestra.

Francisco Santiago (1889–1947), Filipino, studied at the Conservatory of the University of the Philippines and the Chicago Musical College. His graduation composition was a concerto (1924) in the style of Liszt.

Efrem Zimbalist (1889–), Russian-American violinist and teacher, studied at the St. Petersburg Conservatory. While on the faculty at the Curtis Institute of Music, he composed a concerto for pianist William Kapell. The 1953 plane crash that killed the pianist also destroyed the concerto, but Zimbalist attempted to reproduce the composition.

John Tasker Howard (1890–1964) authored the first careful study of music in the United States, *Our American Music*. For piano and orchestra, he composed the *Fantasy on a Choral Theme* (perf. 1929).

Harold Morris (1890–1964) composed music in a neo-classic style that shows influences of impressionism, Scriabin, jazz, blues, and folk music of black and white people of the south. He taught at the Juilliard School of Music and the Teachers College of Columbia University. The concerto (1927) contains the spiritual "I'm a Poor Wayfarin' Stranger." The concerto no. 2 received frequent performances in the 1940s, and the suite (1940) is from the years he taught at Columbia University.

James Philip (1890–1975) was an organist and choir director at New York University. He transcribed Mozart's sonata, K.545, as the concertino (perf. 1932) for piano and orchestra.

Powell Weaver (1890–1951) studied musical composition with Respighi in Rome, played organ, and directed church choirs. He composed the *Dance of the Sand-Dune Cranes* (1941) and *An Ode* for piano and strings.

Frederick Jacobi (1891–1952) studied with Joseffy, Goldmark, Bloch, and Juon, and taught at the Juilliard School of Music. His compositions frequently contain American Indian melodies. He left the concerto (1934–1935), the *Ave Rota* (1939) which is three pieces in multiple styles, the concertino (1946) with strings, and the serenade.

James Johnson (1891/94–1955), the best "stride" pianist in New York City in about 1916, blended classic and jazz idioms in concert works. He composed the rhapsody *Yamekaw* (1927), the *Jasmine* (Jazz-O-Mine, 1934), and the concerto (1935).

Isidor Achron (1892–1948), born in Russia, studied with Liadov at the St. Petersburg Conservatory. In 1922 he settled in the United States, where he accompanied Heifetz and composed two piano concertos, opp. 2 and 47 (1937, 1942). In 1937, he performed the concerto, op. 2, in expanded tonality, with the New York Philharmonic Orchestra.

Ferde Grofé (1892–1972) composed the *Grand Canyon Suite* (1931) for orchestra, and orchestrated Gershwin's *Rhapsody in Blue*. During the years he wrote music for the Paul Whiteman band, he helped establish Whiteman as a leader in merging serious music and jazz into symphonic jazz. Grofé's efforts with the two idioms are in the concerto (1930–1960).

Felix Labunski (1892–1979), brother of Wiktor Labunski, studied at the Warsaw Conservatory and with Boulanger and Dukas at the *École Normale de Musique*, Paris. He directed the Department of Classical Music for Polish Radio, and emigrated to the United States in 1936. In 1945, he joined the faculty at the Cincinnati College of Music (now the Cincinnati Conservatory of Music). His compositional style reflects his Polish heritage and a love of the romantic era. To celebrate its 125th anniversary, Xavier University commissioned the one-movement fantasy *Xaveriana* (1956) for two pianos and orchestra. The one-movement *Music* is tonally free.

John Robb (1892–) studied English at Yale University and Harvard University and music with Parker, Boulanger, Harris, Hindemith, and Milhaud. He likes folk songs of the southwestern United States. He composed the concerto (1951) while on the faculty at the University of New Mexico.

Eugene Goossens (1893–1962) was the internationally recognized conductor of the Cincinnati Symphony Orchestra. The phantasy concerto, op. 60 (1942), is in the tradition of English composers who use modernistic harmonies based on Debussy's style. A four-note motive stated by trumpets at the beginning is the basis for the entire composition.

Clifford Vaughan (1893–) trained at the Philadelphia Conservatory of Music, directed choirs in Philadelphia, and worked in Hollywood as a church organist and film composer. He composed a concerto in Hollywood or Philadelphia.

Robert Russell Bennett (1894–1981) composed film music in Hollywood, and in New York City he scored more than 300 Broadway musicals, including some for

Berlin, Friml, Gershwin, Kern, Loewe, Porter, and Rogers. He may have composed the *Charleston Rhapsody* (1926) for small orchestra and piano in New York City. While in Paris as a student of Boulanger, he composed the *March* (1930) for two pianos and orchestra, revised as the *Three Marches* (1947). Bennett's compositional style for Broadway musicals is evident in his concert works. Other works for piano and orchestra are the concerto (1948), the concerto (1962) for violin and piano, and the *Party Piece*.

Mana-Zucca (ca. 1894–1981), born Augusta Zuckermann, changed her name by rearranging letters of her last name. She studied with Godowsky and Busoni in Berlin, and performed a Beethoven concerto with the New York Symphony at about age 10. Various sources give different birth dates and conflicting ages for the debut. In a romantic style, she composed two concertos, the first is op. 49 (1907).

Edna Pietsch (1894–) studied in Milwaukee and at the Chicago Conservatory. In Milwaukee, she composed two concertos for piano and orchestra.

Walter Piston (1894–1976) studied with Boulanger and Dukas in Paris, and joined the faculty at Harvard University. Many of his musical compositions display classic structures, expanded harmonic ideas, and a personal concept of the twelve-tone method from about 1965. The one-movement concertino (1937) is in three sections, with the opening section having two themes—the adagio functions somewhat as a development in a sonata form, and the large coda balances the opening section. The concerto (1959) for two pianos and orchestra begins in mixolydian mode, and the second movement is a theme and ten variations based on various techniques from French impressionism to chord clusters.

Hans Spialek (1894–1983) studied with Glière at the Moscow Conservatory and settled in New York City in 1924. He orchestrated 147 Broadway shows, including Gershwin's *Strike Up the Band* (1930). He may have composed his concerto in New York City.

Albert Stoessel (1894–1943) trained at the *Hochschule für Music* in Berlin and succeeded Walter Damrosch as the conductor of the Oratorio Society of New York. He helped establish the music department at New York University and taught at the Juilliard School of Music. The concerto grosso (1935) is neo-classic with traditional forms, and various instrumentalists perform in different solo groups.

Wesley La Violette (1894–1978) studied music at Northwestern University. While on the faculty at DePaul University, he composed the *Concert Piece* (1937).

Wiktow Labunski (1895–1974), brother of Felix Labunski, studied music at the St. Petersburg Conservatory. He was the head of the piano department at the conservatory in Cracow, Poland, went to the United States in 1928, and performed in Carnegie Hall, New York City. He joined the faculty at the Nashville Conservatory and the College of Music in Memphis, Tenn., where he composed the concertino (1932). From 1937, he taught at the Conservatory of Music in Kansas City, and while there he composed the concerto, op. 16 (1937), and the variations (1945). A version of the concerto is for two pianos and orchestra as the concerto, op. 16B (1937–1951), but some sources list it as op. 16A. Labunsky had a performing repertoire of more than 1,500 piano compositions.

Alexander Laszlo (1895–1970), Hungarian, trained at the Budapest Academy. In 1915, he went to Berlin to work as a pianist, emigrated to the United States in 1938, and settled in Hollywood in 1945. He invented the "color pianoforte" (*Farblichklavier*), which projects colors. He developed the sonchromatoscope to produce colors of proportional wavelengths, and sonchromagraphy, a system of musical notation for the sonchromatoscope. The *Ghost Train in Marshall Pass* is for the color piano. Other compositions are the concerto (1944), the *4D-122,* and the *Mana Hawaii.*

Karol Rathaus (1895–1954) studied in Vienna at the university and at the Academy of Music and at the Berlin *Hochschule für Musik.* In 1938, he settled in New York City and joined the faculty at Queens College. His compositional style uses expanded tonality, rhapsodic writing, romanticism, and twentieth-century techniques. He composed the concertino, op. 16 (1927), in Berlin and the concerto, op. 45 (1939), in New York City.

Dane Rudhyar (1895–1985), born Daniel Chennevière, changed his name in 1917 based on old Sanskrit roots and astrology. He studied philosophy at the Sorbonne and music at the Paris *Conservatoire,* and emigrated to the United States in 1917. His interest in astrology prompted him to write *The Astrology of Personality,* which became an important document in the field. His lack of musical success caused him to seek fulfillment in theosophy, astrology, and nonrepresentational painting. Musically, he was fond of thick chord textures over pedal points, late-romantic chromaticism, and polytonality. For piano and orchestra, he composed the symphonic poem *The Warrior* (1921), the *Tripthong* (1948, rev. 1977) in Nambe, New Mexico, and the *Encounter* (1977).

Frederick Schreiber (1895–) trained in Vienna as a pianist and composer, taught at the Vienna Conservatory of Music, and settled in New York City in 1939. He played organ and directed the choir at the Reformed Protestant Church. He has two concertos, a concertino for two pianos, and the harpsichord concerto.

Leo Sowerby (1895–1968) played organ at the Cathedral of St. James and directed the College for Church Musicians at the National Cathedral in Washington, D.C. Most likely, he composed the concerto no. 1 (1916, rev. 1919) for piano, soprano obbligato, and orchestra in Chicago. The *Ballad of King Estmere* (1922) for two pianos and orchestra is from the years Sowerby was at the American Academy on a *Prix de Rome.* When he was on the faculty at the American Conservatory, he composed the concerto no. 2 (1932) for piano and orchestra.

William Grant Still (1895–1978) is the first black composer to write a symphony performed by a major orchestra, the Rochester Philharmonic Orchestra. He studied at the Oberlin Conservatory and with Chadwick at the New England Conservatory in Boston, and received a Guggenheim Fellowship. He often took ideas from black culture and American culture. The League of Composers commissioned *Kaintuck* (Kentucky, 1935) for piano and orchestra.

Howard Hanson (1896–1981), director of the Eastman School of Music, composed music with elements of Sibelius and Grieg, his Scandinavian heritage, his teacher Respighi in Rome, American composers of MacDowell's vintage, neoromantic ideas, and clearly structured forms. He left the *Concerto da Camera,* op. 7 (1917), for piano and string quartet; the symphonic poem *Exaltation,* op. 20 (1920), with piano obbligato; the symphonic poem *Pan and the Priest,* op. 26 (1925–1926), with piano obbligato; the concerto, op. 36 (1948); and the *Variations on a Theme of Youth,* op. 40 (1951). After a slow orchestra introduction, the piano enters with a passage that contains cross accents against the orchestra part.

Walter Helfer (1896–1959) trained at Harvard University, in Paris with Caussade, and in Rome with Respighi, and taught at Hunter College in New York City. He composed *A Fantasy on Children's Tunes* (1935), the *Concerto Elegiaco* (1939), and the concertino (1947) with chamber orchestra.

Vladimir Polívka (1896–1948), Czech pianist, taught at the Prague Conservatory and in Chicago. He began his concerto (1930–1934) in Chicago. In 1938, he returned to Prague to teach at the conservatory.

Leroy Robertson (1896–1971) studied with Chadwick and Converse at the New England Conservatory, with Bloch in Switzerland, and with Leichtentritt in Berlin. After returning to the United States he joined the faculty at Brigham Young University in Provo, where he composed the rhapsody (1944). In 1948, he became the head of the Music Department at the University of Utah, and while there he composed the concerto (1966).

Roger Session (1896–) studied with Parker at Yale University and, while an assistant to Bloch at the Cleveland Institute of Music, probably composed the *Strophes* (1927–1929). The composition is an incomplete set of sketches for piano and orchestra in which each strophe is like a variation. The three-movement concerto (1956) is a personal treatment of a row, and influenced by Bloch's neo-classicism.

Hans Barth (1897–1956), student of Reinecke at the Leipzig Conservatory, became interested in quarter-tone scales. He worked with the Baldwin Piano Company on the development of a two-keyboard piano with an upper keyboard tuned to 440 and a lower keyboard tuned to 427.5. This tuning allows intervals as small as quarter tones. Barth premiered the concerto, op. 11 (1928), for quarter-tone piano in Carnegie Hall with Leopold Stokowski and the Philadelphia Orchestra. The concerto, op. 15 (1930), and the Etudes, op. 26 (1942–1944), are for quarter-tone piano, and the concerto (1928) is for piano with normal tuning.

Henry Cowell (1897–1965), originator of the term "tone clusters," composed the concerto (1928) in Havana using tone clusters played by the fist, palm, or forearm. He may have composed the *Irish Suite* (1928–1929) for plucked piano strings and chamber orchestra in San Francisco. He composed the *Tales of Our Countryside* (1940), also titled *Four Irish Tales,* originally piano solo pieces (1922–1930), in four different states: California, along the Hudson River Valley in New York or New Jersey, Iowa, and Kansas. The suite (1941) for piano and string orchestra or band exists in a version as the *Little Concerto* (1945) or *Concerto Piccolo.*

Quincy Porter (1897–1966) studied with Parker at Yale University, with d'Indy in Paris, and with Bloch in the United States. After teaching at several prestigious institutions, he joined the faculty at Yale University in 1946. His compositional style displays influences of German and French music, polytonality, chromaticism, and counterpoint. His string quartets are among the most important examples of the genre by an American composer. Porter won a Pulitzer Prize in 1954 for the concerto *concertante* (1952–1953) for two pianos and orchestra. He left the harpsichord concerto (1959).

Ernst Bacon (1898–), composer of lyric songs, presented piano concerts in the United States and Germany. He taught at Converse College, South Carolina, and at Syracuse University in New York. While studying with Bloch in San Francisco or while in Rochester, New York, he composed the symphony no. 1 (1932) for piano and orchestra, and the symphonic fugue (1932) for piano and strings. Other works are the concerto no. 1 *Riolama* (1963) and the concerto no. 2 (1982).

Nicolai Bolin (1898–), born in the Ukraine, studied music in Kiev and at the University of California, Berkeley. *Los Angeles Concerto* and *Big Town Concerto* may be different titles for the same composition.

George Gershwin (1898–1939) composed the *Rhapsody in Blue* (1924) for Paul Whiteman's concert "An Experiment in Modern Music," presented at Aeolian Hall, New York City. During the three weeks Gershwin composed the work, he handed each page to Ferde Grofé, who wrote the orchestration for piano and jazz band in ten days and, later, a version for symphony orchestra. Originally, Gershwin intended the title *American Rhapsody,* but his brother Ira suggested *Rhapsody in Blue* after attending an exhibition of Whistler's paintings with titles such as *Harmony in Grey and Green* and *Nocturne in Blue and Green.* Gershwin's interest in the loose organization of Liszt's *Hungarian Rhapsodies* is the source for the free structure in his rhapsody. Originally, articulated notes formed the opening scale for clarinet, but during the first rehearsal, clarinetist Ross Gorman performed the passage as a glissando, as he might do in jazz, and Gershwin liked the idea so much he wrote the glissando into the music.

Gershwin's musical roots are in Tin Pan Alley, jazz, and music of black Americans. Feeling inadequate about his compositional skills, he asked Ravel and Boulanger for compositional lessons. Both declined the request because they felt that Gershwin's unique musical creativity might be harmed by their instruction.

Walter Damrosch's request for a work for the New York Symphony Orchestra caused Gershwin to try writing a concerto, but first he had to purchase several books to learn about concertos. The effort resulted in the *Concerto in F* (1925). The first movement has a Charleston rhythm, the second movement is slow and meditative in the style of a nocturne, and the third movement is similar to the rhythmic activity of the first movement. This was Gershwin's first orchestration effort, and he instructed the trumpets in the symphony orchestra to use hats in the blues passages. Due to the popularity of the *Rhapsody in Blue,* conductors quickly contracted Gershwin to perform the unfinished concerto.

The *Second Rhapsody* (1931) was not well received at its premiere, and since then musicians have not given the work much attention. Gershwin composed the Variations on *I Got Rhythm* (1934), based on the song of the same title from the show *Girl Crazy* (1930), for his tour with the Leo Reisman orchestra.

Roy Harris (1898–1979) studied with Farwell and Boulanger. His compositional style uses classic models, polychords, folk songs, dance rhythms, and jazz. The concerto, op. 2 (1926), for piano, clarinet, and string quartet, is a product of his studies with Boulanger at Harvard University. In New York City or Oregon, he arranged the concerto (1936) for piano and strings from the piano quintet (1926). While on the faculty at Cornell University, he composed the concerto (1941) for piano and band, the concerto (passacaglia, 1942), and the fantasy (1943). When on the faculty at Colorado College, Colorado Springs, he completed the *Radio Piece* (1946) and the three-movement concerto (1946) for two pianos and orchestra, with the second and third movements respectively based on the folk songs *True Love Don't Weep* and *Cod Liver Ile*. At the Peabody Conservatory of Music or Chatham College in Pittsburgh, he composed the fantasy (1951) for piano and popular dance band, and at Chatham College the concerto (1953), *Abraham Lincoln Walks at Midnight* (1953) for soprano, piano, and orchestra, and the fantasy (1954) based on three folk songs. While on the faculty at the University of California in Los Angeles, he composed *These Times* (1964) and the concerto (1968) for amplified piano, brass, percussion, and string basses.

Reuven Kosakoff (1898–) studied at Yale University, the Juilliard School of Music, and piano with Schnabel in Berlin. He played organ, directed music, and composed at the Jenesis Hebrew Center in Crestwood. The concerto (1941) is on Hebrew themes.

Mish Levitsky (1898–1941), born in Russia, studied with Stojowski at the Institute of Musical Art (now the Juilliard School of Music) and with Dohnányi at the Berlin *Hochschule für Music*. He was a touring concert pianist and probably wrote the cadenza for Beethoven's concerto no. 3 for his own use.

Vittorio Rieti (1898–), Italian, student of Respighi and Casella, divided his time in the 1920s and 1930s between Rome and Paris. His compositional style is neo-classic, with various contemporary influences. In Europe, he composed two concertos (1926, 1930–1937). In 1940, he settled in New York City and joined the faculties at Queens College and Hunter College. He composed the concerto (1951) for two pianos; the harpsichord concerto (1952–1955) revised as the concerto (1955–1960) for harp; the concerto (1955); and the triple concerto (1971) for violin, viola, piano, and orchestra.

Beryl Rubinstein (1898–1952) toured the United States as a child pianist, studied with Busoni in Berlin and joined the faculty at the Cleveland Institute of Music in 1921. Her book *Outline of Piano Pedagogy* is an important source of information for piano teachers. The concerto (1935) is among the finest piano concertos by an American composer, and the three-movement concerto no. 2 has polytonal techniques in the third movement.

David Broekman (1899–1958) took music training at the Royal Conservatory in The Hague, and went to the United States, where he played violin in the New York Philharmonic Orchestra under Toscanini. In 1929, he settled in Hollywood to write film music, including *All Quiet on the Western Front*. He composed a concerto for piano and orchestra and a concerto for piano, percussion, and orchestra.

Otto Cesana (1899–) wrote film music. He composed three concertos: one for one piano, one for two pianos, and one for three pianos.

John Duke (1899–1984), song composer, studied at the Peabody Conservatory in Baltimore and with Schnabel and Boulanger in Europe. While on the faculty at Smith College, he composed the concerto (1938) for piano and strings.

Antonio Lora (1899–1965), born in Italy, taught at a branch of Ohio State University. His concerto (1948) is highly chromatic and impressionistic.

Harl McDonald (1899–1955) toured England, Germany, and the United States as a pianist and conductor. He may have intended the concerto (1919) for his concert tours. While on the faculty at the University of Pennsylvania, he received a Rockefeller grant to work with a physicist and two electrical engineers on acoustical problems; the research provided material for the book *New Methods of Measuring Sound.* The concerto (1936) for two pianos and orchestra is in a free tonal style influenced by Hispanic-American music. One piano has a solo part and the other piano has an accompanying role.

Robert Schmitz (1899–1949) authored the book *The Piano Works of Claude Debussy,* trained at the Paris *Conservatoire,* and settled in San Francisco in 1934. He left at least one concerto.

Randall Thompson (1899–1984) joined the faculty at Harvard University, where he taught Adler, Bernstein, Foss, Kraft, and I. Tcherepnin. While at Wellesley College, he composed the *Jazz Poem* (1927) for solo piano and revised it in 1928 for piano and orchestra.

Nicolay Berezovsky (1900–1953), born in Russia, played violin in orchestras at the Opera House in Saratov and the Bolshoi Theater in Moscow. In 1922, he emigrated to the United States, studied at the Juilliard School of Music, and played violin in the New York Philharmonic Orchestra. Features of Russian music are evident in the *Theme and Variations,* op. 7 (1926), for clarinet, piano, and strings, and the fantasy, op. 9 (1931), for two pianos and orchestra.

Aaron Copland (1900–1990) is the distinguished composer of *Appalachian Spring, Fanfare for the Common Man,* and numerous other works important in American music. His concerto (1926), in one movement with two parts, displays a strong influence of jazz.

Isadore Freed (1900–1960), Russian born, studied with Bloch, Hoffman, d'Indy, Vierne, and Boulanger, and in Paris he gave joint concerts with Honegger and Tansman. As an organist, he worked at the Keneseth Israel Temple in Philadelphia, the Temple Israel on Long Island, N.Y., and taught at the Hebrew Union School of Sacred Music in New York City. He composed many important Jewish sacred works and the ballad (1926) for piano and small orchestra of five winds and five strings; the ballet *Vibrations* (1930) for two pianos and chamber orchestra; the concerto (1952); and the concertante (1953) for piano and strings.

Anis Fuleihan (1900/01–1970) taught composition at Indiana University. His travels through the Middle East, particularly Cairo, Beirut, and Tunis, influenced his music. There are three concertos (1936, 1937, 1963); the concerto (1940) for two pianos; the epithalamium (1941); the concerto (1943) for piano and violin; and the toccata (1960).

Ernst Krenek (1900–) was born in Vienna and trained in Berlin with Schrenker. His earliest musical compositions show an interest in atonality and polytonality, and in 1933, he adopted the twelve-tone method, while closely associated with Schoenberg, Berg, and Webern in Vienna. Other influences are neo-classicism, serialism, jazz, aleatoric techniques, and electronic devices. In Berlin, Krenek composed the concerto no. 1, op. 18 (1923), and the concertino, op. 27 (1924), for flute, violin, harpsichord, and string orchestra. He composed the concerto no. 2, op. 81 (1937), in Vienna just before leaving for the United States. The *Little Concerto,* op. 88 (1939–1940), for piano, organ, and chamber orchestra is a product of his years in Poughkeepsie, New York, teaching at Vassar College. The concerto no. 3, op. 107 (1946), composed in St. Paul, Minnesota, is not on the twelve-tone method. In Los Angeles, he composed the concerto no. 4, op. 123 (1950), for two pianos and orchestra, the seven-movement double concerto, op. 124 (1950), for piano, violin, and chamber orchestra, and the concerto, op. 127 (1951), for two pianos and orchestra.

Colin McPhee (1900–1964), born in Canada, studied at the Peabody Conservatory and, while there, he composed the lost concerto no. 1 *La mort d'Arthur* (1920). Also lost is the concerto no. 2 (1923, perf. 1924) which he composed in Toronto while studying with Friedheim. After studies in Paris with Le Flem and Philipp, he settled in New York City. The concerto (1928) for piano and wind octet is a neo-classic work in three movements. After hearing recordings of Balinese gamelan music in the late 1920s, McPhee moved to Bali. In Bali, he composed the *Tabuh-Tabuhan* (1936) for two pianos and orchestra with gongs and cymbals. His book *Music in Bali* is the most important study on Balinese music before the influx of Western music. He lived in Mexico, then joined the faculty at the Institute of Ethnomusicology at the University of California in Los Angeles.

Vladimar Padwa (1900–) studied at the Imperial Conservatory in St. Petersberg and with Busoni at the Berlin *Hochschule für Musik*. He taught at the State Conservatory in Tallinn, Estonia, and the New York College of Music. He has the *Concerto in the Form of Variations* (1950).

Tibor Serly (1900–1978), born in Hungary, immigrated to New York City in 1905. In 1922, he returned to Budapest to study with Kodály at the Royal Academy. As a close friend of Bartók, he completed Bartók's concerto no. 3 for piano and orchestra according to the composer's directions. Serly adopted the medieval term *modus lascivus* to describe his own division of the chromatic scale into two segments, producing a multimodal chromatic scale. He composed the first movement (1940) of the concerto for two pianos and waited years before composing the last two movements (1955–1958). His *modus lascivus* appears in the last two movements of the concerto and the *Concertino 3 X 3* (three times three, 1965) for piano and chamber orchestra.

Homer Simmons (1900–1971) studied piano with Paderewski and composition with Respighi, Boulanger, and G. Jacob. For piano and orchestra, he composed the *Phantasmania* (1923–1924), the *Liturgy* (1940), the *Partita Americana* (1945), the *California Nights,* and the *Spanish Caprice*. The sections in the *Liturgy* are "Prelude," "Processional," "Venite," "Te Deum Laudmus," "Sanctus," "Benedictus," "Agnus Dei," "Gloria," "Pax Dei," and "Recessional." Titles for the sections in the *Partita Americana* are "Prelude e Fughetta," "Blues," "Fox Trot," "Waltz," "Rumba," and "Tango at Midnight."

Alexander Steinert (1900–1982) studied at Harvard University and in Paris with Koechlin and d'Indy. He orchestrated the film score for Walt Disney's *Bambi*. French modernists influenced his concerto *sinfonico* (1934).

Joseph Wagner (1900–1974) studied with Converse and Casella in Boston, with Boulanger and Monteux in Paris, and with Weingartner in Basel, Switzerland. The miniature concerto (1919), sometimes called a concertino, also is in a version as the concerto (perf. 1930). The rhapsody (1925, rev. 1940) is for piano, clarinet and strings; *A Fugal Triptych* (1937, rev. 1954) is for piano, percussion, and strings; and the *Fantasy in Technicolor* (1959) is for piano, winds, and percussion.

Victor Young (1900–1956) studied in Warsaw, Poland, and played violin in Warsaw, Chicago, New York City, and Los Angeles. His compositions include the *Manhattan Concerto,* based on a film score, and *Stella by Starlight,* based on the film music for *The Uninvited.*

Daniele Amfitheatrof (1901–1983) studied in Rome with Respighi, who influenced his orchestrations and style. He began the concerto (1937–1946) while an associate conductor of the Minneapolis Symphony Orchestra and finished it in Hollywood. He composed music for more than fifty films.

Alfredo Antonini (1901–1983) studied at the Conservatory in Milan, Italy, and immigrated to the United States in 1923. He worked as a conductor under Toscanini and became the conductor of the Tampa Philharmonic in 1957. The *Study in Baroque* (1968) is for harpsichord and strings.

Ruth Crawford (1901–1953), married to composer Charles Seeger, used Schoenberg's twelve-tone method when she composed the suite no. 2 (1929) for piano and strings. She taught in Chicago.

Boris Koutzen (1901–1966) studied with Gliere at the Moscow Conservatory and settled in 1922 in the United States, where he played violin in the Philadelphia Orchestra and taught at the Philadelphia Conservatory. The concerto (1959) for piano and strings owes much to the Russian romantic style.

Celius Dogherty (1902–) was a member of the Dogherty-Ruzicka two-piano team that premiered Hindemith's *Sonata 1942* and Stravinsky's concerto and sonata. Dogherty's concerto (1922) fulfilled a degree requirement at the University of Minnesota. Later, he studied piano with R. Lhévinne and composition with Goldmark at the Juilliard School of Music.

Michal Kondracki (1902–) studied with Szymanowski in Warsaw and with Dukas and Boulanger in Paris. He composed the lost concerto (1935) in Warsaw. It has been described as dissonant, percussive, and based on Polish folk melodies. Roussel, Ravel, and Prokofieff influenced the concertino (1944) Kondracki composed in New York City.

John Vincent (1902–1977) studied at the George Peabody College in Nashville, with Piston at Harvard and with Boulanger at the *École Normale de Musique* in Paris. His compositional style draws from classic forms, twentieth-century techniques and a concept of tonality he calls "paratonality." While on the faculty at the University of California at Los Angeles, he composed the concerto (1957–1960) for piano and string orchestra or quartet. Early titles of the composition were concerto *grosso* and *Piano Quintet.* He revised the work as the symphony no. 2 (1976) for piano and orchestra.

Stefan Wolpe (1902–1972), born in Germany, studied with Juon at the Berlin *Hochschule für Musik* and with Webern in Vienna. The main influences on his music are Webern, atonality, and folk melodies of the region around Palestine. In 1938, he settled in New York City, supporting himself by teaching; there he composed *For Piano and Sixteen Players* (1960–1961).

Vernon Duke (1903–1969), born in a railroad station as Vladimir Dukelsky, trained with Glière at the Kiev Conservatory and immigrated to New York City in 1922. He dedicated the concerto (1924) to pianist Arthur Rubinstein. The ballad (1931) is for piano and small orchestra and the *Dedicaces* (1938) is for soprano, piano, and orchestra.

Irwin Fischer (1903–1977) joined the faculty at the American Conservatory in 1928. The one-movement concerto (1935) employs Fischer's concept of polytonality he called "biplanal."

Jerzy Fitelberg (1903–1951) studied at the Berlin *Hochschule für Musik* and moved to the United States in 1940. In a style based on neo-classicism, baroque motor rhythms and Polish folk music, he composed the *rhapsodie* (1926) for four pianos and orchestra, two concertos (1929, 1934) in Berlin and Paris, and the concerto (1947) for trombone, piano, and strings.

Vittorio Giannini (1903–1966) studied with Martini, Trucco and Goldmark, and taught at the Juilliard School of Music. In a nineteenth-century style, he composed the concerto (1932–1935) in Rome and the concerto (1940) for two pianos in New York City. He became head of the North Carolina School of the Arts in Winston-Salem.

Bozidar Kunc (1903–1964), Yugoslav, taught at the Zagreb Music Academy and immigrated to the United States in 1950. His one-movement, five-part concerto (1934) is rhapsodic. The *3 Episodes* (1955) uses bitonal and polymetric techniques. The first episode is an impressionistic toccata, the second episode is a romantic pastorale, and the third episode has a modern motor rhythmic style. The concerto (1962) is for small hands.

Nikolay Lopatnikoff (1903–1976), born in Russia, trained at the Imperial Conservatory in St. Petersberg. He moved to Helsinki and later to Heidelberg, Germany, to study civil engineering and musical composition with Toch. His early compositions, including the concerto, op. 5 (1921), show the influence of Borodin and Mussorgsky. In Berlin, he composed the concerto, op. 15 (1930), influenced by Stravinsky and Hindemith. After living in London, he moved to the United States and, while on the faculty of the Carnegie Institute of Technology, he composed the concerto, op. 33 (1950), for the duo pianists Vronsky and Babin.

Hermann Parris (1903–1973), born in Russia, immigrated to the United States in 1901. He studied medicine at the Jefferson Medical College in Philadelphia and music at the University of Pennsylvania, and became a physician and surgeon. He composed eight piano concertos (one each year between 1946 and 1953) and the suite for piano and strings.

Frederick Piket (1903–1974) was born in Istanbul, Turkey, and educated at the Berlin *Hochschule für Musik* and the Vienna State Conservatory. He settled in the United States as a teacher at the Hebrew Union College, New York College of Music, and New York University. He left at least one concerto.

Nancy van de Vate (pseud. Helen Huntley, 1903–) composed the concerto (1968) as part of a doctoral dissertation at Florida State University. She taught in Tennessee, Mississippi, and Hawaii.

Herbert Inch (1904–) studied with Hanson at the Eastman School of Music in

Rochester, N.Y., and taught there and at Hunter College. In New York City, he composed the concerto (1940) in a contrapuntal style.

Tadeusz Kassern (1904–1957), Polish, studied music at the Lwów Conservatory and law in Paris. Polish folk music and classic models are the main influences on his music. Among his many musical compositions lost in World War II is the concertino (1940). In 1945, he joined the Polish Consulate in New York City as the cultural attaché, and there he composed the *Teen-Age Concerto* (1950–1955).

José Pedreira (1904–1959), pianist, studied in San Juan and New York City. He returned to Puerto Rico in 1932 and established the Academia for Piano. He composed the concerto (1936) following classic form and harmony.

Marc Blitzstein (1905–1964), student of Boulanger in Paris and Schoenberg in Berlin, wrote mostly theater music carrying a social message in a vocal style closely resembling speech patterns in the United States. He followed Hanns Eisler's philosophy that an artist must not live as a parasite drawing from society but should contribute to society. He composed the concerto (1931) before learning Eisler's philosophy. Blitzstein died of brain damage caused during a fight in a bar.

Ulric Cole (1905–) studied composition with Goetschius, Goldmark, and Boulanger, and piano with J. Lhévinne. While a student at the Juilliard School of Music, he composed the concerto (1924) for two pianos. While a faculty member at the Master's School in Dobbs Ferry, immediately north of New York City, he composed the divertimento (1938) with string orchestra and the concerto no. 2 (1941).

Dante Fiorillo (1905–1970s) apparently ceased his musical activities in the early 1950s to run an antique shop in Brooklyn. While most of his musical compositions appear lost, there is an extant concerto for harpsichord and strings.

Clark Harrington (1905–) trained at the New England Conservatory of Music, Boston, and worked as a performance rights inspector for CBS. *Alas, That Spring Should Vanish with the Rose* (1920) is for voice, piano, and orchestra.

Eric Zeisl (1905–1959) trained at the Vienna State Academy and immigrated to the United States in 1939. He taught at the Southern California School of Music and Los Angeles City College. His music follows the Viennese romantic style. While best known for song cycles, he also composed the concerto (1951–1952) for piano and orchestra.

Paul Creston (1906–1985) played organ at St. Malachy's Church and taught at the New York College of Music and Central Washington State College. His compositions have free tonality, classic forms, changing rhythms, and impressionistic sonorities. Frequently, Creston writes for the piano as an orchestra instrument. He composed the fantasy (1942), the concerto (1949), the concerto (1951) for two pianos, and the concertino (1969) with woodwind quintet.

Antal Dorati (1906–1988) gained an international reputation as the conductor of the Minneapolis Symphony Orchestra, the Dallas Symphony Orchestra, and other orchestras. He studied with Bartók and Kodály at the Budapest Liszt Academy and championed Bartók's music. He moved to Washington, D.C., to conduct the National Symphony Orchestra, and there he composed the concerto (1974) based on contemporary techniques.

Ross Lee Finney (1906–) studied with Ferguson at the University of Minnesota, with Boulanger in Paris, with Hill at Harvard University, with Berg in Vienna, and with Malipiero in Venice. He was on the faculty at Smith College in Northampton, Mass., when he composed the concerto (1934), originally a sonata, and the concertino (1941). The concerto I (1948) is from an era in Finney's life when he composed music for solo instruments or chamber ensembles. In 1949, he joined the faculty at the University of Michigan and from 1950 he leaned toward the twelve-tone method with some tonal thinking. The concerto II (1968) is atonal and serial.

Gunnar Johansen (1906–) toured Europe as a pianist and joined the faculty at the University of Wisconsin. He demonstrated an amazing feat by learning the piano version of Beethoven's violin concerto in thirty hours for a performance with the Philadelphia Orchestra. He recorded 246 improvisations of piano sonatas on LP records (1952–1970). Johansen championed the music of Busoni who influenced his two concertos (1930, 1970).

Gertrud Kuenzel (1906–) studied at the University of Minnesota and the Leipzig Conservatory. Since 1946, she has been living in Hawaii, where she was the first person to perform a harpsichord recital. Among her harpsichord compositions are the concerto (1973) and the double concerto (1976) for two harpsichords or harpsichord and piano.

Oscar Levant (1906–1972), capable pianist with performances of both serious and popular music, was a friend of Gershwin and a noted interpreter of Gershwin's *Rhapsody in Blue* and *Concerto in* F. He composed a concerto (1936).

Normand Lockwood (1906–) studied at the University of Michigan, with Respighi in Rome, with Boulanger in Paris, and at the American Academy in Rome. He taught at several institutions and the University of Denver. In Denver, he composed the concerto (1973).

Louise Talma (1906–) taught at the Manhattan School of Music, Hunter College and the American University in Fontainebleau, France, where she was the first American teacher. The *Dialogues* (1963–1964) has the piano in an obbligato role.

Franz Waxman (1906–1967) studied at the Berlin Conservatory and worked for the Universal and M-G-M film studios after immigrating to the United States in 1934. Late German romantic music, motor rhythms, and dissonance influenced his music. The *Goyana* (1960) is for piano and string orchestra.

Josef Alexander (1907–) attended Harvard University to study composition with Piston and orchestration with Hill. In Paris, he worked with Boulanger and later with Copland at the Berkshire (now Tanglewood) Music Center. The concerto (1938) is from the year he received his B.A. degree from Harvard.

Gene Gutche (1907–), born in Berlin, Germany, immigrated to the United States in 1926 and studied at the University of Minnesota and the University of Iowa. His compositions owe much to neo-romantic composers, and among his works is the twelve-tone concerto, op. 24 (1955), the serial *Rites in Tenochtitlàn,* op. 39, no. 1 (1963, rev. 1965), the symphonic poem (1965), and the *Gemini,* op. 41 (1965), for two pianos and orchestra, with movement titles "9..8..7..6..5..4..3..2..1 0," "Walk into Space," containing microtones and "Earthbound."

Salvador Ley (1907–), Guatemalan, studied in Guatemala City and with Petri and Leichentritt in Berlin, and directed the National Conservatory in Guatemala. He composed the concertino (1942) in New York City.

Burrill Phillips (1907–), student of Hanson and Rogers at the Eastman School of Music, taught at Eastman, the University of Illinois at Urbana, the Juilliard School of Music, and Cornell University. In a style that merges jazz and neo-classic ideas, Phillips composed the concerto (1943) and the triple concerto (1952) for piano, clarinet, viola, and chamber orchestra.

Miklos Rózsa (1907–1995), Hungarian, studied in Leipzig and went to Paris in 1932. In 1935, he traveled to London and, in 1939, to the United States, where he settled in Hollywood to write film music. He joined the faculty at the University of Southern California in 1945. His music has neo-classic elements, polyphony, rhythmic and melodic features of Hungarian folk music, and elements reminiscent of Bartók. He composed the *Spellbound Concerto* (1946) for two pianos, ondes Martenot, and orchestra based on the Academy Award-winning musical score for the film *Spellbound* (1945). The concerto, op. 31 (1967), for the pianist Leonard Pennario, has the motive of the first movement presented by the timpani (See ex. 16–2). By motivic development Rozsa builds many of the passages in the first movement (See ex. 16–3).

Victor Babin (1908–1972), student of Schnabel and member of a piano duo with his wife Vitya Vronsky, taught at the Cleveland Institute of Music. For two pianos and orchestra, he composed the concerto (1937) in four movements at La Ciotat, France, the concerto (1956), three *Concerto da Cameras* (1965, 1967, 1971), and the *Fantasies on Old Themes* (after 1942). He prepared the "Russian Village" from the fantasies as an individual work. His style is post-romantic.

Elliot Carter (1908–), important avant-garde composer, received training from Piston, Hill, Holst, and Boulanger. After teaching at the Peabody Conservatory in Baltimore and Columbia University in New York City, he went to Yale University. The one-movement double concerto (1961) for harpsichord, piano, and two chamber orchestras has a palindromic-like form, and the harpsichord and piano each have a cadenza. Stravinsky called Carter's piano concerto (1965) the first American masterpiece of the genre. The two-movement composition is on two twelve-tone chords, with one chord in the piano part and the other in the orchestra part. This complex composition uses Carter's ideas on the serialization of all elements and metric modulation. He composed the work partly or totally in Berlin, Germany.

John Green (1908–) trained in economics at Harvard University, left a successful business to work in music, and began writing film music for M-G-M. In 1951,

Example 16–2. Rózsa Concerto, op. 31, mvt. 1, mm. 1–4

Example 16–3. Rózsa Concerto, op. 31, mvt. 1, mm. 45–47

he worked on the score for Gershwin's *An American in Paris,* and 1961 Bernstein's *West Side Story.* His concert music includes the fantasy *Music for Elizabeth* (1942) and the six impressions *Night Club* (1932) for three pianos and orchestra, sometimes listed as *Six Impressions.*

Ray Green (1908–) studied at the San Francisco Conservatory, the University of California at Berkeley, and in Paris. He believes modulations are disturbing elements in music, so he composes without key changes. The music shows influences of jazz, hymns, dance music, modality, and American culture. He composed the concertino (1937); the *3 Inventories of Casey Jones* (1939), revised as the *3 Inventories on a Texas Tune* (1952); and the *Jig Theme and 3 Changes* (1948).

Eloise Koelling (1908–) taught at the University of Wisconsin. She composed the *concertante* no. 2 (1961) and two concertos.

Joaquin Nin-Culmell (1908–), born in Germany, trained at the *Schola Cantorum* in Paris and studied with Cortot, Dukas, Granada, and Falla. In 1936, he immigrated to the United States and joined the faculty at Williams College in Williamstown, Mass. Spanish cultural elements represent the strongest influence on his music, which contains contemporary harmonies, asymmetrical rhythms, and neoclassic forms. He has the concerto (1943).

Halsey Stevens (1908–) is a noted authority on Bartók and author of the book *The Life and Music of Bela Bartók.* While on the faculty at Syracuse University he composed the withdrawn concertino (1936). Since 1948, he has been teaching at the University of Southern California at Los Angeles, where he composed the allegro (1956) for piano and orchestra and the concertino (1966) for piano four hands, strings, and timpani.

John Verrall (1908–) studied with Ferguson in the United States, at the Royal College of Music in London, and with Kodály in Budapest. He taught at Hamline University in St. Paul, Minn., Mount Holyoke College in South Hadley, Mass., and the University of Washington. Verrall developed a nine-pitch scale of two tetrachords with a middle central pitch, striving for symmetry in harmonic, melodic, rhythmic, and metric relationships. The score of the concerto (1949) shows the synthetic scales used.

Robert Van Eps (1909–) played piano for Red Nichols, Freddie Martin, the Dorsey brothers, MGM Paramount, Columbia Pictures, Disney, and Warner Brothers. He composed two concertos.

Edwin Gerschefski (1909–) studied piano with Matthay at the Pianoforte School in London and with Schnabel in Como, Italy, and musical composition with Schillinger. The concerto, op. 5 (1931), on some lists as a concertino, is a conservative, academic work from the year he graduated from Yale University.

Paul Nordoff (1909–1977), author of books on music theory, studied piano with Samaroff and composition with Goldmark at the Juilliard School of Music. The concerto (1932–1936) is a student work from Juilliard. He taught at the Philadelphia Conservatory and at Michigan State University, where he composed the concerto (1948) for violin, piano, and orchestra. After joining the faculty at Bard College, he composed the *Gothic Concerto* (1959). There may be another piano concerto from the 1930s. After leaving Bard College, he went into music therapy and worked for the betterment of retarded children in Germany, Finland, and England.

Elie Siegmeister (1909–) studied with Riegger and Boulanger, taught at Hofstra University, Long Island, and helped establish the American Composers Alliance in 1937. Generally, his compositions use dissonance of minor seconds and ninths and major sevenths. The concerto (1974) has ragtime features, and the double concerto *An Entertainment* (1976), for violin, piano, and orchestra, has elements of jazz.

Samuel Barber (1910–1981) entered the Curtis Institute of Music in Philadelphia at age 13, and later taught composition there. The G. Schirmer Publishing Company commissioned the concerto (1962) to commemorate 100 years of publishing. Barber composed the second movement first, and based it on a canzone he was writing before receiving the commission. The concerto is for pianist John Browning, and Barber used many technical elements of Browning's training with R. Lhévinne, including long passages of parallel sixths in both hands (See ex. 16–4). Barber sought Horowitz's advice concerning various technical demands and, at the suggestion of the conductor Erich Leinsdorf, he changed the original quiet ending of the first movement to an exciting ending by adding a coda. Less than two weeks before the premiere of the concerto, Barber found an ostinato and motive for the last movement (See ex. 16–5). Barber received a Pulitzer Prize for the concerto. His compositional style is tonal, with a liberal use of chromaticism and contrapuntal devices.

Julius Chajes (1910–), Polish, won a prize at the International Concert for pianists in Vienna. In 1940, he immigrated to the United States and became the music director at the Jewish Community Center in Detroit, Mich. His musical compositions include the romantic fantasy (perf. 1928) and the concerto (1953) for piano and chamber orchestra.

Arthur Cohn (1910–) studied with Goldmark at the Juilliard School of Music. The *Quintuple Concerto for Five Ancient Instruments with Modern Orchestra,* op. 31 (1940), for treble viol, viola d'amore, viola da gamba, bass viol, and harpsichord comes from when he directed the Edwin A. Fleisher Collection at the Free Library of Philadelphia. Later, he was the head of symphonic and foreign music at Mills Music Company and MCA Music, and the director of serious music at Carl Fischer from 1972.

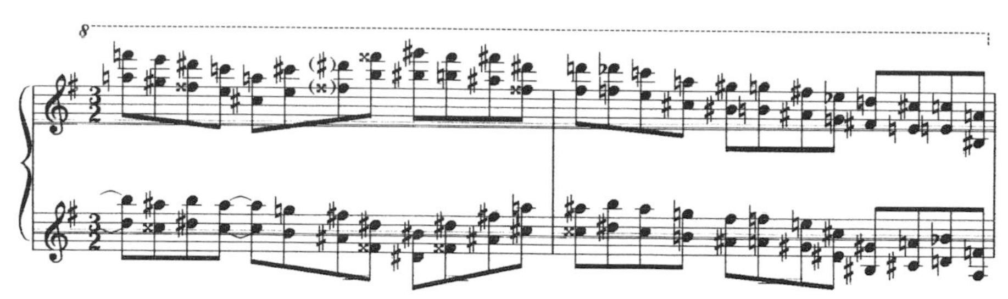

Example 16–4. Barber Concerto, op. 38, mvt. 1, mm. 41–42

Berhard Heiden (1910–) studied with Hindemith at the Berlin *Hochschule für Musik* and in the United States with Grout at Cornell University. He joined the faculty at Indiana University in 1946. The concerto (1956) for piano, violin, cello, and orchestra is a neo-classic composition.

Paul Reif (1910–1978), born in Czechoslovakia, trained at the Vienna Academy of Music with Walter and R. Strauss, and arranged music in Hollywood. The *Pentagram* (1969) is for piano and orchestra.

Earl Robinson (1910–) studied with Copland and wrote songs in Hollywood. The one-movement, four-section concerto *The New Human* (1973) has chromatic harmony.

William Schuman (1910–1992) was the president of the Juilliard School of Music and Lincoln Center. His style has chromaticism, slow themes, nonfunctional triads, and polytonality. He composed the concerto (1938, rev. 1942) with small orchestra while on the faculty at Sarah Lawrence College in Bronxville, just north of New York City; he withdrew the early version of the concerto.

Alan Hovhaness (1911–) studied with Converse at the New England Conservatory and with Martinu, Bernstein, Copland, and Foss at Tanglewood. Amateur artist Hermon di Giovanni is responsible for focusing Hovhaness' interest on his Armenian heritage. His music owes much to the melorhythms of Armenian music and the musical thinking of India and the Orient. In the 1960s, the music of Japan and Korea played a strong role in his compositions; more recently he turned toward Western styles. Many compositions have Armenian titles and numerous works have religious significance. The concerto no. 1 *Lousadzak* (Coming of Light), op. 48 (1944), for piano and string orchestra uses the composer's "rhythmless" technique; the result is a sound of indefinite pulse. The *Artinis,* op. 59, no. 5 (1945), for piano and chamber orchestra is version no. 5. The concerto no. 2 *Ardos* (1947) is for piano, timpani and strings, and the symphony no. 8 *Arjuna,* op. 179 (1947), is for piano and chamber orchestra. The *Sosi* (The Forest of the Prophetic Sound), op. 75 (1949), is for violin, piano, percussion, and strings, and the concerto *Zartik Parkim* (Awake My Glory), op. 77 (1949), is for piano and small orchestra. The *Janabar* (Journey), op. 81 (1950), is "Five Hymns

Example 16–5. Barber Concerto, op. 38, mvt. 3, mm. 1–18

of Serenity" for violin, piano, percussion, and strings. The *Khaldis,* op. 91 (1951), is a concerto for piano, four trumpets or any multiple of four instruments, and percussion. The partita, op. 98 (1953), is for piano and strings. The concerto no. 5, op. 179 (1947), is for piano and orchestra, and the symphony no. 45, op. 342 (1979), is for two pianos and large orchestra.

Boris Kremenliev (1911–), musicologist of Bulgarian birth, settled in the United States, where he studied with Hanson at the Eastman School of Music and joined the faculty at the University of California, Los Angeles. The one-movement concerto (1950) has a traditional style.

Gian Carlo Menotti (1911–), Italian born, immigrated to the United States, where he studied at the Curtis Institute of Music in Philadelphia. He established himself as a leading opera composer with *The Medium, The Consul,* and *Amahl and the Night Visitors.* The concerto (1943) has traditional forms and a strong Italian influence. The *Triplo Concerto a Tre* (1970) is for nine soloists forming three trios of piano, harp, and percussion, and oboe, clarinet, and bassoon, and violin, viola, and cello.

Lionel Nowak (1911–) studied with B. Rubinstein, Fischer, Porter and Sessions; after graduating from the Cleveland Institute of Music, he directed music for the Humphrey-Weidman Dancers. While on the faculty at Converse College, he composed the concerto (1944). He taught at Bennington College in Bennington, Vt., and, after suffering a stroke, began to compose music for the right-hand alone.

Stephen Park (1911–) studied with Finney at the University of Michigan and with Milhaud at the Aspen Music Center. He joined the faculty at the University of Tampa in 1939. He probably composed the *Jubilate* (1961) for two pianos and orchestra while in Tampa.

Albert Sendrey (1911–) studied at the *École Normale* in Paris and with Schoenberg, and orchestrated more than one hundred film scores. The concertino is for piano and orchestra.

Paul Sifler (1911–), born in Yugoslavia, studied at the Chicago Conservatory and Westminster Choir College. He worked in Chicago and New York City as an organist, then settled in Hollywood. His musical compositions include a concerto and *From Barn to Boogie* for piano and band.

Julia Smith (1911–) studied with Friedberg at the Juilliard School of Music and with Bauer at New York University. When she heard the 1938 premiere of Copland's *Billy the Kid,* she saw the potential of authentic American music as the basis of serious musical compositions. The concerto (1938–1939) contains elements of American folk music and jazz.

Vladimir Ussachevsky (1911–) founded, along with Luening, Babbitt, and Sessions, the Columbia-Princeton Electronic Music Center. Ussachevsky and Luening together composed the first important musical composition for tape recorder and orchestra. Among Ussachevsky's conventional works is the intermezzo (1951) for piano and chamber orchestra, and the *Interlude* (1952), which he originally intended as a concerto movement.

Rayner Brown (1912–), educated at the University of Southern California, played organ at the Wilshire Presbyterian Church and joined the faculty at Biola College. Among his compositions is the concerto (pub. 1972) for two pianos, brass, and percussion, a concerto for two pianos and orchestra, and a concertino for piano and band.

John Cage (1912–1992) is an internationally acclaimed avant-garde composer influential on composers in the United States. The concerto (1950–1951) for prepared piano and chamber orchestra contains tone clusters and passages performed directly on the piano strings. The prepared piano has small objects on and between the piano strings to alter the normal piano sound. The concerto (1957–1958) is an aleatoric composition with various instrumentalists in the orchestra given short musical segments that can be played or omitted. Information in the score directs the orchestra members to use their instruments in non-conventional ways, such as playing only on the mouthpiece. The only determined factor in the composition is the duration the conductor indicates by slowly lifting his arms over his head in a clockwise fashion so that the performance ends when the hands touch. Audience reaction at the premier was similar to the riotous response to Stravinsky's *Rite of Spring*.

Don Gillis (1912–1978) was a producer with the National Broadcasting Company and worked with Toscanini and the NBC Symphony Orchestra. He joined the faculty at Dallas Baptist College and became a composer-in-residence at the University of South Carolina. He composed two concertos (no. 2, 1966) in Dallas.

Peggy Glanville-Hicks (1912–), Australian, studied at the Melbourne Conservatory, in London with Vaughan Williams, Benjamin, Lambert, Sargent, and Morris, and in Paris with Boulanger. She composed the concerto (1936) in London and most of her other musical compositions in New York City. The inspiration for the *Etruscan Concerto* (1956) for piano and chamber orchestra is D. H. Lawrence's *Etruscan Places* and *The Painted Tombs of Tarquinia*. She tried to create feelings of ancient Etruscans by using old scales.

Violet Archer (1913–) studied with Champagne at the McGill *Conservatorium* and with Bartók and Hindemith at Yale University, and taught at North Texas State University, the University of Oklahoma, and the University of Alberta. At the MacDowell Colony, she composed the concerto (1957) using a sonata form for the first and third movements and a sonata rondo for the middle movement. The composition has tertian chords with some added tones and triplet motives in the melody.

George Barati (1913–) studied with Kodály at the Ferenc Liszt Academy of Music in Budapest and with Sessions at Princeton University. He was a cellist in the San Francisco Symphony and conductor of the Honolulu Symphony Orchestra. After settling in Saratoga, Calif., he composed the concerto (1973) and the *Branches of Time* (1981) for two pianos and orchestra.

John Barrows (1913–1974) played horn in the Minneapolis Symphony and the New York City Opera and Ballet orchestras. After studies at the Eastman School of Music, he attended Yale University, where he composed the concertino (1937) for piano and orchestra.

Margaret Bonds (1913–1972) was the first black musician to perform a solo composition with the Chicago Symphony Orchestra, and one of the best-known black musicians in serious music. She studied at Northwestern University and the Juilliard School of Music. In the 1930s, she established the Allied Arts Academy in Chicago, performed as a pianist in the United States and Canada, and taught piano in Chicago, New York City, and Los Angeles. The *Nile Fantasy* is her only work for piano and orchestra.

Henry Brant (1913–) studied at the Juilliard School of Music with Goldmark for composition and Friskin for piano. He worked for a radio station and orchestrated compositions for Benny Goodman and Andre Kostelanetz. The *Five and Ten Cents*

Store Music (1932) is for piano and chamber orchestra. He was an early composer in spatial-antiphonal music. The *Spatial Piano Concerto* (perf. 1978) is for piano, sixteen women's voices, and orchestra.

Norman Dello Joio (1913–) writes music in a style influenced by nineteenth-century Italian opera, Catholic church music, and popular music and jazz of the 1920s. He withdrew the concertino (1938) for piano and chamber orchestra. He probably composed the concerto (1941) before beginning a teaching career. While on the faculty at Sarah Lawrence College, Bronxville, N.Y., he composed the three ricercars (1946), and the year he joined the faculty at the Mannes College of Music he composed the *Ballad of the Seven Lively Arts* (1957). The fantasy and variations (1961) has a strong jazz influence. After becoming the dean of Fine Arts at Boston University, he composed *Notes from Tom Paine* (1975) for piano and band.

Vivian Fine (1913–) was a scholarship student in piano at the Chicago Musical College at age 5, and later a student of Sessions, Whiteside, and Szell. She taught at the Juilliard School of Music, New York State University at Potsdam, and Bennington College in Vermont from 1964. The Concertino (1943–1944), frequently listed as a *concertante,* is neo-classic with some twentieth-century idioms. Other compositions are the concertino (perf. 1965), the concerto (1972) for piano and strings, and the *Poetic Fires* (1984). She helped found the American Composers Alliance.

Grant Fletcher (1913–) studied with Krenek, Hanson, B. Rogers and Szell, and joined the music faculty at Arizona State University. He has the concerto (1953), the *Regency Concerto* (1966), and the *Dances from the Southwest* (1966) for piano and strings.

Morton Gould (1913–1996) composed popular Broadway music and probably has the only tap dance concerto for tap dancer and orchestra. He served on the board of directors of the American Society of Composers, Authors, and Publishers (ASCAP). He uses the terms "symphonette" and "concertette" for small musical forms to offset negative images symphonies and concertos might have with the public. Much of his music draws from jazz, Broadway musicals, folk music, American culture, and serious European music. The *Chorale and Fugue in Jazz* (1933) is for four pianos, brass, and percussion, and the concerto (1937) is for piano and twenty-four instruments. The *Interplay* or *American Concertette* (1943) is for a radio concert, and contains elements of jazz, American popular music, and classic form. *Interplay* is the title of Jerome Robbin's choreographic version of Gould's *American Concertante,* where the interplay in dance is between ballet and contemporary dance. The concerto (1944) is for piano and orchestra, and the *Dance Variations* (1953) for the two-piano team of Whittemore and Lowe is in four sections titled "Chaconne," "Arabesques," "Pas de Deux," and "Tarantella," which contains the *Dies irae*. Dimitri Mitropoulos suggested the *Inventions* (1953) for four pianos, winds, brass, and percussions in four sections: "warmup" in a style similar to the *concerto grosso:* "ballad" with various piano sonorities; "Schottische" in the manner of a round dance; and "toccata" with the pianos treated as the caller in a square dance. The dialogues (1958) for piano and strings is a serial work in four sections of "Recitative and Chorale," "Embellishments and Rondo," "Dirge and Meditation," and "Variations and Coda." The suite no. 1, op. 9, for orchestra contains writing for piano as a solo instrument.

Kent Kennan (1913–) trained at the University of Michigan, the Eastman School of Music, and with Pizzetti in Rome. In 1963, he revised the concertino (1946) for piano and wind ensemble. His books include *The Technique of Orchestration* and *Counterpoint Based on 18th-Century Practice.*

Gardner Read (1913–) studied with Hanson, B. Rogers, Sibelius, and Copland. While on the faculty at the Cleveland Institute, he composed the *Music for Piano and Strings,* op. 45a (1946), and the concerto, op. 130 (1977), while on the faculty at Boston University.

Cecil Effinger (1914–) was a student of Boulanger in Paris. He became first oboist with the Denver Symphony Orchestra, and joined the faculty at the University of Colorado in Boulder. His compositional style depends on a personal use of atonality and tonality. He composed the concerto (1946) for piano and chamber orchestra while on the faculty at the American College in Biarritz, France, and the symphonie *concertante* (1954) for harp, piano, and orchestra in Boulder, Colo. He invented the widely used "musicwriter" that he modeled on the typewriter.

Rober Goeb (1914–) studied agriculture before seriously turning to music, performed in jazz bands, and went to Paris for studies with Boulanger. He taught at various institutions, and while on the faculty at Stanford University, composed the *Concertant* IV (1951) for piano and chamber orchestra, which is in a version for clarinet, piano and strings; the concerto (1954); and the fantasy (1955) for two pianos and strings.

Gail Kubik (1914–1984) studied with B. Rogers at the Eastman School of Music, where he composed the *American Caprice* (1933) for piano and thirty-two instruments. He studied with Sowerby at the American Conservatory of Music, and went to Harvard University for instruction from Piston and Boulanger. Kubik received a Pulitzer Prize for the symphonie *Concertante* (1952, rev. 1953) for piano, trumpet, viola, and orchestra. The composition is an attempt to find a middle ground between the grandeur of the symphony and the virtuoso elements of the concerto. He taught at Scripps College in Claremont, Calif., and while there he composed the concerto (1976–1977). His style is neo-classic with influences of jazz and bitonality.

Charles Mills (1914–1982) studied with Czech composer Max Garfield, Copland, Sessions, and Harris. His style merges baroque techniques and American music, and in an output of principally instrumental music is the concerto, op. 75 (1948).

Esther Ballou (1915–1973), student of Luening, Wagenaar and Riegger, used classic models, thematic development, seventh and ninth chords, and seconds. She probably composed the concerto no. 1 (1945) in California and the prelude and allegro (1949), for piano and strings, in New York City. While on the faculty at American University in Washington, D.C., she composed the concerto (1964).

David Diamond (1915–) uses chromatic harmonies and neo-classic ideas, and later a personalized version of the dodecaphonic method. About the time Diamond studied with Sessions, he composed the divertimento (1935) for piano and small orchestra. After settling in Florence, Italy, he composed the concerto (1949–1950).

Homer Keller (1915–) studied with Hanson and B. Rogers. He may have composed his concerto (perf. 1949) while on the faculty at the University of Michigan.

Leslie Kondorossy (1915–) trained at the Budapest Academy of Music and settled in Cleveland. While praised for his short operas, he also composed the harpsichord concerto (1972).

Robert Palmer (1915–) studied with Rogers, Harris, Copland, and Porter at the Eastman School of Music, and taught at Cornell University. His compositional style is neo-classic, with influences of his teachers and Milhaud, Hindemith, Tippett, Petrassi, and Bartók, and the Rimsky-Korsakov scale. His concerto is for two pianos.

George Perle (1915–), student of Krenek, was among the first composers in the United States to follow the styles of Schoenberg, Berg, and Webern, but he modified the twelve-tone method to include some tonal patterns. While on the faculty at Queens College, he composed the concertino (1979) for piano, winds, and timpanis, and the serenade no. 3 (1983) for piano and chamber orchestra.

Vincent Persichetti (1915–1987) composed music that is dependent on various traditions of the classic and romantic eras. The concerto, op. 12 (1940), sometimes listed as the *concertato,* is a student work from the Philadelphia Conservatory, and the concertino, op. 16 (1941), is from the year he graduated and joined the faculty to teach composition. While a faculty member at the Juilliard School of Music, he composed the concerto, op. 90 (1962), using a motto opening as the basis of the melodic and harmonic writing.

Joseph Wood (1915–) studied with Wagenaar at the Juilliard School of Music and Luening at Columbia University and joined the composition faculty at the Oberlin Conservatory of Music. In a romantic style, Wood composed the divertimento (1958) for piano and chamber orchestra and the double concerto (1970) for piano, viola, and orchestra.

Milton Babbitt (1916–) is a noted composer of the twelve-tone method, serialism, and electronic music who worked on the Mark II RCA synthesizer during the 1950s. He taught at Princeton University and the Juilliard School of Music. He has the concerto (1985) for piano and orchestra.

Philip Bezanson (1916–1975) taught at Iowa State University and composed music in a diatonic style influenced by Stravinsky, Bartók, and Hindemith. Dimitri Mitropoulos commissioned the concerto (1952, rev. 1960).

Scott Huston (1916–) studied with Phillips, Rogers and Hanson at the Eastman School of Music. In a style evidencing romantic and impressionistic influences, he composed the toccata (1952) as a Ph.D. requirement. In 1952, he joined the faculty of the College-Conservatory of Music in Cincinnati.

Carlos Surinach (1916–), Spanish, trained at the Cologne *Hochschule* and in Berlin at the Prussian Academy, and settled in the United States in 1951. His music blends features of Spanish music with ideas learned in Europe. The *Doppio Concertino* (1954) is for violin, piano, and nine instruments, and the concertino (1956) is for piano, strings, and cymbals. The concerto (1973) contains dissonance and twentieth-century notation, material with a romantic influence, and an imitative passage based on a characteristic rhythm in the last movement.

Ben Weber (1916–1979) took training in medicine at the University of Illinois before attending De Paul University in Chicago to study musical composition. He adopted the twelve-tone method after meeting Schoenberg, but he modified the technique to allow for tonally oriented ideas. The concerto, op. 32 (1950), is for piano, cello, and woodwind quintet.

Claus Adam (1917–1983) played cello in the Juilliard String Quartet and taught at the Juilliard School, the Mannes College of Music, the Philadelphia College of Performing Arts, and the American Academy in Rome. He composed a concerto for piano and orchestra.

Edward Cone (1917–), theorist, critic, and writer, has been on the faculty at Princeton University since 1947. For piano and orchestra, he composed the nocturne and rondo (1955–1957) and a concerto.

Robert Erickson (1917–) was on the faculty at the San Francisco Conservatory when he composed the concerto (1963) for piano and seven instruments. He is fond of electronic techniques and serialism. In 1967, he joined the faculty at the University of California, San Diego.

Ulysses Simpson Kay (1917–), important black composer and relative of "King" Oliver, probably was at Columbia University when he composed the *Ancient Saga* (1947) for piano and string orchestra. The work is a revision of *The Rope*.

Louis Palange (1917–1979) studied at Mills College in Oakland, Calif., and settled in Los Angeles. He became the conductor of the Beach Cities Symphony Orchestra and founded the Southwest Symphony in 1965. He contributed the romantic concerto (1949) to the literature.

Robert Ward (1917–) studied with Hanson and B. Rogers at the Eastman School of Music and with Jacobi at the Juilliard School of Music. He taught at Juilliard, was the vice-president and editor for the Galaxy Music Corporation, then joined the faculty at the North Carolina School of the Arts. He won a Pulitzer Prize and the New York Music Critic's Circle Award for his opera *The Crucible* (1961). American folk songs and jazz are important influences in his music. The concerto (1970) is for piano and orchestra.

Richard Yardumian (1917–), student of Iturbi and Stokowski, composed works influenced by Armenian music, Appalachian ballads, and Debussy. He devised a system of composition based on what he termed "quadrads" which are twelve notes of superimposed thirds built from alternate black and white notes of the piano. The *Passacaglia, Recitative and Fugue* (1957) appears in several sources as a concerto.

Leonard Bernstein (1918–1990) was among the world's finest conductors and a composer of serious and light music. At Harvard University, he studied musical composition with Hill and Piston, then attended the Curtis Institute of Music. He learned conducting with Reiner, who took an interest in Bernstein's conducting career. Bernstein conducted the New York Philharmonic and retired as the laureate conductor. He joined the faculty at the Tanglewood Music Center (formerly Berkshire Music Center) in Lenox, Mass. For the symphony no. 2 *The Age of Anxiety* (1947–1949), Bernstein drew inspiration from W. H. Auden's poem *The Age of Anxiety: A Baroque Ecolgue*. The work is in two parts of six sections: Part I—"The Prologue," "The Seven Ages" (seven variations, nos. 1–7), and "The Seven Stages" (seven variations, nos. 8–14); and Part II—"The Dirge," "The Masque," and "The Epilogue." The piano has a solo part throughout the symphony. The variety of styles includes jazz and row-like passages. In 1950, Bernstein used material from the symphony for a ballet of the same title.

George Rochberg (1918–) studied at the Mannes College of Music and with Menotti at the Curtis Institute of Music. While on the faculty at the Curtis Institute, he composed the *Concert Piece* (1950) for two pianos and orchestra with elements of Bartók, Hindemith, and Stravinsky. In 1950, he worked with Dallapiccola in Rome, then turned toward serialism.

Arnold Scharzwald (1918–) studied composition with Castelnuovo-Tedesco and composed music for Hollywood films. He composed two *rhapsodies* for piano and orchestra.

Paul Dunlap (1919–) studied with Toch at the University of California at Los Angeles. He composed more than two hundred scores for film and television and a concerto for piano and jazz bands.

Leon Kirchner (1919–), distinguished pianist and conductor, received the Naumberg Award for the concerto no. 1 (1952–1953), which he composed while on the faculty at the University of Southern California, Los Angeles. In 1961, he joined the faculty at Harvard University, and there he composed the concerto no. 2 (1962–1963). His style shows an interest in Bartók, Schoenberg, and Stravinsky.

Harold Zabrack (1919–) studied piano with Ganz at the Chicago Musical College and composition with Boulanger in Fontainebleau, France. In St. Louis, he composed the one-movement concerto no. 1 (1964) and the concerto no. 2 "Symphonic Variations," both in a romantic style. In 1974, he joined the faculty at the Westminster Choir College in Princeton, New Jersey.

Earl Kim (1920–), American composer of Korean descent, studied with Schoenberg at the University of California at Los Angeles and with Bloch and Sessions at the University of California at Berkeley. Although he rarely uses the twelve-tone method, his music shows the influence of Schoenberg's ideas. While on the faculty at Princeton University, he composed the dialogues (1959). In 1967, he joined the faculty at Harvard University.

John La Montaine (1920–) took training with Ganz in Chicago, Hanson and B. Rogers at the Eastman School of Music, Wagenaar at the Juilliard School of Music, and Boulanger in Paris. He holds the Richard Nixon Chair at Whittier College, and received a Pulitzer Prize in 1959 for the concerto, op. 9 (perf. 1958). His interest in various sounds of nature caused him to write works such as the *Birds of Paradise,* op. 34, for piano and orchestra.

Harold Shapero (1920–) studied with Slonimsky, Krenek, Piston, Hindemith, and Boulanger. In 1952, he joined the faculty at Brandeis University, and there he composed the partita (1960) for piano and chamber orchestra, based on the twelve-tone method and neo-baroque ideas.

William Bergsma (1921–) studied at Stanford University and the Eastman School of Music, and taught at the Juilliard School of Music, eventually becoming associate dean. In Oakland, Calif., he composed the concerto (1936).

Matt Doran (1921–) studied with Toch at the University of Southern California and composed the concerto (1975) while a faculty member at Mount St. Mary's.

Andrew Imbrie (1921–) studied with Ornstein, Boulanger, and Sessions. He joined the faculties at the University of California, Berkeley, and the San Francisco Conservatory. His music includes the *Little Concerto* (1956) for piano, four-hands, and two concertos (1973, 1974).

Leo Smit (1921–) trained at the Curtis Institute of Music in Philadelphia and worked with Balanchine in the preparation of Stravinsky's ballets. He writes music in a neo-classic style akin to Stravinsky. While on the faculty at the State University of New York, he composed the concerto (1968).

Héctor Campos-Parsi (1922–) studied at the New England Conservatory in Boston, with Boulanger in Paris and Copland at Tanglewood. In 1932, he began working for the government for the advancement of music in the schools and later directed the Puerto Rico Conservatory. In the 1950s, his music drew upon neo-classicism, and in the 1960s from various contemporary techniques, including electronic and aleatoric devices. The Standard Oil Corporation commissioned the *Duo Tragico in Memoriam John* F. *Kennedy* (1965) that is in ABA form.

Robert Evett (1922–1975) studied with Harris in Colorado and at the Juilliard School of Music, and then settled in Washington, D.C. In a classic style with a contemporary level of dissonance, he composed the concerto (1957) for piano and orchestra and the harpsichord concerto (1961) based on baroque models.

Leo Kraft (1922–) studied with Thompson at Princeton University and with Boulanger in Paris. His music includes baroque rhythms and jazz. Since 1947, he has been on the faculty at Queens College, where he composed the concerto no. 4 (1979, rev. 1982) for piano and fourteen instruments.

Allen Sapp (1922–) studied with Piston, Hill, I. Fine, R. Thompson, Copland, and Boulanger, and aligns himself with neo-classic thinking. The concertino no. 1 (1942) is for piano and chamber orchestra. While Sapp was at the State University of New York, Buffalo, he composed the *Colloquies* no. 1 (1963). While on the faculty at the Cincinnati College-Conservatory, he completed *Colloquies* no. 3 (1980) for piano and ten winds and the *Imaginary Creatures* (1980) for harpsichord and orchestra.

Francis Thorne (1922–) studied with Diamond in Florence, Italy, and Hindemith at Yale University. His avant-garde musical compositions include elements of jazz. For piano and orchestra, he composed the *Rhapsodic Variations* (1964–1965), the concerto no. 1 (1965–1966), the concerto no. 2 (1973) with chamber orchestra, and the *Pop Partita* (1978) with chamber orchestra. His own personal wealth is the financial basis of the Thorne Music Fund to aid impoverished atonal composers.

Roy Travis (1922–) composed the concerto (1957–1968) while on the faculty of the University of California at Los Angeles. His attraction to Greek drama and African tribal music influenced many of his compositions.

George Walker (1922–) is a graduate of the Oberlin Conservatory of Music, a piano student of R. Serkin at the Curtis Institute of Music, and a composition pupil of Menotti, Boulanger, Casadesus, and Curzon. While on the faculty of the Peabody Conservatory of Music he composed the concerto (1975).

Iannis Xenakis (1922–), born in Romania, avant-garde composer of Greek heritage, studied in Paris with Honegger and Milhaud at the *École Normal de Musique* and with Messiaen at the *Conservatoire*. He taught at the University of Indiana and uses mathematical ideas when composing music. Information in the score of the *Synaphai* (Connexities, 1969) directs the pianist to play as many notes as possible. The *Erikhthon* (concerto, 1974) is on a grand scale with some percussion sounds performed on the piano.

Leslie Bassett (1923–) trained with Finney at the University of Michigan and with Boulanger and Honegger in Paris. She was a member of the faculty at the

University of Michigan when she composed the *Forces* (1972) for piano, cello, violin, and orchestra and the concerto (1976) for two pianos and orchestra. Directions in the concerto score require the two pianos to be on the right and left sides of the conductor and at least ten feet apart.

Frederick Koch (1923–) grew up in Cleveland where he studied with B. Rubinstein at the Cleveland Institute of Music and at Case Western Reserve University. After studying composition with B. Rogers at the Eastman School of Music, he returned to Cleveland. His compositions for piano and orchestra are the suite, op. 48 (1961–1962), the *Short Symphony* I (1965), the *Concerto Sonica* (1977), and one or more concertos.

William Kraft (1923–) joined the Los Angeles Philharmonic Orchestra as a percussionist. His composition studies were with Cowell, Luening, Ussachevsky, I. Fine, and L. Bernstein. As a percussionist, he imbued the concerto (1972–1973) and the *Double Play* (1982) for violin, piano, and chamber orchestra with effective rhythmic ideas.

Peter Mennin (1923–1983) taught at the Juilliard School of Music, directed the Peabody Conservatory of Music in Baltimore, and became the president of the Juilliard School of Music. His concerto (1958) is neo-classic and has some thematic development.

H. Luis Antonio Ramirez (1923–) studied at the *Academia del Perpetuo Socorro*. In 1957, he traveled to Madrid, Spain, to study with C. Halffter, and upon returning to Puerto Rico in 1964, worked as a teacher and composer. He began the *Cuatro Homenajes* (1963–1965) for piano and string orchestra in Spain and finished it in Puerto Rico.

Ned Rorem (1923–), song composer, studied at the American Conservatory in Chicago with Sowerby, at Northwestern University, the Curtis Institute in Philadelphia, and the Juilliard School of Music. In New York City, he composed the *Concertino da Camera* (1946) for harpsichord and seven instruments, and possibly the withdrawn concerto (1948). In Morocco, he worked on the concerto no. 2 (1950) using expanded tonality. In 1951, he moved to Paris to work with modern Parisian composers, until departing for the United States the same year. He taught at the University of Buffalo and the University of Utah, then probably settled in New York City. The basis of the *Concerto in Six Movements* (1969) is the first two measures of the first movement. The Cincinnati Symphony Orchestra commissioned Rorem to compose a concerto for piano, cello and orchestra; the resulting work is *Remembering Tommy* (1979).

Clifford Taylor (1923–) studied with Lopatnikoff at Carnegie-Mellon University in Pittsburgh and at Harvard University with I. Fine, Hindemith, Piston, and R. Thompson. He joined the faculty at Chatham College in Pittsburgh and, in 1963, the faculty at Temple University in Philadelphia where he composed the concerto (1974).

Lester Trimble (1923–) studied with Lopatnikoff, Milhaud, Copland, and Boulanger, and served as a composer-in-residence with the New York Philharmonic Orchestra under Bernstein. He composed the harpsichord concerto (1978).

Chou Wen-Chung (1923–), born in Cheefoo, China, immigrated in 1946 to the United States, where he attended the New England Conservatory and Columbia University, then joined the faculty. His compositions join Chinese musical traditions with Western musical elements. Beginning in the 1960s, he used the idea of *I Ching* in musical compositions, particularly in *Pien* (1966) for piano, percussion, and winds. *Pien* means to transform and change in a manner of constant mutation within something. Other compositions are *The Dark and Light* (1964) for piano, percussion, and strings, and the *Yün* (1969) for piano, percussion, and winds.

Russell Woolen (1923–), composition student of Boulanger in Paris, taught at Catholic University and Howard University, and played organ at the Arlington Unitarian Church in Virginia. He used the *Concerto Movement* (1962) as the first movement of the *2 Pieces* (1962–1976).

Hugh Aitken (1924–) studied composition with Wagenaar and Persichetti at the Juilliard School of Music. While on the Juilliard faculty, he composed the concerto (1953) and the *15 Short Pieces* (1960) for piano and strings in a conservative, eclectic style.

Thomas Beversdorf (1924–1981) was a trombonist with the Rochester Philharmonic, the Houston Symphony and the Pittsburgh Symphony. In 1949, he joined the faculty at Indiana University and, while there, he composed the concerto, op. 14A (1951), for two pianos and orchestra. He studied composition with Kennan, Rogers, Hanson, Copland, and Milhaud.

Benjamin Lees (1924–), born in China, trained at the University of California at Los Angeles with Stevens, Dahl, and Kanitz, and privately with Antheil. His style contains expanded tonality with influences of Prokofieff, Bartók, and classic structures. He composed the concerto no. 1 and, in Longpont-sur-Orge, France, the *concertante breve* (1959) for oboe, two horns, piano, and strings. The concerto no. 2 (1966) is a product of when Lees taught at the Peabody Conservatory. He composed the *Five Etudes* (1974) while on the faculty at the Manhattan School of Music, the variations (1976) during his teaching years at the Juilliard School of Music, and the double concerto (1982) for cello, piano, and orchestra, probably after retiring to Long Island.

Lejaren Hiller (1924–) studied music with Sessions and Babbitt while pursuing a major in chemistry at Princeton University. He probably composed the concerto (1949) during his time at Princeton. In 1952, he joined the chemistry faculty at the University of Illinois and the music faculty in 1958.

Stanley Hollingsworth (1924–) studied with Milhaud at Mills College in Oakland, Calif., and with Menotti at the Curtis Institute of Music, Philadelphia, and at the American Academy of Music in Rome, Italy. Since 1963, he has been on the faculty at Oakland University. He dedicated the concerto (1980) to Menotti, and the music shows Menotti's influence. Hollingsworth sometimes composes under the name Stanley Hollier.

Robert Parris (1924–) studied with Mennin at the Juilliard School of Music, with Ibert and Copland at the Tanglewood Music Center, and with Honegger in Paris. The concerto (1954) is for piano and strings. The concerto (1967) for percussion, violin, cello, piano, and orchestra is a product of when Parris taught at George Washington University in Washington, D.C.

Leonard Rosenman (1924–) studied composition with Schoenberg, Sessions, and Dallapiccola. The concertino (1948) is for piano and winds.

Will Gay Bottje (1925–) studied with Giannini at the Juilliard School of Music and in Paris with Boulanger. In 1957, he joined the faculty at Southern Illinois University and established an electronic music studio. He has the concerto (1960), the rhapsody variations (1962) for piano, viola, and strings, and the *Facets* for piano and band.

Margaret Fairlie (1925–), pianist and writer, began composing the concerto (1959–1969) while on a fellowship at Bennington College.

Richard Hoffmann (1925–) graduated from Auckland University College, New Zealand, immigrated in 1947 to the United States where he studied with Schoenberg and became Schoenberg's copyist, and joined the faculty at the Oberlin Conservatory in 1954. He evolved a compositional style that serializes intervals, meters, rhythms, and other musical elements. The concerto (1953–1954) is on a row and a rhythmic serialization of the Morse code of part of a letter from Mozart to his father.

Robert Linn (1925–) studied with Milhaud at Mills College in Oakland and with Stevens, Sessions, and Dahl at the University of Southern California at Los Angeles, where he joined the faculty. The *Hexameron* (1963) for piano and orchestra is a reworking of Liszt's *Hexameron,* which is a set of variations on a theme by Bellini.

Gunther Schuller (1925–) played French horn in the Cincinnati Symphony Orchestra and the Metropolitan Opera Orchestra, taught at Yale University and became the president of the New England Conservatory of Music in Boston. In 1957, he originated the term "third stream" for serious music that incorporates elements of jazz. Part of his musical output is the *Concertino for Jazz-Quartet* (1959) for clarinet, piano, vibraphone, percussion, and orchestra, two concertos (1962, 1981), and the *Colloquy* (1966) for two pianos and orchestra.

Ruth Slenczynska (1925–) studied piano with Hofmann, Petri, Schnabel, Cortot, and Long, and became a member of the faculty at Southern Illinois University. She wrote cadenzas for Beethoven's concerto nos. 1 and 2.

Hale Smith (1925–) trained at the Cleveland Institute of Music and taught at the University of Connecticut. The serial *Concert Music* (1972) has traditional forms.

Earle Brown (1926–), trained in engineering and mathematics at Northwestern University, found serialism limiting, so he evolved a system of metric notation. Two compositions featuring piano are the *Folio* (1952–1953) and the *4 Systems* (1952–1953). He is a member of the "New York" school of composers that includes Cage, Tudor, Feldman, and Wolff.

Barney Childs (1926–) studied with Ratner, Chávez, Copland, and Carter. While on the faculty at the University of Arizona, he composed the *Music for Piano and Strings* (1965).

Morton Feldman (1926–) studied with Riegger and Wolpe, and was influenced by Cage and Webern. The concerto (1975) has changing meters and avoids strong beats.

Karl Kohn (1926–), Austrian, immigrated to the United States with his parents in 1938. At Harvard University, he studied with Piston, I. Fine, and R. Thompson, and composed the sinfonia *concertante* (1951). He taught at Pomona College and the Claremont Graduate School of Music. His compositional style is serial, with elements of diatonicism and pandiatonicism. Other compositions are the *Concerto Mutabile* (1962), with full orchestra or chamber orchestra; the *Episodes* (1964); the Interludes *II* (1969), titled *Intermezzo* in some sources; the *Esdras—Anthems and Interludes* (1969–1970) for flute, piano, mixed chorus, and orchestra; and *The Prophet Bird* (perf. 1982). He is a member of a two-piano team with his wife Margaret.

Marga Richter (1926–) studied at the Juilliard School of Music with Bergsma, Persichetti, and Tureck. Her concerto (1955) for piano and low strings is in five movements. The *Landscapes of the Mind I* (1968–1974), a concerto, has an Indian raga and an orchestra with electric guitar, electric bass guitar, and a novel variety of percussion instruments.

Mary Jeanne van Appledorn (1927–) teaches music literature and theory at Texas Tech University. Her teachers were B. Rogers and Hovhaness. She has the *Concerto Brevis* (1954, rev. 1958).

Dominick Argento (1927–) studied at the Peabody Conservatory, with Dallapiccola in Florence, Italy, and with Hanson and B. Rogers at the Eastman School of Music. The concerto (1954) is from the year he graduated from Peabody. In 1959, he joined the composition faculty at the University of Minnesota.

Joseph Castaldo (1927–), trained by Giannini and Persichetti, was the president of the Philadelphia Music Academy (now the Philadelphia College of Performing Arts). The *Epigrams* is for piano and orchestra.

Emma Lou Diemer (1927–) studied with Hindemith at Yale University and with Toch, Sessions, Rogers, and Hanson. She taught at the University of Maryland and the University of California, Santa Barbara. She composed the concerto (1954) while working with Toch and Sessions at the Berkshire (now Tanglewood) Music Center. At the Eastman School of Music, she composed the concerto (1958) for harpsichord and orchestra.

John Downey (1927–) studied with Rieti, Krenek, A. Tcherepnin, Milhaud, Boulanger, and Messiaen and joined the faculty at the University of Wisconsin. Using a modified serial style, he composed the *Discourse* (1984) for oboe, harpsichord, and strings.

Donald Erb (1927–) studied with Boulanger in Paris and worked as a jazz trumpeter. His music from the 1950s shows influences of jazz, neo-classicism and, from 1953, the serialism of the Second Viennese School. While on the faculty at Indiana University, he composed the chamber concerto (1961) for piano and chamber orchestra, and the *concertante* (1962) for harpsichord and strings. Since 1966, he has been on the faculty at the Cleveland Institute of Music, where he composed the concerto (1970) for keyboards and orchestra.

Walter Hartley (1927–) trained at the Eastman School of Music with Rogers and Hanson. His concertino (1950–1952) and concerto (1952) display expanded tonality and elements of Bartók, Busoni, Hindemith, Honegger, and Stravinsky. In 1969, he joined the faculty at the State University of New York, Fredonia.

Richard Swift (1927–) received a master of arts degree from the University of Chicago (1965), and joined the music faculty at the University of California at Davis. There he composed the concerto no. 1, op. 26 (1961), for piano and chamber ensemble. He is fond of serial techniques, electronic and aleatoric devices, and baroque structures. He composed the concerto no. 2 (1980) for piano and ensemble while on the faculty at Princeton University.

Wallace Berry (1928–), author of *Form in Music,* wrote the well-known vocal orchestra composition *Spoon River*. His concerto (1963) is in five sections to be played without pause.

Arthur Cunningham (1928–) writes music using jazz, serialism, and tonal ideas. He has the dialogue (1966), the concerto, op. 26 (1968), and the *Paladitas* (1970), meaning "little kicks," taken from the *Harlem Suite* (1969).

Nicolas Flagello (1928–), neo-romantic composer, joined the faculty at the Manhattan School of Music. The concerto no. 1, op. 7 (1950), is a student composition from the Manhattan School of Music, and the concerto no. 2, op. 18 (1956), probably is a student work from the Santa Cecilia Academy in Rome. In New York City, he composed the concerto no. 3, op. 36 (1962), the concertino, op. 40 (1963), for piano, brass, and timpani, and the concerto no. 4, op. 73 (1975).

Beverly Grigsby (1928–) studied with Krenek at the Southern California School of Music and Arts. Her style depends on serialism, free tonality, and aleatoric techniques. In 1983, she was working on a concerto for piano, orchestra, and computer generated tape.

Ray Luke (1928–) took training at Texas Christian University and the Eastman School of Music with B. Rogers. He taught at Texas A&M University-Commerce and at Oklahoma City University. His concerto (1968) won the gold medal in the 1969 Queen Elizabeth International Competition in Belgium.

Donal Michalsky (1928–1975) studied with Stevens and Dahl at the University of California at Los Angeles, and with Fortner in Freiberg, Germany. His compositional style has traditional structures, dissonant counterpoint, and dodecaphonic techniques. The sinfonia *concertante* (symphony no. 2, 1969) is for clarinet, piano, and orchestra.

William Russo (1928–) played trombone in Stan Kenton's band and later worked at the Center for New Music in Chicago. The *Street Music* (1975) is a concerto in blues style for piano, harmonica, and orchestra.

Peter Sacco (1928–) was born into a family where most males were tenors, and trained as a tenor before switching to the piano. He studied with B. Rogers and Hanson at the Eastman School of Music and joined the faculty at San Francisco State University in 1959. He writes music using traditional harmonies and some dodecaphony. Among his compositions is the concerto, op. 19 (1964).

William Sydeman (1928–) studied with Salzer at the Mannes College of Music and joined the faculty in 1959. His compositional style has motivic development, atonality, and influences of Mahler and Berg. Sydeman composed the concertino (1956) for oboe, piano, and string orchestra; the chamber concerto (1961) for piano, two flutes, and string quartet; and the concerto (1967) for piano, four-hands, and chamber orchestra.

Constantine Constantinides (1929–), born in Greece, studied at the Greek Conservatory in Athens and violin with Galamian at the Juilliard School of Music. She probably was at Michigan State University while composing the concerto (1968) for violin, cello, piano, and orchestra.

James Drew (1929–) studied musical composition with Varèse and Riegger. While on the faculty at Yale University, he composed the concerto (1968) for two pianos and strings. In 1980, he became the director of the Contemporary Arts Center in New Orleans. There he composed the *St. Mark Triple Concerto* (1981) for violin, cello, piano, and brass or winds; the *Faustus* (1983) for two pianos, cello, and orchestra; and the *Faustus, An Epilogue* (1984) for two pianos, viola, and chamber ensemble.

Eugene Hemmer (1929–1977) of the University of Cincinnati faculty composed *The Voice of the Grand Piano* (1955) and the concerto (1956) for two pianos and orchestra. *The Voice of the Grand Piano* is in two sections, with the first section using a narrator to describe the construction of a grand piano, while a construction crew enacts the making of a piano; the second section is a concertino for piano and orchestra.

Donald Keats (1929–) studied with Porter and Hindemith at Yale University and with Luening and Cowell at Columbia University. In 1975, he joined the faculty at the Lamont School of Music at the University of Denver. He composed the dialogue (1973) for piano and wind instruments in Denver or Europe, and the concerto (1981–1985) in Denver.

Richard Moryl (1929–), founder of the New England Contemporary Music Ensemble, studied at Columbia University and with Blacher at the Berlin *Hochschule für Musik.* When on the Smith College faculty, he composed the *Volumes* (1971) for piano, organ, and large orchestra.

Robert Muczynski (1929–), Polish descent, was studying with A. Tcherepnin when he composed the divertimento, op. 2 (1951–1952), as a graduation work at DePaul University. His music shows the influence of Russian music, neo-baroque elements, Bartók, Piston, and Barber, and he is fond of irregular meters and varied accents. He taught at Iowa College and joined the faculty at the University of Arizona in 1965. While at Iowa College, he composed the concerto no. 1, op. 7 (1956), using neoromantic ideas.

Ruth Schonthal (1929–), born in Germany was, at age 13, the youngest student enrolled at the Royal Academy of Music in Stockholm, and began studies with Hindemith at Yale University in 1946. She taught at New York University and the Westchester Conservatory, and she composed the *Concerto Romantico* (1942) and the concerto no. 2 (1977).

James Woodard (1929–) composed the concerto (1965) for two pianos and orchestra as a DMA requirement at Florida State University in Tallahassee.

Yehudi Wyner (1929–), born in Canada, took training at the Juilliard School of Music, Yale University, and Harvard University. He joined the faculty at Yale, and became chairman of the music department in 1969. In 1976, he began teaching at the Berkshire (now Tanglewood) Music Center in Tanglewood. His music depends on serial devices and neo-baroque forms. The *Concerto da Camera* (1967) is the first part of a planned larger work.

David Amram (1930–), horn player, uses elements from jazz, serious music, and music of other cultures. He wrote music for several successful films, including *The Manchurian Candidate. En memoria de Chano Pozo* (1977) is for flute, electric bass guitar, piano, and orchestra.

Larry Austin (1930–) student of Imbrie, Milhaud, and Shifrin, composes music with his concept of "open style" which allows performers a degree of choice in what they perform; his system of analog notation controls the total composition. While on the faculty at the University of California, Davis, he composed the *Open Style for Orchestra and Piano Soloist* (1965).

Eric Stokes (1930–) studied at Lawrence College (now University) in Appleton, Wis., the New England Conservatory of Music, and the University of Minnesota.

His compositions display an influence of Ives, Brant, jazz, hymns, and American folk music. He composed the *Concerto Music* (1982) while on the faculty at the University of Minnesota.

Federick Tillis (1930–) writes music in a style that blends jazz, serial techniques, and elements of black music. He composed the concerto (1977) for piano and jazz orchestra while on the music faculty at the University of Massachusetts.

Frank Ahrold (1931–) trained at the University of California, Los Angeles, and played piano with the Oakland Symphony Orchestra. He composed a concerto.

David Baker (1931–), jazz cellist, incorporates jazz in serious musical compositions, and has been the chairman of the jazz department at Indiana University. The concerto (1976) is for two pianos, jazz band, chamber orchestra, and percussion.

Lucia Dlugoszewski (1931–), painter and poet, trained in physics at Wayne State University. Her love of mathematical elements in music and studies with Varèse led her to invent several percussion instruments, including a timbre piano, which is a conventional piano played by striking strings with various objects and bows. For timbre piano and orchestra, she composed the *Dazzle on a Knife's Edge* (1966), the *Agathlon Algebre* (1968), and the *Instants in Form and Movements* (1957) with chamber orchestra.

Donald Martino (1931–), student of Bacon, Babbitt, Sessions, and Dallapiccola, taught at Princeton University, Yale University, the New England Conservatory of Music, and Harvard University. The New Haven Symphony commissioned the concerto (1958–1965), which contains written cadenzas connecting the three movements. This serial work has numerous meter and tempo changes, a large percussion section, and elements of romanticism.

Michael Colgrass (1932–), percussionist, studied with Milhaud, Foss, Riegger, and Weber. In an atonal style with elements of jazz, he composed the concerto (perf. 1958), the divertimento (1960) for eight drums, piano, and strings, the collage *Letter From Mozart* (perf. 1976), the *Memento* (1982) for two pianos, and the *Demon* (1984) for amplified piano, percussion, tape, and radio orchestra.

Karl Kroeger (1932–) composed the *Five Bagatelles* (1967) for piano and chamber orchestra while a Ford Foundation composer-in-residence in the public schools in Eugene, Ore. In 1972, he became the director of the Moravian Music Foundation in Salem, N. C., and joined the faculty at the University of Colorado in Boulder in 1982.

Henri Lazarof (1932–), Bulgarian-born, studied with Ben-Haim in Jerusalem, at the Santa Cecilia Academy in Rome, and at Brandeis University. In an atonal style containing serialism, he composed the concerto (1956) in Rome, the concerto (1960–1961) for piano and twenty instruments, the *Ricercar* (1968) for viola, piano, and orchestra, and the *Textures* (1970) for pianos and five instrumental groups.

Marvin Levy (1932–) studied with Philip James at New York University and with Luening at Columbia University. His music has expressionistic ideas, atonality, and asymmetrical rhythms. The concerto (1970) contains sections where the pianist improvises.

Joel Mandelbaum (1932–) studied with Blacher, Dallapiccola, I. Fine, Piston, and Shapero. The concerto (1953) is from the year he graduated from Harvard University. In 1961, he joined the music faculty at Queens College, New York City. Microtonality is an important part of his style.

Lalo Schifrin (1932–), born in Argentina, studied with Koechlin and Messiaen at the Paris *Conservatoire*. He moved to New York City, and later taught at the University of California, Los Angeles. He has the *Pulsations* (1971) for electric piano, jazz band, and orchestra, and a concerto.

Ramon Zupko (1932–) studied at the Juilliard School of Music with Persichetti and at the *Hochschule für Musik* in Vienna. While on the faculty at Western Michigan University, he composed the *Windsongs* (1979).

Leonardo Balada (1933–) writes music displaying his Spanish heritage and training at the Barcelona Conservatory. In the United States, he took training with Copland, Tansman, and Persichetti. The concerto (1964) is from the era he taught at the United Nations International School. He joined the faculty at Carnegie-Mellon University and, while there, he completed the concerto (1974) for piano, winds, and percussion.

Easley Blackwood (1933–) studied with Messiaen, Heiden, Hindemith, and Boulanger, and joined the faculty at the University of Chicago. As a pianist, he performs Ives, Boulez, Schoenberg, Berg, and Webern. The concerto, op. 24 (1969–1970), displays his interest in contemporary compositional techniques.

Rod McKuen (1933–) studied with Stravinsky and Mancini, and composed music for the Kingston Trio, Glenn Yarbrough, and Frank Sinatra. His serious works include the concerto, op. 20, for four harpsichords, the piano concerto *The Cathedrals of England,* op. 27 (1972), and possibly another piano concerto.

Morton Subotnick (1933–), student of Milhaud and Kirchner, has been on the faculty at the California Institute of the Arts since 1969. The *Liquid Strata* (1982) is for piano, orchestra, and electronically manipulated sounds.

Roger Dickerson (1934–) studied with Heiden at Indiana University and in Vienna, worked as a jazz pianist in the French Quarter of New Orleans, and composed concert music blending contemporary compositional devices with jazz and blues. The New Orleans Bicentennial Commission sponsored the *New Orleans Concerto* (1976).

Theodore Antoniou (1935–), Greek, studied at the Hellenic Conservatory in Greece with Papaioannou and the *Hochschule für Musik* in Munich. His compositional style uses a modified serial technique influenced by Penderecki and, after 1961, a Bartók-like use of folk music. In Munich, he composed the concertino, op. 16a (1962), for piano, string orchestra, and percussion, the concertino, op. 21 (1963), for piano, nine winds, and percussion, and the *Events* I, op. 36 (1967–1968), for violin, piano, and orchestra. In 1969, he immigrated to the United States, and taught at Stanford University and the Philadelphia Musical Academy. In Philadelphia, he composed *Fluxus II* (1975) for piano and chamber orchestra. In 1974, he became the director of contemporary music at the Berkshire (now Tanglewood) Music Center, and began teaching at Boston University in 1979.

Jack Behrens (1935–) studied with Bergsma, Persichetti, and Mennin at the Juilliard School of Music, and with Kirchner and Sessions at Harvard University. He taught at the University of Saskatchewan, California State College in Bakersfield, and the University of Western Ontario in London, Canada. The triple concerto (1971) is for clarinet, violin, piano, and orchestra.

Charles Shere (1935–) was a critic, editor and staff member with various radio stations. He composed the *Small Concerto* (1964) that is an arrangement of the *3*

Pieces (1963) for solo piano. He started the concerto (1984) while on the faculty at Mills College.

Alexandru Hrisandis (1936–) studied at the Bucharest Conservatory and with Boulanger at the American Conservatory in Fontainebleau, France. He taught at the Bucharest Academy of Music, the Bucharest Conservatory, and the University of Oregon. The *Sonnets* is a concerto for harpsichord and orchestra based on modified techniques of serialism. In 1974, he settled in the Netherlands.

Carman Moore (1936–) trained at the Oberlin College Conservatory, Ohio State University, and the Juilliard School of Music, and taught at Yale University, Queens College, and Brooklyn College. His compositions merge concert music, jazz, gospel, and rock. Critics praised the *Concerto for Blues Piano* (1982).

Elliott Schwartz (1936–) trained at Columbia University and taught at the University of Massachusetts and Bowdoin College. His compositional style depends on complete freedom and a variety of techniques. The *Magic Music* (1967) is an avant-garde work with directions for the orchestra musicians to leave their chairs and attack the piano. The orchestra performers produce many unconventional sounds, including vocalizations, and the pianist performs some passages at an organ. The *Janus* (1976) has three untitled movements and cadenzas for piano and oboe. The chamber concerto III (1977) requires all musicians to read from full score, and the piano writing is percussive, with some passages plucked and stroked on the piano strings.

Robert Suderburg (1936–) studied at the University of Minnesota, Yale University, and the University of Pennsylvania. He composed the concerto *Within the Mirror of Time* (1974) while on the faculty of the University of Washington. In 1974, he became the chancellor of the North Carolina School of the Arts, and in 1985 he joined the faculty at the Cornish Institute in Seattle.

Gregory Kosteck (1937–) has the capriccio (1958) and the concerto fantasy (1967) for violin, piano, and orchestra. He was on the faculty at a branch of Ohio State University.

William Bolcom (1938–) studied with Milhaud and Messiaen. He composed the *Fives* (1966) for violin, piano, and three string groups while on the faculty at the University of Washington, Seattle, or Queens College, New York City. He joined the faculty at the University of Michigan, and while there he worked on the concerto (1975–1976) commissioned by PONCHO, a Seattle music organization. The composition has expanded tonality, atonality, and passages reminiscent of Gershwin. The last movement has various national melodies and original melodies by Bolcom that sound like national tunes.

David Borden (1938–) studied with Rogers and Hanson at the Eastman School of Music and with Kirchner and Thompson at Harvard University. He composed the *Trudymusic* (1967) while a Ford Foundation composer-in-residence with the Ithaca public school system.

Ramiro Cortes (1938–1984) studied with Stevens and Dahl at the University of Southern California at Los Angeles, and with Giannini at the Juilliard School of Music. From 1972, he taught at the University of Utah. He left the concerto (1970–1971) for harpsichord and string orchestra and the concerto (1975) for piano and orchestra.

Ellsworth Milburn (1938–) studied at the College-Conservatory of Music in

Cincinnati, the University of California, Los Angeles, and with Milhaud at Mills College. While studying with Milhaud, he composed the concerto (1967) for piano and chamber orchestra.

Joan Tower (1938–) studied at Bennington College and Columbia University with Luening, Ussachevsky, and Chou Wen-Chung. In 1972, she joined the faculty at Bard College, and became a composer-in-residence with the St. Louis Symphony Orchestra in 1985. The year she moved to St. Louis, she finished the concerto *Homage to Beethoven* (1985), which shows an influence of Beethoven.

Charles Wuorinen (1938–) studied with Luening at Columbia University, and taught at Columbia and the Manhattan School of Music. The *Concert Piece* (1956) is for piano and string orchestra, the concerto (1966) has a row and serial elements, and the concerto (perf. 1974) is for amplified piano and orchestra.

Jon Appleton (1939–) joined the faculty at Dartmouth College in 1971. *The Bremen Town Musicians* (1971) is a concerto for toy piano and 12 toy instruments. He composes electronic music and spends time in Sweden.

Phillip Ramey (1939–) studied with A. Tcherepnin and became the program editor and annotator for the New York Philharmonic Orchestra. The concert suite (1962) is from the year he graduated from DePaul University. At the MacDowell Colony, he composed the serial concerto (1969–1971) and the tonal concerto (1976).

Tomas Svoboda (1939–), son of the famous mathematician Antonín Svoboda, studied at the Prague Conservatory, the Prague Academy of Music, and with Dahl and Stevens at the University of Southern California, Los Angeles. He joined the faculty at Portland State University and, while there, composed the concerto (1947).

Ellen Zwilich (1939–) was the first woman to win a Pulitzer Prize in music, for her symphony no. 1, and the first woman to graduate from the Juilliard School of Music with a doctor of musical arts degree in composition. A commission in 1984 resulted in a piano concerto.

Mark DeVoto (1940–) studied with Piston and R. Thompson at Harvard University and with Sessions, Babbitt, and Cone at Princeton University. He is a scholar on Berg, revised Piston's book *Harmony,* and composed music using ideas of Schoenberg, Berg, and Varése. The concertos are four in number: no. 1 (1956), no. 2 (1965–1966), no. 3 *The Distinguished Thing* (1968), and no. 4 (1983) for piano, symphony orchestra, wind ensemble, female voices, and viola obbligato. DeVoto composed the concerto nos. 2 and 3 while on the faculty at Reed College in Portland, and the concerto no. 4 while on the faculty at Tufts University in Medford, Mass.

David Cope (1941–) cellist, pianist, bassist, and percussionist, uses numerous compositional devices, including traditional techniques, avant-garde ideas, and instruments he invented. The year he graduated from the University of Southern California, he composed the *Variations* (1965). He composed the concerto (1980) while on the faculty at the University of California in Santa Cruz.

Curtis Curtis-Smith (1941–) taught at Western Michigan University. The *Bells* (*Belle du Jour,* 1974–1975) is in a chromatic style.

Ulf Grahn (1942–) trained at the Royal College of Music in Stockholm and taught at Catholic University. He probably composed the *Ancient Music* (1970) for piano and chamber orchestra in Stockholm. The concertino (1979) is for piano and string orchestra.

Joseph Schwantner (1943–) studied at the American Conservatory and Northwestern University. Since 1970, he has been teaching at the Eastman School of Music, where he composed *And the Mountains Rising Nowhere* (1977) for amplified piano, winds, brass, and percussion, and the *Distant Runes and Incantations* (1983) for piano and orchestra.

James Sellars (1943–) studied musical composition with Giannini, Flagello, and Diamond, and, since 1976, has been teaching at the University of Hartford. Among his compositions are the concerto (1980) and the *Concertorama* (1984).

William Benjamin (1944–) studied with Babbitt and Cone. While on the faculty at Wellesley College, he composed the concerto (1970–1973) in a serial style.

Bruce Saylor (1946–), school teacher, uses twelve-tone ideas in tonal compositions. The *Notturno* (1969) is a student work from the Juilliard School of Music.

Robert Xavier (1946–) studied with Johnson and Kennen at the University of Texas in Austin, with Stevens and Dahl at the University of Southern California, and with Boulanger in Paris. He may have composed the concerto (1968) in Los Angeles or Austin, Tx. The concerto II (1972) is for piano and seven instruments, the concerto III (1973) is for piano, thirteen winds, percussion, and strings, and the sinfonia *concertante* (1974) is for saxophone, harpsichord, and chamber orchestra.

John Adams (1947–), student of Kirchner at Harvard University, is on the faculty at the San Francisco Conservatory and, since 1978, with the San Francisco Symphony Orchestra as the new-music adviser. The *Grand Pianola Music* (1981–1982) for two sopranos, two pianos, and small orchestra is in a minimalist style.

Ran Shulamit (1949–) may have composed the capriccio (1963) while studying with Ben-Haim in Israel or with Dello Joio at the Mannes College of Music in New York City. Her location could not be determined for the composition of the *Symphonic Poem* (1967) and the *Concert Piece* (1970, rev. 1973). She joined the faculty at the University of Chicago and, while there, she composed the concerto (1977).

Tobias Picker (1954–) studied at the Manhattan School of Music and the Juilliard School of Music and became a composer-in-residence with the Houston Symphony Orchestra. Among his compositions based on serial and tonal ideas are the concerto no. 1 (1980), the *Nova* (perf. 1981), and the concerto no. 2 *Keys to the City* (1983).

Paul Romero (1966–) has a concerto with elements of jazz similar to Gershwin.

Rafael Aponte-Ledée (?–) studied at the Madrid Conservatory and in Buenos Aires with Ginastera at the Latin American Center of Advanced Musical Studies at the Di Tella Institute. With Francis Schwartz, he established in San Juan the *Fluxus* music group for the performance of contemporary music. He joined the faculty at the University of Puerto Rico in Río Piedras and, while there, he composed the *Elvira en Sombras* (1973).

Gladys Nordenstrom (?–), married to Ernst Krenek, composed at least the concerto (1947).

Table 37 Additional Composers in the United States

Names	Dates	Compositions
Abramson, Robert	1928–	*Dance Variations* (1965)
Adams, Ernest	1886–1959	*Concerto Impromptu*
		Concertino
Adams, Leslie	1932–	Concerto
Adler, James	1950–	Concerto
Adler, Sam	1928–	Concerto (1983)
Alden, John	1852–1935	Concerto
Alfidi, Joseph	1949–	Concerto II
Allen, Creighton	1900–1969	Concerto
Ames, William	1901–	Concerto
		Nocturne and Scherzo (1942)
Anderson, Gerland	1933–	Concertino (pub. 1969)
Anderson, John	1948–	Concerto no 3
Anson, George	1904–	Concertino (1936)
Applebaum, Edward	1937–	*When Dreams Do Show Thee Me* (1972)
Babin, Stanley	1932–	Concerto (1967)
Babits, Linda	1940–	Concerto *Western Star*
Balsam, Arthur	1906–	Cadenzas, Beethoven & Mozart concs
Barlow, Samuel	1892–1982	Concerto (1930)
Barr, Raphael (Ray)	1912–	Variations
Barthelson, Holloway	1908–	Concerto, 2 pnos
Bazelon, Irwin	1922–	Concerto (1983–84)
Beach, Perry	1917–	Concerto (1952)
Beall, John	1942–	Concerto
Beckon, Lettie	1953–	Intregrated Concerto (1978)
		Fantasy
Belaka, O'sai	1933–	Concerto
Bellamann, Henry	1882–1945	Concerto
Benejam, Luis	? –	*Iberian Preludes* (1965)
Benjamin, Thomas	1940–	*Concert Music* (1968)
Bergen, Hans	1920–	*Three Sketches*
Berkowitz, Leonard	1919–	Concerto (1967)
Berlin, David	1943–	Concerto
Berlinsky, Herman	1910–	For the Peace of Mind (1952)
Bernstein, Seymour	1927–	Concerto *For Our Time* (1972)
Best, Harold	1931–	Concerto
Bilotti, Anton	1906–1963	2 Concertos
Binder, Abraham	1895–1966	*King David*
Biscardi, Chester	1948–	Concerto (1983)
Bley, Carla	? –	3/4 (perf 1974)
Boehle, William	1919–	Concertino
Bonde, Allen	1936–	Fantasia
Bonner, Eugene	1889–	Concertino (1945)
Bowles, Paul	1910–	Concerto (1946)
Boykin, Helen	1904–	2 Concertos
Bracali, Giampaolo	1914–	Concerto
Bradshaw, Merrill	1929–	Concerto (1955)
Braggiotti, Mario	1909–	*Pianorama*
Brandt, William	1920–	Concerto (1972)

Table 37 Additional Composers in the United States—Continued

Names	Dates	Compositions
Brehm, Alvin	1925–	Concerto (1977)
Brenner, Walter	1906–1969	Concerto
Brickman, Joel	1946–	*Thousands of Days*
Briggs, George	1910–	*20th Century Gavotte*
Brings, Allen	1934–	*Concerto da Camera*
Brisman, Heskel	1923–	Concerto
Britain, Radie	1899–1994	Rhapsody (1933)
Brockway, Howard	1870–1951	Concerto, lost
Brody, Wee Kee	? –	Concerto (1983)
Brogue, Roslyn	1919–1981	*Andante and Variations* (1954–56)
Brook, Gwendolyn	1930–	*Précis: Concerto* (1952)
Burge, David	1930–	Concerto (1956)
Burgstahler, Elton	1924–	Concerto
Burton, Eldin	1913–	Concerto
Callender, Charles	1911–	Concerto
Campbell, Henry	1926–	*Folk Song*
Cantrell, Byron	1919–	Concerto
Carlos, Wendy	1939–	*Sphere* (1962)
Carranza, Gustavo	1897–1975	Concerto *Medieval* Concerto *American*
Carroll, Frank	1928–	Concerto
Cassels-Brown, Alastair	1927–	Little Concerto (1961)
Casvant, Charles	1945–	Concerto (1975)
Cazden, Norman	1914–1980	Conc for Ten Instruments, op 10 (1937)
Cervone, Donald	1932–	Sinfonia tutti clavier (1973)
Chance, John	1932–1972	Introduction and Capriccio (1966)
Chanler, Theodore	1902–1961	*Pas de Tois* (1942)
Charkovsky, Willis	1918–	Concerto
Chasins, Abram	1903–	2 Concertos (1928/31)
Chenowet, Wilbur	1899–	*Fiesta*
Chobanian, Loris	1933–	Capriccio (perf 1974)
Clafin, Avery	1898–1979	Pop Concerto (1958)
Clarke, Rosemary	1921–	2 Concertos Fantasy
Clayton, Laura	? –	Sagarama (1968)
Cohen, Joseph	1917–	Concerto
Cohn, James	1928–	Concertino, op 8 (1946)
Coller, Jerome	1929–	Concerto (1971)
Collins, Edward	1889–	Concerto Piece
Cook, Peter	1923–	*River Boat Fancy*
Corbett, Richard	1942–	*Music for Pno and Orch*
Corigliano, John	1938–	Concerto (1968)
Cory, Eleanor	1943–	Concertino
Cotel, Morris	1943–	Concerto (perf 1968)
Cowles, Walter	1881–1959	Concerto
Cox, Michael	? –	Concerto (1984), 2 pnos
Coyner, Lou	1931–	Concerto
Cunningham, Michael	1937–	Concerto (1968)
Cuppett, Charles	1894–1967	*Lament for the Living*
Demarest, Clifford	1874–1946	Rhapsody

Table 37 Additional Composers in the United States—Continued

Names	Dates	Compositions
Diebel, Wendel	1914–	Concerto Piece (1938)
		Concerto (1940)
Dudley, Majorie	? –	Concerto
Dupage, Florence	1910–	Concerto
Dushkin, Dorothy	1903–	Concerto (1960)
Dydo, Stephen	1949–	Capriccio
Eckstein, Maxwell	1905–1974	*Conc for Young Americans*
Elie, Justin	1883–1931	Concerto
Ellstein, Abraham	1907–1963	*Negev Concerto*
Epstein, Alvin	1926–	Concerto
Evans, Billy	1938–	Concerto
Evensen, Bengt	1944–	Divertimento *Concertante* (1967)
Faith, Richard	1926–	2 Concertos (1964–69/75)
		Concerto (1974), 2 pnos
Farberman, Harold	1929–	*Paramount Concerto*
		Variations
Fennimore, Joseph	1940–	Concerto Piccolo
Fenstock, Belle	1939–	American Rhapsody
Fink, Myron	1932–	Concerto
Fitch, Theodore	1900–	Concerto
Flanagan, William	1923–1969	*Another August* (1967)
Flores, Bernal	1937–	*William* (1963)
Floyd, Monte	1941–	Concerto (1970), 2 pnos
Fornuto, Donato	1931–	Concerto
Fortner, Clarke	1904–	*Blue Waters*
Franco, Johan	1908–	*Serenade Concertante* (1938)
		Symphonic *Concertante* (1940)
		Concerto Lirico III (1967)
Frank, Marcel	1909–	*Golden Gate Concerto*
Frank, Marco	1881–	2 Concertos (1930/38)
		Youth Concerto
Freed, Walter	1903–	Concerto in Miniature
Fremder, Donald	1920–	Concerto (1970)
Freud, Donald	1947–	Concerto (1970)
Froom, David	? –	Concerto (1984)
Gaber, Harley	1943–	*Three Ideas for a Film* (1970)
Gabriel, Charles	1892–1934	Concerto
Gaburo, Kenneth	1926–	Sinfonia *Concertante* (1949)
Gangware, Edgar	1921–	Concerto
Gates, Crawford	1921–	Concerto
Gehlhaar, Rolf	1943–	*Tokamok* (1982)
Geissler, Fredrich	1946–	Concertino
George, Earl	1924–	Concerto (1958)
George, Thom	1942–	2 Concertos
Ginn, Jim	1935–	Concerto
Gioe, Joseph	1890–1957	Concerto
Giuffré, Gaetano	? –	*New York Concerto* (1978)
Godowsky, Leopold	1870–1938	Cadenzas, Beethoven's Conc no 4
Gold, Ernest	1921–	Concerto (1943)

Table 37 Additional Composers in the United States—Continued

Names	Dates	Compositions
Gold, Morton	1933–	Concerto (1960)
Gould, Edward	1911–	Concerto
Gould, Elizabeth	1904–	Concerto (1953) *Games* (1962)
Graham, Robert	1912–	Suite, hpd Concerto
Grant, Allan	1892–	Concerto
Grantham, Donald	1947–	Chamber Concerto (1973–74), hpd
Griebling, Margaret	1961–	*Atlanta* (ca. 1978)
Griffis, Elliot	1893–1967	*Montevallo* (1945)
Gruen, Rudolph	1900–1966	*Alpine Concerto* (1962)
Guarnieri, John	1917–	Concerto
Hagan, Helen	1893?–	Concerto
Haieff, Alexei	1914–	2 Concertos (1950/76)
Haimsohn, Naomi	1894–	Concerto no 2 (1966)
Harnell, Joseph	1924–	Concerto
Harris, Larry	? –	Concerto
Harris, Margaret	1943–	Concerto (perf 1972)
Harris, Theodore	1912–	Concerto
Harrison, Lou	1917–	Suite (1951)
Hartley, Gerald	1921–	*Sonatine*
Hartway, James	1944–	Dialogue
Haufrecht, Herbert	1909–	Suite (1934)
Haussermann, John	1909–	Rhapsodic Overture (1939)
Hendriks, Francis	1881/3–1969	Concerto
Hively, Wells	1902–1969	*Priscilla Variations* (1939) Concerto (1958)
Hodkinson, Sydney	1934–	Dialogue (1963)
Hoiby, Lee	1926–	2 Concertos (1957/80)
Holden, David	1911–	*Music for Piano and Strings* (1936–37)
Homes, Markwood	1899–	Symphonic episode
Hovey, Serge	1920–	Intermezzo
Hruby, Frank	1918–	Concertino (1941)
Huffman, Spencer	? –	Concerto (perf 1946) Concerto (1959), hpd
Hugo, John	1873–1945	2 Concertos
Hutchins, Farley	1921–	Concerto, hpd
Hyman, Richard	1927–	*Concerto Electro* *Ragtime Fantasy*
Jackson, Duke	1946–	Concerto, 2 pnos, hpd
Jackson, John	1919–	*Themes and Explorations* *The Capacabana Cakewalk*
Jameson, Robert	1947–	3 Concertos (1965/67/69) Symphonic Cadenza
Jenni, Donald	1937–	Concertino (1955)
Johnson, Hunter	1906–	Concerto (1935–36)
Johnson, Roy	1933–	Concerto (1960)
Johnston, Albert	1925–	Rhapsody
Kahmann, Chesley	1930–	Concerto (1955–66)

Table 37 Additional Composers in the United States—Continued

Names	Dates	Compositions
Kalmanoff, Martin	1920–	Concerto III *Climax*
Kasschau, Howard	? –	Concerto (1940)
		Concerto Americana (1950)
		Candlelight Concerto (1957)
		The Legend of Sleepy Hollow (1964)
		Country Concerto
Katz, Erich	1900–1973	Toy Concerto (1950)
Kempinski, Leo	1891–1958	Victory Concerto
Kessler, Minuetta	1940–	*New York Concerto* (1942)
		Alberta Concerto (1947)
Kinney, Gordon	1905–	Piece (1935)
Kirk, Theron	1919–	Concerto *Grosso*
Kiss, Janos	1920/21–	Concerto
Klein, Leonard	1929–	Concerto
Kohs, Ellis	1916–	Concerto (1945)
Korn, Clara	1866–1940	Concerto
Korte, Karl	1928–	Concerto (1976)
Kraehenbuehl, David	1932–	*Rhapsody in Rock* (1974)
		A Short Piano Concerto for Young People
Kupferman, Meyer	1926–	2 Concertos (1948, 1977)
Kurka, Robert	1921–1957	Concertino, op 31
Kurtz, Arthur	1929–	Concerto (1972)
Labounty, Edwin	1927–	*Excursus* (1962)
Laderman, Ezra	1924–	3 Concertos (1936/57/78)
Lamb, Hubert	1900–	*Concerto da Camera* (1943)
Lapham, Claude	1890–1957	*Concerto Japonesa* (1935)
Lee, Noel	1924–	*Capricies sur le nom de Schoenberg* (1975)
Leichtentritt, Hugo	1874–1951	Concerto
León, Tania	1944–	*Concerto Criollo* (1977)
Leonard, Clair	1901–	Concerto (1933)
Leonardi, Leonid	1901–	*Blue Ridge Rhapsody*
Levey, Harold	1898–1967	Concerto
Levine, Jeffrey	1942–	Concerto (1971)
Lévy, Heniot	1879–1946	Concerto
Lewis, Alfred	1925–	Classical Concerto (1939)
Lewis, Leon	1890–1961	*Jessica—A Portrait*
Lewis, Peter	1932–	Capriccio *concertato*, 2 pnos (1960, rev 1962)
Lieberson, Goddard	1911–1977	Tango (1936)
Liebling, Georg	1865–1946	*Concerto Eroico* (1925)
Lieurance, Thurlow	1878–1963	Titles unknown
Lindenfeld, Harris	1945–	Concerto (1972)
Lipsky, Alexander	1901–	Concertino
Liter, Monia	? –	*Prelude Espagnole*
Lloyd, Gerald	1938–	Concertino (1965)
Lomardo, Mario	1931–	*Blue Interlude*
Loth, Louise	1888–	2 Concertos

Table 37 Additional Composers in the United States—Continued

Names	Dates	Compositions
Lundborg, Charles	1948–	Concerto
Lynn, George	1915–	Concerto
Mamorsky, Morris	1910–	Concerto (1943)
Maneri, Joseph	1927–	Concerto *Metanoia*
Manning, Kathleen	1890–1951	Concerto
Manton, Robert	1894–1969	Concerto
Marcus, Ada Belle	1929–	Concertino (1963)
Markaitis, Bruno	1922–	Concerto (1968)
		2 Concertinos (1968/69)
Maslanka, David	1943–	Concerto (1974–76)
Masters, Juan	? –	Concerto
Mayer, William	1925–	*Octagon* (1967)
McBride, Robert	1911–	*Ill Tempered "Apologies of J.S.B."*
McCollin, Frances	1892–1960	*Variations on an Original Theme* (1942)
McKay, Ivan		See Mikhashoff
Meister, Christopher	? –	Concerto
Meneely-Kyder, Sara	1945–	Concerto (1966–67)
		Time (1969–71), 2 pnos
Meyers, Emerson	1910–	Concertino
Meysenberg, Agnes	1922–	Suite
Middleton, Robert	1920–	Variations (1965)
Mikhashoff, Ivan	1941–	Concerto (1965)
Milano, Robert	1936–	*Concierto Pegueño* (1973)
Miles, Harold	1908–	Concerto (1946)
Miller, Harvey	1934–	Concertino, hpd
Mineo, Antoinette	1926–	Concerto
Mineo, Samuel	1909–	*California Rhapsody*
Mollicone, Henry	? –	Fantasy (1967)
Monello, Spartaco	1909–	Concerto
Montani, Nicola	1880–	Fantasia
Moody, Philip	? –	*The Luna Concerto*
Moore, George	1918–	Concerto
Moore, Thomas	1933–	*A Quality of Spring*
Mopper, Irving	1914–	*Patterns*
Moritz, Edvard	1891–1974	2 Concertos
Mossman, Ted	1914–	2 Concertos
		Central Park New York
Mulfinger, George	1900–	Symphonic variations
Munger, Shirley	? –	Concerto
Myover, Max	1924–	Concerto
Neiburg, Al	1922–1978	*Scenario Music to a Matinee Idol*
Nelhybel, Vaclav	1919–	Concertino (1949)
		Passacaglia (1965)
		Concertino da Camera (1972)
		Toccata (1972)
		Cantus and Ludus (1973)
		Dialogues (1976)
		Two Movements

Table 37 Additional Composers in the United States—Continued

Names	Dates	Compositions
Nero, Peter	1934–	Fantasy and Improvisation
Nevin, Arthur	1871–1943	Concerto
Newell, Dika	? –	Chamber Concerto
		Concerto
Niemack, Ilza	1936–	2 Concertos
North, Alex	1910–	Rhapsody (1939–40)
Norton, Spencer	1909–	Partita for Two Solo Pianos and Orch (1950)
O'Meagher, Hugh	? –	Concerto (1956), hpd
		Concerto grosso (1967)
O'Sullivan, Patrick	1871–	Fantaisie Irlandaise
Ohlson, Marion	? –	Little Concerto
Olds, Gerry	1933–	Concerto (1960)
Olsen, Loran	1898–	Concertino
Ostroff, Ester	1909–	Cadenzas (1932), Mozart K.466 & Beethoven Conc 4
Owen, Blythe	1898–	Concerto, op 24 (1953)
Pace, Pat	1930–	Concertino
Panetti, Joan	1941–	Concerto
Parchman, Gen	1929–	12 Variations on an Original Theme (1960)
		Concerto (1963), 4 hds
		Concerto (1963), 2 pnos
Parks, Gordon	1930–	Concerto
Partch, Harry	1901–1947	Concerto (destroyed)
Pasquet, Jean	1896–1977	Concertino
Pearl-Mann, Dora	1905–	Symphony Concerto
		Concerto
Penman, Lovington	1895–	Prelude
Pennario, Leonard	1924–	Concerto
Perkinson, Coleridge–Taylor	1932–	*Grass* (1956)
Perry, Julia	1924–	2 Concertos (pub 1964?/65?)
Phillips, Robert	? –	*Three Pieces* (pub 1978)
Pickhardt, Ione	1900–	2 Concertos
Polifrone, Jon	1937–	Concerto
Ponce, Ethel	? –	Three Dialogues
Powell, John	1882–1963	2 Concertos
		Rhapsodie Negre, op 27
Powers, Maxwell	1911–	2 Concertos
Prendergast, Roy	1943–	Concerto (1971)
Press, Jacques	1903–	*Disconcerto*
Preyer, Carl	1863–1947	*Concertstück* (1908)
Price, Florence	1888–1953	3 Concertos (1934?/53/ca. 40)
		Rhapsody
Price, John	1935–	*The Jeweled Sword* (1947)
		Atoms (1947)
		The Wheel (1948)
		Rhapsody Symphonique (1950)
		Serenade for Tulsa (1950)

Table 37 Additional Composers in the United States—Continued

Names	Dates	Compositions
Price, John (cont.)		*For L'Overture* (1951)
		March (1951)
		Second March (1953)
		Episode (1956–57)
		Concerto (1969)
Prigmore, James	1943–	Concerto
Quilling, Howard	1935–	Concerto (1969)
Ralston, Fanny	1875–1952	*Rhapsodie*
Raphling, Sam	1910–	5 Concertos
		Minstrel Rhapsody
		Israel Rhapsody
Rapopart, Eda	1886–1968	Concerto (1938)
Redewill, Gene	1881–	Concerto
Reich, Bruce	1948–	Concerto
Reilly, Jack	1932–	Concerto
		Rhapsody
Réti, Rudolph	1885–1957	2 Concertos (1944/54)
Reynolds, Charles	1931–	Concerto
Riley, Ann	1928–	Concerto
Rodgers, Richard	1902–1979	*Nursery Ballet* (1938)
Roger, Kurt	1895–1966	Sinfonia *Concertante,* op 66 (1951)
Rollins, Robert	1947–	*By a Child Seven Sound-Images on Seven Stanzas*
Rosco, Jeannie	1932–	Concerto
Rose, Griffith	1936–	Concerto
Rosenthal, Manuel	1904–	*Aesopi Convivium* (1948)
Rosette, Marion	? –	*Busy Bar Rag*
Rovics, Howard	1936–	Concerto (1960)
Rozin, Albert	1906–	Little Concerto
Russell, Craig	1951–	Concerto (perf 1973)
Sandoval, Miguel	1903–1953	*Spanish Dance*
Sanjuan, Pedro	1886–1976	Concerto (1942)
Santos-Ocampo de Francesco, Amanda	1927–	Concerto (1957)
Sapieyevski, Jerzy	1945–	Concerto (1977)
Savino, Domenico	1882–	Concerto
		Cuban Concerto
Saxton, Stanley	1904–	Concerto
Schaum, John	1905–	*Mountain Concerto*
Schickele, Peter	1935–	Conc for Pno vs Orch
		Three Girls, Three Women
		Simple-Minded Theme
		Fantasieshtick
Schlein, Irving	1905–	Concertino (1942)
Schmidt, William	1926–	Concerto
		Concertino
Schoenfeld, Henry	1857–1936	Concerto
Schroeder, William	1888–1936	Concertino
Schubel, Max	1932–	Divertimento (1982)

Table 37 Additional Composers in the United States—Continued

Names	Dates	Compositions
Schuyten, Ernest	1881–	Concerto
Schwartz, Paul	1907–	Chamber Concerto (1944)
Seuel-Holst, Marie	1877–	*In Elfland,* op 26
Seymour, John	1893–	Concerto
Shackford, Charles	1918–	Serenade (1942)
		Fantasy on Vysehard (1969)
Shaffer, Lloyd	1901–	*Three Etchings*
Shakarian, Roupen	1950–	Concerto (1977), hpd
Sheinfeld, David	1906–	Fantasia (1951)
Sheinkman, Mardechai	1926–	Konzert, op 3 (1955)
Shelley, Harry	1858–1947	Fantasia
Shreve, Susan	1952–	Concerto (1972)
Sinatra, Ray	1904–	Concerto
Slyck, Nicholas Van	1922–1983	3 Concertos (no 2, 1957)
		Variations (1947)
		Concert Music (1954)
Smith, Clifford	1945–	Toccata *Perpetua*
Smith, Ladonna	1951–	*Orchestrophes* (pub 1975)
Smith, Russe	1927–	2 Concertos (1952/56)
Smolanoff, Michael	1942–	Concerto, op 29
Snyder, Randall	1944–	*Hegemony* (1973)
Songer, Lewis	1935–	Concerto
Sprecher, William	1924–	*Jerusalem Concerto* (1967)
St. Clair, Richard	1946–	*Amen Concerto* (1972)
St. John, Kathleen	1942–	*Fragrances*
Stabile, James	1937–	Concerto
Starer, Robert	1924–	3 Concertos (1947/53/72)
Stearns, Peter	1931–	Concerto (1952)
		Reminiscence
Steiner, Gitta	1932–	Concerto (1967)
Stepper, Martin	1948–	Concerto (1973)
Stokowski, Leopold	1882–	3 Concertos
Straight, Willard	1930–	Concerto
Stuessy, Joseph	1943–	Concerto
Suchy, Gregoria	? –	*Symphonic Piece* (1972)
		Three Lovers, 2 pnos
Suesse, Dana	1911–	Concertino in Three Rhythms (pub 1932)
		Eight Waltzes (1937)
		Concerto (1934–41), 2 pnos
		Concertino (pub 1946)
		Concerto *Romantico* (1946)
		Jazz Concerto (pub 1955)
		Concerto
Suszczynska, Anna	1931–	*Piesn o Pokoj*
Swisher, Gloria	1935–	3 Pieces (1954)
		Suite
Tanner, Peter	1936–	Introduction and Allegro
Taubman, Paul	1911–	Concerto for Toy Piano
Tautenhahn, Gunther	1938–	*Numeric Serenade* (1978)

Table 37 Additional Composers in the United States—Continued

Names	Dates	Compositions
Taxin, Ira	1950–	Concerto (1972)
Taylor, William	1921–	Suite
Templeton, Alec	1909–1963	Concertino lirico (1942) Gothic Concerto (perf 1954) *Rhapsodie Harmonique* (1954)
Tessier, Albert	1900–	*Symphonic Concerto*
Thome, Diane	1942–	*Three Movements* (1962)
Thompson, John	1889–1963	Concerto
Tonsing, Evan	? –	*Conc for a Young Pianist*
Townsend, Douglas	1921–	Chamber Concerto (1971)
Truesdell, Donald	1920–	Concerto (1951)
Tucker, Gregory	1908–1971	2 Concertinos (both 1958)
Turner, Godfrey	1913–1948	Sonata *Concertante*
Turok, Paul	1929–	*Ragtime Caprice* (1976)
Twombly, Mary	1935–	*Symphonic Statments* (1971)
Twombly, Preston	1945–	Chamber Concerto (1975)
Vamos, Grace	?–	Fantasy Concerto (1951)
Vars, Henry	1902–1977	Concerto
Vauclain, Constant	1908–	Symphony (1948) Suite (1956)
Vyner, Mary	1936–	21? Concertos
Wagner, Thomas	1931–	Concerto Concerto, 2 pnos
Ward, Edward	1896–	Concerto
Ward, Louise	? –	Concerto
Ware, Harriet	1877–1962	Concerto
Warkentin, Larry	1940–	Concertino (1964)
Waxman, Ernest	1918–	Concerto
Wegner, August	1941–	*Ice-Nine* (1975)
Weinberger, Jaromir	1896–1967	*Under the Spreading Chestnut Tree* (pub 1931)
Weingarden, Louis	1943–	Concerto (1974)
Wendelburg, Norma	1918–	Suite *To Nature* (1964–72)
Wessel, Mark	1894–1973	*Scherzo Burlesque* (1926) 2 Concertos (1933–42/42)
Wheeler, Gayneyl	? –	Concerto
Whitcomb, Robert	? –	Variations
White, Louis	1921–	Concerto, hpd
Whittaker, Howard	1922–	Concerto
Wigham, Margaret	? –	Concerto, 2 pnos
Wild, Earl	1915–	Concerto
Wilding-White, Raymond	1922–	Concerto (1949)
Williams, David	1932–	Concerto, op 39 (1963–64)
Williams, Jean	? –	5 Concertos (ca. 1942–1955)
Willis, Richard	1929–	Concertino (1969)
Wilni, Monica	? –	Concerto (1949)
Wilson, Olly	1937–	*Akwan* (1972)
Wirtel, Thomas	1937–	Music for Winds, Perc and Prepared Piano
Wirth, Carl	1912–	Rhapsody

Table 37 Additional Composers in the United States—Continued

Names	Dates	Compositions
Wolf, Kenneth	1931–	2 Concertos
Wolfsohn, Juliusz	1880–	Suite
Woltmann, Frederick	1908–	Concerto (1937)
		Variations on an Old English Folk Song (1938)
Worth, Frank	1903–	Concerto
Wright, Nannie	1879–	Concerto, op 42
Wykes, Robert	1926–	Concertino
Yaysnoff, June	1918–	*Islam: Symphonic Suite,* op 61 (1939)
Zaimont, Judith	1945–	Concerto (1972)
Zeckwer, Camille	1875–1924	Concerto, op 8 (1897)
Ziskin, Victor	1937–	*San Francisco Rhapsody*

Chapter 17

Canada

Louis Waizman (1863–1951), born in Salzburg, Austria, attended the *Mozarteum,* settled in Canada in 1893, and joined the Toronto Symphony Orchestra as a performer and later as the librarian. The *Concert Caprice* (perf. 1906) is for piano and orchestra. The *Song Without Words* (1948) and the *Impromptu* (1950) are for piano and strings.

Emiliano Renaud (1875–1932), called the Canadian Paderewski, may be the first person in Canada to compose a work for piano and orchestra—the *concertstück* (perf. 1900). After training in Montreal, Vienna, and Berlin, he returned to Montreal in 1899 to pursue a career as a pianist, composer, organist, and teacher. The date he returned to Canada suggests that he may have composed the *concertstück* in Europe. He joined the faculty of the McGill Conservatory in 1914, and toured North America with the singer Emma Clavé.

Healey Willan (1880–1968), English-born, was the most influential composer in English-speaking Canada during the first half of the century. He studied at St. Saviour's Choir School in Eastbourne, and played organ in London churches until immigrating to Canada in 1913. He directed the theory departments at the Royal Conservatory in Toronto and the University of Toronto. In 1967, he was the first musician to be awarded the Companion of the Order of Canada. The concerto (1944, rev. 1949) is on some lists as B76, meaning work number 76 in Giles Bryant's *Healey Willan Catalogue* (Ottowa: National Library of Canada, 1972). The third movement is on an unfinished finale to the piano concerto (ca. 1910) and interludes connect the three movements. Willan's conservative style comes from Brahms, Franck, Holst, R. Strauss, Tchaikovsky, Elgar, Stanford, and Parry. He used Liszt's practice of modulating to lower mediant keys.

Federic Lord (1886–1945), organist at the First Baptist Church, left two concertos (before 1936) for piano and orchestra based on nineteenth-century virtuosity.

Rodolphe Mathieu (1890–1962), father of composer André Mathieu, studied in Montreal and Paris, where he knew d'Indy, Durey, Roussel, and Aubert. The incomplete concerto (1955) lacks an orchestra score and contains elements of French music.

Claude Champagne (1891–1965) was among the best-known Canadian composers during the first half of this century. Among his many composition students were Duchow, Archer, Dela, Matton, Pepin, and Morel. Champagne studied in Montreal, Brussels, and, with Gedalge and Koechlin at the Paris *Conservatoire*. His style has harmonies of Franck, Fauré, and Debussy and Canadian folk melodies. One of his important contributions was a Canadian compositional style based on French influences. The concerto (1948) is conservative, with neo-baroque contrapuntal features. He taught at McGill University and the Conservatory of Quebec.

Alfred Mignault (1895–1961) was an organist in churches around Montreal, a pianist for a radio station, and a teacher at the Quebec Provincial Conservatory. The *Divertissement sur Deux Thèmes* (perf. 1938) is for piano and orchestra.

Quintin Maclean (1896–1962), English-born, trained in Leipzig with Straube and Reger, worked as a theater organist in London until moving to Toronto, and taught at the University of Toronto and the Toronto Conservatory of Music. His traditional musical style has modal influences. The *Concerto Romantico* (1953) is for piano and orchestra, and the *Theme and Variations* (1954) is for harpsichord and orchestra.

Paul de Marky (1897–) studied in Budapest, Hungary, and immigrated to Canada in 1924. He taught at McGill University and performed as the soloist in Franck's symphonic variations in the inaugural concert (1930) of the Montreal Orchestra. His own compositions include the ballad (perf. 1944) and the concerto *Trans Atlantic* (1948).

Sophie-Carmen Eckhardt-Gramatté (1899/02–1974), born in Russia, made a Berlin debut at age 11 as a violinist and pianist performing Beethoven's *Kreutzer* and *Appassionata* sonatas in one recital. She lived in Paris, Barcelona, and Vienna, and immigrated to Canada in 1953. Gramatté is the name of her first husband and Eckhardt is the name of her second husband. Among her many friends were Busoni, D'Albert, Schnabel, and Casals. Generally, her style shows evidence of nineteenth-century romantic ideas, including motives, tonality, and virtuoso piano writing. In Barcelona, she composed the concerto no. 1 (1925) using the virtuoso style from the days she concertized as a pianist. In Germany, she composed the concerto no. 2 (1946) and probably the *Markantes Stück* (1950) for two pianos and orchestra. In Canada, she composed the concerto no. 3 (1966–1967) which appears in some sources as the symphonic concerto.

Arnold Walter (1902–1973), born in Hannsdorf, Germany (now Moravia, Czechoslovakia), graduated in law from Prague University and studied musicology, piano, and harpsichord at the University of Berlin. After finding too many pianist-composers working in Berlin, he chose to write about music. He emigrated to Canada in 1937, and directed the music faculty at the University of Toronto. While his reputation rests on teaching and administration, he composed the one-movement *Music* (1941) for harpsichord and orchestra based on nineteenth-century romanticism.

Gordon Fleming (1903–1959), organist, pianist, and arranger, studied composition with Paul de Marky in London, Ontario. He worked at radio station CKLW in Windsor. The concerto (1948) is for piano and orchestra.

Horace Lapp (1904–), organist, conductor, and writer, worked as a pianist in theater orchestras and as an accompanist during a revival of silent films in the 1960s. His compositions include the *Poem* (1951) for piano and orchestra and the concerto (1958) for piano and voices.

Murray Adaskin (1906–) studied violin in Toronto and Paris, viola with Primrose, and composition with Weinzweig and Milhaud. In 1952, he became the head of the music department at the University of Saskatchewan. The capriccio (1961) shows neo-classic and contrapuntal techniques.

Walter Kaufmann (1907–1984) was born in Germany. He studied composition with Schrenker in Berlin and musicology in Prague. He conducted in Europe, India, England, and Canada with the Winnipeg Symphony Orchestra. He taught at the Halifax Conservatory and at Indiana University in Bloomington. He composed the concerto (1934) with orchestra or strings in England, the *Andhera* (1942–1949) in India, England, and Winnipeg, and the suite *Navartnam* (1945) for piano and orchestra in Bombay, India. In Halifax, he composed the concertino (1947) with strings, the fantasy (1949), the concerto no. 2 (1949), and the *Arabesques* (1952) for two pianos and orchestra.

Jean Coulthard (1908/09–) studied with Vaughan Williams at the Royal College of Music in London, England, and with Benjamin, Milhaud, Bartók, Wagenaar, Boulanger, and Jacob. In 1947, she took a teaching position at the University of British Columbia. She is the first composer in western Canada to develop an international reputation. She composed the *fantasie* (1960–1961) for piano, violin, and chamber orchestra, the concerto (1961–1963, rev. 1967), and the *Burlesque* (1977) for piano and strings. The concerto has unprepared and unresolved secondary dominants and modal writing in a post-romantic style.

Keith Bissell (1912–), educator and conductor, studied with Orff, and introduced Orff's ideas to the Scarborough School System, in a suburb of Toronto, while the chief coordinator of music. He believes musical compositions should be provided for semiprofessional and amateur musicians, and many of his compositions draw upon Canadian folk music. The concertino (1962) for piano and strings contains mediant key relationships of the romantic era, and unresolved seventh, ninth, eleventh, and thirteenth chords and added tones.

Fraser MacDonald (1912–) studied composition with Weinzweig at the Toronto Conservatory of Music and worked for the CBC. His compositions for piano and orchestra are the *Concerto on French Canadian Themes* (1933–1937), the capriccio (1935–1936), and the fairy tale *Adventures of a Piano* (1941–1948).

Barbara Pentland (1912–) studied with Jacobi and Wagenaar at the Juilliard School of Music and with Copland at the Berkshire (now Tanglewood) Center. While on the faculty at the Royal Conservatory of Music in Toronto, she composed the *Colony Music* (1947) for piano and strings during a stay at the MacDowell Colony in New Hampshire. The work has three movements of "Overture," "Chorale," and "Burlesque." The *Colony Music* is from a period when Pentland rejected the harmonic system in favor of serial ideas, but serialism is not in the composition. While on the faculty at the University of British Columbia, Vancouver, she composed the concerto (1955–1956) in the serial style of Webern. The pointillistic composition has mirror techniques in the treatment of the row, and a portion of the row is in the right-hand part and the rest is in the left-hand accompaniment. The fantasy (1940) for piano and orchestra remains unfinished.

Lucio Agostini (1913–), born in Italy, emigrated to Canada with his parents in 1916. He wrote film scores for Associated Screen News, radio, and television. The concerto (1948) is for piano, voices, and orchestra.

John Weinzweig (1913–) is one of Canada's most successful composers. He studied at the University of Toronto and with B. Rogers at the Eastman School of Music. He joined the faculty at the Toronto Conservatory in 1939 and the University of Toronto in 1952. In 1951, he organized the Canadian League of Composers and served as the first president. Much of his style follows Stravinsky's *Rite of Spring* and Berg's *Lyric Suite*. The twelve-tone concerto (1965–1966) has a five-part arch form. Jazz influences include blues rhythms, melodic phrases, and elements of bebop and swing rhythms.

Marvin Duchow (1914–1979) studied at McGill University, the Curtis Institute of Music, the Eastman School of Music, and the Chicago Conservatory. While on the faculty at McGill University, he composed the *Bandinerie* (1947). He was one of Canada's leading musicologists; as a composer he felt an attraction to Hindemith's style and serialism.

Morris Surdin (1914–1979) studied in Toronto, Philadelphia, and New York City. He worked as an arranger with the CBC in Toronto and CBS in New York City. After returning to Canada, he continued working in film and television. The *Short!* no.1 (1969) is for piano and strings and the *Short!* no. 2 (1969) is for piano, wind quartet, and strings. Surdin's style is traditional, with elements of folk music.

Alexander Brott (1915–) trained at the McGill Conservatory and the Juilliard School of Music and taught at McGill University. *The Vision of Dry Bones* (1958) for baritone voice, piano, and string orchestra is on *Ezekiel* 37:1–14.

Jean Papineau-Couture((1916–) studied at the New England Conservatory of Music in Boston and with Boulanger at the Longy School in Cambridge, Mass. He was the first president of the *Société de Musique Contemporaies de Quebec* and the dean of the music faculty at the University of Montreal. His musical compositions through the 1940s exhibit romantic and impressionistic features, works of the 1950s show expressionism and serialism, and during the 1960s he leaned toward the styles of Bartók and the late Stravinsky. While a student at the New England Conservatory, he composed the concerto *grosso* (1943, rev. 1955) in a style reminiscent of Debussy and Ravel. In several works titled *Piece Concertantes,* no. 1, "Repliment" (Folding Back, 1956), for piano and string orchestra, is on a row, and the "folding back" signifies that the entire composition is in retrograde beginning at the center. The one-movement concerto (1965) is a rondo-like composition, with the emotional elements de-emphasized. The concerto (1967) displays Messiaen's fondness for exotic instruments and sounds.

Eldon Rathburn (1916–) taught at the University of Ottawa and, after studies at the Royal Conservatory in Toronto, he took a position in 1947 with the National Film Board of Canada. Several of his approximately 185 film scores received international awards. While at the National Film Board he composed the nocturne (1953) for piano and small orchestra. In 1972, he joined the faculty at the University of Ottawa and, while there, he composed the *Rhythmette* (1973) for two pianos and rhythm band. He writes music in a style pleasing to varied tastes.

Samuel Dolin (1917–) studied composition with Weinzweig and Krenek, and joined the faculty at the Toronto Conservatory in 1945. Much of his importance comes from teaching numerous successful Canadian composers. His compositional style is highly chromatic, with thematic development and frequent ostinatos. The fantasy (1967) is for piano and chamber orchestra, and the concerto (1974) is for piano and orchestra.

William McCauley (1917–) studied composition with Willan at the Royal Conservatory in Toronto, with B. Rogers and Hanson at the Eastman School of Music, and with Hovhaness. In 1970, he became the head of the music department at Seneca College. Among his compositions is the concerto no. 1 (1977).

Oskar Morawetz (1917–), self-taught composer, trained at Prague University, and emigrated in 1939 to Canada where he studied at the University of Toronto and taught at the Royal Conservatory and the University of Toronto. At age 19, George Szell recommended Morawetz as an assistant conductor of the Prague Opera. The one-movement concerto (1960–1963) has a classic design, a romantic mood, and impressionistic harmonies.

Lorne Betts (1918–) was a principal at the Hamilton Conservatory of Music, wrote music criticism, and played church organ. He studied composition with Krenek, Rawsthorne, and Harris. He composed the concertino (1950) for harpsichord and orchestra while a student of Weinzweig. Neo-classic features are evident in two concertos (1955, 1957) and the double concerto (1976) for cello, piano, and orchestra.

Godfrey Ridout (1918–1984), respected teacher at the University of Toronto, is an example of English musical tradition in Canada. The concerto *grosso* (1974) for piano, violin, and string orchestra is tonal and based on short rhythmic motives. The slow movement is built on a tone-row and permutations suggested by Schoenberg.

Gerald Bale (1919–), choirmaster and teacher, studied at the Toronto Conservatory of Music and composes music in a style influenced by Willan. While employed as an organist at the Rosedale United Church, he composed the fantasy (1939) for piano and orchestra.

Maurice Dela (1919–1978) studied composition with Champagne at the Montreal Conservatory and orchestration with Sowerby in Chicago. He worked as a church organist and an arranger and composer for the CBC. His music displays the conservative style of his teacher Champagne, baroque and classic elements, and French transparency. The *Ballade* (1945) has a nineteenth-century style, and the concerto (1946, rev. 1950) is freely tonal. The concertino (1961–1962) is a three-movement work performed without breaks between movements. The forms are sonata and ternary, the harmony contains seventh chords, unprepared and unresolved dissonances, modality, seconds and thirds, and the rhythm incorporates syncopation and irregular accents.

Udo Kasemets (1919–) is among the few Canadian composers to maintain close contact with avant-garde composers in the United States. He trained at the Tallin Conservatory in Estonia and the State Music Academy in Stuttgart, Germany, and attended avant-garde music courses at Darmstadt. He immigrated to Canada in 1951, and joined the faculty at the Ontario College of Art in 1970. The Poetic Suites, op. 37 (1954), for soprano, piano, and string orchestra is a twelve-tone work on poems by the English poet Kathleen Raine.

Talivaldis Kenins (1919–), born in Latvia, studied musical composition at the State Conservatory of Riga and with Messiaen at the Paris *Conservatoire*. In 1951, he went to Canada, where he became the music director of the Latvian Lutheran Church and taught music at the University of Toronto. His musical compositions follow classic design and employ folk material from Latvia and Canada. During the 1940s and 1950s, his style showed elements of romanticism and the neo-classicism of his French training, while in the 1960s he used more transparent textures. The concerto (1946) is a student work from the Paris *Conservatoire*. In Toronto, he worked on the *Duo* (1951) and the one-movement *Fantasies Concertantes* (1971), which contains motor rhythms.

Edmund Assaly (1920–) worked as an organist in Saskatoon. In Winnipeg, he composed the *Red River Valley* for two pianos and orchestra for the CBC presentation *Canadian Party*. He composed the *Mount Royal Fantasy* (1948) in Montreal. In 1970, he joined the faculty at the University of Wisconsin, Milwaukee.

Neil Chotem (1920–) performed as a pianist with many Canadian orchestras and on the BBC and the CBC. At age 13, he soloed with Saint-Saëns' concerto no. 2 with the Regina Symphony Orchestra, and, in 1950, he premiered Champagne's concerto. Chotem composed the *Scherzo Tarantelle* (1936) in Saskatoon, and arranged Spanish folk melodies into the *Rhapsody on El Vito* (1963) in Montreal.

Robert Turner (1920–) studied with Champagne at McGill University in Montreal, with Howells and Jacob at the Royal College of Music in London, England, with Messiaen at the Berkshire (now Tanglewood) Music Center, and with Harris in Nashville. He worked for the CBC in Vancouver and taught at the University of British Columbia and Acadia University in Nova Scotia. His compositional style follows the conservative direction of Champagne and contains elements of jazz, modal and quartal harmony, and the twelve-tone method. In 1969, he joined the faculty at the University of Manitoba in Winnipeg and, while there, composed the concerto (1971) for two pianos and orchestra and the *Capriccio Concertante* (1975) for cello, piano, and orchestra. In the concerto, the pianist plucks and beats the piano strings. Themes taken from other works by Turner appear in the cadenza in the third movement.

Robert Fleming (1921–1976) took piano with Benjamin and composition with Howells at the Royal College of Music in London, England; after World War II he studied at the Toronto Conservatory. In 1946, he began working at the National Film Board, composing more than 250 film scores. Many films on Canadian subjects caused him to add features of folk songs to his style, which is based on tonality, traditional forms, and a mild level of contemporary dissonance. In 1970, he moved to Ottawa to teach music at Carleton University. His concert works include the *Short and Simple Suite* (1959) for piano and strings, the concerto (1963), and the *Concerto '64* (1964).

William Rogers (1921–) studied at the Juilliard School of Music, with Boulanger in Paris, and with Toch at the Berkshire (now Tanglewood) Music Center. He composed the concertino (1949) for piano and small orchestra while on the faculty at the Hamilton Conservatory.

George Fiala (1922–), born in the Ukraine, studied at the Kiev Conservatory and in Berlin. He moved to Belgium, then immigrated in 1949 to Canada where he worked in the Russian section of Radio-Canada International. Many of his musical compositions contain Russian and Ukrainian elements. Up to the 1960s, his music was tonal, then he turned to the twelve-tone method. He composed the concerto (1946) in Brussels, Belgium, while a student of Jongen. The concertino, op. 2 (1950), is for piano, trumpet, timpani, and strings. Other compositions are the capriccio (1962) in twelve-tone style, the *Musique Concertante* (1968), and the *Sinfonietta Concertata* (1971) for accordion, harpsichord, and strings.

Michel Perrault (1925–) studied at the Montreal Conservatory and with Honegger and Boulanger in Paris. He was a percussionist and assistant conductor with the Montreal Symphony Orchestra, and now he owns the publishing house Publications

Bonart. Mozart, Bach, and Ravel are strong influences on the *Berubee* (1959) for piano and orchestra.

Harry Somers (1925–) studied at the Royal Conservatory in Toronto and with Milhaud in Paris. He received the Companion of the Order of Canada in 1971, and became a commentator for radio and television. He learned the twelve-tone method from Weinzweig, and he uses ancient, national, and exotic materials. The concerto no. 1 (1947) is on a twelve-tone row with motives taken from the row. The concerto no. 2 (1956) has a triple canon in augmentation in a style similar to Messiaen, two rows, classic and romantic harmonies, and atonality. Sometimes the triadic accompaniment suggests Rachmaninoff or Prokofieff. To obtain sufficient, untroubled time for musical composition, Somers chose to drive a taxi for a living.

Gerhard Wuensch (1925–) studied composition and piano at the State Academy of Music in Vienna, and worked in Austria and Germany as a pianist and accompanist. Most of his musical compositions display neo-classic features. He composed the concerto, op. 17 (1961), while on the faculty at Butler University in Indianapolis, Ind. When he was on the faculty at the University of Calgary, a branch of the University of Alberta, he composed the concerto, op. 57 (1971), for piano and chamber orchestra, and the scherzo, op. 58 (1971).

François Morel (1926–) studied composition and piano at the Conservatory of Music, Montreal, worked at CBC radio and joined the faculties at the University of Montreal and Laval University. With Joachim, Garant, and Landry, Morel is a founding member of *Musique de Notre Temps* for performances of contemporary music. After studies with Schoenberg, Morel evolved his own concept of serialism while keeping features of Debussy, neo-classism, and Varèse. The *Melisma* (1980) is for piano and orchestra.

Clermont Pépin (1926–) graduated from the Curtis Institute of Music at age 19. The two concertos (1946, 1949) are conservative, tonal works he composed before going to Paris; the second concerto contains serial themes. In Paris, he studied with Jolivet, Honegger, and Messiaen, and ideas he learned in Paris are evident in the nocturne (1950–1957) for piano and strings. He based the serial *Nobres* (1962) for two pianos and orchestra on mathematical procedures structured by Boulez. The ensemble is in twelve groups, with the two pianos being a group, and microphones and speakers surround the audience. The *Nobres* is for the two-piano team of Victor Bouchard and his wife Renée Morisset. Pépin taught at the Montreal Conservatory.

John Beckwith (1927–) received training at the Conservatory of Toronto and with Boulanger in Paris. He wrote music criticism for the Toronto *Star* and taught at the University of Toronto from 1952. His other activities include being an associate editor of the *Canadian Music Journal* and a writer and commentator for the CBC radio series the *World of Music*. Influences on his compositional style include French neo-classicism, R. Thompson, Copland, and Canadian folk materials. The concerto fantasy (1958–1959) is tonal and shows neo-classic thinking akin to Stravinsky. The finale of the three-movement work has an all-interval, twelve-tone row taken from United States composer Henry Leland Clarke. The *Circle, with Tangents* (1967) is for harpsichord and thirteen solo strings.

Adrian Butler (1929–), church organist, composed the concerto no. 1 (1945) for piano and strings and the concerto no. 2 (1950) for piano and orchestra.

Serge Garant (1929–) studied composition with Champagne in Montreal and Messiaen in Paris. Returning to Canada, he worked as a pianist and arranger, and taught at the University of Montreal. A performance of Stravinsky's *Rite of Spring* sparked his interest in musical composition. The *Adagio et Allegro* (1948) for piano and band is from the period when he studied with Champagne. The *Musique pour la Mort d'un Poete* (1954) for piano and strings is serial and pointillistic in a style similar to Webern. Along with Morel, Jachim, and Landry, he helped organize the modern music group *Musique de Notre Temps*.

Alfred Kunz (1929–) was in Toronto when he composed the *Student Concerto* (1950) for piano and small orchestra. He studied with Stockhausen in Darmstadt, and held several teaching posts in Ontario. *In the Park of October Colour* (1969) is a love song for solo piano, chorus, and orchestra. The concerto (1975) contains tonal material, tone clusters, and aleatoric devices.

André Mathieu (1929–1968) composed the concertino nos. 1 and 2 (perf. 1936 and 1941). An abridged version of the concerto no. 3, *Romantic* (1944), is the *Quebec Concerto* (pub. 1948) for use in the Canadian film *La Forteresse* (Whispering City). The concerto no. 4 (1949) exists in sketches, with the third movement intact.

Roger Matton (1929–) studied with Champagne at the Conservatory of Music in Montreal and with Boulanger and Messiaen in Paris. In Paris, he worked on the concerto (1953–1955) for two pianos and percussion using elements of Bartók's style. The finale is on the lumberman song *Les Raftsmen*. In 1956, he returned to Canada as a researcher and ethnomusicologist at the *Archives de Folklore* at Laval University in Quebec. The concerto (1963–1964) is for the piano team of Victor Bouchard and his wife Renée Morisset.

Ronald Collier (1930–) studied in Vancouver and went to Toronto to study jazz composition with Gordon Delamont in 1951. He played trombone with the National Ballet Orchestra, the Toronto Symphony, and various radio and television orchestras, and became the resident composer at Humber College in Toronto. Collier collaborated with Duke Ellington to compose the *Celebration* (1972) for piano and orchestra.

Milton Barnes (1931–) studied at the Conservatory of Toronto, the Berkshire (now Tanglewood) Music Center, and the Vienna Academy. He conducted the University of Toronto Orchestra, the Toronto Repertory Ensemble, the Niagara Falls (New York) Philharmonic, and directed the Toronto Dance Theater. For piano and orchestra, he composed the *Classical Concerto* (1973).

Paul McIntyre (1931–) composed the concerto (1952) while studying in Toronto. Later, he studied piano with Arrau in Stratford and composition with Messiaen at the Paris *Conservatoire*. He served as the department head at the University of Alaska, the University of Minnesota, and the University of Windsor, Ontario.

Lothar Klein (1932–), German-born Canadian, studied at the Free University of Berlin and with Blacher at the *Hochschule für Musik*. He taught at the University of Minnesota, the University of Texas at Austin, and the University of Toronto. His early compositional style is tonal, with neo-baroque features, and later works have serial elements. The concerto (1954) may have been a graduation piece from the University of Minnesota. *Le Trésor des Dieux* (1972) is a suite for guitar or harpsichord and orchestra that Klein composed while on the faculty at the University of Toronto.

Michael Miller (1932–) took training at the Eastman School of Music, the University of New York, and Vassar College, and joined the faculty at Mount Allison University in Sackville, New Brunswick. He writes music in a chromatic and polytonal style, and has the *Two Pieces* (1975) for piano and orchestra.

Walter Buczynski (1933–) studied at the Conservatory of Toronto and with Milhaud and Boulanger in Paris, and took piano with R. Lhévinne. In 1962, he joined the faculty at the Conservatory of Toronto. Piano studies in Warsaw, Poland, brought him into contact with Polish music. The *Berztitula* (1964) and the *Lyric* (1976) are for piano and orchestra. The *Four Movements* (1969) for piano and string orchestra requires the pianist to play clusters and pluck and strike the strings with mallets. Theatrical techniques appear in the *Zeroing in No. 4* (*Inwards and Outwards,* 1972) for soprano, flute, piano, and orchestra.

R. Murray Schafer (1933–) studied at the Royal Conservatory of Music in Toronto, where he composed the concerto (1954) for harpsichord and eight wind instruments. This polytonal composition shows influences of his teacher Weinzweig and postwar serialism. He studied in Vienna, and began working for the CBC in 1962.

Srul Glick (1934–) began composition studies with Weinzweig at the University of Toronto and continued with Milhaud in Aspen, Colo., and taught at the Conservatory in Toronto. His compositional style incorporates chromaticism and polytonality. For piano and orchestra, he composed the *Symphonic Dialogues* (1963) and the concertino (1977).

Ben McPeek (1934–1981) enjoyed a highly successful career as a composer of more than 2,000 jingles. He trained at the Royal Conservatory of Music in Toronto and the University of Toronto. The concerto (1979) contains elements of Canadian folk songs.

Raymond Pannell (1935–) studied at the Juilliard School of Music, and joined the faculty at the Royal Conservatory of Music in 1959. In 1962, he was a contestant in the Tchaikovsky Piano Competition in Moscow. Some of his compositions are the double concerto no. 1 (1957) for piano, voice, and orchestra, and for piano and orchestra the concerto no. 2 (1961), the ballad (1968), the concerto (1966–1967) and the *Elegy* (1967). The London (Ontario) Symphony Orchestra commissioned the last two works.

Malcolm Forsyth (1936–) studied at the University of Cape Town, South Africa, and, in 1968, emigrated to Canada where he played trombone in the Edmonton Symphony and taught at the University of Alberta. In a tonal style, he draws upon African folk tunes and contemporary European ideas, including atonality and ostinatos. The concerto (1973–1975) is for piano and orchestra.

Derek Healey (1936–), English, trained at the Royal College of Music in London, England, and taught at the University of Victoria, B.C., the University of Toronto and the University of Guelph. His music displays elements of Hindemith and Britten. The triple concerto *Noh,* op. 42 (1974), is for flute, piano, synthesizer, and orchestra. In 1978, he took a teaching position at the University of Oregon.

Table 38 Additional Composers in Canada

Names	Dates	Compositions
Ackland, Jeanne	1914–	Concerto, 1st mvt
Angus, Roy	1902–	Concerto (1951)
Baker, Michael	1942–	*Okanagan Landscapes* (1971)
		Contours (1973), hpd
		Concerto (1976)
		A Struggle for Dominion (perf 1976)
Bevan, Richard	1894–	Concerto (1950)
Blackburn, Maurice	1914–	Concertino (1948)
Blair, Dean	1932–	Concerto (1977)
Boivin, Maurice	1918/20–	*Lac champlain* (1962)
Brisson, Gaston	? –	Concertino (perf 1978)
Brown, Allanson	1902–	Fantasy-Prelude (1948)
Chubb, Frederick	1885–1966	Rhapsody
Dainty, Ernest	1891–1947	Romanza
Descarries, Auguste	1896–1958	Rhapsody *Canadienne* (perf 1936)
Dompierre, François	1943–	Concerto (perf 1978)
Edwards, Eric	1913–	*Mexican Rhapsody* (1938)
Gagnon, André	1942?–	*Mes Quatre Saisons* (1960s)
		4 Concertos
Gould, Glenn	1932–1982	Cadenzas (1954), Beethoven Concerto no 1
Gratton, Hector	1900–1970	*Coucher de Soleil* (1947)
		Nocturne (Lune)
		Complainte de la Folle
Higgin, Clifford	1873/76–1951	*Butterfly's Ball*
Hurst, George	1926–	Concertino
Laliberté, Alfred	1882–ca. 1952	*Passacaille et Choeur Final,* unfin
Lowe, John	1902–	*Irish Rhapsody*
		Eastern Fantasy
		Pan's Dance
Morin-Labrecque, Albertine	ca. 1896–1957	2 pno Concerto (*Poéme sur Jeanne d'Arc*)
Morley, Glen	1912–	Scherzo
Raymond, Madeleine	1919–	*Ballade sur l'Eau*
		Danse Sauvage
		Pastorale
Ruff, Herbert	1918–	Rhapsody
Saarinen, Gloria	1934–	Cadenzas, Mozart concs.
Savaria, Georges	1916–	Concerto (1951)
Van Dijk, Rudi	1932–	*Symfonia Concertante* (1959)
Vocelle, Lucien	1910–	Concerto (1936)

Jacques Hétu (1938–) studied at the Montreal Conservatory and with Messiaen in Paris. He returned in 1963 to Canada, where he taught at Laval University. His compositions show elements of neo-classicism and influences of Bartók, Hindemith, and French composers. In 1962, he turned to a serial style akin to Webern. He has the double concerto, op. 12 (1969), for violin, piano, and chamber orchestra, the concerto, op.

15 (1967), the *Cycle,* op. 16 (1969), for piano and wind instruments, and the *Fantasie,* op. 21 (1973), for piano and orchestra.

Victor Davies (1939–) trained at the University of Manitoba, Indiana University, and with Boulez in Switzerland. He is a church organist, composer, arranger, and conductor. *A Mennonite Piano Concerto* (prem. 1957) is a three-movement work based on eleven chorales.

Bruce Mather (1939–) writes music encompassing neo-classicism, expressionism, serialism, and microtonality. This diversity comes from the styles of his various teachers, including Ridout, Morawetz, and Weinzweig at the Royal Conservatory of Music, Toronto, and Plé-Caussade, Messiaen and Milhaud in Paris. Mather develops "fields" of six or seven chromatic notes that provide material for a composition. The concerto (1958) is for piano and a chamber orchestra comprising a wind quintet and a string quartet. Mather and his wife Pierrette LePage concertize as a piano duo.

Ann Marianne Lauber (1943–) studied in Lausanne, Switzerland, and emigrated in 1967 to Montreal, where she joined the staff at the Canadian Music Centre. The *Piece concertante* (1977) is for piano and orchestra, and *L'Affaire Coffin* is a film score for piano and youth orchestra.

Steven Gellman (1948–) combines contemporary compositional ideas of his teachers Milhaud and Messiaen with classic formal designs. While a student at the Juilliard School of Music, he studied with Berio, Persichetti, and Sessions. At age 16, he premiered his own concerto (1974) in Toronto. The *Odyssey* (perf. 1971) for rock group, solo piano, and orchestra blends elements of rock and concert music.

Chapter 18

Mexico, Guatemala, Costa Rica, Panama, Colombia and Venezuela

Mexico

Ricardo Castro (1864–1907) studied at the National Conservatory of Music and in Paris, Berlin, and London. In 1907, he returned to Mexico City to direct his alma mater. The concerto (perf. 1904) merges Mexican musical elements with features of Chopin, Schumann, and Liszt.

Rafael Tello (1872–) studied in Mexico and Europe, taught composition at the National Conservatory, and wrote criticism for various periodicals. The *Fantasia* (1940) for two pianos and orchestra is in four parts titled "Prelude," "Scherzo," "Adagio," and "Finale." The Finale contains material presented in earlier sections.

Julián Carrillo (1875–1965) took training at the National Conservatory and the Leipzig Conservatory. After returning to Mexico in 1905, he frequently performed as a violinist. About 1895, he began experimenting with dividing strings into various proportions and created a "new sound" that is a pitch having a ratio of 1:1.007246. This 1/16-tone replaces the usual twelve divisions of the octave, and Carrillo named it *el sonido trece* (the thirteenth sound). Carrillo may be the first composer to work with microtones. By 1925, he codified the theory and used it in musical compositions. The concertino *Metamorfoseador Carrillo* (1950) is for piano tuned in third-tones and orchestra, and the *Balbuceous* (1960) is for piano tuned in sixteenth-tones and chamber orchestra. With traditional semitones, Carrillo composed the *Fantasia Impromptu* (1930). There may be an earlier fantasy for piano and orchestra. Also, he transcribed compositions of Bach and Beethoven into his quarter-tone system. In 1940, he completed plans for a microtonal piano, and the firm of Carl Sauter in Spaichinger Würt build one of the pianos for display at the 1958 Exposition in Brussels.

Manuel Ponce (1882/1886–1948) studied in Bologna, Berlin, and Paris with Dukas. In Paris, he developed a love of Debussy's music and, after returning to Mexico, introduced Debussy's music to students and concert audiences. His own musical compositions display elements of romanticism, mestizo folk music, and nineteenth-century salon music. Ponce's fondness for the music of Chopin appears in the concerto (1910), which Ruth Schoental completed. The second movement contains themes of a Mexican character. Other compositions for piano and orchestra are the *Balada Mexicana* (1914) and the concerto II *Concierto Romantico*.

José Rolón (1883–1945), symphonic composer, studied with Moszkowski, Boulanger, and Dukas in Paris, and taught at the *Conservatorio Nacional* from 1936.

The concerto, op. 42 (1935), with national rhythms and melodic style, was among the most advanced compositions in Mexican music.

Jacobo Kostakowsky (1893–), born in Odessa, Russia, studied with Schoenberg and d'Indy, played violin in several German orchestras, and emigrated to Mexico in 1925. His music displays his Russian heritage and Mexican melodies. Among his compositions is the *Capricho* (1934), the concerto (1937), and the *marimba* (perf. 1940), which is a *capricho* for piano and orchestra.

Ignacco Fernández Esperón (1894–) studied in Mexico, New York City, and Paris, and earned a living working for the Mexican consul and Mexican radio. *El Zihuateco* (1939) follows a popular musical style.

Antonio Gomezanda (1894–) trained at the National School of Medicine and the National Conservatory, and joined the piano faculty at the Conservatory. He has the *Fantasia Mexicana* (perf. 1923).

Carlos Chávez (1899–1978) is Mexico's most famous composer and the father figure of Mexican music. After becoming the director of the National Conservatory of Music in 1928, he began raising the musical standards. In 1933, he became the chief of the Department of Fine Arts in the Secretariat of Public Education. He founded the National Institute of Fine Arts in 1947 and the Composer's Workshop at the National Conservatory in 1960. The concerto (1938–1940) is in three movements, with material in the first movement appearing later. In much of the concerto, the piano has rhythmic passages (See ex. 18–1) and sometimes large, dissonant chords (See ex. 18–2). Mexican nationalism and Indian influences are notable in the melodies, rhythms, and harmonies.

Example 18–1. Chávez Concerto, mvt. 1, mm. 31–41

Example 18–2. Chávez Concerto, mvt. 1, mm. 101–112

Daniel Ayala (1906–1957) studied at the National Conservatory in Mexico City, and taught at the Yucatán Conservatory, the Veracruz School of Music, and the Veracruz Institute of Fine Arts. He founded the Yucatán orchestra, and worked as a nightclub musician. His music contains ancient Mayan modes and rhythms. The concertino (1974) is for piano and orchestra.

Gerhart Muench (1907–), German-born pianist, studied at the Dresden Conservatory, where he debuted at age 9. He immigrated to the United States in 1947, and to Mexico City in 1953; he taught at the National University. He championed twentieth-century piano music, and introduced the music of Stockhausen, Boulez, and other contemporary composers to Mexican audiences. In Dresden, he composed the *Concerto da Camera* (perf. 1926) and the capriccio *variato* (1941). In Mexico City, he composed the *Vocationes* (1951) for piano and chamber orchestra, the concerto (1957) with string orchestra, and the *Itinera Duo* (1965).

Blas Galindo (1910–) took training with Chávez, Rolón, and Huízar at the National Conservatory and with Copland at the Berkshire (now Tanglewood) Music Center. He taught music, and then became the music director of the *Instituto Mexicano de Seguro Social Symphony Orchestra*. His music blends neo-classic elements and native music. In the 1940s and 1950s, he used chords of fourths and fifths, parallel seconds, fifths, and sevenths, and pandiatonicism. There are two concertos (1942, 1961), with the earlier based on material intended for a concerto for two pianos.

Carlos Jiménez-Mabarak (1916–) studied in Santiago, Chile, and Brussels. His teaching career has been at the National Conservatory and the School of Arts in Villahermosa. He studied dodecaphony in Brussels, and was the first composer in

Mexico to write music using electronic techniques and *musique concréte*. Mexican folk songs provide an important resource for Jiménez-Mabarak's compositions. The *Concierto de Abuelo* (1938) is for piano and string quartet. He composed the concerto (1944) in Mexico City and the sinfonia *concertante* (1966) in Villahermosa.

Ruth Schoenthal (1924–), born in Berlin and trained at the Stern Conservatory, immigrated in 1940 to Mexico, where she took lessons with Ponce, gave piano recitals, and composed for radio programs. She has the concerto *romántico* (1941).

Jorge González-Avila (1925–) trained at the National Conservatory and pursued a teaching career until becoming the director of the Audiotranscription Division of the National Institute of Fine Arts in 1972. His compositions include the *Invention* (1964) for soprano, piano, and orchestra, the *Invention Concertante* no. 1 (1973), the *Invention Interpolar* (1974), and the *Invention* (1975) for English horn, piano, and orchestra.

Manuel Enrizquez (1926–) studied composition and violin at the Guadalajara Conservatory and composition with Mennin and violin with Galamian at the Juilliard School of Music. In Mexico, he was the concertmaster of the Guadalajara Symphony Orchestra, and taught at the Institute of Fine Arts in Mexico City. He believes Mexican folk music does not offer a worthwhile source of inspiration, and since 1960 he has used serial and aleatoric devices. The concerto (1970–1971) shows contemporary techniques.

Eduardo Mata (1942–1995), conductor, studied composition with R. Halffter at the National Conservatory and privately with Chávez. His conducting studies were under Rudolf, Schuller, and Leinsdorf. While the conductor of the Guadalajara Symphony Orchestra, he composed the *Improvisaciones* no. 2 (1965) for strings and two pianos. The piano I has a percussive style and the strings are in four sections, with each division having its own staff in the score. The pianist plays on the strings with mallets, sticks, fingers, and hands. This was among the most advanced dodecaphonic works by a Mexican composer. Mata became principal conductor of the Phoenix Symphony Orchestra in Arizona, and the conductor and music director of the Dallas Symphony Orchestra in Texas.

Maria Teresa Prieto (? –) was born in Spain and trained at the Conservatory in Madrid. In 1936, she moved to Mexico where her teachers were Chávez and Ponce, and Milhaud at Mills College in Oakland, Calif. For piano and orchestra, she composed the *Impresión Sinfonica* (1940) and the fantasia *Sobre una Fuga* (1950).

Table 39 Additional Composers in Mexico

Names	Dates	Compositions
Curiel, Gonzalo	1904–	Concerto
Garcia Ascot, Rosa	1906–	Concerto
Gomez Barrera, Carlos	? –	Fantasia (pub 1964)
Gutiérrez Heras, Joaquin	1927–	Divertimento (1949)
Miramontes, Arnulf	1882–	Concerto
Moncayo Garacía, José Pablo	1912–1958	*Simiente* (unfin)
Vasquez, Jose	1895–	4 Concertos
Zozaya, Carlos	1893–	Concerto

Guatemala

Franz Ippisch (1883–1958), German, studied piano with Hoffman before moving to Guatemala in 1939. The concerto (ca. 1943) is for piano and orchestra.

Ricardo Castillo (1894–1967) went to Paris to study at age 14, and stayed there until age 30. His experiences in Paris provide a strong influence of French impressionism in his compositions, which contain elements of the Indian folk music of Guatemala. He was fond of using one melodic or rhythmic figure as a unifying device. In the years 1950–1951 he worked on a concerto for piano and orchestra.

Jorge Alvaro Sarmientos (ca. 1933–) received a scholarship to the National Conservatory at age 15. Later he studied at the Paris *Conservatoire* and, while in Paris, began and possibly finished the concerto, op. 10 (1956). He probably composed the suite *concertante,* op. 14 (1960), in Guatemala City, where he played timpani and sometimes conducted the National Symphony Orchestra. Indian folk melodies provide musical sources for Sarmientos' compositions.

Enrique Solares (1910–) studied in Guatemala, San Francisco, Prague, Rome, and Brussels. He started the *capricho* (1941–1951) during studies with Casella in Rome, and possibly finished it in Guatemala. For some years, he worked in the diplomatic service for the Guatemalan government, and his experiences in many of Europe's most cosmopolitan cities probably are what caused Solares to turn away from Guatemalan folk music in preference to atonality, free treatment of rows, quartal and quintal harmonies, serialism, and baroque structures.

Costa Rica

Julio Fonseca (1885–1950) studied at the National School of Music in San Jose, the Conservatory in Milan, Italy, and the Brussels Conservatory. In Milan, or perhaps Brussels, he composed the poem *El Cenaculo y el Golgota* (1904) for piano and strings. In 1906, he returned to San Jose, where he taught at the *Colegio Superior de Señoritas* and the National Conservatory. *La Cochita* (1942) contains folk melodies, tonal harmonies, and slow harmonic rhythms.

Carlos Enrique Vargas (1919–) studied in Detroit, Mich., at the *Liceo of Costa Rica,* and at the Santa Cecilia Conservatory in Rome. In San Jose, he taught at the *Colegio Superior de Señoritas,* played organ at the Metropolitan Cathedral, and gave piano recitals and solos with the National Symphony Orchestra. His music is tonal, with both functional and non-functional harmonies. He has the concerto (perf. 1944).

Panama

Luis Delgadillo (1887–1962/64), Nicaraguan teacher and composer, studied at the Milan Conservatory, Italy, became the director of the first National School of Music in

Nicaragua, and went to Panama to teach at the National School of Music. In Panama, he composed the *Fantasía Tropical Panameña* (1943) and the ballet *El Gato Felix* (1945) for piano and orchestra. His music incorporates rhythms and melodies of South America. He taught in Mexico City and, eventually, returned to Managua.

Colombia

Guillermo Uribe Holguín (1880–1971) studied with d'Indy at the *Schola Cantorum* in Paris and, after returning to Bogotá in 1910, he directed the recently established National Conservatory. In 1935, he left the conservatory to compose, conduct, and work the family coffee plantation. His music displays the French impressionism he learned in Paris and various elements of Colombian folk music. The *Villanesca* (1930) for piano and orchestra bears a striking similarity to d'Indy's *Symphony on a French Mountain Air*. Another work for piano and orchestra is the *Concerto a la Manera Antiqua,* op. 67 (1939).

Jose Rozo-Contreras (1894–) trained in Colombia, Vienna, and Rome. The Colombian government officially approved his orchestration of the Colombian national anthem. He conducted the national band and, in 1936, he transcribed Saint-Saëns' *Rhapsodie d'Auvergne* for piano and band.

Roberto Pineda-Duque (1910–), autodidactic composer, became the conductor of the Bogotá Symphony Orchestra and the director of the National Conservatory. He won the Colombian Sesquicentennial of Independence Prize for the concerto (1960).

Fabio Gonzalez-Zuleta (1920–) graduated from the National University, where he joined the faculty. His music has classic forms, polytonality, atonality, and serialism. The concerto *grosso* (1968) is for harpsichord and strings.

Luis Antonio Escobar (1925–) trained at the Bogotá Conservatory, the Peabody Conservatory in Baltimore, and with Blacher in Berlin, and taught at the Bogotá Conservatory. Using contemporary techniques with melodies and rhythms of Spanish-American dances, he composed the concertino (1958) for harpsichord and strings and the concerto (1959) for piano and orchestra.

Venezuela

Juan Vicente Lecuna (1891–1954) studied at the *Escuela Nacional de Musica* and in New York City and Baltimore. He composed the concerto (1941) while a student at the Caracas National School of Music. His style uses Hispanic musical sources, melodies similar to D. Scarlatti, and Venezuelan folklore.

Maria Luisa Escobar (1903–), pianist for several radio stations in Caracas, used Venezuelan tribal and folk music in her compositions. The two-movement *Concierto Sentimentale* (1949) appears as the *Vals Sentimental*.

Evenico Castallanos (1915–), brother of G. Castellanos, composed the concerto (1944) in the year he graduated from the *Escuela Superior de Música*. He played organ at the Caracas Cathedral, conducted the Venezuela Symphony Orchestra, and taught at the *Escuela Superior de Música*.

Rhazes Hernandez-Lopez (1918–) is a musicologist, flutist, critic, teacher, and a founding member of the Venezuela Symphony Orchestra. The twelve-tone *Casualismo* (1967) is for piano obbligato and orchestra.

Gonzalo Castallanos (1926–), brother of E. Castallanos, directed the *Escuela de Musica Juan Manuel Oliveras* and conducted the Venezuela Symphony Orchestra and the *Collegium Musicum*. The *Symphonic Fantasy* (1954) is for piano and orchestra.

Yannis Ioannidis (1930–), Greek, studied at the Athens Conservatory and the Vienna Musical Academy. In 1968, he settled in Caracas to teach at the conservatory and the university. His music in the style of the Second Viennese School includes the *Orbis* (1975–1976) he composed just before returning to Athens.

Chapter 19

Brazil, Uruguay, Peru, Ecuador, Bolivia, Paraguay, Argentina, Chile, Cuba, and the Dominican Republic

Brazil

Alberto Nepomuceno (1864–1920) studied at the Santa Cecilia Conservatory in Rome, the Stern Conservatory in Berlin, and the Paris *Conservatoire*. He returned to Rio de Janeiro in 1895, became the director of the National Institute of Music, and introduced the music of Glazunov, Mussorgsky, and Debussy to audiences. Although his European musical training made his use of Brazilian folk music difficult, eventually he became the first composer to use Brazilian folk music in concert music. The six *Valsas Humoristicas* (1903) are in a post-romantic style.

Heitor Villa-Lobos (1887–1959) studied at the National Institute of Music in Rio de Janeiro, became the director of music education in Rio de Janeiro, and established the Brazilian Academy of Music. He stressed native, folk, and popular music resources of Brazil for concert music. Like Bartók, Villa-Lobos roamed the countryside learning the regional music. Brazilian rhythmic (See ex. 19–1) and melodic (See ex. 19–2) features are in the concerto no. 1.

Villa-Lobos' music for piano and orchestra includes the suite (1913) in three movements of "A Espanha," "Ao Brasil," and "A Italia," the *Folia de um Bloco Infantil* (1919), the *Dansa dos Indios Mesticos* (1920), and the *Rudepoêma* (1926). The generic title *choros* is for a popular Brazilian dance form having an original meaning of "lament" because of the melancholy expression in music performed by a woodwind instrument accompanied by a small ensemble of plucked stringed instruments, including guitars. Villa-Lobos composed fourteen *choros* with each having a different instrumentation. The *choros* no. 11 is for piano and orchestra. The *Mômo Precoce* (Precocious Momus, King of the Carnival, 1929) is a fantasy or suite based on music taken from an earlier composition. The concertos are five in number: no. 1 (1945) in four movements, no. 2 (1948), no. 3 (1952–1957), no. 4 (1952), and no. 5 (1954). Different instrumentations are in each of nine *Bachianas Brasileiras* that merge Brazilian melorhythms and Bach-style counterpoint into works intended as an homage to J. S. Bach. Each composition is a suite of dances having rhythmic ostinatos and motivic writing, while avoiding triadic structures and staying in one tonal center. The *Bachianas Brasileiras* no. 3 has three movements titled "Preludio," "Aria," and "Toccata"—named *Picapao* after a bird akin to the woodpecker. The *Bachianas Brasileiras* no. 4

Example 19–1. Villa-Lobos Concerto no. 1, mvt. 1, mm. 9–12

Example 19–2. Villa-Lobos Concerto no. 1, mvt. 1, mm. 162–169

(1931–1936) has four movements of "Preludio" (1931), "Aria" (1931), "Coral" (1936), and "Dansa" (1936).

Hekel Tavares (1896–1969) was a wealthy plantation owner who learned native folk songs in the work fields. Although he did not receive a formal musical education, he composed vocal and instrumental music influenced by folk songs and dance forms of the region. In São Paulo, he composed the *Concerto in Brazilian Forms,* op. 105, no. 2 (1941), with three movements titled "Modinha," "Ponteio," and "Maracatú" representing three common types of urban, rural, and Negro folk songs. Tavares' original melodies contain elements of native folk music.

Oscar Lorenzo Fernández (1897–1948) was studying medicine when he developed an interest in music. He entered the National School of Music in 1917, later joining the faculty, and helped establish the Brazil Conservatory of Music. He obtained some musical training in Europe, and quickly became a leading figure in the nationalist movement. He liked classic forms, literal quotations of Brazilian folk tunes, harmonies of second, sevenths, fourths, and fifths, and rhythms and ostinatos as organizational elements. Among his compositions are two concertos (1924, 1937) and the *variaçoes sinfônicas* (1948).

Francisco Mignone (1897–) studied at the São Paulo Conservatory and the G. Verdi Conservatory in Milan, Italy, and joined the faculty at the National Music School in Rio de Janeiro. Studies in Milan imbued his music with a European flavor that attracted harsh criticism from Brazilian nationalists. Mignone quickly adapted to Brazilian musical expectations by dropping his European influences and adopting elements of indigenous Brazilian music. Now, he is among the finest Brazilian composers of symphonic music. The four *Fantasia Brasileira* (1929, 1931, 1934, 1936) include some of Mignone's best works of the late 1920s and 1930s. They are rhapsodic in character and technically demanding on pianists. The harmony is triadic with passages of parallel seventh chords, and popular dances and folk music strongly influence the pieces. The *Fantasia Brasileira* no. 1 is Mignone's musical response to criticism leveled at his European style. The concerto (1958) displays virtuoso piano writing, European romanticism, and elements of Portuguese, Indian, and Negro music. The first movement contains the raised fourth and lowered seventh scale degrees common to music of northeastern Brazil. The *Burlesca e Toccata* (1958) has a serial *Burlesca* and a pandiatonic *toccata.* The concerto (1966) for violin, piano, and orchestra is from an era when Mignone's style was eclectic, with polytonality, tone clusters, atonality, and serialism.

Joao de Souze Lima (1898–), founding member of the Brazilian Academy of Music, received a government scholarship to study at the Paris *Conservatoire* with Philipp and Long. In 1923, he began a concert career with piano performances throughout Europe and South America, then he settled in São Paulo to conduct an orchestra and teach at the Carlos Gomes Conservatory. He composed the *Minueto* (1918), the *O Rei Mameluco* (1938), the *Poema dos Americas* (1942), the *Suite Mirim* (1959) in five movements, the concerto (1965), and the *Three Brazilian Dances.*

Dinorá de Carvalho (1905–) studied with Philipp in Paris and toured Italy and Brazil as a pianist. She was the first woman to join the Brazilian Academy of Music, and she established and directed the Women's Orchestra of São Paulo, the earliest all-women orchestra in South America. Her compositional style draws from indigenous music of Brazil and the harmonic vocabulary of Debussy. Among her compositions is the fantasia-concerto (1937), the *Dancas Brasileiras* (1940), the *Contrastes* (1930?, 1969?), and the concerto no. 2 (1972).

Radamés Gnattali (1906–) studied in Rio de Janeiro and conducted the National

Radio Orchestra. He toured Brazil as a pianist, and helped establish the Brazilian Academy of Music. Up to 1945, his nationalistic and post-romantic compositions include the concerto (1933) for violin, piano, and string quartet, the concerto nos. 1 and 2 (1934, 1936), and the concertino (1942) for piano, flute, and string orchestra. From about 1945 into the 1960s, his style had a subtle and reserved use of national resources and a return to neo-romantic and neo-baroque ideas. From those years come the *Três Movementos* (1947) for piano, string orchestra, and timpanis; the *Brasiliana* no. 2 (1948) for piano, string orchestra, and drums in three movements marked "Samba de Morro," "Samba Cançao," and "Samba de Batucada"; the *Variaçao Sôbre uma Série de Sons* (1949) for piano, violin, and orchestra; the *Concêrto Romântico* no. 1 (1949); the *Brasiliana* nos. 6 and 9 (1954, 1960); and the concerto no. 3 (1960). During the 1960s, his compositions contained the folk and popular music of Brazil, and among those works are the *Concêrto Romântico* no. 2 (1964) and the concerto no. 4 (1967).

Camargo Guarnieri (1907–) studied in São Paulo and Paris with Koechlin, joined the faculty at the São Paulo Conservatory, and helped establish the Brazilian Academy of Music. His music is nationalistic, neo-classic, polyphonic, and rhythmic, and the tempo indications are in Portuguese and Brazilian. He has five concertos (1931, 1946, 1964, 1967, 1970), the *Variations on a Theme of the Northeast* (1953), the *chôro* (1956), the concertino (1961) and the *Seresta* (1965) with chamber orchestra. The concerto no. 2 has a sonata form for the first movement, an ABA structure for the second movement, and a rondo for the third movement. He is fond of native instruments, rhythmic and metric changes, ostinatos, and accents out of phase with the meters.

José de Lima Siqueira (1907–) studied at the National School of Music in Rio de Janeiro, established and conducted the Brazilian Symphony Orchestra, founded the Symphonic Orchestra of Rio Janeiro, and taught at the National School of Music. His concert music has elements of folk and Afro-Brazilian music of northeastern Brazil. Siqueira developed theoretical concepts he named "Brazilian tri-modal" and "Brazilian penta-modal" systems based on scales of the region. He composed three concertos (1955, 1965, 1966) and the concertino (1973) in one movement of three sections.

César Guerra-Peixe (1914–) settled in Rio de Janeiro in 1934 as a performer and composer of popular music. He studied composition with Koellreutter, who championed the Second Viennese School, and Guerra-Peixe's early works follow the twelve-tone method of Schoenberg. About 1949, he turned from serialism to a conservative style with triads, traditional forms, homophonic writing, and folk music of northeastern Brazil. The *Pequeno Concêrto* (1956) is in the conservative style.

Eunice Catunda (1915–) played piano concerts and taught at the University of Brasilia. She studied composition with Guarnieri and serialism with Maderna in Europe. In a style that merges elements of folk music with the twelve-tone method, she composed the concerto (1955).

Hans Joachim Koellreutter (1915–) studied in Berlin and Geneva, and in 1937 emigrated to Brazil, where he became a leading exponent of the twelve-tone method and opposed nationalism based on folk music. He taught many Brazilian composers and strongly influenced Brazil's concert music. In 1939, he founded the music group

Musica Viva Brasil to promote contemporary music. His own music frequently has classic forms and the twelve-tone method. The *konzertmusik* (1946), sometimes listed as *musica concertante,* is from when Koellreutter adhered to Schoenberg's ideas.

Claudio Santoro (1919–), Italian descent, learned the twelve-tone method from Koellreutter at the Rio de Janeiro Conservatory. The *música concertante* (1944) is in the twelve-tone style. Boulanger turned Santoro from the twelve-tone method and the concerto no. 1 (1951) has a clear tonal center, polyphonic textures, and conventional forms. The first movement, titled "Chôro," contains two styles of popular Brazilian music, parallel harmonic structures, and triadic chords with added seconds and sevenths. He founded the Music Department at the University of Brasilia, and taught there for several years. He composed two concertos (1958–1959, 1960) in Brasilia. In Rio de Janeiro he taught and probably composed the *Intermitencias* III (1967). He began teaching at the *Hochschule für Musik* in Heidelberg, Germany, and returned to Brazil in 1978. A symphony is for two pianos and orchestra.

Ernst Widmer (1927–), born and educated in Switzerland, settled in Bahia in 1956, and directed the School of Music at the Federal University. Early influences on his music are Stravinsky, Bartók, and Hindemith, and the *Bahia-Concerto,* op. 17 (1958), evidences those elements. Other works are the *Prismas,* op. 70 (1971), and the aleatoric *ENTROnacamentos SONoros,* op. 75 (1972), for piano, five trombones, strings, and tape.

Edino Krieger (1928–) studied with Copland at the Berkshire (now Tanglewood) Music Center, with Mennin at the Juilliard School of Music, with Krenek in Brazil, with Berkeley at the Royal Academy of Music in London, England, and with Koellreutter on serial techniques. In 1953, he adopted neo-classicism and nationalism as evidenced in the *concertante* (1955). Since 1965, he has merged serialism with elements of Brazilian popular music; among these works is the toccata (1967).

Correa de Oliveira (1938–) studied in São Paulo and with Stockhausen and Boulez, composed music with the twelve-tone method and serialism, joined the Musica Nova Group in support of avant-garde music, worked for several firms, and taught at the University of São Paulo from 1969. The *Ouviver a Musica* (1965) for strings and piano is a serial work.

Marlos Nobre (1939–) studied at the Pernambuco Conservatory, and probably with Koellreutter about the time he composed the concertino, op. 1 (1959). He attended the São Paulo Conservatory, and studied with Ginastera in Buenos Aires while working on the divertimento, op. 14 (1963). He composed the *concerto breve,* op. 33 (1969), in Rio de Janeiro or New York City. Nobre uses the improvisational rhythms of the folk music of northeastern Brazil, free serialism since 1964, and aleatory techniques and proportional notation after 1967.

José de Almeida Prado (1943–) studied with Guarnieri and in Paris with Boulanger and Messiaen. From the 1960s, he followed a style similar to post-Weberian serialism, and used elements of Brazilian folk music. Since 1974, he has been on the faculty at the Art Institute of the State University. For piano and orchestra, he composed the *Variaçoes* (1963–1964) and the *Exoflora* (1974). The *Aurora* (1975) is for piano, wind quintet, and orchestra.

Table 40 Additional Composers in Brazil

Names	Dates	Compositions
Almedia, Waldemar de	1904–	*Danza de Indios*
Almedida, Carlos de	1906–	*Introduçao e Dança Brasileira*
Barros Marcarian, Nadile de	1914–	*Poema*
Barroso Neto, Joaquin	1881–1941	*Minha Terra*
Bosman, Arthur	1908–	*Cymbalum*
Cameu, Helza	1903–	Concerto (1936)
Campos, Meneleu	1872–1927	Concerto
Jabor, Najla	1915–	Concerto
Kiefer, Bruno	1923–	*Diálogo* (1966)
Mariz, Vasco	1921–	3 Concertos (1951/58/60)
Morozowicz, Henrique	1934–	Divertimento (1969)
Mussurunga, Bento	? –	*Ondas do Iapó*
Priolli, Maria	1915–	Concerto (1940)
Siqueira, Baptista	1906–	*Northeast Symphony* Concerto
Tacuchian, Ricardo	1939–	Concertino (1977)
Vieira Brandao, José	1911–	Fantasia *Concertante* (1936, rev 1954)

Uruguay

Luis Sambucetti (1860–) went to Paris in 1885 to study at the *Conservatoire* and, after returning to Montevideo, worked as a violinist, composer, and band director. His compositions are triadic, with traditional forms and features of folk music. He composed the *Tarantelle Caprice* for piano and orchestra, and the cadenza (perf. 1913) for Beethoven's concerto no. 1.

Luis Cluzeau-Mortet (1889–1957) was the first Uruguayan to win a prize at the Paris *Conservatoire*. In Montevideo, he worked as a pianist, and played first violin in the Uruguay Radio Symphony Orchestra. His compositional style is romantic, with elements of contemporary techniques. Among his musical compositions is the *burlesca* (ca. 1920–1925), the *fantasia concierto* (1927, rev. 1938) and the *Fantasia Criolla y Burlesca*.

César Cortinas (1890–1918), student of Bruch in Berlin, composed music with elements of nineteenth-century romanticism and his Uruguayan contemporaries. The concerto (pub. 1940) is for piano and orchestra.

Ramón Rodriquez Socas (1890–) trained in Montevideo and at the G. Verdi Conservatory in Milan, Italy. After returning home, he adopted nationalistic traits. Although most of his compositional efforts are in opera, he left the concerto (1943) for piano and orchestra.

Vincente Ascone (1897–1979), born in Italy, emigrated with his family to Uruguay while a child. He directed the Municipal Band of Montevideo, and taught at the Municipal School of Music. His musical nationalism contains Uruguayan folk songs and traditional European forms. The *Rapsodia Criolla* (perf. 1944) is a concerto along classic lines. A much later work is the *Politonal* (1967).

Carlos Giucci (1904–1958) composed music with Uruguayan musical elements. He left the nationalistic fantasia (1920s?) and the contrapuntal *Tierra Adentro* (1938).

Guido Santórsola (1904–), born in Italy, studied at the Conservatory of São Paulo in Brazil and in Europe, took Uruguayan citizenship in 1936, worked as a conductor and string performer, and established the Uruguayan Cultural Association and the Kleiber Quartet. His early musical compositions have elements of Brazilian folk music; later works show features of Uruguayan folk music, then he turned to atonality and serialism. The concerto (1938–1939) is for piano and orchestra.

Carlos Estrada (1909–1970) studied in Paris, established the Chamber Orchestra of Montevideo, worked for the State Radio, taught at the National Conservatory of Music, and conducted the Municipal Symphony Orchestra. The concertino, op. 24 (1944), is neo-classic.

Robert Eugenio Lagarmilla (1913–) wrote music criticism for the newspaper *La Mañana*. The music of Uruguay and Central America provides the inspiration for his music which includes the concerto (1943) for piano and orchestra.

Alberto Soriano (1915–) settled in Montevideo and taught enthnomusicology at the university. His music has the melorhythms of South America, classic forms, and brilliant orchestrations. He composed the concerto (1952) before joining the university faculty.

Jaurés Lamarque Pons (1917–), influenced by Afro-Uruguayan traditions, composed the concerto (perf. 1959) for piano, strings, and percussion.

Héctor Tosar-Errecart (1923–) taught at the Montevideo Conservatory and the Puerto Rico Conservatory. Neo-classic features and elements of Latin American melodies and rhythms occur in the concertino (1941) and the sinfonia *concertante* (1957).

Antonio Mastro-Giovanni (1936–) uses traditional forms and style in his music. The *concierto* (1964) has three movements to be played without pauses.

Peru

Ernesto Lopez Mindreau (1890–) studied in New York City and Berlin with Scharwenka and Leichentritt, and concertized as a pianist in Berlin, London, Paris, Madrid, Brussels, and other European cities. In 1929, he returned to Peru to teach in Lima. The indigenous music of Peru is strong in the *Tema y Variaciones* (1936) for piano and orchestra.

Rudolph Holzmann (1910–) was born in Germany and attended the Klindworth-Scharwenka Conservatory in Berlin. While he was pursuing a concert career in Europe, the Peruvian government invited him to teach at the Lima Conservatory beginning in 1945. He taught oboe at the Alzebo Academy, played violin in the Peruvian National Symphony Orchestra and became very important in Peruvian music during the 1940s and 1950s. Some Peruvian musical ideas appear in his compositions, which feature Hindemith's tonal ideas. The three-movement divertimento *concertante* (1941) for piano and ten woodwinds presents the piano in a solo style, and passages effectively blending with the woodwinds. Other compositions are the concerto or concertino (1947) for two pianos and orchestra, and the *Concierto Para la Ciudad Blanca* (1949). Many of Holzmann's compositions have traditional European forms, developments, canons, and variations.

Enrique Pinilla (1927–), anti-nationalist, recognizes the need for regional composers to evolve a distinct Latin American style by blending European techniques with musical material of South America. He uses polytonality, atonality, serialism, electronic music ideas and shifting meters. The concerto (1970) is for piano and orchestra.

Edgar Valcárcel (1932–) studied at the Lima Conservatory, Hunter College in New York City, and in Buenos Aires with Ginastera, Paris with Messiaen, and Italy with Malipiero, Maderna, and Dallapiccola. In Lima, he taught at the conservatory. Musically, he is anti-nationalistic, and he prefers serialism and aleatoric techniques. Among his compositions is the concerto (1968).

Ecuador

Luis Salgado (1903–) trained at the conservatory and later became the director. He wrote an important study on Ecuadorean folklore and folk music. His musical compositions include the programmatic concerto *Consagracion de las Virgenes del Sol* (1941), the *concierto fantasia* (1948), and the *Tercer Concierto* (1958–1959).

Bolivia

Eduardo Caba (1890–1953) studied in Buenos Aires and in Spain with Turina. In 1942, he settled in La Paz, and composed music using pentantonic scales of Bolivian folk songs. *El Poema del Charange* is for piano and orchestra.

Alberto Villapando (1955–) composed the *Musica para Piano e Pequena Orquesta* (1968) in three parts titled *El Mundo del Amor, El Mundo del Miedo,* and *El Mundo del Silencio.* Tempo indications are in Spanish, and contemporary techniques are chord clusters, string plucking, and harmonics on the piano strings.

Paraguay

Carlos Lara-Bareiro (1914–) writes music influenced by the folk music of Paraguay. He composed the concerto (1949) for piano and orchestra in Paraguay or Rio de Janeiro. He established the Symphony Orchestra in Ascunción in 1951, and later settled in Buenos Aires, Argentina, as a composer, teacher, and conductor.

Argentina

Jamie Pahissa (1880–1969), Spanish composer and musicologist, arrived in Buenos Aires in 1937. In Barcelona he studied musical composition, and, in Buenos Aires, trained as an architect. He devised a compositional style using free tonality and polytonality. The *Somni d'Infant* (1949) is for piano and orchestra.

Alfredo Pinto (1891–1968), born in Italy, where he studied with Longo in Naples, emigrated to Argentina, and established the Wagnerian Association in Buenos Aires. His style displays features of his Italian heritage and elements of Argentinean Indian music. Among his compositions is the *Pezzo di Concerto* or *Concertstück* (1922) and the four-movement suite *Serie Popular Italiana* (1934).

José Maria Castro (1892–1964), cellist and brother of Juan José Castro, trained in Buenos Aires and in Paris with d'Indy. He returned to Buenos Aires in 1930 and conducted the *Orquesta Filharmónica* and the Municipal Band. His concerto (1941, rev. 1956) for piano and orchestra merges traditional forms with neo-classic style.

Juan José Castro (1895–1968), brother of José Maria Castro, organized and conducted the *Orquesta de Nacimiento,* and conducted at the *Teatro Colon.* He and his brother established the Quartet Society and started the *Grupo Renovación.* Like José, Juan studied in Buenos Aires and in Paris with d'Indy. His compositional style depends on characteristics of Spanish music without quoting authentic material, and ideas he learned from d'Indy. The concerto (1941) is neo-classic.

Jacobo Ficher (1896–1978), born in Odessa, Russia, studied at the St. Petersburg Conservatory and settled in Buenos Aires in 1923 as a violinist in theater orchestras. He helped establish the Argentinean Composers' League, joined the faculty at the University of La Plata, and taught at the National Conservatory. He composed three piano concertos: op. 53 (1945), op. 81 (1954), and op. 103 (1960). His style displays neo-classic elements and ideas he learned from Tcherepnin in Russia.

Juan Carlos Paz (1901–1972) studied music in Buenos Aires and in Paris with d'Indy, and helped organize the *Grupo Renovación* to promote new music. Up to ca. 1927, he composed in a neo-classic style akin to Stravinsky. Between 1927 and 1934 his neo-classic style became more contrapuntal, atonal, and polytonal, and in 1934 he began using Schoenberg's twelve-tone method. The concerto no. 1 (1932) is for piano and wind quintet of flute, oboe, clarinet, bassoon, and trumpet. The concerto no. 2 (1934) is for piano with a wind quintet of oboe, trumpet, two horns, and bassoon. The *Musica* (1963) for piano and orchestra has free atonality, aleatoric techniques, and explorations of rhythmic and timbral ideas.

Arnaldo D'Espósito (1907–1945) studied at the *Conservatorio Nacional de Musica y Arte Escéncia* and later taught there. From 1928, he was an assistant conductor at the *Teator Colón.* The concerto (1934) has a lyric style.

Juan Emilio Martini (1910–) conducted important orchestras in several cities, including Lima, Montevideo, Rio de Janeiro, Caracas, Santiago, and São Paulo. He composed the concertino (1939) for piano and orchestra while the conductor at the *Teatro Colón.*

Roberto Garcia Morillo (1911–) taught at the National Conservatory in Buenos Aires, and wrote music criticism for *La Nacion.* He studied at the *Escuela Argentinal de Música,* the *Conservatorio Nacional de Música y Arte,* and in Paris with Yvers Nat. Influences on his early compositional style were Stravinsky, Bartók, and Scriabin. The *Overture Bersserke* (perf. 1932) is for piano and small orchestra. The National Commission on Culture commissioned the concerto, op. 6 (1937–1939), and

La Mascara y el Rostro, op. 33 (1963), which is a choreographed concerto for piano and orchestra.

Alberto Ginastera (1916–1983) studied at the National Conservatory of Music and in the United States on a Guggenheim Fellowship. Returning to Buenos Aires, he joined the faculty at the conservatory and became the dean of the *Facultad de Artes y Ciencias Musicales* at the Catholic University in 1958. His nationalistic style merges Argentinean folk music with twentieth-century European compositional techniques. The concertos for piano and orchestra are three in number: *Concierto Argentino* (1935), no. 1, op. 28 (1961), and no. 2 (1972). Koussevitsky commissioned the four-movement concerto no. 1. The work is on a row and in traditional formal structures. The first movement is the "cadanza e varianti," with the "varianti" being ten microstructures with differing moods. The second movement is a three-section "scherzo" between an introduction and coda, with pointillistic orchestration. The third movement is similar to a ternary form, and the fourth movement is a "toccata concertata" similar to a rondo with a short introduction and coda. The concerto no. 2 has a first movement of thirty variations based on a chord taken from the last movement of Beethoven's symphony no. 9. The second movement is for left hand alone, and the third movement has material from the last movement of Chopin's sonata no. 3.

Marcelo Koc (1918–) was born in Russia and trained at the Lodz Conservatory in Poland. In 1938, he immigrated to Buenos Aires, where he became active in the Association of Young Argentine Composers and the Union of Argentine Composers. The concertino (1958) is for piano and ten instruments.

Silvano Picchi (1922–), born in Italy, immigrated to Buenos Aires, where he studied with Ginastera. He writes music criticism for *La Prensa,* and his compositional style has interesting sonorities. The concerto (1965) is in two movements.

Robert Caamaño (1923–), touring concert pianist, was the best Argentinean instrumentalist, according to the Association of Argentine Music Critics. He trained at the *Conservatorio Nacional* and taught there, directed artistic matters at the *Teatro Colón,* and joined the composition faculty at the *Pontifica Universita Catolica Argentina*. His music displays traditional chord progressions, features of folklore, spontaneity, and neo-classic elements. For piano and orchestra, he composed the concerto no. 1, op. 22 (1958), and no. 2 (1971).

Werner Wagner (1927–) was born in Germany and settled in Buenos Aires as a composer and impresario. He served as the president of the Association of Young Composers of Argentina, and helped found the Composers Union. The concerto, op. 12 (1964), is for piano and orchestra.

Alcides Lanza (1929–), avant-garde composer, studied with Messiaen, Malipiero, Copland, Maderna, and Ussachevsky. The concerto (1964) for piano and orchestra displays atonality, sonorities, clusters, and pointillism.

Gerardo Gandini (1936–) established the *Grupo de Experimentacion Musical* to promote avant-garde music and taught at the Catholic University of Argentina, the Buenos Aires Province Conservatory, the Di Tella Institute, and the American Opera Center at the Juilliard School in New York City. In Buenos Aires, he studied with Ginastera and Caamaño, and he studied in Italy and the United States. His compositions

Table 41 Additional Composers in Argentina

Names	Dates	Compositions
Aretz, Isabel	1909–	*Danzas con Interludio* (1933–36)
Arizaga, Rodolfo	1926–	Concerto (1963)
Biondo, Juan Carlos	1933–	4 Concertos (1964/68/70/74)
Bringuer, Estela	1931–	Concerto, op 25 (1963)
Calcagno, Elsa	1910–	Concerto (1935)
		Fantasia Argentina (1941)
		Fantasia y Variaciones Classicas (1942)
Castro, Washington	1909–	Concerto (1960)
Drangosch, Ernesto	1882–1925	Concerto (1912)
Fracassi, Elmérico	1874–1930	Concerto
Franchisena, César Mario	1923–	Concerto (1954)
Garcia Munoz, Carmen	1929–	Concerto
Gianneo, Luis	1897–1968	Concerto (1941)
Guastavino, Carlos	1912–	*Romance de Sante Fe* (1952)
Iglesia Villoud, Hector	1913–	*Embrujo Pampeano* (1952)
Krieger, Armando	1940–	Concerto (1963) 2 pnos
		Metamorphose d'Apres une Lecture de Kafka (1968)
Kuri-Aldana, Mario	1931–	*Pasos* (1963)
Lamuraglia, Nicolás	1896–	Suite (perf 1936)
Lopez-Buchardo, Próspero	1883–1964	*Nidos* (1939)
Maragno, Virtú	1928–	Concertino (1954)
		Dialogos Sin Voz (1968)
Ogando, Eduardo	1933–	Concertino
Patino Andrade, Graziela	1920–	Sinfonia
Pedro, Roque de.	1935–	Concerto (1968)
Pemberton, Carlos	1932–	*Concertino da Camera* (1962)
Rattenbach, Augusto	1927–	Concerto (1956)
Romaniello, Luis	1862–	Concerto
Roqué Alsina, Carlos	1941–	*Approach,* op 30 (1972–73)
		Señales (1977)
Sammartino, Luis	1890–	Suite
Scheller Zembrano, Maria	1917–1944	Concerto (1939)
Sciammarella, Valdo	1924–	*Variaciones concertantes* (1952)
Sebastiani, Pia	1925–	Concerto (1941)
Siccardi, Honorio	1897–1963	Double Concerto (by 1947)
		Concerto (1950)
Tada Paz, Herberto di	1903–	Suite (1930)
Tauriello, Antonio	1931–	*Musica* III (1965)
		Concerto (1968)
		Masion de Tlaloc (1969)
Wilensky, Osias	1933–	Concerto

draw upon serial techniques and interesting timbres. He has the concertino (1959–1960), the *Contrastes* (1968) for two pianos and chamber orchestra, the *Fantasia Impromptu* (1970), the *L'Adiu* (1967) for piano and percussion, and the concertino III (1962–1963) for harpsichord and instruments. The *Contrastes* is an exploration of contrasts in textures, dynamics, and other musical elements. In the *Fantasia Impromptu,* Gandini used a Chopin mazurka to create a musical portrait of Chopin.

Chile

Alfonso Leng (1884/94–1974) trained as a dentist and musician, taught dentistry and joined the Group of the Ten to bring modern musical ideas to Chile. The fantasia (1927) follows German romanticism, and Rachmaninoff influenced the piano writing.

Enrique Soro (1884–1954) studied at the conservatory in Milan, Italy, at age 14, and joined the faculty at the National Conservatory. His music has the Italian lyricism of the romantic era and elements of the folk music of Chile. Among his works are the *Impresiones Liricas* (1908), the concerto, op. 32 (1918), and the *6 Estudios Melodicos* (ca. 1920).

Pedro Humberto Allende (1885–) studied at the National Conservatory and later joined the faculty. He is a musical pioneer, and represented Chile at international musical events. His compositions have traditional harmony and French impressionism. For piano and orchestra, he composed the *Concerto Sinfonico* (1945) and some *tonadas.*

Domingo Santa Cruz (1899–) received a law degree from the University of Chile and, simultaneously, studied musical composition with Soro. While in Spain as a secretary at the Chilean Embassy, he studied musical composition with Campo in Madrid and, after returning to Chile, gave up law to pursue music. In 1928, he began teaching at the National Conservatory, and as the dean of Fine Arts he greatly improved musical training in Chile. His compositions show the dual influences of European neo-classicism and Chilean melodies. On a Chilean song, he composed the variations in three movements, op. 20 (1942–1943), with the dimensions of a concerto; it is the earliest work of this genre to have historical importance in Chile. The sinfonia *concertante* (perf. 1945) is for flute, piano, and strings.

Pablo Garrido (1905–) studied music in Paris, and settled in Santiago in 1934. His ethnomusicological interests prompted field work in several South American countries and in Spain, and his compositions evidence folk music. He composed the fantasia *Submarina* (1932), the *Rapsodia Chilena* (1937–1938), and the concerto (1950).

Jorge Urrutia-Blondel (1905–) studied with Allende and Santa Cruz, and traveled to Paris to study with Boulanger, Dukas, and Koechlin, and to Berlin to study with Hindemith. In 1931, he began teaching at the conservatory in Santiago and, while there, he composed the concerto, op. 30 (1938–1950), for piano and orchestra.

Alfonso Letelier (1912–) studied with Allende at the National Conservatory and later joined the faculty. *La Vida del Campo,* op. 14 (1937), is a symphonic movement in sonata form that displays French impressionism, Chilean folk music, and piano writing akin to Rachmaninoff.

Esteban Eitler (1913–1960) was born in Austria, trained at the University of Budapest, and settled in Santiago in 1945. The concertino (1947) is for piano and eleven instruments.

Table 42 Additional Composers in Chile

Names	Dates	Compositions
Becerra-Schmidt, Gustavo	1925–	Concerto (1958)
Helfritz, Hans	1902–	Concertino, hpd
		Concertino, pno
Mackenna, Carmela	1879–1962	Concerto (1933)
Riesco, Carlos	1925–	Concerto (1961–63)
Sepulveda, Maria Luisa	1898–1959	Suite

Juan Orrego-Salas (1919–) studied architecture at the Catholic University and music with Allende and Santa Cruz at the National Conservatory and with R. Thompson at Princeton University in the United States. He taught at the University of Chile and at Indiana University in the United States. Early compositions have neo-classic traits, baroque rhythms and lines, and his style evolved toward disjunct melodies and rhythms, quartal and altered chords, and clusters. Later, he delved into the twelve-tone method and atonality. Among his compositions are the concerto, op. 28 (1950), the *Concerto a Tre,* op. 52 (1962), for violin, cello, piano and orchestra, and the *Volte,* op. 67 (1971), for piano, fifteen wind instruments, harp, and percussion.

Cuba

José Ardévol (1911–) was born in Barcelona, Spain, settled in Havana in 1930, and became an important composer in the 1940s and 1950s. His style features neo-classic techniques, polyphony, polytonal and pandiatonic harmonies, Cuban folk music and popular melodies. The concerto *grosso* (1937) is for piano, flute, oboe, bassoon, two trumpets, and orchestra; the concerto (1938) is for three pianos and orchestra; and the concerto (1944) is for piano, winds, and percussion. In the 1950s, he turned toward the style of Webern.

Harold Gramatges (1918–) studied with Roldán and Ardévol at the Havana Conservatory and with Copland in the United States. In 1943, he banded together several Cuban composers to found the *Grupo de Renovacón Musical* to promote modern music, and he wrote criticism for the group's bulletin and the *Diario de Cuba.* The neo-classic concertino (1945) is for piano and wind instruments.

Julian Orbón (1925–), born in Spain, moved to Cuba about 1935, studied with Copland in the United States, and directed the Orbón Conservatory. In 1964, he went to New York City and taught at Lenox College, Barnard College, and the Hispanic Institute of Columbia University. His compositional style shows influences of Falla, the two Halffters, neo-classicism, Chávez, and Villa-Lobos. The overture *concertante* (1942) is for flute, piano, and chamber orchestra.

Table 43 Additional Composers in Cuba

Names	Dates	Compositions
Adam, Maria Emma	1875–	*Serenade Andalouse*
Csonka, Paul	1905–	Cuban Concerto I
García Catural, Alejandro	1906–	Concerto (1926)
		Primera Suite Cubana (1931)
González, Hilario	1930–	Concerto (1943)
Jiménez, José	? –	Concerto
Lecuona, Ernesto	1896–1963	*Rapsodia Negra* (1943)
León, Argeliers	1918–	Concertino (1948)
		Sonatas par la Virgen de Cobre
Tomás, Guillermo	1868–1933	*Esbos de Mi Tierra*

The Dominican Republic

Juan Francisco García (1892–), autodidactic composer, draws on elements of Dominican music for his concert music. While he was the director of the National Conservatory, he composed the fantasia *concertante* (1949).

Enrique Mejía-Arredondo (1901–) directed the Dominican Symphony Orchestra and wrote music criticism for *La Opinion*. His compositional style uses conventional forms, traditional harmony, and elements of Dominican folk music. Among his compositions is a concerto for piano and orchestra.

Enrique de Marchena (1908–) studied at the National University and the *Liceo Musical de Santo Domingo,* wrote music criticism for the *Listin Diario,* and became the director of fine arts. His musical style evidences romantic elements and impressionistic sonorities. He was composing a piano concerto in 1946 and 1947.

Chapter 20

Australia, New Zealand, The Philippines, Japan, China, Vietnam, and India

Australia

Alfred Hill (1870–1960) studied at the Leipzig Conservatory with Reinecke and followed the compositional styles of Bruch, Goetz, Mendelssohn, and Schumann. He played violin in the *Gewandhaus* Orchestra under the batons of Brahms, Grieg, and Tchaikovsky, and taught in New Zealand and at the Sydney Conservatory. As a champion of Australian musical nationalism, he added elements of Maori and Australian aboriginal music to his German romantic style. The concerto (ca. 1936) for piano and orchestra has four movements.

Percy Brier (1885–1970) established the Brisbane Chamber Music Society and the Music Teachers' Association of Queensland. He was an important recitalist, adjudicator, lecturer, and author in Queensland. He left the fantasia (1924) for piano, chorus, and orchestra, two *fantasie concertos,* and a concerto.

Hooper Brewster-Jones (1887–1949) debuted as a pianist at the Adelaide Town Hall at age 6, studied with Bridge and Stanford at the Royal College of Music, London, pursued a concert career in Paris, Germany, and London, and settled in Adelaide. As a pianist, he performed French music of the twentieth century, and as a composer he followed a style influenced by Debussy and Ravel. He composed four piano concertos, and the *Australian Concerto* (by 1945) is Brewster-Jones' second and most performed concerto.

Mirrie Irma Hill (née Solomon, 1892–) studied with A. Hill before their marriage, and taught at the New South Wales Conservatorium. For piano and orchestra, she composed the rhapsody (1914) and the *Three Aboriginal Dances* (1950).

Frank Hutchens (1892–1965), born in New Zealand, studied with Matthay and Corder at the Royal Academy of Music in London, taught at the Royal Academy, and joined the faculty of the State Conservatory in Sydney. His compositional interests were in educational music. Among his compositions is the concerto symphonique (1936), the concerto (1940) for two pianos and orchestra, the fantasy concerto (1944) for two pianos and orchestra, and the concerto (1950) for piano and strings.

Margaret Sutherland (1897–) studied in Australia, London, and Vienna; the influences on her music are Bax, Bartók, Hindemith, and baroque forms. The concertino (1940) is for piano and orchestra.

William Lovelock (1899–) studied at the Trinity College of Music, London, and joined the faculty. After returning to Brisbane, he directed the Queensland State Conservatorium of Music, and wrote music criticism for the *Courier Mail*. The concerto (1963) is for piano and orchestra.

Clive Douglas (1903–1977), conductor, studied at the Melbourne Conservatory, and worked for the Australian Broadcasting Commission. While on the faculty at the Melbourne Conservatory, he composed the divertimento no. 2, op. 84 (1962), for two pianos and chamber orchestra. He was fond of using Australian national melodies and rhythms.

Felix Werder (1922–), German-born, was in England at the declaration of war between Germany and England, and the British government interned him in Australia for the duration of the war. He stayed in Australia, taught in Melbourne high schools, and wrote criticism for the newspaper *The Age*. Influences on his compositional style are Hebrew chant, German and Austrian romanticism, Hindemith, the twelve-tone method, serialism, pointillism, and aleatoric ideas. Schoenberg was a family friend, and Werder developed a feeling for the twelve-tone method. He composed more than 500 works, and renounced more than half. The concerto, op. 18 (1955), is for piano and orchestra.

Keith Humbel (1927–), performer of modern music, studied at the Conservatory of Melbourne and with Leibowitz in Paris. He taught at the University of California at San Diego, then returned to Melbourne. His music displays influences of British, French, and American contemporary music. The *Arpes la Legende* (1969) is for piano and orchestra.

Richard Meale (1932–), pianist, studied at the New South Wales Conservatorium. He learned a variety of musical styles when he was a buying agent for a chain of record stores. The sinfonia (1959) for piano, four-hands, and strings is in a conventional style he learned at the conservatorium. In 1960, he took a six-month break to rethink his compositional ideas, and now Meale explores the avant-garde styles of Boulez and Stockhausen, non-western music, and expressionism. In 1971, he joined the faculty of the Music Department of the University of Adelaide.

Colin Brumby (1933–), interested in opera and poetry, taught at the Brisbane Teacher's Training College, and joined the faculty at the University of Queensland. He likes contemporary techniques, including the twelve-tone method. He tried to withhold the *Realisation* (1966), but the composition has been published.

Donald Hollier (1934–) took training at the New South Wales State Conservatorium, the Royal Academy of Music in London, and the University of London. He composed the concerto no. 1 (1966) while the director of music at Newington College in Sydney, and the concerto no. 2 (1972) while on the faculty at the Canberra School of Music.

Barry Conyngham (1944–) studied in Sydney and the United States at the University of California in San Diego and at Princeton University, and taught at Melbourne University. His music has elements of Ligeti and Zenakis, tone clusters, and colorful textures. In Japan, he composed *Water . . . Footsteps . . . Time . . .* (1970–1971) for piano, harp, electric guitar, tam-tam, and orchestra. The *Southern Cross* (1981) is a double concerto for piano, violin and orchestra.

Elena Katz (1957–) was born and trained in Russia. While a student at the New South Wales Conservatorium, she composed the concerto (1978–1979) for piano and orchestra.

Table 44 Additional Composers in Australia

Names	Dates	Compositions
Buesst, Victor	1885–	Concerto, 3 pnos
Butterley, Nigel	1935–	*Explorations*
Davy, Rudy	1883–	Concerto
Eagles, Moneta	1924–	*Diversions* (1951)
		Autumn Rhapsody (1964)
Edwards, Ross	1943–	*Choros* (1971)
Evans, Lindley	1895–	*Idyll* (by 1936), 2 pnos
Gethen, Felix	1916–	Concertino (1955)
Penberthy, James	1917–	3 Concertos (1947/55/74)
Perkins, Horace	1901–	Concertos
Sitsky, Larry	1934–	Concerto (ca. 1978).

New Zealand

Edwin Carr (1926–) studied musical composition with Frankel at the Guildhall School of Music in London, England, with Petrassi in Rome and with Orff at the Munich *Hochschule für Musik*. He returned to New Zealand, taking a position in the Sufform Rural Schools. After 1961, he used the twelve-tone method. The concerto (1959) is for piano and orchestra.

David Farquhar (1928–) studied at Victoria University and in England at Cambridge University and the Guildhall School of Music, London. In 1953, he returned to New Zealand to teach at Victoria University. The concertino (1960) for piano and strings is a highly rhythmic work in a style akin to Prokofieff.

The Philippines

Nicanor Abelardo (1892/93–1934) brought the sonata form to the Philippines. The concerto, op. 23 (1923), is the first piano concerto by a Filipino composer. Folk melodies are an important influence on his music.

Rodolfo Cornejo (1909–) toured the United States, Canada, and Europe giving piano recitals and conducting orchestras. He studied at the Conservatory of Music at the University of the Philippines and the Chicago Musical College, and taught at several institutions in the Philippines. He has three concertos (1933, 1950, 1968), the first of which was a graduation piece at the Chicago Musical College. The *Philippine Rhapsodies* nos. 1–3 (1939, 1942, 1947) and the *Taurus Fantasy* (1957) are for piano and orchestra.

Rosalina Abejo (1922–), nun in the order of the Virgin Mary, studied theory and composition in the Philippines, in Cincinnati, Ohio, at the Eastman School of Music, and in Paris with Boulanger and Milhaud. With the permission of Pope John XXIII,

Table 45 Additional Composers in the Philippines

Names	Dates	Compositions
Gamilla, Alice D.	1931–	Concerto (1972)
Hernandez, Juan d.	1881–1945	Concerto (perf 1935–39)
Kasilag, Lucrecia	1918–	Divertissement (1960)
		Concertante (1969)
Pajaro, Eliseo	1915–	Concerto (1964)
Sacramento, Lucino	1908–	3 Concertos (1969/73/74)
Santos, Rosendo	1922–	2 Concertos (1948, 1956)
Santos Ocampo, Amanda	1925–	Concerto (1957)

she became the first nun to conduct a symphony orchestra. As a composer, she uses neo-classic and impressionistic techniques, quartal harmonies and a variety of scales and modes. For piano and orchestra, she composed the *Aeolian Concerto* (1954), the *Jubilee Concerto* (1958), and the concerto *Golden Foundation* (1959–1960). For two pianos and orchestra, she composed the *13 Variations* (1957) and *Mangima Canyon* (1969).

Jose Balingit (1926–) began writing music in a romantic style, and later adopted the twelve-tone method. His career as a concert pianist ended due to a heart condition, which forced him toward a less strenuous activity like musical composition. He studied at the Conservatory of Music at the University of the Philippines and the University of the East. He composed the concerto no. 1 (1951) while at the conservatory.

Japan

Shukichi Mitsukuri (1895–1971) studied chemistry at the Imperial University and musical composition with Georg Schumann in Berlin. The German romantic style is the strongest element in his music. He established the Society of Japanese Composers, and taught at the Music Academy. He left the concertino (1953) and the concerto (1955).

Saburo Moroi (1903–1977), father of composer Makoto Moroi, read literature at Tokyo University. In Berlin, he studied musical composition at the *Hochschule für Musik,* and there composed the concerto (1933) for piano and orchestra. His compositional style owes much to German romantic traditions. Other works for piano and orchestra are the allegro (1947) and the concerto (1977).

Koji Taku (1904–) studied piano with Cortot and composition with Boulanger in Paris, and taught at the Tokyo Music Academy. The suite (1953) is for harpsichord and chamber ensemble.

Hisatada Otaka (1911–1951) studied in Vienna—composition with Marx and conducting with Weingartner. In Tokyo, he conducted the Nippon Symphony Orchestra. He left the rhapsody (1943) for piano and orchestra.

Akihirô Tsukatani (1919–) studied law at Tokyo University and music with S. Moroi. He taught the history of economics at Tokyo University, and later moved to the Music Department. Among his compositions is the concerto (1961) for piano and orchestra.

Yoshirô Irino (1921–1980), born in Vladivostok, studied economics at Tokyo University and worked at the Bank of Tokyo. Meanwhile, he studied musical composition and joined the faculty at the Tokyo Music School. He is the first Japanese composer to use the twelve-tone method, and he leans toward classic structures. The double concerto (1955) is for violin, piano, and orchestra, and the *Music* (1963) is for harpsichord, percussion, and nineteen string instruments.

Ikuma Dan (1924–) trained at the Tokyo Music Academy, and joined the faculty at the Tokyo Music School. He writes film music and scores for television. His opera *Yuzuru* (The Twilight Heron, 1950) is the best-known opera by a Japanese composer. The concerto *grosso* (1965) is for harpsichord and string ensemble.

Akio Yashiro (1929–1976) studied at the National University in Tokyo and in Paris with Boulanger and Messiaen. French musical characteristics are an important part of his music. The concerto (1964–1967) has expanded tonality and varied meters.

Kazuo Fukushima (1930–), autodidactic avant-garde composer, taught at Darmstadt and the *Ueno Gakuen* College in Tokyo. His music merges Japanese *gagaku* and *noh* music with Western serialism. In 1967, the International Society for Contemporary Music recognized Fukushima for the *Twuki-shiro* (The Spirit of the Moon, 1965) for piano, harp, percussion, and fifty-two strings.

Toru Takemitsu (1930–1996) helped establish the music group Experimental Laboratory to promote contemporary Japanese music. His compositions for piano and orchestra are the *Arc* Part I (1963) in three movements, the *Arc* Part II (1964–1966) in three movements, the *Asterism* (1968) in tone row style (See ex. 20–1), and the *Quatrain* (1975) for violin, cello, clarinet, piano, and orchestra. The *Textures* (1964) is the first movement of the *Arc* Part II and apparently a separate composition.

Akira Miyoshi (1933–) read French literature at the University of Tokyo, studied music composition in Tokyo and Paris, and joined the faculty at the *Toho Gakuen*

Example 20–1. Takemitsu *Asterism,* mm. 4–6

Table 46 Additional Composers in Japan

Composers	Dates	Compositions
Abe, Komei	1911–	Concerto (1945)
		Pastoral (1945)
Goh, Tairjiro	1907–1970	2 Concertos (1936, 1940)
Hachimura, Yoshio	1938–	*The Logic of Distraction*
Hara, Kazuko	1935–	Concertino (1966), fl, hpd
Hattori, Koh-Ichi	1933–	Concertino for Small Hands (pub 1968)
Hayasaka, Fumco	1914–1955	Concerto (1946)
Ichikawa, Toshiharu	1913–	Concerto (by 1983)
Ifukude, Akira	1914–	*Symphonie Concertante* (1941)
		Ritmica Ostinata (1961)
Kiyose, Yasuji	1900–1981	Concerto (1954)
Kondo, Jo	1947–	*A Shape of Time* (by 1984)
Kubota, Minako	1972–	*Cheerful Dumbo* (1984)
Kurokawa, Manae	1966–	Concerto (by 1984)
Makino, Yutaka	1930–	2 Concertos (1953, 1971)
Mamiya, Michio	1929–	2 Concertos (1954, 1970)
Matsudaira, Yoritsuné	1907–	Theme & Variations on a Folksong from the Nanbu District (1939)
		Theme & Variations (1952)
		Concerto (1964)
		Concerto da Camera (1964)
		Dialogo Coreografico (1966) 2 pnos
Matsumura, Terzo	1929–	2 Concertos (1973, 1978)
Matsushita, Shin-ichi	1922–	*Ouvrage Symphonique* (1957)
Mayuzumi, Toshiro	1929–	Pieces for Prepared Piano & Strings (1957)
Morio, Makoto	1930–	2 Concertos (1966, 1971)
Nishimura, Yukie	1968–	Concerto (by 1984)
Noda, Teruyuki	1940–	Concerto (1977)
Ogura, Roh	1916–	Concerto (1946)
Takagi, Toroku	1904–	2 Concertos (1942, 1944)
Takahashi, Yuji	1938–	*Kagahi* (1971)
Tamura, Toru	1938–	Concerto (1979)
Toda, Kuio	1915–	2 Concertos (1944, 1945)
Toyama, Yuzo	1931–	2 Concertos (1962, 1963)
Urakabe, Shinji	1970–	Concerto
Yokoyama, Yukio	1971–	Concerto

School of Music. Experiences in France affected his music. The concerto (1962) contains percussive piano writing and orchestra colors suggesting French music. Among his compositions is the symphonie concertante (1954) and the *Odes Metamorphosees* (1968) for marimba, vibraphone, celesta, piano, harp, and orchestra.

Shin-ichiro Ikebe (1943–) studied at the Tokyo University of Arts and joined the faculties at the University of Tokyo and Tokyo College of Music. He has the concerto (1966–1967) for piano and orchestra.

China

Yip Wai Hong (1930–) trained at Yen-Ching University and Peking Central Conservatory. After settling in Hong Kong, he became the head of the Music and Fine Arts Department at the Baptist College. The *Temptation* (1978) is on the hymn *Jesus Loves Me* and the three temptations of Jesus in Matthew 4:1–11. The movements are the "Desert," where two different melodies portray Jesus and Satan, the "Temptations," describing three temptations, and the "Victory." Eastern and Western musical elements are present.

Hsien Hsing-hai (?–) composed the *Yellow River Cantata* (1939) that a committee revised as the *Yellow River Concerto* (1972). Yin Cheng-chung (?–) possibly prepared the piano part in the style of Liszt and Rachmaninoff. The movements are "The Song of the Yellow River Boatmen," "Ode to the Yellow River," "The Yellow River in Wrath," and "Defend the Yellow River," with the Chinese song *East Is Red* in the last movement.

Vietnam

Louise Nguyen Van Ty (1915–) composed the *Fêtes du Têt* (1954) as a musical portrayal of the annual *Têt* celebrations. The movements are the "Joyeux Cortège," the "Offrande Devant l'Autel des Ancêtres," the "Festin-Echange de Voeux - Année du Dragon," and the "Chant d'Espérance."

India

Bhatia Vanraj (1927–) has the concerto (1955) for piano and strings.

Discography

Concertos and concertinos are for piano and orchestra unless other instruments are listed. After the company name, the letters CD or LP are for compact disc or long playing record. Performers' names are not listed. Recordings with multiple listings have only the composer's last name.

Abel, Carl Friedrich

Concerto in G, op. 11, no. 5. Schroeter Concerto in C, op. 3, no. 3. Haydn Concertino in E-flat, Hob.XIV:1. Gyrowetz Concerto in F, op. 26. Pantheon CD D07639.

Concerto in D for piano four hands and orchestra. Donizetti Concerto for violin, cello and orchestra. Haydn Concerto for cello and orchestra. Melodiya CD MCD 228.

Addinsell, Richard

Warsaw Concerto. Rachmaninoff Concerto no. 2. Litolff Scherzo. London CD 414 348–2.

Warsaw Concerto. Bath *Cornish Rhapsody* for piano and orchestra. China committee *Yellow River Concerto*. Decca LP VIV5.

Albeniz, Isaac

Concerto no. 1. Liszt-Busoni *Rhapsodi Espagnole*. Turnabout LP TV-S 34372.

d'Albert, Eugène

Concerto no. 2. Reinecke Concerto no. 1. Candide LP CE 31078.

Albrechstberger, Johann George

Concerto for harpsichord. See Dittersdorf.

Alexandrov, Anatoli

Concerto-Symphony, op. 102. Melodiya LP C10–15161–2.

Alkan, Charles Valentin

Concerti da Camera, op. 1, nos. 1 and 2. See Henselt.

Amalia, Anna (Duchess of Saxe-Weimar)

Concerto for twelve instruments and cembalo obbligato; Divertimento for piano and strings. See Tailleferre.

Ancelin, Pierre
Concerto for oboe, piano and strings; *Concerto Gioioso* for flute, piano, and strings. Cybelia CD CY 706.
Concerto for flute, piano, and strings; *Lou Riou;* Concerto for oboe, piano, and strings. Cybelia LP CY 706.

An-Lun, Huang
Concerto. Hong Kong CD 8.242108.

Anonymous
Concerto for harpsichord. See Cimorosa.

Arensky, Anton
Fantasie on a Russian Theme, op. 48. See Rimsky-Korsakow.
Concerto; *Egyptian Nights*. Ippolitov-Ivanov *Caucasian Sketches*. Olympia CD OCD 107.
Concerto. See Rubinstein Concerto no. 4.

Babajanian, Arno
Heroic Ballad for piano and orchestra; *Trio* for piano, violin and cello. Melodiya LP M10–36363–64.

Babbitt, Milton
Concerto; *The Head of the Bed*. New World Records CD NW 346–2.

Bacewicz, Grazyna
Concerto for two pianos and orchestra; Concerto for Orchestra; Concerto for viola and orchestra; Divertimento for strings; *Pensieri Notturni*. Olympia CD OCD 311.

Bach, Carl Philipp Emanuel
Concertos, Wq.31 and Wq.33. Opus CD 9350 1618.
Concertos for two harpsichords. Deutsche Grammophon CD 419 256–2.

Bach, Johann Christoph Friedrich
Concerto for harpsichord and string orchestra. C. P. E. Bach *Sinfonie* no. 5. J. C. Bach *Sinfonie* for Double Orchestra, op. 18, no. 3. W. F. Bach Sinfonia. Vox LP STPL 514.070.

Bach, Johann Sebastian
Brandenburg Concerti (six). Deutsche Grammophon 2 CDs 415 374–2.
Concertos for harpsichord, BWV 1052–1054. Deutsche Grammophon CD 415 991–2.
Concertos for harpsichord, BWV 1055–1058. Deutsche Grammophon CD 415 992–2.
Concertos for harpsichord, BWV 1060–1062. Deutsche Grammophon CD 415 131–2.
Concertos (piano), BWV 1051–1056 and 1058. Sony CD SM2K 52591.
Concertos for three and four harpsichords, BWV 1060, 1061, 1063 and 1065. Deutsche Grammophon CD 415 655–2.

Concerto for harpsichord, flute, violin, and strings; Suite no. 2 for flute and strings. Turnabout LP TV 34219.
Concertos (seventeen), BWV 972–987. Editio Laran 3 LPs 7074/5/6.

Bach, Wilhelm Friedemann
Concerto for two cembali and orchestra; Sonata for two cembali. C. P. E. Bach Concerto for two cembali and orchestra. Archiv LP 419256–1.
Concertos in E minor and F minor for harpsichord and orchestra; Sinfonia in D minor. Ricercar CD RIC 069049.

Badinski, Nikolai
Omaggio a Bach (concerto) for harpsichord and chamber orchestra; *Dialog* for viola solo; *Preltan* for viola and clavier. ProViva LP LC 6542.

Baker, Michael Conway
Concerto for piano and chamber orchestra; *Fanfare to Expo '86, A Planet for the Taking;* Suite; *Counterplay* for viola and strings; *Four Songs for Ann;* Concerto for flute and strings. CBC CD SMCD 5107.

Balakirev, Mili
Concerto. Liapunov *Rhapsody on Themes from the Ukraine* for piano and orchestra. Turnabout LP QTV-s 34645.
Concerto no. 1. Medtner Concerto no. 1. Turnabout TV LP 34789.

Balanchivadze, Andrei
Concerto no. 4. Melodiya LP 33 C10–09671–72(e).

Barati, George
Baroque Quartet Concerto for flute, oboe, double bass, harpsichord, and orchestra; *Indiana Triptych* for flute, oboe, violin, and piano; *A Chant to Pete* for flute. Enharmonic LP EN85–008.

Barber, Samuel
Concerto. Copland Concerto. Hanson Concerto. Pantheon CD D14104.

Barsukov, Sergei
Concerto no. 2; Concerto no. 2 for violin and orchestra. Everest LP 3167.

Bárta, Lubor
Concerto. Podést Concerto no. 2. Panton LP 8110 0296.

Bartók, Bela
Concerto nos. 1, 2, and 3; Rhapsody. Phillips 3 CDs 416 831–2.
Concerto for two pianos. Kodály *Dances of Galanta*. Phillips CD 416 378–2.
Concerto for two pianos. See Malipiero.

Bath
Cornish Rhapsody for piano and orchestra. See Addinsell.

Bax, Arnold

Symphonic Variations; Morning Song (Maytime in Sussex), both for piano and orchestra. Chandos CD 8516.

Winter Legends; Saga Fragment, both for piano and orchestra. Chandos CD 8484.

Beach, Amy (Mrs. H. H. A.)

Concerto; Quintet for piano and strings. Vox Turnabout CD PVT 7196.

Beethoven, Ludwig van

Choral Fantasy; Concerto no. 2. Turnabout LP TV-S34500.

Concerto in E-flat (1784); *Tempo di Concerto; Romanza Cantabile;* Rondo, all for piano and orchestra. Orion LP ORS 7016.

Concertos in D major and E-flat (1784). Turnabout LP TV-S34367.

Concerto, op. 61a, (piano version of violin concerto); Romances nos. 1 and 2. Deutsche Grammophon CD 429 179–2.

Concerto nos. 1 and 2. Phillips CD 412 787–2.

Concerto nos. 3 and 4. Phillips CD 412 788–2.

Concerto no. 5; Sonata, op. 110. Phillips CD 412 789–2.

Concerto nos. 1–5. Phillips 3 CDs 411 189–2.

Concerto, op. 56, for piano, violin and cello; *Trio,* op. 121a. Phillips CD 420 231–2.

Rondo in B-flat. See Hoffmeister.

Benda, Jirí Antonin

Concerto in B-flat for harpsichord and orchestra. F. Benda Trio; Sonata for violincello. J. Benda Concerto for violin; Sonata two violins; Concerto. Pantheon LP FSM 68907.

Concerto in B minor; Sonata for two violins and harpsichord. F. Benda Trio no. 6; Sonata for cello and harpsichord. Jan Benda Concerto for violin and strings. Pantheon CD D07167.

Bennett, William Sterndale

Concerto no. 4; Symphony in G minor. Milton Keynes LP MKM 861.

Bentzon, Niels Viggo

Chamber Concerto, op. 52, for three pianos, clarinet, bassoon, two trumpets, double bass, and percussion; Symphonic Variations, op. 92. Turnabout TV-S 34374.

Concerto no. 2. Philips LP DMA 063.

Berezowsky, Nicolai

Fantasie, op. 9, for two pianos and orchestra. See Creston.

Berg, Alban

Concerto for violin, piano, and thirteen instruments. Brahms Double Concerto. Sony CD SK 45999.

Berkeley, Lennox
Concerto; Symphony no. 2. Lyrita LP SRCS.94.
Concerto for two pianos and orchestra; Symphony no. 1. Lyrita LP SRCS.80.

Bernstein, Leonard
Symphony no. 2, *The Age of Anxiety,* for piano and orchestra. Deutsche Grammophon CD 415 964–2.

Berwald, Franz Adolf
Concerto; Concerto in C-sharp minor for violin and orchestra; *The Queen of Golconda:* Overture; *Festival for the Bayadères; Serious and Joyful Fancies*. EMI CD CDM 5 65073 2.
Concerto. See Liszt *Malediction.*

Bettinelli, Bruno
Concerto no. 1; Sinfonia breve; *Varianti per orchestra*. Ricordi CD CRMCD 1026.

Biggs, John
Variations on a Theme of Shostakovich for piano and orchestra. Wolff Symphony no. 4. Dembski *Of Mere Being* for mezzo-soprano and orchestra. Jazwinski *Stryga*. Vienna Modern Masters CD VVM 3003.

Blake, Chistopher
The Coming of Tane-Mahuta (Concerto for piano and orchestra); *The Lamentations of Motuarohia*. John Elmsley Cello Symphony. Ribbonwood CD RCD 1003.

Blake, Howard
Concerto; *Diversions* for cello and orchestra; Toccata. Columbia CD HB 3.

Bliss, Arthur
Concerto; *March of Homage*. Unicorn-Kanchana CD UKCD 2029.

Blitzstein, Marc
Concerto. Picker *Keys to the City*. CRI CD 554.

Bloch, Ernest
Concerto Symphonique for piano and orchestra; Scherzo *Fantasque* for piano and orchestra; Concerto *Grosso* no. 2. Laurel CD LR-851CD.

Blomdahl, Karl-Birger
Chamber Concerto for piano, winds, and percussion; Symphony no. 3; Trio for clarinet, cello and piano; *Sisyphos, Two Dances*. Swedish Society Discofil CD SCD 1037.

Boccherini, Luigi
Concerto for piano-forte. Field Rondo in A-flat. Schobert Concerto in G. EMI CD CDC 7 47527 2.

Boesmans, Philippe

Concerto; *Conversions;* Concerto for violin and orchestra. Ricercar CD RIC 014024.

Concertino; Concert Piece for violin and orchestra; *Songs to French Texts; Ave Maria.* Attacca-Babel LP 8311–4/8315–5.

Boieldieu, François-Adrien

Concerto; Concerto for harpsichord. Turnabout LP TV 34148S.

Concerto. See Lalo.

Bolcom, William

Concerto. Adler Concerto for flute and orchestra. Pantheon LP PFN 2041.

Boldemann, Laci

Concerto; *Sechs Kleine Liebeslieder; Morgenstern Sanger.* Swedish Society Discofil CD SKCD 1.

Bolling, Claude

Suite for chamber orchestra and jazz piano trio. CBS LP FM37798.

Bomtempo, Joao

Concerto nos. 1 and 3. Portugalsom CD 870017.

Concerto nos. 2 and 4. Portugalsom CD 870005/PS.

Borkovec, Pavel

Concerto no. 2. Khachaturian Concerto. Urania CD US 5164-CD.

Bortniansky, Dmitri

Sinfonie concertante for piano, harp bassoon, and strings. Mouravieff *Nativité* for string trio and string orchestra. P. Tchaikovsky *Elegy.* Borodin Nocturnes, Scherzo. Rimsky-Korsakov *Sostenuto and Allegro.* Christophorus CD 74581.

Brahms, Johannes

Concerto no. 1. Deutsche Grammophon CD 413 472–2.

Concerto no. 2. Deutsche Grammophon CD 415 359–2.

Brandenburg-Bayreuth, Markgräfin Wilhelmine von

Concerto for harpsichord; Arias. Concerto Bayreuth LP CB 12 005.

Bridge, Frank

Phantasm for piano and orchestra. Moeran Rhapsody for piano and orchestra. Lyrita LP SRCS.91.

Britten, Benjamin

Concerto. Khachaturian Concerto. Hyperio CD CDA66293.

Diversions for piano left hand and orchestra; *The Prince of the Pagodas.* London 2 CDs 421 855–2.

Young Apollo for piano and orchestra; *Canadian Carnival; Four French Songs; Scottish Ballad.* EMI LP DS- 37919.

Bronsart, Hans von
Concerto. d'Albert Concerto no. 2. Liszt *Malediction.* Vox Turnabout CD PVT 7206.

Bruch, Max
Concerto for two pianos and orchestra; Fantasy for two pianos; *Swedish Dances* for two pianos. Turnabout LP TV-34732.

Brüll, Ignaz
Concerto no. 2; Overture to *Macbeth.* Genesis LP GS 1015.

Bush, Alan
Variations, Nocturne and Finale on a Old English Sea Song for piano and orchestra. Delius Double Concerto for violin and cello. Golden Guinea LP GSGC1.

Busoni, Ferruccio
Concerto. CPO CD 999 017–2.
Concertstück. Raff *Concertstück* (Ode au Printemps), op. 76, for piano and orchestra; Concerto, op. 185. Claves CD 50–8806.
Konzertstück for piano and orchestra, op. 31a; Divertimento for flute and orchestra, op. 52; Concertino for clarinet and small orchestra, op. 48; Rondo *Arlecchinesco,* op. 46. Candide LP CE31003.

Camilleri, Charles
Concerto no. 1 *Mediteranean;* Concerto no. 2 *Maqam;* Concerto no. 3 *Leningrad.* Unicorn-Kanchana CD DKP(CD)9150.

Canfield, David DeBoor
Concerto. Enharmonic LP EN86–009.

Carter, Elliott
Concerto; Variations for Orchestra. New World Records CD NW 347–2.

Casadesus, Robert
Concerto; Concerto for three pianos and orchestra. Col LP M 30946.

Casella, Alfredo
Scarlattinana. Henze *Telemanniana.* Villa-Lobos *Bachianas Brasileiras* no. 9. Schwann CD 11649.

Castelnuovo-Tedesco, Mario
Concerto no. 2. Surinach Concertino for piano, strings, and cymbals. Ginastera *Variaciones Concertantes.* Elan CD 2222.

Castillon, Alexis de
Concerto, op. 12; *Esquisses Symphoniques,* op. 15. EMI LP I27 0334 1.

Chaminade, Cécile
Concertstück for piano and orchestra. See Lalo.

Chausson, Ernest
Concerto, op. 21, for violin, piano and string quartet. Harmonia Mundi CD HMC 901135.

Chávez, Carlos
Concerto. Westminster LP WST 17030.

Chaynes, Charles
Concerto; Concerto for organ, strings, timpani, and percussion. Musical Heritage Society LP 1088.

Chin-Yuan, Kuo
Concertino. See Sung-Jen.

China Committee
Yellow River Concerto. See Addinsell.

Chopin, Frederic
Allegro de Concert. See Liszt *Totentanz*.
Andante Spianato et Grande Polonaise Brillante; Concerto no. 2. Deutsche Grammophon LP 2531 126.
Concerto nos. 1 and 2. Deutsche Grammophon CD 415 970-2.
Fantasy on Polish National Airs, op. 13; Concerto no. 2. Angel LP RL-32093

Chopin-Cortot
Concerto, op. 11. Chopin- Nicodé *Allegro de Concerto*. Tausig-Eibenschütz *Hungarian Gypsy Melodies*. Le Chant du Monde CD LDC 278962.

Chopin-Tausig
Concerto, op. 11. Wieniawski Concerto, op. 20. Le Chant du Monde CD LDC 278.902.

Cimarosa, Domenico
Concerto for harpsichord. Seixas Concerto for harpsichord. Anonymous Concerto for harpsichord. Hungaroton LP SLPX 12392.

Clementi, Muzio
Concerto; Symphonies in D and B-flat. Musical Heritage Society LP 851.
Concerto in C. Kuhlau Concerto, op. 7. Turnabout LP TV-S 34375.

Conyhgham, Barry
Southern Cross; Ice Carving. EMI LP OASD 27 0403.

Copland, Aaron
Concerto. Menotti Concerto. Vanguard Classics CD OVC 4029.

Corigliano, John
Concerto; *Promendade Overture; Gazebo Dances; Voyage; Summer Fanfare; Campane di Ravello*. Louisville CD LCD008.

Corrette, Michel
Concerto for harpsichord, op. 26, no. 6; Concerto for flute; *Les Jeux Olympiques;* Sonata for violincello; *Les Sauvages et le Fürstemberg*. Turnabout LP TV34010S.

Cramer, John
Concerto no. 5. Hummel *Grand Sonata,* op. 81. Turnabout LP TV-S 34608.

Cras, Jean
Concerto; *Journal de Bord; Ames d'Enfants*. Cybelia CD CY 803.

Creston, Paul
Concerto for two pianos. Berezowsky *Fantasie,* op. 9, for two pianos and orchestra. Poulenc Concerto for two pianos and orchestra. Albany CD TROY 112.

Czerny, Carl
Concerto for piano four hands. Mennin Symphony no. 4. Desto LP DC-7149.
Divertissement de Concerto. See *Liszt Malediction*.

Davis, Anthony
Wayang no. 4 for piano and orchestra; *Maps* (Concerto) for violin and orchestra. Gramavision LP 18-8807–2.

Debussy, Claude
Fantasy for piano and orchestra; *Premiére Rapsodie* for clarinet and orchestra; *Rapsodie* for saxophone and orchestra; *Khamma; La Plus que Lente;* Dance. Angel CD CC33–3625.

De Greef, Arthur
Concerto no. 1. Jongen *Symphonie Concertante* for organ and orchestra. EMI CD CDM 5 650752.

Delius, Frederick
Concerto; *Paris; Life's Dance; Dance Rhapsody* no. 1. Unicorn-Kanchana CD DKPCD 9108.

Denisov, Edison
Concerto for two violas, harpsichord, and string orchestra; *Chamber Music* for viola, harpsichord, and strings; *Variations on 'Es ist Genug'*; *Epitaph* for chamber orchestra. Bis CD-518.

Dickinson, Peter
Concerto; Organ Concerto. EMI CD 7 47584 2.

Dittersdorf, Karl Ditters von
Concerto for harpsichord. Albrechstberger Concerto for harpsichord. Werner *Pastorale* for harpsichord. Turnabout LP TV-S 34325.

Djabadary, Heraclius
Concerto; *Rhapsodie Georgienne; La Melopée du Serpent; Tiflisiana*. Quantum CD QM 6915.

Dohnányi, Erno

Concerto no. 1. PRT CD PVCD8398.

Variations on a Nursery Song. Liszt Concerto nos. 1 and 2. Phillips CD 422 380–2.

Variations on a Nursery Song, op. 25. R. Strauss *Burleske*. Litolff Scherzo from Concerto Symphonique no. 4. CBS LP M 35832.

Dorati, Antal

Concerto; *Variations for Solo Piano on a Theme by Béla Bartók*. Turnabout LP TV-s 34669.

Drejsl, Radim

Concerto. Pauper Concerto for trumpet. Panton LP 11 0487H.

Durbovay, László

Concerto no. 4 for piano, synthesizer, and orchestra; Concerto no. 1 for eleven strings; Concerto no. 2 for trumpet and fifteen strings. Hungaroton LP SLPX 12415.

Durante, Francesco

Concerto *La Pazzia*. Pergolesi Concerto for violin; Concerto two harpsichords. Erato LP HUM 75–192.

Dusek, Frantisek Xaver

Concertos in D & E-flat. Surpaphon CD CO-2059.

Dutkiewicz, Andrzej

Concerto for piano and chamber orchestra; *Six Meditations* for piano and electronic sound; *Toccatina 2* for piano. Pro Viva CD ISPV 124.

Dvorák, Antonin

Concerto. Schumann Introduction and Allegro, op. 92. London CD 417 802–2.

Eckerberg, Sixten

Concerto nos. 1 and 3. Big Ben LP 861–003.

Eckhardt-Gramatté, Sofia Carman

Concerto no. 1; Sonatas II and III. World Records LP WRC1–1596.

Markantes Stück for two pianos and orchestra; Duo *concertante; Ruck-Ruck* Sonata for clarinet; Berceuse for flute; Prestos for flute I and II. World Records LP WRC1–1599.

Egge, Klaus

Concerto no. 2; Sonata, op. 4. Philips LP 6507 014.

El-Khoury, Bechara

Poems nos. 1 and 2 for piano and orchestra; Symphonic Suite; *Poem* for orchestra; *Symphonic Image;* Dance for orchestra; Requiem for orchestra; Serenades nos. 1 and 2 for string orchestra. Erato LP ERA 9260.

Englund, Einar

Concerto no. 1. Palmgren Piano Pieces. EMI LP 7491052.

Erdmann, Dietrich

Concerto; *Improvisations; Monodie* for flute. Thorofon LP LC 0065.

Erkin, Ulvi Cemal

Sinfonia *concertante* for piano and orchestra; Symphony no. 2; *Köçekçe*. Hungaroton CD HCD 25180.

Falla, Manuel de

Concerto for harpsichord. Sierra *Concierto Nocturnal* for harpsichord and orchestra; *Con Salsa*. C. Halffter *Tiempo para Espacios; Adieu*. Marco *Herbania; Torner*. Adda CD 581235.

Concerto for harpsichord. See Newman.

Concerto for harpsichord (piano version). RCA LP ARL1-3004.

Nights in the Gardens of Spain. See Orbón and Milà.

Fauré, Gabriel

Ballade; *Fantaisie* for piano and orchestra; *Élégie* for cello and orchestra; Berceuse for violin and orchestra; *Les Djinns; Caligula; Pénéope*. EMI CD CDC 7479382.

Ballade. See Sauguet.

Fantaisie for piano and orchestra. Debussy *Fantaisie* for piano and orchestra. Barclay LP 995 027.

Feld, Jindrich

Concerto. See Fischer.

Fennimore, Joseph

Concerto Piccolo; Quartet for violin, viola, violincello, and piano. Hear America First, vol. 2, LP SR-119.

Ferdinand, Louis. Prince of Prussia

Rondo, op. 9; Rondo, op. 13, both for piano and orchestra; Octet, op. 12. Thorofon CD CTH 2088.

Ferguson, Howard

Concerto; *Amore Langueor* for tenor, chorus, and orchestra. Finzi *Eclogue* for piano and string orchestra. EMI CD CDC 7 49627 2.

Field, John

Concerto nos. 1 and 2. Musical Heritage Society MHS LP 1578.

Concertos (seven). Fidelio 4 LPs SPH 9940/43.

Rondo A-flat. See Boccherini.

Filippis, Conrad de

Dialogue for piano and orchestra; Symphonic Rhapsody. Moss Music Group LP D-MMG 116.

Fine, Vivian

Concertante for piano and orchestra. Franco Symphony no. 5. CRI LP SD135.

Finzi, Gerald

Eclogue for piano and string orchestra. See Ferguson.

Fischer, Jan

Seven Letters (to the Sonatori); *Sonatori de Praga*. Feld Concerto. Panton LP 110622G.

Flosman, Oldrich

Symphonic Plays (double concerto) for bass clarinet, piano, and orchestra. Lucky Fantasia *Concertante* for bass clarinet, piano, and string orchestra. Panton LP 8110 0419.

Symphony (concerto for piano and orchestra); Concertino for guitar and strings; Fugues for strings. Panton LP 8110 0220.

Foulds, John

Dynamic Triptych, op. 88, for piano and orchestra. Vaughan Williams Concerto. Lyrita LP SRCS 130.

Francaix, Jean

Concerto. See Lalo.

Concerto for two pianos and orchestra; *Variations on a Pleasant Theme; Five Portraits of Young Girls*. Wergo CD WER 6087–2.

Concertino; Concerto. Saint-Saëns Concerto no. 2. Arabesque CD Z6541.

Franck, César

Concerto; Variations Brillantes. Musique en Wallone LP MW80047.

Concerto no. 2, op. 11; *Variations Brillantes sur la Rondo Favorite de Gustave III,* op. 8, both for piano and orchestra. Koch-Schwann CD 311 111.

Symphonic Variations; *Les Djinns,* both for piano and orchestra. See Grieg.

Frumerie, Gunnar de

Variations and Fugue for piano and orchestra. Larsson Concerto for saxophone and string orchestra. Caprice LP 1259.

Furtwängler, Wilhelm

Symphonic Concerto for piano and orchestra. Marco Polo CD 8.223333.

Gade, Niels W.

Spring Fantasy, op. 23, for soprano, alto, tenor, bass, piano, and orchestra; Symphony no. 8. EMI LP D.M.A. 046.

Symphony no. 5 for piano and orchestra; Symphony no. 6. Bis CD-356.

Galuppi, Baldasare

Concerto for harpsichord and strings; *Concerti a Quattro* nos. 1–4; Sinfonia *della Serenata;* Sinfonia. Claves CD 50–8306.

Genzmer, Harald

Concertino no. 2 for piano and string orchestra. Mozart Concerto, K.415. Schubert

Adagio and Rondo *concertante,* D.487, arranged for piano and orchestra. Bayer LP 100205.

Gerber, René
Concerto; Concerto in D-flat for chamber orchestra; Concerto in A. Gallo CD 548.

Gershwin, George
Concerto in F; Second Rhapsody; *I Got Rhythm Variations; Rhapsody in Blue;* Preludes. Sony CD MPK 47681.
Rhapsody in Blue for piano and orchestra; Second Rhapsody for piano and orchestra (original version); Preludes for piano; unpublished piano works. Sony CD MK 39699.

Ginastera, Alberto
Concerto (1961); Concerto for harp and orchestra; *Estancia.* ASV CD DCA.
Concerto no. 2; Quintet for piano and strings. Orion LP ORS76241.

Glazounov, Alexander
Concerto nos. 1 and 2; Concerto in A minor for violin and orchestra. Chant du Monde CD LDC 278 925.

Goldberg, Johann
Concertos (two) for harpsichord. Dabringhaus und Grimm CD MD+G L 3250.

Goetz, Hermann
Concerto, op. 18. Bronsart Concerto op. 10. Candide LP CE31075.

Golubev, Evgeni
Ukrainian Rhapsody; Concerto no. 1. Melodiya LP C10 27953 004.

Gordelli, Otar
Concerto, op. 2. Taktakishvili Concerto. Westminster LP XWN 18171.

Gottschalk, Louis Moreau
Grand Tarantelle for piano and orchestra; *The Union* for piano and orchestra; *Fantasy on the Brazilian National Anthem; Triumphal March* for orchestra and band. Turnabout LP TV-S 34449.

Gould, Morton
Concerto *Concertante* for violin, piano, and wind quintet; *Cellos* for eight cellos; *Pavanne* for wind quintet. Music Masters CD MMD 60140K.
Rhapsodies for piano and orchestra. Col LP ML 4657.

Gounod, Charles
Fantasy on the Russian National Hymn. See Massenet.

Grieg, Edward
Concerto. See Schumann Concerto.

Concerto. Franck Symphonic Variations; *Les Djinns,* both for piano and orchestra. EMI LP ASD3960.

Grofe, Ferde

Concerto; *Grand Canyon Suite*. Everest LP 3044.

Guarnieri, Camargo

Concerto nos. 3 and 4. ProMemus LP 3–56-404–004.

Gyrowetz, Adalbert

Concerto in F, op. 26. See Abel.

Hába, Alois

Symphonic Fantasy, op. 8, for piano and orchestra; *The Way of Life,* op. 46; *The New Land:* Overture, op. 47; String Quartets nos. 11, 12, 15, and 16; Quartet for four bassoons; Suite for four trombones; Fantasy no. 1 for nonet; Suite for cello solo; Partita for alto saxophone; Suite no. 1 for quarter-tone clarinet and piano; Suite for bass clarinet and piano; Suite for quarter-tone piano; Sonata for quarter-tone piano; Suite for dulcimer. Supraphon 3 CDs 11 1865–2.

Hachimura, Yoshio

The Logic of Distraction for piano and orchestra. Sato Sinfonia III. Irino Symphonia. Mori *The Groom is Gloomy*. Noda *Mutation*. Camerata LP CMT-3004–5.

Halffter, Dolfo

Overture *concertante* for piano and orchestra. Enríquez Concerto no. 2 for violin and orchestra. Sarrier Symphony. RCA CD MRS-020.

Hall-berg, Bengt

Lyric Ballad for two pianos and orchestra. Numerous other compositions by a variety of composers are in this set. MAP 3 LPs R 8717.

Haieff, Alexei

Concerto; *Five Pieces for Piano; Four Juke Box Pieces*. M-G-M Records LP E3243.

Hannikainen, Ilmari

Concerto; *Three Piano Pieces; Three Waltzes,* op. 17. Palmgren *Nocturne in Three Scenes;* Prelude-Nocturne. Sibelius *Esquisses,* op. 114. Finlandia CD FACD 811.

Hanson, Howard

Concerto. See Barber.

Concerto da Camera for piano and string quartet; *Two Yuletide Pieces* for piano; Concerto for organ, harp, and strings; *Nymphs and Satyr*. Bay Cities CD BCD-1005.

Harbison, John

Concerto. Stock *Inner Space* for orchestra. CRI LP SD440.

Harrison, Lou

Concerto; Suite for violin, piano, and small orchestra. New World Records CD NW366–2.

Harris, Roy

Concerto for piano and strings; *Elegy and Dance;* Toccata; Chorale and Fantasy; *Cimarron Overture*. Bay Cities CD BCD-1002.

Harty, Hamilton

Concerto; *In Ireland; With the Wild Geese*. Chandos CD CHAN 8321.

Haydn, Franz Joseph

Concerto nos. 3, 4, and 11. Sony CD SK 48383.

Concerto in D. See Hummel Concerto, op. 85.

Concertos 12 (piano). Telefunken 3 LPs 6.35604.

Concertino in E-flat, Hob.XIV:1. See Abel.

Haydn, Michael

Concerto for harpsichord, viola, and strings, P 55; Concerto for clarinet and orchestra, P 54; Concerto for violin and orchestra, P 53. Olympia CD OCD 406.

Hegdal, Mage

Concerto II; Sinfonia; *Three Prunes* for piano. Folke Stromholm *Samiaedan; Noai'di; Farewell to the Piano; Water—A Phenomenological Study*. Aurora CD NCD-B 4951.

Heider, Werner

Bezirk for piano and orchestra. Kagel *Sur Scène -Theater Piece* in one act; March for two cellos and percussion. Huber *Parusie* for large orchestra. Henze *Elegy for Young Lovers; Hespose Dschen* for saxophone and string orchestra. Schnebel Chorale Prelude no. 1 for organ, trombone ensemble, and tape; *Atemzuge*. Zimmermann *Crucifixion* for choir. Schönbach *Canticum Psalmi ad Laudes* for soprano and orchestra. Deutsche Harmjonia Mundi 3 LPs DMR 1016–18.

Heininen, Paavo

Concerto no. 2; Symphony no. 2; *Arioso*. Finlandia CD FACD 373.

Concerto no. 3. Englund Concerto no. 1. Musica Nova Academiae LP (1982).

Heinio, Mikko

Through the Evening (Concerto no. 4) for piano, chorus and string orchestra. Rautavaara *Cantos* I -III for string orchestra; *Die Liebenden*. Finlandia CD FACD 378.

Henselt, Adolf

Concerto, op. 16; Variations *de Concert,* op. 11. Alkan *Concerti da Camera,* op. 10, nos. 1 and 2. Hyperion CD CDA66717.

Concerto in F. See Liszt *Totentanz*.

Henze, Hans Werner

Tristan for piano and orchestra. EG LP 2530 834.

Hill, Alfred

Concerto. Lovelock Concerto for flute and orchestra. Penberthy Concerto for saxophone and orchestra. Festival LP L 27016.

Hiller, Ferdinande

Concerto, op. 69. Raff Concerto, op. 185. Candide LP CE 31058.

Concerto, op. 113. See Mosonyi.

Hindemith, Paul

Concerto Music for piano, brass, and harps. Janacek Capriccio for piano left hand and winds. Vackar Concerto for trumpet, percussion, and keyboard. Nimbus CD NI 5103.

Concerto. Zwilich Symphony no. 2. Lawhead *Aleost*. Louisville CD LCD002.

Hoffmeister, Franz Anton

Concerto, op. 24. Beethoven Rondo in B-flat. Auditorium LP BX 207.

Concerto, op. 24. Haydn Concerto Hob.18:3. Koch-Schwann CD 316 027.

Hoiby, Lee

Concerto, op. 17. V. Thomson Symphony no. 3. David *Music for Shakespeare's Romeo and Juliet*. Bay Cities CD BCD-1003.

Honegger, Arthur

Concertino; *Prelude, Arioso et Fughette; Pastorale d'Ete;* Symphony no. 4. Chandos CD CHAN 8968.

Horky, Karel

Preludes on Fate for piano and orchestra; Symphony no. 3. Panton LP 11 0457.

Hovhaness, Alan

Concerto no. 1 *Lousadzak* for piano and string orchestra; *Mysterious Mountain* (Symphony no. 2). Harrison Elegiac Symphony. Music-Masters CD MM 60204.

Khaldis (piano concerto); *The Spirit of Ink*. Poseidon Society LP 1011.

Hummel, Johann Nepomuk

Concerto in A minor; Concerto for piano and violin. Turnabout LP TV 34028S.

Concertino, op. 73; *La Galante* (*Rondeau*), op. 120, for piano and orchestra; Concerto for bassoon and orchestra. Turnabout LP TV 34348.

Concertos, opp. 85 and 44. Schwann CD 11099.

Concerto, op. 85. Haydn Concerto in D. Turnabout LP TV 4073.

Concertos, opp. 85 and 89. Marco Polo CD 8.223107.

Grand Concerto *Les Adieux*. See Kalkbrenner.

Hurlstone, William

Concerto; *Variations on a Swedish Air*. Lyrita LP SRCS.100.

Ichikawa, Toshiharu
Concerto; Symphonic Movement; *Gyo-no-sho*. Denon LP OX-1240-ND.

Ifukube, Akira
Ritmica Ostinata for piano and orchestra. Koyama *Kobitk-Uta*. Toyama Rhapsody. Victor CD VCD-5505.

Ikege, Sin-Ichiro
Concerto no. 2. Matsumura Concerto for cello and orchestra. Hosokawa *Jenseits der Zeit*. Camerata CD 32CM-85.

d'Indy, Vincent
Concerto, op. 89, for piano, flute, cello, and string orchestra; Suite, op. 24; *Kradec,* op. 34. Erato LP STU71423.
Symphony on a French Mountain Air. Ravel Concerto in G. RCA CD 6805.

Ireland, John
Concerto; *Mai-Dun; Legend,* all for piano and orchestra. Chandos CHAN CD 8461.
Concerto; *These Things Shall Be*. Lyrita LP SRCS 36.
Concerto. Rubbra Concerto for violin and orchestra. Unicorn-Kanchana CD DKP 9056.

Ivanov, Janis
Concerto; Concerto for violin. Melodiya LP 33 C 10-11829–30(a).

Janácek, Leos
Concertino. Dvorák Concerto. RCA 60781.
Capriccio for piano left hand and winds. See Hindemith.

Jezek, Jaroslav
Concerto; Bagatelles; *Petite Suite;* Etude. Panton LP 8180 0375.

Jing-jing, Luo
Concerto; Piano Solo Pieces Based on three Dunhuang Poems; *Two Movements* for piano, mezzo-soprano, and orchestra. HK LP 6.340–161.

Jirko, Ivan
Concerto no. 3. Kabalevsky Concerto no. 3. Martinu Quintet for piano and strings. Urania CD US 5176-CD.

Jolas, Betsy
Stances for piano and orchestra; *Points d'Aube* for alto and thirteen winds; *J.D.E.* for fourteen instruments; *D'un Opera de Voyage*. Musique Française CD ADES 14.087–2.

Jolivet, André
Concerto. See Milhaud.

Joly, Suzanne
Fantaisie concertante for piano and orchestra; *Petite Suite; Rupestra* for orchestra;

Triptyque for string quartet; *Thème, variations et allegro fugato* for piano; *Ode à la Jeune Fille* for girls' choir and instrumental ensemble. Cybelia CD CY 873.

Jordan, Sverre

Concerto Piccolo for piano and orchestra; *Fever* Poems; *Holberg Silhouette;* Seven Songs. Simax CD PSC 3107.

Juon, Paul

Concerto for violin, violincello, and piano. Tcherepnin Concertino for violin, violincello, and piano. Thorofon LP 76.26209.

Kabalevsky, Dmitri

Concerto nos. 2 and 3. Melodiya LP 33 C10–08015–16(a).

Concerto no. 3. See Muczynski and Jirko.

Concerto no. 4 *Prague;* Rhapsody *School Years* for piano and orchestra. Melodiya LP C10–18261–2.

Kadosa, Pál

Concerto; Concertino for viola and orchestra; Concerto for string quartet and chamber orchestra. Hugaroton LP SLPX 11859.

Concerto no. 4, op. 63; Symphony no. 6, op. 62; Symphony no. 7, op. 64. Hungaroton LP LPX 11456.

Kalabis, Viktor

Concerto. See Pálenícek.

Kalkbrenner, Friedrich

Concerto no. 1. Hummel Grand Concerto *Les Adieux*. Turnabout LP TV-S 34561.

Kalomiris, Manolis

Symphonic Concerto for piano and orchestra. ERT LP 1982.

Katzer, Georg

Concerto for harpsichord. Goldmann *Sing', Lessing*. Schenker *Titilijubili*. Nova LP 8 85 222.

Kaufmann, Dieter

Für Clara for piano and orchestra; *Concertomobi* for violin, tape, and orchestra; *Serenade for a Potentate* for cello and band; *Three Poems of Stéphane Mallarmé* for soprano and five instruments. Amadeo LP 419 557–1.

Kelemen, Milko

Mirabilia for piano ring modulator and two orchestras; *Love Song* for orchestra; *Mareia* for orchestra; *Infinity* for orchestra. Eterna LP 8 27 977.

Keuris, Tristan

Concerto; Movements for orchestra. Composers' Voice LP 8304.

Khatchaturian, Aram

Concerto. See Britten and Brokovec.

Konzertrhapsodie for piano and orchestra; *Konzertrhapsodi* for violincello and orchestra. Melodiya LP 28 730KK.

Kirchner, Leon
Concerto no. 1. Piston Symphony no. 6. New World Records LP NW286.

Kiysoe, Yasuji
Concerto; *Primitive Dance; Élágie*. Fontec CD FOCD3266.

Klami, Uuno
Concerto no. 2. Jolivet Concertino for trumpet, string orchestra, and piano. Shostakovich Concerto no. 1 for piano, trumpet, and string orchestra. Finlandia CD FACD 393.

Köhler, Siegfried
Concerto, op. 46; *Dritte Sinfonie,* op. 57. Nova LP 8 85 126.

Kondo, Io
A Shape of Time for piano and orchestra; *Strands III* for violin and piano; Duo for harp and guitar; *Still Life* for eight violins. ALM LP AL-27.

Korngold, Erich Wolfgang
Concerto for piano left-hand and orchestra; Symphonic Overture, *Sursum Corda; Much Ado About Nothing*. CPO CD 000 046.

Korte, Oldrich Frantisek
Concerto grosso for trumpets, flutes, piano and strings; *Philosophical Dialogues* for violin and piano; *Wonderful Circus* for orchestra. Panton LP 81 0742.

Kubík, Ladislav
Concerto. Riedlbauch Sonata for winds and percussion; *Fiala* for organ. Zámecník *Musica Concertante* for orchestra. Panton LP 11 0580.

Kucera, Václav
Obraz for piano and orchestra. Páenicek *Symfonické Variace ne Imaginárhí Portrét Ilji Erenburga*. Panton LP 11 0391.

Kuhlau, Friedrich
Concerto in C; Concertino for two horns and orchestra; *Elf Hill:* Overture. Unicorn-Kanchana CD DKPCD9110.

Kulenovic, Vuk
Word of Light for soprano, piano, and orchestra; *Icarus* (Symphonic Postlude). RTB LP 2330024.

Kurokawa, Manae
Concerto. See Urakabe.

Kyurkchiyski, Krassimir
Concerto; *Salutatory Overture*. Balkanton LP BCA 1300/420.

Lalo, Edouard

Concerto. Chaminade *Concertstück,* op. 40. Boieldieu Concerto. Massenet Concerto. Pierné Concerto. Roussel Concerto. Françaix Concerto. Vox Box 2 CDs CDX5110.

Lambert, Constant

Concerto. Bax *Nonet.* Rieti Serenade for violin and small orchestra. AS Disc CD AS 5005.

Landowski, Marcel

Concerto; Concerto for flute and orchestra; Concerto for Ondes Martenot and orchestra; *Improvisations* for trombone and orchestra. Koch-Schwann CD 311 175.

Larsson, Lars-Erik

Sinfonietta, op. 10; *Little Serenade,* op. 12. Bluebell CD ABCD 012.

Lazarof, Henri

Tableaux (after Kandinsky) for piano and orchestra; *Icarus*—Concerto no. 2 for orchestra; *Poema.* Delos CD DE 3069.

Leduc, Jacques

Concerto; *Instantanées* for chamber orchestra; *Summer Overture* for concert band. EMI LP 063–23990.

Legrand, Hervé

Concertino; *Piece pour Cordes;* Andante; *Attila.* Arcobaleno CD SBCD-7300.

Leigh, Walter

Concertino for harpsichord and strings; *Music for Strings; A Midsummer Night's Dream-Suite;* Overture and Dance (The Frogs). Lyrita LP SRCS.126.

Leimer Kurt

Concerto. EMI LP SME 91 753.

Lentz, Johan Nicolaas

Concerto no. 2 for harpsichord and strings. Wilms Symphony. Fodor Symphony no. 4. Graaf Symphony. Fesch Concerto *Grosso,* op. 3, no. 2. Blanckenburg Cantata *l'Apologie des Femmes.* Buns Sonata *Finalis* no. 15. Hacquart *O Jesu Splendor.* Sweelinck *Psalm* 150. Conradus *Canzon à* 8. Hague Philharmonic 2 LPs 6818 531/2.

Levinas Michaël

Concerto—*Space* no. 2; *Ouverture pour une Fete Étrange; Les Ries du Gilles; Clov et Hamm; Contrepoints Iréels-Rencontres.* Adés CD 14.072–2.

Liapunov, Sergei

Concerto no. 2, op. 38. Glazunov Concerto no. 1, op. 92. Russian Disc CD RD CD 11 024.

Rhapsody on themes from the Ukraine. See Balakirev.

Lieberson, Peter
Concerto. New World CD NW 325–2.

Ligeti, György
Concerto; Concerto for cello and orchestra; Chamber Concerto for 13 Instruments. Sony CD SK 58945.

Linde, Bo
Concerto no. 1. Liljefors *Festspel; Frithiof och Ingeborg*. Hägg *Nordische Symphonie*. Berlioz *La Damnation de Faust*, act 3. Sterling LP S 1007.
Concerto no. 2. Eklund *Facce; Lamento*. Caprice LP CAP 1275.

Lipatti, Dinu
Concertino in Classical Style; Nocturne. Bach transcriptions. Dynamic CD CDS 57.

Liszt, Franz
Concerto nos. 1 and 2. Deutsche Grammophon CD 423 571-2. See Dohnányi.
Concerto no. 3; *De Profundis; Totentanz*. Academy Sound and Vision CD DCA 778.
Malediction. Czery *Divertissement de Concerto* for piano and orchestra. Berwald Concerto. Alkan *Concerto da Camera* no. 2 for piano and strings. Turnabout LP TV 34740.
Malediction. See Bronsart.
Totentanz. Mendelssohn Capriccio *Brillant*. Chopin *Allegro de Concerto*. Turnabout LP TV 34735.
Totentanz. Rubinstein Concerto no. 4. Henselt Concerto in F. Scharwenka Concerto no. 2 (Finale). LP Col MG35183.

Liszt-Busoni
Rhapsodie Espagnole. See Albeniz.

Litolff, Henry
Concerto Symphonique no. 3. Rheinberger Concerto, op. 94. Candide LP QCE 31112.
Concerto Symphonique no. 4; Trio for violin, cello, and piano. Genesis CD GCD 101.

Lloyd, George
Concerto nos. 1 and 2. Albany CD TROY 037–2.
Concerto no. 3. Albany CD TROY 019–2.
Concerto no. 4. Conifer Records LP CFRA 119.

Lopes-Graça, Fernando
Concertino for piano, strings, brass, and percussion; Concertino for viola and orchestra; Divertimento. Portugalsom CD 870013/PS.
Concerto no. 2. HMV LP 069–40586.
Concerto no. 2. EMI LP 069–40586.

Lora, Antonio
Concerto. Weiss Theme and Variations for orchestra. CRI LP 113.

Luchy, Bárta
Concerto for violin, piano, and orchestra; Concerto for violin and orchestra. Panton LP 110454.

Lucky, Stepán
Fantasia *Concertante* for bass clarinet, piano, and string orchestra. See Flosman.

Lutoslawski, Witold
Concerto; *Chain* 3; *Novelette*. Deutsche Grammophon CD 431 664–2.
Variations on a Theme of Paganini for piano and orchestra; *Trauermusik* for string orchestra; *Livre* for orchestra. PWM 8 27 796.

MacDowell, Edward
Concertos (two). Archduke Recording CD DARC 1.

Malipiero, Gian Francesco
Concerto for two pianos and orchestra. Martinu Concerto for two pianos and orchestra. Bartók Concerto for two pianos and orchestra. Olympia CD OCD 270.

Mamiya, Michio
Concerto no. 2. See Moroi.

Marbe, Miriam
Concerto for harpsichord and eight instruments; Serenata; *Time Found Again*. Electrecord LP ST-ECE 02105.

Martin, Frank
Concerto for harpsichord; *Ballade* for piano and orchestra; *Ballade* for trombone and orchestra. Jecklin-Disco CD JD 529–2.
Concerto nos. 1 and 2; Ballade for piano and orchestra. Claves LP D 8509.

Martincek, Dusan
Dialogues in the Form of Variations for piano and orchestra; Sonata no. 4; Invention; Concerto *Étude;* Prelude. Opus LP 9111 1009.

Martinez, Mariana
Concerto for harpsichord; Sinfonia. Etnos LP 02-A-XI.

Martinu, Bohuslav
Concerto no. 3; Rhapsody-Concerto for viola and orchestra. Supraphon CD 11 0374–2.
Concerto no. 4; Sinfonietta *Giocosa* for piano and orchestra. Artia LP ALPS712.
Concerto no. 5; Concerto for two pianos and orchestra. Supraphon LP 1110 2338.
Concerto for two pianos and orchestra; Fantasia for two pianos; Three Czech Dances. Britten *Scottish Ballad*. Phoenix CD PHCD 104.
Concerto for two pianos and orchestra. See Malipiero.

Concerto for violin, cello, piano, and string orchestra; Concertino for piano trio and string orchestra. Thorofon CD CTH 2013.

Concerto da Camera for violin, piano, timpani, percussion, and strings; Divertimento for violin, viola, two oboes, piano, and strings; Partita. Amati CD SRR 9004/1.

Concertino for piano trio and string orchchestra; Sinfonietta *Giocosa*. Supraphon LP 4 10 2198.

Divertimento (sometimes called Concertino) for piano left hand and orchestra; Sinfonietta *Giocosa* for piano and orchestra. Supraphon CD 11 0374–2.

Triple Concertos (two) for piano, violin, and violincello; *La Bagarre*. Thorofon CD CTH 2013.

Martucci, Giuseppe

Concerto. Mignone *Symphonic Impressions of Four Brazilian Churches*. dell'Arte LP DA9017.

Concerto no. 2; Canzonetta; *Tempo di Gavotta; Giga;* Serenata; *Minuetto; Momento Musical*. ASV CD DCA 691.

Masek, Václav

Concerto in D for three harpsichords and wind octet. Druecky *Parthia* no. 3 for wind octet. Jirovec *Parthia* (*Concertante*) for wind instruments. Vranicky *Three Marches in French Style* for wind instruments. Supraphon CD CO-2060.

Mason, Daniel Gregory

Prelude and Fugue for piano and orchestra. See Beach.

Massenet, Jules

Concerto. Saint-Saëns Fantasy *Africa*. Gounod *Piano Fantasy on the Russian National Hymn*. Candide LP QCE31088.

Concerto. See Lalo.

Matacic, Lovro von

Confrontation Symphony for two pianos and orchestra. Denon CD CO-1004.

Matsudaira, Yoritsune

Theme and Variations after a Berceuse by Nanbu for piano and orchestra. Hirao *Cantilene Antique*. Ogura *Dance Suite*. Kataoka *Composition on Batou;* Sinfonia *concertante* for accordion and orchestra. Fontec CD FOCD3246.

Matsumura, Teizo

Concerto nos. 1 and 2. Victor LP SJX-1175.

Matsunaga, Michiharu

Divided Elaborate Maps for piano and orchestra. Shimoyama *Yugenism*. Okasaka *Kei*. Yoshizaki *New Heaven and Earth* for soloists, electronic organ, and orchestra. ALM 2 CDs ALCD-3034/35.

Mayer, William

Octagon for piano and orchestra. Rudhyar *Paeans, Stars; Granites*. CRI CD 584.

McKinley, William Thomas

Silent Whispers for piano and orchestra. Kelly *Alden's Retreat*. Whitaker *Prayers of Habakkuk*. Hoose *Rights to Passage*. Giobbi *Khe Sanh*. Stanley Fanfare. MMC Recordings CD MMC2004.

McKuen, Rod

Concerto no. 1 for four harpsichords; *Four Statements from Three Books*. Stanyan LP 10009.

McPhee, Colin

Concerto. Sessions String Quartet no. 2. Columbia LP ML 5105.

Medtner, Nicolas

Concerto no. 1; Piano Pieces. Melodiya CD SUCD 10–00175.

Concerto no. 2. Medodiya LP C10–08099–8100.

Concerto no. 3; Sonata *Tragica*, op. 39; Sonata, op. 22. Candide LP CE 31092.

Meier, Jost

Esquisses for piano, strings, and percussion. See Zbinden.

Mendelssohn, Felix

Capriccio Brillant. See Liszt *Totentanz*.

Concerto nos. 1 and 2. London CD 414 672–2.

Concerto in A minor for piano and strings; Serenade; Allegro *Giocosa*. Turnabout LP TV 34170S.

Concerto in D minor for violin, piano, and strings; Concerto for violin and orchestra. Deutsche Grammophon CD 427 338–2.

Concerto no. 1 for violin, piano, and string orchestra. See Viotti.

Concertos in E-flat and A for two pianos and orchestra. Schwann CD 11088.

Duo *Concertante* for two pianos and orchestra, co-composed with Moscheles. Chopin Rondo. Saint-Saëns Polonaise. Liszt *Les Préludes*. Turnabout LP TV 34821.

Mennin, Peter

Concerto. Yardumian Passacaglia, Recitatives and Fugue for piano and orchestra. RCA LP LSC-3243.

Menotti, Gian Carlo

Concerto. See Copland.

Merikanto, Aarre

Concerto no. 2; Concerto Piece for cello and orchestra. EMI LP 063–36024.

Meriläinen, Usko

Concerto no. 2. Krami Concerto for violin and orchestra. Kokkonen Concerto for cello and orchestra. Finlandia CD FACD 702.

Messiaen, Oliver

Oiseaux Exotiques; Reveil des Oiseaux, both for piano and orchestra. Candide LP CE 31002.

Univtrail et des Oiseaux; Oiseaux Exotiques; Couleurs de la Cité Céleste; Sept Haikai, all for piano and orchestra. Disques Montaigne CD WM 332.

Meynaud, Michel
Concerto no. 1. See Mozart, K.459.
Concerto no. 2. Tcherepnin *Bagatellen,* op. 5. Wagner *Lohengrin Vorspiel,* act 1. Colosseum LP SM 802.

Mieg, Peter
Concerto for harpsichord and chamber orchestra; *Triple Concerto in the Italian Style* for violin, viola, cello, and strings. Ex Libris LP EL 16879.

Mignone, Francisco
Fantasia Brasileira no. 3 for piano and orchestra; *The Auction; Musica* no. 1; Concertino for bassoon and orchestra. Funarte LP 3–56-404–003.

Milhaud, Darius
Carnaval d'Aix; Suite *Provencale;* Suite *Francaise.* EMI LP 1731861/PM375.
Concerto no. 1; *La Création du Monde.* Jolivet Concerto. Columbia LP MS7432.
Concerto no. 2; Concerto no. 1 for viola and orchestra; Suite *Cisalpine* for cello and orchestra; Concerto for percusssion small orchestra; Six *Petites Symphonies; L'Homme et Son Désire; Le Boeuf sur le Toit; La Muse Ménagère; Le Carnaval d'Aix.* Vox Box 2 CDs CDX5109.

Minchev, Georgi
Concerto; Symphonic Prologue; Concerto Breve for ten instruments; Three *Poems* for soprano, strings, and percusssion. Balkanton CD 030066.

Minkofski-Garrigues
Klaviermusik, op. 15. J. S. Bach Partita no. 2. Teldec TST 76780.

Miyoshi, Akira
Concerto; Concerto for violin and orchestra. Victor CD VDC-5509.

Moeran, E. J.
Rhapsody for piano and orchestra; First Rhapsody; Second Rhapsody; *In the Mountain Country.* Chandos CD CHAN 8639.

Moevs, Robert
Concerto *Grosso.* Druckman *Windows.* CRI LP SD457.

Monn, Johann Matthias
Harpsichord Concerto in D. Turnabout LP TV-S34324.

Montaine, John La
Concerto. Stevens Symphonic Dances. CRI LP SD166.

Montsalvatge, Xavier
Concerto *Breve.* See Surinach.

Moroi, Makoto
Concerto. Mamiya Concerto no. 2. Noda Concerto. Seven Seas CD KICC 2016.
Concerto no. 1; Three Concerto Movements for shakuhachi, percussion, and strings. JVC LP KVX-5515.

Moross, Jerome
Symphony no. 1 for piano and orchestra. Herrmann *Welles Raises Kane*. Premiere Records LP PR-1202.

Mortensen, Finn
Concerto; Fantasy for piano and orchestra; Per Orchestra, Fantasy and Fugue for piano; Studies I and II for flute. Aurora CD NCD-B 4942.

Moscheles, Ignaz
Concerto no. 3; Concerto for flute, oboe, and orchestra; *Bonhonnière Musicale* for piano. Supraphon CD CO-1326.
Concerto for piano and 5 strings. Kalkbrenner *Effusio Musica Grande Fantaisie.* Turnabout LP TV 34678.
Duo Concertante. See Mendelssohn.

Mosolov, Alexander
Concerto no. 1; *Iron Foundry; Soldiers' Songs*. Melodiya CD MCD 176.

Mosonyi, Mihaly
Concerto; Symphony no. 1. Marco Polo CD 8.223539.

Moszkowski, Moritz
Concerto, op. 59; *Caprice Espagnol,* op. 37; Etude, op. 72; *Etinselles,* op. 36. *Venusberg Bacchanale,* Danse *Bohéme*. Candide LP CE 31030.

Mozart, Franz Xaver
Concertos, opp. 14 and 25. Koch-Schwann CD 311 004.

Mozart, Wolfgang Amadeus
Concertos, K. 37, 39, 40, and 41. Sony CD SK 39225.
Concertos, K.107, nos. 1–3. Schröter Concerto op. 3, no. 3. Sony CD SK 39222.
Concertos, K.175 and 503. Sony CD SK 37267.
Concertos, K.242, for three pianos in Mozart's version for two pianos, and K.365 for two pianos. Phillips CD 426 241–2.
Concertos, K.238 and 415. Sony CD SK 39223.
Concertos, K.365 and K.242, for two and three pianos. London LP CS6937. See K.242.
Concertos, K.414/K.595. CBS LP M35828.
Concerto, K.415. See K.238.
Concertos, K.271 and K.467. Sony CD SK 34562.
Concertos, K. 413, K.414, and K.449. Sony CD SK 42243.
Concerto, K.414. See K.413.
Concerto, K.449. See K.413.
Concertos, K.450 and K.451. Sony CD SK 37824.

Concerto, K.451. See K.450.
Concertos, K.453 and K.456. Sony CD SK 36686.
Concertos, K.459 and K.488. Sony CD SK 39064.
Concerto, K.459. Meynaud Concerto no. 1. Colos LP SM801.
Concertos, K.466 and K.595. Sony CD SK 42241.
Concertos, K.467 and K.595. Sony CD SK 46485.
Concerto, K.467. See K.271.
Concertos, K.482 and K.491. Sony CD SK 42242
Concerto, K.488. See K.459.
Concerto, K.491. See K.482.
Concerto, K.503. See K.175.
Concerto, K.537; Rondos, K.382 and K.386. Sony CD SK 39224.
Concerto, K.595. See K.466, and K.467.
Concertos; Rondos K.382 and K.386. Sony 12 CDs SX12K 46441.

Muczynski, Robert
Concerto no. 1; *A Serenade for Summer;* Suite, op. 13. Kabalevsky Concerto no. 3. Centaur CD CRC 2089.

Muldowney, Dominic
Concerto; Concerto for saxophone. EMI CD CDC7 49715 2.

Müller-Siemens, Detlev
Concerto; Variations on a Ländler by Schubert; *Under Neonlight* I. Wergo CD 60503.

Nenov, Dimitar
Concerto. Balkanton LP BCA 10899.

Newman, Anthony
Concertino. Falla Concerto for harpsichord. Poulenc Concerto for organ, strings, and timpani. Newport Classic CD NC 60017.

Nikisch, Mitja
Concerto. Graunke Symphony no. 7. Marco Polo CD 223194.

Nikolov, Lazar
Concerto no. 2; Symphony no. 1. Balkanton LP BAC 1300/435.

Nishimura, Akira
Concerto no. 3. See Yokoyama.
Heterophony two pianos and orchestra. Yoshimatsu *Threnody to Toki.* Mizuno *Orchestra 1966.* Hosokawa *Ferne-Landschaft* I. Seven Seas CD KICC 2015.

Nobre, Marlos
Divertimento for piano and orchestra; Concerto *Breve; Rhythmic Variations* for piano and Brazilian percussion; *In Memoriam* for orchestra; *Mosaico; Convergencias; Biosfera; O Canto Multiplicado* for voice and string orchestra; *Ukrinmakrinkrin* for voice, winds, and piano; *Rhythmetron* for percussion; *Sonancias* I and II. Léman Classics CD LC44100.

Noda, Teruyuki

Concerto; Eclogue for flute and percussion; *Trois Dévelopements; Ode Capricious* for piano; Serenade I; *Poems* I and II for septet. Camerata CD 3CM-58.

Concerto. See Moroi.

Norton, Spencer

Partita for 2 pianos and orchestra. See Pozdro.

Nyman, Michael

Piano Concerto; *MGV* (*Musique à Grande Vitesse*). Argo CD 443 382–2.

Ogdon, John

Concerto no. 1. Shostakovich Concerto no. 2. Angel LP S-36805.

Ohana, Maurice

Sarabande for harpsichord and orchestra; *Plainte pour Ignacio Sanchez Mejias*. Musidisc LP RC697.

Synaxis for two pianos, percussion and orchestra. Malec *Oral* for speaker and orchestra. Musical Heritage Society LP MHS 1082.

Oldham, Kevin

Concerto. Hampton Variations on *Amazing Grace*. Hirsch *Tango Bittersweet*. Gannon *Triad-O- Rama* for oboe, clarinet, horn, and bassoon. Catalyst CD 09026-61979–2.

Olsen, Ole

Little Suite for piano and string orchestra. NKF CD 50024–2.

Orbón, Julian

Partita no. 4 for piano and orchestra. Falla *Noches en Los Jardines de Espana*. Olympia LP OCD 351.

Otte, Hans

Passages for piano and orchestra. Zimmermann *Musique pour les Soupers du Roi Ubu,* ballet; *Photoptosis*—prelude for large orchestra; *Stille und Umkehe*—orchestral sketches; *Monologue* for two pianos; *Four Short Etudes* for cello. Stockhausen *Kantakte* for electronic sounds, piano and percussion. Becker *Stabil-Instabil* for large orchestra. Lachenmann Air for large orchestra and percussion. Biel String Quartet no. 2. Wittinger *Om* for orchestra. Kelemen *Changeant* for cello and orchestra. Deutsche Harmonia Mundi 3 LPs DMR 1013–15.

Pade, Steen

Concerto. Nielsen *Il Giardino Magico*. Norby *Rilke Lieder*. Point CD PCD 5083.

Paderewski, Ignacy Jan

Concerto. Sound CD 3446.

Polish Fantasy; Symphony in B minor. Olympia CD OCD 302.

Paisiello, Giovanni

Concerto in C. K. Stamitz Concerto in F. Turnabout LP TV 34001S.

Concerto nos. 1, 5, 7, and 8. ASV CD DCA 873.
Concerto nos. 2, 3, 4, and 6 are available on the ASV label.

Pálenícek, Josef
Concerto no. 3. Kalabiv Concerto. Supraphon LP 1 10 1680 G.

Palmgren, Selim
Concerto nos. 2. *The River,* 3. *Metamorphosos,* and 5. Finlandia CD FACD 379.

Paulson, Gustaf
Concerto no. 2. Fernström *Den Kapriciöse Trubaduren.* Dahl *Maison de Fous.* Carprice LP CAP 1238.

Pergolesi, Giovanni Batista
Concerto for two harpsichords; Concerto for violin. See Durante.

Perle, George
Serenade no. 3 for piano and orchestra; *Ballade;* Concertino. Nonesuch LP 979 108–1.

Perrenoud, Jean-Frédéric
Contrées (concertino) for piano. See Gerber.

Persichetti, Vincent
Concerto; Symphony no. 5. New World CD NW 370–2.

Pfitzner, Hans
Concerto. Marco Polo CD 8.223162.

Pierné, Gabriel
Concerto, op. 12. See Lalo.

Pijper, Willem
Concerto; Symphony no. 2; Six Adagios; String Quartets nos. 4 and 5. Composers' Voice CD 1.

Piston, Walter
Concertino. See Schuman.
Concerto for two pianos and orchestra. Gould *Dance Variations.* Copland *Danzón Cubano; Rodeo; El Salón México.* Koch International Classics CD 3–7002-2.

Pixis, Johann Peter
Concerto for piano, violin, and string orchestra. Moscheles *Grande Sonata Symphonique,* op. 112. Turnabout LP TV-S 34590.

Pololáník, Zdenek
Concerto Grosso for flute, guitar, harpsichord, and strings. Podesva Sonatina *Drammatica* for oboe and piano; *Homage to Leos Janácek.* Panton LP 8110 0294.

Porter, Quincy
Concerto for harpsichord. Barati Harpsichord quartet. CRI LP 226USD.

Poulenc, Francis

Aubade; Concerto; Concerto for two pianos. EMI CD CDM 7 647142.

Concerto for two pianos; *Elégie;* Capriccio *L'Embarquement pour Cythìre;* Sonata *a quatre mains* (four hands). Philips CD 426 284–2.

Concerto *Champetre;* Concerto for harpsichord. Supraphon LP 50 926.

Previn, André

Concerto; Concerto for guitar and orchestra. London CD 425 107–2.

Prokofiev, Sergei

Concerto no. 1; Toccata; Sonata no. 8. Hungaroton LP SHLX 90048.

Concerto no. 1. See Tedeschi.

Concerto no. 3. Tchaikovsky Concerto no. 1. Deutsche Grammophon CD 415 062–2.

Concerto no. 3. See Rachmaninoff Concerto no. 4.

Concerto no. 4. Britten *Diversions,* op. 21. Ravel Concerto for the left hand. Sony CD SK 47188.

Concerto no. 5. Rachmaninoff Concerto no. 2. Deutsche Grammophon CD 415 119–2.

Puccini, Domenico

Concerto. Michele Puccini *Concertone* for flute, clarinet, trumpet, horn, and orchestra. Bongiovanni CD GB 2048–2.

Rachmaninoff, Sergei

Concerto nos. 1 and 2. Phillips CD 412 881–2.

Concerto no. 2. See Prokofieff.

Concerto nos. 2 and 3. Sony CD SK 47183.

Concerto no. 4. Prokofief Concerto no. 3. Melodiya LP C 01417–18.

Rhapsody on a Theme of Paganini. Saint-Saëns Concerto no. 2. Phillips CD 410 052–2.

Raff, Joachim

Concerto, op. 185. See Hiller.

Concerto; *Ode to Spring* for piano and orchestra. Ferruccio Busoni *Konzertstück.* Claves CD 50-8806.

Konzertstück, op. 76; Concerto. See Busoni.

Rajna, Thomas

Concerto no. 1; *Music* for violin and piano. Claremont LP GSE602.

Rautavaara, Einojuhani

Concerto nos. 1 and 2. Ondine CD ODE 757–2.

Ravel, Maurice

Concertos (two). Pro-Art CD CDD265.

Concerto for left hand. See Prokofieff Concerto no. 4.

Rawsthorne, Alan

Concerto nos. 1 and 2. Lyrita LP SRCS.101.

Reinecke, Carl
Concerto nos. 1 and 2. Genesis CD GCD 102.

Reger, Max
Concerto, op. 114. Koch-Schwann CD 311058.

Reizenstein, Franz
Concerto *Popolare* for piano and orchestra. Angel LP 35500.

Rejcha, Antonín and Josef
Concerto in E-flat by A. Rejcha. Concerto, op. 2, no. 1, for viola and orchestra by J. Rejcha. Supraphon CD CO-1969.

Remenkov, Stefan
Concerto no. 1; Concertino for violin and orchestra; Suite for flute and string orchestra. Balkanton LP BCA 1300/430.

Respighi, Ottorino
Concerto in Modo Misolidio; Three Preludes on Gregorian Themes. Marco Polo CD 8.220176.
Concerto in A minor; *Concerto in Modo Misolidio*. Chandos CD CHAN9285.

Revutsky, L.
Concerto, op. 18. Melodiya LP C10 28549 004.

Rheinberger, Joseph
Concerto, op. 94. See Litolff.

Ritchie, Anthony
Concertino; J. Ritchie *Aquarius* for string orchestra. Moon *Shadows*. Elmsly *Neither from nor Towards*. Kiwi LP SLD-71.

Riegger, Wallingford
Concerto for piano and woodwind quintet; *Romanza; Dance Rhythms; Music* for orchestra; *Music* for brass choir; Movement for two trumpets, trombone and piano; *Nonet* for brass; Symphony no. 3. CRE CD 572.

Rieti, Vittorio
Concerto for harpsichord; Partita for harpsichord, flute, oboe and string quartet. CRI LP SD312.

Rimsky-Korsakoff, Nikolai
Concerto, op. 90. Arensky *Fantasie on a Russian Theme,* op. 48. A. Tcherepnin Concerto no. 5 for piano and orchestra. RBM LP 3016.

Rodrigo, Joaquin
Concierto Heroico; Cinco Piezas Infantiles; Soleriana. EMI LP 270397 1

Romero, Paul
Concerto. See Urakabe.

Rorem, Ned

Concerto for piano left hand and orchestra; *Eleven Studies for Eleven Players*. New World 80445–2.

Concerto in six movements; *Eagles; Air Music*. Albany CD TROY 047.

Ross, Walter

Mosaic (Concerto) for piano and orchestra. Johnson *Letter to the World;* Suite for orchestra. Ward Concertino for strings. Rendleman Concertino for tenor saxophone and orchestra. Albany TROY 111.

Rossum, Frederik

Concerto; *Requisitore* for brass and percussion; *Eloquences* for horn and orchestra. Polygram 1980 015.

Roussel, Albert

Concerto, op. 36; Concertino for cello and orchestra; *Petite Suite; Bacchus et Ariane*. Cybelia CD CY 2002.

Concerto. See Lalo.

Rózsa, Miklós

Concerto, op. 31; Concerto for violin. Pantheon CD DO7124.

Spellbound Concerto for two pianos, ondes Martenot, and orchestra; *New England Concerto* for two pianos and orchestra; Overture to *The World; The Flesh and the Devil;* Overture to *Because of Him*. Varese Sarabande LP 704.260.

Rozycki, Ludomir

Ballade for piano and orchestra; Symphonic Scherzo; *Stanczyk;* Symphonic Poem; *Anhelli; Pan Twardowski*. Olympia CD OCD 306.

Rubinstein, Anton

Concerto no. 1. Orion LP ORS 79347.

Concerto no. 3. Orion LP ORS 74149.

Concerto no. 4. Rimsky-Korsakov Concerto. Arensky *Fantasy on a Russian Folk Song,* op. 48. Price- Less CD D24797.

Concerto no. 4. See Thalberg.

Concerto no. 5. Genesis CD GCD-103.

Fantaisie; Concertstück, both for piano and orchestra. Marco Polo CD 8.223190.

Ruzicka, Peter

Rapprochement and Silence—Four Fragments of Schumann for piano and forty-two strings; *Satyagraha;* Preludes for piano. Koch-Schwann CD 311082.

Saegusa, Shigeaki

Symphony *Do-Ran* for piano and orchestra. Kitty Records CD H30K20077.

Saeverud, Harald

Concerto; *Peer Gynt Suite* nos. 1 and 2. Aurora CD NCD-B 4954.

Saint-Saëns

Carnival of the Animals. Ravel *Ma Mére l'Oye*. Phillips CD 400 016–2.

Concerto no. 1; *Wedding Cake; Rapsodie d'Auvergne; Allegro Appassionato; Africa*. Angel CD 49757.

Concerto nos. 2 and 4. Angel CD 47816.

Concerto no. 2. See Françaix and Rachmaninoff *Rhapsody on a Theme of Paganini*.

Concerto nos. 3 and 5. Angel CD 49051.

Salieri, Antonio

Concerto; Concerto for flute, oboe and orchestra. Francesco Salieri *La Tempesta di Mare;* Sinfonia. Erato CD R32E-1031.

Concertos (two). Italia LP ITL 70028.

Sarközy, Istaván

Confessioni (*Anno 1853*) for piano and orchestra; concerto *Semplice* (*Ricordanze* II) for violin and orchestra. Hungaroton LP SLPX 12515.

Sauguet, Henri

Concerto no. 1. Fauré *Ballade* for piano and orchestra; Nocturne no. 1; Impromptu no. 2. Chant du Monde CD LCD 278330.

Saygun, Ahmed Adnan

Concerto; Symphony no. 3; Lento. Erkin Concerto for violin and orchestra; Symphony no. 2. Melodiya LP D 011581–84.

Scambati, Giovanni

Concerto, op. 15. Genesis LP GS 1020.

Schafer, R. Murray

Concerto for harpsichord and eight wind instruments. Forsyth Fanfare; *Three Masquerades*. Kulesha Chamber Concerto no. 3. Centrediscs CD CMC CD-3488.

Scharwenka, Xavier

Concerto no. 1. Chopin Concerto no. 1. Collins Classics CD 12632.

Concerto no. 2 (Finale). See Liszt *Totentanz*.

Concerto no. 2; Scherzo, op. 4; *Erzaehlung am Klavier* no. 2; *Novelette,* op. 22; Polonaise, op. 42. Candide LP CE31046.

Schmitt, Florent

Symphonic *concertante,* op. 82, for piano and orchestra; *Reves,* op. 65; Soirs, op. 5. Valois CD V 4687.

Schnittke, Alfred

Concerto; Concerto *Grosso* (1977); Concerto for oboe. BIS CD 377.

Schobert, Johann

Concerto in G. See Boccherini.

Schoenberg, Arnold
Concerto, op. 42. Schumann Concerto. Deutsche Grammophon CD 427 771–2.

Schoenfield, Paul
Four Parables for piano and orchestra; *Klezmer Rondos* for flute and orchestra. Argo CD 440 212–2.

Schröter, Johann-Samuel
Concerto, op. 3, no. 3. See Mozart, K.107
Concerto in C, op. 3, no. 3. See Abel.

Schubert, Franz
Adagio and Rondo *concertante,* D.487, arranged for piano and orchestra. See Genzmer.

Schuman, William
Concerto. Piston Concertino. Turnabout LP TV 34733.

Schumann, Clara
Concerto; Trio; 3 Romances for violin and piano. Pro- Arte CD CDD 395.

Schumann, Robert
Concerto. Grieg Concerto. Deutsche Grammophon CD 410 021–2.
Konzertstück; Concert Allegro; Concerto. Turnabout LP Qtv S 34559.
Introduction et Allegro Appassionato for piano and orchestra. See Dvorák.

Scott, Cyril
Concerto no. 1. Lyrita LP SRCS.81.
Concerto no. 2; *Early One Morning*. Lyrita LP SRCS.82.

Scriabin, Alexander
Concerto, op. 20; *The Poem of Ecstasy; Prometheus*. London LP 417 252.

Segerstam, Leif
Concerto no. 1; Concertino-Fantasia for violin, piano, and small orchestra; *Orchestral Diary Sheet* no. 34. Kontrapunkt CD 32184.
Concerto no. 3 *So It Feel;* Symphony no. 13; *Moments of Peace* III. Bis CD 484.

Seixas, Carlos de
Concerto harpsichord. See Cimarosa.
Concertos in A major and G minor; Sinfonia in B-flat major. Portugalsom LP 860002/PS.

Sessions, Roger
Concerto. Thorne Concerto no. 3. New World CD 80443–2.

Shchedrin, Rodion
Concerto no. 1; Sonata; Three Pieces from *The Humpbacked Horse;* Eight Pieces for piano. Melodiya CD MCD 259.
Concerto nos. 1 and 2. Melodiya LP 149 001.

Shostakovich, Dimitri
Concerto nos. 1 and 2. Nimbus CD 5308.
Concerto no. 2. See Ogdon and Klami.

Sierra, Roberto
Concierto Nocturnal for harpsichord and orchestra. See Falla.

Simonis, Ferdinando
Concerto. Banchieri 3 Canzones. Bongiovanni LP GB 5006.

Sinding, Christian
Concerto in D-flat major; Symphony no. 1. NKF CD 50016–2.

Siqueira, Baptista
Concerto in E. Uirapuru LP LPU 10015.
Concerto in D; *Murmúrios da Tarde*. Uirapuru LP LPU-10015.
Nordeste (Symphony) for piano and orchestra; *Jandaia*. Uirapuru LPU-1001.

Smalley, Roger
Concerto; Symphony. Oz Music CD OZM1001.

Smith, Russell
Concerto no. 2. Hoiby Concerto, op. 17. CRI LP 214.

Söderlundh, Lille Bror
Suite from *Havang* for piano and string orchestra. Nilson *Meditation* for viola and string orchestra; *Six Popular Tunes; Three Swedish Folk Songs*. Debussy four piano preludes arranged for string orchestra. Bluebell CD ABCD 038.

Sommerfeldt, Oistein
Towards a Yearning (concerto) for piano and ochestra; Sinfonia *La Betulla; Fable Suite* no. 3 for piano; *From William Blake's Poetry;* Three Songs. Norwegian Composers LP NC 4902.

Soriano, Enrique
Concerto. Santa Cruz *Preludios Dramáticos*. Letelier *Preludios Vegetales*. Interamerican Musical Editions LP OEA–011.

Stamitz, Karl
Concerto in F. See Paisiello.

Stanford, Charles Villiers
Concerto no. 2; *Concert Variations Upon an English Theme* for piano and orchestra. Chandos CD CHAN 8737.

Stavenhagen, Bernard
Concerto, op. 4. Sinding Concerto. Candide LP QCE 31110.

Stenhammar, Wilhelm
Concerto no. 1. Sterling CD CDS 1004–2.
Concerto no. 2; *Chitra*. Bis CD 476.

Stephenson, Allan
Concerto; Toccata *Festiva*. Claremont LP CTSO 2.
Concertino; Concerto for oboe. Claremont LP GSE 601.

Stevens, Bernard
Concerto, op. 26; *Dance Suite,* op. 28; Variations, op. 36. Marco Polo CD 25470.

Stoikov, Todor
Concerto no. 1; Concerto for violin and orchestra. Balkanton LP BCA 1300/445.

Stoyanov, Vesselin
Concerto no. 1. Vladigerov Concerto no. 3. Gega CD GD 107.

Strauss, Richard
Burleske for piano and orchestra. See Dohnányi.
Burleske for piano and orchestra; *Paregon* for piano left hand and orchestra; *Stimmungsbilder*. Arabesque CD 6567.

Stravinsky, Igor
Concerto for piano and wind instruments; Movements for piano and orchestra; Capriccio for piano and orchestra; Concerto for violin and orchestra. Sony CD SMK 46295.

Suder, Joseph
Concerto; *Ariette and Burlesque* for clarinet and piano; *Four Dances in Traditional Style; Two Lyric Pieces;* Scherzo; *Four Piano Pieces*. Calig CD CAL 50888.

Suderburg, Robert
Concerto, *Within the Mirror of Time*. Schuman Symphony no. 8. Col LP 34140.

Sung-Jen, Hsu
Concerto. Chin-Yuan Concertino. Shue-Long *A Sketch of the Rainy Harbor* (concerto) for piano and orchestra. Thorofon CD CTH 2024.

Surinach, Carlos
Concerto. Montsalvatge Concerto *Breve*. London LP CS6990.
Concertino for piano, strings, and percussion. See Castelnuovo-Tedesco.

Svetlanov, Evgeni
Concerto; Preludes-Symphonic *Reflections; The Red Guelder-Rose*. Russian Disc CD RD CD 11 043.

Sydeman, William
Concerto for piano four hands. Spiegelman *Morsels*. Moss *Homage*. Wuorinen *Making Ends Meet*. DESTO LP DC-7131.

Szymanowski, Karol
Symphonie concertante (Symphony no. 4) for piano and orchestra; Concerto nos. 1 and 3 for violin and orchestra. Pantheon CD D18401.

Tailleferre, Germaine
Ballade for piano and orchestra. Chaminade *Concertstück.* Amalia Concerto for twelve instruments and cembalo obbligato; Divertimento for piano and strings. Turnabout LP TV 34754.

Takemitsu, Toru
Asterism for piano and orchestra; Requiem; *Green; The Dorian Horizon.* RCA LP LSC03099.
Arc I and II for piano and orchestra; Requiem for strings; *The Dorian Horizon.* Victor CD VDC-5507.
Riverrun for piano and orchestra; *Water-Ways* for clarinet, violin, cello, piano, two harps, and two vibraphones; *Rain Spell* for quintet; *Rain Coming; Three Line* for chamber orchestra. Virgin Classics CD VD 7 91180–2.

Taktakishvili, Otar
Concerto no. 1; Concerto for violin. Melodiya LP 33 10–10115–16(a).
Concerto no. 3; Five *Vocal Poems.* Melodiya LP 33 C 10–09347–48(a).

Tanev, Alexander
Divertimento-*Concertante* for piano and orchestra; *Building Music;* Concerto for winds. Nimbus LP ATD 8205.

Tavares, Hekel
Concerto, op. 105, no. 2; Suite *Sinfonica André de Leao* e *o Demonio de Cabelo Encarnado.* Estúdio Eldorado LP (no number).
Concerto in Brazilian Forms; André de Leao and the Crimson-Haired Demon. Estúdio Eldorado LP 63.82.0355.

Tchaikovsky, Alexander
Concerto no. 2 for piano and string orchestra; Concerto for violin and orchestra. Art & Electronics CD AEC-10273.

Tchaikovsky, Boris
Concerto. Melodiya LP 33 C 10–06427–8.

Tchaikovsky, Peter
Concerto no. 1. See Prokofieff Concerto no. 3.
Concerto nos. 1, 2, and 3. Sony 2 CDs M2YK 46460.

Tcherepnin, Alexander
Bagatelles, op. 5, for piano and orchestra. Mouravieff *Nativité.* Shostakovich Chamber Symphony, op. 110. Turnabout LP TV-S 34545.
Concerto no. 2. Honegger Suite *Archaïque.* Louisville Orchestra Series LP 615.
Concerto no. 5. See Rimsky-Korsakoff.

Triple Concertino for violin, cello, piano, and orchestra; Symphony no. 3; *Georgian Rhapsody* for cello and orchestra. Thorofon CD CTH 2021.

Tedeschi, Alberto Bruni

Fantasia, Recitativo Quasi una Danza for piano and orchestra. Prokofiev Concerto no. 1. Edition Brockhoff LP FSM 68211.

Tellefsen, Thomas

Concerto, op. 8. Winter-Hjelm Symphony no. 2. Polygram LP NKF 30058.

Thalberg, Sigismund

Concerto. Rubinstein Concerto no. 4. Vox CD VU 9014.

Thorne, Francis

Concerto no. 3. See Sessions.

Tippett, Michael

Concerto; Concerto for Double String Orchestra; *Fantasia Concertante on a Theme of Corelli;* Piano Sonata nos. 1 and 2; String Quartet no. 1. EMI 2 LPs EX29 0228 3.

Tomasek, Jan Vaclav

Concerto no. 1. Wenzel Symphony no. 1. Candide LP CE 31073.

Trajkovic, Vlastimir

Duo for piano and orchestra; *Arion* for guitar and strings; Ten Preludes for Solo Guitar. RTB LP 2330016.

Tubin, Eduard

Concertino; Sinfonietta on Estonian Motifs; Symphony no. 7. Bis CD 401.

Tveitt, Geirr

Concerto no. 5. Aurora LP AR 1906.

Urakabe, Shinji

Concerto. Kurokawa Concerto; *Rainbow Fantasy*. Romero Concerto. Yoguchi *Fantasy of Chateau; Silhouette*. Iwauchi *The Hunters; The Milkyway Train*. Yamashita *Dance of a Comic Doll*. Yamaha 2 LPs 19–282.

Vackár, Tomás

Concerto *Recitativo; Tri Dopisy Dívkám; Metamorfózy*. Supraphon LP 1 10 0409.

Válek, Jirí

Symphony *Revolutionary* for piano trio, wind quintet, and orchestra. Vacek *Poem of Fallen Heros*. Panton LP 110528.

Van Baaren, Kees

Concerto. Vlijmen Serenata II for flutes and four instrumental groups. Kruyf *Einst dem Grau*. Donemus LP DAVS 6603.

Vaughan Williams, Ralph

Concerto; Symphony no. 9. Chandos CD CHAN 8941.

Concerto for 2 pianos; Symphony no. 8. Angel LP S-36625.

Velehorschi, Alexandru

Concerto in E. Popa Concerto for trumpet; Concerto for clarinet. Electrecord LP STM-ECE 01546.

Villa-Lobos, Hector

Concerto nos. 1–5. London 2 CDs 430 628.

Momoprecoce for piano and orchestra; Concerto no. 5; Symphony no. 4; Choros nos. 2, 5, 10, and 11; *Bachianas Brasileiras Invocaçao em Defesa da Pátria.* EMI 6 CDs CZS 7 67229 2

Viotti, Battista

Concerto for piano, violin, and strings. Mendelssohn Concerto no. 1 for piano, violin, and strings. Koch-Schwann CD 311 047.

Vladigerov, Pancho

Concerto no. 3. See Stoyanov.

Concerto no. 4. Melodiya LP 33 M10–39759–60.

Concertos (five); Concertos for violin and orchestra; *Bulgarian Rhapsody; Song; Burlesque; Three Bulgarian Paraphrases;* Five *Silhouettes* for piano; Concerto-Fantasy; *Elegiac Romance,* both for cello and orchestra. Balkanton LP BCA 10630/87.

Vogel, Wladimir

Hörformen for piano and string orchestra. See Zbinden.

Volkmann, Robert

Konzertstück for piano and orchestra; Concerto for violincello. Turnabout LP TV-S 34576.

Vorísek, Jan Hugo

Introduction et Rondeau Brillant, op. 22; *Variations de Bravoure,* op. 14, both for piano and orchestra; Symphony. Supraphon CD CO-1787.

Wagner, Henrikh

Concerto. Podkovyrov Quartet for four flutes. Kaminsky Concert Fantasia for piano and orchestra. Melodiya 33A 023793–94(a).

Ward, Robert

Concerto; Symphony nos. 2 and 3. Bay Cities CD BCD-1001.

Weber, Ben

Concerto, op. 52. Wuorinen Concerto. CRI LP 239 USD.

Weber, Carl Maria von

Concerto nos. 1 and 2; *Konzertstück.* Europa Musica CD 350238.

Weiner, Stanley

Conciertos de Sanlúcar nos. 3, 4, and 5; no. 5 is for violin, piano, and orchestra; no. 3 is for violin, flute, and orchestra; no. 4 is for violin, cello, and orchestra. Koch-Schwann 311154.

Werner, Gregor Joseph
Pastorale for harpsichord and string orchestra. See Dittersdorf

Wieniawski, Jósef
Concerto. See Chopin-Tausig.

Wiklund, Adolf
Concerto nos. 1 and 2. Caprice CD CAP 21363.

Williamson, Malcolm
Concerto no. 2; Concerto for two pianos and strings. EMI LP EMD 5520.
Concerto no. 3; Organ Concerto. Lyrita LP SRCS.79.

Wilson, Thomas
Concerto; Introit (*Towards the Light*). Chandos CDP 8626.

Wismer, Pierre
Concerto no. 3; Symphonic Suite. Quantum CD QM 6908.

Wuorinen, Charles
Concerto. See B. Weber.

Yashiro, Akio
Concerto; Concerto for cello and orchestra. Miyoshi Concerto for Orchestra. Matsumura Prelude for Orchestra. Denon CD COCO-6721.

Yokoyama, Yukio
Concerto no. 2; *Hope*. Nishimura Concerto no. 3. Mochizuki *As Time Goes By*. Kubota *Cheerful Dumbo*. Yamaha LP 19–298.

Zarins, Margeris
Concerto *Grosso* for harpsichord, piano, and orchestra. Kalnins Suite of Latvian Folk-Songs. Melodiya LP C10 19181 008.

Zbinden, Julien François
Concerto da Camera, op. 16, for piano and orchestra; Meier *Esquisses* for piano, strings, and percussion. Vogel *Hörformen* for piano and string orchestra. Bloch Concerto *Grosso* no. 1. Gallo CD-728.

Zelezny, Lubomír
Concertante Music. Drejsl Symphony for String Orchestra. Panton LP 11 0344.

Bibliography

Abraham, Gerald. *Chopin's Musical Style*. London: Oxford University Press, 1939; reprinted and corrected, Westport, Conn.: 1980.
Abraham, Gerald, ed. *Handel: A Symposium*. 3rd ed. Westport, Conn.: Greenwood Press, 1980.
Abraham, Gerald. *This Modern Music*. 3rd ed. Boston: Crescendo, 1955.
Adams, Frank John Jr. "The Place of the Piano Concerto in the Career of Mozart: Vienna 1782–1786." Ph.D. dissertation, Harvard University, 1972.
Aiken, Ruth Karin. "Karl-Birger Blomdahl." M.M. thesis, University of Cincinnati, 1968.
Allison, Rees Stephen. "The Piano Works of Alan Rawsthorne." Ph.D. dissertation, Washington University, 1970.
Almeida, Renato. *Historia da Musica Brasileira*. Segunda Edicao. Correta e Aumentada. Rio de Janeiro: F. Briguiet & Co., 1942.
Ammer, Christine. *Unsung, A History of Women in American Music*. Westport, Conn.: Greenwood Press, 1980.
Anderson, E. Ruth. *Contemporary American Composers: A Biographical Dictionary*. Boston: G. K. Hall & Co., 1976.
Anderson, E. Ruth. *Contemporary American Composers: A Biographical Dictionary*. 2nd ed. Boston: G. K. Hall & Co., 1982.
Anderson, Owen. "New Works." *Music Journal* 24 (March 1966): 141.
Andreis, Josip. *Music in Croatia*. 2nd enl. ed. Zaqreb: Institute of Musicology, Academy of Music, 1982.
Apel, Paul H. *Music of the Americas North and South*. New York: Vantage Press, 1958.
Apel, Willi. *Harvard Dictionary of Music*. Cambridge, Mass.: Harvard University Press, 1956.
Appleby, David P. *The Music of Brazil*. Austin: University of Texas Press, 1989.
Appleby, David Percy. "A Study of Selected Compositions by Contemporary Brazilian Composers." Ph.D. dissertation, Indiana University, 1956.
Arizaga, Rodolfo. *Enciclopedia de la Música Argentina*. Buenos Aires: Fondo Nacional de las Artes, 1971.
Arnold Bax, A Catalogue of His Music. Compiled by Graham Parlett. London: Triad Press, 1972.
Arozamena, Jesus M. De. *Jesus Guridi*. Madrid: Editora Nacional, 1967.
ASCAP Biographical Dictionary. Compiled by Jaques Cattrell Press. 4th ed. New York: R. R. Bowker Co., 1980.

Asow, Erich H. Mueller von. *Richard Strauss, Thematisches Verzeichnis*. 3 vols. Wien: Verlag L. Doblinger (B. Herzmansky) K. G., 1974.

Asow, Hedwig, and Mueller E. H. von. *Kurschners Deutscher Musiker-Kalender 1954*. Berlin: Walter de Gruyter & Co., 1954.

Austin, William W. *Music in the 20th Century*. New York: W. W. Norton & Co., 1966.

Bach, Carl Philip Emanuel. *Essay on the True Art of Playing Keyboard Instruments*. Translated by William J. Mitchell. New York: W. W. Norton & Co., 1949; reprint, London: Eulenburg Books, 1985.

Badura-Skoda, Eva and Paul. *Interpreting Mozart on the Keyboard*. Translated by Leo Black. New York: St. Martin's Press, 1957.

Baker, David N., Lida M. Belt, and Herman C. Hudson, eds. *The Black Composer Speaks*. Metuchen, N.J.: Scarecrow Press, 1978.

Balough, Teresa. *A Complete Catalogue of the Works of Percy Grainger*. Nedlands, Western Australia: The University of Western Australia, 1975.

Bals, Karen Elizabeth. "The American Piano Concerto in the Mid-Twentieth Century." D.M.A. dissertation, University of Kansas, 1982.

Bator, Victor. *The Béla Bartók Archives, History and Catalogue*. New York: Bartók Archives Publication, 1963.

Baum, Richard. "Joseph Wölfl (1773–1812), Leben, Klavierkammermusik, und Klavierkonzerte." Inaugural-Dissertation zur Erlangung der Doktörwurde der Philosophischen Fakultat (I. Sektion) der Ludwig-Maximilians-Universität zu Munchen vorgelegt von Richard Baum aus Esslingen. Kassel: Bärenreiter, 1928.

Beck, G. H. *Darius Milhaud; Etude Suivie du Catalogue Chronologique Complet du son Oeuvre*. Paris: Heugel & Cie, 1949.

Behague, Gerard. *Music in Latin America: An Introduction*. Englewood Cliffs, N.J.: Prentice Hall, 1979.

Behague, Gerard. *The Beginnings of Musical Nationalism in Brazil*. Detroit, Mich.: Information Coordinators, 1971.

Bell, Carla Huston. *Olivier Messiaen*. Boston: Twayne Publishers, 1984.

Bennett, Clive. "A Record Review." *Tempo* 125 (June 1978): 37–38.

Benton, Rita. *Ignace Pleyel: A Thematic Catalogue of His Compositions*. New York: Pendragon Press, 1977.

Bergaas, Mark Jerome. "Compositional Style in the Keyboard Works of Hugo Distler (1908–1942)." Ph.D. dissertation, Yale University, 1978.

Berger, Arthur. *Aaron Copland*. New York: Oxford University Press, 1953.

Billaudot, Gérard, ed., M. Fedorov, M. Guinard, and M. M. Seymour. *Andre Jolivet: Catalogue of Works*. Paris: Billaudot, 1969.

Bird, John, Alan Woolgar, and David Tall. *Percy Grainger*. London: Schott & Co., 1982.

Blair, Ted M. "Henry Charles Litolff: (1818–1891): His Life and Piano Music." Ph.D. dissertation, University of Iowa, 1968.

Bloch, Suzanne. *Ernest Bloch: Creative Spirit*. New York: Jewish Music Council, 1976.

Blom, Eric, ed. *Grove's Dictionary of Music and Musicians*. 9 vols. New York: St. Martin's Press, 1960.

Blom, Eric. "Works for Solo Instrument and Orchestra." *The Music of Tchaikovsky*. Edited by Gerald Abraham. New York: W. W. Norton & Co., 1946; reprint, 1974.

Blume, Friedrich. *Die Musik in Geschichte und Gegenwart*. 14 vols. Kassel und Basel: Im Barenreiter, 1949–1951. 3 vols. Supplement, 1973.

Blume, Friedrich. "The Concertos: (1) Their Sources." In *The Mozart Companion*. Edited by H. C. Robbins Landon and Donald Mitchell. Translated by H. C. Stevens. New York: W. W. Norton & Co., 1969.
Boelza, Igor. *Handbook of Soviet Musicians*. Edited by Alan Bush. London: The Pilot Press, 1943.
Bolen, Jane Moore. "The Five Berlin Cembalo Concertos, P. 390, of John Christian Bach: A Critical Edition." Ph.D. dissertation, Florida State University, 1974.
Boretz, Benjamin, and Edward T. Cone, eds. *Perspective on American Composers*. New York: W. W. Norton & Co., 1971.
Borrás, Tomás. *Conrado del Campo*. Madrid: Instituto do Estudios Madrileños, 1954.
Boyd, Malcolm. *Grace Williams*. n.p.: University of Wales Press, 1980.
Branson, David. *John Field and Chopin*. New York: St. Martin's Press, 1972.
Brawley, Thomas Michael. "The Instrumental Works of Robert Volkmann (1815–1883)." Ph.D. dissertation, Northwestern Unversity, 1975.
Bennecke, Dietrich. *Das Lebenswerk Max Buttings*. Leipzig: VEB Deutscher Verlag fur Musik Leipzig, 1973.
Broder, Nathan. "Mozart and the Clavier." *Musical Quarterly* 27 (October 1941): 422–432.
Broder, Nathan. "The First Guide to Mozart." *Musical Quarterly* 42 (April 1956): 223–229.
Brofsky, Howard. "The Instrumental Music of Padre Martini." Ph.D. dissertation, New York University, 1963.
Brofsky, Howard. "The Symphonies of Padre Martini." *Musical Quarterly* 51 (October 1965): 649–673.
Brook, Barry S., ed. *The Breitkopf Thematic Catalogue: The Six Parts and Sixteen Supplements 1762-1787*. Facsimile edition with introduction and indexes by Barry S. Brook. New York: Dover Publications, 1966.
Brown, Maurice J. E. *Chopin: An Index of His Works in Chronological Order*. 2nd rev. ed. New York: Da Capo Press, 1972.
Browning, John. "Samuel Barber's Piano Concerto Turns Twenty-Five." *Clavier* 26 (September 1987): 24–27.
Bruhns, Svend, and Dan Fog. *Finn Hoffding Kompositioner*. Copenhagen: Dan Fog Musikforlag, 1969.
Bryant, Giles. *Healey Willan Catalogue*. Ottawa: National Library of Canada, 1972.
Cage, John. *John Cage: Catalogue of Compositions*. New York: C. F. Peters, 1993.
Callaway, Frank, and David Tunley. *Australian Composition in the Twentieth Century*. Melbourne: Oxford University Press, 1978.
Calvocoressi, M. D. *A Survey of Russian Music*. Westport, Conn.: Greenwood Press, 1974.
Canadian Broadcasting Corporation. *Thirty-Four Biographies of Canadian Composers*. St. Clair Shores, Mich.: Scholarly Press, 1964; reprint 1972.
Canadian Music Centre. *List of Canadian Orchestra Music—Supplement*. Toronto: Canadian Music Centre, 1968.
Canteloube, Joseph. *Anthologie des Chants Populaires Français*. 4 vols. Paris: Durand & Cie, 1951.
Carlson, Effie B. *A Bio-Bibliographical Dictionary of Twelve-Tone and Serial Composers*. Metuchen, N.J.: Scarecrow Press, 1970.

Carpentier, Alego. *La Musica en Cuba*. Pánuco, Mexico: Fondo de Cultura Economica, 1964.
Carrell, Norman. *Bach the Borrower*. Westport, Conn.: Greenwood Press, 1980.
Caso, Fernando H. *Héctor Campos Parsi en La Historia de la Musica Puertorriqueña*. n.p.: n.p., 1980.
Catalogue of Works by Mario Castelnuovo-Tedesco. Compiled and edited by Nick Rossi. New York: International Castelnuovo-Tedesco Society, 1977.
Chase, Gilbert. *A Guide to the Music of Latin America*. Washington: Pan American Union & Library of Congress, 1962.
Chase, Gilbert. *America's Music*. New York: McGraw-Hill Book Co., 1966.
Chase, Gilbert. *The Music of Spain*. 2nd rev. ed. New York: Dover Publications, 1959.
"A Chicago Grad Student Strikes a Career High Note, Finding a Long-Lost Liszt." *People* 31 (April 10, 1989): 113.
Clarke, Frederick Robert Charles. *Healey Willan: Life and Music*. Toronto: University of Toronto Press, 1983.
Clarke, Garrye E., ed. *Essays on American Music*. Westport, Conn.: Greenwood Press, 1977.
Clarkson, Austin. "The Works of Stefan Wolpe: A Brief Catalogue." *Notes* 41 (June 1985): 667–682.
Cobin, Marian W. "Aspects of Stylistic Evolution in Two Mozart Concertos: K.271 and K.482." *Music Review* 31 (February 1970): 1–20.
Coeuroy, Andre. *La Musique Francaise Modern*. Paris: Librairie Delagrave, 1924.
Cohen, Aaron I. *International Discography of Women Composers*. Westport, Conn.: Greenwood Press, 1984.
Cohen, Aaron I. *International Encyclopedia of Women Composers*. 2nd ed., rev. and enl. New York: Books and Music USA, ca. 1987.
Cohn, Arthur. *Twentieth-Century Music in Western Europe*. New York: Da Capo Press, 1972.
Collaer, Paul. *A History of Modern Music*. Cleveland: World Publishing Co., 1961.
Colles, H. C. *Walford Davies: A Biography*. London: Oxford University Press, 1942.
Collier, James Lincoln. *The Making of Jazz: A Comprehensive History*. Boston: Houghton Mifflin Company, 1978.
A Complete Catalogue of Compositions by Edmund Rubbra to June 1971. London: Alfred Lengnick & Co., 1971.
The Compositions of Nikolai Lopatnikoff: A Catalogue. Complied by William Critser. Pittsburgh: n.p., 1979.
Contemporary Concert Music by Women: A Directory of The Composers and Their Works. Compiled and edited by Judith Lang Zaimont and Karen Famera. Westport, Conn.: Greenwood Press, 1981.
Contemporary Norwegian Orchestral and Chamber Music. Compiled by The Society of Norwegian Composers. Oslo: Johann Grundt Tanum Forlag, 1970.
Cooper, Martin. *French Music*. London: Oxford University Press, 1951.
Cope, David H. *New Directions In Music*. n.p.: Brown and Bencham, 1993.
Copland, Aaron. *Our New Music*. New York: W. W. Norton, 1968.
Cosma, Viorel. *Muzicieni Români, Compozitori si Muzicologi Lexicon*. Bucharest: Editura Muzicala, 1970.
Covell, Roger. *Australia's Music: Themes of a New Society*. Melbourne: Sun Books, 1967.

Craggs, Stewart R. *William Walton: A Thematic Catalogue of His Musical Works*. London: Oxford University Press, 1977.

Craw, Howard Allen. "A Biography and Thematic Catalog of the Works of J. L. Dussek (1760–1812)." Ph.D. dissertation, University of Southern California, 1964.

Creative Canada, A Biographical Dictionary of Twentieth-Century Creative and Performing Artists. Compiled by Reference Division, McPherson Library, University of Victoria, BC. Toronto: University of Toronto Press, Vol. 1, 1971; Vol. 2, 1972.

Crichton, Ronald. *Manuel de Falla: Descriptive Catalogue of His Works*. London: J. & W. Chester Music, 1976.

Crickmore, Leon. "C. P. E. Bach's Harpsichord Concertos." *Music and Letters* 39 (July 1958): 227–241.

Cudworth, Charles L. "Cadence Galante: The Story of a Cliché." *Monthly Musical Record* 79 (September 1949): 176–178.

Czigány, Gyula, ed. *Contemporary Hungarian Composers*. Budapest: Editio Musica, 1970.

Czigány, Gyula, ed. *Contemporary Hungarian Composers*. Budapest: Editio Musica, 1979.

Dallin, Leon. *Techniques of Twentieth Century Composition: A Guide to the Materials of Modern Music*. 3rd ed. Dubuque, Iowa: William. C. Brown Co., 1974.

Davies, Laurence. *César Franck and His Circle*. New York: Da Capo Press, 1977.

Davies, Laurence. *Franck*. London: J. M. Dent & Sons, 1973.

Davis, Shelley George. "The Keyboard Concertos of Johann Georg Lang (1722–1798)." Ph.D. dissertation, New York University, 1971.

Dawney, Michael. "Edmund Rubbra and the Piano." *Music Review* 31 (August 1970): 241–248.

Delente, Gail Buchanan. "Selected Piano Music in France Since 1945." Ph.D. dissertation, University of Washington, 1966.

Del Mar, Norman. *Richard Strauss: A Critical Commentary on His Life and Works*. Ithaca: Cornell University, 1986.

Demuth, Norman. *Musical Trends in the Twentieth Century*. London: Rockliff Publishing Corp., 1952.

Dent, Edward J. *Ferruccio Busoni*. London: Eulenberg Books, 1974.

Dickinson, P. "Contemporary Hungarian Composers." *Recorded Sound* 12 (April-July 1971): 42–43, 782.

D'Indy, Vincent. *César Franck*. Translation and introduction by Rosa Newmarch. London: Bodley Head, 1910; reprint ed., New York: Dover Publications, 1965.

Dipiazza, Joseph Anthony. "The Piano Sonatas of Clementi." Ph.D. dissertation, University of Wisconsin-Madison, 1977.

Doyle, John G. *Louis Moreau Gottschalk 1829–1869: A Bibliographical Study and Catalog of Works*. Detroit: Information Coordinators, 1983.

Drummond, Pippa. "Johann Sebastian Bach" and "Handel." In *The German Concerto: Five Eighteenth-Century Studies*. Oxford: Clarendon Press, 1980.

Dubbiosi, Stelio. "The Piano Music of Maurice Ravel: An Analysis of the Technical and Interpretative Problems Inherent in the Pianistic Style of Maurice Ravel." 2 vols. Ph.D. dissertation, New York University, 1967.

Eagon, Angelo. *Catalog of Published Concerto Music by American Composers*. Metuchen, N.J.: Scarecrow Press, 1969.

Eastman, Sheila, and Timothy J. MeGee. *Barbara Pentland.* Toronto: University of Toronto Press, 1983.
Edel, Theodore. "Piano Music for the Left Hand Alone." D.M.A. dissertation, Manhattan School of Music, 1980.
Edmunds, John, and Gordon Boelzner. *Some Twentieth Century American Composers.* Washington: Pan American Union & Library of Congress, 1962.
Edwards, Owain. "Charles Avison; English Concerto-Writer Extraordinary." *Musical Quarterly* 59 (July 1973): 399–410.
Einstein, Alfred. *Music in the Romantic Era.* New York: W. W. Norton & Co., 1975.
Engel, Hans. *Dis Entwicklung des Deutfchen Klavierkonzerts von Mozart bis Liszt.* Leipzig: Breitkoff & Härtel, 1927.
Engel, Hans. *The Solo Concerto.* Translated by Robert Kolben. Cologne: Arno Volk Verlag, 1964.
Eschman, Karl Henry. *Changing Forms in Modern Music.* 2nd ed. Boston: E. C. Schirmer Music Co., 1968.
Evans, Edwin (Sr.). *Handbook to the Pianoforte Works of Johannes Brahms.* London: William Reeves, (1936).
Evans, Lee. "Morton Gould: His Life and Music." Ed.D. dissertation, Columbia University Teachers College, 1978.
Evans, Peter. *The Music of Benjamin Britten.* London: Dent, 1989.
Ewen, David. *European Composers Today.* New York: H. W. Wilson, 1954.
Ewen, David. *The Complete Book of 20th-Century Music.* New York: Prentice-Hall, 1952; reprint, n.p.: Blond, 1961.
Ewen, David. *The World of Twentieth-Century Music.* 4th ed. Englewood Cliffs, N.J.: Prentice-Hall, 1968.
Falck, Martin. *Wilhelm Friedemann Bach: Sein Leben und Seine Werke.* Leipzig: C. F. Kahnt Nachfolger, 1913.
Farmer, Henry George. *A History of Music in Scotland.* New York: Da Capo Press, 1970.
Farwell, Brice, ed., B. Farwell, S. F. Milbert, E. Farwell, J. Farwell, and C. F. Hensch. *A Guide to the Music of Arthur Farwell and to the Microfilm Collection of His Work.* Briarcliff Manor, NY: Stein & Day, 1972.
Ferguson, Linda. "The Concertos of Johannes Brahms: An Historical and Analytical Approach to the Compositional Process." M.M. thesis, Texas Christian University, 1969.
Fink, Robert, and Robert Ricci. *The Language of Twentieth Century Music.* New York: Schirmer Books, 1975.
Fischer, Wilhelm, ed. "Matthias Georg Monn." Band 39: *Denkmäler der Tonkunst in Osterreich.* Graz: Akademische Druck, 1959.
Fiske, Robert. *Beethoven Concertos and Overtures.* BBC Music Guides. London: British Broadcasting Corporation, 1970.
Forbes, Elliot, ed. *Thayer's Life of Beethoven.* 2 vols. Princeton, N.J.: Princeton University Press, 1964.
Foreman, Lewis. "A Catalogue of Autograph Manuscript Sources of Music by Sir Arnold Bax." *Royal Musical Association Research Chronicle* 12 (1974): 91–105.
Foreman, Lewis. *Arthur Bliss: Catalogue of the Complete Works.* London, Great Britain: Novello & Co., 1980.
Foreman, Lewis, ed. *British Music Now.* London: Paul Elek, 1975.
Forman, Denis. *Mozart's Concerto Form.* New York: Da Capo Press, 1983.

Friskin, James. "The Text of Tchaikovsky's B-Flat Minor Concerto." *Music & Letters* 50 (April 1969): 246–251.
Fukui, Masa Kitagawa. "Japanese Piano Music, 1940–1973: A Meeting of Eastern and Western Traditions." D.M.A. dissertation, University of Maryland, 1981.
Garden, Edward. *Balakirev: A Critical Study of His Life and Music*. New York: St. Martin's Press, 1967.
Garden, Edward. "Three Russian Piano Concertos." *Music & Letters* 60 (April 1979): 166–179.
Garofalo, Robert Joseph. "The Life and Works of Frederick Shepherd Converse (1871–1940)." Ph.D. dissertation, Catholic University of America, 1969.
Gavoty, Bernard. *Frederic Chopin*. Translated by Martin Sokolinsky. New York: Charles Scribner's Sons, 1977.
Gavoty, Bernard. *Louis Vierne, La Vie et L'Oeuvre*. Paris: Editions Buchet/Chastel, ca. 1980.
Geiringer, Karl. *Haydn: A Creative Life in Music*. New York: W. W. Norton & Co., 1946.
Geiringer, Karl. "W. A. Mozart the Younger." *Musical Quarterly* 27 (October 1941): 456–473.
Geiringer, Karl and Irene. *Johann Sebastian Bach: The Culmination of An Era*. New York: Oxford University Press, 1966.
Geotschius, Percy. *Mrs H. H. A. Beach*. Boston: Arthur P. Schmidt, 1906.
Giazotto, Temo. *Giovan Battista Viotti*. Milan: Edisioni Curci, 1956.
Girdlestone, Cuthbert Morton. *Mozart and His Piano Concertos*. Norman: University of Oklahoma Press, 1952.
Glennon, James. *Australian Music and Musicians*. Adelaide, Australia: Rigby, 1968.
Goldman, Richard F. "The Music of Wallingford Riegger." *Musical Quarterly* 16 (January 1950): 39–61.
Goléa, Antoine. *Marcel Landowski: L'homme et son Oeuvre*. Paris: Editions Seghers, 1969.
Golos, George S. "Some Slavic Predecessors of Chopin." *Musical Quarterly* 46 (October 1960): 437–447.
Gradenwitz, Peter. *Music and Musicians in Israel: A Comprehensive Guide to Modern Israeli Music*. 3rd ed., rev., rewritten and enl. Tel Aviv: Israeli Music Publication, 1978.
Gradenwitz, Peter. *The Music of Israel*. New York: W. W. Norton & Co., 1949.
Graue, Jerald Curtis. "Muzio Clementi and the Development of Pianoforte Music in Industrial England." Ph.D. dissertation, University of Illinois at Urbana-Champaign, 1971.
Greer, David, ed. *Hamilton Harty, His Life and Music*. New York: Da Capo Press, 1980.
Green, Mildred Denby. *Black Women Composers: A Genesis*. Boston: Twayne Publishers, 1983.
Grierson, Mary. *Donald Francis Tovey*. Westport, Conn.: Greenwood Press, 1970.
Griffiths, Paul. *The Master Musician Bartók*. London: J. M. Dent & Sons, 1984.
Grinde, Nils. *Contemporary Norwegian Music 1920-1980*. Translated by Sandra Hamilton. Oslo: Universitetsforlaget, 1981.
Grossman, Orin Louis. "The Piano Sonatas of Jan Ludislav Dussek (1760–1812)." Ph.D. dissertation, Yale University, 1975.

Guerry, Jack Edwin. "Bartok's Concertos for Solo Piano: A Stylistic and Formal Analysis." Ph.D. dissertation, Michigan State University, 1964.
Haas, Robert Bartlett, ed., P. H. Slattery, V. Arvey, W. G. Still, L. and A. Kaufmann. *William Grant Still, and the Fusion of Cultures in American Music*. Los Angeles: Black Sparrow Press, 1975.
Hansen, Peter S. *An Introduction to Twentieth Century Music*. 4th ed. Boston: Allyn & Bacon, 1978.
Hanson, Lawrence and Elisabeth. *Prokofief*. London: Cassell, 1964.
Hartog, Howard, ed. *European Music in the Twentieth Century*. Westport, Conn.: Greenwood Press, 1976.
Headington, Christopher. *Britten*. New York: Holmes & Meier, 1982.
Hedley, Arthur. *Chopin*. 4th printing. New York: Farrar, Straus & Cudaby, 1957.
Heitor, Luiz. *Música e Musicos do Brasil*. Rio de Janeiro: Livraria-Editôra de Casa do Estudante do Brasil, 1950.
Helm, E. Eugene. *Thematic Catalogue of the Works of Carl Phillip Emanuel Bach*. New Haven: Yale University, 1989.
Helm, Ernest Eugene. *Music at the Court of Frederick the Great*. Norman: University of Oklahoma Press, 1960.
Henderson, Donald Gene. "Hans Pfitzner: The Composer and His Instrumental Works." Ph.D. dissertation, University of Michigan, 1963.
Hertel, Sister M. Romana. "The Keyboard Concertos of Johann Wilhelm Hertel (1727–1789)." Ph.D. dissertation, Catholic University of America, 1964.
Hess, Willy. *Verzeichnis der Nicht in der Gesamtausgabe Veröffentlichten Werke Ludwig van Beethovens*. Wiesbaden: Breitkopf & Hártel, 1957.
Higgins, Thomas. "Tempo and Character in Chopin." *Musical Quarterly* 59 (January 1973): 106–120.
Hill, Cecil. *Ferdinand Ries, A Thematic Catalogue*. Armidale, Australia: University of New England, 1977.
Hill, Jackson. "The Music of Kees van Baaren: A Study of Transition in the Music of the Netherlands in the Second Third of the Twentieth Century." Ph.D. dissertation, University of North Carolina, 1970.
Hill, Thomas H. "Ernest Schelling (1876–1939): His Life and Contributions to Music Education Through Education Concerts." D.M.A. dissertation, Catholic University of America, 1970.
Hinds, B. Wayne. "Leo Sowerby: A Biography and Descriptive Listing of Anthems." Ed.D. dissertation, George Peabody College for Teachers, 1972.
Hinson, Maurice. "Long Lost Liszt Concerto?" *Journal of the American Liszt Society* XIII (June 1983): 53–58.
Hinson, Maurice. *Music for Piano and Orchestra*. Bloomington: Indiana University Press, 1981.
Hitchcock, H. Wiley, and Stanley Sadie, eds. *The New Grove Dictionary of American Music*. 4 vols. London: Macmillan Press, 1986.
Hoboken, Anthon van. *Joseph Hayden: Thematisch-Bibliographisches Werkverzeichnis*. Band I. Mainz: B. Schott's Söhne, 1957.
Holcomb, Dorothy Regina. "Philip Greely Clapp: His Contribution to the Music of America." Ph.D. dissertation, University of Iowa, 1972.
Hold, Trevor. "The Music of William Alwyn—2." *Composer* 44 (1972): 15–20.
Holmberg, Mark L. "Thematic Contours and Harmonic Idioms of Mario Castelnuovo-

Tedesco, as Exemplified in the Solo Concertos." Ph.D. dissertation, Northwestern University, 1974.

Holt, Richard, ed. *Nicolas Medtner*. London: Dennis Dobson, 1955.

Honegger, Marc, ed. *Catalogue des Oeuvres Musicales de Georges Migot*. Strasbourg: Institut de Musicologie, 1977.

Hopkinson, Cecil. *A Bibliographical Thematic Catalogue of the Works of John Field 1782-1837*. London: printed for the author, 1961; Bath: Harding & Curtis, n.d.

Horstman, Jean. "The Instrumental Music of Johann Ludwig Krebs." Ph.D. dissertation, New York University, 1949.

Howard, John Tasker. *Our Contemporary Composers, American Music in the Twentieth Century*. Salem, N.H.: Books for Libraries, 1975.

Howe, Ann Whitworth. "Lily Strickland: Her Contribution to American Music in the Early Twentieth Century." Ph.D. dissertation, Catholic University of America, 1968.

Howes, Frank. *The English Musical Renaissance*. Briarcliff Manor, New York: Stein & Day, 1966.

Hudson, Frederick. "A Catalogue of the Works of Charles Villiers Stanford (1852–1924)." *Music Review* 21 (February 1964): 44–57.

Hudson, Frederick. "A Revised and Extended Catalogue of the Works of Charles Villiers Stanford (1852–1924)." *Music Review* 37 (May 1976): 106–128.

Hunt, Jon Leland. "The Life and Keyboard Works of Giovanni Paisiello (1740–1816)." Ph.D. dissertation, University of Michigan, 1973.

Husarik, Stephen. "Joseph Hofmann (1876–1957), the Composer and Pianist, with Analysis of Available Reproductions of His Performances." Ph.D. dissertation, University of Iowa, 1983.

Hutchings, Arthur. *A Companion to Mozart's Piano Concertos*. 2nd ed. London: Oxford University Press, 1950; 5th impression, 1974.

Hutchings, Arthur. "The Keyboard Concerto." *Music and Letters* 23 (July 1942): 298–311.

Iglesia, Antonio. *Oscar Espla*. Madrid: Servicio de Publicaciones del Ministerio de Educación y Ciencia Secretaria General Técnica, 1973.

Igor Stravinsky: A Complete Catalogue. Compiled by Clifford Ceasar. San Francisco: San Francisco Press, 1982.

Igou, Orin Lincoln. "Contemporary Symphonic Activity in Mexico with Special Regard to Carlos Chavez and Silvestre Revueltas." Ph.D. dissertation, Northwestern University, 1946.

International Who's Who in Music and Musicians' Dictionary. 10th ed. Cambridge: International Who's Who in Music, 1984.

Jähns, Friedrich Wilhelm. *Carl Maria von Weber in Seinen Werken*. Berlin: Schlesinger'schen Buch- und Musikhandlung, 1871; reprint, 1967.

James, Helga. *A Catalog of the Musical Works of Philip James (1890-1975)*. New York: Judith Finell Music Services, 1980.

Jenkins, Newell, and Bathia Churgin. *Thematic Catalogue of the Works of Giovanni Battista Sammartini*. Cambridge: Harvard University Press, 1976.

A Jewish Composer by Choice, Isadore Freed: His Life and Work. New York: National Jewish Music Council, 1961.

John Ireland: A Catalogue of Published Works and Recordings. Compiled by Ernest Chapman. London: Boosey & Hawkes, 1968.

Johns, Keith T. "De Profundis. Psalm Instrumental: An Abandoned Concerto for

Piano and Orchestra by Franz Liszt." *Journal of the American Liszt Society* XV (June 1984): 96–104.

Johns, Keith T. "Malédiction: The Concerto's History, Programme and Some Notes on Harmonic Organization." *Journal of the American Liszt Society* XVIII (December 1885): 29–35.

Johnson, Edward. *Robert Simpson Essays*. London: Triad Press, 1971.

Johnson, Robert Sherlaw. *Messiaen*. Berkeley and Los Angeles: University of California Press, 1975.

Jordan, Ruth. *Nocturne: A Life of Chopin*. New York: Taplinger Publishing Co., 1978.

Joseph, Charles Mensore. "A Study of Igor Stravinsky's Piano Compositions." Ph.D. dissertation, University of Cincinnati, 1974.

Kallmann, Helmut, ed. *Catalogue of Canadian Composers*. Rev. and enl. ed. St. Clair Shores, Mich.: Scholarly Press; republished 1976.

Kallmann, Helmut; Gilles Potvin, and Kenneth Winters, eds. *Encyclopedia of Music in Canada*. Buffalo: University of Toronto Press, 1992.

Kallstenius, Edvin. *Swedish Orchestral Works. Annotated Catalogue*. Stockholm: Nordiska Musikförlaget, 1949.

Karpel, Alan Marc. "A Comprehensive Project in Piano Performance and An Essay on the Works of Johann Matthias Leffloth Including An Edition of the Concerto in F for Cembalo and Violin." D.M.A. dissertation, University of Iowa, 1974.

Kefferstan, Christine Bane. "The Piano Concertos of Edward MacDowell." D.M.A. dissertation, University of Cincinnati, 1984.

Kelley, Edgar Stillman. *Chopin, the Composer; His Structural Art and Its Influence on Contemporaneous Music*. New York: Cooper Square Publishers, 1969

Kelly, John Dennis. "Three Keyboard Concertos of J. C. Monn (1726–1782) in Two Volumes." Volume I: "Identification and Analysis." Volume II: "An Edition." D.M.A. dissertation, University of Missouri, 1974.

Kendall, Alan. *The Tender Tyrant, Nadia Boulanger*. Wilton, Conn.: Lyceum, 1977.

Kennedy, Michael. *A Catalogue of the Works of Ralph Vaughan Williams*. 2nd ed. Oxford: Clarendon, 1992.

Kennedy, Michael. *Richard Strauss*. London: J. M. Dent & Sons, 1988.

Kennedy, Michael. *The Works of Ralph Vaughan Williams*. London: Oxford University Press, 1964.

Keys, Ivor. *Mozart, His Music in His Life*. New York: Holmes & Meier Publishers, 1980

King, A. Hyatt. *Introduction to W. A. Mozart's Piano Concerto in D, K.40*. Edited by Arthur Balsam. London: Oxford University Press, 1966.

Kinsky, George, and Hans Halm. *Das Werk Beethovens. Verzeichnis Seiner Sämtlich Vollendeten Kompositionen*. Munchen: G. Henle Verlag, 1955.

Kirby, F. E. *A Short History of Keyboard Music*. New York: Free Press, 1966.

Kirby, F. E. "Discography." *Piano Quarterly* 119 (Fall 1982): 47–52.

Kirkpatrick, John. *A Temporary Mimeographed Catalogue of The Music Manuscripts and Related Materials of Charles Edward Ives 1874–1954*. Mimeographed at Yale University. Copyright 1960; reprint, 1973.

Klein, Sister Mary Justina. "The Contribution of Daniel Gregory Mason to American Music." Ph.D. dissertation, Catholic University of America. Washington, D. C.: Catholic University of America Press, 1957.

Kloppenburg, W. C. M. *Thematisch-Bibliografische Catalogus van de Werken van Willem Pijper (1894-1947)*. Assen: Van Gorcum & Co., N. V., 1960.
Knape, Walter. *Bibliographisch-Thematisches Verzeichnis der Kopositionen von Karl Friedrich Abel (1723–1787)*. Cuxhaven, Germany: Herausgebers, 1971.
Köchel, Ludwig Ritter von. *Chronologisch-Thematisches Verzeichnis Sämtlicher Tonwerke Wolfgang Amadé Mozarts*. Wiesbaden: Breitkopf & Härtel, 1983.
Komma, Karl Michael. *Johann Zach und die Tschechischen Musiker im Deutschen Umbruch des 18. Jahrhunderts*. Studien zur Heidelberger Musikwissenschart, Band VII. Kassel: Bärenreiter, 1938.
Kortsen, Bjarne. *Contemporary Norwegian Piano Music*. 3rd ed. Bergen, Norway: n.p., 1976.
Kovacevic, Kresimir. *The History of Croatian Music of the Twentieth Century*. Zagreb: Udruzenje Kompositora Hrvatske, 1967.
Landon, H. C. Robbins. *Haydn: Chronicle and Works*. 5 vols. Bloomington: Indiana University Press, 1980.
Landowski, Marcel, and Guy Morancon. *Louis Aubert*. Paris: Durand et Cie, 1967.
Landreth, Janet. "André Jolivet: A Study of the Piano Works with a Discussion of His Aesthetic and Technical Princples." D.M.A. document, University of Oklahoma, 1980.
Lang, Paul Henry, ed. *Problems of Modern Music*. The Princeton Seminar in Advanced Musical Studies. New York: W. W. Norton & Co., 1962.
Lang, Paul Henry, and Nathan Broder, eds. *Contemporary Music in Europe: A Comprehensive Survey*. New York: G. Schirmer, 1965.
Lange, Kristian. *Norwegian Music, A Survey*. 2nd ed. Oslo: Johan Grundt Tanum Forlag, 1982.
Langley, Robin. "Arne's Keyboard Concertos." *Musical Times* 119 (March 1978): 233–236.
Lanjean, Marc. *Jean Francaix, Musicien Francais*. Paris: Contact Editions, 1961.
Laplante, Louise. *Compositeurs Canadiens Contemporains*. Montréal: Les Presses de L'Université du Québec, 1977.
Lara, Adelina de. *Finale*. Saint Clair Shores, Mich.: Scholarly Press, 1972.
Larese, Dino. *Heinrich Sutermeister*. Amriswiler: Amriswiler Bücherei, 1972.
Larese, Dino, and Willi Schuh. *Conrad Beck, Eine Lebensskizze, Der Komponist un sein Werk*. Amriswiler: Amriswiler Bücherei, 1971.
Larese, Dino, and Jacques Wildberger. *Robert Stuter*. Amriswiler: Amriswiler Bücherei, 1967.
Large, Brian. *Martinu*. New York: Holmes & Meier, 1976.
Lasalle-Leduc, Annette. *La Vie Musicale au Canada Français*. Québec: Ministère des Affaires Culturelles, 1964.
Latham, Peter. *Brahms*. London: J. M. Dent & Sons, 1948; reprint 1975.
Lauth, Wilhelm. *Max Bruchs Instrumentalmusik*. Cologne: Arno Volk-Verlag, 1967.
Lee, Douglas A. *Franz Benda (1709-1786): A Thematic Catalogue of his Works*. New York: Pendragon Press, 1984.
Lee, Douglas Allen. "Christoph Nichelmann and the Early Clavier." *Musical Quarterly* 57 (October 1971): 636–655.
Lee, Douglas Allen. "The Instrumental Works of Christoph Nichelmann." Ph.D. dissertation, University of Michigan, 1968.

Lerma, Dominique-René de. *Charles Edward Ives, 1874-1954: A Bibliography of His Music*. Kent, Ohio: Kent State University Press, 1970.

Lesure, Francois. *Catalogue de l'Oeuvre de Claude Debussy*. Geneva: Minkoff, 1977.

Levey, Joseph. *The Jazz Experience: A Guide to Appreciation*. Englewood Cliffs, N.J.: Prentice-Hall, 1983.

Ley, Salvador. "Cultural Aspects of Music Life in Guatemala." *Latin American Studies 13* (June 14–17, 1951): 73–83. Westport, Conn.: Greenwood Press, 1970.

Liess, Andreas. *Carl Orff*. Translated by Adelheid and Herbert Parkin. London: Calder & Boyars, 1966.

Lindlar, Heinrich. *Hermann Reutter, Werk und Wirken*. Mainz: B. Schott's Söhne, 1965.

Lindlar, Heinrich, ed. *Wolfgang Fortner, Eine Monographie*. Kontrapunkte. Band 4. Rhine: P. J. Tonger, 1960.

Loggins, Vernon. *Where the World Ends: The Life of Louis Moreau Gottschalk*. Baton Rouge: Louisiana State University Press, 1958.

Lomnitzer, Helmut. "Das Musikalische Werk Friedrich Schneiders (1786–1853)." Inauguraldissertation zur Erlangung der Doktorwürde der Hohen Philosophischen Fakultat der Philipps-Universität zu Marburg, 1961.

Longyear, Rey M. *Nineteenth-Century Romanticism in Music*. 3rd ed. Englewood Cliffs, N.J.: Prentice-Hall, 1988.

Louwenaar, Karyl June. "The Keyboard Concertos of Christoph Schaffrath (1709–1763)." D.M.A. dissertation, Eastman School of Music, University of Rochester, 1974.

Lowe, Rachel. *Frederick Delius 1862–1934: A Catalogue of the Music of the Delius Trust, London*. London: Delius Trust, 1986.

Lundahl, Per Olfo. *Katalog over Svensk Instrumentalmusik: Piano*. Stockholm: STIM, 1971.

Luper, Albert T. "Lorenzo Fernândez and Camargo Guarnieri: Notes Toward a Mid-Century Appraisal" *Latin American Studies 23* (June 14–17, 1951): 98–114. Westport, Conn.: Greenwood Press, 1977.

Lyall, Max Dail. "The Piano Music of Gail Kubik." D.M.A. dissertation, Peabody Conservatory of Music, Johns Hopkins University, 1980.

M'Arthur, Alexander. *Anton Rubinstein: A Biographical Sketch*. Edinburgh: Adam and Charles Black, 1889; reprint ed., Ann Arbor, Mich.: University Microfilms, 1979.

McBurney, Gerard. "Howard Ferguson in 1983." *Tempo* 147 (December 1983): 2–6.

MacDonald, Calum. "Luigi Dallapiccola. The Complete Works: A Catalogue." *Tempo* 116 (March 1967): 2–19.

McGee, Timothy J. *The Music of Canada*. New York: W. W. Norton & Co., 1985.

Machado, Manuel. *Joaquin Turina*. Madrid: Editora Nacional, 1956.

MacMillan, Keith, and John Beckwith, eds. *Contemporary Canadian Composers*. Toronto: Oxford University Press, 1975.

The Macmillan Encyclopedia of Music and Musicians. Compiled and edited by Albert E. Wier. New York: Macmillan Co., 1938.

Macomber, Frank S. "Bach's Re-use of His Own Music: A Study in Transcription." Ph.D. dissertation, Syracuse University, 1967.

Malmström, Dan. "Introduction to Twentieth Century Mexican Music." Doctoral dissertation, Uppsala University, Uppsala, Sweden, 1974.

Manuel, E. Arsenio. *Dictionary of Philippine Biography*. Vol. 1. Quezon City: Filipiniana Publications, 1955.
Marco, Tomas. *La Musica de la España Contemporanea*. Madrid: Publicaciones Españolas, 1970.
Mariz, Vasco. *Dicionário Bio-Bibliográfico Musical*. Rio de Janeiro: Erich Eichner & Cia, 1948.
Mariz, Vasco. *Figuras de Música Brasileira Contemporânea*. São Paulo: Universidade de Brasíliá, 1970.
Mark, Michael L. "The Life and Works of Vittorio Giannini (1903–1966)." D.M.A. dissertation, Catholic University of America, 1970.
Martin, William R., and Julius Drossin. *Music of the Twentieth Century*. Englewood Cliffs, N.J.: Prentice-Hall, 1980.
Matthay, Jessie Henderson. *The Life and Works of Tobias Matthay*. London: Boosey and Hawkes, 1945.
Matthews, David. *Michael Tippett: An Introductory Study*. London: Faber and Faber, 1980.
Matthey, Jean-Louis, and Louis-Daniel Perret. *Catalogue de l'Oeuvre de Hans Haug*. Lausanne: Bibliotheque Cantonale et Universitaire, 1971.
Mayer-Serra, Otto. *Musica y Musicos de Latinoamerica*. 2 vols. Mexico City: W. M. Jackson, 1947.
Mekota, Beth Anna. "The Solo and Ensemble Keyboard Works of Johann Christian Bach." Ph.D. dissertation, University of Michigan, 1969.
Melville, Derek. *Chopin: A Biography, with a Survey of Books, Editions and Records*. Hamden, Conn.: Linnet Books, 1977.
Merkl, Josef. "Josef Riepel Als Komponist (1709–1782)." Ph.D. dissertation, Universität zu Erlangen, 1935. Kellmünz: Buchdruckerei von Michael LaBleben, 1937.
Michel, Francois, ed. *Encyclopedie de la Musique*. 3 vols. Paris: Fasquelle, 1958.
Michelitsch, Helga. *Das Klavierwerk von Georg Christoph Wagenseil, Thematischer Katalog*. Tabulae Musicae Austriacae, Band III. Vienna: In Kommission Bie Herman Böhlaus, 1966.
Mies, Paul, and Joseph Schmidt-Görg. *Beethoven-Jahrbuch*. Jahrgang 1965/68. Bonn: Beethovenhaus, 1969.
Milhaud, Darius. *Notes without Music*. New York: Da Capo Press, 1977.
Milligan, Thomas B. *The Concerto and London's Musical Culture in the Late Eighteenth Century*. Ann Arbor, Mich.: UMI Research Press, 1983.
Mishkin, Henry G. "Incomplete Notation in Mozart's Piano Concertos." *Musical Quarterly* 61 (July 1975): 345–359.
Mishkin, Henry G. "The Published Instrumental Works of Giovanni Battista Sammartini: A Bibliographical Reappraisal." *Musical Quarterly* 61 (July 1975): 345–359.
Mitchell, Donald, and Hans Keller, eds. *Benjamin Britten*. Westport, Conn.: Greenwood Press, 1952.
Mitchell, Francis Humphries. "The Piano Concertos of Johann Nepomuk Hummel." Ph.D. dissertation, Northwestern University, 1957.
Moldenhauer, Hans. "A Newly Found Mozart Autograph: Two Cadenzas to K.107." *Journal of the American Musicological Society* 8 (Fall 1955): 213–216.
Muñoz, Maria Luisa. *La Musica en Puerto Rico*. Sharon, Conn.: Troutman Press, 1966.

Murdoch, James. *Australia's Contemporary Composers*. Melbourne: Sun Books, 1975.
Myers, Rollo. *Modern French Music*. London: Blackwell, 1972.
Myers, Rollo H. *Ravel, Life and Works*. London: Duckworth, 1971.
Nelson, Jon Ray. "The Piano Music of Francis Poulenc." Ph.D. dissertation, University of Washington, 1978.
Nelson, Wendell. *The Concerto*. Dubuque, Iowa: William C. Brown Co., 1969.
Nettl, Paul. *Beethoven Handbook*. New York: Frederick Ungar Publishing Co., 1956, 1967.
Newman, William S. *The Sonata in the Classic Era*. 3rd ed. New York: W. W. Norton & Co., 1983.
Newtyev, Israel. *Prokofiev*. Stanford, Calif.: Stanford University Press, 1971.
Nick, Edmund. "Georg Göhler." *Musica* 8 (1954): 208.
Niemann, Walter. *Brahms*. Translated by Catherine Alison Phillips. New York: Cooper Square Publishers, 1969.
Nordyke, Diane. "The Piano Works of Carlos Chavez." Ph.D. dissertation, Texas Tech University, 1982.
Northcott, Bayan, ed. *The Music of Alexander Goehr*. London: Schott & Co., 1980.
Offergel, Robert. *The Centennial Catalogue of the Published and Unpublished Compositions of Louis Moreau Gottschalk*. Prepared for *Stereo Review*. New York: Ziff-Davis, 1970.
Ogdon, Brenda Lucas and Michael Kerr. *Virtuoso: The Story of John Ogdon*. London: Hamish Hamilton, 1989.
Olmstead, Andrea. *Roger Sessions and His Music*. Ann Arbor, Mich.: UMI Research Press, 1985.
Orenstein, Arbie. *Ravel, Man and Musician*. New York: Dover, 1991.
Orga, Ates. *Chopin, His Life and Times*. 2nd ed. Neptune City, N.J.: Pagannininana Publications, 1978.
Owen, Stephanie Olive. "The Piano Concerto in Canada Since 1955." Ph.D. dissertation, Washington University, 1969.
Pan American Union. *Composers of the Americas: Biographical Data and Catalogs of Their Works*. 19 vols. Washington, D. C.: Organization of American States, 1955–77.
Parker, Craig Burwell. "John Vincent (1902–1977): An Alabama Composer's Odyssey." Ph.D. dissertation, University of California at Los Angeles, 1981.
Parrish, Carl G. "The Early Piano and Its Influence on Keyboard Technique and Composition in the Eighteenth Century." Ph.D. dissertation, Harvard University, 1939.
Parthun, Paul. "Concord, Charles Ives, and Henry Bellamann." *Student Musicologists at Minnesota* (1975–76): 66–86.
Pauly, Reinhard G. *Music in the Classic Period*. Englewood Cliffs, N.J.: Prentice-Hall, 1988.
Peare, Catherine Owens. *Aaron Copland: His Life*. New York: Holt, Rinehart & Winston, 1969.
Pepin, S. N. J. M. and Sister M. Natalie. "Dance and Jazz Elements in the Piano Music of Maurice Ravel." D.M.A. dissertation, Boston University, 1971.
Perdomo, Escobar and Jose Ignacio. *Historia de la Música en Colombia*. Volumen CIII: *Biblioteca de Historia Nacional*. Tercera Edicion. Bogota: Editorial A B C, 1975.

Perger, Lothar Herbert. *Michael Haydn: Instrumentalwerke I*. Vol. 29: *Denkmäler der Tonkunst in Österreich*. Graz: Akademische Druck-U. Verlagsanstalt, 1959.
Peter, Philip Henry. "The Life and Work of Cipriani Potter (1792–1871)." Vols. I and II. Ph.D. dissertation, Northwestern University, 1972.
Peyser, Joan. *Boulez*. New York: Schirmer Books, 1976.
Piggott, Patrick. "John Field, The Piano Concertos." An article accompanying the recording *John Field, The Complete Piano Concertos*. Claddagh Records CSM55–58.
Piggott, Patrick. *Rachmaninov*. London: Faber & Faber, 1978.
Pirani, Max. *Emanuel Moor*. London: P. R. MacMillan, 1959.
Plantinga, Leon. *Clementi: His Life and Music*. New York: Dover, 1985.
Pollack, Howard. *Walter Piston*. Ann Arbor, Mich.: UMI Research Press, 1982.
Poos, Heinrich (Herausgegeben). *Festschrift Ernst Pepping*. "Junge Komponisten," by Adam Adrio. pp. 38–45. "Systematisch-chronolotgisches Verzeichnis der im Druck erschienenen Werke Ernst Peppings" by Heinrich Poos. pp. 345–361. Berlin: Verlag Merseberger, 1971.
Porte, John F. *Sir Charles V. Stanford*. Reprint of the 1921 edition. New York: Da Capo Press, 1976.
Posner, Bruce. "Sorabji." B.S. dissertation, Fordham University, New York, 1975.
Proctor, George A. *Canadian Music of the Twentieth Century*. Toronto: University of Toronto Press, 1980.
Raabe, Peter. *Liszts Schaffen*. Tutting: Hans Schneider, 1968.
Radcliffe, Philip. *Mendelssohn*. London: Dent, 1990.
Radcliffe, Philip. *Mozart Piano Concertos*. BBC Music Guides. n.p.: Ariel Music, 1986.
Ramsay, Alice Box. "Aurelio de la Vega, His Life and His Music." M.A. thesis, San Fernando Valley State College, 1963.
Rapoport, Paul. *Opus Est: Six Composers from Northern Europe*. New York: Taplinger Publishing Co., 1979.
Rapoport, Paul. *Vagn Holmbor: A Catalogue of His Music, Discography, Bibliography, Essays*. 2nd ed., rev. and enl. Copenhagen: Hanson, 1979.
Rauth, F. *Contemporary British Music 1945-1970*. London: MacDonald, 1972.
Reeser, Eduard, and Wouter Papp. *Contemporary Music from Holland*. Translated by W. van Maanon and Elizabeth Sherman Swing. Amsterdam: Donemus, 1953.
Reich, Nancy B., ed. *A Compendium of Piano Concertos of William Sydeman*. 2nd ed. New York: Division of Music Education, New York University, 1968.
Reif, Jean Frances. *A Compendium of Piano Concertos*. Hawthorne, N.J.: Publication Arts, 1981.
Reis, Claire R. *Composers in America: Biographical Sketches of Living Composers with a Record of Their Works 1912-1937*. Rev. and enl. ed. New York: Macmillan Co., 1947.
Riedel, Johannes. *Music of the Romantic Period*. Dubuque, Iowa: William C. Brown Co., 1969.
Ringenwald, Richard Donald. "The Music of Esther Williamson Ballou: An Analytical Study." M.A. thesis, American University, 1960.
Roberts, Maynard Wesley. "An Introduction to the Literature for Two Pianos and Orchestra, 1915–1950." D.M.A. dissertation, Southern Baptist Theological Seminary, 1981.
Robinson, Forrest T. "The Works of Darius Milhaud for Piano and Orchestra." D.M.A. document, Boston University, 1965.

Rosen, Charles. *The Classical Style: Haydn, Mozart, Beethoven*. London: Faber, 1976.

Rosen, Lydia. "Guide to the Understanding and Performance of Contemporary Piano Literature of Holland." Ed.D. dissertation, Columbia University, 1959.

Rosner, Arnold. "An Analytical Survey of the Music of Alan Hovhaness." Ph.D. dissertation, University of New York at Buffalo, 1972.

Rotharmal, Marion. *Bernd Alois Zimmerman, Werkverzeichnis*. Mainz: B. Schott's Söhne, 1971.

Routh, Francis. *Contemporary British Music: The Twenty-Five Years from 1945–1970*. London: Macdonald & Co., 1972.

Royal Swedish College. *Three Aspects of Music*. Stockholm: Nordisk Musikforlaget, 1968.

Rózsa, Miklós. *Double Life, The Autobiography of Miklós Rózza*. London: Baton Press, 1984.

Rudolf Moser (*Composer 1892–1960*): *Short Biography and List of Printed Works*. Arlesheim, Switzerland: n.p., (ca. 1982).

Rush, Laura Rhoades. "The Harpsichord Concertos of Johann Schobert." D.A. dissertation, University of Northern Colorado, 1983.

Russell, John. "Howard Ferguson's Concerto for Piano and String Orchestra." *Tempo* 24 (1952): 24–26.

Russian Composers and Musicians, A Biographical Dictionary. Compiled by Alexandria Vodarsky-Shiraeff. New York: H. W. Wilson Co., 1940; reprint, Westport, Conn.: Greenwood Press, 1969.

Russian Composers and Musicians, A Biographical Dictionary. Compiled by Alexandria Vodarsky-Shiraeff. New York: Da Capo Press, 1969.

Rust, Ezra Gardner. "The First Movements of Beethoven's Piano Concertos." Ph.D. dissertation, University of California, Berkeley, 1970.

Ryom, Peter. *Verzeichnis der Werke Antonio Vivaldis*. Leipzig: VEB Deutscher Verlag Für Musik, 1985.

Sachs, Joel. "A Checklist of the Works of Johann Nepomuk Hummel." *Notes* 30 (1974): 732–754.

Sachs, Joel. "Hummel and The Pirates: The Struggle of Musical Copyright." *Musical Quarterly* 59 (January 1973): 31–60.

Sachs, Joel Alan. "Hummel in England and France: A Study in the International Musical Life of the Early Nineteenth Century." Ph.D. dissertation, Columbia University, 1968.

Sadie, Stanley. "The Chamber Music of Boyce and Arne." *Musical Quarterly* 46 (October 1960): 425–436.

Safranek, Milos. *Bohuslav Martinu: His Life and Works*. Translated 1962. London: Allan Wingate, 1961.

Safranek, Milos. *Bohuslav Martinu: The Man and His Music*. New York: Alfred A. Knopf, 1944.

Salgado, Susana. *Breve Historia de la Musica Culta en el Uruguay*. 2nd ed. Montevideo: A. Monteverde y Cia. S. A., 1980.

Salzman, Eric. *Twentieth-Century Music: An Introduction*. Englewood Cliffs, N.J.: Prentice-Hall, 1988.

Samazeuilh, Gustave. "Sylvio Lazzari." *Musiciens de Mon Temps*. Paris: Éditions Marcel Daubin, 1947.

Samson, Helen F. *Contemporary Filipino Composers*. Quezon City: Manlapas Publishing Co., 1976.
Samson, Jim. *The Music of Szymanowski*. New York: Taplinger Publishing Co., 1981.
Sarrautte, Jean-Paul. *Catalogue des Oeuvres de Joao Domingos Bontempo*. Lisbon: Fondation Calouste Gulbenkian, 1970.
Schäfer, Albert. *Chronologilch-Lylthematilches Verzeichnis der Werke Joachim Raffs*. Tutting: Verlegt Bei Hans Schneider, 1974.
Schaffrath, Christoph. *Concerto in B-Flat for Cembalo and Strings*. Edited by Karyl Louwenaar. Collegium Musicum: Yale University, 2nd series, vol. 7. Madison, Wis.: A-R Editions, 1977.
Schauffler, Robert Haven. *The Unknown Brahms*. New York: Dodd, Mead & Co., 1934.
Schmieder, Wolfgang. *Thematisch-Systematisches Verzeichnis der Werke von Johann Sebastian Bach*. Leipzig: Veb Breitkopf and Härtel, 1966.
Scholz-Michelitsch, Helga. *Das Orchester und Kammermusikwerk von Georg Christoph Wagenseil, Thematischer Katalog*. Vienna: Ernst Becvar, 1972.
Schreiber, Flora Rheta, and Vincent Persichetti. *William Schuman*. New York: G. Schirmer, 1954.
Schwartz, Charles. *Gershwin: His Life and Music*. New York: Bobbs-Merrill Co., 1973.
Schwarz, Boris. "Karol Rathaus." *Musical Quarterly* 41 (October 1955): 481–495.
Schwerke, Irving. *Alexandre Tansman*. Paris: Editions Max Eschig, 1931.
Searle, Humphrey. *The Music of Liszt*. 2nd rev. ed. New York: Dover Publication, 1966.
Searle, Muriel V. *John Ireland: The Man and His Music*. London: Midas Books, 1979.
Shanet, Howard. "Why Did J. S. Bach Transpose His Arrangements?" *Musical Quarterly* 36 (April 1950): 180–203.
Shead, Richard. *Constant Lambert*. Revised and corrected. London: Simon Publications, 1986.
Sheerson, Grigory. *Aram Khachaturyan*. Moscow: Foreign Languages Publishing House, 1959.
Shere, James. *Dane Rudhyar 1895-: A Brief Factual Biography with a Listing of Works*. Printed in the United States, n.p.: copyright 1972.
Simo, Rita. "Stylistic Analysis of Piano Music of Latin America since 1930." Doctoral dissertation, Boston University of Fine and Applied Arts, 1975.
Simon, Edwin J. "Sonata into Concerto." *Acta Musicologica* 31 (1959): 171–185.
Simon, Edwin Julien. "The Double Exposition in Classic Concerto Form." Ph.D. dissertation, University of California, Berkley, 1954.
Simpson, Ralph Ricardo. "William Grant Still—The Man and His Music." Ph.D. dissertation, Michigan State University, 1964.
Sjoerdsma, Richard Dale. "The Instrumental Works of Franz Christoph Neubauer (1760–1795)." Vols. I and II. Ph.D. dissertation, Ohio State University, 1970.
Slonimsky, Nicolas. *Baker's Biographical Dictionary of Musicians*. 6th ed. Completely revised. New York: Schirmer Books, 1978.
Slonimsky, Nicolas. *Music of Latin America*. New York: Thomas Y. Crowell Co., 1945. Second printing 1946.
Smith, Catherine Parsons, and Cynthia S. Richardson. *Mary Carr Moore, American Composer*. Ann Arbor, Mich.: University of Michigan Press, 1987.

Southall, Geneva Handy. "John Field's Piano Concertos: An Analytical and Historical Study." Ph.D. dissertation, University of Iowa, 1966.
Spitta, Phillip. *Johann Sebastian Bach.* Translated by Clara Bell and J. A. Fuller-Maitland. 3 vols. Wiesbaden: Breitkoph & Härtel, 1979.
Steffan, Joseph Anton. *Piano Concerto in B-Flat.* Edited by Howard Picton. Madison, Wis.: A-R Editions, 1980.
Stevens, Halsey. *The Life and Music of Bela Bartók.* 3rd ed. Prepared by Malcolm Gillies. New York: Oxford University Press, 1964.
Stevens, Jane R. "The Keyboard Concertos of Carl Philipp Emanuel Bach." Ph.D. dissertation, Yale University, 1965.
Stevenson, Robert. *Music in Mexico.* New York: Thomas Y. Crowell Co., 1952.
Stookes, Sacha. *The Art of Robert Casadesus.* London: Fortune Press, 1960.
Sucoff, Herbert. "A Catalog and Evaluation of Stefan Wolpe's Music." M.A. thesis, Queens College, City University of New York, 1969.
Swiss Composers' League. *40 Contemporary Swiss Composers.* Amriswil: Bodensee-Verlag, 1956.
Terry, Charles Sanford. *Bach.* London: Oxford University Press, 1928. 2nd rev. ed., 1933; reprint, 1940.
Terry, Charles Sanford. *John Christian Bach.* 2nd ed. London: Oxford University Press, 1967. First published 1929; reprint, Westport, Conn.: Greenwood Press, 1980.
Terry, Charles Sanford. *The Music of Bach: An Introduction.* Oxford University Press, 1933; reprint, New York: Dover Publications, 1963.
Thal, Marlene. "The Piano Music of Igor Stravinsky." D.M.A. dissertation, University of Washington, 1978.
Thematic Bibliographical and Critical Catalogue of the Works of Luigi Boccherini. Compiled by Yves Gérard. Translated by Andreas Mayor. London: Oxford University Press, 1969.
Thematisches Verzeichniss im Druck erschienener Compositionen von Ignaz Moscheles. Leipzig, 1885. London: Reprinted for H. Baron, 1966.
Thompson, Kenneth. *A Dictionary of Twentieth-Century Composers (1911–1971).* New York: St. Martin's Press, 1973.
Thompson, Kenneth L. "For Arthur Bliss's 75th Birthday, Catalogue of Works." *Musical Times* 107 (1966): 666–673.
Thompson, Oscar. *The International Cyclopedia of Music and Musicians.* 9th ed. Edited by Robert Sabin. New York: Dodd, Mead & Co., 1964.
Thorp, Keith Andrew. "The Twentieth-Century Harpsichord: Approaches to Composition and Performance Practice as Evidenced by the Contemporary Repertoire." D.M.A. dissertation, University of Illinois at Urbana-Champaign, 1981.
Threlfall, Robert, and Geoffrey Norris. *A Catalogue of the Compositions of S. Rachmaninoff.* London: Scolar Press, 1982.
Tischler, Alice. *Fifteen Black American Composers: A Bibliography of Their Works.* Detroit, Mich.: Information Coordinators, 1981.
Tischler, Alice. *Karel Boleslav Jirák: A Catalog of His Works.* Detroit, Mich.: Information Coordinators, 1975.
Tischler, Hans. *A Structural Analysis of Mozart's Piano Concertos.* Brooklyn: Institute of Medieval Music, 1966.

Tovar, Andrés Pardo. *La Cultura Musical en Colombia*. Historia Estensa Colombia. Vol. 20. Tomo 6. Bogotá: Ediciones Lerner, 1966.
Tovey, Donald Francis. *Essays in Musical Analysis*. Vol. III: *Concertos*. London: Oxford University Press, 1989.
Trickey, Samuel Miller. "Les Six." Ph.D. dissertation, North Texas State University, 1955.
Truscott, Harold. "Dussek and the Concerto." *Music Review* 16 (February 1955): 29–53.
Tschupp, Räto. *Hugo Pfister*. Zurich: Atlantis, 1973.
Tupper, Janet Eloise. "Stylistic Analysis of Selected Works by Frank Martin." Ph.D. dissertation, Indiana University, 1964.
Turrentine, Herbert Charles. "Johann Schobert and French Clavier Music from 1700 to the Revolution." Vols. I and II. Ph.D. dissertation, State University of Iowa, 1962.
Tyson, Alan. *Thematic Catalogue of the Works of Muzio Clementi*. Tutting: Hans Schneider, 1967.
Ujfalussy, Józef. *Béla Bartók*. Boston: Crescendo Publishing Co., 1971.
Upper, Henry A. "An Historical and Analytical Study of Selected Works for Piano Obbligato with Orchestra." D.M. document, Indiana University, 1971.
Vallas, Leon. *César Franck*. Translated by Hubert Foss. London: George G. Harrap & Co., 1951.
Veinus, Abraham. *The Concerto*. New York: Dover Publications, 1944; revised, 1964.
Vise, Sidney R. "Ray Green: His Life and Stylistic Elements of His Music from 1935 to 1962." D.M. dissertation, Conservatory of Music at University of Missouri-Kansas City, 1975. Boston: Carl Fischer, n.d.
Vogel, Jaroslav. *Leos Janáncek: A Biography*. Revised and edited by Karel Janovicky. New York: W. W. Norton & Co., 1981.
Waddington, Patrick. "Charles Avison, English Concerto Writer." *Musical Quarterly* 59 (July 1973): 382–398.
Wade, Rachel W. *The Keyboard Concertos of Carl Philipp Emanuel Bach*. Ann Arbor, Mich.: UMI Research Press, 1981.
Wagner, Hermann. *Hans Poser, 1917-1970*. Hamburg: n.p., 1972.
Walker, Alan, ed. *Franz Liszt, The Man and His Music*. New York: Taplinger Publishing Co., 1970.
Walker, Alan, ed. *The Chopin Companion*. New York: W. W. Norton, 1966, 1973.
Wallace, David Edward. "Alberto Ginastera: An Analysis of His Style and Techniques of Composition." Ph.D. dissertation, Northwestern University, 1964.
Wallerstein, Gerry. "Happy Birthday to Alexander Tcherepnin." *Clavier* 13 (January 1974): 10–17.
Walter, Arnold, ed. *Aspects of Music in Canada*. Toronto: University of Toronto Press, 1969.
Weinstock, Herbert. *Chopin, The Man and His Music*. New York: Alfred A. Knopf, 1965.
Wellesz, Egon, and F. W. Sternfeld. "The Concerto." In Vol. VII. "The Age of Enlightenment, 1945–1970." Chapter VII. *The New Oxford History of Music*. London: Oxford University Press, 1973.
Werner, Eric. "Two Unpublished Mendelssohn Concertos." *Music and Letters* 36 (April 1955): 126–138.

Werner, Warren Kent. "The Harmonic Style of Francis Poulenc." Ph.D. dissertation, University of Iowa, 1966.

White, Alton Duane. "The Piano Works of Anton Eberl (1765–1807)." Ph.D. dissertation, The University of Wisconsin, 1971.

White, Chappell. "Did Viotti Write Any Original Piano Concertos?" *Journal of the American Musicological Society* 21 (Summer 1969): 275–284.

White, Chappell. *Giovanni Battista Viotti (1755–1824): A Thematic Catalogue of His Works*. New York: Pendragon Press, 1985.

White, Chappell. "The Violin Concertos of Giornovichi." *Musical Quarterly* 58 (January 1972): 1–24.

White, Eric Walter. *Stravinsky, The Composer and His Works*. Berkeley and Los Angeles: University of California Press, 1966.

Wiebusch, Janice M. "The Piano Concerto Since 1950." M.M. thesis, University of Nebraska, 1969.

Wild, Stephen. *E. J. Moeran*. London: Triad Press, 1973.

Wilder, Robert D. *Twentieth-Century Music*. Dubuque, Iowa: William. C. Brown Co., 1969.

Wohlfarth, Hannsdieter. *Johann Christoph Friedrich Bach*. Munich: A. Francke, 1971.

Wolff, Konrad. "Johann Samuel Schroeter." *Musical Quarterly* 46 (July 1958): 338–359.

Wörner, Karl H. "Edmund von Borck." *Musica* 5 (1951): 402–405.

Wotquenne, Alfred. *Thematisches Verzeichnis der Werke von Carl Philipp Emanuel Bach (1714-1788)*. Wiesbaden: Breitkopf & Härtel, 1972.

Wouters, Jos. *Dutch Composers' Gallery: Nine Portraits of Dutch Composers*. Amsterdam: Donemus, 1971.

Wuellner, Guy. "Alexander Tcherepnin, 1899–1977." *Piano Quarterly* 100 (Winter 1977–78): 29–33.

Wuellner, Guy. "The Piano Concertos of Alexander Tcherepnin." *American Music Teacher*. Part I (June/July 1978): 11–13; Part II (September/October 1978): 18–21.

Yasser, Joseph. "The Opening Theme of Rachmaninoff's Third Piano Concerto and Its Liturgical Prototype." *Musical Quarterly* 55 (July 1969): 313–328.

Yates, Peter. *Twentieth-Century Music: Its Evolution from the End of the Harmonic Era into the Present Era of Sound*. New York: Random House, 1967; reprint, Westport, Conn.: Greenwood Press, 1980.

Young, Percy M. *A History of British Music*. New York: W. W. Norton & Co., 1967.

Zaimont, Judith Land, ed. *The Musical Woman: An International Perspective*. Westport, Conn.: Greenwood Press, 1983.

Zimmerschied, Dieter. *Thematisches Verzeichnis der Werke von Johann Nepomuk Hummel*. Hofheim: Friedrich Hofmeister, 1971.

Index of Composers

About the Author

John M. Harris was born in Chicago in 1939. He holds a B.S. from San Jose State University, B.S. and M.S. degrees from the Juilliard School of Music, and a D.M.A. from the University of Texas at Austin. In 1964, he joined the faculty at Texas A&M University—Commerce.